GLADSTONE

By the same author:

Gladstone, Volume I: 1809–1865

RICHARD SHANNON

GLADSTONE

VOLUME II
1865–1898

THE UNIVERSITY OF NORTH CAROLINA PRESS
CHAPEL HILL

First published in the United States in 1999 by the University of North Carolina Press.

First published in Great Britain in 1999 by the Penguin Group

Library of Congress Cataloging-in-Publication Data
Shannon, Richard.
Gladstone/Richard Shannon
v. 2 : ill.; 24 cm.
Originally published: London : Penguin, 1999.
Includes bibliographical references and index.

ISBN 0-8078-1591-8 (v. 1)
ISBN 0-8078-2486-0 (v. 2)
1. Gladstone, W. E. (William Ewart), 1809–1898. 2. Great
Britain—Politics and government—1837–1901. 3. Prime
ministers—Great Britain—Biography. 4. Liberal Party (Great
Britain)—Bioigraphy. I. Title.
DA563.4 .S5 1984
941.081'092'4—ddc19
[B] 83-19860 CIP r95

Set in 10/12 pt PostScript Adobe Palatino
Typeset by Rowland Phototypesetting Ltd, Bury St Edmunds, Suffolk
Printed in Great Britain by the Bath Press, Bath

03 02 01 00 99   5 4 3 2 1

Contents

Contents

List of Illustrations

Photographic Acknowledgements

Dudley W. R. Bahlman: 7

Flintshire Record Office: 22, 23

The House of Lords, by kind permission: 6

Hulton Getty: 3, 4, 8, 9, 10, 12, 13, 16, 18, 19

Illustrated London News: 20

Mary Evans Picture Library: 17

National Portrait Gallery, by courtesy: 1

Popperfoto: 11, 14

Public Record Office Image Library: 21

Städtische Galerie im Lenbachhaus, Munich: 15

Topham Picturepoint: 2, 5

Acknowledgements

My words of gratitude for encouragement and assistance in the preface to the first volume of this reading of Gladstone must bear repetition in certain instances. Firstly, I renew my acknowledgements to Sir William Gladstone – in the centenary year of his great-grandfather's death – for the generosity with which he and his family have freely made available the immense Gladstone documentary archive at the Clwyd Record Office, Hawarden, and at the British Library. I should like once more also to record my gratitude to the Council of the University of Wales Swansea for their allocations of study leave. There is no source of materials bearing on Gladstone's life and career more consequential and indispensable to Gladstone scholarship in general and Gladstone biography in particular than his diaries, housed at Lambeth Palace Library and published by Oxford University Press, under the editorship (for the years covered in this volume) of Professor H. C. G. Matthew. I am accordingly under very great obligation to Oxford University Press for their generous permission to publish substantial extracts from *The Gladstone Diaries* in the present work.

New obligations of gratitude must now be acknowledged. Bruce Hunter of David Higham Associates has exerted his expertise on my behalf invaluably. So have also Simon Winder, Martin Toseland, Cecilia Mackay and Lindeth Vasey of Penguin Press. Peter Phillips, especially, deserves praise for his indefatigable editorial labours. To John Vaio I am much obliged for material relating to Heinrich Schliemann and Gladstone. I am grateful to my colleague Professor D. George Boyce for his judicious assistance in matters Irish. And, not least, I continue to be indebted to Janet Toft, June Morgan, and Jane Buse of the Swansea History Department Office.

Richard Shannon
London, 30 June 1998

Prologue

The thirty-three years that elapsed between William Ewart Gladstone's election to the House of Commons in 1832 and his promotion in 1865 to be the Leader of that House encompassed, in Gladstone's interpretation of his own times, two distinct phases. These phases had little to do with the fact that he was first elected as a promising young reactionary Tory, fresh from scholastic success at Eton and Oxford, just before his twenty-third birthday, as the Duke of Newcastle's candidate for the Duke's borough of Newark; or with the fact that by the time of his Leadership of the Commons he was not only a member of a Liberal Cabinet but judged widely to have in him the makings of a dangerous Radical. Rather, the contrasting epochs identified by Gladstone had about them each a general character epitomized in the former, beneficent instance by the Conservative Sir Robert Peel and in the latter, deleterious instance by the Liberal Lord Palmerston. The Crimean War of 1854–6, and its destruction of the government of Peel's senior inheritor, Lord Aberdeen, and its destruction therewith of the financial plan of Peel's junior inheritor, Gladstone himself, and its allowing public and parliamentary ascendancy for the following decade to the deplorable Palmerston, was the fatal, disastrous turning point.

Gladstone's criteria of judgement in drawing out his eulogistic assessment of Peel and his scarifying indictment of Palmerston had to do with the energies of government and administration which they embodied. With Peel it was a case of heroic energy and high intensity. With Palmerston it was a case of flaccid and ignoble negativity. Gladstone was perfectly willing to associate with Peel the achievements of the Whig administrations of Lord Grey, of Lord Melbourne, and of Lord John Russell. Though a political opponent, Gladstone could recognize their active good will and their reforming zeal. Above all, he could applaud the manner in which, as he saw it, they exerted themselves to inculcate distinct party lines and strong party discipline as the indispensable foundations of efficient governmental power. He was equally willing, conversely, to indict along with Palmerston Lord Derby's readiness as Peel's successor as Conservative leader to collude in dissolving party lines and in subverting party discipline; and, particularly, he was very ready to identify in Derby's henchman in the House of Commons, Benjamin Disraeli, the man who would be Palmerston's political inheritor in terms both of domestic flaccidity and reckless foreign adventure.

Thus, as Gladstone contemplated in 1865 the long-delayed and blessed departure of the unlamented Palmerston and his own elevation as the designated heir to the new prime minister, the veteran Lord Russell, he envisaged not so much an inauguration of new times as a retrieval of old times. He was indeed a very odd and idiosyncratic Liberal.

How was this so? In the intervening thirty-three years Gladstone's political life had been shaped by three profoundly formative influences. Most obvious, and well understood in the public domain, was his devotion to the principles and policies of Sir Robert Peel, prime minister in 1834–5 and 1841–6. Gladstone served Peel in both these ministries, and was brought by Peel into the Cabinet in 1843 as President of the Board of Trade. Secondly, there was Gladstone's discovery of 'the people' as a great resource of beneficent public energy to be mobilized and manipulated to good political ends. His excursions among the masses on Tyneside and Merseyside were matters of grave disquiet among the political classes. Not at all well understood in the public domain, but more profoundly formative than either, was Gladstone's Anglican Christianity: his unswerving conviction, whether as young Evangelical or mature High Churchman, of the manifest providential government of the world, and his growing sense of his own assigned role as an instrument, however unworthy, of God Almighty.

It was this Christian providentialism which was, primarily and ultimately, most significant in explaining the contours and courses of Gladstone's life. It was necessarily, in the nature of the case, occult: revealed in the privacy of his diaries, rarely alluded to in public. It would not be in fact until 1878 that Gladstone finally satisfied himself that the intimations he had received throughout his career hitherto of his accredited servitude to the 'deep and hidden agencies' of God's providential plan had accrued into an evident reality. But his awareness of those deep and hidden agencies had been of long existence. In the years before 1865 he was feeling his way as a Christian statesman determined to fulfil the will of God in Christ through political struggle, anxious all the while to discern correctly what that will was and to find the appropriate mode of action to realize it.

Gladstone asserted throughout his life that his true vocation was for the Church; he entered politics at his father's behest, not unwillingly, yet ever with an awareness that for him politics uninformed and undirected by religion would be a vain and futile exercise. He determined that he would consecrate his political career to an ideal of service to the Church. He set out the lineaments of this ideal in his book, *The State in Its Relations with the Church*, in 1838. He promised both himself and his closest ecclesiastical friends, James Hope-Scott and Henry Manning, that should this ideal turn out to be impractical, he would abandon politics and devote himself to service of the Church outside Parliament. When, however, that impracticality very soon became manifest, Gladstone never quite nerved himself to fulfil his undertaking to retire. Instead, he resigned with a certain emphatic deliberation from Peel's Cabinet in 1845 over the highly abstruse question of his own published doctrinal incompatibility with the government's policy of extending the subsidy to the Roman Catholic seminary at Maynooth, in Ireland. He determined, in effect, to stay in politics, as a churchman still, but serving religion through service of the state. The theological materials with which he constructed this golden bridge were supplied by Bishop Joseph Butler's *Analogy of Religion, Natural and Revealed, to the Constitution and Course of Nature* (1736). In 1845 Gladstone began work on an edition of Butler's works which he eventually completed and published in 1896: a life's effort dedicated to the theological lodestar of his political career.

The deep and hidden agencies which Gladstone sensed sustaining and directing that career were integrally linked to the surface phenomena which it exhibited. He was in no doubt that Peel's great ministry of 1841–6 had about it all the cogent marks of providential ordination. Working for Peel at the Board of Trade, amid the intricacies of tariffs and the fiscal revolution commenced in Peel's epochal budget of 1842 and consummated with the repeal of the Corn Law in 1846 and the inauguration of the era of free trade, was in Gladstone's estimation working to fulfil God's purposes. Peel was ever his mentor and master within this divine frame of reference. Gladstone's own epochal first budget of 1853 was modelled deliberately on Peel's precedent of 1842. The lessons Gladstone learned from Peel were those of masterful government and executive prerogative over Parliament. Above all, Gladstone learned from Peel the supreme lesson that the highest exigencies of the state might well require heroic sacrifice of the interests of party. Gladstone was to lead an often resentful and disaffected Liberal party very much in the imperious spirit he had observed in Peel's leadership of an often resentful and disaffected Conservative party. Peel's disgusted abdication of leadership in 1846 prefigured with an almost uncanny appositeness Gladstone's disgusted abdication of leadership in 1875. The great difference between Peel and his disciple Gladstone was that Gladstone discovered an immense political power outside Parliament by which

Parliament, and party, might eventually be brought politically to heel: 'the people'.

For Peel it had been a matter, as he explained to Prince Albert in 1850, of trusting to the 'quiet good sense and good feeling of the people' to provide a 'powerful instrument on which Executive government may rely for neutralising the mischievous energies of the House of Commons'.* Gladstone was to find such reliance on quiet good sense and good feeling of the people an inadequate resource. Nor would it be a matter merely of neutralizing parliamentary mischiefs. With Gladstone eventually it was going to be a matter of active and coercive manipulating and directing of noisy popular energies; of nothing short indeed, as his critics bitterly remonstrated, of 'demophilic' agitation and even intimidation.

Appropriately, Gladstone's first, rather trepid yet thrilling, encounter with the people en masse was at Manchester in 1853, when the city saluted the author of the great budget of that session by inviting him to inaugurate the statue of the late lamented Sir Robert Peel. Already Gladstone was rather giddily aware of ground shifting beneath him. At Naples in 1850 he had been jolted out of his habitually counter-revolutionary attitudes in foreign policy. Without relaxing in any essential degree his inherited Conservative loyalties or predispositions, Gladstone was starting to look to wider horizons. His first hope was that means to higher political ends might be supplied by the coalition government led by Peel's successor Aberdeen. He was devastated by the collapse of that hope under the cruel impact of the Crimea. From 1855 to 1859 Gladstone denounced Palmerston relentlessly as the political profiteer from the nation's calamity. He was even prepared to give the benefit of the doubt to Derby and Disraeli when they fortuitously and briefly replaced Palmerston in 1858–9.

Yet at the same time Gladstone was beginning to work at an alternative seam of political resource represented by his experience at Manchester. What Manchester taught Gladstone was that the fundamental terms of political trade in which he had been brought up were being turned upside down. When he first entered Parliament in 1832 government feared the people and was feared by them. Now it was becoming evident that the governed were reconciling themselves to government as a beneficent agency. For Gladstone that was the immense legacy attributable to Peel more than to any other. Through the 1850s into the 1860s Gladstone explored this new terrain of popular energies no longer subversive or dangerous, allowing renewed hopes for auspicious promises of a better age when those energies could be harnessed and directed by the right kind of leadership.

---

* N. Gash, *Sir Robert Peel* (1972), 673.

Meanwhile, in 1859, Gladstone was confronted by the wrong kind of leadership, in the person of the detestable Palmerston, offering him a return to the Exchequer in the first 'Liberal' ministry. In the vote of confidence which had led to the formation of that ministry Gladstone voted for Derby and Disraeli. Yet a few days later he was shamelessly installed once more at the Treasury under a premier he despised and deplored. Why? Derby and Disraeli had often enough tried to lure the Peelite Gladstone back to the body of the Conservative party. Gladstone could always find adventitious reasons for refusal. But the reason that really counted for him was that in the series of general elections which had taken place since 1846 the Conservative party had failed conspicuously to recover the confidence of the electorate. It could not be the foundation of the kind of energetic government Gladstone was in quest of. There was of course no energy to be had from Palmerston; yet Palmerston was old and could not last long. From any point of view joining Palmerston was a better bet than rejoining the Conservatives, hopelessly in a permanent minority and with the suspect Disraeli, only five years older than Gladstone, as their Leader in the Commons. Gladstone could conveniently find in the cause of Italy, the one issue on which he and Palmerston were agreed, a second golden bridge, over which he could cross from being a Conservative with dim prospects to being a Liberal with bright prospects.

This juncture requires attentive refinement and close definition. Gladstone became a kind of Liberal without renouncing his Peelite inheritance: a Peelite, in short, in Liberal guise. In due time Gladstone would declare that the first Liberal government of which he was a member was that of Lord Aberdeen in 1852–5. It was a matter of adaptation, not of conversion. He did not need Liberalism to teach him the merits of free trade. He did not need Liberalism to teach him the virtues of liberty not only for the Italians, but also for the Romanians (in the teeth of Palmerston's 'Crimean System'). He did not need Liberalism to formulate for him the key to the politics of the future, the articulation between executive potency and responsive opinion. The attraction of Liberalism for Gladstone was in essence that it offered him the only plausible prospect of Peelite government. He became a Liberal, in short, the better to be a Peelite. Once Palmerston was gone (he lasted obstinately long) there was the logic of joining with Russell, Palmerston's heir, to resuscitate a new version of the Aberdeen government.

While Palmerston doddered on certain things had to be done. One was to prepare appropriate policy. With his budgets of 1860–63 Gladstone substantially fulfilled the financial programme he had set out in 1853, with the one exception of failing to dispense with the income tax. Perhaps occasion would offer itself in the future for that. However that might be, a new stock in political trade had to be assembled. In those years in the early 1860s Gladstone presented himself on Tyneside and Merseyside to be saluted by the millions; their energies would be his means. The question of how these energies would be articulated to the machinery of politics and government suggested itself urgently. Hitherto Gladstone had been an enemy or a lukewarm friend to extension of the franchise. Peel had not been in need of it; and Gladstone regarded Russell's insistence on a second Reform Bill at the time of the Aberdeen government as merely a pointless obstacle in the way of his much more important financial plans. When Derby and Disraeli produced their anodyne Reform Bill in 1859 Gladstone supported it against the expansive amendments of Russell and John Bright. He still regarded Reform as an irrelevance, but was willing to accept a measure which preserved the influence of beneficial property in the counties and nomination seats in the boroughs if only to clear the issue away and leave room for more serious matters.

Once Gladstone cleared his own financial matters out of the way in 1863 the question of Reform took on a different aspect. The budget of 1853 Gladstone was to put into a category of providentially inspired insights generating in his mind a conviction that the 'materials' existed for 'forming a public opinion and directing it to a particular end'. Gladstone's great task now was to formulate the elements of the second in a series of 'insights' which would take upon itself the grandeur and ineluctability of that accreditation. Eventually, with considerable trepidation, he declared in 1865 that it would be the disestablishment of the Anglican Church of Ireland. This, he knew well, would involve a great heave in the body politic; it would be a very serious matter indeed. So serious would it be that he deprecatingly assured the shocked political classes that it would be a matter perhaps five or ten years distant. The necessary materials existing for forming a public opinion and for directing it to that particular end, the corresponding conviction wrought by his intentions upon the public mind, would require the harnessed energies of a public opinion and a public mind much more imposing than that needed for financial policy. Accordingly Gladstone had prepared the way in 1864 by declaring in principle – again, it was not a question lightly or wantonly to be entered upon – his willingness to admit a fitting proportion of the people into the 'pale of the constitution'.

Tentatively, thus, the keys to the future were formulated and proclaimed. Thus, also, the reading of Gladstone which emerges from this story of his first thirty-three years in politics is one which is studious first to reconnect and reintegrate his religion with his politics, and second, within that frame, to reallocate the component elements of his adaptation to a populist Liberalism as modified by his deeper abiding loyalties to his Peelite inheritance. What is hoped will come of this is a view which gives full and proper value to the stark singularity of his situation as a truly astonishing phenomenon in his time and among the political classes: wielding the mandate of heaven in an age of burgeoning democracy.

CHAPTER 1

'MAKING HISTORY': THE STRUGGLE FOR REFORM, 1865–6

[1]

In the autumn of 1865, as the political nation began to habituate itself to Palmerston's passing, Gladstone became more than ever the focus of intense speculation, partly in foreboding, partly in hope. As Lord Stanley had remarked, Gladstone had become 'the central figure in our politics'; and his importance was manifestly increasing rather than diminishing.[1]* The veteran Whig, Charles Wood, lamented on departing from Palmerston's funeral: 'Our quiet days are over; no more peace for us.' It was Wood who, after Gladstone's notorious 'pale of the constitution' declaration in 1864 on popular moral entitlement to the franchise, judged that, after Palmerston, Gladstone was 'inevitable, but most dangerous'.[2]† Wood and Lord Clarendon were notable among Gladstone's colleagues in making little scruple about letting their detestation of him be known. Perhaps a recrudescence of malicious rumours about Gladstone's 'benevolent nocturnal rambles' (in Clarendon's words)[3] was not to be wondered at. Sir John Acton, immensely hopeful about the intentions Gladstone had disclosed to him at Cliveden as to Ireland and the Catholics, wrote in November 1865 to his mentor Döllinger: 'Gladstone's standing is now very high, but I am expecting any day to hear that the dark stains in his private life, about which I once spoke to you, have been discovered; for I hear that men are lying in wait for him.' Acton feared that this 'might mean his downfall'.[4] As yet, however, Gladstone eluded his ambushers. His standing did not slip. There was a general if reluctant collegiate consensus about Gladstone: 'He must lead, there is no one who can compete with him, and yet his temper and restlessness make him entirely unfit.'[5] Clarendon's gloomy prediction – the 'inevitable political future' being Russell and Gladstone, with the latter having 'all the real power'[6] – now seemed on the point of realization.

---

* Stanley succeeded as fifteenth Earl of Derby in 1869.
† Wood created Viscount Halifax in 1866.

As for Russell, now at last emancipated from Palmerston's shadow as the nominal Whig chief, and about to undertake his second if rather lame tour as prime minister, the assumption was that the object of his career since 1850, a second Reform Act, must be his immediate concern. 'If Johnny is the man', Disraeli remarked, 'there will be a Reform Bill – very distasteful to the country. The truce of parties is over. I foresee tempestuous times, and great vicissitudes in public life.'[7] An expectation of Reform as the signal harbinger of new and better times was at the centre of the hopes of the 'advanced Liberals', the Radicals, the leaders and activists of social-political 'movement'. As early as 1861 John Bright had identified Gladstone as 'the man' destined 'to guide a wiser policy, and to teach a higher morality'.[8] Since that time, Gladstone's public deeds – his grand oratorical tours among the masses of Tyneside and Merseyside, his epochal statement about their moral entitlement to the vote, his portentous pointing to Ireland's ecclesiastical emancipation as the fittest work to which such an enfranchised popular energy should be set, his dismissal of the clerical and reactionary voters who had expelled him from Oxford University and his consequent advent 'unmuzzled' in industrious South Lancashire – seemed to provide ample evidence of a new order and a new evangel.

In reality, as to either hopes or forebodings, things were far from being as clear and straightforward as might appear on the surface. Gladstone had indeed sensed then the horizon enlarging, the sky shifting, about him. He had become aware of an 'age of shocks: a discipline so strong, so manifold, so rapid & whirling', that only when it was at an end could he hope to comprehend it.[9] He had indeed detected 'some better gleams of light' amid the lowering gloom of the later Palmerstonian epoch.[10] He had indeed expressed himself oracularly on the theme of the 'revenge' which the 'future' would wreak on what Oxford represented in the way of the culpable blindness of those who had eyes to read the signs of the times and who yet would not see. He had talked ominously of a great death or transmigration of spirit probably about to come in his political existence.[11]* He would before long be talking about having to connect himself 'with silent changes which are advancing in the very bed and basis of modern society'.[12] And, for practical purposes, above all, he had indeed declared himself to Russell, in accepting Russell's leadership and a place in his Cabinet, as being quite clear that any government now to be formed could not be wholly a continuation, but must be 'in some degree a new commencement'.[13]

Yet there are countervailing considerations. 'Wholly' and 'in some

---

* W. T. Stead was still puzzling over the deep meaning of this omen in 1892. There is no trace of any explanation by G.

degree' express them in a kind of adequate generality. But with Gladstone the specifics always have the greater explanatory weight. In the first place there are questions about readiness and preparation. Gladstone was surprised and disappointed by Palmerston's healthy majority in the 1865 general election. Gladstone had been in hopes of a modest and short-lived Conservative interval somewhat perhaps on the lines of the 1858–9 Derby ministry, for the continuance of which Gladstone had very deliberately voted at the opening of the new Parliament in 1859. He had now been for six years in strenuous office and badly felt the need of a recuperative break. He was quite sure that the political health of the Liberal party would benefit greatly from a spell in opposition. He was, in 1865, in fact, far from having a clear view of what his 'cause' or his 'followers' precisely consisted. He was far from trusting himself, especially in his new role as Leader of the Commons. He had but a tentative sense of the direction which a general advance would take. It was a question for him whether reorganization of the Treasury should take precedence of Reform. There would be memories of bitter conflict on that theme with Russell in 1853. Added to which are considerations as to the equivocality and ambiguity in many crucial respects of Gladstone's Liberalism and his relationship to the Liberal party.

When Gladstone, a refugee from Oxford, introduced himself to the electors of South Lancashire in 1865, he saluted what he persuaded himself was their industrious, enterprising, philanthropic, tolerant, and freedom-loving spirit; but at the same time he insisted that the primary duty incumbent upon the public men of England was 'the duty of establishing and maintaining the harmony between the past of our glorious country, and the future that is still in store for her'. Gladstone avowed being 'a member of a Liberal Government'. He avowed being 'in association with the Liberal party'. But he avowed equally that he had never swerved from what he conceived to be 'those truly Conservative objects and desires' with which he entered political life.[14] This was a Peelite declaration. It defined accurately what would be, solidly and consistently, the elements forming the matrix of Gladstone's politics for the rest of his life.

Such considerations in turn invite a retrospective reconsideration of what might be termed the specifics of the manner in which Gladstone in 1859 had trimmed himself from being a Conservative with dim prospects to being a Liberal with bright prospects. There were acute observers at that time, not unsympathetic, who commented on what seemed to be the 'secondary, and almost accidental, character of Gladstone's Liberalism'; who discerned an essentially adaptive quality about it.* That charac-

---

* For a discussion of this crux, see *Gladstone*, 168–9.

ter and quality stemmed from Gladstone's laying the foundations of his 'association with the Liberal party' on distinctly Peelite grounds. He set out his basic formula in 1856 when he identified the shape of future politics as an articulation between the executive power ('the doings and practical intentions of the minister') and the response to those doings and intentions from the people ('a corresponding conviction wrought by them upon the public mind').[15] Lord Aberdeen took the point perfectly when, in 1857, he advised Gladstone that 'in this age of progress the liberal party must ultimately govern the country'.[16] Liberalism clearly was where the 'public mind', 'opinion', was, and where the big political action was going to be; and therefore, again, where Gladstone would want to be.

There were yet deeper foundations, further back. For Gladstone his great budget of 1853 was the first occasion in which his 'doings and practical intentions' as minister of executive government wrought a corresponding conviction on the 'advanced intelligence' of the public mind, as represented most immediately in that case by Manchester. It was his first, rather thrilling, excursion among 'the *people*'.[17] In due time, in mature retrospect of his life, Gladstone would elevate that bright moment in 1853 as the first of a series by which a presumed 'striking gift' of 'insight' vouchsafed to him by divine providence led him to awareness that the 'materials' existed for 'forming a public opinion, and for directing it to a particular end'.[18] Such revelations would remain veiled and occult from public awareness. Yet both the causes and consequences of Gladstone's increasingly intense intercourse with the Almighty would, however incongruously, form part of the data bearing upon analyses of the 'secondary, and almost accidental' character of Gladstone's Liberalism.

They would have to do, in short, with ways of being a Liberal characterized most saliently by two fundamental premises. The first was a revised version of his doctrine of the 1840s, that while 'opinion' had power, it had not authority. In the 1840s the Tory Gladstone had feared opinion; now the Liberal Gladstone did not. 'I was brought up to dislike and distrust Liberty,' he remarked in 1891. 'I learned to believe in it. That is the key to all my changes.'[19] But it was also the key to things that did not change. For Gladstone, liberty made opinion bigger and better, but not the less to be formed and directed to ends not chosen by itself. No more later than earlier did Gladstone ever admit that the virtue and righteousness of the freedom-loving people was translatable into directive popular political prerogative. His position invariably was that virtue and righteousness and love of freedom were the energizing forces in popular materials available to him on occasions defined by him, to be formed, mobilized, manipulated, and directed for purposes also defined by him. He was always clear that the nature of the popular vote would be moral and ethical rather than intellectual.[20] He had put that point accurately on the lovability of the people after his speaking tour in 1864: 'God knows I have not courted them: I hope I do not rely on them: I pray I may turn them to account for good.'[21]

Gladstone's second premise bore upon his view of the status and function of party in politics, with special reference to the Liberal party. Gladstone was ever a disciple of Peel in this respect as in others. From this point of view it might well be said that party was relegated by them both to a 'secondary, and almost accidental', status in politics. As Gladstone succinctly put it in 1877, party was the 'instrument by which a great work is to be carried out'.[22] This 'instrumental' view of party was quite essentially Peelite. The treatment the Liberal party was to get at Gladstone's hands in the later nineteenth century had distinct affinities with the treatment the Conservative party got at Peel's hands in the earlier nineteenth century. Gladstone's predisposition to a high view of executive prerogative was notorious; his bent to hector and drive had led to a crisis in the Commons in 1860. Already there was much complaint among Gladstone's colleagues of his being overbearing and dictatorial beyond even what was allowed to men of his unquestioned eminence. Where Gladstone differed from Peel was in his coming to have a charismatic or 'priest-king' role in the popular political culture, a 'leadership of the nation' and an effective control of party 'out of doors', which Peel never had.[23] Gladstone's genius was to instrumentalize the Liberal party into being the hinge which articulated his doings and intentions as minister to the corresponding conviction wrought by them upon the popular mind. The Liberal party, like the public mind, would never be consulted by Gladstone as to what his doings and intentions should be. His very idiosyncratic Liberalism, made all the more idiosyncratic by his conviction of an assigned providential vocation, would make him in many ways a very problematic Liberal.

To these considerations of preparation and readiness, equivocation and ambiguity, must be added, in 1865, some attention to Gladstone's sense of the relationship to his recent experiences in the past of the political issues confronting him in the immediate future. The financial vocation which he had inaugurated in 1853 he declared substantially fulfilled in 1863, with one reservation as to eventual repeal of the income tax. That the two issues on which he now thought 'action possible' were franchise reform and dealing with the Irish Church establishment was well known.[24] On the face of it, with Palmerston's departure, the way seemed clear. Moreover, Russell, the new prime minister, had been a good enemy to the Irish ecclesiastical establishment since the 1830s and a good friend to an extension of the Reform Act of 1832 since the 1850s.

Surely Gladstone's prospects were of a brilliance unprecedented in the nineteenth century? Peel, Free Trade, and the great works of state in Gladstone's own budgets of 1853 and 1860 had achieved the greatest fact yet of the times: the conciliation of the governed with government. Those words and that fact had borne their fruits, manifested famously on the Mersey and the Tyne, constituting a mighty new social and political popular energy. How could it be otherwise than that he was appointed to form and direct such materials to his declared ends? A new generation, emancipated yet appreciative of the beneficence of its political heritage, was correspondingly responsive to the claims of that heritage for loyalty and deference. Gladstone could well be excused for seeing himself on the verge of presiding over a grand synthesis of cause and effect.

All that was true enough; but Gladstone also had painful memories of earlier times when things had looked invitingly propitious, only to be betrayed by circumstances. Peel's great ministry of 1841 was ever for Gladstone the model of heroically commanding government. Yet its catastrophic end still gave pause after twenty years. The fortunes of the attempt to resuscitate that commanding model in the form of the Aberdeen coalition – 'the first Liberal Cabinet to which I belonged'[25] – gave even more pause. In 1857 Gladstone had congratulated himself immoderately on the definitive political exit of the detestable Palmerston, only to find himself two years later trapped into Palmerston's harness, with little to do but wait for the coming of better times. One can readily read into Gladstone's obsessive and almost hysterical love affair during these years with the Arthurian symbolism of Tennyson's *Idylls of the King* a kind of emotional compensation for his undergoing the dark night of Palmerstonism.[26]

Yet even now when better times were at last come Gladstone still had to attend to ungrateful circumstances. The damage the Liberal party had done to itself in its grapplings with the Irish Church in the 1830s was very much in his mind as he contemplated a fresh bout of hostilities. Gladstone had spent most of his political life only too keenly aware of that bristling question, and keeping a prudent distance from it. Very much the same cautionary imperative applied to the Reform question. It had helped to wreck Russell's first ministry. It had destabilized Aberdeen's ministry. Palmerston had evaded it only by surprise electoral victory in 1857 and then by surprise parliamentary defeat in 1858. Derby and Disraeli discredited their ministry by failing to secure it in 1859. And for all Palmerston's repressive talents, it persisted, in 1860, 1864, and 1865, in disturbing the peace of his last years. The attitude Gladstone took in 1859, supporting the Derby–Disraeli bill against radical amendments proposed by Russell and Bright, was entirely applicable to his attitude in 1865: it was a question containing 'all the elements of a false position'. On the one hand, the 'good sense and practical turn' of the English people suggested confidence in a 'tolerable solution'. But on the other, 'what ministries it will scatter on its road may be very uncertain'.[27] It was by no means clear to Gladstone, quite apart from his own personal equivocal 'Liberal-Conservatism', that Bright's contention of 1861 that 'Towns and great populations' would be a match for the 'traditions of the last century', was an accurate assertion about 1865. Gladstone was anything but an impatient and eager reformer in 1865-6. And not the least of the elements of a false position now was that in 1865 a new Parliament was elected without the slightest reference, allusion, veiled commitment or shrouded mandate on the part of responsible ministers to the effect that in any sense or time it was bound to undertake Reform.

[2]

All the same, Russell's first act after kissing hands on undertaking the government was 'to tell the Queen that he would want to bring in a Reform Bill, and his second was to tell Gladstone that it would be a life or death question'.[28] Gladstone later assured the Commons as evidence of bona fides that ministers gathered in the first cabinet after the death of their 'lamented leader' agreed that they would prepare a Reform bill to be introduced without any arts of delay. As designated Leader of the Commons, Gladstone was assured by Russell that 'the most frequent and unreserved communications must take place between us – such as always took place between Lord Grey and Lord Althorp, and between Lord Melbourne and me'.[29] In fact, Whig clannishness made Russell prone to confide more readily with his connections in the cousinhood than with Gladstone;[30] but the important point in their new relationship was that both men were studious to avoid any recurrence of their old quarrels. Russell's handing over the Foreign Office to Clarendon removed the only likely impediment to their entente. Russell and Gladstone were now on converging political tracks. If Reform was to be the great thing, that convergence would consist essentially in foisting Reform on a largely unwilling Liberal party in a largely hostile House of Commons.

The Reform issue became entangled with the problem of party unity, which in turn became entangled with the problem of filling ministerial places. Clarendon had vacated the Duchy of Lancaster. If foisting was to be the order of the day, some tactful management would be requisite. Would it not be politic to placate one of the leaders among the Liberals who had in 1865 joined with the Conservatives to defeat Baines's Borough

Franchise Bill?[31] Russell favoured Horsman; Gladstone, together with Granville and Wood, preferred Lowe. Gladstone also pressed Russell to attract Derby's heir, Stanley, across from the Conservatives as a gesture to sustaining the 'truce of parties'. There was talk of Russell's asking Gladstone to stand down from the leadership in favour of Grey, in the interests of tact and management; but Gladstone could not see it that way. John Bright was a big problem. Now that the 'reign of humbug' had ended with Palmerston's death,[32] he did not have Cobden's excuse for refusing ministerial place. On the other hand, even if he could be induced, his presence inside might do more harm to the cause of Reform than his agitation outside. Gladstone thought he might be feasible for the Duchy, but was more concerned to keep his distance and deprecate public notions of a Gladstone–Bright partnership leading the way to better times. In the end it was agreed to leave the place vacant for the time being. Then Chichester Fortescue's promotion to the Irish Office* left the Colonial Under-Secretaryship available. Russell, who had vetoed Bright, was willing to accept Gladstone's advocacy of the pro-Reform 'advanced' Liberal W. E. Forster as a kind of Bright-substitute.

Gladstone, meanwhile, had his hands full. Not only would there be no blessed repose from office, as he had hoped: now, piled on top of his responsibilities at the Exchequer and his Leadership responsibilities, was to be responsibility for framing the Reform measure. Before the formidable sequence of November cabinets he squeezed in a visit to Scotland. In Glasgow he was honoured with the freedom of the city. In Edinburgh he delivered his valedictory address as Rector of the University, in which he took the opportunity to expand his old Homeric theme of the place of the ancient Greeks 'in the Providential order, aye, and in the Evangelical Preparation, as truly and really as the children of Abraham themselves'. As ever, Gladstone was studious to connect the ancient and the modern; to trace in the ancient world not only evidences of the Evangelical Preparation and providential purpose but evidences also bearing directly on the controversies of his own time about science and faith.

And therefore it is well that we should look out over the field of history, and see if haply its records, the more they are unfolded, do or do not yield us new materials for the support of faith. Some at least among us experience has convinced that, just as fresh wonder and confirmed conviction flow from examining the structure of the universe, and its countless inhabitants, and

---

* Fortescue had been Colonial Under-Secretary 1857–8, 1859–65; reputed, as husband of Lady Waldegrave, to have 'dined his way into the Cabinet'. Created Lord Carlingford in 1874.

their respective adaptations to the purposes of their being and to the use of man, the same results will flow in yet larger measure from tracing the footmarks of the Most High in the seemingly bewildered paths of human history.[33]

Even after omitting '40 or 45 minutes worth of matter', his lecture lasted two hours. 'And so ends, apparently, my Academic life.'[34]

Back in the seemingly bewildered paths of human history in Whitehall there was for Gladstone the annoyance of Austrian unreasonableness in negotiations for a commercial treaty. True to his instinctive Austrophobia, Gladstone was all for a 'peremptory' response, rather in the hope that the matter would be abandoned. A cabinet on 1 December was 'chiefly on Jamaican horrors & on U.S. correspondence'. News was coming in of the grisly consequences of Governor Eyre's stern repression of an alleged insurrection of former Negro slaves. Gladstone told Argyll that the intelligence was so 'horrible and sickening' that 'one hopes against hope that some of it is fabulous'.[35] Dining at the sculptor Woolner's on 8 December, Gladstone found himself in conflict on the issue with Tennyson. Gladstone condemned Eyre for needless and illegal brutality; Tennyson defended him as dealing faithfully with a savage mob. The intellectual fault-line opened by the shock of the Jamaica case took on a public dimension in the agitation and counter-agitation it engendered, with J. S. Mill versus Thomas Carlyle to the fore. Their arguments for and against legal and moral absolutism and *raison d'état* aligned with the intellectual debate over the American Civil War, and prefigured in many ways the issues raised in the much more extensive public excitement over the 'Bulgarian horrors' of 1876.[36]

The American correspondence also prefigured events in the 1870s with a very direct bearing on Gladstone's political fortunes. As one recent visitor to the United States had put it to Gladstone (being assured that Gladstone would 'not shrink from hearing that you have yourself become an object of unpopularity and obloquy among the Americans'), the United States government really did intend to press its demand for compensation from Britain for the depredations inflicted by the *Alabama* and the other Confederate commerce-raiders let loose by British negligence during the Civil War.[37]* This was the beginning of what was to prove a fraught and wearisome negotiation.

The fraught and wearisome negotiation immediately confronting Gladstone was trying to get the details of Reform straight. The bill, as in 1832, would be for England and Wales. Separate subsequent bills were envisaged for Scotland and Ireland. A meeting of the Home Office on

* G was being plagued at this time by forgeries representing him to have been a subscriber to Confederate war loans.[38]

22 November on 'Reform Information' started detailed work. Uniformly reliable and extensive figures and statistics were never to be available, bedevilling the whole operation. There were many who had a view to influencing Gladstone. Milner Gibson, the token Radical in the Cabinet, was one who got in early.

I rather liked old Henley's notion of a franchise qualification i.e. Household franchise. I think people are tired of the rental franchise of £6, £8 and the like. Household franchise with the proper qualification of payment of rates, length of residence etc. would give a good constituency, and the idea is thoroughly English of the settled heads of families being voters.[39]

Gibson was certainly correct in supposing that public and parliamentary patience would soon wear thin over rental or ratal scholastics. 'Household suffrage' was also urged by Forster. He and Gibson went to see Gladstone, who let Forster talk 'as much', as Forster ruefully recorded, 'as he lets anyone; but he does as much of the talking as Johnny [Russell] does little'. Forster 'went over the reform question with him, up and down, and I think he really took in what I said'.[40] This episode can be seen as a kind of microcosmic exemplar of the shape of things to come in 1866 and 1867: Gladstone talked rather than listened. What Gladstone did not take in, then or ever, was the expediency of the householder criterion. When it came to rental or ratal scholastics, no one could surpass him.

In that time of 1865, the idea of a householder franchise was associated dangerously with John Bright, who held it to be the ancient privilege of the English folk. When, in December, Russell finally abandoned his efforts to appease Whig doubters and denied their demands for an evasive commission of inquiry, he settled for a reduction of the £10 borough rateable-value level set in 1832 to £6 as the point of equilibrium on the franchise calibration where the resisters and the advancers would be politically balanced. There would be a measure of lateral extension of the 'beneficial property' franchise in the counties to offset the new weight of 'heads'. There would be a modest degree of redistribution of seats. This seemed a prudent calculation when Bright was agitating the country on Reform, appealing, as he did at Birmingham, to that 'auguster thing' than Parliament or Crown, 'the almost voiceless millions of my countrymen'.[41] The £6 level was transmitted to Gladstone as the datum for his considerations; and so began the long comedy of the quest for the golden lip on the rating-rental ratchet. Gladstone was already conscious of difficulties about rating figures, which varied from place to place. And he soon became aware of even greater difficulties about the £6 level. Such estimates as he could fairly calculate suggested that £6 might prove dangerously democratic.

At Hawarden over the Christmas season Gladstone worried away at this problem. It did not crowd out entirely his usual concerns and avocations. There were further anxious compilations about the burdens of purchasing the reversion of the Hawarden estate from Sir Stephen Glynne. Calculations of the value of real property, credits, stocks and shares, and unproductive personalty, less debts, obligations, and funds for charity and religion, left Gladstone with a surplus balance of £270,000 as at 31 December 1865;[42] but of this only £125,000 was clear capital available for the heavy undertaking. The intellectual point of substance was reading the anonymous and rather scandalous *Ecce Homo,* a life of Jesus interpreting His public career as a grand exercise in the science of politics. Startled, but not repelled, Gladstone detected 'a vitality, an earnestness, an eloquence, a power, all of them derived from the deep and overflowing life of the wondrous Figure which it contemplates and sets forth'. Given his own theological adventurousness with the ancient Greeks, Gladstone was better placed than most believers to welcome such a work as salutary in times when there was a disposition either to deny outright the authority of the Christian Church or to slight it silently and pass by. Gladstone particularly mentioned the new popular edition of Strauss's *Leben Jesu* as a deplorable case in point.[43] In his retrospect of the year, Gladstone marked the passing of 'another gift of God, an allotment of precious time, wherein to work out His will and our own discipline and salvation'. After church on the morning of 9 January he set off for London. 'Vale! May that calm holy atmosphere abide around me.'

The atmosphere abiding in the capital was anything but calm and holy. The first shock on arriving at Carlton House Terrace ('Saw, before I reached home, not less than 5 or 6 faces of much beauty, all astray') was news that Russell, with all his old 'rapidity', had lost patience with the toilsome negotiations over the Duchy of Lancaster place, and peremptorily appointed G. J. Goschen. An import from the world of banking and finance, Goschen was a backbencher of only three years' standing. It was a deliberate snub to the recalcitrant Whigs; already shocked by Russell's frequenting Bright's society at Woburn and Chesham Place, and who now were even more offended at the passing over of their candidate for promotion, Lord Hartington. Gladstone thought the Prime Minister's 'precipitancy amounts to a disease'.[44] Such was the fuss that in the end Russell had to reshuffle the Cabinet to slot Hartington in at the War Office. Soreness among Russell's colleagues made the pre-sessional cabinets even more strained affairs than ever. Gladstone produced his memorandum on the £6 borough franchise.

Meanwhile Gladstone was determined to avoid getting Reform entangled with Redistribution. '*Why* is a good enfranchisement to be condemned unless with a good redistribution?' he demanded of one of the advocates of combination.

We have an Opposition of say 290. Suppose Mr Lowe and Mr Horsman with their tail to be only 10. That gives 300. Then suppose we have only a Schedule B, taking one member from each of 30 boroughs. How do you suppose the votes of the 60 Representatives of those Boroughs will go? What margin will remain for carrying a Bill?[45]

Most of Gladstone's colleagues supported this stand, though Russell always held to the model of 1832. Redistribution would offer a wider target to Reform's enemies or false friends. Bright and his friends 'out of doors' mainly agreed. Redistribution would be better done by the new Parliament. To persistent complaint that without Redistribution the government's plan lacked a vital component, Gladstone struck back robustly:

With regard to [a] thorough general approach, I will at once say boldly the case does not admit of it. Cherubim and Seraphim, if they had to frame a Bill, could not obtain it, in the present state of things. If the Government show: 1. Care. 2. Courage, and the party: 1. Forbearance. 2. Loyalty (and of these last I have little doubt) we may come through; but at the best be with some wry faces, some shrugging of shoulders, and divers hairbreadth scapes.[46]

Another memorandum to the Cabinet Committee on Reform from Gladstone in February dealt with the counties and with a variety of refinements for the boroughs. But what was by now exercising the Cabinet's attention were the stark implications seemingly emerging from the £6 level. It would appear that out of 440 boroughs in England and Wales 260 would be materially dominated by working-class 'occupier' voters. The 'balance of the constitution' would be upset. The level was promptly raised to £7.

By this time the first session of the 1865 Parliament was well launched. Gladstone did his best as Leader to 'conciliate' the Commons, as he had promised Harriet Sutherland he would.[47]* He was preparing legislation also on the vexed Church Rates question (a tea party with a 'conclave of Dissenters' at Newman Hall's on 25 January suggested to Gladstone that 'the teeth and claws are not very terrible').† Gladstone actually

---

* The Queen wrote to G on 19 February of her gratification 'at the accounts she hears from all sides of the admirable manner in which he has commenced his Leadership of the House of Commons'.[48]
† But G was presumably not aware that the aggressive Edward Miall was carefully not invited.[49]

missed the reading of the Speech from the Throne ('Hustled out of the Speaker's Courtage and unable to reach the House of Lords'), which informed Lords and Commons that their attention would be called 'with a view to such improvements in the laws which regulate the Rights of Voting in the Election of Members of the House of Commons as may tend to strengthen our free institutions and conduce to the Public Welfare'.

As Leader Gladstone threaded his way carefully through such preliminary matters as Cattle Plague and Jamaica scandals. He spoke on Irish disturbances, on the dangers of Fenianism in America, and defended the suspension of habeas corpus in Ireland. He announced a renewed legislative effort to reconcile Irish Roman Catholicism to an improved system of unsectarian higher education. Chief Secretary Fortescue would introduce legislation to ameliorate the relations between Irish landlords and tenants. There was the 'delicate duty' of provision for Princess Helena's marriage and Prince Alfred's settlement on becoming Duke of Edinburgh. Then there was the 'far more delicate and difficult one of the Speech on Lord Palmerston'. Given Gladstone's deep-rooted antipathy to the subject of his memorial tribute, it is perhaps not surprising that he received no acknowledgement from the widowed Lady Palmerston ('Not a word of Lord P. One or two allusions of mine fell dead').[50]

A cabinet on 8 March 'settled after discussion but with harmony the final form of the main points of our Bill'. Gladstone introduced the Reform Bill on 12 March to a Commons chamber 'much crowded both with members and strangers' and buzzing with curiosity.[51] Ministers had in view enfranchising some 400,000 new voters, half of them of the skilled labouring class, in order to lay the political foundations of the nation on a broader and more secure foundation. The principal mechanisms would be a £7 borough occupier rating and a £14 county rating. Gladstone could not avoid explaining the change from the original £6 level, since that figure featured in some earlier draft versions of the bill. He made an anti-democratic virtue of this necessity. His tone on the whole was indeed apologetic, congruent with the expectations he had sketched as to wry faces, shrugging of shoulders, and divers hairbreadth scapes to come. He dwelt on the wreckage of earlier bills littering the political landscape. He pleaded with the House not to see this bill as a 'Trojan horse approaching the walls of the sacred city, and filled with armed men, bent upon ruin, plunder, and conflagration'. 'I believe that those persons whom we ask you to enfranchise ought rather to be welcomed as you would recruits to your army or children to your family.' It was a bill which comprehended the 'just limits of prudence and circumspection'; it accorded with the 'beneficent process of the law of nature and of Providence'; it was a boon which would be 'reciprocated in grateful attachment' of the people to the throne.[52]

Wry faces, shrugging shoulders, and threats of hairbreadth scapes to come quickly assumed the form of hostile notices of amendments. Most notable among them was one from Lord Grosvenor, heir to the Westminster marquessate and a prominent Liberal member, regretting that the government's 'whole scheme', including proposals for redistribution, was not before the House. He was seconded by Lord Stanley, from the Conservative front bench. This was immediately taken to be an ominous shot across Gladstone's bow.

Then came the series of debates which made the 1866 session illustrious in parliamentary annals. Roundell Palmer, the Attorney-General, judged them 'remarkable as a display of intellectual power'.[53] Gladstone, after recovery from a somewhat recessive opening, he thought 'magnificent'. Bright emerged 'a great humorist as well as an orator'. Bright's sally at Horsman, one of the leading recalcitrants, as a skulker in the 'political cave of Adullam', where gathered 'everyone that was in distress, and everyone that was discontented',[54] coined two new terms in the political currency: 'cave' for a dissident group in a party, and 'Adullamite' for the particular group of Liberal dissidents in 1866 and 1867. John Stuart Mill was, in Gladstone's estimate, 'admirable'. But it was one of the most prominent Adullamites, Robert Lowe, who raised his reputation most conspicuously. He launched two powerful and brilliant assaults on the bill which took the Commons by storm.

Lowe's central point was simple: virtue, morality, justice and right had no bearing whatever on the franchise question; it was consequences that mattered, not motives; 'it is purely a question of State policy'.[55] In terms of beneficial political consequences, the existing franchise answered all requirements. Gladstone recorded some 'lively skirmishing' on 23 March, when he counter-attacked Lowe's notorious invective about democratic venality, ignorance, and drunkenness with admonitions that they were not talking of an invading army, they were talking of 'our fellow-subjects, our fellow-Christians, our own flesh and blood'.[56] Lowe made himself vulnerable by his provocative, oligarchic ferocity; but Gladstone equally exposed himself to charges of sentimental cant and enquiries as to how it was that flesh and blood ceased to obtain below the £7 ratchet lip.

[3]

The Easter recess was now at hand. Gladstone had matters other than Reform to attend to. He introduced, as a private member, his Compulsory Church Rates Abolition Bill, as the 'best practical solution' to a long-running irritation not only between Church and Dissent but among churchmen.[57] He aimed to restore churches in urban areas to the control of churchmen in return for surrendering non-Church income. This problem was to prove far more troublesome than he bargained for. The imminent budget was not likely in itself to be troublesome except as yet another battle in his long war of attrition against rising public expenditure. It was in accordance with that policy of attrition that Gladstone in 1866 was a party to smuggling through the renewal of the 1864 Contagious Diseases Act. That act provided for compulsory medical inspection of prostitutes in dockyard and garrison towns. Gladstone approved it on expedient grounds: the cost of non-prevention of venereal disease added enormously to the services estimates.[58] He was to find himself, once Josephine Butler's agitation to repeal the act got under way, accused embarrassingly of condoning both prostitution and scandalously oppressive policing.

It was, however, a brush with Lord Clarence Paget, Secretary of the Admiralty, on the naval estimates, which raised an issue of more long-term significance. Gladstone insisted on reductions in peremptory terms which harked back to the times of his skirmishes with Palmerston. But far more resonantly they presaged and anticipated the issue of his break with his colleagues and his final resignation in 1894.

To present an increase to the New Parlt. in the present circs. of the world, & especially viewing what America is about, wd. be an affirmation in substance that our present state of naval Expre. is really normal . . . I believe we shall become deeply responsible to the world if we continue to set other ctries the example wh. our enormous naval force now places before them.[59]

Willingness so resolutely to recur to the challenges with which he had so often affronted Palmerston was not, however, matched by readiness on Gladstone's part to recur to his challenge to Palmerston in 1858 on the question of Romanian freedom. The Romanians, led by Bratiano, were now braving the Ottoman suzerainty by preparing to elect as hereditary prince Charles of Hohenzollern, and hoped to enlist Gladstone's moral support for their cause. Gladstone's response was not at all a prevision of the spirit of his advocacy of Bulgarian freedom in 1876. It was, rather, entirely in line with his reluctant compliance to pressure from Palmerston and Brand, the Whip, in 1863, to defend the status quo of the 'Crimean System'.[60] His tone in 1866 was entirely consistent. His motives, at one level, were transparent. The last thing he could afford to do was to provoke more wry faces and shrugging shoulders from among those many 'moderate' Palmerstonians and Whiggish men in his party susceptible to Adullamite lures. Gladstone announced flatly to the

Commons that he was 'not here to declare any departure from the policy which the British Government has heretofore pursued with regard to the Eastern question'. The best he could do for Bratiano was to offer some equivocal remarks on hopes that the local institutions of the principalities might be developed in accordance with the well-ascertained opinions of their inhabitants.[61]

What is most interesting at this point is Gladstone's feeling the need to wrap his decidedly grudging response within a curious kind of moral doctrine of the positive benefits of not being independent. Here there are echoes of Gladstone's preference in 1859 that Lombardy-Venetia become devolved within an Italian framework under Austrian suzerainty on the model of the Ottoman suzerainty of the Danubian principalities.[62] There is even a distant glimmer of Irish Home Rule. It is possible that certain disillusioning aspects of the experience of independent Italy may have prompted Gladstone's advice to Bratiano on the theme of peaceful progress.

In no instance can this desire I think be more natural and suitable than in the case of the Danubian Principalities: where the relation to the Ottoman Porte established by the public law of Europe entails as I trust and believe no danger and no impediment either to the attainment of material prosperity or to the development of political freedom in all the points of practical self-government: while it ought to relieve them from much of the burden of an absolute independence, and from those heavy charges which are so burdensome and even so perilous, to young states, and yet which as we see young states find it difficult to avoid.[63]

The insurrectionary Cretans were to get nothing less grudgingly bleak from Gladstone in 1867* than the Romanians perforce had to make the best of in 1866. It is likely that Gladstone's recent bruising experiences with respect to the American Civil War reinforced the exigencies he felt pressing upon him from the large Palmerstonian constituency in the Liberal party to inhibit adventures in foreign policy. Certainly, as things turned out, a new initiative on the 1858 model would have to wait until 1876.

---

* See below, page 31.

[4]

The Easter recess found Gladstone, after a refreshing break at Brighton, among his constituents in Liverpool. There he was tempted into an adventurous 'out of doors' manner, somewhat in the style of John Bright. Lowe's astonishing success in the Commons nettled and disconcerted him. Nor was it merely a matter of Adullamites. The Conservative party, hitherto reserved and waiting to see how things would go, was now in the field, openly hostile, with visions of the larger possibilities suggested by a replay of the 1865 combination against Baines's bill. Disraeli, impressed also by Lowe's impact on the Commons, and by the evident extent to which Grosvenor was prepared to go, turned away from notions of a compromise Reform settlement towards ambitions to do damage – perhaps mortal – to Liberal unity and Gladstone's prospects. Clearly Gladstone could not rely simply upon the 'forbearance' and 'loyalty' of his party to see him through. What he decided to do was to summon the genius of the people, as represented by Liverpool, to put Parliament straight. For all that Argyll and Goschen were present as tokens of public decorum, Gladstone's populist purpose was unapologetic, constituting the first occasion on which a responsible minister directly agitated public support for a measure being considered in Parliament.[64]

In a general perspective of Gladstone's later career, the Liverpool episode in 1866 simply establishes itself as a premonitory anticipation of what was to become Gladstone's grand formula of political action: the imposition of his will as 'leader of the nation' over the will of his parliamentary party in particular and of Parliament in general.[65] At the time it was merely a scandal. The seismic shock was palpable. John Bright had often enough menaced Parliament from 'out of doors'; but this was the Chancellor of the Exchequer and the Leader of the House of Commons. Gladstone's rhetoric at Liverpool on 5 and 6 April blazed with images of unswerving fixity of purpose: Rubicon crossed, bridges broken, boats burned. The words that caused most offence were Gladstone's regret that two great names honoured among the aristocracy – Grosvenor and Stanley – should be setting up impediments to the popular will, possibly with results ultimately detrimental to their order, and his summoning the people to vindicate 'not only a fitness but in a moral sense a right' against Lowe. 'It is not in our power to secure the passing of the measure: that rests with you', Gladstone confided to his enthusiastically responsive audience, 'and more with those whom you represent, and of whom you are a sample, than it does with us.'[66]

Back at Westminster, Gladstone retreated in a flurry of deprecatory assertions of innocence of any intent to intimidate. In the Commons he moved the second reading of his Reform Bill on 12 April with much more restrained rhetoric. He was nervous of the Conservatives. He declared his motive to be to avoid all issues either of party or of class. He would be studious to avoid 'any statement of principle, any argument, any suggestion, any reference to the past, which could in any manner raise even so much as a flutter of hostile emotion on the part of Gentlemen who sit opposite'. He denied that his Liverpool speeches were direct responses to Lowe in the Commons. 'I beseech you to be wise; and, above all, to be wise in time.'[67]

Lowe seized eagerly on the provocation offered by Gladstone at Liverpool's 'inappropriately named Philharmonic Hall'. It was idle and absurd for Gladstone to 'pretend that the influence of agitation was not resorted to', and it was not the fault of some of those who took part in that agitation that it did not 'develop into an influence of terrorism'. Gladstone had given explanations to the people of Liverpool he had not deigned to give to the House of Commons. He had returned thither and delivered 'a languid *rechauffe* [*sic*] of the arguments of Liverpool; and thus the baked meats of the Philharmonic Hall did coldly furnish forth the tables of the House of Commons'.[68]* Lowe, as defender of the dignity and independence of the House of Commons against Gladstone's threats, did good service to his cause as enemy of Gladstone's bill.

The particular danger of the Grosvenor–Stanley amendment was its ostensibly being not hostile to Reform in principle; and by dragging in Redistribution it provided pretext and cover for a good many Liberals to break ranks. They could always cite Russell's authority and the sacred model of 1832. Brand, the Chief Whip, warned Gladstone of ominous instances of backsliding. While still expecting to win a second reading, Brand told Clarendon: 'You will be shocked at some of the names scored as voting against us.'[69] Gladstone himself pleaded with the veteran Peelite, Lord Ernest Bruce, invoking the shade of Sir Robert: '*every man* who shared his labours, who possessed his confidence to the end of his life, who knew his mind, has recommended and supported larger measures of extension than those which we now bring forward'.[70] Russell ordered capitulation. Redistribution would immediately be introduced. The true character of Grosvenor's amendment was revealed when he declined implacably to withdraw it.

One of Gladstone's flanks was now turned. Disraeli launched his charge. He extolled the 'English spirit' of the constitution as against the spirit of the American constitution. He incautiously extolled Gladstone's

* It was actually G's second speech, on 6 April, at the Amphitheatre, at which he spoke 'wholly on the Bill'.

speech as a passionate young Tory against the first Reform Bill at the Oxford Union in 1831. More slyly, he extolled the late, lamented Sir George Cornewall Lewis, who, had he lived to succeed Lord Palmerston as Leader of the Commons, would not have counselled the Whigs 'to reconstruct their famous institutions on the American model'.[71] This, in the context both of Lowe's unforgiving invective and Grosvenor's unforgiving 'Adullamry', provoked from Gladstone one of his supreme oratorical performances.

In his diary for 27 April Gladstone recorded: 'Spoke from 1 to past 3 following D. It was a toil beyond my strength: but I seemed somehow to be sustained and borne onwards I knew not how.' Here Gladstone referred obliquely to his earlier commendation of the bill as integral to a 'beneficent process of the law of nature and of Providence'. Gladstone's sense of his being sustained and fortified by a higher, unworldly power, for a purpose congruent with 'that great and all-embracing plan for the rearing and training of the human children of our Father in heaven, which we call the Providential Government of the world',[72] would become increasingly a theme of his diary commentaries and self-analysis. Certainly, for this high moment of almost desperate political crisis, it fuelled powerfully his rebarbative talents. He mocked Disraeli's 'American' argument. It was absurd to contend that in a country of five million adult males an additional 200,000 middle class and a mere 200,000 respectable artisan voters were the materials for reconstructing the constitution on 'American principles'. He denied that the Cabinet was in thrall to Bright. He defended his Liverpool speeches. He withered Lowe. As to Disraeli's taunts at the 'political errors of my boyhood', his response was devastating. He apologized for having been at that time 'bred under the shadow of the great name of Canning'. 'I grant my youthful mind and imagination were impressed with the same idle and futile fears which still bewilder and distract the mature mind of the right hon. Gentleman.'

There were touching, but also in a curious way revealing, words comparing his relationship to the Liberal party with Russell's (to which Disraeli had invidiously alluded). Gladstone allowed that his position in regard to the Liberal party was 'in all points the opposite of Earl Russell's'. 'I am too well aware of the relations which subsist between the party and myself. I have none of the claims he possesses. I came among you an outcast from those with whom I associated, driven from them, I admit, by no arbitrary act, but by the slow and resistless forces of conviction.' The classical tag from Virgil with which Gladstone illustrated this point was perhaps infelicitous. Aeneas, shipwrecked on Carthage shore, turned out not to be a lucky find for those who rescued and succoured him. And that Gladstone should then proceed to preface his peroration with an invocation of Peel was highly characteristic, but again not without its aspect of infelicity. 'Elevate your vision', was his Peelite text for the benefit of the sulky ranks of his adopted party. They must understand 'the enormous and silent changes which have been going forward among the labouring population'. The working classes were not adequately represented 'in proportion to their intelligence, their virtue, or their loyalty'. Gladstone pointed to the 'magnificent moral spectacle' of working-class fortitude in Lancashire at the time of the cotton-famine distress. He urged the House to see that they were now 'making history', laying the foundations of much that was to come. This battle for Reform was the same battle as that for removing civil disability for religious opinions; as that for the first Reform Act; and as that for the cause of Free Trade. 'You cannot fight against the future. Time is on our side.' The 'banner which we carry in this fight' was the banner of the 'great social forces which move onwards in their might and majesty', ensuring a 'certain and not too distant victory'.[73]

It was unquestionably, in Palmer's word, magnificent. But the implications of Gladstone's emphasis on Parliament's duty to bow to forces outside it and greater than it would have been ungrateful to many parliamentarians of perfect good faith in the matter of Reform. It was not difficult for Whigs and Palmerstonians of sceptical turn to observe uncomfortably the way in which Gladstone's well-known 'inclination to religious enthusiasm' became translatable through his doctrine about 'profound and uniform tendencies, associated with the movement of the public mind – with the general course of events, perhaps I should say the providential government of the world',[74] into a kind of ungainsayable spokesmanship both for 'the future' and for 'the people'. The scandal of the Liverpool episode was not forgotten. Wry faces and shrugging shoulders enough in any event made a hairbreadth scape likely in the division for the second reading. 'The House was charged with electricity like a vast thundercloud; and now the spark was about to be supplied.'[75] The Cabinet stipulated for a majority of ten (Clarendon wanted it fifteen) to sustain the bill's credibility. With 631 members voting (the largest division so far recorded) the majority was just five.

Frantic scenes of near delirium erupted in the chamber and the galleries. Lowe was in a kind of ecstasy, his albino colouring mantling to something like bishop's purple. His Adullamite cave numbered thirty-five. There rose a 'wild, raging, mad-brained shout from floor and gallery such as has never been heard in the present House of Commons'.

But see, the Chancellor of the Exchequer lifts up his hand to bespeak silence, as if he had something to say in regard to the result of the division. But the more the great orator lifts his hand beseechingly, the more the cheers are renewed and the hats waved. At length the noise comes to an end by the process of exhaustion, and the Chancellor of the Exchequer rises. Then there is a universal hush, and you might hear a pin drop. He simply says, 'Sir, I propose to fix the committee for Monday, and I will then state the order of business.' It was twilight, brightening into day, when we got out into the welcoming fresh air of New Palace Yard ... It was a night long to be remembered. The House of Commons had listened to the grandest oration by the greatest orator of his age; and had then to ask itself how it happened that the Liberal party had been disunited, and a Liberal majority of sixty 'muddled away'.[76]

[5]

The Cabinet was summoned for 28 April. 'Much discussion & division about resigning' Gladstone recorded; 'but all ended as Ld R & I strongly urged.' Gladstone would fight on and trust to the new Redistribution Bill to turn the tide. The message Gladstone now delivered to the party was calculated to make it clear that the option of trusting that Reform might be conveniently abandoned would simply not be available. 'If the Bill falls we fall.' Lady Trevelyan sent word of cheer by enclosing Macaulay's account of the crucial division on the first Reform Bill in 1831 which was carried by one vote: 'a good omen for the future'.[77] Introducing his budget on 3 May, Gladstone took the opportunity to rejoice that it involved nothing likely to raise angry controversy after the 'warm debates and sharp crisis of last week'.[78] By the same token, it could do nothing to restore party morale. (The only point of interest was Gladstone's ruminating on coal as a finite resource.) Gladstone grimly introduced Redistribution on 7 May. It was prudently anodyne. Forty-nine seats only would be affected, with a system of grouping to avoid any borough's being absolutely extinguished. The session would be extended into an autumn sitting to accommodate the new measure. A sullen mood now prevailed in the Commons. Gladstone's prestige as a parliamentary manager was severely compromised. The bloom of invincibility had faded.

With the government in travail its friends out of doors hastened to its relief. A letter from Gladstone to a pro-Reform demonstration on Primrose Hill gave Disraeli occasion to protest at the 'reign of terror' with which the Leader of the House was 'continually threatening us'.[79] Gladstone's temper no longer served any 'conciliatory' purpose. Lord Robert Montagu complained at Gladstone's 'tone of dictation'.[80] The waters of Reform were now muddied by an Elective Franchise Bill introduced by the Radical member for Hull, James Clay. The point of this bill was to set up an educational test for aspirant voters. Clay's intention was honest and innocent; but his bill took on importance only because it helped fortuitously to fill the space vacated by Gladstone's shrinking authority. Clay provoked John Bright into furious denunciation of fancy tests for the franchise, and into correspondingly candid advocacy of the good old solid principle of household suffrage. This in itself, again, might not have mattered had not Roundell Palmer, the Attorney-General, been provoked in turn to give Bright his wholehearted approval and support. Palmer argued prophetically that the existing municipal franchise – settled heads of families inhabiting rated houses – was 'the point to which we must ultimately advance'. 'I, for one, should be well pleased to advance now.'[81]

Hitherto, Palmer had been looked upon wistfully by the Palmerstonians as the last hope, after the demise of Cornewall Lewis, of heading off Gladstone. And in times to come Palmer would indeed distinguish himself as an obstacle to Gladstone's plans. For the moment, his urging the case of household suffrage as a 'reasonable basis' in contrast to arbitrary calibration, as an ideal of a 'definite status, and the stake of one who was or might be the head of a family in the social system', was ungraciously received by Gladstone as insubordinate and rash.[82] Nonetheless, coming from a senior member of the administration, it was to prove the pebble that began to set loose the avalanche which eventually buried Gladstone's stubbornly entrenched £7 fixation.

By early June Gladstone had effectively lost control of the Commons. A deliberate challenge to his authority was set up in the form of an amendment to be proposed by Lord Dunkellin to alter the rating incidence of the £7 level. Dunkellin was well regarded (unlike his father, Clanricarde); as with Grosvenor, his amendment did not deny the principle of Reform. Its point was to restrict eligibility for the franchise. Gladstone sensed danger looming. He threatened: 'any triumph which may be gained will recoil with tenfold force upon the heads of those who may achieve it'.[83] By now the House had relapsed into procedural chaos. Members rushed en masse in and out of lobbies and in and out of the chamber in a confusion of divisions ('Then followed what the Americans call a "skedaddle" ').[84] Then a lull before resumption of the combined Reform and Redistribution Bills gave time for manoeuvres and calculations. Gladstone was now limping, vulnerable. His relentlessly high-minded stiffness in refusing to bend in any detail of his proposals laid him open to being made by the Opposition the scapegoat for their own obstructive tactics.[85] He was ambushed by a 'most bare-faced proposal' that he build into the Reform and Redistribution measure provisions to repress bribery and corruption. He protested wearily to Russell:

'The Franchise Bill alone I might have managed, but to arrange, put into shape, to prepare for the Cabinet the multitude of points that arise upon the combined measure is physically as well as in every other way impossible for me.'[86]

Dunkellin moved his amendment on 18 June. The Cabinet was incoherent in its response. Neither Russell nor Gladstone gave an early, decisive lead. Brand by now was more a spokesman for Whig and Palmerstonian dissidence than an effective Chief Whip. It was not until 2 a.m. on the 19th that Gladstone announced that the amendment was incompatible with the plan of enfranchisement proposed by ministers, who could not engage to accept an adverse vote. Childers held that had Gladstone made this declaration at 8 p.m. the previous evening, the slide of defectors towards the cave would have been halted. Gladstone recorded: 'Spoke on Lord Dunkellin's motion fully. After much anxious communication with Colleagues, & a little pressure on some, made a short declaration at the close.' One of Gladstone's critics thought it the case that 'Gladstone lost his temper sadly and bullied his party', and did himself and his cause much harm.[87] Ministers were defeated in the division, 304 to 315. The cave was now crowded with forty-four Adullamites. 'With the cheering of the adversary there was shouting, violent flourished hats & other manifestations,' Gladstone noted frowningly, 'which I think novel & inappropriate.'[88]

'If the Bill falls, we fall.' These words now came home. The Cabinet reconvened on the afternoon of the 19th. 'Decided to resign: not without difference and in the teeth of the Queen.' Gladstone always doubted the wisdom of this decision. He was reluctantly a party to it, preferring a dissolution and an appeal to the constituencies. He put it to Russell that a general election was the only way to 'keep faith with the people' in the matter of Reform and the only way to redeem the 'honour of Parliament'. Even were the Liberal party to be returned in reduced numbers, this would be well worth while if the reduction was also a 'purging'. The main thing was the amount of real strength 'available for great public purposes'.[89] Russell, furiously unforgiving of the treachery of the 'forty thieves' of the cave, and infinitely reluctant to see his second long-yearned-for premiership crumble away, had only Argyll and Gibson staunchly with himself and Gladstone for making a fight of it. The majority of the Cabinet held that 'the apathetic state of the people at that date' ruled out this recourse.* Bright, naturally, was loud and long in his demands for a dissolution; but by now not a few of Gladstone's colleagues were weary of being hectored and lectured by Bright. The Queen, horrified at losing her ministers on the eve of war in Germany

---

* As G later recounted in an analogous instance in 1886.[90] See below, pages 436, 441.

and Italy, put every obstacle in the way of their departure. Queasy at the ungallantry of deserting her, Russell summoned a 'Conciliabulum' at Pembroke Lodge on 24 June: 'many plans still afloat'. Why not a vote of confidence? Russell proposed 'rehabilitating' the clause technically at the centre of the trouble. But a 'small dinner of Ministers' at Granville's on the 25th was by way of 'winding up'. There was much division of opinion still, but resignation remained always that which divided least. Brand advised against dissolution as a 'fatal mistake'.[91] Russell in the end was obliged to press his resignation on the Queen.

Gladstone announced the government's resignation to the Commons on 26 June. 'I kept to facts without epithets; but I thought as I went on that some of the words were scorching.' The wreckage of yet another Reform Bill now littered the political landscape. Gladstone told the Queen: 'from all the miscarriages attending the past history of this question, not ministers alone, & leaders of parties, nor parties alone, but Parliament itself & Parliamentary Government were discredited'.[92] On 6 July Gladstone 'finished in Downing Street. Left my keys behind me. Somehow it makes a void.'

CHAPTER 2

'IN THE PATH OF RIGHT': FROM REFORM TO IRELAND, 1866–8

[1]

Derby took over as prime minister and Disraeli took Gladstone's places as Chancellor of the Exchequer and Leader of the Commons. (Clarendon declined Derby's invitation, endorsed by the Queen, to stay on at the Foreign Office.) For his part, Gladstone adopted the stance of one passing on the baton of Reform. On 20 July he informed the new Conservative front bench: 'I shall only say with regard to our successors in office, that it would be a matter of great satisfaction to myself and my colleagues when the Government shall feel themselves in a position enabling them to deal with this matter in an effectual manner.' Support would gladly be forthcoming for any measure under Conservative auspices which was yet 'prudent and effectual'; but resistance would be uncompromising to anything 'illusory or reactionary'.[1] It was Gladstone's settled conviction that the rod the Conservatives had pickled for their own backs would be their being obliged to offer a larger rather than a smaller enfranchisement than the one they had helped defeat. Disraeli was indeed ready to take up Gladstone's challenge out of hand by taking over the Reform Bill 'where it stops'. Redistribution could be handled in a conciliatory way. 'You could carry this in the present House', Disraeli promised Derby, 'and rapidly.' It would prevent all agitation in the recess; and it would 'cut the ground entirely from under Gladstone'.[2] But Derby was unprepared for anything so boldly and blatantly precipitate. Things would be left over until the 1867 session.

The friends of Reform out of doors, however, were not patient enough even to wait for the recess before launching a revived campaign of agitation. The inaugural Cobden Club dinner, on 21 July, when J. S. Mill proposed Gladstone's health with laudations ('and was almost overcome with tears'),[3] was a kind of inaugural also of a season of counter-attack by 'opinion' unhappy at the way Reform had been made the plaything of parliamentary factions. The Reform League, led by Edmund Beales and George Howell, organized an enormous demonstration on 23 July to protest against the Commons' dereliction of its duty to the people. The plan was to march to the upper-class precinct of Hyde Park for a massively climactic assertion of the people's sense of betrayal. The authorities feebly attempted to ban the use of the park, but its frail railings were no obstacle to the surging mass of demonstrators. Watching from a Bayswater Road balcony, Matthew Arnold witnessed what was to be the inspiration of *Culture and Anarchy*. Gladstone, riding in the park on the 24th to view the devastated shrubberies and trampled flower beds – the 'field of battle' – could only comment sadly, 'Alack for the folly that made it.'

Gladstone's last major contribution to the session was in a debate on the Habeas Corpus Suspension (Ireland) Bill. This was a coercive response to the flare-up of 'Fenian' activity. Gladstone signalled his readiness to explore implications bearing upon conciliatory responses compatible with ideas of a 'new commencement'. He declared that he shared 'the conviction that questions relating to the tenure of land in Ireland and the relations between landlord and tenant lie at the root of the condition of the country'.[4] Ireland begins to assume the status of a persistent subtext to the Reform question, though for the time being the Irish Church side of the matter was left to one side. The Conservative government was preparing legislation on the landlord–tenant issue; the Church question would be at this stage entirely premature.

Which is not to say that it did not feature at a post-sessional gathering called by Russell at Woburn on 14 September. 'Morning *sederunt* with Lord R & Brand on Reform & other matters. We agreed neither to egg on the Government nor the reverse.' Russell, thwarted on the Reform leg, was quite apt for giving a lead on the Irish Church leg. Brand set off on a round of visits with a view to getting the Liberal party back on an even keel. Gladstone thought this might best be left to the 'healing power of nature' (there was a touching assumption that the Adullamites were 'more or less ashamed of themselves') and set off with Catherine, Agnes and Mary at the end of September for a long, recuperative sojourn in Rome. The Russells also had the benefits of wintering in the warm south in mind, and settled in Florence, the new capital of the kingdom of Italy, where Lady Russell's brother, Sir Henry Elliot, was ambassador. It was in many respects a piquant moment for those two statesmen famously friendly to the cause of the Risorgimento. Now that Austria had withdrawn from Venetia, Rome remained invidiously the last gap to be filled by the Italian state. A nervous sense of an ending ('the world turned upside down', in the anguished words of Antonelli, the Cardinal Secretary of State) pervaded the Roman atmosphere. The French presence in the Patrimony of St Peter alone sustained the temporal power of Pius IX. (Garibaldi would make a premature bid in 1867 to put an end to it.)

There was a curious appropriateness in the context of the Cavourian ideal of a 'Free Church in a Free State' of Gladstone's calling on Russell in Florence to discuss an Irish version of that ideal. Russell observed with satisfaction that Gladstone was 'as little disposed as I to maintain Protestant ascendancy in Ireland'.[5]

Rome was a place in which Gladstone never found any difficulties in being busy. He and Catherine and Mary and Agnes settled in the Piazza di Spagna. Stephen Glynne joined the party a little later.* The intense world of grand society beckoned. So did the world of sermonizing, audiences with cardinals ('the atmosphere of Antonelli's room stifled me'), sightseeing and excursions and porcelain and antique-hunting. Nor was there any stint of collegial society: Clarendon, Cardwell, and Argyll were also keenly observing the latter days of the papacy as a temporal power. The Vatican made itself receptive to the English statesmen who had been damaging to its interests in the past but of whom hopes might now be entertained. Manning, since 1865 Archbishop of Westminster, assured his agent in Rome, Monsignor Talbot, that Gladstone was *'much* softened' from of old. Gladstone had been keeping silence on the temporal power; and 'he has been helping us' in Ireland. It would be well to cultivate him with a view to future benefits.[6]

The Gladstones were received *en famille* to be blessed by His Holiness, and Gladstone in a personal audience as well. Accoutred in 'household uniform', Gladstone knelt and kissed the papal hand, and reluctantly obeyed the papal order to sit. Conforming studiously to etiquette, Gladstone volunteered nothing; and commented on the Pope's remarks as they ranged widely over Italy, Europe, and the British colonies. Ireland was a matter of particular and mutual interest.

He spoke warmly against Fenianism and declared the decided hostility to it of his clergy in Ireland; which hostility, in any point that might come before him, he always approved and seconded.

He said the Irish Bishops were true to the existing order of things, though in some points they would wish for a change – and in some points I replied *hanno ragione.*[7]†

Much absurd rumour about this audience got about: that the Pope and Gladstone plotted the destruction of the Irish Church; or that Gladstone was conspiring to provide the Pope with a refuge, perhaps in Ireland, should he be dispossessed in Rome.[8] The duller reality of the matter was that for all the 'exceedingly genial & simple & kindly manner

---

* The three elder sons, Willy, Stephen, and Harry, joined them on 16 December.
† 'they have reason', 'they are right'.

of His Holiness', Gladstone found no opening into 'Roman affairs' and the preparatory stages of the Vatican Council or into any areas where his theological intimacy with Döllinger* would be material, or into the question of higher education for Roman Catholics in Ireland.

Gladstone lingered long in Rome. The life of London, even of Hawarden to a degree, had lost its savour. There was much of the same sense of escape from personal crisis as there had been on his previous Roman visits in the late 1830s and 1849, and of course in the case of the Neapolitan visit of 1850. His own world, in its way, had been as much turned upside down as Antonelli's. Antonelli had used that phrase apropos of the battle of Königgrätz; Gladstone might well have used it in the aftermath of the Dunkellin division on the early morning of 19 June. Socializing with the Argylls, the Cardwells, and the Clarendons provided him with as much domestic political company as he cared for.† More important was Sir John Acton's presence. His intellectual sympathy and friendship with Gladstone ripened in the Roman atmosphere in the wake of the papal fulminations against the Liberal world of the *Syllabus Errorum* of 1864 and the preliminaries of the Vatican Council of 1870.

Rome was reluctantly relinquished at the beginning of the new year. 'Would that the old year sped away from me with wings less charged,' wrote Gladstone, '& may God grant that the new one may be a year of true gladness.' The Gladstones, with the Argylls and the Cardwells, journeyed back via Florence, where there was much hobnobbing with the Italian political class and an audience with King Victor Emmanuel. Leisurely travel (there were six crowded days in Paris) meant that Gladstone was not back in the London scene until near the end of January. It was a matter of much observation that he did not give the customary pre-sessional dinner to his Commons colleagues. Granville remarked to Halifax: 'He dares not ask Bright, and funks omitting him.'[11] Grosvenor underlined the point by ostentatiously dining the Adullamites.

Bright had indeed been making himself a problematic guest amid the official Liberals. After the Hyde Park shock had subsided he launched his own series of giant demonstrations with a view to intimidating the Conservative government. Of Bright's campaign Gladstone wrote from Rome to Brand: 'I do not like what I hear of Bright's speeches.' The scandal of his own Liverpool indiscretion no doubt made Gladstone all

---

* J. J. I. Döllinger, Roman Catholic theologian and historian; Professor at Munich. Admired by G for his liberal and historical ecumenicism.[9]

† Another story that got around was the 'quadrilateral' joke of the Pope's collation of his audiences with the English political notables: that he liked Mr Gladstone but did not understand him; that he understood Mr Cardwell but did not like him; that he both liked and understood Lord Clarendon; and that he neither liked nor understood the Duke of Argyll.[10]

the more concerned to establish a fitting distance between himself and the people's tribune. He urged upon Brand the desirability of a parallel campaign in the Liberal press to make it clear to Lord Derby and his friends that they would have to pay dearly for their triumph of June: 'that a bill from them, to be accepted by the people, must be larger, and not smaller, than would have been, or even would be, accepted from us'.[12] Derby had already come reluctantly to the conclusion, as he told Disraeli, 'that we shall have to deal with the question of Reform'. The Queen was anxious about European instability in the aftermath of the war; anxious that destabilizing agitation in the country about Reform be contained. 'The Queen', Derby told Disraeli, 'wants "us" to settle it.'[13]

Conservatives could see the point that Bright's agitation might become dangerous. But they could see also that it might well become far more dangerous to the integrity of the Liberal party than to themselves. There were many 'moderate' men who, in Bagehot's words, really wished for 'a large infusion of popular strength, but also did not want to see the flavour of the wine quite destroyed by the quantity of alcohol introduced into it'. They were outraged by Bright's scarcely veiled appeals to popular intimidating force and his insistence on a 'monopoly of the right to do justice' being accorded to but one party.[14] There were many also who judged that, with Gladstone having 'dished' himself with Bright, a 'fusion' between Tories and Palmerstonians would be the likeliest result in consequence.[15]

[2]

Derby and Disraeli approached the Reform question with every intention that 'settling' it would not be incompatible with some such outcome. Derby wrote to Disraeli in December 1866: 'Of all possible hares to start, I do not know a better than the extension to household suffrage coupled with plurality of voting.'[16] Plurality of voting, much canvassed in the coming debates about Reform, meant electors qualifying for more than one vote in a constituency. It was the standard 'safeguard' formula in relation to the household criterion. Derby did not envisage a hasty exercise. Reform was to be made palatable to a wide catchment by sugaring the pill by a preliminary commission of enquiry. There was need, after the sad experience of the Liberal government, for politic deliberation, for feeling the 'pulse of Parliament and the country'. The best procedure would be by the tactic of resolution: tentative, exploratory, avoiding an immediate declaration of details. The Queen's Speech at the opening of the 1867 session on 5 February included a reference to measures 'which, without unduly disturbing the Balance of political Power, shall freely extend the Elective Franchise'. Gladstone responded with guarded blandness. He welcomed the Canadian Union and measures to improve landlord–tenant relations and to terminate arbitrary coercion in Ireland. On Reform he merely observed that the proposal was 'enigmatical'. Gladstone proposed no amendment to the Address.

This blandness came probably out of two considerations. First, there seemed no compelling reason to suppose that the minority Conservative government's Reform Bill could not be shepherded by the bulk of the Liberal party in the Commons into an acceptable form – that is to say, acceptable to Gladstone; and 'larger, and not smaller, than would have been, or even would be, accepted from us'. Gladstone certainly assumed that he could command its salient features. His revenge for 1866 would be a Conservative measure on his terms, somewhat larger in scope but in all essentials a revised version of his 1866 bill. It was the received explanation of Gladstone's failure in 1866 that he fought 'on party lines against any important modification of the measure which he brought forward'.[17] Gladstone never had been, nor ever would be, a ready conceder to important modifications in any measure with which he identified his own prepossession. That would apply, party lines or no party lines, as much to the forthcoming Conservative measure as to his own in the last session. He would stamp his authority on the 1867 session. If the old year had sped away with wings all too charged, surely the new year would unfold itself as 'a year of true gladness'.

The second likely consideration bearing upon Gladstone's assurance at this point was a feeling of security in having weapons in reserve. The persistent subtext of his politics had become Ireland, with reference increasingly to the future of the Church of Ireland. The land question in Ireland was already the subject of Conservative attention. Defending an Anglican establishment catering for twelve per cent of the people of Ireland was a task the Conservatives would prefer not to have to undertake. Gladstone himself had spent most of his career to date being cautiously circumspect on the matter. He still had to circumvent his declaration of 1865 that dealing with the Irish Church would be a matter five or ten years in the future. It was helpful here that Russell was prepared to lead the way. Gladstone was still innocent of the revelations that would later strike him that the seven centuries of English tutelage of Ireland had been an unmitigated and intolerable disgrace. Sensitive to later accusations that his Irish initiative of 1868 had been prompted as the 'outcome of Fenian disturbances', Gladstone was studious to emphasize that 'in the end of 1866 I declared publicly my opinion that the time had come when religious equality might forthwith be established in Ireland'.[18] That was the fruit of Florentine discussions with Russell. It was a kite flown to test the winds of opinion. Here was an issue which, if handled carefully, was calculated to unite the always fragile and fissile Liberal party. Even Bright stood in quite a different aspect as disestablisher of the Irish Church from Bright the tribune of the plebs. Russell decided in January 1867 to set the Irish ball rolling. Preparations were put in hand to pre-empt possible resistance from influential dissidents: Clarendon was deputed to soften up Roundell Palmer. It remained Palmer's opinion that the effect of any ambitious measure on the Irish Church would do more 'to create than to solve difficulties', because it would unavoidably call into question the Act of Union of 1800.[19] But it seemed that Palmer would be safely among a decided minority of Liberals in that opinion.

Gladstone was studious also in the early days of the 1867 session to continue his 1866 tactic of not rocking the Palmerstonian foreign-policy boat. He was blandness itself in trusting once more that the Ottoman government would not be found blameworthy in the matter of the Cretan insurrection.[20] He was hopeful a little later that the Turks would be ready to listen to friendly counsel. In any event he was willing to bow to Lord Stanley's judgement as Foreign Secretary if Lord Stanley were satisfied with Turkish fulfilment of the 1856 undertakings to Christian subject peoples. To carpers Gladstone was quite forthright: 'I would not venture to say one word which would have the effect of encouraging the people of Crete to throw off the Ottoman rule.'[21]* This, again, was politic with a view to Liberal unity. Urgent representations from Lord Clarence Paget in Malta, detailing the horrors of the situation in Crete, did not budge Gladstone. Paget's insistence that the 'Eastern question' was evolving rapidly to crisis point and that there was need of speedy intervention by the Great Powers to stop wholesale Turkish butchery of Cretans[22] did no more than to move Gladstone to consult the erstwhile 'Grand Elchi', Lord Stratford de Redcliffe,[23] with the result that Gladstone abided by his readiness to leave the affair in the official hands of the Foreign Office.

Thus conducing towards at least an approximation to an amenable and undisturbed Liberal party, Gladstone confronted the principal issue of the day. 'Spoke after Disraeli after his extraordinary scheme & position,' he recorded on 11 February. 'It was difficult in many ways.' The essence of Gladstone's difficulty was his fixed determination to impose upon Disraeli a version of the 1866 bill, whereas Disraeli was advertising to the Commons that he sought any bill precisely not of Gladstonian provenance that could catch majority acquiescence. Hence his exploratory procedure by resolutions. Since the Conservatives preferred to leave the counties alone, it would be a question of the boroughs. Disraeli began

---

* This declaration was to cause G some embarrassment in 1877. GBA, 91.

his quest clumsily. This was partly because of the old problems of want of reliable statistical information. It was also because Disraeli was an amateur in the field compared with Gladstone. Paradoxically, this proved to be to Disraeli's advantage and Gladstone's disadvantage. Gladstone, unequalled for his intimacy with complex minutiae, was in a position to savage and devastate Disraeli's feckless initiatives. But not the least part of Gladstone's difficulty was that, being so well versed in the intricacies of the details that had led him to the conclusion he had reached early in 1866, it had become virtually impossible for him to remain other than inflexibly bound by them. Disraeli was made free by his ignorance and incompetence.

Nonplussed, Gladstone moved warily, declaring his wish to be cooperative and charitable to ministers. 'We are here embarked upon a common cause.'[24] He kept his temper and handled the party with tact. Villiers reported to Delane of *The Times*: 'His judgment & moderation are astonishing everybody.'[25] He trailed behind Lowe and Bright in their insistence that the resolutions unveiled by Disraeli on 25 February be converted without delay into a definite bill. Gladstone insisted still: 'I am not taking the part of an opponent of the Government.'[26] Disraeli flailed about trying to reconcile Derby's insistence on Reform in 'no niggard spirit' with acceptance by Cabinet sceptics led by Cranborne.* In the end, he failed. On 4 March Disraeli announced to the Commons the resignations of Cranborne, Carnarvon, and Peel.

Fatally, Gladstone misconstrued Disraeli's discomfiture as his great opportunity to strike. He revelled all the more in the commanding ease with which he could demolish Disraeli's improvisations. On 5 March Gladstone dug in his heels. He insisted obdurately that his £7 occupation formula must obtain.[27] But already he was being overtaken by the pace of events. The first point was that the Conservative party remained steady behind Derby. There would be no Conservative 'cave' behind the resigned dissidents. Furthermore, it was by now also clear that the Adullamites were not prepared to 'fuse' with Conservative doubters to go for a restrictive, minimal compromise settlement. To that extent the logic of the parliamentary situation became clear and open. This would give Disraeli scope for flexible manoeuvre.

But what gave Disraeli most scope for flexible manoeuvre was his simple discovery that, on some very plausible figures which in fact had been available since March 1866, it was 'possible that a Bill giving even household suffrage on the proof of full payment of rates would not add more votes to the lists than Mr Gladstone's Bill'.[28] This set Disraeli loose.

---

* Viscount Cranborne, earlier Lord Robert Cecil, succeeded in 1868 as third Marquess of Salisbury.

At a meeting of 150 Conservative MPs on 1 March – including most of the borough members – Disraeli disclosed his revelation. The strength of feeling among the borough members was clear: four fifths of them found the sense of 'finality' attractive in a suffrage of resident house-holders who personally paid rates.[29] This feeling neutralized Cranborne and his friends; and Disraeli was now equipped with a formula which even Bright was prevailed upon to disown as too expansive. Lowe put his finger unwittingly on the crux: he pointed out that for the first time the minister had pronounced 'the fatal and ominous words, "household suffrage"'.[30] The fact that Cranborne and his friends elevated them into a tocsin of betrayal[31] gave them the very best kind of publicity from Disraeli's point of view. Gladstone assembled his forces for a frontal assault, not disdaining to woo Adullamites with dire prognostications. 'We are very near the point for our final plunge,' he warned Lord Elcho on 7 March.

It may soon be too late for deliberation. I am sure that if Household Suffrage were proposed with 'securities', you would not wish the securities to be adopted as such by those who did not believe in them. And here I think is the responsibility of encouraging even negatively the launching of a proposal even wider than we think – nay, as we know that Bright thinks, the circumstances demand or warrant.[32]

When Disraeli introduced what he now at length concocted as his Representation of the People Bill on 18 March, he proposed 'a most popular principle', the enfranchisement of 'male occupiers of dwelling houses'. For all that some 723,000 householders not presently voters in England and Wales would thereby be added to the registers, Disraeli was at pains to insist (with his 'American' theme of 1866 in mind) that such an extension of popular privilege was quite at odds with acceding to any idea of 'democratic rights'. He dismissed the familiar formulas of rating or rental (there would be 'no Serbonian bog deeper than a £5 rating would prove to be'). There were to be safeguards and securities: payment of rates would be personal, alternative franchises would be made available, and there would be plurality of voting. But the essence of the matter was an appeal to what was put forward as a simple, commonsensical, readily acceptable criterion.[33] Lowe in fact put the attractions of household suffrage to members most tellingly: 'they believe they find in it a new principle, going lower, perhaps, than they would themselves like to go, but still giving them something that would afford rest and tranquillity after the storms of the last fifteen years – something so low they cannot fall lower'. Lowe warned, of course, that all this was a deceptive mirage. It might seem 'natural', but it was not 'accurate';

household suffrage would prove rather to be 'quicksand', and 'quag-mire'.[34] It was Gladstone's absurd fate to allow himself to become a kind of adjutant spokesman for Lowe's doctrine.

Gladstone's first essay in this Lowean theme was on the incongruities which a franchise 'which is close upon universal suffrage – equal to it or to manhood residential suffrage' – would lead to in certain rural districts, where 'a peasant, or common hodman, or day labourer' would get the vote, while leaving many workmen in boroughs unbenefited.[35] Confronted with the alluring temptations of household suffrage, the Liberal party in the House of Commons began to betray symptoms of being enticed. Gladstone swiftly took steps to call them sternly to order on 21 March, at Carlton House Terrace: 'Meeting of the party 2½–4: the end as good as I could hope.' Fortified by such hopes (in hard fact rather self-delusory)* Gladstone soon expounded a more spacious objection: 'it does not appear to me that we are required either by the state of the population, by the wishes of the country at large, by the opinion of this House, by previous pledges, or by any single consideration that can be brought to bear on the question to assent to that very broad principle'. Gladstone did not apprehend ruin or destruction from household suffrage; he was too much a believer that the 'good sense of the country and the strength of its institutions and traditions would effectively qualify and restrain the evil consequences of such an error'. But Gladstone could see no reason to assent if a better and safer proposal were devisable. Gladstone fastened upon what was the greatest weakness in Disraeli's position: offering a popular principle so hedged with 'pretended safe-guards' as to be virtually negated. Gladstone pointed precisely to Disraeli's admitting 'a principle of needless breadth' while removing it from the reach of perhaps two thirds of its professed beneficiaries.[37]

This was indeed true criticism. But in the way things happened, Gladstone tangled himself up, not Disraeli. Disraeli accurately pointed to Gladstone's dilemma: 'half alarm, half derision – alarm at the revolu-tionary proposal, derision at the petty consequences it will produce'.[38] Disraeli, aware of the isolation of both the Conservative dissidents and the Adullamites, was prepared by now to be quite candid on the theme of 'no niggard spirit', while Gladstone was declaring his implacable hostility to any notion of plural or dual voting as a safeguard.[39] In no niggard spirit Disraeli was prepared to barter away safeguards which Gladstone derided as 'pretended' to a proposal which Gladstone thought 'needless, and therefore unwise', requiring to be qualified and restrained in the 'evil consequences' of such an 'error'.

---

* Disraeli quite accurately judged the amount of 'murmuring, round robins, and scuffling of feet' in the sulky Liberal ranks directed at 'iracundus Achilles'.[36]

This incoherence was a cue for so acutely critical a colleague and observer of Gladstone as Roundell Palmer. On 26 March the former Attorney-General reminded the House of his intervention of 30 May 1866; and therefrom that members must be 'aware that I am not one of those who entertain any alarm at the idea of household suffrage. Upon a former occasion, when there were many reasons why I might have abstained from making a declaration on the subject . . . I felt it to be my duty not to conceal from the House that my own mind had for some time been travelling in the direction of household suffrage.' Palmer defended the principle as combining a liberal element of 'large and satisfactory admission' with a conservative element of heads of families inhabiting rateable houses embodying a 'natural principle of finality'. Palmer shared what he judged evidently to be a widely held wish that 'something, if possible, may be made of this Bill' in committee.[40]* In 1866, Palmer had put himself behind Bright; now Bright, embarrassed and fast-retreating, was nowhere in sight. Palmer had helped materially to sabotage Gladstone's 1866 bill; now he was helping to sabotage Gladstone's resistance to Disraeli's 1867 bill. He was challenging directly Gladstone's call to order of 21 March.

Disraeli in turn took Palmer's cue. Palmer, as a soundly Oxonian High Churchman, was as good a parliamentary specimen of that genre as Cranborne, and a counterweight encouragement both to doubting Whigs and Conservatives as much as to opportunist Liberals and Radicals. Disraeli candidly opened the bidding. At the end of the second night of the second reading debate on 26 March, in a bravura speech of astonishing brazenness and knockabout histrionics, Disraeli invited the House: 'Act with us cordially and candidly, assist us to carry this measure. We will not shrink from deferring to your suggestions so long as they are consistent with the main object of this Bill . . . Act with us, I say, cordially and candidly, you will find on our side complete reciprocity of feeling. Pass the Bill, and then change the Ministry if you like.'[41] Disraeli did not invite in vain. The Commons, bemused by his consummate effrontery, let him have his way. The following night, 27 March, saw the 'droll situation', as Gladstone watched in astonishment, of the bill's passing its second reading without a division.[42]

To Gladstone it was imperative that this bizarre and absurd trend of events be summarily stopped. He arranged another party meeting for 5 April at Carlton House Terrace, to lay down the law for dealing with the committee stage. But even as Gladstone stamped his foot and summoned his legions, Disraeli presented his budget on 4 April, dripping with cordial and candid signals to Liberal backbenchers, who applauded

* For Palmer on 30 May 1866, see above, page 22.

while the Conservative benches sat silent. Gladstone could find no fault with it. One angry Conservative indeed denounced Disraeli for appearing to have 'consulted the wishes of the party opposite rather than those of his own party'. The government's friends had been 'shirked'; what was due to the agricultural interest had been ignored.[43]

More bemused than ever, 250 Liberal members gathered at Carlton House Terrace the following day to be harangued by their leader. There were, ominously, something like seventy absentees. There had been resistance to the summons by many who resented Gladstone's driving. Gladstone, as he himself recorded, 'spoke at length'. There was no room for anyone else's speaking. What Gladstone proposed to do was no less than bind Liberal members with an instruction to proceed in committee 'with a view to fix a line for the borough franchise' for such prospective electors who passed a 'defined test of social and moral worth'. In short, Gladstone proposed to replace Disraeli's bill in effect with a version of his own 1866 bill by tying the hands of his party and marching them into parliamentary battle as an infinitely manipulable phalanx. The instruction scheme was sprung at the meeting without prior notice in order to prevent opposition. Gladstone's behaviour and demeanour was entirely characteristic. It was in many ways one of his finest Peelite moments. Members complained of dictatorial behaviour, that 'Gladstone always monopolised the discussion', that members 'had never been asked to give [their opinion]'.[44] Having been obliged to swallow the second reading, Gladstone now compensated by refusing to accept amendments to his plan. He seemed to be oblivious of the danger. He was loyally supported throughout by Bright; but by now Bright sounded rather hollow.

Some Liberals, disliking Gladstone's dictatorial manner and proposed method of procedure, conferred at the Reform Club on 7 April. A further gathering met in the Commons' tearoom on 8 April, giving rise to the definition of the 'Tearoom Cave' as a kind of counter-version of the 1866 Cave of Adullam. This was mutiny. Something near fifty Liberal MPs were prepared to defy their Whip. Brand's position had become untenable. A delegation was dispatched to Gladstone with demands that he drop features of his instruction.[45] (Some of the Tearoomers would have been perfectly ready to see Gladstone fall on his face without warning.) Gladstone had become aware on 6 April of the ground beginning to slip beneath his feet. 'Conclave on the situation & on Disraeli's foolish amendments.' It was no longer really a matter of the foolishness of Disraeli's amendments. Offended and affronted, Gladstone nonetheless conceded the demands of the Tearoom mutineers: 'the retreat was effected, perhaps "as well as could be expected"'.[46] His retreat was in fact but a cunning feint. Gladstone counter-attacked with a series of 'crafty amendments' which would in effect have replaced the part of his planned instruction which he had ostensibly agreed to drop.[47] He appeared to be unteachable. His attack was a disaster. His friend Phillimore observed on 9 April: 'Entire collapse of Gladstone's attack on Government yesterday . . . Disraeli's insolent triumph.'[48]* Disraeli was now in a position to declare that he deeply appreciated the behaviour of the House. It showed that the House was resolved to support the government in passing its bill, behaving in a 'generous and candid manner'. Disraeli conveyed the sense of his colleagues 'of the generous candour with which they have been treated by the House'. Gladstone professed to find the 'tone of the House better' on 11 April, 'but issue not yet certain'.

The issue became critical on 12 April, when Gladstone, doggedly and tenaciously unwilling to yield a jot or a tittle, persisted with his offensive. Gladstone was more than ever master of the intricacies; but the House was more than ever weary of them. Gladstone apologized for the 'mingled difficulty and dryness' of the details, but went on relentlessly.[49] To Gladstone's immense indignation, Disraeli abruptly refused to accept the amendments ('a declaration of war'). Disraeli held that 'they would entirely alter and would completely supersede the policy which we recommend the House to adopt'. Disraeli unctuously underlined the peril of Gladstone's position: 'It is a disagreeable thing to distinguish between the House generally and the right hon. Gentleman opposite.'[50] It was astonishing indeed that only now was Gladstone beginning to have inklings. Disraeli was willing to accept almost any amendment provided it was not from Gladstone. Phillimore met Gladstone and Catherine as events were moving to the brink of a division. 'His *disgust* and *deep mortification* at the defection of his party mingled with due sense of loyalty of the greater number, and especially of his old cabinet.' Phillimore's tendentious comment that, 'if deserted, he will abdicate, and leave them to find another leader', was 'fully responded to by him'.[51] The expectation was still, nevertheless, that Gladstone would carry the day, even with 'hairbreadth scape'. As Big Ben struck two in the morning, Gladstone found himself invidiously in a minority in the division, 289–310. Forty-five Liberals voted or paired against their party. Given the natural Liberal majority in the Commons, revived and as it was hoped repaired after the fissure of 1866, Gladstone's rueful comment was apt: 'A smash perhaps without example.'[52]

---

* Robert Phillimore, Admiralty Advocate, Judge of the High Court of the Admiralty, 1867. Created baronet in 1883.

[3]

If in Disraeli's accurate reading of the House of Commons there were the fruits of long, hard, and often bitter experience of the patient wiles concomitant with minority status and its exigencies, so with Gladstone's wilful self-sufficiency there was exemplary indication of imposition of inherently executive values on Parliament, of ministerial and magisterial impatience with mere parliamentary skills, with more than a touch of Peel's superb political self-regard. Gladstone's failure to read his party with anything like accuracy either in 1866 or 1867 spoke eloquently both of his 'instrumental' view of party as such and of the problematic deeply embedded in the manner and motives of his becoming 'associated' with the Liberal party in the first place. Gladstone's uneasy relationship with the Liberal parliamentary party was to a great extent inherent in his much more comfortable relationship with 'opinion' out of doors. The echoes of Liverpool in the Easter recess of 1866 still reverberated, dimly but insistently. It was a very 'Gladstonian' admirer of Gladstone, Frederick Temple, Headmaster of Rugby, who wrote supportively after the 'smash' in 'hearty admiration' of Gladstone's efforts: 'I do not feel that the present Representatives of the Liberal Party in Parliament can be taken as a fair expression of the Liberal feeling in the country.'[53]

Certainly the mutineers of 1867 were not a fair expression of the feeling of the parliamentary Liberal party. Mostly they were not the 'Tearoom Cave' people; they were rather more of the old Adullamite cast. Gladstone had been 'thrown overboard', as one member put it, '– not by the Radicals . . . but by the timid men, the Adullamites and the "moderate" Conservatives'.[54] Thomas Hughes (of *Tom Brown's Schooldays* fame), Liberal MP for Lambeth, no doubt spoke accurately for the loyal majority when, apologizing to Gladstone for words he used on the stairs leading to the Lobby after the 'humiliation' of the division, Hughes insisted that Gladstone should not in any way draw back or leave the ' "free lances" to get what may yet be got out of this Government'. Gladstone and Gladstone alone could rally the 'true Liberals'.[55]

Yet it was going to be the case that 'free lances' – as it happened of a rather different stripe from those of 12 April – were very much out to get what might yet be got from the Conservative government. The circumstances were such that Gladstone was now incapable of rallying the 'true Liberals' for his franchise cause. The message to that effect was put to Gladstone with candid brutality by George Denman, former colleague of Palmerston in Tiverton. Household suffrage was inevitable: 'we should recognize the fact that, so far as *this* question is concerned, there is no such thing as a Liberal Party, and that every one is at liberty to act and speak for himself without reference to the convenience of his Party'.[56] The point was underlined by Argyll. 'I fear that any effort on your part now to get rid of "Household Suffrage" would again divide and proclaim the division of the Liberal party.'[57] Many Liberal MPs feared that if Gladstone succeeded in blocking Disraeli, Derby might advise a dissolution and force the Liberal party to go to the country as the enemies of household suffrage.

Phillimore recorded anxiously of the division: 'a surprise, I believe, to both parties'. What would Gladstone do? '*Query.* – Ought he on account of the defection of 20 to leave so considerable a party?'[58] Gladstone's indignant readiness to consider abdication was no doubt a genuine emotion, but there is no evidence that he contemplated seriously anything more than a marked withdrawal of his presence for a time from the front bench. Even so, there is more than a hint of 1874–5 to come. He left much of the routine business after the Easter recess to juniors such as Ayrton and Palmer. While Gladstone commenced a new volume of his diaries by quoting Bunsen's resolution not again to 'enter into public life', but devote the years yet remaining to 'great objects of eternal significance',[59]* Palmer proudly observed that *The Times* paid him the compliment of coupling his name with Gladstone's as 'the twin leaders of the Opposition'.[60] There was the awkward matter of Henry Brand's retirement as Chief Whip. A dinner and a presentation of plate had to be deferred, ostensibly on grounds of Brand's health, but 'really because at present Gladstone refuses to take the chair at the dinner, though attached to Brand, because many who had deserted him (G.) would attend the dinner'. Gladstone would not 'countenance the appearance of a sham union when the party is discredited'.[61]†

The remainder of the session, so far as Reform was concerned, had to do with the working out of the logic defined positively by Denman and negatively by Hughes in the context of Gladstone's admission: 'I have been ... definitely overruled.'[62] The 'free lances' of the Liberal party were at liberty, acting and speaking for themselves without reference to the convenience of their party or its leader in the Commons, going for what could yet be got. Given that household suffrage in itself was 'inevitable', the questions remaining had to do with the securities and safeguards of plurality of voting and personal and direct payment of rates encompassing it. Could the Conservative government uphold them as Disraeli had promised he would do? Or would there emerge a majority willing to disown them for a mixture of motives? One kind of motive

---

* Baron C. C. J. Bunsen, Prussian Ambassador in London, 1841–54; admired for a time by G for his ecumenical Protestantism.
† Brand later, 1872–84, became Speaker and Viscount Hampden.

was that of the opportunist Radical wing of the Liberals, willing to offer Disraeli their support in return for 'democratic' concessions: no plural voting (that in itself was no great difficulty) and votes for 'compounders', tenants who compounded with landlords to include their rates in their rent. The number of such compounders in the boroughs was calculated to increase enfranchisement by four times the numbers originally contemplated. It was a very serious matter, going far beyond the 'just limits of prudence and circumspection' recommended by Gladstone in 1866 or the image of the sturdily independent heads of families conjured hitherto by the household-suffrage advocates. The other kind of motive was that emerging among Conservatives who had no great love for the idea of borough democracy for itself but a considerable fondness for it as a means of keeping the Liberal party in turmoil and of further undermining Gladstone's authority. Gladstone noted: 'The underground tone of the House most unsatisfactory.'[63] Moreover, in the larger electoral frame, so long as counties were left alone, what had they to lose? Given that the existing borough franchise gave the Conservative party little joy, a radical extension of it might conceivably benefit them. This was a notion Disraeli did nothing to discountenance.

As the session wound its exhausting way into the doldrums of summer, an amendment in the name of a member of the 'Tearoom Cave', Grosvenor Hodgkinson, became the focus of attention in the crucial matter of giving the vote to 'compounders'. In the calmer times of the autumn recess, Gladstone could recall that the 'true initiative, on the capital point of the Reform Bill, was the initiative of Mr Hodgkinson. A provincial solicitor (to his honour be it spoken) reversed the plan of the Queen's Advisers, and determined the essential character of the New Reform Act.'[64] At the time, Hodgkinson was an obscure MP for Newark who got in the way of Gladstone's plan to remodel the bill. For Disraeli, that was precisely Hodgkinson's great utility. Conceding willy-nilly Denman's doctrine on the inevitability of household suffrage, Gladstone's plan was to get hold of the details. He was also reviving into something like his normal contentious form. Protests obliged him to withdraw the word 'fraud' to describe the bill.[65] He was now, despite being 'much fatigued by heat & work', in furious competition with Hodgkinson on behalf of the compounders. He commanded resources unavailable to the Newark solicitor.

On 11 May a 'monster deputation' from the Reform Union waited on Gladstone at Carlton House Terrace to declare confidence in his leadership. 'Spoke at some length: a quasi-manifesto.' In what was described as an 'angry speech', Gladstone threatened that unless stipulations about personal rating were removed from the bill he would not reconcile himself to the legislation but would endeavour by all legitimate means to alter it.[66] Under fire from Disraeli's raillery at 'spouters of stale sedition' (there had recently been another Hyde Park rally which successfully defied the Home Secretary's feeble interdiction), Gladstone weighed the implications of recourse to 'the people' in aid of his offering 'a decided resistance' in Parliament. The Liverpool echoes now resonated once more. He informed the Commons on 17 May: 'I must consider what is taking place and what is likely to take place out of doors.' He could not contemplate without the greatest pain 'the probable recommencement and continuance of a most resolute opposition out of doors of a character which I cannot pronounce to be illegitimate'. Those 'agencies out of doors, which are intended to form, to develop, and to mature public opinion, are the legitimate expressions of the people, by which bad legislation is to be corrected'. Gladstone deplored 'circumstances by which the business of governing this country' would be 'taken from within the walls of this House and transferred to places beyond them'. But he could see that 'that is the state of things at which we are likely to arrive, unless some measures be adopted to prevent it'.[67]

Over the years to come this style of argument would become Gladstone's grand leitmotiv: that danger to the state and the constitution came from those who resisted his proposals. The Commons at this moment had its own retort to such terrors. Gladstone was attempting to upstage Hodgkinson by smothering the obscure solicitor with the warm embraces of the millions. He recommended Hodgkinson's amendment (having in reserve a much better-drafted version in Childers's* name), making much of the point that his appeal was 'upon our part a complete waiving of the ground upon which we have stood'.[68] It would, of course, involve an even more complete waiving of the ground upon which Disraeli and the government stood. But the curious situation obtained that by now Disraeli was on the path of victory through surrender.

After speaking Gladstone left the chamber along with most of the members on his way to dinner. There had been much toing and froing in procedural confusion. In a thin House of fewer than a hundred members Disraeli thereupon upstaged Gladstone comprehensively by taking him simply at his word. Without prior consultation with his colleagues, Disraeli casually yet dramatically accepted Hodgkinson's amendment without a division as 'the quickest way out of the maze'.[69]† Many a 'snug dinner party' prematurely broke up in consternation as the wire agencies sent forth the startling news.[70] Gladstone himself hastened back to the chamber, stunned at Disraeli's coup. His bitterness comes through in a later comment he made on the event: 'even as a dog

---

* H. C. E. Childers, former Financial Secretary to the Treasury, 1865–6.
† The amendment would probably have been defeated in a division.

loves and follows his master drunk not less than his master sober, so the 250 Conservative gentlemen, who had hailed the measure in its narrow and reactionary form, continued to support it with equal fidelity when it had assumed its present wide and, as some would say, democratic proportions'. 'It was short, rapid, noiseless. Two hours of conversation, no debate – and all was over.'[71]

All was indeed over. Disraeli had his bill as good as in the bag. The utter unconvincingness of his assertion that ministers had intended all along to spring this surprise at the right moment hardly mattered in the heat both of events and the sticky temperature. Childers, bereft of Gladstone's presence, could only declare his sincere satisfaction at the government's third reversal of policy. John Stuart Mill was gratified at this 'great and splendid concession', which doubtless encouraged him in his efforts to tack female suffrage on to the bill. Cranborne denounced a 'change of startling magnitude', which he later interpreted as Disraeli's obsequious yielding to Gladstone's 'imperious dictation'.[72] Gladstone declaimed in futile indignation at Disraeli's 'astounding declaration of consistency'.[73] This moral ascendancy availed Gladstone as little as had his ascendancy hitherto on all matters of fact and detail. The nub of Gladstone's rebuke was that there remained 'no sufficient case for disputing the plan offered by the Government . . . considering how fully the Government plan involves the attainment of most of the substantial objects for which we on this side of the House have contended'.[74] As Lowe later put it in despairing exasperation: 'Was it in human foresight to have imagined such a thing?'[75]

[4]

'So strange is the *bouleversement* of this session and so willing are the more extreme men on the Liberal side to yield to the fascinations of the great actor, whose baits seem to be especially spread for them.' So wrote Roundell Palmer to Frank Faber on 12 June. To Palmer the implications of the *bouleversement* looked likely to strike deep. The spectacle of Gladstone's failure to lead and win in two successive sessions with all the advantages stacked behind him looked portentous, something far beyond mere fortuity. 'It seems to me that all political distinctions which we have hitherto known are, or shortly will be, broken up . . . and future political combinations will be formed with a freedom of choice unknown since the interregnum, after Sir Robert Walpole's fall was terminated by Pitt's first ministry.'[76] Palmer's wish very possibly fathered his thoughts. But even so, the condition of the Liberal party to all appearances was unprecedentedly dire. Gladstone had to endure Lady Waldegrave's reporting to him 'from friends the errors & defects they notice in me': an office she rather eagerly specialized in.[77] Then he had also to excuse himself to the Duchess of Sutherland for his withdrawal from front-bench leadership ('for me to be present and interfere continuously, or so far continuously as I might in other circumstances, would exhibit needlessly from day to day the divisions and consequent weakness of the Liberal party').[78] When it came to the closing debate on the third reading on 15 July Gladstone thought it best not to take part, 'for fear of doing mischief on our own side'. He left Cranborne to launch a philippic at Disraeli's treachery and Lowe to lament the coming dominion of the multitude ('I believe it will be absolutely necessary that you should prevail on our future masters to learn their letters').[79] Bright summed up the Liberal sense of disillusionment: 'It is curious that there is no exultation in the passing of the Reform Bill. The whole thing has been so unpleasant & so discreditable, that we who gain by it seem to have no satisfaction in it. It was very different in 1832 – & in 1846 when we won after great fights.'[80]

When it came to considering amendments from the Lords (where Derby famously avowed that the Reform Bill was 'a leap in the dark', and where Russell talked wildly of throwing household suffrage out) and winding up the session, Gladstone detected that the Liberal party 'was more healthy than of late'.[81] Gladstone did not care for Lord Cairns's proposal for a cumulative voting system in the larger boroughs to protect minority interests; and it was in its way only appropriate that he should end up losing the division on that issue. But what was really of consequence for Gladstone in the first session of 1867 had to do not with the Reform question but with the Irish question. In an intervention on matters concerning the Queen's University, he sketched a notion of a policy for Irish Catholic higher education: a foreshadowing of one foot of the tripod of his Irish reforms in his first administration.[82] Gladstone also made a parliamentary utterance which prepared the way for the Irish subtext to promote itself into an enhanced status, preparatory to metamorphosis. On 7 May he intervened in a debate on the Irish Church question launched by the Liberal MP for Kilkenny, Sir John Gray, with much the same purpose in view that Dillwyn had entertained in 1865.[83] Gladstone could hardly avoid the implied invitation; but in view of his earlier reservations about the necessary lapse of time in relation to the ripeness of the case, he had to introduce himself in a manner but little less reserved. He declared that he felt no difficulty about the issue as such; but he felt bound to question 'whether the time has come when a practical plan upon this subject can with advantage be submitted to Parliament'. But then, after piling abuse on those deprecating Gray's initiative, Gladstone executed a distinct transmutational shift: 'the time is not far distant when the Parliament of England, which at present undoubtedly has its hands full of other most important business and engagements, would feel it its duty to look this question fairly and fully in the face'.[84]

Thus Gladstone had left an imprint of auspicious purpose on the otherwise (for him) wholly forgettable session of 1867. No doubt the question was already forming in his mind: what would be the most fitting object to which the enormously enhanced power of popular opinion could be formed and directed? Once back at Hawarden in August, his primary concern was to acquit himself of an account of the last session for the *Edinburgh Review* which adequately delineated Disraeli's delinquencies and the dishonour they had imposed on the Conservative party. The 'good sense of the public', Gladstone had no doubt, 'has sickened at attempts alike despicable and ridiculous to claim originality and consistency in the very act of plagiarism and of tergiversation'. But the central thrust of his denunciation of that whole sad episode was to point to what yet remained to the future: 'Time, as it has thus far been, so it will continue to be', the 'vindicator and avenger' of the Liberal party; there was 'nothing to show that the Liberal party within the walls of Parliament, as it is at present composed has disabled itself from resuming, quite apart from any question as to the resumption of office, the command of public affairs and of Parliamentary legislation'. And, given that resumption of command and legislation, what then? The 'very air is full of the presage of events to come,' insisted Gladstone, 'and to exigencies, duties, and opportunities of the State, enlarged in proportion to the widening of its basis'. The public was 'impressed with the belief that within these last years a real arrears of work has accumulated'. There was education, there was economy, there was the Army, there were the colonies. Above all there was Ireland. 'What is our arrear in Ireland? That pregnant word suggests a whole range of painful misgivings, and of a work which, if much longer delayed threatens to become impracticable.'[85]

The unspoken definition of 'the work' for Ireland Gladstone left eloquently suspended in the autumnal atmosphere of the last days of the old politics. Otherwise, as balm to his wounds, there was Homer. He was nursing a plan to produce a revised edition of his *Studies on Homer* of 1858. The work he started on this plan in the 1867 recess would eventually emerge in 1869 as *Juventus Mundi. The Gods and Men of the Heroic Age*. But these were early days. He was eloquent at the first Lambeth Conference of representatives of the world of Anglicanism on the claims of the Church of England to stand 'in the very centre of all the conflicting forms of Christianity'.[86] His more substantial undertaking in these Hawarden weeks was to renew consideration of *Ecce Homo* –

authorship now acknowledged by Professor Seeley of University College, London – for *Good Words*. This he achieved by December, despite the interruption of an emergency session in November, occasioned by the government's decision to send an expedition to Abyssinia to rescue Consul Cameron and other British subjects who were being held captive by King Theodore, and to take countermeasures against the organized violence and assassinations of the 'Fenian' conspiracy.

The opening of the new session was marked by one of Gladstone's rare personal exchanges with Disraeli. Socially they were on a footing of somewhat contrived amiability, by means of reciprocal enquiry about the welfare of spouses.[87] Now Mary Anne Disraeli's serious illness prompted a truce. Disraeli wrote to Gladstone on 20 November regretting that his emotions had made it impossible for him the previous day to thank Gladstone adequately for his 'considerate sympathy' in kind words in his speech on the Address. 'My wife had always a strong personal regard for you, & being of a vivid & original character, she could comprehend, & value your great gifts, & qualities.'[88] Gladstone 'chivalrously' abstained for the time from political hostilities,[89] though was somewhat captious about the Palmerstonian style of the Abyssinian expedition. But Gladstone on the whole refrained from the minatory vindicating and avenging tone of the *Edinburgh Review* article. He trusted that the Scottish and Irish Reform bills would be put in hand without delay. He trusted also that the legislative responses to the Irish land question and to Fenian outrages could be equally efficacious. He deprecated as 'premature' (and by implication as likely to be obstructive to more immediately consequential objects) Lord Russell's resolution in the Lords about the 'moral right' of every child to an education.[90] He trusted that rumours were unfounded that the Irish Church Commissioners had been assigned the duty of drawing up plans for the reorganization of the Irish Church.

This last somewhat more specific hint of things to come hung in the air of the Christmas and New Year recess. Then in December came the most violent of the series of Fenian atrocities which had occurred throughout 1867 – in Canada, in Ireland itself, Chester, and Manchester (where a policeman was killed). Now, in London, an attempt to achieve a breakout of prisoners from Clerkenwell gaol by means of explosives led to many deaths and injuries. It happened that Gladstone was to speak at Oldham (with 'remarkable courage') on trade unionism, restraint of trade, and strikes, in terms provoking considerable offence in the trade-union movement. He included in his address an allusion to the Irish case: 'We must not get on the high horse and say we will entertain no questions with regard to the measures of relief until what is called Fenianism is extinguished. No: when you attack social evils, don't attack them in their manifestations, but attack them in their roots and in their causes.'[91]* He repeated the point the following day at Southport. Gladstone's connecting of Fenian outrages with attacking their roots and causes was later alleged to be, and interpreted as, the point of departure in his bringing forward the Irish Church issue. Lord Grey in particular pressed the case that this was the most deplorable incitement to 'the disposition of the Irish people to act on the fears of Government and Parliament' as the 'readiest mode of obtaining anything they desire'.[92]

Obviously Gladstone would have no difficulty in countering such criticisms by citing his declaration in the Commons of 7 May about the duty of looking the Irish Church question fairly and fully in the face,† or his *Edinburgh Review* article of October on the pregnant word arrear in the case of Ireland. Still, there is no doubt that it was Fenian terrorism at the end of 1867 which enabled Gladstone to begin to transmute into immediacy the process since 1865 which had passed from 'five or ten years' through to 'not far distant'. Gladstone later told the Queen's Secretary, General Grey, that he 'made up his mind' that the Irish Church '*must* be dealt with, when reading, in the railroad, the account of the rescue of the Fenian prisoners at Manchester'. So far from supposing that this would embarrass the government and strengthen himself with the Liberal party, Gladstone 'believed at the time that it would have the effect of weakening his personal position, and he had been *astonished* by the way it had been taken up'.[93]

Then at Christmas another event occurred which, while it might not have tended to the quickening of the pace of things notably, certainly promised a sharpening of the edge of things. Russell confided what could be interpreted (and Gladstone very promptly did so interpret) as an intention to retire from the Liberal leadership. On 26 December he assured Russell that his 'title to repose' could not be questioned. More to the immediate point: 'Nor am I sanguine as to what is to take place in the Liberal party when your decision is known.'[94] Perhaps, from Gladstone's point of view, this was just as well. Ambiguity about the leadership would be helpful while he was restoring his credit and authority in Parliament and in the party. Russell undertook to make his decision public at the end of his projected pamphlet on the Irish Church question (in which he argued, across Gladstone's line, for concurrent endowment of Roman Catholicism and Presbyterianism in Ireland, along with the Church of Ireland, by appropriating three quarters of the ecclesiastical revenues for the Catholics, and dividing the other quarter between

---

* On the trade-union issue, see below, page 96.
† See above, page 44.

the Anglicans and Presbyterians). But when it was published in February Russell's pamphlet was silent as to any such promise.[95] There remained the possibility that the quirky Whig chief might make a nuisance of himself by demanding the Foreign Office in a new Liberal ministry. Gladstone himself, in his birthday ruminations of 29 December, inaugurated a motif which was to become as insistent and as long-lived as it was to be unfulfilled: 'I long for the day of rest.'

If Gladstone was to have no rest, neither was he stinted for advice. The new leader of the party had the benefit of Argyll's agreeing with the *Daily News* that Gladstone's 'hold over the country is a very different thing' from his hold over the present House of Commons. 'My own view', he advised Gladstone, as one of the few who felt in a position, rather like Lady Waldegrave, to proffer candid counsel, 'is decidedly that during this coming session no attempt should be made to test party fidelity.' Argyll admitted the necessity 'sooner or later of putting an end to the condition of things in which a normal leader is regularly deserted by his men at the moment when he orders a charge'. Argyll urged Gladstone to 'postpone till the new Parliament all attempts to rally or to test party allegiance, and above all else choose a vote on which the tendencies of our party are as far as possible undivided'.[96] Clarendon analysed well the problem to Granville:

You must be a far better judge than myself, but I cannot discover a germ of appreciation towards Gladstone, or an attempt to discover how he can be done without; there seems a determination to distrust him, and to find fault with whatever he does or does not do. His genius and eloquence enable him to soar high above the heads of his party, who are always suspicious of what he may devise when he gets into higher or unknown latitudes.[97]

Gladstone, with due humility, could no doubt reflect that the qualities which made him such a problem to his political friends were precisely the same qualities which had projected him unerringly to the leadership. It was indeed, as Clarendon suggested, and would remain, an insoluble conundrum. For the moment, Gladstone could trust that his moving the second reading of his Compulsory Church Rates Abolition Bill would not test party allegiance too straitly. Then on 25 February he heard from Stanley that Derby was resigning from ill health, and that Disraeli was 'at work upon a Cabinet'. This was important. Derby commanded respect and forbearance among Whigs and Palmerstonians and Liberals generally which Disraeli did not. Derby, as a battle-hardened veteran in the Irish political and ecclesiastical wars, would not in 1868 have been the object of any enthusiastically united Liberal assault on Irish ground. Disraeli would provide a much more eligible target upon which Liberal unity could be focused. Gladstone on the 28th 'considered a good deal on the personnel of our party with a view to contingencies'.

Argyll's criterion of an issue on which the tendencies of the Liberal party were as far as possible undivided pointed of course to the Irish Church question. Gladstone continued to caution zealots like Bright that the cause of Irish disestablishment 'may again lead the Liberal party to martyrdom' as it did in the 1830s.[98] In this respect Russell's departure was even more apropos than Derby's. Russell's urging concurrent endowment chimed in well with Conservative dispositions on the same lines towards pre-emption, building on the existing provision for Roman Catholicism of the Maynooth grant and of the *Regium Donum* for the Presbyterians. Gladstone was now set free to push for the more radical course of straightforward disestablishment and disendowment all round. Cairns put the case accurately from the Conservative point of view: 'If Gladstone and his friends go for anything *like* Ld Russell's proposition they will fail signally. If they throw it over, & go for a complete disendowment of everybody, they may catch voluntaries, radicals, & anti-poperymen, & make a formidable phalanx.'[99]

That kind of formidable phalanx was very much what Gladstone had in mind when on 12 March he summoned a 'Conclave 12–2 on the Irish question'. The ball had been set rolling with nicely connived timing by Maguire, Liberal MP for Cork, on 10 March: the Irish Church was becoming 'the question of the day'; there was 'foreboding and alarm', not merely anxiety, as Parliament came to find itself 'on the eve of a great struggle'.[100] Gladstone prepared himself for his incisive stroke. On 16 March he launched his attack. Disraeli described it as an 'announcement of startling importance'.[101] Gladstone took up Maguire's theme: the government had 'failed to realise in any degree the solemn fact that we have reached a crisis in the affairs and in the state of Ireland'. The land question and the education question needed attention; but most urgent was the Church. If any good was to be done for the Church of Ireland it must be by putting an end to its futile existence as a state Church. This would be 'a great and formidable operation', but not beyond 'the courage and statesmanship of the British legislature'.[102]

After further conclaves on the 19th and 20th, Gladstone on 23 March reinforced the startling importance of his general advance with the stunning specifics of notice of three resolutions. They constituted a peremptory stroke which quite unnerved Disraeli's Cabinet. Disraeli had cause to lament his ill fortune at being early the head of a government so suddenly struck with a fateful crisis which its striker had less than two years previously defined as a matter of remote contingency. He protested at the suddenness and 'unseasonable' nature of Gladstone's assault, with the session well advanced, with much business to transact, on an issue which would better be left to the new Parliament. Argyll privately explained to enquirers as to the urgency: 'There really was no other way of getting Dizzy out of office.'[103]

Although many Whigs found Gladstone disturbing in general and distasteful in many particulars, they could not deny the validity of the tradition of Whiggish despite for the Church of the Irish Ascendancy. The year 1868 was undoubtedly a time, rather like 1859, when the centripetal tendencies of the Liberal groups and interests took command against their rather more accustomed centrifugal habits. Curious echoes recurred from the past. Lord Derby and Gladstone were respectively at the opposite poles of their positions in the 1830s and 1840s.[104] Gladstone reread his speeches of the 1830s. There were Liberals with doubts and reservations. Their spokesman was Roundell Palmer: reluctantly accepting the unavoidability of disestablishment, but balking at disendowment. Gladstone grappled with him as Derby (then Stanley) had grappled with Gladstone over Maynooth; Palmer now echoing the Gladstone then: 'I cannot separate myself in feeling from my fellow-churchmen in Ireland.'[105] But Palmer represented a decided minority of Liberals. Granville commented on the 'almost unanimous opinion of the Liberal party'.[106] Gladstone pressed on with introducing his resolutions on the 30th and carried the House brilliantly on 3 April: 'Spoke 1½ hours after D (who was tipsy) in winding up the debate.' The divisions consistently of a near sixty majority were 'wonderful'. He walked home with Harry and Herbert, 'a crowd at our tail'. 'The counts are big: and I, how little.'

It was at this moment of public triumph that a disturbing element privately intruded. The peremptory tone of Gladstone's resolutions offended the Queen. She visited Derby at St James's Square on 3 April, speaking 'in the most unreserved terms of condemnation of Gladstone's motion and conduct'. She was especially offended that she had not been offered prior consultation with respect to Gladstone's third resolution, which prayed that the Crown put all its interest in Irish Church temporalities at the disposal of Parliament. She felt her prerogative being touched disrespectfully. Derby reported to Disraeli: 'I took it upon myself to say that I had strongly urged you in the event of defeat, not to think of resigning, to which H.M. answered, "Quite right".'[107] As Granville explained to the Queen, in his role as tactful smoother, Gladstone had consulted relevant precedents, and felt himself unable, as being no longer a servant of the Crown, to make any confidential communication. This was rather straining the niceties of the case. The office of personal explanation was just as open to Gladstone as it was to Granville. Gladstone, made aware of the Queen's sense of hurt, declared himself 'really curious to know what *is* the course which it is supposed ought to have been taken in order to satisfy the principles of the Constitution, and the claims of personal loyalty and faith'.[108] There was never much doubt in any case of the course Gladstone was likely to take as between constitutional principle and personal claims. The episode had bearings not only immediately on Disraeli's decision not to resign, but also for the longer term marked a moment of sharp deterioration in Gladstone's relations with the Queen.

With painful memories of the previous two sessions of the 1865 Parliament, Gladstone trusted that the Irish Church question would not be 'degraded into a warfare of trick and contrivance'. He defended his past record with respect to the question. He denied sudden 'apostasy'. The burden of his argument was that the time had come when there was a prospect of carrying the issue to a successful conclusion: circumstances were now 'ripe'.[109] This ripeness in the time bore for Gladstone much deeper import than the mere 'right-timing' or opportunism or the expediency of gathering the Liberal party back into unity. 'Religious equality for Ireland' would later be cited by Gladstone as the second occasion, after the 1853 budget, of his special gift of insight at critical junctures of appreciating the general situation and its result. The very air presaging great events to come, the exigencies, duties, and opportunities of the state, enlarged in proportion to the widening of its electoral basis, all conjoined within Gladstone's appointed office in the divine economy, now assumed potent urgency in an articulation between the doings and intentions of the minister (or in this case, of the minister-to-be) and the corresponding conviction wrought by them upon the public mind.

As the pace of events quickened, Gladstone responded to an appeal for less precipitate advance: 'I should acknowledge the justice of your claim that I should pause & meditate, were it not that I had paused long, meditated often, & thoroughly convinced myself by the experience & reflection of many years that I am in the path of right, & therefore doing what does honour, as far as so poor a creature may, to God, as the God of truth & justice.'[110] On Easter day, in exalted mood, Gladstone confided to his diary: 'And this day, all unworthy as I am, I solemnly offered before the Eternal Throne, with the perpetual sacrifice of the great High Priest, the arduous public work in which I am engaged.'[111] Thus fortified, Gladstone pressed onward after the recess. By now Disraeli and his colleagues were reeling, on the run. Neither Ward Hunt's budget nor Turkish atrocities in Crete deflected Gladstone from his arduous and high purpose. On 27 April he put his first resolution forward for formal adoption by the Commons. 'Much oppressed in *nerve*, only by the bigness of the subject: & with a great sense of giddiness.' Here, as with the Reform issue, Gladstone was absolute master of the intricacies; but this time his mastery of detail was translated into mastery of the political arena. On 30 April Gladstone carried the division with crushing decisiveness, 330 to 265. Disraeli announced that the vote had altered the relations between Her Majesty's Government and the House of Commons. It would be necessary for Her Majesty's Government to consider its position.

Now began the comedy mingled a little with farce and not untouched by a hint of tragedy, whereby the Conservative government offered the Queen its resignation; and upon that offer, or any contingent advice as to a dissolution and general election, being declined, stayed in office until, in December, Disraeli judged the results of the November general election to be tantamount to dismissal. Gladstone and his friends confidently assumed that, in the conventional manner, upon having manifestly lost the confidence of the Commons on a matter of the highest public import, ministers would either resign, whereupon Gladstone would be summoned and requested to form a new government, or would dissolve the Parliament. On 1 May: 'Conclave 2–4 on the Situation. Almost agreed to resist an appeal for the loss of a twelve month: but to allow with Censure an immediate dissolution.' Which, being translated, meant that the Liberals would have preferred office immediately, but were willing to accept in lieu an immediate appeal to the constituencies: though whether on the old or new registers was not at that time entirely clear.

That was precisely the thin end of the obstructive wedge which Disraeli put in the way of Gladstone's plans. Disraeli in the Commons and Malmesbury in the Lords announced on 4 May that Her Majesty had been pleased to decline the government's proffered resignation, and that the 1865 Parliament would be dissolved 'whenever the state of public affairs would permit'.[112] The justifications were first that the Irish Church resolutions were 'unseasonable' and improperly the occasion of resignation; they had been forced forward with minimal notice and startling suddenness and would be much more appropriately dealt with by the new Parliament. Second, the government's Reform measures for Scotland and Ireland were still in train. Third, the registers for the hugely expanded new electorate would take time to prepare. The unspoken presumption here was the supreme undesirability, after the drama of Reform in 1866 and 1867, of dissolving in 1868 on obsolete 1865 registers. That quickly became designated as the 'penal' option. The nub of the affair, constitutionally, was Disraeli's deliberate restriction of the case to the Queen's response to advice as purely that of declining resignation and to agreeing to a future dissolution, without any reference to the readiness of registers. In other words, Disraeli had at his disposal a 'penal' dissolution with which to blackmail Gladstone and the Liberal majority of the Commons. To indignant Liberals, this seemed – which it was – the dragging of the

Queen into partisan politics. But the point, which Disraeli potently knew and Gladstone had good cause to suspect, was that Victoria was perfectly prepared to play a high game. That she disliked Gladstone's Irish Church policy was hardly a secret in the political world. That she found offensive Gladstone's manner of pursuing it was but little more occult. Gladstone's introduction of a bill to suspend all new preferments in the Irish Church exacerbated this sense of offence. She certainly agreed with Disraeli's opinion that Gladstone's initiative was sudden and unseasonable, and that the Irish Church, if it had to be touched, would better be touched by a new Parliament.

Given her and Disraeli's readiness to play the high game together, there was little the Liberals could do but fulminate against Disraeli's clinging to office and emoluments. Gathorne Hardy recorded Gladstone's being 'in a white heat with an almost diabolical expression of counten-ance'.[113] Bright's 'rabid rage' at Disraeli's being at once 'pompous and servile' ended their personal relationship. Disraeli was able to crush Lowe witheringly by challenging him: 'If you want to have a vote of Want of Confidence, propose a vote of Want of Confidence.'[114] Confronted with the prospect of a 'penal' dissolution, Gladstone prudently declined a vote either of confidence or censure.

Therefore it was that Disraeli's minority government held on until necessary business was completed and the Parliament was prorogued on 31 July. Disraeli was soon able to announce that a dissolution on the new registers would be possible in November. He had assurances from Spofforth, his party agent, that Gladstone would be defeated in South Lancashire. In any case, Disraeli was at pains to convince his colleagues (several of whom were very doubtful about the whole proceeding) that he possessed most reliable information that Gladstone, 'instead of wishing to upset us, has no Cabinet ready, & though sanguine as to his future, is at present greatly embarrassed'. Gladstone wished, alleged Disraeli, to 'build us a golden bridge, and if we announce a bona fide attempt to wind up, he would suggest Bills to extend the time of regis-tration, which would be necessitated by the passing of the Scotch and Irish Bills'. It was true that while some of Gladstone's following, led by Bright and Ayrton, were demanding instant and violent action, the 'commercial Liberals' looked with the greatest alarm to Lord Russell's return to the Foreign Office, or even Lord Clarendon's. Never was there a moment when a Want of Confidence vote would have a worse chance. All intentions to humiliate the government, Disraeli insisted, were 'quite superficial'. An immediate dissolution was quite unnecessary and would be unpopular in the House.[115]

That there was a certain kind of crude plausibility for this is undeniable: though whether owing more to Disraeli's necessities than to Gladstone's convenience is a moot question. Certainly Russell was being refractory and troublesome.[116] Certainly Gladstone did not embark upon any 'violent action'. And certainly Gladstone had grounds for supposing that Spofforth might not be all that far out in his estimate of the electoral chances in South Lancashire. On the other hand the government became subject to what Hardy described as 'no wholesale censure, but retail humiliation' as the 'miserable session' wound its way out.[117]

First and foremost, naturally, was the triumphant conclusion to the issue of Gladstone's Irish Church resolutions on 7 May: 'The Resolutions were passed: & then we had stirring scenes. All ended well, very well. Thanks be to God.' Much bad temper and altercation was displayed on all sides. Clarendon commented that while confidence in Gladstone seemed on the increase throughout the country, it remained 'feeble and stationary in the H. of C.'.[118] Then on 16 June the Irish Church Suspensory Bill went through, 'in all but silence: except the cheers'. Gladstone also got his Compulsory Church Rates Abolition measure through, though hardly as a matter of his exerting imperious mastery over cowed ministers, helpless to stem or stay. The government granted Gladstone sessional accommodation partly because they had to, but partly also because they wanted to. Cairns in the Lords together with a majority of the bishops made amendments which in fact represented a distinct rebuff to Gladstone's plan. However, faced with ministerial unwillingness to extend their accommodation, Gladstone settled reluctantly for what he could get.[119] (He thought Archbishop Tait had 'gone stark mad'.)[120]

The bench of bishops was also to the fore in the division in the Lords which threw out the Irish Church Suspensory Bill at the end of June. This in turn provoked a demonstration which marched from Clerkenwell through to Hyde Park Corner, occasioning tremors of 'some excitement' within the clubhouses of Pall Mall and St James's. Parliament once again was made aware of the displeasure of the people. A deputation addressed Gladstone at Carlton House Terrace. Gladstone expressed his pleasure at this manifestation of 'real working men'.[121]

[5]

For the rest, it was a matter mainly of preparing for the general election in November and the likely shape of things following. Gladstone was in no doubt that Liberalism's habitual political hegemony would be confirmed and reinforced by the expanded electorate. On 10 July there was a conversation with Granville, 'long & large, including possible ministerial arrangements'. 'Puss' Granville, easy and amenable, was establishing his place as an agreeably supportive confidant. Gladstone saw also Clarendon 'on all questions & especially respecting the coming Govt.'. It was now held out of the question that Russell might return to the Foreign Office, but Gladstone's invitation to Clarendon to do so would cause yet another difficulty with the Queen. Then there was a complication about the South Lancashire seat. A second two-seat division had been created under the new redistribution arrangements, and Gladstone was allocated to a South-West division. At the time when Disraeli's resignation or a dissolution was expected in May, Rathbone in Liverpool had assured Gladstone that as far as the old registers were concerned, 'I certainly consider our prospects more encouraging than previous to the last election & particularly so on the resignation of ministers. I believe a minister was never defeated in Liverpool & a Liverpool Lancashire prime minister would be a difficult man to beat.'[122] But the problem was that there had been no resignation of Conservative ministers and no dissolution by Liberal ministers. And as to an election on new registers in November, or January 1869, 'it is too soon to speak'. Sir C. Armitage 'has been giving an unfavourable opinion'. Lord Sefton was willing to fund his brother-in-law, H. R. Grenfell, as Gladstone's Liberal partner in the new division, which it was held ensured 'brilliant prospects'.[123] Gladstone declared his candidacy on 3 August, and began his campaigning at the Adelphi Hotel in Liverpool and at St Helens. It was thought prudent nonetheless to provide a fall-back refuge at Greenwich should South-West Lancashire turn too Orange on the Irish Church.

Over late summer and early autumn Gladstone relaxed at the family's old resort at Penmaenmawr on the north Wales coast ('But *public* business takes half my working day or near it'). Much of this business was wrangling correspondence with critics who accused Gladstone of apostasy on the Irish Church, with lengthy quotations from the 1830s and 1840s. Back at Hawarden on 17 September Gladstone began 'what may be "A Chapter of Autobiography"'', in which he envisaged setting out the whole history of his personal concern with the Irish Church question in order to demonstrate his good faith and good intentions. Within a month he had it prepared for the press. As he pointed out, a great cause can suffer in credit for the real or supposed delinquencies of a person especially associated with it. Gladstone's concern was to defend himself from two principal accusations: first, his alleged intellectual and ecclesiastical betrayal of his doctrine in *The State in Relation to the Church* of 1838; and second, his alleged tactical opportunism – 'You would never have heard anything about the Irish Church question from Mr Gladstone if the Tories had not been in power, and he had not wanted to get their place.'[124]

On neither indictment was Gladstone in great difficulties in pleading innocence. He could demonstrate how the Irish Church question had over the decades 'continually flitted, as it were, before me'. He could demonstrate that, with Palmerston's demise in 1865, the 'calm was certain to be succeeded by a breeze, if not a gale'. He could cite the testimony of Roundell Palmer, no less, as a witness to his innocence in the matter of political opportunism. He circulated pre-publication copies to selected colleagues. Granville judged it 'perfectly unanswerable', 'admirable', and was 'all for its publication'.[125] However, Gladstone instructed the publishers, Murray's, to hold it back until after the election so as to avoid giving it a partisanly apologetic character. Gladstone was quite justified in thinking that, as an account of the mental history of a rather intensely engaged Christian Churchman and politician of his time, the *Chapter* deserved more than to be remembered merely as electoral propaganda.

Serious campaigning work began in October, with an appearance at the Liverpool Amphitheatre as the star turn. Apart from the Church issue, Gladstone's Address confined itself to the standard clichés of economy and rating. Clarendon professed anxiety that 'Merry-pebble' would be 'worked up by his meetings to a state of excitement which Christmas will hardly cool'.[126] Certainly, 'unmuzzled', Gladstone was leaving fang marks on the body politic which he had not done in 1865. The mood of his *Edinburgh Review* article of October, with its themes of vindication and vengeance, of vast arrears to be overcome, of the presagements of great events in the air, of the exigencies, duties, and opportunities of the state, set the tone. There were irritating diversions. A steely letter from the Liverpool feminist activist Josephine Butler intruded: how did Gladstone propose to vote on Mr Shaw-Lefevre's proposed Married Women's Property Bill, and on admitting women to the parliamentary suffrage? Great numbers, he was assured, were 'waiting anxiously' for his answer. Gladstone warily declined to give pledges. His attitude in 1867 to John Stuart Mill's attempt to tack female suffrage on to the Reform Bill had been gnomic. He did not speak directly on the question, but was understood to think it impracticable.[127]* Of far greater moment to Gladstone was the death of his Egeria, Harriet, Dowager Duchess of Sutherland: 'the warmest and dearest friend, surely, that man ever had'.[129] He was one of the pallbearers at the funeral at Trentham ('my very dear friend, whom I hardly yet can believe to be dead, so inaccessible to the last enemy appeared one who lived so intensely').[130] This death left a serious gap in Gladstone's recourse to female intellectual and spiritual companionship.

---

* In 1870 G cast his vote 'cheerfully' against Jacob Bright's bill to remove women's disabilities.[128]

A welcome telegram on 17 November from Greenwich announced that Gladstone had safely secured the second seat there. But Milner Gibson's defeat at Ashton – a seat he had held without contest since 1857 – indicated that hitherto secure Liberal seats in Lancashire were vulnerable to what the mortified Gibson called 'Murphyism or Orangeism'.[131]* This vulnerability was confirmed by Hartington's defeat in North Lancashire. Sure enough: the poll at Liverpool on 21 November left Gladstone and Grenfell trailing behind the two Conservative candidates. The apologetic Liberal managers could only cite the 'effect of the result of the other Lancashire Elections'.[132] Defeat in South Lancashire was irritating, considering the cult Gladstone had made of its civic virtues since his expulsion from Oxford. But the ignominy of retreating to the second Greenwich seat was more than compensated for by the enlarged Liberal majority overall. Its likely dimensions of near one hundred worried sceptical Whigs like Clarendon. 'Heaven knows, however, of what materials it will be composed, and one can only feel sure that such a team will require to be driven by a more skilful Jehu than Gladstone.' Clarendon, in his mischievously gossiping way, was in hopes that the Queen might upset the apple-cart by summoning Russell; but reflected that 'for her interest' she must ask Gladstone in order 'to give no colour to the notion that is rife of his being utterly repugnant to her'.[133]

Given the somewhat anomalous status of the government since its defeats at Gladstone's hands in April, there was a certain logic and fitness in Disraeli's unprecedented act of immediate resignation when the electoral fact of his government's dismissal became manifest. The conventional procedure would have been to wait to meet the new Parliament. Disraeli's resignation was widely deplored on the grounds that it recognized the ascendancy of electoral power out of doors at the expense of the constitutional role of the House of Commons in deciding the fate of ministries. As it happened, it was not until Lord Salisbury met the new Parliament of 1885 in 1886 that the conventional procedure was resumed. It is a matter of some interest that Gladstone, conservative as he was on almost all niceties of parliamentary and constitutional usage, made no complaint at the compliment thus implicitly accorded to the judgement of the people. In due course he would declare that it was 'admitted by all' that Disraeli had 'exercised a sound judgment'.[134] In fact, he had plans to emulate Disraeli's radical innovation by instantly summoning the new Parliament before the end of the year, to underline his earlier complaints about lost time. He was immediately in touch with

---

* Another conspicuous though unrelated Liberal casualty was J. S. Mill, ousted at Westminster by the free-spending newsagent W. H. Smith.

Disraeli about the new Speaker of the Commons, Denison; and with compliments also for Mary Anne Disraeli's peerage of Beaconsfield.[135] At Hawarden on 1 December Gladstone was alerted by the Queen's secretary, Grey, on her intention to invite him to undertake the government. Grey assumed Gladstone would come to London, but Gladstone proposed Hawarden 'as attracting less attention'. At church, as he awaited Grey, Gladstone observed: 'The Lessons, as usual in times of crisis, supplied all my need. "The Lord shall give thee rest from thy sorrow, & from the hard bondage wherein thou was made to serve ... The whole earth is at rest, & is quiet: they break forth into singing". '[136]

Thus it was on 2 December that Evelyn Ashley, Shaftesbury's son and former private secretary to Palmerston, attended Gladstone while he felled an ash in the park. He recollected, some thirty years later, that as he held Gladstone's jacket, the telegram was delivered announcing Grey's intended arrival that evening. Gladstone remarked: 'Very significant.' 'I said nothing, but waited while the well-directed blows resounded in regular cadence. After a few minutes the blows ceased, and Mr Gladstone, resting on the handle of his axe, looked up, and with deep earnestness in his face, exclaimed: "My mission is to pacify Ireland." He then resumed his task, and never said another word till the tree was down.'[137] As he awaited Grey, Gladstone adjured himself: 'The Lord is in his holy temple; the Lord's seat is in heaven.' Grey was astonished, on arriving at Chester station at 4.15 p.m., to be met by Catherine and to find out from her on the drive to Hawarden 'that Mrs G. knew everything that had passed! The Queen's objections, etc. etc.' On arrival Grey was taken at once by Catherine 'into an almost dark room – the only light being the fire, and the two candles by which Mr Gladstone was working'. It was already clear that there would be a difficulty about Clarendon, to whom the Queen had strong objections, never precisely defined. Both Grey and Clarendon were concerned to avoid anything that would give the appearance of a '*Court* manoeuvre'. Clarendon was an assiduous gossip and Gladstone assumed the problem had to do with some 'rashness of speech', and that there was 'likewise the idea of some indelicacy', repeated to the Queen 'with carelessness or malignity'.[138]* Gladstone promptly turned to Dean Wellesley of Windsor to apply his talents as intermediary.

At Windsor on 3 December (to which he walked unnoticed from Eton, having called in to see Harry, thereby also avoiding a large demonstration at the station) Gladstone found the Queen 'kind, cheerful, even playful'.

---

* G seems to have been unaware that he had himself great cause to be offended by Clarendon's malicious gossip.

No doubt Victoria was impressed with the need to put the best face on things. This was the worst moment for her, in such matters, since 1841, when she was confronted by the unwelcome figure of Sir Robert Peel. On her question as to whether he would undertake to construct an administration, Gladstone replied: 'Madam, I have no choice: & I have only to regret that my powers whether of body or mind are not better suited for the purpose.' No allusion was made to the Irish Church question. Gladstone did notice, however, a curious constraint in her manner. It was not until 5 December, on going through the budget figures with her, with the Queen 'perfectly kind and accessible', that he asked 'whether I ought not to kiss hands: she said yes & it was done'. The Queen raised the Church question, he noticed, only 'when the time for the train was fast approaching'.[139] Clarendon for the Foreign Office was still a problem, but Granville deployed his famed 'tact and conciliatoriness' to good effect in the background, along with Wellesley and Grey. Granville and the Queen were trying hard to get Halifax in to represent 'the *Old Whigs*'.[140]

In fact, Gladstone had far greater problems about Bright than he had with the Queen about Clarendon. As he assured Wellesley, Gladstone had exchanged not a word thus far upon coming events with any 'advanced Liberal of whatever school'. Now came the moment to confront the task of offering a Cabinet place to a man he had been chary of offering a pre-sessional dinner place to in 1867. Cobden had proudly refused Palmerston's offer of office in 1859. 'Mr Bright 10–12: a very stiff conversation.'[141] Milner Gibson, Cobden's substitute in 1859, was now out of the running. And Bright's stiffness had much to do with his stipulation that the new ministry must take up the secret ballot.[142] Bright would sit uncomfortably among the great official Whigs. Indeed, some of them found Bright far too close for comfort, and refused offers from Gladstone. Bright had no administrative talent. But his presence in the government as the first non-Anglican Radical was felt by Gladstone to be inescapably the seal of good faith between the new ministry and the new electorate. Gladstone had been favoured with gratuitous advice from the ancient Lord Brougham, a victim of the Whigs in 1834. 'You alone ought to be Prime Minister – & being so, I earnestly advise you to have as little as possible to do with the Brooks's Clique.' Brougham recommended Bright for either the Home or the Colonial Offices.[143] Gladstone, after a long struggle, persuaded Bright to accept the Board of Trade.

By late on the 6th, dispositions were beginning to emerge with something like clarity. Palmer was ineligible for the Lord Chancellorship because of the Church question. Gladstone dropped Stanley of Alderley. He took pains to keep Delane of *The Times* in the picture.

You may like certainty at a time such as this.
The appointments actually made to the Cabinet are

    Mr Gladstone – First Lord has kissed hands
    Ld Justice Page Wood – Chancellor*
    Ld Clarendon – Foreign Secretary
    Ld Granville – Colonies
    Duke of Argyll – India
    Mr Cardwell – War
    Mr Lowe – Chancellor of the Exchequer
    Mr Childers – Admiralty
    Mr Bright – President Board of Trade
    Mr Fortescue – Secretary for Ireland

Mr Bright has declined the rank and office of a Secretary of State.

A seat in the Cabinet has been offered to Lord Russell & declined with the most friendly assurances of his disposition towards the Government. Sir G. Grey is in the north and his intentions are not yet known . . .

Should there be more intelligence tonight – Mr Glyn will be in a condition to let you know.[145]†

There was much observation on the 'ominous absence of many supposed candidates'.[146] Somerset, Halifax, and Grey declined offers from Gladstone.[147] But the big surprise was Lowe. Lowe himself was not surprised – 'my sins in 1866 notwithstanding'. Gladstone had approved of Lowe in general. He approved Lowe's cost-cutting Revised Code in the Education Department. He thought highly of Lowe's financial capacity. He liked Lowe's penchant for being 'effectively disagreeable'.[148] Now Lowe's parliamentary reputation was enormous. Gladstone in due course would have reason to lament his choice, especially after revelations of Lowe's 'abject poverty of powers of defence'.[149] Gladstone's great mistake was to overlook Goschen. Edward Hamilton, who later became Gladstone's private secretary at the Treasury, thought Gladstone's preference for Lowe in 1868 was 'certainly an instance of the mistaken estimate which Mr Gladstone has often made of men'. Hamilton came to rank Goschen with Peel and Gladstone himself as the premier financiers of the time.[150] However, in December 1868 Lowe's appointment seemed an apt stroke both of political forgivingness and shrewdness. De Grey accepted the Lord Presidency, and added some Whig weight.

---

* Lord Westbury's comment on Page Wood (created Lord Hatherley): 'The Lord Chancellor's character is unredeemed by a single vice.'[144]
† G. G. Glyn, MP for Shaftesbury, was Brand's successor as Chief Whip. Succeeded as Lord Wolverton, 1873. An ever-present figure in the G entourage.

H. A. Bruce, who became Home Secretary, recalled Carlton Gardens on 7 December: de Grey asleep, 'and Gladstone, Glyn, and I walked up and down for half an hour, Gladstone walking home with us as far as Piccadilly. He was in high spirits.'[151]

Bruce, a Merthyr coal and ironmaster, represented something of what has been described as 'moralised commercial efficiency';[152] again considered apt for the time and the political circumstance. Goschen also belonged to that category; but his time would come later and under different auspices. The appointment outside the Cabinet in 1868 that occasioned most notice in this category of *novi homines* was that of the Bradford worsted manufacturer W. E. Forster, who, an ex-Quaker brother-in-law of Matthew Arnold, was an interesting appointment as vice-president of the Committee of the Council on Education. Forster was an entirely new and different kind of Radical from the anti-state, laissez-faire tradition of Cobden. Meanwhile Cobden's heir, Bright, was being house-trained at Osborne by Granville.[153]

For Gladstone there were also certain preparatory visits and missions. He devoted the first weekend of the session to Hatfield, seat of the new Marquess of Salisbury, erstwhile Cranborne and Lord Robert Cecil. He and Gladstone were much apart in their politics, but much together in their churchmanship. They were also, now, much together in their hostility to Disraeli. But beyond that there was the question of the House of Lords and its relationship to the new government's legislation. Gladstone wanted his Irish Church Suspensory Bill pushed through promptly. Derby had resigned the Conservative leadership in the Lords on his retirement; and Malmesbury was a reluctant temporary replacement. Cairns was resisting Disraeli's pleas to take it on and save Disraeli from the intense embarrassment of having Salisbury elected to the post by the Conservative lords: he and Salisbury were on the worst possible personal terms.* This was precisely where Gladstone came in. He moved up to Hatfield after a Windsor audience ('Saw the Queen at one & stated the case of the Irish Church. It was graciously received').[154] He walked on the Saturday with Salisbury across to Brocket Hall to pay respects to the widowed Lady Palmerston. It was on that day that Gladstone also commenced his preparatory intercourse with the Irish Establishment. To Archbishop Trench of Dublin he trusted, on Hatfield notepaper, that their present degree of personal relationship would continue. All views held by the Irish Anglican episcopate 'will at all times have my most respectful attention'.[155]

No doubt it would colour the Hatfield visit too highly to allow in it

---

* The Duke of Richmond eventually agreed to take it on. Salisbury succeeded Derby as Chancellor of Oxford University.

the material reality of anything like a working anti-Disraeli axis between Gladstone and Salisbury. Yet the victim of Disraeli's treachery and the victim of Disraeli's plagiarism and tergiversation were curiously linked by Lowe, a habitué of Hatfield. It had been to the new dowager Lady Salisbury that Lowe had written in September: 'I wish that they would make me Chancellor of the Exchequer.' It was with some such sense of community of spirit that Gladstone thanked Lady Salisbury for her kindness and hospitality, adding some words about her husband of extraordinary, and in some ways poignant, prescience.

I feel it the more because although in public discussion on recent events his name comes to the mind of everyone I dare not pronounce it, for fear I should not myself be satisfied to leave it without a mark, & on the other hand I do not know how much harm I might do by a word of civility to him, that is to the interest which England has in him.

In one way or another, if he is spared, his time must come.[156]

The long-drawn-out process of administration-making was now almost complete. Gladstone very characteristically apologized to Lord Lansdowne for carelessly addressing him 'in terms of familiarity' when offering him a Lordship of the Treasury.[157] Hartington had to wait to scramble back into the Commons by courtesy of Mr Greene-Price's exchanging his Radnor District seat (for an ultimate baronetcy) in February 1869, when he could not be accommodated with anything better than the Post Office. But in a certain way, Gladstone's most significant appointment in December 1868 was of Robert Peel's son Arthur as Parliamentary Secretary to the Poor Law Board.* Gladstone wrote to Sir Robert's daughter:

I tread the footsteps of greater men. It is now just 34 years since yr. father did for me what I have been doing for your brother Arthur . . .

And whatever seem the seeming changes of name or measures of this I am inwardly sure, that I am as loyal as ever to your father's principles, & that if he had been alive I will not say he wd have been with us, but we with him, in the very work & purpose we are now about.[158]

* A. W. Peel, MP for Warwick 1865–95; Speaker of the Commons 1884–95. Created Viscount Peel 1895.

CHAPTER 3

'THE ALMIGHTY SEEMS TO SUSTAIN AND SPARE ME . . .': HEROIC PEELITE GOVERNMENT, 1869–71

[1]

The intensity and authenticity of Gladstone's evocation of Peel as the tutelary genius of the work and purpose he was now about leave no doubt as to his sense of the reality and material relevance of that filiation. It was of a piece with his earlier *Edinburgh* manifesto of 1867. In surveying the 'merits and services' of the Parliaments between the Great Reform Act of 1832 and the Crimean War, Gladstone concluded unequivocally: 'It was a golden age of useful legislation, and of administrative improvement.'[1] Gladstone saw himself at the end of 1868 as the restorer and fulfiller of that golden age. The epoch which followed Peel's smash and the smash of the Aberdeen effort to resuscitate Peelism had been – as Gladstone most fervently so denounced it in many a polemic and invective in the 1850s – an epoch of political bad faith, an epoch most fittingly characterized by the name of Palmerston, and fittingly also capped by that ultimate exponent of bad faith, Disraeli.

Now came all the Tennysonian promise of the golden years returned. The air was full of auspicious presagements. Finance, happily, under Gladstone's care in 1853 and 1859–66, was one responsibility of the state which had been to a great extent honoured; though even here the fearful pressures on economical management had not abated, and would be as important as ever to resist. Economy, as Gladstone later put it, had been 'out of fashion' for the latter twenty years of his political life 'as it was in fashion for the first twenty'. Otherwise, it was a picture of 'immense deficiency' (as with popular education), of matters 'crying aloud for the most vigorous handling' (as with the organization of the Army), of matters, in Ireland especially, of a supreme urgency brooking no further delay. It was this statesmanship, curiously mingling old-fashioned references to the days of Peel with the most modern exigencies of the instant, which confronted Gladstone's new private secretary and head of his secretariat, Algernon West. He recalled Gladstone wearing a dark frock coat, with a flower in his buttonhole; a pair of brown trousers with a dark stripe down them, 'after the fashion of twenty years earlier'; a 'somewhat disordered neckcloth and a large collar'. West particularly noticed the black leather finger-stall which Gladstone 'invariably adjusted over the amputated finger on his left hand before he began to write'.[2] But most of all West was impressed by Gladstone's air of potent energy and high seriousness of purpose.

Nothing had been lacking in Gladstone's *Edinburgh* prevision of 1867 of awareness of those most modern exigencies of the instant. The reformed Parliament 'must be an ambitious, and may be an impatient and exacting Parliament'. The picture he drew, Gladstone felt, 'seems to show that more strain is wanted for the engine of the State; and, to say nothing of the counties, the profound change that has been made in the borough franchise of itself suffices to warrant the belief that the stimulus will be supplied'. The great question then was, who would be the directing and controlling power? 'From whence is this to come? The strain will be supplied; the engine will be started; who is to appoint the drivers?'[3]

Events had supplied the answers. It need not be supposed that Gladstone had any doubts as to his own appointed role in the ordering of those events. Power was now his to direct and control. The strain would soon be supplied; the engine started. Power was exciting. On Christmas Eve: 'At night went to work on draft of Irish Church measure, feeling the impulse.'[4] Other impulses were felt. Four nights later: 'Saw Mrs. Thistlethwayte – Gringer – and three more.' Laura Thistlethwayte was the mystic lady, formerly of the *demi-monde* and not received in general society, whom Gladstone had met earlier under the auspices of the Duke of Newcastle.[5] In the lamented absence now of his Egeria, Harriet Sutherland, Gladstone seems to have been attracted by certain qualities in Mrs Thistlethwayte to a degree of an analogous kind. At all events, the gap left by Harriet Sutherland would be partially filled.

In these highly intense circumstances, Gladstone's birthday and end-of-year self-admonitions in 1868 were correspondingly intense. 'This birthday opens my 60th year,' he recorded on 29 December at that 'very happy home' of the Lytteltons at Hagley. 'I descend the hill of life. It would be a truer figure to say I ascend a steepening path with a burden ever gathering weight. The Almighty seems to sustain and spare me for some purpose of His own deeply unworthy as I know myself to be. Glory be to his name.'

On New Year's Eve he listed ('rather a frivolous enumeration') the notable Decembers of his life, culminating in the premiership: his birth, his Oxford honours, his election to Parliament in 1832, his Lordship of the Treasury in 1834, his first book in 1838, his becoming a Secretary of State in 1845, the Exchequer in 1852. A special joy of this December was

Stephy's being given to the Church. Yet Gladstone now was all the more conscious of burdens to right and to left. The absorption of political life, with its insatiable demands, left not 'the smallest stock of moral energy unexhausted and available for other purposes'.

Swimming for his life, a man does not see much of the country through which the river winds . . .

But other years as I hope are to come a few at least in which yet ampler mercy will permit to learn more of my own soul and to live for that kind of work which perhaps (I have never lost the belief) more specially belongs to me . . .

Farewell great year of opening, not of alarming, change: and welcome new year laden with promise and with care.[6]

[2]

Hawarden provided three weeks of combined repose and preparations for the new session. The signal social event of the season was the first visit of Sir John Acton, who arrived in company with his stepfather Granville. Unfortunately for Acton, he arrived at a time when Gladstone was deep in what was to become *Juventus Mundi*. Acton described the occasion to his wife: 'Before dinner I had a dreadful hour, listening to Gladstone's theories about Homer, and this morning I have been reading a manuscript book of his, which he is going to publish . . . a hard trial.'[7] For all such trials, Acton henceforth was not deterred from a near lifetime's assiduous courtiership within the Gladstone entourage. Gladstone himself was having hard trials with the Queen. Having heard and read, disapprovingly, his explanations of the Irish Church measure, she felt it most inappropriate that she should open the Parliament in which it would be revealed to the people.[8] Gladstone fell back on the recourse of proposing that the Queen at least receive addresses from the two Houses, as he informed Disraeli, 'on the occasion of the meeting of the Parliament of which the House of Commons has been chosen by a greatly enlarged constituency'.[9] Victoria was in no mood to collaborate, and set her physician, Jenner, to put up a barrage of reasons and objections. Gladstone had occasion later to remark acidly on the way 'fanciful ideas of a woman about her health, encouraged by a feeble-minded doctor, became realities'.[10]

It was somehow in fated conformity with this inauspicious commencement of his relationship as first minister with his sovereign that Gladstone should soon become embroiled in a fuss raised by her cousin the Duke of Cambridge, General Officer Commanding-in-Chief, about remarks deemed offensive by one of the new junior ministers, G. O. Trevelyan. Trevelyan had incautiously observed on the 'tremendous influence of the Court' as an obstacle to War Office reform.[11] Facing his first working session as prime minister, Gladstone was anxious that the best of impressions be made. One of his backbenchers noted: 'Gladstone looks somewhat worse thro' care and labour. Evidently, the smallest and greatest matters beget anxiety in him . . . Will he bear his work?'[12]

That inauspicious commencement, from the angle of the Queen's viewpoint on the new House of Commons and its new constituency, had much to do with Victoria's sense of unease about the fate of the Irish ascendancy as intermingled with the Irish Church. Another suspensory bill on the lines of the 1868 bill was now unnecessary; temporalities would be included in the wider frame of disestablishment. In offering good wishes for the new year to his Irish Solicitor-General, Sullivan, Gladstone added: 'I *hope* before that has again to be said that ascendancy will have received a deadly blow.'[13] His private language about the Church of Ireland and its partisans in the Church of England was triumphally aggressive. 'It is greatly to our interest,' he told Sullivan, 'to nurse and develop the party of "Surrender".'[14] 'As they mean to fight,' he remarked to Granville of the Irish bishops, 'I am not sure that it is a bad thing for us to have so little handiness in Dublin, and so little ability in Armagh.'[15] On the English side, 'the party of concession, from amongst those who have hitherto resisted', was shepherded in Convocation by the Bishop of Peterborough and by Wilberforce of Oxford. The Bishop of Gloucester assured Gladstone early in March that the 'wiser bishops' would accept the national verdict.[16]

On such a momentum of success Gladstone launched his great legislative centrepiece in a crowded and intent Commons on 1 March – 'perhaps the most grave and arduous work of legislation that has ever been laid'. The Cornish MP Trelawny, from the Liberal backbenches, in 'the fullest House I ever saw', was impressed with Gladstone's 'marvellous exposition'. 'It seems to me he revels in distinctions. The use of his intellect is evidently not merely a delight but a necessity of his nature . . . The orator's exordium and peroration were both excellent.'[17] The Church of Ireland, 'if not the home and the refuge, the token and symbol of ascendancy', Gladstone announced, evocative of 'painful and bitter memories', would be disestablished and disendowed as from 1 January 1871. All other public endowments of religion in Ireland, whether to Presbyterians (the *Regium Donum*) or to Catholics (the Maynooth grant), would likewise cease. The bishops and representative clergy and laity would constitute a self-governing body for the new Church of Ireland: truly a free church in a Free State. The proceeds of disendowment (calculated

at £16 million), once existing interests and obligations were fairly discharged, would be devoted to a fund (Gladstone estimated at nearly half
the total) for beneficial measures of relief not eligible under the existing
Poor Law. Gladstone claimed to be acting in the spirit of Pitt and the
Act of Union, recognizing the incompatibility of legislative union with
religious inequality. He was confident of the 'approving verdict of civilized mankind'.[18]

This was heroic government engaging in a set-piece frontal assault on
a deeply entrenched historic vested interest. Something of this awareness
of having provoked a kind of profound cultural resentment came upon
Gladstone when returning thanks for ministers at the Royal Academy
banquet, where all on the surface was decorously proper: 'But the *noise*
was Tory.'[19]

Understandably, with painful memories of the Liberal mutinies in
1866 and 1867, Gladstone did not take the seemingly conclusive majority of the 1868 election for granted. He anxiously reinforced the Whips
before the first big division. 'Now that measure will not be carried by
a simple announcement that "The Ayes have it" ', he sternly reminded
Sir John Ramsden, MP for Monmouth, 'but by the unanimity of the
Liberal party, and by the commanding character of the majority.' The 'first
signs of faltering purpose' were not to be betrayed 'without incurring
a heavy responsibility'.[20] Trelawny detected Gladstone 'uneasy as his
conduct on the Maynooth grant was dissected; his pallid and passionate
lineaments lie exposed to full observation of every change'.[21] Gladstone's
uneasiness came less from worries about the official Conservative opposition – Disraeli and Stanley accepted that the elections had given Gladstone a presumptive right to deal with the question, and were relying
on the Lords to mitigate the consequences – than from worries about his
own ranks. It became clear that his biggest problem was going to be
Roundell Palmer, who offered the most effective opposition to the bill
in the Commons.

Palmer's arguments were in the main reconditely legalistic, but they
centred dangerously around the implications of Irish Church disestablishment for the Union. That was certainly a widespread way of reading
the matter in Ireland. Gladstone's supreme concern was to keep an
equilibrium between a sustained momentum for his measure while at
the same time restraining and confining the energies radiating from that
momentum from invading contiguous political tissue. Cardinal Cullen,
the head of the Irish Catholic hierarchy, assured Gladstone that the Irish
Church Bill was 'very well adapted to promote the interests of Ireland',
and that it would 'inaugurate an era of peace and prosperity'.[22] What,
however, it was immediately inaugurating was an era of Irish agrarian
agitation. The mass of Irish had little direct concern with the Church of

Ireland. But they had an immense concern with what the Church issue seemed to promise in relation to the land issue. A vast swell of excited and deluded hopes and expectations for the disestablishment of the landlords was beginning to build up. For Gladstone the danger was that this swell could get out of control. Bright gave the swell an extra impulse when he let slip indiscreetly his candid opinion that there would be no peace in Ireland until far greater numbers of the population were put in possession of the soil of the country.[23] Gladstone, embarrassed, 'spoke on Irish Land, trying to cover Bright'.[24]

Gladstone conceded that the 'land question' was a 'branch of the great question of Protestant ascendancy' in Ireland. He conceded also that, in dealing with the Church question, Parliament was 'in a certain sense, dealing with the land; for it has been the maintenance of Protestant ascendancy, in the form of the religious Establishment which has been one great and permanent cause of the mode in which the power of the landlord has been used, and his relations to his tenant have been habitually and vitally affected by that which, in its first aspect, seems only to be a religious or ecclesiastical question'. However, Gladstone insisted that nothing had been said to shake the general principle of property or the actual state of possession or settlement in Ireland. But he felt himself also obliged to undertake 'to cap the great task, in which we are now engaged, in respect to the Irish Church, with another equally great task', that of applying effective remedies to the grievances of the 'occupiers of the soil in Ireland'.[25]

That there would be a big Irish land measure for 1870 was not in itself surprising; but what was awkward for Gladstone was the appearance of being hustled into the matter and the way that entanglement of questions about the Union and questions about 'tenant right' and indeed 'landlordism' as such with the Church measure gave stimulus and stiffening to resistance, especially in the House of Lords. In fact this was helpful to Gladstone in the Commons as it had the effect of rallying his party behind him. On seeing the third reading through on 31 May Gladstone delivered a clear threat with respect to the 'future progress of this measure in "another place" ', very much in the style and spirit of his quarrels over the paper duties in 1860 and 1861. He added, with characteristic extra menace, that the wishes and desires of the nation at large were not adequately represented even in the great majorities of its several stages in the Commons.[26] Throughout the whole process of his measure, Gladstone had displayed an extraordinary parliamentary mastery. ('Gladstone calmly awaits the fray, his arms crossed, and his eyes tranquilly fixed on the stained glass windows. He looks ash-pale and sharp-visaged. On his right Cardwell, on his left Childers – who occasionally appear to take instructions.')[27] Now, as he threatened the

Lords, his mastery seemed all the more impressive. 'Gladstone is unusually forcible and calm,' observed Trelawny. 'I never knew a speech of his more terse. He is speaking like a winning man.' At his peroration there were 'cheers and clapping of hands'.[28] On 7 June: 'On entering the House tonight Mr Gladstone was received with a burst of cheers, which were intended as a note of warning to the Lords.'[29]

In the Lords it was Salisbury – 'young Sarum', as Granville dubbed him, aware of Gladstone's 'personal regard for him'[30] – who helpfully led the way to an uncontroversial second reading. But then, incited by a furious Lord Derby, hostile amendments flew thick and fast. 'Sad work in the Lords,' Gladstone recorded on 6 July. He was already in touch with Dean Wellesley of Windsor with a view to mediation with Archbishop Tait and the Queen. When the Lords' amendments duly came back to the Commons Gladstone was in no humour to concede. As he put it indignantly to Manning, those relating to disendowment would convert the bill into an 'imposture'.[31]

After much bad-tempered toing and froing Gladstone was desired by the Cabinet to see the Queen at Windsor, 'for the sake of peace and of the House of Lords', with one final concession.[32] Tait had already been squared. Gladstone was in hopes that Palmer could be of use through Salisbury or the bishops. Disraeli made overtures through Bessborough to help ease the strain. For Gladstone the strain became in truth quite seriously stressful. He had welcomed assurances of prayers from the Roman Catholic Bishop of Limerick and the great London Baptist preacher Spurgeon: 'I think that in these and other prayers lies the secret of the strength of body which has been given me in unusual measure during this very trying year.'[33] Stanley, always a shrewd observer of Gladstone, recorded at this time:

Gladstone's own temper is visible and audible whenever he rises to speak: but he has so far restrained the expression of it so as to have said nothing particularly offensive, though the mixture of anger and contempt in his voice and look is almost painful to witness. With all his splendid talents, and his great position, few men suffer more from the constitutional infirmity of an irritable nature: and this is a disease which hard mental work, anxiety, and the exercise of power, all tend to exacerbate. Disraeli is quite aware of the advantage which he possesses in his habitual calmness: and takes every opportunity to make the contrast noticeable.[34]

On entering the Commons on 20 July, Gladstone was 'loudly cheered' by his party. On 22 July the Lords prudently gave way on the most contentious amendments. 'The favourable issue left me almost unmanned, in reaction from a sharp and stern tension of mind.' Gladstone took to his sofa and left Granville to transact the settlement with Cairns. 'The news was brought to me on my sofa and between 5 and 6 I was able to telegraph to the Queen . . . that "a general satisfaction prevailed".' Back in the Commons on the 23rd Gladstone 'felt very weak' up to the moment of his statement 'but all this vanished when I spoke, and while the debate lasted. Then I went back to bed.' He retreated to the soothing hospitality of Lord Richard Cavendish at Chislehurst: 'Weak still, I presumed over much in walking a little, and fell back at night to my lowest point.' His physician, Clark, was in constant attendance while Granville sent notes of the Cabinet council over which he presided in Gladstone's absence.

The Conservative party and the House of Lords had been overawed and overborne. The Irish ecclesiastical ascendancy had been humiliated. The engine of the state had, as Gladstone foresaw, taken and borne a tremendous strain. As Granville put it: 'Who can write history? You however can make it.'[35] But Gladstone's collapse in the aftermath of these triumphs raised again the question Trelawny had asked at the opening of the session: 'Will he bear his work?' Gladstone had run his government, and to an extent his party, almost as much into a state of exhaustion as he had himself. Thus commenced a pattern which Gladstone would repeat, with diminishing returns, every year until his majority collapsed in 1873. For the moment, it was enough to have prevailed and survived. The 1869 session faded away with reprimands from Gladstone to Lord Otho Fitzgerald, Treasurer to the Household, on the 'thin attendance of official persons' in divisions early in August.[36] It was a great relief to get away to Walmer with Granville, 'the most delightful of colleagues'.[37]*

September was a time of recuperative travel and visits: Raby Castle (Duke of Cleveland), Balmoral (where he drafted a memorandum for the Queen on improving the House of Lords with new peerages, and found her 'exceedingly easy and gracious'),† Fasque (a 'family party, very good and homelike'), Camperdown House in Forfarshire (where he discussed Irish and Oxford matters with Dr Jowett), until Hawarden was gained at the end of the month. Apart from his preoccupation with the Irish land problem, which he would need to get into some kind of shape for the coming series of preparatory cabinets in November, Gladstone's principal concern was to prepare *Juventus Mundi* for publication. In it he addressed such puzzles as the relationship of the

---

* Russell had made Granville Lord Warden of the Cinque Ports vice Palmerston in December 1865.
† She was less easy and gracious in her report to her daughter, the Crown Princess of Prussia: 'Mr Gladstone left this morning. I cannot find him very agreeable, and he talks so very much. He looks dreadfully ill.'[38]

Phoenicians to the Homeric text, and continued his argument against Grote, incorporating Lenormant's Egyptological research, which in his view indicated Homer's historicity through a revised chronology of the second millennium, BC.[39] As with the reception of *Studies on Homer*, learned mockery was excited: 'When William shows himself a Johnny Raw, Right honourable is the loud guffaw.'[40] Gladstone remained, as ever, serenely unperturbed by scholarly disapproval.

[3]

Behind the grandeurs of 'making history' remained the prosaic obligations of administration. Matters of patronage in the old style of rewards and inducements for party services were by no means despised by Gladstone, but he was determined to shift the bulk of official preferment in the directions he had indicated in the Northcote–Trevelyan report on the reform of the civil service in 1853. That report he imbued with his vision of a Coleridgean ideal of a clerisy of guardians of a higher notion of the duties and functions of the state.[41]* He wanted to make preferment to office less a matter of 'prizes' and more a matter of meritorious qualifications for service. Reforms of Oxford and Cambridge had begun to show the way. The Crimean War and its Palmerstonian aftermath had stifled such plans; but now the return of the conditions of the 'golden age of useful legislation, and of administrative improvement', opened up new opportunities. In Lowe at the Exchequer Gladstone had a zealous collaborator in his old quest to 'strike a real blow at Parliamentary Patronage'. In November 1869 Lowe pressed Gladstone to act. 'As I have so often tried in vain, will you bring the question of the Civil Service before the Cabinet today – something must be decided – we cannot keep matters in this discreditable state of abeyance. If the Cabinet will not entertain the idea of open competition might we not at any rate require a larger number of competitors for each vacancy?'[42] Gladstone had more expansive ideas. He proposed to appoint a Cabinet committee so as to leave the two 'obstacles' to reform (from very different viewpoints), Clarendon and Bright, 'so insulated that their ground would be untenable'.[43]

Resuscitating the Northcote–Trevelyan reform proposals from their 1853 limbo would be one of the more pleasurable aspects of the 1870 session. Meanwhile Gladstone pressed ahead with his ideas of a new

---

* G appointed his son Willy, MP for Chester and Whitby since 1865, to a junior Lordship of the Treasury in 1868.

ethos of peerage preferments. His brush with the Lords over the Irish Church Bill had made Gladstone sensitive to the question of the constitutional role of the peers. He put it to the Queen that the Lords' evident tendency to become averse to the Liberal party would necessitate counteractive measures. It would not be in the best interests either of the Lords or of the country 'that their assembly should stand in marked combat with the steady and permanent judgment of the country which on every occasion since 1830 except one has returned a Liberal majority'.[44] Gladstone urged the need for more working peers. He canvassed John Bright for information as to 'any representative men who might go into the House of Lords on behalf partly of trade and manufactures but especially of Nonconformity'.[45] Victoria was reluctant to approve any marked change in the general character of peerage creations. She refused Gladstone's proposal of a Jew, Nathan Meyer Rothschild, as she might well have done also, had not Gladstone been dissuaded by Granville, of the infidel John Stuart Mill.* On the other hand she accepted Gladstone's recommendation for Sir John Acton, eighth baronet. Roman Catholic peers had not been created since 1688. Acton was away in Rome at the time, a kind of unofficial observer for Gladstone at the Vatican Council. Quite apart from the religious aspect, his peerage remained an oddity. He was certainly nothing of a working peer, and contributed little to the Lords beyond an occasional aura of the exotic world of middle-European high culture. Gladstone's motives in advising the creation probably had most to do with honouring Döllinger through his prize pupil and thereby making a point to the ultramontane party at the Vatican.

It says something for Gladstone's generosity of spirit that he offered a peerage to George Grote, his old enemy in Homerology. While praising Gladstone for having 'entered in the work of reform with a sincerity and energy hitherto unparalleled', Grote felt that he could not allow new duties to disturb his work.[46] Perhaps the most characteristic creation by Gladstone at this time in terms of a new ethos was the Blachford peerage for Frederic Rogers, the Under-Secretary for the Colonies. By this unprecedented honour for a civil servant, Gladstone signalled his commitment to an ideal of the higher service of the state. Otherwise, Gladstone's creations of these years were conventional enough; and although he was by no means jealously restrictive in the matter of peerages,† he failed, then and later, to make any marked impression on the political complexion of the House of Lords. His problem in this respect is best illustrated in the difficulties he had in distributing the

* G does not seem to be aware at this time of Mill's earlier advocacy of birth control. See below, page 127. Rothschild got his peerage eventually in 1885.
† By 1891 he was prepared to sell peerages for contributions to the Liberal party fund. See below, pages 512–13.

higher honours. The Dukes of Norfolk and Leinster and Lords Bessborough and Portsmouth declined Garters on the grounds of unwillingness to offer political support; and Lord Meath likewise declined an Irish Patrick.

It was to ecclesiastical patronage, however, that Gladstone characteristically gave his most devoted attention. 'A vacant see', wrote one of his secretaries, 'is a great excitement to Mr Gladstone. Indeed I believe it excites him far more than a political crisis.' In 1869 Gladstone set out the seventeen qualities which he considered needed to be looked for in candidates for promotion to the episcopal bench.[47] His prime intention was to rescue the higher ecclesiastical preferments from what he held was the woodenness of the kind of sub-evangelical prelates favoured by Palmerston and the Queen. His first episcopal vacancy was for Exeter. His choice was Temple, Headmaster of Rugby.* This Gladstone knew would be controversial. Temple had been one of the notorious *Septem contra Christum* of *Essays and Reviews*. Gladstone would have preferred Temple for Oxford, a see also now vacant; but knew that there this row would be too damaging. Failing that, St David's or another Welsh see was in Gladstone's mind. For the Church, Wales was now, with the onset of aggressive Nonconformity, 'the point of danger and weakness'. Temple might do there what the scholarly but ineffectual Connop Thirlwall had failed to do.[48] However, Exeter it was to be: 'when the hour comes', as Gladstone told T. D. Acland, 'there will be a great outcry'.[49] Outcry there was, but Gladstone could reflect thankfully: 'Today the first Bishop recommended by me is consecrated. May the richness of all holy life be given to him.'

In the richness of all holy life, Oxford always had a special place in Gladstone's eyes. It was a pleasure to prefer Keble's old Oxford ally J. B. Mozley to a Canonry of Worcester, and then in 1871 to the Regius Chair of Divinity at Oxford. He was able to promote Samuel Wilberforce at last from Oxford to Winchester in 1869 at a time when vacant sees began to multiply. 'Is it not extraordinary', Gladstone remarked to Dean Ramsay of Edinburgh, 'to see this rain of Bishoprics upon my head?'[50] What Gladstone no doubt had in mind here were memories of his strictures upon the right reverend brethren at the time of the Gorham affair as well as his more recent strictures in the matter of the Irish Church. George Moberly for Salisbury,† James Fraser for the new see of Manchester, and Harvey Goodwin for Carlisle were among Gladstone's more noteworthy preferments at this time. The vexed case of St Asaph made him aware

---

* See above, page 38.
† On the death of G's old friend W. K. Hamilton, father of his future private secretary, E. W. Hamilton.

that preferments in Wales were becoming problematical because of demands that they be filled by Welsh-speakers.

Another of his Oxford chairs was the Regius Professorship of Modern History, to which he preferred the Rev. Dr Stubbs, whose high ambition it was to build up a seriously *wissenschaftlich* historical school. This appointment soon had a knock-on effect at Cambridge, where the Regius Professor, Charles Kingsley, was the object of a campaign of despite by Stubbs and his acolyte, E. A. Freeman. Kingsley, avowedly an 'amateur', resigned the chair and thus placed upon Gladstone the task of finding for Cambridge its first *ernst* historical professor. After several false starts, Gladstone eventually lighted upon the author of *Ecce Homo*, J. R. Seeley. Possibly Gladstone was impressed with Seeley's Coleridgean ideal of historians as a kind of Christian clerisy.[51] At all events, neither Seeley nor Gladstone was aware in 1869 that Seeley's quest to make history the foundation of a science of politics would work its way through to the immensely influential prophetic text of imperialism, *The Expansion of England*.*

These dealings with historians were in fact in their way quite apropos of Gladstone's concern with what was going on in the preparations for the Vatican Council. Both Seeley and Acton (who succeeded Seeley in the Regius Chair at Cambridge in 1895) agreed with Gladstone as to the 'teaching of history and experience, respecting the methods of God in dealing with his Church'. This was part of Gladstone's current polemic with Archbishop Manning, by now England's accredited exponent of ultramontane values, in defence of Döllinger, the leading clerical resister in Germany to Pius IX's intention to promulgate the dogma of Papal Infallibility. To Manning's complaints about 'rationalism', Gladstone cited the authority of 'Bishop Butler (one of my four great teachers)'.[52] It was to another of his great teachers† that Gladstone appealed in a letter to Döllinger: 'May the *Curia Romana* prove to be other than Dante thought it, and other than what now for many years it has been trying to be with consequences so disastrous to the hopes of those who desire that knowledge and liberty should ever abide in holy union with Reason and Faith.'[53] It would come to the point in 1870 of Döllinger's pleading that the British government intervene against 'the infatuated proceedings of the Roman Court'. Gladstone's cautious response was that the two agencies most likely to avail against a 'light-minded, and hot-headed Pope, with his satellites, in their deplorable career', remained France and the Catholic episcopate. And it was particularly painful for Gladstone to reflect on the 'singular phenomenon' of the mind of Newman. Gladstone

* See below, page 320.
† The two others were Aristotle and Augustine.

knew Newman to be in 'fear and dismay' at the prospect of the Council and Infallibility ('what have we done to be treated as the Faithful never were treated before?'); yet Newman's position was one of 'impotence before the world at the cardinal moment which others have been showing him how to use'.[54]

Nor were these Catholic and Roman matters without their immediate and practical bearing on the question of university education for Irish Roman Catholics. Gladstone had been scandalized in 1866 at the way the Liberal government's well-meant efforts in this direction had been sabotaged by the Irish Catholic bishops. He had tried, ineffectually, to make a point about it to Pius IX. He was determined to do something about it in the current Parliament as a coping stone on his Church disestablishment measure and his planned land measure. To both Acton and Döllinger Gladstone expatiated on the deleterious influences 'conspicuously exhibited' by ultramontanism on the question of education in Ireland. They were 'most injurious', he told Döllinger, 'to the prospects of any future legislation in this country which may have for its object the rendering of full justice, in matters of Education and otherwise, to the members of the Roman Communion'.[55] To Acton Gladstone's fears about the ultramontane contagion in Ireland led him to use words curiously prophetic of the ultimate legislative catastrophe in 1873: 'Indeed, we have already had a taste of it in the very powerful opposition which was raised against the very moderate measure of justice which we attempted to carry in 1866 with respect to the Irish colleges and the Roman Catholic University, and the storm will rise again when we come back, as we must before long, to the subject of the higher education in Ireland.'[56]*

[4]

Rather further in the rear of Gladstone's concerns in 1869, but not less laden with prospective political significance, was the question of United States claims for reparations for the depredations in the Civil War of the British-built Confederate privateers, especially *Alabama*. Gladstone was nettled at the appointment of J. L. Motley as the American Minister in London. Motley had made himself troublesome at the time of Gladstone's Newcastle declaration in 1862 about the Confederacy.[58] Gladstone was

---

* However, by the time Döllinger differed from G on the issue of Irish Home Rule, G asserted that Döllinger 'mistook the nature of the Irish question, from the erroneous view that Irish Catholicism is ultramontane, which it certainly is not'.[57]

indignant at what he held to be Motley's imputations on the veracity of his explanations on that point. Granville's and the Duchess of Argyll's combined skills in emollient mediation[59]* soothed Gladstone and opened the way for constructive initiatives. Gladstone saw the opportunity to convert a rather bad-tempered bilateral negotiation on to a higher moral plane of international arbitration, as an example to a civilized world stunned by Bismarckian 'blood and iron' in 1866. To Clarendon Gladstone urged the expediency of a wide frame of reference for an arbitration so as to give it a more substantial profile as a 'very solemn proceeding of authority'.[61] It also struck Gladstone, after examining some specimens of the 'bunkum' being produced in Washington, 'how necessary it is to have the case brought before some third person for trial'.[62]

That very solemn proceeding of authority would, like the Irish university issue, be a question of some years hence. More immediately, Gladstone was anxious to lay early foundations for the major initiative on popular education in England, which he had identified in 1867 as one of the country's more conspicuous 'arrears'. Early in October 1869 Gladstone alerted de Grey, the Lord President, that it was 'desirable that we should avail ourselves of some *early* occasion on our gathering in London to lay the foundation stone of our Education measure in England'.[63] He had in mind also the possibility of a big initiative against the drink trade, for which Bruce prepared schemes for restricting opening hours and reducing licences. But overwhelmingly in these latter months of 1869 Gladstone began to address his huge appetite for strenuous politics to grappling with the conundrum of Irish land.

As Gladstone put it when he moved the first reading of the Irish Land Bill in February 1870, he and his colleagues had been sensible that behind the 'heavy labour' of the Irish Church legislation 'there remained for us a labour probably heavier still'. On the land question the Liberal government would 'not have the advantage of that definite guidance and support which, in relation to the Church question, we thought and found we should derive from the clear, established, and familiar convictions of the majority of the people'. Gladstone could but hope that those 'who then thus spoke' would speak accordingly in the matter of Irish land tenures.[64]

As events were to prove, Gladstone had good reason for anxiety on that point. Whereas the struggle over the Irish Church had given purpose and strength to his government and party, the Irish land issue would

---

* 'I do not know that I can explain well the feeling I have that there was excuse for great irritation about your Newcastle Speech because it had a sound of *exultation* in it, coupled with your declaration of wishing them [the Confederacy] well as a people. It would have been better if you had said what Palmerston felt – "It is safer for England that it should be divided, and I believe that it will be".'[60]

damage and weaken them. Not the least part of the heaviness of the problem was the rising tide of Irish expectations. These expectations took on increasingly the colour of what in Britain were conventionally derided as 'Irish ideas': that is to say, ideas in conflict with orthodox notions of absolute property rights, individualism, and classical political economy. In the context of 'Irish ideas', the fall of the Irish Church portended the return of the land to the people. One heir to an Irish landlord at this time (Lord Stanley) had reports of Tipperary tenants: 'peasantry full of vague hopes, which perhaps they hardly define to themselves'.[65] Gladstone, by September 1869, observed the way in which the Irish land question had 'altered its aspect a good deal', and was 'afraid lest the subject should have outgrown them'.[66] Gladstone devoted himself to 'three months of hectic consultation and hard political bargaining'[67] in framing his Irish land measure within a political landscape of shifting ground and uncertain, slippery footing.

A further weight bearing on Gladstone was that, whereas he had entered on the Church question possessed of confident expertise, he was now having to learn his way in a question bristling with controverted intricacies. Unfortunately, in this case, once he was clear in his own mind, he was not less intractable than he had been (successfully) in the Church question or (disastrously) in the Reform question. His broad approach on Irish land was to smother 'Irish ideas' with English goodwill and the warm embrace of a reformed landlordism but yet to recognize them just sufficiently to engender Irish goodwill in return. His policy was in fact the opposite of his Church policy. There his disendowment had been absolute, and he had dismissed all alternatives of concurrent establishments. Now Gladstone would attempt to engineer a kind of concurrence between an official establishment of compulsorily benign landlords and an unofficial establishment of assumably grateful tenants. The mechanics of this social engineering would be concessions to 'tenant-right' in the matters of compensation for improvements initiated by tenants, evictions, and fairness of rents; all to be subject if necessary to appeal to special commissioners sitting in Land Courts. Irish landlords, in other words, were to surrender from one quarter to one third of the value of their estates in return for a new lease of life being given to Irish landlordism. Precisely: re-establishment purchased by part-disendowment.

Critics of Gladstone's scheme would indeed denounce it in due course as a system of 'dual ownership', and, as such, an offence to 'English ideas'. For the economics of the market were substituted judicial proceedings about 'fairness'. Rights of property were deeply compromised by 'tenant-right'. Yet Gladstone wanted to be seen as the defender and upholder of property-rights. His model was the mutually beneficial landlord–tenant relationship he knew on his own ground in Flintshire. He wanted this steadily to obtain in Ireland so as eventually to obliterate the 'inveterate mischiefs' of a 'tradition & marks of conquest, & of forfeiture'.[68] It was while he grappled with his Irish land measure that Gladstone negotiated to purchase the Dundas property, near Hawarden, a transaction completed in November 1869, for £57,000. 'If I have an ambition,' Gladstone commented, 'it is to make an Estate for my children.'[69]

The alternative argument about Irish land in the field at the time was for disestablishing landlordism by providing an endowment wherefrom occupiers could purchase their tenancies from landlords. This line of policy was associated with the names of John Bright and John Stuart Mill. It was ideologically anti-landlord and posited the social benefits of many small landowners – a 'peasant proprietary'. It had the great merit of going with the grain of Irish social trends: particularly the trend which linked Irish nationalistic sentiment to an agrarian campaign against 'English' landlordism. It could well be attractive on the other hand to many struggling landlords confronted by a fatal combination of falling agricultural prices together with the task of extracting rents from tenants who saw the Land Court as the halfway house to expropriating the landlords.

Gladstone was and remained (apart from one eccentric and curious episode, 1877–9) deeply hostile to all land-purchase schemes. He wanted to restore and sustain Irish landlordism, not conduce to its abolition. He disliked particularly the implications for the British Treasury in putting up huge sums of money to facilitate Irish 'jobbing' in land. He had no love in principle for 'peasant proprietaries', which he judged likely to be undercapitalized and inefficient. Very reluctantly in the end he allowed Bright to tack on to his bill the 'Bright Clauses' providing for purchase of tenancies; but he saw to it that they were cast in grudgingly restrictive form. The Irish Land Bill as it emerged for the beginning of the 1870 session was essentially his own work, aided on the technicalities by the Irish Law Officers. (To Solicitor-General Sullivan he wrote: 'I shall never again live to see such a pair of Irish Law Officers as you and Lawson.')[70] He selected carefully the Cabinet Committee on the bill: Clarendon was the only one likely to be seriously sticky; Granville and Cardwell would have their doubts, but were unlikely to be stiff; Kimberley and Bright were generally amenable and supportive; Fortescue knew much more than anyone else about Irish land problems, but had no influence on Gladstone and for his pains was treated as a nuisance who kept raising difficulties. The important thing was to keep Argyll and Lowe out. It was a committee which did little to temper Gladstone's bent for being indomitably undeflectable.

[5]

As with the case of the Irish Church, the political excitements of the preparation of the Irish Land Bill transferred themselves into Gladstone's old pattern of religio-sexuality. Laura Thistlethwayte became increasingly through 1869 an object of intense interest and concern for Gladstone. Over the period from January 1869 to June 1871 he wrote 112 letters to her and met her on forty-five occasions. It was in certain respects a tortured as well as a tortuous liaison, an odd mix of the spiritual and the erotic. Something of a critical moment arrived in October 1869, sparked off possibly by the use of the word 'love' on her part.[71] She was sending him batches of her autobiography. 'A letter from Mrs. T. much wounded disturbed me. I have a horror of giving inner pain to a woman.' It was next day, 21 October, that 'Dear Mrs. Thistlethwayte' became 'Dear wounded Spirit'. This prompted from her a 'touching, but bewildering' letter; he felt himself 'astonished, though interested, and bound in honour to do the best for her if she really needs it'. He wrote to her on 28 October: 'in great gravity of spirit. Duty and evil temptations are there before me, on the right and left. But I firmly believe in her words "holy" and "pure", and in her cleaving to God.' On 18 November they talked of 'deep matters'. 'I have only known you in an inner sense within the last two months', he wrote to her at this time. In December Gladstone visited 'Dear Spirit' ('Dear trustful Spirit' was another variation in the theme) at a house she had taken in Boveridge, Dorset.

Mrs Th. came to my room aft. and at night. Walk with her. Miss Fawcett let down her hair: it is a robe. So Godiva

> 'the rippled ringlets to the knee'. (Tennyson)

How very far I was at first from understanding her history and also her character.[72]

One of life's relaxing yet inspiriting fascinations now for Gladstone was reperusing Mrs Thistlethwayte's 'really marvellous and most touching tale'.[73] Gladstone was eloquently understanding of her 'hunger of the heart', and of the problem that her 'measure of married life could not be filled up'.[74] In 1869 he accepted from her the gift of a ring which he wore[75] ('Let it be "L" only if you like').[76] This became known between them as the 'Mizpah ring'.[77] Over the years there would be many presents, occasionally embarrassingly ostentatious. As with his 'rescue' work, Gladstone seems to have been entirely secure in a consciousness of the beneficial and innocent necessity of the relationship. He declined her offer in May 1870 to return his letters, except one: which he wanted to expand and develop the 'egotistical' part of. Quite what Catherine and the family made of all this is not clear. No doubt Catherine knew Gladstone well enough not to attempt to intervene in the inner needs and recesses of his religious life. There are indications, however, in later years that the daughters, especially Mary and Helen, spoke out on the 'subject' with respect to the feelings of their mother.* It is probable that Gladstone for his part never quite fully appreciated the depth of Laura Thistlethwayte's feelings for him. She docketed a letter from him in 1871: 'He can *care* for *nothing* of mine, or nothing from me. Oh how madly I love March 16th.'[78]

By late 1869 Gladstone was clearly feeling the strain of his Irish land preparations. He found difficulty in combining physical effort with measured words in his Guildhall speech on 9 November. The discussion raised by Professor Huxley at the Metaphysical Society 'fatigued' his 'poor brain sadly'.† He kept to his bed all day on 16 December, finding in Tennyson's latest volume 'Much beauty but a downward movement'. He found he could obtain 'brain rest' by the sorting of books. But it was the new intensity of the Laura Thistlethwayte relationship which seems to have been most efficacious in a tonic way. The birthday retrospect for 1869 was accordingly fraught with a solicitude which mingled in an inimitably Gladstonian manner the personal and the political. 'My review this year includes as a prominent object LT: the extraordinary history, the confiding appeal, the singular arousal. It entails much on me: and as I saw most clearly of all today, first to do what in me may lie towards building up a true domestic community of life and purpose there.' On the political side: 'My retrospect brings one conclusion. "Mercy Good Lord is all I seek," for the past: for the future grace to be Thine instrument if scarcely thy child.'[79]

[6]

Seeking grace to be the Good Lord's instrument would pile pressures on the parliamentary session of 1870 very much in the style of 1869. Gladstone's efforts to coax the Queen into opening the Parliament in person were as ungraciously received now as then. Soon Disraeli was protesting at the exigencies demanded by this further exercise in strenuous government. Gladstone later denied accusations of 'dragooning';

---

* See below, page 486.
† For the Metaphysical Society see below, page 117.

but admitted frankly that 'blame is assignable to us for having undertaken so much business'.[80] Part of the trouble was, as had been the case also in 1869, the eagerness of Liberal backbenchers to take advantage of the slipstream caused by governmental momentum. Thus P. A. Taylor of Leicester, for example, pressed his case for the 'ancient constitutional usage' of payment for Members of Parliament, to Gladstone's disdain ('To see this House composed and constituted of men who have received a limited education and are in dependent circumstances would be a most calamitous thing').[82] There was Wilfred Lawson's bill against the liquor trade. There was Jacob Bright's bill about women's disabilities, which Gladstone, while gracefully deploring Mill's absence from the Commons, thought it 'would be a very great mistake to proceed with'.[82] On certain such matters to which hitherto he had been resistant, Gladstone now signalled, in consideration of 'the movement of opinion', a more concessionary line: the perennial deceased wife's sister question, for example (causing much mockery among Conservative churchmen),[83] and the secret ballot for parliamentary elections. On this latter question Gladstone's rather sudden change of front made some of his supporters anxious: 'It is rather alarming to some to observe the agility with which he conforms his opinions to those which he had but lately opposed.'[84]*

Certain valuable things were achieved in the early weeks. The Order in Council setting in place the 1853 recommendations for reform of the civil service was approved on 4 June. This was mainly Lowe's work. Cardwell had in place also his preliminary dispositions relating to the reform of the military system. But by that time Gladstone was in a state of near collapse. The Queen had observed him before the session looking 'wretchedly ill and seeming weak – a bad beginning'.[86] He launched the Irish Land Bill on 15 February without anything of the atmosphere of triumphant *éclat* that had attended the Church Bill in the previous year. He escaped for an interlude of retreat with Granville at Walmer. Granville seized the opportunity for a day at the Epsom races on 1 June to see the Derby run ('I was immensely interested in the scene, and the race. Conversation with Prince of Wales – Admiral Rous – and many more. The race gave me a tremor'). This appears to have been Gladstone's only appearance at a race meeting.

His colleagues were equally under stress. To Irish Land would be added a coercion measure to damp down the swell of Irish agrarian unrest. 'If Ministers deal successfully with all three Bills now before the country', a Liberal member remarked, ' – on Irish Land, Irish Crime and English education – Ministers must be more than human.' It was said

* For G's old opinion of the ballot as 'trash', see C. S. Parker.[85]

'the first outrages Political economy, the 2nd the Constitution, the 3rd the conscience!'[87] 'This Cabinet', Gladstone told Russell, 'is the most laborious as a whole I have ever seen.'[88] The Queen had already expressed concern at Clarendon's health. Bright, who detested Forster's Education Bill cordially, broke under the strain. So nearly did Cardwell and Childers. Lowe was quarrelsome and angular. One junior minister, Acton Smee Ayrton, was fabulous for brutish offensiveness in the name of economy against the high-minded exponents of state expenditure in aid of the arts and sciences and public health. To Mrs Cardwell, who had protested on behalf of her husband, Gladstone responded: 'I quite appreciate the toil, the sacrifice, even the apprehension. But pray consider the reward. He will leave behind him, and that justly in my consideration the name of the best War Minister in our age and country.'[89] The Liberal MP Trelawny noted as early as 31 March: 'The work of Parliament has beaten us. Its magnitude even in peace is beyond our powers . . . double sittings are already to be held even before Easter. Many subjects are in [the] charge of select committees . . .'[90]

Clarendon died on 27 June while Gladstone was deeply enmeshed in assisting Forster to get his Education Bill past the large and enraged Nonconformist section in the Liberal ranks. Halifax consented to come in to fill the Whig gap, while Granville took Clarendon's place at the Foreign Office. The Cabinet regrouped but Gladstone failed to save the initial proposals in Forster's bill (to provide elementary education for hitherto unschooled children together with religious education in any shape or form which the local school boards to be set up might provide or assist out of rate income). Gladstone's central concern with the question of providing a national system of elementary education was always that, directly or indirectly, an education bill would need to be 'conducive to the most effectual propagation of religion'.[91] He fought to save the dimension of 'Anglican dogmatic vitality'[92] in the Education Bill. An observer in the Public Gallery at the Commons described him in this quest: Gladstone, 'thin-haired, with gaunt penetrating face, is restless; talks to this one and that; wipes his spectacles; unfolds clean pocket handkerchief suggestive of womankind. Lowe, a parson's son: Gladstone, a trader's; Forster, a manufacturer; Stansfeld, a brewer. Mais il faut descendre encore, un peu!'[93] But Anglican dogmatic vitality was not consistent or compatible with the Liberal majority elected in 1868. Gladstone and Forster were obliged to concede that the Liberal party in general simply would not consent to the notion that the Church of England had historic claims as the national Church to be supported and assisted by public funds to realize its educative vocation. Gladstone and Forster retreated to a compromise – the 'Cowper–Temple clause' – providing for strictly 'undenominational' religious teaching at Board Schools.

The parliamentary spectacle here unfolded in the Education issue was of the Liberal party largely at odds with the Liberal government. Gladstone's 'compromise' did not appease the more embattled Nonconformists, who claimed to have been marched by Gladstone 'through the Valley of Humiliation'.[94] Gladstone, for his part, complained at the grievous wounds he had received at the hands of the Disestablishment agitator Edward Miall. Stanley recalled hearing Gladstone say to Clarendon, 'If I am going to be baited much longer in this way, I will take off the gloves.'[95] The Liberal government, Gladstone declared, did not exist for the benefit of any section of the community; 'we are the government of the Queen'. This Peelite note rang bravely. But what it meant was that Gladstone was having to appeal for the Education Bill to the whole House, to all groups and parties to join together for the common purpose of aiming 'at making elementary education universal in an efficient form throughout the country', and at not allowing religious differences to stand in the way of that 'great and essential public good'.[96] Disraeli seized very caustically and adroitly on Gladstone's predicament. 'I hardly know any occasion since I have sat in Parliament that can be compared with the present.' The country demanded that 'National education' be 'religious education'. The Conservative party were ready to support the government's Education Bill on that ground. Now they are told suddenly there are to be great changes. 'This appears to me to be a most extraordinary course for a great Minister and Leader of the House to take,' both for its importance in itself and the 'rarity of the circumstances'.[97] Disraeli deftly exploited Liberal dissensions. Trelawny recorded on 8 July: 'Fawcett haranguing at 20 minutes to 6. How he rants! Poor ministers! There is Forster looking with eye glass most wistfully at the clock, Gladstone next, arms crossed over his legs with a look of fatigued resignation, Bruce wishing Fawcett to the devil.'[98]

Ministers got their Education Bill through by grace of the Conservative Opposition. Unquestionably this compromised their prestige. No doubt it was no small matter and worth much 'after all to have before us a measure which proclaims the title of every child to be educated'.[99] But in some ways the great point of the matter is what Disraeli made of it. Gladstone's hot resentment at Gathorne Hardy's mocking comments on Liberal divisions was eloquent of an awareness that the aura of invincibility of 1868 was now fading. This new vulnerability was important because it was contagious and infected the concurrent Irish Land debates. Bright had very sensibly advised postponing the Education Bill to the 1872 session to give it more ease. There is no doubt that its absence in 1870 would have eased the way of the Irish Land Bill.

Gladstone introduced the Irish Land Bill to a House of Commons overwhelmingly composed of members who more or less agreed with

Clarendon's view of the situation: that it was 'an attempt to bribe the tenant into obedience to the laws by subsidizing [him] out of the pocket of the landlord'.[100] Standing on shifting political ground, with uncertain, slippery footing, Gladstone had to present his bill as a measure not only of good will but also of good faith, securely framed in principles which were politic but not merely expedient. The delicacy of the equilibrium which he was trying to maintain behind the façade of things between bad good faith and good bad faith was well illustrated in an exchange with Cardwell on the theme that '"a careful regard for the security of property and the just rights belonging to it" or something of that kind' would be preferable as a descriptive formula to '"the strictest regard" to the rights of property'.[101] The reception in the House given to Gladstone's eloquently plausible exposition reflected an underlying discomfiture and unease. 'Even if the measure were devised by an angel', as one Liberal commented, 'it is doubtful whether, in the existing state of opinion in Ireland, there is enough respect for the laws to insure the measure fair play.' He observed the Conservatives 'listening very tranquilly' to Gladstone's explanation of the complex judicial apparatus of commissioners and land courts. 'The Liberals occasionally cheered him – but not with as much confidence as one has witnessed.' The 'naked fact' was staring them in the face: 'we have turned our backs on Political economy. The science appears to have broken down.' The fact was, 'both sides feel that a measure of some sort is indispensable, yet the vastness of the difficulty repressed hasty conviction; still more, enthusiasm'.[102]

The tranquillity of the Conservatives had much to do with a shrewd awareness that, as with the Education measure, they could rely on Liberals to do most of their work for them. It was an ominous moment for Gladstone when Roundell Palmer opened up on 10 March with the point that the success of the bill would depend entirely on the success of the coercive Peace Preservation (Ireland) Bill which Fortescue would shortly be introducing. Palmer's line in 1869 over the Church bill had been to the effect that the House ought honestly to acknowledge what was being done: 'we ought to say so if we do it'.[103] The damage he did then to Gladstone was limited, because the vast majority of the Commons could not honestly see that disestablishing the Church of Ireland did in fact call the Union into question. But over Irish Land in 1870 Palmer was far more dangerous. He articulated what the House felt, but was reluctant to admit. He greatly offended Gladstone on the issue of 'compensation for disturbance' for evicted tenants.[104] Cardwell soon observed on Palmer's 'offering a most dangerous opposition to important parts of the Bill'. Gladstone fulminated against Palmer as 'the means of bringing into focus the scattered elements of disapproval'. To Gladstone it was a scandal that opposition to his measure was being 'led and officered from the Liberal party'.[105] He expounded to Spencer on Palmer as 'our only formidable antagonist'.[106]

All Disraeli needed to do was to take Palmer's cues. Amendments piled in. By 6 April Gladstone noted: 'The crisis is sharp.' The 7th was 'a most anxious day from end to end'. There was but feeble support from the Irish, who mostly regarded Gladstone's elaborate scheme as irrelevant to the real issue ('It is extraordinary how little good one hears of the Bill from Irishmen of any party').[107] By 8 April: 'Very anxious: Irish Land Bill not yet out of danger. H. of C. again 9½–10¼. Visited Mrs Thistlethwayte after. She is indeed an excepted person: and strangely corresponds with me in some of the strangest points.' What the Conservatives would offer most saliently by way of opposition was to take up the cue given earlier by Clarendon: that English tenants were taking an unhealthy interest in Irish developments.[108] Gladstone wrote to Russell: 'The fear that our Land Bill may cross the water, creates a sensitive state of mind among all Tories, many Whigs, and a few Radicals. Upon this state of things comes Palmer with his legal mind, legal point of view, legal aptitude and *in*aptitude . . . and stirs these susceptibilities to such a point that he is always near to bringing us to grief.'[109] To Manning Gladstone reported that he had been 'obliged to resort to something like menace' to assert his authority. The 'strain thus far had been extreme: and I regret to say it is not yet over'. *When* it was settled, Gladstone assured Manning, 'I shall begin to detach my hopes and interests, if I may, from the political future'.[110] Here, fleetingly but tellingly, in Gladstone's response to Liberal parliamentary reluctance, was a reminiscence of his thoughts of abdication in 1866 and a prevision of abdication in 1875.

On Easter Day: 'At the Altar this day it was the Irish Land question that I presented before God more than aught else living or dead.'[111] Gladstone expended such tremendous quantities of his public and parliamentary credit in ramming through the Irish Land Bill that neither he, nor his ministry, were anything like as formidable thereafter. Gladstone himself put it with uncanny prescience when he told Clarendon that he felt about the imperativeness of his bill 'as a bee might feel if it knew that it would die on its sting'.[112] On 18 April he 'loosed off' a letter of mingled expostulation and threat to Palmer. Gladstone could foresee with numbing clarity a reprise of the 1866 disaster. In which case he predicted – for Clarendon's benefit – that Disraeli, as with the Reform question then, would go on to carry a stronger measure.[113] But for Disraeli Irish Land in 1870 offered none of the enticements Reform offered in 1866. Much better to help the Liberal government limp through the Commons stages and get it up to the Lords for bracing treatment. Gladstone carried his party and his bill in the end because enough

Liberals agreed, reluctantly, with one of their number: 'Economically, the measure is, I fear, wrong. Imperially, it is, I think, necessary.'[114]

Getting the Irish Land Bill through the Lords was almost as fraught as getting it through the Commons. The Lords were less intimidated than they had been in 1869, but they were aware that any replacement bill would be for the worse. Gladstone appealed to Samuel Wilberforce: the Irish bill 'stands by itself'; 'it really appertains not so much to the well-being as to the being of civilized society'.[115] Tensions led even to ruffled relations between Gladstone and Granville.[116] The Lords were 'unexpectedly stubborn' on certain points.[117] The Duke of Argyll played something of the same role for the Liberal peers as Palmer had played for the Liberal commoners. Gladstone commented acidly on Argyll's being 'not infrequently misled by the rapid facility of his active mind' on the question of tenant-right;[118] but, like many another, Argyll had shrewd suspicions that Gladstone's Land Bill was going up an Irish dead end. Salisbury approved of the 'Bright clauses' providing for purchase by tenants: a germ of the policy eventually adopted by successive Conservative and Unionist governments between 1885 and 1905 which abandoned Gladstone's efforts to sustain Irish landlordism and converted Ireland into an overwhelmingly owner-occupier agrarian society.

Thus it was that what actually happened to Irish land in the later nineteenth and early twentieth centuries is by far the most cogently dismissive judgement on Gladstone's heroic effort of 1870 (and its supplementary version of 1881). As was often predicted, it proved to be 'a boon to the lawyers of Ireland', while the legal wrangles in the land courts poisoned relations between landlords and tenants.[119] For much of rural Ireland it was irrelevant. At the same time, as Clarendon gloomily predicted, it would encourage opinion in Ireland that British government was on the run, and that repeal of the Union was the obvious next step. Isaac Butt, the Irish Conservative MP, launched his 'Home Rule' movement while the Land Bill was still going through the Commons. By the 1874 general election the majority of Liberal MPs in Ireland had been obliged to adopt Home Rule colours. Gladstone himself was shocked and disappointed by the absence of any widespread response of acceptance and gratitude in Ireland. To Cardinal Cullen he complained that a 'perverse and vengeful spirit seems to meet every pacific and just indication on the part of Parliament, by . . . outrages and an extension of terrorism, which create on this side of the channel not apprehension, but disgust'.[120] Palmer's ultimate reflection on the matter stands indisputable: 'it may be said with certainty that it would never have passed if what were to follow had then been foreseen'.[121]

[7]

Though it took time for the symptoms to manifest themselves, Gladstone's ministry had wounded itself mortally. His remark to Clarendon about the bee dying on its sting was indeed uncannily prescient. For all that *The Times* could point to the advantage Gladstone derived from the impact of a democratized electorate in 1868 in making Members of Parliament less able to resist the executive power led by a leader who could claim a people's mandate,[122] Gladstone's imperious driving of an 'instrumental' parliamentary party would sooner or later bring it and himself to grief.

More insidious maladies infected the Liberal wounds of the 1870 session. Gladstone's stipulations for reductions in the Army estimates over the period of the new Parliament were marked conspicuously by withdrawals from colonial commitments. In 1865 Gladstone had peremptorily curtailed military operations in New Zealand.[123] Now came the time to call home the legions.[124] The Canadians and others were also targets for military and naval economies. The Colonial governments complained of niggardly 'Little Englandism'. Granville, at the Colonial Office, prudently censored documents relating to the new Canadian dominion so as to veil the government's desire, while not wishing to change 'abruptly' Britain's relationship with the self-governing colonies, to 'gradually prepare both countries, for a friendly relaxation of them'.[125] Gladstone was incautious enough, on the question of that relationship, to formulate the very Cobdenish notion that it should be on such a footing that 'if separation should occur, it should be in a friendly way'.[126] This and similar official declarations caused a stir of discomfort in British opinion at what seemed the disturbing implications of imperial abdication in the aftermath of Palmerston's departure and Bismarck's arrival on the European scene. At Windsor in November 1869 Granville was confronted with the Queen's complaints that England was 'being reduced to the state of a second-rate power'.[127] Russell revealed himself in the 1870 session as restless on the question of defence and the security of the colonies. Disraeli began to sniff the air of politics for the fragrances of what would soon be defined as reactive sentiment of 'empire'.

With all this Gladstone was perfectly serene. He had shown himself unwilling to mount any direct doctrinal challenges to the prevalent Palmerstonian orthodoxy either in foreign or colonial policy; but he was ready all the same to chip away at their financial foundations wherever possible and feasible. As he had suffered so much at Palmerston's hands in matters of military and naval expenditure over the period from 1859 to 1865, it would be of the essence of his own ministry's policy that

'Palmerstonism' be decisively discounted. Offering the Americans an international arbitration over the *Alabama* dispute was a signal case in point.[128] In any case, as he put it in February 1870, 'In truth the period since we came into office has been one of universal and almost total silence in the H. of C. with regard to foreign affairs.'[129] Gladstone's greatest concern by far on the international front was, of course, the nefarious machinations of Pius IX in the Vatican Council. When Granville arrived to replace Clarendon at the Foreign Office in June 1870 he was famously assured by his Permanent Under-Secretary that there never was such a quiet time in Europe's affairs.

That all changed with startling and brutal suddenness in July when France declared war on Prussia. The swiftness and magnitude of the catastrophe of Napoleon III and the Second Empire stunned the world. 'Indeed I have laughed but little for weeks past,' Gladstone told Laura Thistlethwayte on 13 August.[130] 'The news which has been so exciting every day, became overpowering,' Gladstone recorded on 3 September. He had been looking forward to the grateful possibilities of mediation such as he had been unable to impose upon the Washington regime at the time of the American Civil War. In rejecting Disraeli's call for an 'armed neutrality', Gladstone extolled the 'totally different' ideal of 'a secured neutrality, a neutrality backed and sustained by an adequate condition of defensive establishments'. This was necessary for 'the moral authority by which the peaceful offices of neutrals may be discharged', taking the 'form of friendly mediation'.[131]

Two considerations bore upon Gladstone's thinking during these events. The first was a perfect readiness to put Britain forward as an active power in the frame of European power politics, provided that active forwardness assumed the character of the 'moral authority' of some form or degree of an authentic international concert or community. Gladstone had been a reluctant but convinced maker of war in such terms in 1854. He had been quite prepared to intervene on the side of Piedmont-Sardinia against Austria in 1860. In the American case in 1861–2, even Palmerston thought Gladstone too eager to press the weight of international moral authority on Washington which he had been ready to impose on Vienna. Gladstone had been entirely ready to join with France to confront the Germanic powers in their war against Denmark in 1864. Indeed, he put it on record that Napoleon III's unwillingness to concert with Britain at that time was his greatest mistake, for had there been war in 1864, 'France with Great Britain on her side would never have undergone the crushing defeat which she had to encounter in 1870–1 . . . That is to say the whole course of subsequent European history would in all likelihood have changed.'[132] The misconceived public reputation as a Manchester isolationist under which Gladstone then suffered was a consequence of the failure of a policy to intervene, not the success of a policy not to intervene.

The second, more particular, consideration bearing on Gladstone's thinking was the question of Belgian integrity and neutrality as guaranteed by the Great Powers in London in 1839. The problems here were that that guarantee had been aimed overtly at the Dutch and covertly at the French. Gladstone was a convinced exponent of Belgian neutrality less as a capital British interest as a power than as the fruit of the moral authority of Europe. The Belgian issue was highlighted when Bismarck disclosed the project of a treaty with France in 1866 purporting to show that Napoleon III had designs to annex Belgium and Luxembourg as compensation for Prussian aggrandizement. Gladstone found the explanations given by the French for the 'Secret Treaty' of 1866 'unsatisfactory', and advised the Queen that the best response would be a 'new point of departure'. Gladstone's interpretation of Palmerston's doctrine on the matter was that the 1839 guarantee was a collective one; and that though Britain had the right to intervene unilaterally there was no obligation so to do.[133] The 'new point of departure' accordingly was to set Granville to the task of shifting Britain's position on to a revised foundation of international moral authority. France and Prussia were both approached with an undertaking of British belligerent alliance: Britain would prosecute war within 'the limits of Belgium' in alliance with Prussia against France if France invaded Belgium; and vice versa should Prussia invade Belgium. Gladstone pushed Granville keenly to get these treaties in place before any great battle altered the relative positions of the belligerents.[134] All that Parliament was told before the event was that the government had 'taken into consideration the whole state of the case', and that they had 'adopted such steps as appeared to them best calculated to establish confidence and security'.[135]

Parliament was informed by Gladstone and Granville of these treaties involving possible belligerence in the last minutes of the last day of the session, 10 August.[136]* There was little that startled members could do apart from complain about not being consulted and point out that confining British obligations within Belgium might be difficult. Gladstone envisaged his new departure as a preliminary stage on the way to a brilliantly expansive exercise in mediation. In which case, no doubt, the prestige and authority of his government would have been immensely enhanced. As it happened, however, the Prussians thwarted Gladstone by the speed of their victorious campaign, as Lincoln had earlier thwarted him by his bloodthirsty obstinacy. As he put it to Laura Thistlethwayte, 'Here I am the slave of events.'

* In 1890 King Leopold II of the Belgians told G of his act in 1870 over Belgium: 'you saved it'.[137]

By September, all Gladstone could do was to scrape together some sherds from the wreckage of his hopes. These he focused on Prussian intentions with respect to annexing French territory. 'I think it well deserves attention', he told Granville, 'whether we ought to make any remarks upon Bismarck's bold paper about Alsace and Lorraine.' Silence would be tantamount to acquiescence.[138] Gladstone's memorandum on the French appeal to the neutral powers was, as Granville assured Gladstone, 'the sort of thing Thiers ought to have said but did not'. Granville nonetheless had no wish that Gladstone should square up to Bismarck on Thiers's behalf. The Foreign Secretary and his colleagues were alarmed at Gladstone's hankering for some kind of intervention, and particularly his persistence in being 'much oppressed with the idea that this transfer of human beings like chattels should go forward without any voice from collective Europe if it be disposed to speak'.[139]*

In a heated and fractious cabinet on 30 September Gladstone struggled hard and long to persuade his colleagues 'to speak with the other neutral powers against the transfer of A. & L. without reference to the populations'.[141] He failed. Granville tenaciously resisted any form of intervention not substantiated by will and capacity, if necessary, to employ force. Laying down the moral law would expose Britain to an even more humiliating snub than Palmerston's 'brag' over Denmark had been subjected to in 1864. Granville found Gladstone quite alarmingly indefatigable in his restless moral urges to make Britain speak for Europe. Gladstone had already written an article on Bismarck's proposed peace terms which Granville deprecated as dangerously indiscreet. There are indications that Gladstone was prepared to go into some form of 'armed neutrality' such as Disraeli had earlier urged if the other neutral powers could be so persuaded.[142] Gladstone told Granville that he found the Cabinet's refusal to follow his European lead 'rather indigestible'.[143] He would counter-attack by publishing his article in the *Edinburgh Review*.[144] He would be careful, of course, to preserve anonymity. Behind his phrases extolling the claims of a European moral order against 'any mere assertion of power' was Gladstone's sense of outrage at the Prussian intent to annex Alsace and much of Lorraine. He later told the Queen in a 'much excited' manner that there would never be a cordial understanding with Germany if she took that million and a quarter people against their will; and that he 'wished they could know this'.[145] That was substantially the point of his article.

Gladstone's authorship was very soon leaked in the *Daily News*. This

---

* Thiers, then head of the French provisional government, was contemptuous of and bitter at G for what Thiers considered was G's refusal to aid France. 'One word would have sufficed . . . "M. Bismarck n'aurait jamais traversé La Manche."'[140]

unfortunately exposed Gladstone and his government to mockery. That the efforts of the British government in relation to cataclysmic European events should take the form ultimately of a furtive review article lent an air of absurdity to the proceedings. The *éclat* that would have attended mediation turned sourly into bathos. Gladstone predicted accurately to Granville that the 'violent laceration and transfer of Alsace-Lorraine is to lead us from bad to worse, and to be the *beginning* of a new series of European complications'.[146] Gladstone's eloquence against 'Bismarck-ism, militarism, and retrograde political morality' was soon lost in the din of recrimination. The air became thick with fantastic notions (much canvassed by the unfortunate French) as to what Britain might have achieved by a forceful policy of armed neutrality at the head of a European league. Disraeli and the Conservatives benefited from the domestic political fallout of the resounding French crash. These benefits accrued enormously in November 1870 when the Russians took the opportunity to repudiate the clauses in the Treaty of Paris of 1856 forbidding them to maintain a war fleet in the Black Sea. These 'Black Sea clauses', hobbling Russian power against the Ottoman Empire and the Straits, had been the jewel of Palmerston's 'Crimean system'. Anti-Russian war fever instantly ignited, with Russell, to Gladstone's disgust, 'leading the mad'.[147]

This was a particularly cruel blow to Gladstone, who had consistently, since 1856, decried the futility and impolicy of Palmerston's imposing humiliating restrictions on Russian sovereignty. Now Gladstone found himself being blamed by excited 'national' opinion for failing to respond adequately by reimposing treaty provisions he had always denounced as mischievously counter-productive nonsense. Disraeli, in fact, in 1856, had quite agreed with Gladstone on that point;[148] but prudently in 1870 said nothing to discourage the public agitation's demands that the Russians be punished for their insolent provocation. All that Gladstone could do was to set Granville to covering the nakedness of realpolitik with a 'European' fig leaf by persuading the Russians to go through the forms of getting their case accepted by a conference of ambassadors in London.

Even more unfortunate for Gladstone was the way this ebullience of 'national' or 'Crimean' agitation fed into the concurrent mood of perplexity about the question of Britain's problematic relations with the self-governing colonies. Both had to do with invocations of 'empire'. There were parliamentary expressions of 'uneasiness and uncertainty' as to those relations having taken on a 'tone of irritation, dissatisfaction and distrust sadly in contrast with the spirit of mutual respect and confidence which had hitherto generally characterised that inter-course'.[149] Such expressions now mingled with questions as to the adequacy of the armed services to fulfil their functions; which mingled in turn with resentful complaints at Britain's humiliatingly feeble role in Europe, and the necessities which bound her to what Salisbury would characterize as a *'rôle d'effacement'*.[150]

[8]

Maimed by Irish Land, wounded by dissension and faction on English education, infected by doubts and suspicions on foreign and colonial policy, Gladstone's party and government were nonetheless to be called to order by their leader for yet another gruelling exercise in legislative heroism. Once more the strain would be supplied to the engine of the state. There were great arrears still to be redeemed. There were entrenched interests to be confronted and worsted. The Army was going to be subjected to drastic and economic reorganization, with special attention paid to abolition of purchase of commissions. The Universities of Oxford and Cambridge would be made more conformable to progressive requirements. The drink trade would feel the stern hand of licensing limitation and restriction. Another social problem, the trade unions, still smarting under Gladstone's strictures at Oldham in December 1867, would be enfolded within the civic law. The secret ballot would be introduced for parliamentary and municipal elections. All these matters promised to be contentious. Was Gladstone well advised to push for another heavy session? For the first time he would be leading the government and the Commons without a commanding legislative centrepiece to hold Parliament either in awe or in terror. A Liberal member noted early in April 1871 that 'Ministers must have worked very hard in the recess', but he had doubts that the backbenches would reciprocate in the session. 'I have doubts whether their recent measures will have the success which the Irish Church Bill, the Land and Education Bills had. Pressure will be less strong. Interests more divided. It takes time for measures to ripen.'[151]

Preparations in the later months of 1870 were not as hectic as they had been for Irish Church or Irish Land, but they were hectic all the same. Cardwell at the War Office had the most daunting task in making the Army both better and cheaper. John Bright had had enough. His naturally indolent disposition[152] could not stand the Gladstonian pace. In November he requested that what Gladstone had recommended as 'judicious abstinence from public cares' be converted into definitive resignation.[153] Forster and Stansfeld had earned promotion to Cabinet. Halifax now played Clarendon's part in adding steadying dignity to the administration, which meant mainly trying to damp down Gladstone's proneness to moral excitement. Hartington, as he recounted to his father Devonshire, was 'bullied' by Gladstone into accepting the Irish Office vacated by Fortescue's being shifted to fill Bright's place at the Board of Trade.

In what was by now something of an annual ritual, the Gladstones were 'most kindly received' by the Salisburys at Hatfield in November, where Gladstone was gratified by the decorum in the chapel ('careful and seemly service: rare in private chapels').[154] Doubtless university reform matters were aired. As he had revealed in debates on the issue in the 1870 session, Salisbury by no means shared Gladstone's confidence that abolition of religious tests at Oxford and Cambridge would not weaken their Christian character. Foreign affairs would also have been much in mind. Salisbury too had struck out fiercely against Bismarck in the previous month, in the *Quarterly*; but he could share nothing of Gladstone's faith in the European moral order. In the decades to come Bismarck was to find both of them puzzlingly but differently irritating.

Another matter on Gladstone's mind in the closing weeks of 1870 was the 'royalty' problem. The scandalous Mordaunt divorce case earlier in 1870 had exposed the Prince of Wales to a damaging appearance in the witness box. The damage would have been much greater had not Gladstone used his influence to shield the Prince and the monarchy from the possibility of the Prince's being cited as a co-respondent.[155] The Queen asked Gladstone 'to speak to the P. seriously'.[156] The task of easing the Queen out of her obstinate clinging to widowed seclusion was to prove far more difficult. Gladstone had scored a coup over Jenner in 1869 by getting Victoria to open the new Blackfriars bridge. It turned out to be a splendidly successful event. Gladstone hoped now to build on that success. 'I cannot help continually revolving the question of the Queen's invisibility,' he told Granville.[157] Speaking 'in rude and general terms, the Queen is invisible, and the Prince of Wales is not respected'. The fund of credit built up by the Crown was diminishing. Gladstone feared the outlook ten, twenty, thirty, forty years hence 'is a very melancholy one'.[158]

Gladstone's immediate tactic was to use Ireland as a lever. Sentiment in Ireland was growing for the establishment of a royal residence in the country (nor was there lack of embarrassed owners of expensive piles eager to unload them for the purpose).[159] It was expedient to counteract grievances about Ireland's being deliberately neglected in the matter of the royal presence. The expedient also suggested itself that the Prince of Wales might be advantageously employed in some capacity in Ireland; perhaps attached to the Lord-Lieutenant, or in some other capacity in the event of planned change in the government of Ireland consequent on abolishing the lord-lieutenancy. It was for Gladstone an auspicious sign that the Queen consented to open the 1871 parliamentary session in person, 'at an epoch of such moment in the future fortunes of Europe'.[160] But Gladstone was soon confronted with the 'ugly' problem of opposition to financial provision for Victoria's third son, Prince Arthur, the future Duke of Connaught. 'We now begin to see', Gladstone commented to Halifax, 'the first results in a practical form of the Queen's retirement from London, which has grown to be, to so serious an extent a retirement from business.'[161]

Public stirrings of republican sentiment, associated particularly with the name of the Liberal MP for Chelsea, Sir Charles Dilke, made Gladstone increasingly anxious in 1871 to lance the boil. He considered Dilke's campaign 'part of a most serious question': how to allay the public dissatisfaction with the Queen's reclusiveness, 'of which the absurd republican cry is an external symptom'? He thought stern language from the government against the republicans inadvisable, as tending to 'establish rather than end the controversy'.[162] Much of the public stir had to do with an aggrieved sense of not getting royal value from the royal Civil List. An influential 'Tract for the Times', *What Does She Do with It?*, explored the mysteries of the royal finances. As Gladstone wrote to Lord Chancellor Hatherley, the writer 'exaggerates extremely; but on the other hand he omits *much* that would be in favour of his case'.[163]* Gladstone ordered copies to be secretly distributed to the Cabinet. He nerved himself with preparations for what he hoped would be a decisively remedial confrontation with the Queen. On 21 June: 'Conclave in Downing Street on the anxious subject of Royalties and Residence in Ireland.' At Windsor on the 25th there was a 'long conversation with H.M. Wrote Memm of the past on residence in Ireland.' But Gladstone found the Queen in a disconcertingly strong position. She quite approved of plans afoot to abolish the lord-lieutenancy. And her trump card was her quite accurate opinion that the Prince of Wales would never consent to go into what would be tantamount to a Dublin exile.

The other, and much more decisive, side of the case of the Queen's strong position was, however, the steep slide in Gladstone's own position. The 1871 session very quickly took a disastrous turn. Ministers trusted that issues abroad would 'not greatly abate the energy' with which the Commons and Lords had heretofore applied themselves to the 'work of general improvement in our domestic legislation'.[164] They trusted in vain. After two sessions of prudently deliberate reserve, Disraeli judged the moment right for a signal intervention. As Gladstone himself remarked,

---

* The author was G. O. Trevelyan, who had resigned from the administration in 1870 over the Education Bill.

Achilles had emerged from his tent. Trelawny, the Cornish Liberal MP, recorded the occasion.

Disraeli made a long speech on the neutralization of the Black Sea. He appears to have annoyed Gladstone exceedingly. The speech was, in my judgment, a good one. Gladstone has been wanting, of late, in temper, discretion & straightforwardness . . . It seems to me that he lost his temper – & Disraeli, who is provokingly calm, actually shone by contrast. It is not clear to me that the Tories will not soon put govt. in a minority by proposing a vote in wh. the radicals will join . . . We, Liberals, are in a sad plight – under a cloud, at least.[165]

Derby recalled Gladstone being so exasperated at Disraeli's attack that 'some unparliamentary violence was feared'.[166] Gladstone had cause to resent Disraeli's exploitation of the government's undeserved vulnerability in the fudging over of the Russian repudiation. He had cause also to be anxious about the rather unforgiving attitude of the Americans over the *Alabama* negotiations. On returning from the marriage at Windsor in March of the Queen's daughter Louise and Argyll's son Lord Lorne ('the spectacle beautiful: some things should have been otherwise'), Gladstone held a 'Cabinet in G.W.R. carriage' to revise a response to the American demands that might have provoked hostility in Parliament.[167]

Within a fortnight the Tories very nearly put the government in a minority. On 10 March Disraeli had to lead fifty or sixty Conservatives out of the House to 'prevent a catastrophe': he needed much more time to ripen the prospect of Conservatism's return to office. Gladstone's majority was in a distempered condition. The Nonconformists had not forgiven him for the Education Act. The 'advanced Liberals' were observed meditating revolt. 'They have lost their chief watchwords.' W. V. Harcourt led an attack on the government's failure to make any ground in reducing expenditure. Gladstone could only respond defensively and apologetically. At the Irish Office Hartington was thought to be less than impressive. 'The course of Ministers, in every respect,' seemed to be 'weak and inapposite.' Gladstone was 'falling in the estimation of his party'. The government was 'going down hill'.[168] Derby noted on 3 March: 'The House is tired of Gladstone: inclined to magnify his mistakes.' Disraeli was in 'high spirits' about the problems and blunders of ministers as much as about his Black Sea success.

The business of the Commons became hopelessly clogged. In a kind of saturnalia of indiscipline Liberal members put forward ever more private bills: there were no fewer than ninety-eight in 1871, compared with eighty-two in 1869.[169] Gladstone now found himself being regularly harassed by the Contagious Diseases Act abolition sect. There were also disturbing background influences. There was something of a public panic in May 1871 set off by the Paris Commune. Then Scott Russell's 'New Social Alliance', aimed at bridging the gulf between the possessing classes and the labouring masses, raised many perturbing questions about a new ordering of social policy. The stimulus for this project was an unprecedented outbreak of industrial unrest in the North and Midlands. Gladstone's Irish Land Act itself contributed to anxiety about challenges to the rights of property, and to a sense of a general unsettlement of all opinions, social, political, and religious. Disraeli was intrigued by Russell's ideas, seeing in the Alliance 'a new method of outbidding the Whigs, or rather Gladstone'.[170] Gladstone, in his old-fashioned way, dismissed the whole affair as quackery.*

Meanwhile Gladstone pleaded misfortune. 'During the course of nearly 40 years', he told the Commons on 14 March, 'I can remember no case in which, separately, and one by one, over the short period of eight months, three of the most important members of the Government have been struck down either by death or by illness.' The loss of Clarendon and Bright and the unsureness of Cardwell's health had 'considerably impoverished the resources with which the government was originally formed'.[171] He claimed that the 'affairs of Scotland and England have been suffered to reach a legislative dead-lock solely through the anxiety of this House to deal with the affairs of Ireland'.[172] Gladstone allowed that the government was 'overcharged with measures of deep importance', but insisted that it was 'admitted' that they were 'legitimately within the desires of the House, and also most pressing in their urgency'.[173] The item Gladstone himself pressed most urgently was that of the voting by secret ballot; but since he was but a recent and not entirely convinced convert to it ('spoke on Ballot and voted in 324:230 with mind satisfied & as to feeling a lingering reluctance'),[174] his advocacy lacked commanding cogency. The 'hands of Parliament are too full', he declared apropos of failing to make way on the Ballot, 'and the time of the Parliament is too limited'.[175] Gladstone threatened obstructors with an extended October sitting. It was Gladstone's driving a second reading of the bill on the day when quarter sessions were to get under way which provoked Disraeli to deny charges from his own party that he was complicitous with the Treasury Bench as to procedure and to the 'deleterious influence exercised over this House by the two front benches'.[176]

With Gladstone a propensity to drive came swiftly upon resistance. Peter Rylands protested against the way ministers were trying to force through the Army Regulation Bill. There was a scene with a Conservative member, Bentinck, who accused Gladstone of being a 'Bismarck', of

* See below, pages 101–2.

applying 'offensive' and 'unconstitutional' pressures to stifle debate.[177] Trelawny observed on 'Ministerial dawdling and inefficiency', with ministers being 'more frequently carped at in this year than in last'. The want of decision in a scandalous case of voter intimidation in a by-election at Westmeath had 'an ugly appearance'. Goschen's bill on local taxation was 'hardly a project describable as one presenting a definitive settlement'. Bruce's Licensing Bill 'will never pass as it stands'. 'Whether Cardwell will succeed is a question by no means solved. The budget may not add to any good temper still remaining in the Public mind.'[178]

This was precisely the point where Lowe stumbled badly. Hitherto, in his 1869 and 1870 financial statements, Lowe had performed solidly and sustained well the cherished reputation he inherited from Gladstone for the financial soundness and expertise to be expected from Liberal governments. Now the spell was broken. Lowe and his colleagues blundered, particularly on the issue of levying a tax on matches (*'ex luce lucellum'*, in Lowe's clever quip), which 'struck the House with some astonishment'.[179] It was seen as an imposition on the poor; and Lowe's plan had no chance once pathetic processions of 'match girls' from Messrs Bryant & May's establishment began petitioning Parliament. Formidable in advance, Lowe had no resource in retreat; and Gladstone was obliged to take over and replace the abandoned indirect tax with another hoist of the income tax.

Derby noted: 'On the whole this business is a heavy blow to the ministry – the first they have had.'[180] Within a few days there was a defeat in a division. 'The state of the House is indescribable: ministers have managed to offend nearly every important interest in the country.' Derby listed them: the Army, with purchase abolition; the publicans, with Bruce's Licensing Bill to discourage drinking; the country gentlemen, by Goschen's rating plans; the middle classes, by the increase of the income tax; the farmers, by another of Lowe's projects, a tax on horses; the East End, by the match tax; the Dissenters, not yet reconciled on the Education question; the clergy, on the university religious tests question; and property holders, by the proposed succession duty.[181] Derby might well have added the extreme annoyance of the Trades Union Congress at the Trade Unions and Criminal Law Amendment Bills, which the Congress thought, by treating unions as a form of social disease, like drink, made far too much of intimidating 'rattening' and unreasonably made picketing illegal.[182]

It was all rather reminiscent of the bad days of 1866 and 1867. Nothing Gladstone did seemed to strike the right note. On Jacob Bright's Women's Disabilities measure it was held that 'Gladstone trimmed his sails, which evolution was pointed out by Mr Henry James and Lord John Manners'.[183] As Gladstone, with his back to the wall, fought indomitably to save the budget and his income tax, Trelawny declared himself 'really tired of hearing the Lancashire twang of our verbiose and diffusive leader'.[184] Gladstone was obliged to withdraw several bills wholly or in part: Local Rating and most of Licensing, against which the trade had drummed up a very effective agitation in recent by-elections. There was laughter in the House at references to the government's 'very narrow and decreasing majority'.[185] Cardwell came under ambush from the Liberal side over the Purchase issue: 'these repeated shocks are disintegrating the strength of the Government seriously'.[186] On 28 May Gladstone suffered a sharp collapse and kept his bed for several days. He was judged as suffering seriously in encounters with Disraeli, 'who surpasses his rival in calm & premeditation – also, in point. His allusion to Gladstone's change on the Ballot was a very palpable hit.' With the government unable to keep the House in hand, Trelawny felt it 'difficult to believe that either the Army Bill or the Ballot Bill will pass this year'.[187]

The Army Bill and the Ballot Bill became the nodal testing issues of the session. Gladstone summoned a party meeting at Downing Street on 6 July to rally his forces. 'It sounded very comical in the Premier to counsel abstention from speeches.' But Trelawny was in no doubt Gladstone did a 'very wise thing in proposing to leave the conduct of the Ballot Bill to Ed. Forster'. Perhaps Gladstone would have done better to have arranged the meeting at the Reform Club, as more in keeping with the desired spirit of party solidarity. But Gladstone was never clubbable in that way. Although the committee of the Reform had elected him to membership in 1869 for distinguished eminence in public service[188]* (and as a required attribute in a Liberal leader), he never much frequented the place and resigned with indecent promptitude after defeat in 1874. Enough solidarity was rallied to get Cardwell's Army Bill through and up to the Lords. But the Commons soon fell once more into a 'very unruly state', with Gladstone's prestige waning. 'He wants several of the happy qualifications in a leader, which Palmerston had.'[189] In the Lords Grey complained of lax sessional management.[190] There were complaints in the Commons about an unsatisfactory and deplorable state of business: 'business confused, legislation abortive, Estimates postponed till they cannot be fairly debated, a loss of influence and authority on the part of the Government which is actually unprecedented', bringing the parliamentary system into 'discredit'.[191] Gladstone did not get his third reading of the Ballot Bill until 8 August.

There was clearly going to be trouble with the Lords over both the Army and Ballot Bills. The government now lacked the confidence and

---

* It was also thought expedient that G alter his profession of party allegiance for the 1871 edition of *Dod's Parliamentary Companion* from 'Liberal Conservative' to 'Liberal'.

authority necessary to intimidate and overcome the Lords as it had done in 1869 and 1870. Gladstone's waning prestige invited attack. Gladstone took steps. 'We were most kindly received and very happy at Hatfield – Army Bill not withstanding.'[192] Although not the Conservative leader in the Lords, Salisbury was more influential than the nominal leader, Richmond. He was, moreover, Chancellor of Oxford University, and it was most helpful for Gladstone that, despite misgivings, Salisbury was willing to shepherd through the University Tests Abolition Bill as an issue not between Church and Dissent but between Christianity and unbelief. Gladstone could not persuade Salisbury, however, to adopt the same understanding attitude towards the Army Regulation Bill. The sticking point was abolition of the system of purchase of commissions, with large financial implications for compensation. Abolition was a long-desired Radical objective. It was desired also by those who criticized the 'gentleman-amateur' ethos of the officer corps. Gladstone had not been tactful in his quest to let the nation 'buy back its own army from its own officers', declaring that it was 'undoubtedly alleged that under the present system generals and others in high command were rather wooden-headed'.[193] The Duke of Cambridge was indeed a great obstacle. Gladstone warned the Lords that the government was relying 'upon the known and proved views of a large majority of the members of this House'; he warned them also that they must not be deluded by misapprehension and rumours that ministers were prepared to abandon the Ballot Bill.[194] At the second reading in the Lords on 17 July the Lords passed a resolution detaching the purchase-abolition provisions from the bill. In a very excited Commons on 20 July Gladstone announced that since the existence of the purchase system depended on a royal warrant, the government had advised the Queen to cancel that warrant.

With this ruthless stroke of retaliation against the Lords Gladstone at least recovered his Peelite poise and retrieved something from the general wreckage of the session. Disraeli accused him of defying the opinion of Parliament and appealing to the prerogative of the Crown 'to assist him in the difficulties which he himself has created'.[195] For all his pious insistence on due 'observance of constitutional usage', Gladstone in fact was very ready to defy the opinion of a Parliament which, as in 1866 and 1867, had failed to live up to the high legislative requirements he had demanded of it; and nothing was more characteristic of him than to resort to high-executive prerogative. He was ever ready to make a joke of the 'numerous proofs of my domineering disposition'.[196] He was quite unapologetic to the remonstrative Lyttelton. 'What method of putting an end to it remained to us, except that which we adopted?'[197] Liberals of Palmerstonian tendency, like Trelawny, might well lament: 'How different would have been the conduct of some of the Premiers whom it has been my lot to observe &, generally, follow!'[198] For Gladstone that was, precisely, begging the point. It was not for avoiding confrontation with the Lords or for having 'several of the happy qualifications in a leader, which Palmerston had', that Gladstone in 1868 had invoked the tutelary genius of Peel, or the potent image of the straining engine of the state.

[9]

It was thus with more of a spring in his step that Gladstone set off on 22 July for a weekend with the Tennysons at Aldworth, Haslemere, in the Surrey hills. There were long conversations ('chiefly of religion and metaphysics'). Gladstone was intent on assuring Tennyson of his truly conservative predispositions, about which the Laureate was likely to be having some qualms. He certainly had qualms about such things as the Black Sea and *Alabama* affairs; but, as Hallam Tennyson later observed, Gladstone was adept at managing Tennyson with a mastery and flow of words and with 'a certain persistence in dwelling on those topics which he had himself started for discussion'.* Gladstone found Aldworth 'a characteristic and delightful abode'. 'Afternoon walk over the hill, and much conversation morning noon and night.' In Tennyson Gladstone found 'singularly mixed true greatness, genuine simplicity, and some eccentricity'. The latter he thought from 'habit and circumstance'; 'the former is his nature'. Gladstone could feel assured that the ideal of partnership between art and politics which he had cherished since 1859 remained in being.

Back at Westminster Gladstone finally got the Ballot Bill through its third reading on 8 August. The Lords countered by abruptly dispatching it two days later; or, as Gladstone contemptuously put it, 'stooped to reject it on the miserable plea of time'.[199] Gladstone did not repine. It would be ready for the next session. And no doubt he derived some satisfaction from the circumstance that, once purchase of commissions had been abolished, the Lords were forced to scramble the Army Bill through so as to provide the funds (Gladstone calculated £8 million over thirty-five years to settle claims) for compensating vested interests. More irritating was the squabble with the Queen in a conflict between the government's need for an extra three days of session before prorogation and her need to get up to Balmoral. Gladstone confided to Catherine the Queen's 'saying things you would not believe'.[200] Undeniably the

* See below, page 318.

government ended the 1871 session in a much weakened state; 'the prestige and success which belonged to them in 1869–70 is vanished'.[201] On the other hand, as Disraeli himself admitted, the Conservative opposition was as yet entirely unconvincing as an alternative government. In May 1870 Disraeli looked forward to 'Gladstone becoming useless to the Radicals & a disruption. Gives two years or more.'[202]

Almost certainly Gladstone himself would have acknowledged that estimate as reasonable and well founded. Two by-elections in 1871 provided indications of important shifts of opinion away from the Liberal government. The first was at Westmeath in Ireland, a traditional Liberal seat.

In Westmeath, the priests have thrown over the government candidate, and give their support to a Mr. Smyth, whose only claim is that he is styled a 'nationalist' or 'home rule candidate' which means a repealer. The priests cannot control the movement, and therefore put themselves at its head. If this precedent is to be followed (and that it will be, appears probable) a new Irish difficulty had arisen, more serious than any we have yet dealt with.[203]

Derby's account was accurate and prescient. Gladstone and Glyn could well envisage Liberal MPs or candidates in Ireland being pushed aside as at Westmeath or being defeated by the new 'home rulers' unless they adopted 'home rule' colours. Liberalism in Ireland was at great risk.

The second by-election was at East Surrey. There, just after the end of the session, a brewer, Watney, defeated one of the members of the Whig clan of Leveson-Gower. Gladstone viewed it as a portent possibly indicative of analogy with the fading of the Grey–Melbourne majority after 1831. There were 'untoward incidents' involved in this case: to be beaten by the Licensed Victuallers was disagreeable but not dishonourable. 'It is another matter', he told Glyn, 'if our own bettermost friends are falling away or cooling.'[204] Derby, again prescient, asked: 'Is this a beginning of the middle-class reaction against Gladstone?'

Gladstone retreated with Catherine to the refreshing sea breezes of Whitby, for which his son Willy was MP. 'I fell all to pieces, in mind more than in body,' he confessed to Granville, 'but I hope that if allowed to vegetate here for a little while mental life will return to me.'[205] There was much bathing; but the big event was a speech at the Congress Hall on 2 September. Return of mental life took the form of recasting the story of the late unfortunate session in terms reminiscent of his declaration at Liverpool in April 1866. Then he had summoned the genius of the people against a recalcitrant Parliament. Now he identified the London press as the medium of the animus against his government; an animus expressive of the class interests concentrated in London, of the power and influence of metropolitan plutocracy. It was to the people that he looked 'to redress the balance of the Press if the Press goes wrong'. Wealth had taken 'desperate offence because the Government has recommended to Parliament that power in the English Army should no longer be the prize of wealth but the reward of merit'.[206] To Glyn Gladstone reported of the 'large & enthusiastic' Whitby meeting: 'I fear the Metr^n Press will not be pleased with what I said of them; but it was time I think to say something for the purpose of reminding people that that press is not the country.' To Lord Houghton's warning that 'there is a Demon, not of Demagogism, but of Demophilism, that is tempting you sorely', Gladstone responded on the theme of the growth of 'plutocracy', the power of property and wealth, its 'domination in the Clubs, and in the Army'. He was sure that 'in a political view the spirit of plutocracy requires to be vigilantly watched and checked. It is a bastard aristocracy, and aristocracy shows too much disposition, in Parliament especially, to join hands with this bastard.'[207]

For Gladstone there was no lack of evidence, as he progressed from Whitby to Hawarden, of the responsiveness of the 'people' to his summons. Great crowds and deputations thronged his way at Wakefield (where he delivered an address on the virtues of Sir Robert Peel) and elsewhere. Then at Aberdeen, where he was honoured with the freedom of the city, there was 'much enthusiasm for the Government'. His address there gained the reputation of being a 'distinct and manly repudiation' of the objects of the Home Rule agitation in Ireland. In fact it was a rather incoherent and ambiguous statement which Gladstone would later cite as material to his case for conceding Home Rule.*

It is surprising that Gladstone seemed to be surprised at his chilly reception at Balmoral at the beginning of October. 'The repellent power which she so well knows how to use, has been put in action towards me on this occasion for the first time since the formation of the Government. I have felt myself in a new and different footing with her.' Possibly this chill disposed him to be much more restrained in his speech to a vast multitude at Blackheath in his Greenwich constituency later in the month. Here he justified his conduct of the session, adding a sideswipe to put a stop to the 'Social Alliance' nonsense. Granville assured him that the scheme of a Conservative 'coalition with the workmen' would 'do Dizzy harm with his practical and sensible friends, and cannot have much

---

* 'You would expect, when it is said that the Imperial Parliament is to be broken up, that at the very least a case should be made out showing there were great subjects of policy, and great demands for the welfare of Ireland which representatives of Ireland had united to ask, and representatives of England, Scotland, and Wales had united to refuse ... There is no such grievance. There is nothing that Ireland has asked, and which this country and this Parliament have refused.'[208]

political effect'. Scott Russell's group had put forward the idea of 'a decent house and wholesome food at a fair price'. Gladstone thought this 'Manifesto Internationale and something more, ought to make some sport for us. Is it Dizzy?' Gladstone was sure 'the wizard of Hughenden Manor is behind the scenes'. His attack on the Social Alliance was an attack mainly on Disraeli: 'I will say they are quacks; they are deluded and beguiled by a spurious philanthropy.'[209]

At Hawarden in November, Bright presents an attractive picture of the domestic Gladstone.

I think him most liberal, & very far ahead of any minister this Country has had in times of which I have any knowledge. He is very happy in his family, & nothing can be more amiable & cheerful than his home & family character. He has a good library, & reads much, & he takes good exercise in walking 'rain or shine' as the Americans say. He seems to delight in felling trees – which is an exercise I think a little hazardous, and too violent for a man of his age. I walked out in the park with Mrs. Gladstone. We came to a small plantation. 'Here is our woodman' she said.

I saw a man – without coat – without waistcoat – with *braces* thrown back from off the shoulders, and hanging down behind – engaged with a large axe in cutting down a tree, – it was not a large one – but it fell with a certain crash, & with the dignity which became it. The 'woodman' was the 'Prime Minister' of the Queen!

He lives carefully – in eating, drinking, & in exercise, & thus is able to sustain the tremendous strain which is upon him.

I think they will have a better Session in 1872 than that of 1871 . . .[210]

Gladstone's purpose in inviting Bright to Hawarden was to entice him back to the Cabinet, with remission for late-night attendances and such like. He found Bright rather a mellowed character, with no points of sharp difference. At a time when certain Whigs were complaining bitterly about being denied a 'quiet life',* Bright, as a totem of Radicalism and Nonconformity, would stand as a symbol of the Liberal government's earnestness of purpose with regard to the 1872 session. Bright, however, was not enticeable at that time.

The notion that a Liberal government existed to provide Liberals with

---

* 'A Whig' wrote to *The Times* from Brooks's Club on 24 November: 'Conservative reaction is very small but Liberal discomfort is very great. All that the Liberal party with a majority of eighty or one hundred ask is a quiet life; but that is not allowed us . . . During the last twelve months we have seen a want of tact, of true liberality, of good taste, of good manners, of consideration for the permanent officials (who, after all are the true executive), of sympathy with public opinion, of common sense in treating questions of the day, that has worn out our patience and made us angry and hostile.'[211]

a quiet life Gladstone regarded as a preposterous denial of its vocation to restore and fulfil the 'golden age of useful legislation and of administrative improvement' of the earlier part of the century. He was already proposing 'to hold a little Autumn Session of Cabinets' to start preparing bills and estimates 'so that they may be thoroughly matured and early'.[212] The lesson of the 1871 session was not to recoil from strenuous effort, but to make sure that the procedural shambles be not repeated. The Ballot and Licensing would be at the front. Bruce found himself in difficulties on Licensing. 'Unfortunately Gladstone cares for nothing but "Free Trade", which the House won't have, and I cannot get him really to interest himself in the subject.'[213] One of the subjects Gladstone found himself impelled to take an interest in was 'that plaguy ship': the *Alabama* case now began to take on a menacing and urgent immediacy. A Court of International Arbitration had been established at Geneva. Tenterden at the Foreign Office informed Gladstone that the US claims, 'swollen in every possible way', amounted in total to £4,479,463 ($22,397,305).[214]

Another subject of keen attention in these last weeks of 1871 was the disagreeableness of colonial governments in their demands for fiscal independence. Gladstone was shocked to discover from Kimberley how far things had gone in this respect. Gladstone was still at heart the schoolman he had been when at the Colonial Office in 1845–6.[215] His encouragement of self-government presumed the existence of a clear-cut distinction between questions of a local and of an imperial character, which in turn implied logically the necessary supremacy of the metropolitan centre over colonial dependencies. Despite his rhetoric about freedom and Hellenic ideals, he was an imperialist in what by the 1870s was an old-fashioned way. His notions were not entirely remote from recommendations, as to the Romanians, that suzerain status had its advantages over independence. Self-government meant, for Gladstone, strictly internal liberty of action. He was annoyed to discover that the colonies interpreted it at full face value as involving the liberty to alter fiscal arrangements among themselves and with Britain. He thought the possibility of New Zealand's admitting shoes from Sydney free but taxing those from Northampton 'brings us near the *reductio ad absurdum* of colonial connection'.[216] He was contemptuous of sentimental colonial verbiage about their wanting 'the closest & most affte relations with this country. (So does the Boa constrictor with the rabbit; but they are one-sided.)' He found Kimberley alarmingly lax in the matter, especially when confronted with the 'insolence' of Mr Gavan Duffy in Australia.

Frankly I do not yet see my way. I think that I am not like you if you are more or less prepared to concede everything except neutrality in war, & then stop at that point . . . I really do not see upon what foundation any duty of military

& naval protection on our part is to rest, if the foreign relations of Colonies are to pass out of our hands into theirs. Would Mr. Duffy be kind enough to give us a definition of the Colonial relation, as to rights and duties, on the one side and on the other, as he would have it. *What* will be the remaining duties of the Colony towards the mother State?[217]

This hankering after a definition of rights and duties was entirely characteristic of Gladstone. On the strength of insisting on it as a matter of equity for British interests (he was worried about the implications for Britain of commercial treaties with foreign powers) he 'opposed the Canadian attempt; and fought the Australians to a standstill'.[218] In the end he had to concede. There was no way of forcing colonial governments to be logical and consistent in definitions of right and duties. In a curious way Gladstone's rhetoric came to look far-sighted, prophetic of the Statute of Westminster and the Commonwealth ideal; quite at odds with what he actually tried to do. The point of greatest interest in this episode is the attempt he would make, in the case of Home Rule for Ireland, to return to the quest to realize a logical and consistent definition as to reciprocal rights and duties of imperial and subordinate jurisdictions. He would then, quite illogically and inconsistently, cite the self-governing colonies as instances wholly relevant to and supportive of his Irish cause; and one of the most influential professors of the appropriate definition of rights and duties would be that former Young Irelander, Sir Charles Gavan Duffy.*

Alarming news about the very serious illness of the Prince of Wales at Sandringham brought Gladstone back from Hawarden to London on 9 December. On the 11th the Cabinet, confronted with news of 'another sad change, almost shutting the door of hope', considered the contingency of the Prince's death. But with his slow recovery, Gladstone began to see the possibility of turning the matter to account in the 'royalty question'. The idea was floated in Conservative quarters of 'a public recognition say at St. Paul's', and the Duke of Cambridge was enlisted to approach Gladstone.[219] A 'long and interesting conversation' with the Duke on 20 December put Gladstone in hopes of squashing the republicans with a grand manifestation of national and popular solidarity with the monarchy. 'We have arrived at a great crisis about Royalty,' he told Granville; the 'last opportunity to be given us of effecting what is requisite'. A national Thanksgiving Service would scatter 'that disagreeable movement with which the name of Sir C. Dilke has been connected'.[220] Gladstone wanted something as elaborate as possible; and the precedent of the service for the recovery of George III in 1789 was examined.

* See below, page 371.

Ministers were under the impression that the Queen was agreeable to going solemnly in state to St Paul's Cathedral. At an audience at Windsor on 21 December, however, Gladstone was dismayed to find her averse to cathedral services, pomp, and 'false and hollow' ceremonial display in the name of religion. Gladstone put up a tremendous fight, not shirking the argument that 'principal personages' might well 'properly cast aside all thought of themselves, and their own feelings, in the matter', and consider the 'great religious importance of such an act for the people at large'. This 'appeared to tell very much with the Queen'; and Gladstone relentlessly wore down her resistance to the point of discussing details, the most salient of which was her stipulating for a short service. 'The upshot of the whole was that the Queen is in no way committed, and that the whole idea is subject to consideration of health, but it is entertained, and not unfavourably.' Gladstone enlisted Dean Wellesley of Windsor to keep working on the Queen and improve the shining hour by getting an opening of Parliament as well as a Thanksgiving.

Gladstone could return to Hawarden reasonably confident that the grand occasion would duly take place at some date to be fixed after the opening of the parliamentary session on 6 February. (The emergency visit to London had not otherwise been without its incidents. On 19 December Gladstone recorded: 'Saw Mrs Th.: a painful scene: my fault perhaps.') The theme of his birthday and end-of-year meditations now began to take on a decided consistency of lament at his life's confinement in arduous public duties and his yearning for release. In 1870 he recorded that the sentiment had deepened in his mind that his life 'can attain neither its just balance nor its true basis till it shall please God to give me a lawful opportunity of escape from the present course of daily excess which is for me inseparable from my place and calling'.[221] Perhaps he recalled his words to Manning in April 1870 about beginning to detach his hopes and interests from the political future.* In 1871, his words reflected the even more intense excesses of the year: 'And yet my life is but half life while it is oppressed entangled and bent as it now is with the heavy burdens upon me which exhaust in public affairs the moral force of the soul.'[222] Gladstone hoped, perhaps in view of the rapid decline of his political fortunes, that 'God in His mercy may soon deliver me into a freer and purer air'.

* See above, page 84.

CHAPTER 4

'THE FUTURE OF POLITICS HARDLY EXISTS FOR ME': THE STRAIT WAY TO ABDICATION, 1872–5

[1]

The unfortunate session of 1871 put Gladstone himself, among many others, in mind of possible developments more consequential even than those implied in the current talk of 'Conservative reaction' or 'middle class reaction'. Gladstone later explained his doctrine of the legitimacy of governments in relation to the lifespan of parliaments. It was not enough, he held, that a government should command a majority in the Commons. There were 'signs and currents' of public opinion which had to be taken into account.

We recognize the title of the country to be governed in conformity with its wishes and its intelligence; and the mere possession of a Parliamentary majority, satisfactory as it is when it is a true indication of the actual current of feeling and opinion of the country, is no adequate support and no adequate warrant for the continuance of a government in office if it has become clear, or when there is reasonable ground for supposing that the desires of the country are in an opposite direction.

It was the duty of government 'never to continue to carry on the business of the country unless it is convinced that it is possessed of the strength necessary for carrying on with dignity and credit'. Without that 'reasonable ground', without such conviction, a government is bound either to resign or dissolve.[1]

Strength necessary for 'dignity and credit' as opposed to 'mere possession of a majority' of course Gladstone interpreted in strenuously Peelite terms. What was good enough for Palmerston for virtually the whole period of his premiership was not by any means good enough for the inheritor and expositor of the dynamic values and requirements of the 'golden age'. It is true that Gladstone expounded this doctrine by way of extenuating to his rather bruised and bewildered party the precipitancy of his dissolving the 1868 Parliament in January 1874. But

neither regret nor apology was, in the nature of his interpretation of
the case, necessary or appropriate. As instruments of strenuously high
purposes, governments and parliaments in his view had either to fulfil
those purposes or break in the attempt. There was no question of the
flexible bend, the expedient relaxation of pace and pressure, the 'quiet
life'. What was at the heart of it was the imperative mood: 'that careful
comparison of the work we had to do with the strength we possessed
for doing it'.[2] From 1872 Gladstone's central purpose at the head of the
government was to discover the elements of a renewed legitimacy that
would provide strength for dignity and credit as had been supplied
copiously in 1869 and sufficiently in 1870: a 'special call' as he put it to
Manning at the time of his resignation in 1873;[3] a regaining of *'vital
power'*, as he put it to Ripon at the same critical phase;[4] some *'positive*
force to carry us onward as a body', as he put it to Bright;[5] and again,
'some one issue, clear, broad & straight'.[6]

In the want of such, Gladstone examined the consequential signs and
currents of public opinion and the actual current of feeling and opinion
in the country. Most stark was the run of by-election losses, which
threatened to take on the character of a haemorrhage. There had been
'no parallel within the Parliamentary experience of the present century',
declared Gladstone.[7] It was in 1872, as he later recounted, that he observed
to his Chief Whip, Glyn, that 'the indications of single elections in the
country were becoming considerably marked that, if they continued to
run in a similar direction, and to maintain a great degree of force,
they must end in abbreviating the existence of the late Parliament'.[8] A
Conservative gain in the West Riding in February 1872 suggested that
'great towns and manufacturing villages' could no longer be counted
on as safe Liberal terrain.[9] The Conservatives held Preston in September
1872: a notable win, as it was the first constituency to poll on the new
secret ballot. That by-election confirmed Gladstone, as he told Glyn, in
his impressions 'that our hold over the Constituencies is weakened, &
that the Conservatives may begin soon to think of another advent to
power, although unless they do much more than they have yet done in
laying f[urther] grounds for confidence, it will only be for a short lease'.[10]
It was true that Gladstone's major political asset remained the unconvincingness of the Conservatives as an alternative government. Still, that
was a meagre consolation with the prospect of a possible repeat of 1866 in
view. In 1872 Conservatives captured seven Liberal seats and lost none.
By the end of 1873 Disraeli could proclaim the reduction of the Liberal
majority by thirty votes in the lobbies.

For 1872, in any case, Gladstone had to do without 'vital power' or
'positive force' meanwhile. The Parliament he met in February was
fractious and distempered. Reintroducing the Ballot Bill was hashing

the old mutton, and in any case it was the issue in which Gladstone impressed least. On Licensing there had been a placatory and appeasing retreat, but no guarantee of better fortune. It was hopeless now to expect Lowe to restore prestige on the financial front. Gladstone was disgusted at Lowe's supineness in the battles over the estimates during the pre-sessional cabinets. ('For 2½ hours we discussed Army Estimates, mainly on reduction & the C. of E. did not speak one word!')[11] Speaker Denison had had enough in 1871, and Gladstone pressed Henry Brand, his former Whip, to take the chair. This was thought by many to be improper. Disraeli was in hopes that it might be a spark which could ignite 'a good deal of combustible material'.[12]

Other patronage improprieties exposed Gladstone's vulnerability to accusations of want of 'judgment and moderation', of proneness to 'vehemence & excitability'.[13] He ingeniously circumvented the statutes of the University of Oxford to appoint to the Rectory of Ewelme: he had a case, but his procedure was reckless and imperious. Again, with the appointment of the Attorney-General, Sir Robert Collier, to the Judicial Committee of the Privy Council, Gladstone rather brazenly chicaned his way through statutes and conventions. He survived a bad-tempered debate in the Lords by a majority of one, with difficulties exacerbated by disagreeableness on the part of Lord Chief Justice Cockburn.[14] In the Commons he was querulous that members collated the Ewelme and Collier affairs. He got the majority he demanded; but manifestly Glad-stone was getting 'intensely unpopular with the House: much more so this year than the last', with his 'increasing irritability and violence, itself the effect of overworked brain'. There was talk among Liberals that Forster should take over the leadership.[15] A reference by Gathorne Hardy to the Hyde Park riot of 1866 'caused such an explosion of passion & temper from Gladstone as even he has seldom exhibited'. There were 'storms' and 'abuse'. 'He could scarcely get it out for rage. What a Leader of the House.'[16] These were all bad omens for the session.

Another matter in which Lord Cockburn was thought to be unhelpful was the *Alabama* case. His opinion was that Britain was unequivocally liable. The arbitration at Geneva now loomed over the 1872 session like a lowering and threatening cloud. What promised so well had turned sour. Tennyson wrote cheeringly to Gladstone on the eve of the session: 'Heaven help you fair through the Session – like enough to be a rough one – but – if you let these Yankee sharpers get anything like their way of you in the Alabama Claims, I won't pay my "ship money" any more than old Hampden.'[17] The following day Gladstone recorded of the opening of Parliament: 'The Alabama question lay heavy on me – till the evening. Even during the Speech I was disquieted and had to converse with my colleagues.' What could the government do if the Court accepted the American interpretation of the Treaty of Washington and allowed the claim for 'indirect' damages? John Bright thought it 'monstrous to propose an arbitration on a question, – say the prolongation of the war, – on which no proof is possible'. He feared 'our friends on the other side have been "trying it on" as people here say of those who are sometimes rather too sharp'.[18] Gladstone assured the Queen that the conduct of the Americans was the most 'disreputable' he had ever known in his recollections of diplomacy – which included the Russian behaviour over the Black Sea in 1870.[19] But the crux was that Gladstone could well see himself, like Napoleon III in 1870, confronted with the options of humiliation or war. That 'plaguy ship' was deeply troubling: 'all the bunkum and irrelevant trash', as Gladstone commented to Granville, 'might be handled in some degree as "Americanism" due to want of knowledge of the world and of European manners'. But one of the features of the 'Yankee sharpers' was that their replies to British rejoinders about the inadmissibility of indirect claims came in 'much too quick'.[20]

[2]

Amid all the gloom and tension, the one bright spot for Gladstone was the brilliant success of the Thanksgiving Service at St Paul's on 27 February for the recovery of the Prince of Wales. Even at 'half-state', as the Queen grudgingly conceded, the arrangements, Gladstone thought, were excellent, the spectacle magnificent, and 'the behaviour of the people admirable (to us very kind)'.[21] There were observers who thought the reception the Disraelis got was even kinder, marking yet another point in Disraeli's re-emergence from the political reserve into which he had withdrawn himself since 1869. But unquestionably Gladstone would have felt a public ovation to Disraeli a small price to pay for getting some positive movement on the way to improving 'relations between the Monarchy and the Nation'. Gladstone set out determinedly to exploit the occasion by 'framing a worthy and manly mode of life, *quoad* public duties, for the Prince of Wales', Ireland being once more the designated locale, linked to the issue of a royal residence in Ireland.[22]

'It will be a calamity if we fail, either with the Queen, the Prince, or both.'[23] Fail Gladstone duly and comprehensively did. 'There is a manifest *twist*, in the Queen's mind', he complained to Spencer, 'with respect to Ireland.' The responses Gladstone got from the Queen were not only tart, but shrewd in her assessment of the Prince's deep reluctance to devote himself to the affairs of Ireland.[24] Gladstone, both exasperated and exasperating, persisted in spite of all her efforts to fend him off. He probably did more harm than good in his attempt to stifle Dilke's motion in March 1872 for a complete reform of the Civil List. The month of July 1872 was largely taken up with a 'formidable letter to H.M.: by wh I am willing to live or die'.[25] Softened in detail and manner by both Granville and Catherine, it nevertheless failed to breach the royal defences. Gladstone asked Halifax to hint to Victoria that he, Gladstone, was 'rather obstinate or tenacious'. She had no need of such information; and besides, she was well aware that the balance of advantage had tilted her way. Gladstone was by no means as formidable a force in politics as he once had been. Gladstone confessed to the Duke of Cambridge in August the 'entirely barren' results of his efforts to convince the Queen of the need to give the Prince 'a plan of life' as against 'a driblet of business coming up now and then'.[26] And, as he assured the Duke, it was 'not for want of plainness of speech'.

Were it well settled, I could lay down my office on the morrow of the settlement with perfect satisfaction. I never can hold that office with anything like satisfaction while the subject continues in its present state . . . It is painful to think that a reign which for 25 years tended so much to the strengthening of foundations, may in its latter portion be found to have been marked by an opposite process.[27]

As things turned out, there was no 'calamity' arising from Gladstone's failure and no 'opposite process' from the tendencies of the Queen's reign. The 'melancholy prospect' which Gladstone discerned ten, twenty, thirty, forty years on in 1869 did not eventuate. Ironically, the fortunes of the monarchy prospered steadily as those of Gladstone underwent extreme vicissitudes and then went into marked decline. Monarchism and imperialism would become foundations of a 'modernized national ideology'.[28] Even in the context of 1872, as the monarchy became seen as a force for social stability, Gladstone came to be associated with Dilke as 'dangerous'. The Queen made no bones of it. She told her daughter, now the German Crown Princess: 'Mr. Gladstone is a very dangerous Minister – and so wonderfully unsympathetic. I have felt this very much, but find his own followers and colleagues complain fully as much.'[29]

The Queen remained stiff and assured. She had made it clear to Derby that she expected 'a political crisis'; which gave Derby the 'opportunity of saying that we, the Opposition, could not think of taking office while in a minority of 100, but that while remaining where we were, we would do what was possible to prevent embarrassment and help in working the machine'.[30] At a 'rather long audience' after a Council at Windsor Gladstone recorded her manner as being 'as usual, kind and pleasing: nevertheless the whole helped to show me yet more that the occurrences

& correspondence of this year have led & will lead her to "shut up" (so to speak) towards me'.[31] On the other hand, Gladstone came to be on increasingly good terms with the Prince. The Gladstones were invited to Sandringham late in 1872: 'This is a pleasant interior: the chief personages carry themselves becomingly, but there is none of the stiffness of a Court. I like the house too, the place, & the air.'[32] The Prince and Princess Alexandra were actuated in no small degree by an acute sense of the dangers to the monarchy's position should it become identified with a partisanly anti-Liberal stance. It becomes evident through the years to come how carefully they balanced the Queen's antipathy with a sympathetic solicitude for the Gladstones.

The pity of the matter, no doubt, is the way the notion of a royal residence in Ireland rather dropped out of sight between Gladstone's tactless obstinacy and tenaciousness, the Queen's narrowness of outlook and tart resentment, both within the frame of the waning of his prestige, and the Prince's unwillingness in any case to embrace the 'plan of life' which Gladstone devised for him. Would a royal residence in Ireland have aided materially the cause of popular 'unionism'? The Unionists in Britain as well as Ireland certainly came to think so.[33] As events in Ireland were showing, the new 'home rule' movement and the link with politicized priests were undermining the traditional influence of the 'gentry and quality'. All the evidence indicated that Gladstone's Church and Land measures of 1869 and 1870 had stimulated rather than pacified this process. As events more particularly in 1873 would show, the collision between British Liberalism and Irish Romanism (with more than a whiff of the late Vatican Council in the Irish air) suggested the urgency of the need for countervailing initiatives to temper the drift of Irish sentiment in directions contrary to reconciliation with the British connection.

[3]

The faded and threadbare issues of the Ballot and Licensing proved ungrateful tasks. Licensing got through with aid from the Conservatives, and not without comment on Bruce's 'moral prostration before the victuallers'.[34] The *Licensed Victuallers Gazette* proclaimed the Trade's message of revenge: 'we shall hail with delight the advent of a Conservative Ministry'.[35] Little could be done to bind the party's wounds in the Education imbroglio. 'The education question is all wrong', as Bright put it, '– & so wrong that it cannot now be put right.'[36] There were Conservative fears still about the Ballot, but they were counterbalanced by considerations that too stout a resistance might give Gladstone a handle for a Liberal rally. The Lords were given no encouragement to stick with their amendments when Gladstone threatened an autumn session and a November dissolution. On that latter point Glyn's advice to Gladstone was that on a dissolution 'without a cry' the government's existing majority of eighty-six would decline by thirty-two seats: sixty-four votes in a division. A new register would possibly gain ten seats; and with the Ballot and Licensing as 'cries' there would assumably be a much better showing by the party, though Glyn found this difficult to quantify with any certitude.[37]* These drastic recourses were not, in the end, needed.

Bright's view was that the Liberal government was 'weak & blameable on the Expenditure question, & this will damage it greatly at a General Election'. A 'good budget' from Lowe would help; but Bright 'had not much faith in the Chancellor of the Exchequer', and he feared the Prime Minister was 'not enough master in his Cabinet'.[39] Lowe was greatly aided by buoyant revenues, but he was by now a fast depreciating asset. Gladstone and his ministry appeared to be helplessly becalmed in a political doldrums. There was the simmering aftermath of the patronage 'scrapes'. There was the implacable Nonconformist disaffection. There was continued failure to prune the Estimates. Junior ministers, with the irrepressible Ayrton in their midst, brawled with each other as Gladstone remonstrated ineffectively. Disraeli chose his moment well to launch his strategic counter-attack at Manchester early in April. He denounced the 'principle of violence' behind Gladstone's policies. He pointed out the 'portentous birth' in Ireland of 'sedition rampant, treason thinly veiled'. He criticized Liberal harassment of 'every institution and every interest, every class and calling in the country'. He taunted Liberal ministers with having subjected themselves as well as the country to humiliation over the Black Sea and *Alabama* questions. Above all, his picture of the spectacle of the jaded Liberal Cabinet well deserved Morley's tribute to 'one of the few classic pieces of oratory of the century'.[40]

The unnatural stimulus is subsiding. Their paroxysms end in prostration. Some take refuge in melancholy, and their eminent chief alternates between a menace and a sigh. As I sit opposite the Treasury Bench, the ministers remind me of one of those marine landscapes not very unusual on the coasts of South America. You behold a range of exhausted volcanoes. Not a flame flickers on a single pallid crest. But the situation is still dangerous. There are occasional earthquakes, and ever and anon the dark rumblings of the sea.

---

* Current Conservative estimates were for thirty to forty gains: good, but not enough for a majority.[38]

All eyes now were on the *Alabama* issue. For the time being it guaranteed the survival of the government. The last thing Disraeli and the Conservatives wanted was to inherit it as long as it remained unsettled. It was now clear that the American claims for indirect damages would go forward to be considered by the Court of Arbitration at Geneva. The alternatives of humiliation or withdrawal and war loomed ever more starkly. Gladstone had every reason for feeling aggrieved as well as *désœuvré* ('What am I now?' he wrote to 'Dear Spirit'. 'As Dizzy says an exhausted volcano . . .').[41] The public mood waxed excitable. In the Lords Russell declared that Her Majesty's honour must not be sacrificed to improving President Grant's prospects of re-election to the presidency. Gladstone wanted from Granville answers to questions about the military and naval strength of the United States.[42] In public he did his best to spread calm and reason. He was grateful to Disraeli and the bulk of the Conservatives for holding fire and declining to follow Russell's lead. 'Dizzy was perfect,' Gladstone reported to Granville. 'I understand he was much pleased with my having called to inquire after Lady Beaconsfield a few days ago. Perhaps this helped a little.' Russell he regarded as exhibiting a 'spectacle melancholy to those who have known and admired him when he was himself'.[43]

Early in June 1872 Granville's offer of what the American Minister in London, General Schenk, called an 'olive branch' was promptly rejected in Washington.[44] 'The House behaved *well*' on Gladstone's statement of 3 June. On the 6th Gladstone could allow that the Commons were even '*too* well pleased' with the government's handling of the crisis. By 13 June the matter was acutely critical. Was there justification for breaking off from the Geneva proceedings? Gladstone had reached the point of opting for that drastic recourse. 'My determination upon it is now firmly rooted & tested by all the mental effort I can apply.' He began to prepare the Queen's mind for the shock. The '*root* of the probable difficulty' in the Cabinet was the reluctant trio of Halifax, Kimberley, and Cardwell. But Gladstone was determined to go ahead regardless: 'if anything like a Government can be held together, I will not shrink'.[45] On 15 June: 'Cabinet 12–2¼ & with brief intervals to 7½.' Word was expected from Geneva as to the American indirect claims. 'Thank God that up to a certain point the indications on this great controversy are decidedly favourable.'[46]

So in the end it proved. On 27 June Gladstone in the Commons and Granville in the Lords announced that the indirect claims had been withdrawn by the Americans. Disraeli again behaved well. At the Crystal Palace at Dulwich on 24 June he famously banged the drum of Empire but he was notably reticent on the *Alabama* matter. The eventual award to the United States (14 September 1872) Gladstone considered too punitive – 'harsh in its extent and unjust in its basis' – yet 'as dust in the balance compared with the moral example set' of two proud nations going 'in peace and concord before a judicial tribunal' rather than resorting 'to the arbitrament of the sword'.[47]* These were words Gladstone used in 1880 after the dust had settled. But at the time, once the initial feeling of relief passed, and for long, it left a sense of public unease and rancour about Britain's 'truckling to the Yankees'.

That unease and rancour permeated in many directions. It reached back to the captiousness about Britain's effacement in 1870. It linked to the current fashion for Empire, much drummed up by Disraeli as a kind of consolation and compensation for the grateful public. It related to Gladstone's stubborn resistance to 'the licence now demanded by the Australian colonies to regulate their Tariffs with the absolute discretion of independent Powers'.[48] All of which contributed to the exposing of what was being increasingly identified as an area of Liberal deficiency. The sense of general dissatisfaction at the existing relationship between the colonies and the 'mother-country' spurred the Scottish Liberal MP, MacFie, to move for arrangements for colonial governments to participate in the conduct of affairs concerning the general interests of the Empire.[49] This accorded with the programme of Dilke's influential *Greater Britain*. McFie was almost certainly emulating Disraeli's initiative; but he evoked no sympathetic governmental response. Just as Disraeli's evocation of the social-reform ethos of the New Social Alliance merely incited Liberal mockery, so his high note in foreign and imperial affairs found as yet no echo in the upper, directive circles of Liberal government.

Instinctively, Gladstone reacted against both the 'new imperialism' and the 'new social reform'. He prompted Kimberley to withdraw from West African responsibilities in Ashanti, and to fob Gambia off on to the French. But he found himself impeded by resistant influences. Humanitarian, missionary, and commercial interests combined to thwart his policy. By February 1873 the Colonial Office conceded that in 'the present tone and temper of the public mind no abandonment of territory would . . . be permitted by Parliament, or sanctioned by public opinion'.[50] Soon Gladstone would find himself the official espouser of Sir Garnet Wolseley's expedition to subdue the King of the Ashanti. He also took prudent steps to dissociate himself from Henry Richard's motion in the Commons extolling the principles of Cobden and of international arbitration. Granville had warned him that the extent of the award to the Americans would 'not be popular here – & will create an angry debate in each house'.[51] Lowe (who of course had to find the money) was embarrassingly indiscreet in grumbling openly about the burden.[52] In answer to Richard's

* The award was for the equivalent of £3¼ million, about a third less than the American claim (not including the indirect claims).

evocation of Cobden Gladstone made great play with the name of Palmerston. Facts must be faced. Those facts included a 'portentous development of armaments' and a recognition that 'insular' powers like Britain and America were in a quite different position from the 'continental' powers of Europe. Let the idea of arbitration make its natural way in the world as free trade had done.[53]

These were expedient tactical retreats from positions which circumstances made exposed. They did not divert Gladstone from attending to domestic and Irish questions as the core of his proper concerns. He persisted in his attempt to cajole Bright back into the Cabinet. There was daylight at last visible on the Army estimates. He could congratulate Cardwell on having accomplished a 'large, & I hope a permanent and salutary work'.[54] The 1872 session was in the end surmounted. Derby conceded that 'on the whole the Cabinet has got through its difficulties safely but not triumphantly'.[55] On the strength of such achievements Gladstone felt himself entitled to be 'absolutely governed by a clamorous demand for rest'. When that demand was in some degree satisfied, 'I know not as yet which way my face will turn'. Homerology beckoned enticingly for the moment. But then so did the question of what next to do in the great world of politics. There was no question of scrambling through another session in the somewhat disreputable manner of 1872. Given his survival, Gladstone could see the prospect only in terms of a reversion to the high Peelite strenuousness of 1869 and 1870. There would be no less than a third pod to the Irish question; a return to the Irish higher-education issue of 1866, but now in such a manner of ruthless frontal assault as would put petty grievances and minor irritations in their place. With a rising new confidence in the benefits of shock effect Gladstone slapped down Nonconformist requests that something be done on the Burials question. He informed their spokesman: 'we do not in consequence of the great labours of Parlt. during the past years find ourselves confronted by a less formidable array of demands than in former years'.[56] 'You had come in as a lamb', as Granville helpfully put it, 'and gone out as a lion.'[57]

[4]

While contemplating that formidable array of demands during the latter months of 1872 Gladstone found much to concern him on the domestic side. The signal event was the death in July 1872 of the Rev. Henry Glynne, Catherine's brother and Rector of Hawarden since 1834. 'What a breach & wrench of all our calmly settled life.' Gladstone reflected that in thirty-three years he had not had from Henry an unkind word. Perhaps Henry's thoughts, in the matter of his aborted adventures in matrimony with a view to heading off the Gladstones by providing Hawarden with a male Glynne heir, might have verged on the unkind.[58]* However that may have been, the immediate question arose as to how the late Henry's brother Sir Stephen, as patron of the lucrative living, might dispose of it. Even with curacies incumbent, Hawarden was a considerable place, worth nearly £3,000 a year. With his sister Catherine and her husband – the 'grand people' as Sir Stephen in his mood of slightly mocking deference called them – in residence on his own ground, there was little doubt that the call would come to his nephew, the Gladstones' son Stephen, since 1868 a curate in Lambeth. The Rev. Stephen had his own doubts about returning to Hawarden to live in the shadow of the 'grand people'. But in the end, as the patron had bowed, so the son and nephew bowed: 'an event in his history', as Gladstone noted, '& ours'.[60]

There were the distractions of current literature: the memoirs of the late Baron Stockmar, mentor to Prince Albert, Gladstone found remarkable for want of tact, taste, and insight. He was tempted by the idea of a review.[61] But it was at this time on the ecclesiastical and theological side that Gladstone's interests were ever most lively. The fortunes of Döllinger and the 'Old Catholics' who refused to submit to the Infallibility dogma of 1870 were much, and painfully, on his mind. An invaluable source of information was Robert Morier, at the British Legation in Munich. The fortunes also of the schismatic Bulgarian Church in its quarrels with the Greek Orthodox patriarchy he found absorbing, in relation particularly to Döllinger's initiatives for union with Orthodoxy.[62] Gladstone devoted an enormous amount of time to a correspondence on religion and belief with the young and rather untoward Earl of Pembroke. But a much more formidable problem confronting him in these years of the early seventies was to examine more closely than hitherto Darwin, whose *The Descent of Man* was one of the major intellectual events of 1871.

One of the intellectual characteristics of the day, in Gladstone's view, was a 'mental rashness', which infected the mind and the criticism of the time. 'To form an adequate judgment of such subjects', Gladstone thought, 'my first step must be to resign, & divest myself of every other thought or care, & spend some undivided years on them.'[63] In default of resignation, all Gladstone could do was to grapple as best he could, using the inadequate notions he was able to form. With respect to Darwin, he thought it 'something truly portentous' in the 'avidity' with which

---

* Henry appears to have been struck by lightning: in Catherine's view an incongruous end for so matter-of-fact a person.[59]

the age 'leapt' to 'ulterior conclusions' which the *Origin of Species* was thought 'scarcely to hint, & which his physiological theory did not even require'. Gladstone remained confident that it had not been 'given to Mr. Darwin or Mr. Buckle to sweep away that fabric of belief which has stood the handling of 1800 years & of stronger men perhaps than any now alive'.[64]*

There were problems of the demands of science on the state. Gladstone had misgivings. He greatly respected individual scientists, but had 'little sense of what science or scientific method represented'.[65] He was a member of the Metaphysical Society, founded in 1869 by James Knowles, editor of the *Contemporary Review* and later founder of the *Nineteenth Century* review, 'to unite all shades of religious opinion against materialism'. Over the years he engaged in many controversies with Tyndall, Lubbock, and especially Huxley, 'Darwin's bulldog'. To Max Müller, the Oxford orientalist and philologer, Gladstone confessed that he lacked the 'physical knowledge really necessary to deal with the Darwinian question'. But Gladstone felt 'less unable to deal with the non-physical part of the subject'. Here, his 'ever-strengthening conviction' was that 'strength of belief lies in – Butler'. The *'method of handling'* of Gladstone's supreme theological mentor was, he was sure, 'the only one known to me that is fitted to guide life, and thought bearing upon life, in the face of the nineteenth century'. But Gladstone felt he could do little 'until I abandon politics, which God in his mercy grant me before long'.[66] His fervid loyalty to Bishop Butler helped make Gladstone proof against the newer trends of thought to which many of the younger generation of his contemporaries were turning, seeking means of revitalizing Millian individualism through idealist metaphysics. He was not impressed by the kind of Hegelian theory of a higher vocation of the state taking root in Oxford. 'German philosophy', he told Manning, 'has added but little to the stock of our knowledge of the mind & nature of men, if indeed it has added anything.'[67]

Of men of science in general, Gladstone could see 'nothing in their pursuits, or in their words as a body, to invest them with special authority in regard to the greatest questions of history, philosophy, & religious belief'. With respect to questions about the progress of Christian belief and the loss of belief since 1845, as he wrote to Döllinger, it was the 'fashion to ascribe the change to science, i.e. physical science, and to criticism and research'. Such was not Gladstone's view. By the side of the scientific 'counter-movement' the 'original religious and dogmatic movement' had continued, constantly assuming a more Catholic

---

* H. T. Buckle, immensely influential author of *The History of Civilisation in England* (1857–61), was inclined to free thought in religion.

character, and with the beneficial loss of some traditional superstitions.[68] His reading of George Eliot's *Middlemarch* (1871) in late 1874 was no doubt informed with this kind of resistant response to the Comtist implications of the translator of Strauss's deplorable *Leben Jesu*. Gladstone always professed himself as being a 'firm adherent of the principle of dogma, & under strong conviction as to the central elements of the dogmatic system of Christianity'.[69] These were indeed the uncompromising doctrines of an address he delivered in December 1872 at Liverpool College, asserting that the major duty of the times was to repel threats to religious faith from speculative rationalism. He remained also, consonantly, in touch with his old 'other worldly' interest in spiritualism (via, at this time, the group around Henry Sidgwick and Arthur Balfour).[70] He corresponded with one of the *Planchette* providers of the 'spiritual requirement of a scientific age',[71] offering to put him in touch with 'a friend', probably Laura Thistlethwayte. Nor had he lost touch with the phrenologists, one of whom thought he had cause to comment on Gladstone's 'over-active mind'.[72]

A collision with the quintessential social evolutionist, Herbert Spencer, late in 1873 illustrated well Gladstone's rather prickly and uneasy relationship with most 'men of science'.[73] Preparing a new edition of his *Principles of Sociology*, Spencer alluded to Gladstone as 'typical of the anti-scientific view in general', on the strength of Gladstone's Liverpool College address. Gladstone challenged Spencer for misunderstanding his providentialist argument that the 'functions of the Almighty as Creator and Governor of the world' were being denied on insufficient grounds. Spencer allowed that he had interpreted Gladstone perhaps too narrowly; but insisted on his 'scientific view' that the power manifested in the universe 'from the movements of the stars to the unfolding of individual men' worked 'in ways that are absolutely uniform'.[74]

Much more agreeable to Gladstone was Stanley Jevons's treatment of scientific method in his *Principles of Science* of 1874. Gladstone welcomed it as being cautious and circumspect in its ulterior conclusions. He accorded Jevons, indeed, his supreme intellectual accolade. 'I hope you will not be shocked if I designate it by an epithet which to my mind conveys the highest commendation: it seems to me eminently *Butlerian*.' As to evolution and Darwinism: 'I must say that the doctrine of Darwin, if it be true, enhances in my judgment the proper idea of the greatness of God, for it makes every stage of creation a legible prophecy of all those which are to follow it.' But Gladstone remained certain that there was 'gross ambiguity & latent fallacy in much that we hear about "uniformity of laws"'. He set out a series of sceptical propositions about the claims of science.

That we are not warranted in predicating, of time & space themselves, that they are necessarily conditions of all existence.

That there is real insoluble mystery in some of the formulae of mathematics.

That we are in danger from the precipitancy & intellectual tyranny of speculation.

That the limits of our real knowledge are (if I may use the word) infinitely narrow.

That we are not rationally justified in passing our own inward perceptions of things inward, & confirming the sphere of knowledge & things outward.

These, Gladstone explained to Jevons, were his 'old convictions which I live in the hope of doing something before I die to sustain and illustrate'.[75]

Darwinist speculation, however, impinged upon Gladstone in a manner bearing important and immediate political implications. He recorded reading in December 1872 Walter Bagehot's recently published *Physics and Politics, or Thoughts on the Application of the Principles of 'Natural Selection' and 'Inheritance' to Political Society*. This was Bagehot's speculative exercise in accounting for human prehistory in terms of the survival of the fittest and in terms of the role of the crucial 'hereditable excellence' in national life of what he termed 'animated moderation', the key element in mankind's most successful achievement in social evolution, the 'polity of discussion'. Gladstone made no comment on Bagehot's 'ulterior conclusions', which were no less than to cite the late Lord Palmerston as the best example of the progressive and efficient quality in English statesmanship.[76] In this respect Bagehot, very much an intellectual bell-wether of his time, contributed influentially to a rising new cult of the lamented Palmerston, a potent symbol of past stability and sureness to set against the present image of the frenetic and flailing Gladstone. This invidious evocation of Palmerston's memory and reputation was a conspicuous feature of the attitudes of exasperated Liberal MPs such as Trelawny.[77]

[5]

The central feature of the formidable array of demands contemplated by Gladstone for the 1873 session was going to be the imposition by strenuous main force of the means of providing the Irish with a system of higher education designed to foster a native ruling gentry class, Catholic yet pacified. Gladstone had long been foremost in guiding the Anglican elites of Oxford and Cambridge to a better appreciation of and adaptation to the requirements of the progressive and liberal nineteenth century. Now the same possibilities and potentialities must be established for the culture of an Irish elite to conduce to the benefit of a progressive and liberal Ireland. 'Give us now', as one Irishman had pleaded in 1870, 'Christian education. Though last in time, it is the first in our minds, *believe me.*'[78] The measure had long been promised and expected. 'The Government', Gladstone declared in the Commons in 1870, 'has taken office for a variety of purposes connected with the profession of what is called the Liberal creed in politics; but the first of these purposes was and is to find a solution to the Irish question, meaning thereby the great question of which the three branches are, the Irish Church, the Irish land, and the Irish education questions – this latter including especially the subject of higher education in that country.'[79] In 1871, apropos of the question of abolishing religious tests at the Anglican Trinity College, Dublin, Gladstone likewise reaffirmed that 'he had always stated that the higher education of Ireland required the attention of Parliament, so as to apply to it those principles of religious equality that had been applied to the Church of Ireland'.[80]

The great problem was that by 1873 an Irish Catholic demand for their definition of 'Christian education' sat ill with the Liberal party. That party had, largely, welcomed the disestablishment of the Irish Church. It had accepted with more or less resignation the partial disestablishment of the Irish landed Ascendancy. It was, however, decidedly unhappy at the prospect of partly disestablishing the principle of non-denominational higher education in Ireland, now including the University of Dublin (Trinity College) and the Queen's University colleges at Cork, Galway, and Belfast, and the setting up of denominational colleges, including Roman Catholic ones under the control of priests. To many Liberals this was a profound contradiction of the great point of Liberalism. The Roman Catholic Church of late years had flaunted the triumph of the counter-revolution of 1849 and after by proclaiming the dogma of the Immaculate Conception of the Virgin. It had insulted every value held dear by Liberals in the Syllabus of Errors. And it had, ultimately, flouted the progressive nineteenth century with the dogma of papal Infallibility. Moreover, what the British public had been witnessing recently in Ireland were disturbing indications that the reactionary aggressiveness characteristic of the Roman Curia had its manifestations on the soil of the United Kingdom. A virulent campaign against a judge, Keogh, who had dared to denounce clerical manipulation in a Galway election, was seen as a distressing sign of the times. So was the case of a dissident Roman Catholic priest, O'Keeffe, manager of mixed educational schools, whose liberties as a British subject were seemingly suppressed by the legatial prerogatives of the Cardinal-primate. Gladstone himself became involved in an enormously voluminous controversy over one

Gordon, in Scotland, who remarried as a Catholic after his Anglican marriage was declared null by the Holy Office.

Gladstone was well aware of all these considerations and of all the inhibitions inherent in them. He took care to be publicly discreet. He was aware that several of his colleagues saw the question as offering, in Granville's words, 'an admirable opportunity for an honourable defeat'.[81] Argyll retreated to Scotland rather than sit through the dreary preparatory cabinets for a measure he regarded as hopeless. Hartington, an unwilling Irish Chief Secretary in any case, threatened resignation when his own alternative scheme was rejected by Gladstone. Liberal opinion was attuned to what had been the prevailing principle hitherto applied to public education in Ireland of 'mixed' or 'united' non-denominationalism. This principle was espoused by many prominent Roman Catholics of the older Irish tradition: Archbishop Murray of Dublin, President Russell of Maynooth. As the Declaration of members of Dublin University in favour of 'United Academical Education' put it to Gladstone in 1870, 'the association of young men of different religious persuasions in the same Lecture Halls, and at the same Commons Table, is productive of the best results of religious creed, and in teaching all to tolerate and respect the conscientious opinions of others'.[82]

What observers of the Irish scene were now becoming aware of was the coming of new and chillier Irish Catholic winds. Murray's successor at Dublin, Paul Cullen, was a very different kind of prelate. He wrote to Gladstone in 1872 making it clear that the Irish Hierarchy were convinced that non-denominational education – as most notably supplied by Trinity College, Dublin – was too dangerous to the faith of Irish Catholic youth. Any new initiative must be such that 'Catholics could be fully instructed in the doctrines and practices of their religion, and at the same time trained to be good and faithful subjects of the state, and to hate those revolutionary principles now so prevalent, which are strongly condemned by the Catholic Church'.[83] Behind these phrases was as ultramontane a mentality as any in the Curia; and, more to the Irish point, it was a mentality which flatly equated Irish nationality with Roman Catholicism. 'How the Cardinal romances,' remarked Gladstone to Granville.[84] It would not be long before Gladstone was startled by an 'impudent' statement in the *Osservatore Romano* praising the work of Irish priests for the 'autonomy of Ireland'.[85]

For the challenges of the 1873 session Gladstone braced himself with his usual sojourn with the Salisburys at Hatfield ('There are no kinder hosts than here').[86] 'And so falls the curtain of another anxious and eventful year', he recorded on New Year's Eve; 'probably the last one of the present cares, and coming near the last of all. How I feel myself bound to earth: but whenever the command comes, with whatever awe misgiving and remorse, I hope to yield it a prompt obedience.'

[6]

The crucial challenge for Gladstone in 1873 was to restore his personal authority by imposing on both the British Parliament, and more particularly its Liberal component, and the Irish Roman Catholic Church a measure which neither of them liked. It would be an act of magisterial potency, proclaiming the revival of the heroic Peelite spirit of 1868 and 1869. The inherent difficulty of the operation was in a way its greatest recommendation for Gladstone.

There were other matters aplenty. Goschen's unfairly traduced local rating measure would be reintroduced. A Supreme Court of Judicature Bill in the charge of former Attorney-General Roundell Palmer, now promoted to replace Hatherley as Lord Chancellor Selborne, aimed to confer on the public the benefits of more cheap, certain, expeditious, and effectual administration of justice. There would be an attempt to appease the Nonconformists with an Education Act Amendment Bill. It was to be hoped that Lowe's budget would finally restore his and the government's financial reputation. There was a moment of unaccustomed good feeling when Gladstone offered Disraeli condolences on the recent death of Lady Beaconsfield. Disraeli responded with 'sincere regard' that he was 'much touched'. Gladstone well knew what Disraeli also well knew: that marriage was 'the greatest earthly happiness when founded on complete sympathy'.[87] Not the least of the pities of Mary Anne's death was that it removed the last personal element concerned to preserve a degree of civility in the relations of the two political leaders. Catherine Gladstone was much less inclined to see herself in that emollient role.

But overwhelmingly the 1873 session, and Gladstone's fortunes and the fortunes of his government, would be determined by the fate of the Irish University Bill. The prospect, as he could reasonably assert, was not utterly bereft of grounds for confidence. He had Manning in support. And 'even as to Irish University education', as he put it to his brother Robertson, 'I am not without hope of obtaining fair play, which I trust is all we want'.[88] His plan was to separate Trinity College from the University of Dublin, which was to become purely an examining body to which teaching institutions would be affiliated. Three of these would be denominational: Magee in Ulster for the Presbyterians, and Maynooth and a college to be established in Dublin for the Catholics. The teaching of religion was to be separated from secular education (this was calculated to reconcile the Nonconformists). In the Catholic institutions certain areas of secular teaching would be under strict reservation; and certain 'controversial' areas would not be examinable. Gladstone unfolded his scheme on 13 February in a speech of 'prodigious length' and 'dazzling eloquence'. He argued that the well-being of Ireland depended ultimately on the 'moral and intellectual culture of her people'. But when he disclosed restrictions as to teaching and examining – there were to be no chairs in theology, philosophy, and modern history in the denominational colleges – he raised a laugh.[89] This was ominous of trouble. The 'gagging clauses', as they were dubbed, provoked the obvious response that they would precisely prove fatal to high mental culture.[90]

It looked for the while, however, that Gladstone had pulled it off. He was gratified by the generally 'favourable reception'. 'It seems likely to pass, so far as judgment can be formed thus early.'[91] Bruce and other ministers were disappointed at the receding vision of escaping from office. 'Alas! I fear all prospect of ministerial defeat is over.'[92] But soon the initial spell of Gladstone's potency faded. Doubts emerged as to 'whether the ultramontane priesthood in Ireland would accept it'.[93] Trelawny was of opinion that the debate on 3 March was 'most damaging' to the government. By the 4th he diagnosed the bill as being in 'a very weak & sickly condition'.[94] The ultramontane Irish priesthood insisted on full and entire control of publicly funded institutions. Gladstone circulated to Cabinet a report of negotiations with Cullen. 'Overhead it is dark, & underfoot a chaos, but our course is perfectly clear & straight & as far as real criticism is concerned the Bill has stood it well.' The most serious danger and difficulty Gladstone foresaw was mutilation in the Lords, 'as I do not see how the Government could resign on it'.[95] On 5 March Gladstone assured the Queen that 'no apprehension was at present entertained with respect to the immediate impending division'.

But by 8 March defeat was anticipated ('Cabinet 2¾-5½. Most harmonious, at this critical time'). To Manning Gladstone declared defiantly: 'I shall fight to the last against all comers, but much against my inclination which is marvellously attuned by the vision of my liberty dawning like a sunrise from beyond the hills. For when this offer has been made, and every effort of patience employed to render it a reality, my contract with the country is fulfilled, and I am free to take my own course.'[96] An onslaught from Harcourt on 10 March gave the cue to the Liberal pack. The 'gagging clauses' were the 'anathema of the Vatican against modern civilization'. They breathed the 'spirit of the "Index"'. They comprehended the 'whole Dunciad of the Syllabus'. They 'wounded the free intellect of England'. The House would never accept them.[97] Which was the simple truth. Disraeli, confronted with the highly unwelcome prospect of premature and minority office, might well have tried to aid

Gladstone once more, despite his own misgivings about the 'nonsense' of the measure. But though the Conservative party shared certain concerns with the Catholic Church about the benefits of denominational education, it was too affronted both by the brazen content of Gladstone's measure and the dragooning of Gladstone's vote-of-confidence procedure to be amenable to any such expedient manoeuvre.

The bill crashed by 284 votes to 287. A Liberal member such as Trelawny was summoned by peremptory whips but could not bring himself to obey. Thirty-eight Irish Liberals voted or paired against. Ten British Liberals opposed and nine abstained. Trelawny was scathing but misapprehending. 'It seems to me that this defeat is mainly the effect of bad judgment and mismanagement.' The measure was not one 'on which the existence of a Government ought to turn'. That also was Disraeli's opinion. 'Gladstone ought to have been more sure of his ground before committing his party so far.' That was entirely to miss the point of Gladstone's imperious bid to impose his will by sheer main force. 'And now – the Deluge?'[98]

Gladstone repaired immediately to the Queen to prepare her for contingencies. 12 March: 'Cabinet 1–2¾. Confab. on my own position with Granville & Glyn: then joined by Bright. To the Queen again at 6.' At the cabinet: 'Glyn called in: reported conversation with Sir G. Grey who recommended resignation & thought the other side would fail to form a Govt.' There was a discussion as to the course to be taken: ignore the vote (which would have suited Disraeli); revise the measure; propose another vote of confidence in general terms; but the debate was mainly as to resignation of the government or dissolution of the Parliament. Gladstone put the argument for resignation. Divisions within the Liberal party were now to be seriously apprehended: from a 'factious spirit'; on 'questions of economy'; on 'questions of education in its relation to religion'; on questions of 'further Parliamentary change' – that was to say the county franchise; on 'the Land Laws'. On these questions generally Gladstone felt his sympathies were with 'what may be termed the advanced party, whom, on other & general grounds, I certainly will never head or lead'. This was in fact a preview and a misprophecy of his role between 1876 and 1880. But in 1873 his sense of the situation was: 'There is now no *cause*. No great public object on wh. the Liberal party are agreed & combined.' The 'constitutional argument' no doubt was for dissolution. But Gladstone was 'quite willing to resign'. The 'inequality' as to himself personally was 'not so great as it may at first seem'. The time was come for him 'at least to *prepare*'; '(always subject to a reserve)'.

Here in fact was an accurate preview of his entire conduct in politics from 1875 to 1894: preparing to retire but always subject to a reserve as to a *'cause'*. The immediate likelihood seemed at first for dissolution; but at a cabinet on 13 March Gladstone made clear his own preference for a 'temporary rest'. The Cabinet, 'without any marked difference, or at least any positive assertion to the contrary, determined on our tendering our resignations'. On that day, having seen the Queen, Gladstone announced in the Commons that he had tendered his government's resignation. He denounced a factious and malignant combination of Romanism and Toryism.

Now Gladstone could fairly assume that he was indeed free, and that his vision of liberty was dawning like a sunrise from beyond the hills. In his elation he visited Mr Millais's studio, attended at Christie's, and read Trollope's *The Eustace Diamonds*. As he put it to Manning: 'You give no heed to the wailings and pleas of my old age: but I do, & the future of politics hardly exists for me, unless some new phase arise and, as in 1868, a special call may appear: to such call, please God I will answer; if there be a breath in my body.'[99] Here was another version of the course of Gladstone's life and career for the next twenty years or more: all would turn on that question of a 'new phase' arising and a 'special call' appearing. But the immediate twist of events was that Disraeli declined to accept the Queen's request for him to form a government and by implication recommended that she take recourse again to Gladstone (who found himself unable to grasp Disraeli's line that Disraeli 'could not tender advice to Your Majesty ... without being Your Majesty's adviser').[100] Disraeli's position was that Gladstone had been constitutionally ill-advised to make the issue one of confidence, and that the elements of the adverse majority, being fortuitous, bore no constructive responsibility for consequences.

To Gladstone, Disraeli immediately took on the character of the 'artful dodger'. Gladstone fought tenaciously to stay out; but Disraeli foiled him. 'Disraeli as usual escapes the real point and argues against a proposition which I have nowhere stated or implied viz. that the Opposition are unconditionally bound to take office.' Disraeli twisted and swerved to evade the poisoned chalice. Victoria, for all that she was anxious to be rid of Gladstone, blamed him for the difficulty: he had no 'tact'; 'he has been very tiresome and obstinate in this business'.[101] Gladstone confessed defeat and allowed himself to be 'foisted in' on 17 March. During explanations in the Commons on the 20th Gladstone 'advisedly let pass Mr. Disraeli's speech without notice'. There were Liberals like Trelawny who thought Disraeli 'had the best of it' in explanations about 'the late interregnum'.[102] Gladstone persisted in thinking that there was no good reason for Disraeli's refusal 'except that a portion of his party were determined not to be "educated" again, & more certain that if he got in he would again commence his educating process'. Gladstone added with profound misapprehension: 'The Conservative Party will never assume its natural position until Disraeli retires: & I sometimes think he & I might with advantage pair off together.'[103]

[7]

At one unhappy moment in the speech which Gladstone advisedly let pass, Disraeli slipped into the admission that his party could 'not appeal to the country without having a policy'. This was greeted with a roar of laughter from the Liberal benches. Liberals were used to being the party of great measures. Gladstone, however, was well aware that his own position was not all that different. He was now leader of a limping government without a cause or great public object upon which the Liberal party were agreed and combined. Kimberley, surveying the plight of that government after the ministerial crisis, concluded shrewdly: 'Our old programme is completely exhausted: and Gladstone is not the man to govern without "measures", nor is he at all suited to lead a party in difficulties. He must have a strong current of opinion in his favour.'[104] Gladstone was eloquent to Ripon on the 'great difficulty of the loss of *vital power*' with questions such as education and economy hanging over awkwardly. Cardwell's estimates were looking less promising than had been hoped. Although Gladstone could hope that Lowe's budget in April might do much to make 'a real onward step in the Session',[105] it could hardly be the means of restoring 'vital power' to a flaccid and effete administration. Part of the fractiousness among Liberals was a grievance at the increase in public expenditure. Gladstone had pinned great hopes on Cardwell's reforms eventually achieving material reduction. He was vulnerable to this line of criticism. There was always, therefore, the likelihood that if obliged to stay in office and see the session through, and then dissolve the 1868 Parliament, Gladstone would recur to the spirit of 1853 to shape a 'special call' to generate vital power out of some big issue of finance. The one thing he most decidedly would not do was simply to preside over seeing both the session and his own official career slide quietly and dimly into historical oblivion.

Meanwhile there was little enough to sustain a sense of drive and purpose. Lowe's budget did nothing to help. He clumsily dragged up the *Alabama* affair again, and put Gladstone on the defensive. Goschen's local taxation and rating reform also failed to make the desired impact. The sequence of by-election losses continued relentlessly. 'Gladstone looked very pale and ill,' observed Trelawny. 'They say he cannot sleep.'[106] There were troubling personal problems. Over the Easter recess he had been at odds with Robertson over the Seaforth accounts.[107] Hope-Scott's death later in April evoked many poignant memories. Then came the shock of J. S. Mill's death on 8 May, and, in its way, the greater shock of Gladstone's discovering that he could not after all take part in any project of a public memorial until the question of Mill's part in the 'loathsome' matter of birth control was cleared up.[108] Gladstone looked even iller. 'All conscientious statesmen are living too fast. It is self-murder.'[109] Gladstone lost his Chief Whip, Glyn, who succeeded to the Wolverton peerage. He appointed Arthur Peel to replace Glyn; but all Peel could do was continue the glum litany of reports of by-election disasters: 'since the first Licensing Bill we have . . . gained no seat from the Tories and have lost 15'. Dover was causing great anxiety.[110] Even the Conservatives were astonished at winning Dover. Derby noted: 'This really looks like winning at the general election, if we make no blunder.'[111]

There were galling defeats for the government in the Commons and losses of temper on Gladstone's part. Welcome relief came in another Hatfield weekend (Gladstone sent Salisbury a 'little book on prayer as a memento').[112] But there were more 'scrapes' with brutish Ayrton at the Board of Works and, of more moment, with Lowe over the Zanzibar contract with the Post Office, a project whereby the Sultan was to be bribed with a regular mail service in return for suppressing the slave trade. Lowe's defence was thought to be 'not only maladroit but petulant'. The government 'lost character in the transaction'. Gladstone's handling was judged 'imprudent & fussy'.[113] Ministers seemed to be tottering in a vicious cycle of lucklessness and terminal discredit. But it mattered little. There was no danger from the Conservative opposition. The death of Bishop Wilberforce of Winchester in a riding accident was another great personal shock: 'a sad sense of a great void in the world'.[114] Gladstone collapsed on 23 July: 'Gave way under great heat, hard work, & perhaps depression of fever.'

It was on that day, in fact, from his sickbed, that Gladstone made the first initiative discernibly and definably within the frame of generating 'vital power'. He authorized Forster to declare his (Gladstone's) personal approval of Trevelyan's County Franchise Bill to extend the borough occupier franchise of 1867 to the counties. This declaration, for all that it involved no pledge on behalf of the government, sent a frisson through the political world. Ripon immediately offered his resignation at this imprudently democratic outburst. To many Liberals of 'moderate' per-suasion it seemed that Gladstone was striking out as a discredited politician with nothing to lose. Trelawny's reaction was typical of many such: 'One is tired of chronicling our leader's faux pas. Will he hold his office next session?'[115] The county franchise was a very long-term matter.

It would not be until 1877 that Hartington accepted it on behalf of the Whigs and it would not be until 1884 that Gladstone effected it in the third Reform Act. In the context of 1873 Gladstone's commitment looked a forlorn enough hope; but it was a portent all the same. It was part of Gladstone's thinking about where next vital power and a strong current of opinion would come from: certainly not from the majority of 1868.

There were many Liberals who, like Ripon, read into it much more than a faux pas. In the background in 1873 of continued industrial strife and then in June of the 'revolt of the labourers' against the squires and the farmers, Gladstone's declaration of 23 July looked like part of a plan ominously deep. Derby was approached by a Liberal MP representing a group of colleagues looking to the Conservatives for a 'policy of repose'. 'The explanation: that they are alarmed by the attitude of the working men, and at the power acquired by the trade unions: and belief that Gladstone, half out of ambition and half out of sentimental sympathy, is ready to throw all the influence of the State into the scale against the employer.'[116] This was to misread Gladstone rather grossly. But even so, those disaffected Liberals seeking 'repose' from Gladstone's strenuous politics would not have been reassured by his serene response to Lowe's anxieties at the Home Office about trade-union demonstrations against the government's recent 'labour' legislation. He had no fears of the labouring classes, Gladstone confided to Lowe, if only because of the hard limits bounding their lives (Gladstone himself was soon to assist in reducing wages at the Aston Hall colliery near Hawarden);* 'except the fear of being embarked against them in a bad cause'.[117] Such a 'bad cause' clearly, for Gladstone, would be embarking on resistance to the occupier county franchise. The 'faux pas' of 1873 was in fact the germ of what was accomplished in 1880: of Gladstone's leading 'the people' and 'the country' to reimpose his authority by main force on the parliamentary Liberal party, once for all.

All that was a long time ahead. For the rather miserable future immediately at hand Parliament was prorogued on 5 August until 22 October. It was indicative of the general collapse of the ministry that Parliament did not reassemble on 22 October. There was a further prorogation until 16 December; then postponement yet again to 5 February 1874. But even that date was to be overtaken by events.

By the beginning of August it had become clear that the scandals of irregularities and overspending in the Post Office and the Department of Works had implicated Lowe too deeply to be overlooked. The session was abruptly truncated to relieve ministers of an intolerable sequence of humiliations. Ripon's resignation of the Lord Presidency in any case

* See below, page 144.

opened up the question of reconstruction. Gladstone consulted Granville, Wolverton, and Cardwell ('repeatedly'). For it was upon Cardwell that Gladstone imposed the task of 'breaking to Lowe the necessity of changing his office'. August the 2nd was an 'anxious day'. Bruce was to take a peerage (Aberdare) and replace Ripon in the Lords. Lowe was shunted across to the Home Office to replace Bruce. After thinking of Goschen, or possibly bringing Childers back, Gladstone decided to take over at the Exchequer himself. That was where the big strategic opportunities were likely to be available. Hartington was sore at being left stranded in the Irish Office; but Gladstone now was thinking of remaking the Exchequer the great hinge of state, a task for which he could not see the amiable Whig as being in the least fitted. In deference to the magnitude of the crisis, Bright consented to come back to the Duchy of Lancaster. Lowe was not an amenable man. He made the business excessively painful. Before a cabinet on 6 August Gladstone underwent a 'sad escapade of Lowe's'. To Gladstone it was an immense strain. He assured the Queen that he hoped 'to come through it without breaking down'.[118]

As the case of Carlingford was later to show,* Gladstone had no stomach for ruthless excision of redundant colleagues. As he had initially appointed Lowe, he now kept him on out of an excessive respect for Lowe's intellectual eminence. 'I always hold', he wrote to Lowe, 'that politicians are the men whom as a rule it is most difficult to comprehend, i.e., understand completely; & for my own part, I never have thus understood or thought I understood above one or two, though here & there I may get hold of an isolated idea about others.' The isolated idea he had about Lowe was Lowe's having 'too prompt an intellect'; seeing everything in a 'burning, almost scorching' light. 'Is your light too much concentrated? Does not its intensity darken the surroundings?'[119]

It was a characteristic specimen of Lowe's promptness of intellect and capacity to darken surroundings that he should almost eagerly have assured Gladstone that by taking over at the Exchequer he had vacated his Greenwich seat; and that in a contested by-election Gladstone's chances of adding yet another item to the Liberal party's grisly roster of losses would be only too good. This embarrassment would remain for the remainder of the Parliament a constant irritation.[120] Gladstone took counsel of the Attorney-General, Sir George Jessel, who advised him that adding an office to his existing office would not require him 'to notify his acceptance of office to the Speaker'.[121] This opinion was endorsed by the Solicitor-General; but still certain punctilious critics were not content, and Speaker Brand felt himself obliged to raise the question. Gladstone

* See below, page 344.

held his ground, 'advised by high legal authority'. But the shadow of a doubt made his position increasingly uncomfortable.

The recess at least offered respite. Ministers could regroup, the better to face the planned October session. Gladstone had time to attend to Dr Schliemann's latest discoveries at Troy, which provided Gladstone with what he took to be decisive evidence justifying his faith in the 'basic historicity of the Homeric epics'. He set out to make himself Schliemann's 'prophet' in England: two amateurs in battle against the ranks of pro-fessional scholarship.[122] He had time also to preside at the Welsh National Eisteddfod at Mold, where he had sympathetic things to say about the Welsh people and their claims as a nation.

Above all he needed time to rethink options and try to discern a straight path through the political thickets. He could indulge a little in freedom of action. If he had pleased the advanced Liberals over the county franchise issue, he could make his personal position equally clear in favour of denominational voluntary schools. Provided Bright could be kept from 'bolting' the Cabinet,[123] he would, it was to be hoped, help to keep the compromise of 1870 reasonably stable. Gladstone confided to Granville his fear that the education controversy would 'eventually either split the party, or fatally cripple it for a time in regard to Parliamen-tary action'. The Nonconformists, he was sure, meant 'mischief for the future'. They had the power, he pointed out to Lord Frederick Cavendish (whom he had just appointed to join Willy as a Treasury Lord), 'to throw us into a minority, & they probably will use it; but they have not power to do more'. There was nothing to be done for the present other than to 'avoid sharp issues'.[124] Gladstone had no fears of the 'secular system'; but he could not join in any measures of 'repression' against voluntary schools.[125] That remark was occasioned by the widespread public com-ment Gladstone raised by a speech at a Hawarden parish meeting, when he indicated his support for voluntaryism at Hawarden to obviate the need for a local school board.[126] This unabashed assertion of Anglican interests scandalized John Morley, editor of the *Fortnightly Review*, who saw himself as J. S. Mill's successor as promoter of secular Liberal values. To his Radical friend and collaborator, Mayor of Birmingham and orchestrator of the Nonconformist agitation in the Education League, Joseph Chamberlain, Morley pointed out that Gladstone's words 'commit him to Voluntary Schools & Church Supremacy for the rest of his life'.[127]

[8]

The important thing now was to light upon an issue which would tend to override such divisive matters and pull Liberals and Liberalism, both in and out of doors, together. Now that he was back at the Exchequer, Gladstone was in immediate charge of a potential engine of regeneration. At the heart of the Treasury he had initiated and fulfilled his first great political vocation, stemming from his taking up Peel's great work in the epochal budget of 1853. Gladstone was back again, in a sense, on familiar, home ground. He wrote to 'Dear Bright' ('Let us bid farewell to *Misters*') on 14 August: 'What we want at present is a *positive* force to carry us onward as a body.' This was not to be had out of local taxation or education. 'It may possibly, I think, be had out of *Finance*.' Now that the government had got over their scrapes of the last session, 'we have now before us a clear stage for the consideration of measures for the Autumn. We must, I think, have a good bill of fare or none.'

That 'good bill of fare' would depend crucially on the services estimates. Gladstone was once more in consultation with Cardwell, 'to whom at the W.O. I told in deep secrecy my ideas of the *possible* finance of the next year: based upon abolition of Income Tax & Sugar Duties with partial compensation from Spirits & Death Duties. This *only* might give a chance.' Having sketched the elements of a reversion to the high tone of 1853, Gladstone thereupon set out for Hawarden 'with a more buoyant spirit and greater sense of relief than I have experienced for many years'. Gladstone explained to himself that 'this gush is in proportion to the measure of the late troubles & anxieties'.[128]

There was in truth little that was new in the elements Gladstone thus sketched. Debates throughout the 1873 session had rehearsed them thoroughly. Deepest in the background was the uncomfortable fact simply but tellingly put by the Lancashire Radical Peter Rylands: 'The present Government came into power on the promise of great economy, yet they have accomplished but very little.'[129] This prompted the Conservative Leeds MP Wheelhouse to enquire: why not abolish income tax altogether? Gladstone himself had often enough denounced it as temptingly and fatally cornucopic for the revenues. A few days later Gladstone made reference in the Commons to his having received a deputation urging the repeal of the income tax: 'he had as much reason as any gentleman in the deputation for desiring the repeal of the income tax'.[130]

Had not that projected repeal been the very foundation of Gladstone's grand financial plan of 1853–60? That was the point made by Stafford Northcote, Disraeli's designated Chancellor of the Exchequer in a new

Conservative ministry, in a series of debates on direct and indirect taxation. Northcote hailed Gladstone's 1853 budget as 'perhaps the greatest, of all his financial statements'; but with the wrecking of that long-term financial plan by the Crimean War, the income tax had remained uneasily suspended between temporary and permanent footing, 'a sort of Mahomet's Coffin'.[131] In his own contribution to that debate Gladstone had made clear his ideas as to the correct relationship both of direct to indirect, and of the correct incidence of indirect taxation, making any simple reduction of indirect taxes on the poor a difficult match for abolition of the income tax on the rich. 'Let me point out an ineffaceable distinction between the labouring and wealthy classes, a distinction to which I do not advert invidiously, for I believe it to be inevitable.' The hard fact remained that on grounds of the 'working of sound principles', the luxuries of the wealthy must be lightly taxed whereas the luxuries of the poor – spirits, beer, and tobacco – 'are and must remain heavily taxed'.[132]

In preparation for this debate, Gladstone had already taken soundings from the trade about sugar-duty abolition.[133] 'My view about finance is this,' he told Bright from Balmoral on 27 August. 'It is in finance *only* that I see a possibility – I will not yet say more – of our being able to do something that may raise us to a higher and firmer level.' Gladstone studiously tailored his message to suit Bright's specific requirements. At a time like this of 'comparative depression' men see all in 'dark colours'. But if once the government could be thus raised, 'if we feel that we are breathing a more healthy and "nimble" air, then I think will be the time when there will be the best hope, the best likelihood, of an improved understanding among ourselves about the question, Education'.[134]*

At Hawarden on 13 September Gladstone convened Bright, Wolverton, and Granville to help him thrash the matter out. Over four days – Gladstone lamented the strain on his 'half-exhausted brain' – they waded through the figures. Gladstone felt himself in want of £8 million 'to handle' for his 1874 budget, to replace remissions on income tax, sugar duties, and local taxation. Where to find the leeway? As he ruefully pointed out earlier to Stansfeld, the Army estimates for 1872–3 were up on the 1870–71 level and not far short of the 'Derby–Dizzy' level of 1869. And that was not inclusive of the cost of abolishing purchase.[135] Disraeli had had his Abyssinian bill; but now Gladstone was threatened by his Ashanti bill. (Bright would reassure his people: 'The stuff you read in the papers is mostly rubbish – the instructions are pacific, & there is no idea of invading Ashantee, or making a raid on its capital.'[136] But Sir

---

* Bright: 'The Education question is a very ugly question with a State Church & its interests & superstitions & politics.'

Garnet Wolseley went ahead to do those two very things.) An October session now seemed impracticable. Not until the last quarter of the year were estimates reliably formed. Much would depend on the surplus available. Looking forward to a start early in 1874, Gladstone informed Speaker Brand: 'The Financial question looms large & probably will be the hinge of the Session – possibly of the Election too.'[137]

A lull followed while the necessary figures were awaited. Gladstone was enthralled by the photographs of the 'Troy' excavations, sent by Schliemann via the British Museum 'expressly for your inspection'. Schliemann's offer of a sale of his collection to the Museum for £50,000 was 'of course not to be entertained'.[138] There were lamentations about not being able to get down to some Homerology. As Gladstone put it to Lord Crawford, the 1858 *Studies on Homer* was 'so crude that I cannot reprint it', while the *Juventus Mundi* of 1869 was 'only a summary'.[139] A cost-cutting exercise in eliminating the flanking towers on the designs for the new fronts for the Home and Colonial Offices drew a pained protest (at Rome) from Sir George Gilbert Scott.[140] There was the practical question of an alternative constituency, given Greenwich's unreliability, for the general election after the 1874 session. Gladstone consulted Peel with a view to Newark, should South-West Lancashire be unavailable, but would settle for 'that which the general interests, & general advisers, of the party recommend'. Wolverton preferred Chester, for which Lord Westminster was willing to lend his influence.[141] The happy event, on 27 December, was Gladstone's giving away Agnes in marriage to the Rev. E. C. Wickham, Fellow and Tutor of New College, Oxford ('A superior man: perhaps his appearance does not do him full justice').[142]*

Given the imminence of great undertakings and great events in view, Gladstone's birthday and end-of-year reflections were even more fraught than usual with solemn introspection. 'Sixty-four years complete today,' he recorded on 29 December, 'what have they brought me? A weaker heart, stiffened muscles, thin hairs: other strength still remains in my frame. But what inwardly? Continued strain and tossing of the spirit: I dare not say solid improvement: but a hope of release, recollection, and penitence, growing more eager as the time gets nearer.' On the eve of the new year: the year 'ends as it were in tumult'. Gladstone's 'constant tumult of business makes other tumult more sensible'. He could hope that his 'spirit instead of grovelling may become erect, and look at God'. For he could not, as he now was, 'get sufficiently out of myself to judge myself, and unravel the knots of being and doing, of which my life seems to be full'.

---

* G made Wickham Headmaster of Wellington College, 1873–93. Dean of Lincoln in 1894.

[9]

When he wrote to Lord Westminster early in the new year to acknowledge his offer of the Grosvenor influence for the Chester seat, Gladstone professed himself unable to accept as yet. 'I cannot even pretend to give any information on the probable course of politics which could be of material use: but I should say about next May is the time when it is most likely, or least unlikely, that we may see our way better than at present.'[143] Gladstone at that point envisaged a signal and masterful budget in April, which would be the spearhead of a dissolution and an appeal for the renewed confidence of the constituencies. No other remedy for the present state of affairs seemed feasible. The 'ordinary remedies' of resig-nation or dissolution, as he put it formally to Granville on 10 January, were unavailable. Resignation was out of the question following the events of 1873. Dissolution at present would mean coming back with a uselessly small majority consisting of Irish home rulers. As the 'signs of weakness multiply' upon the government, things were getting to the point of its ceasing to have the confidence of the country. What was needed were measures to 'reanimate' some portion of the 'vital force' of 1868. The supreme remedy was the model of 1853: to 'frame a budget large enough and palpably beneficial enough'. Gladstone was 'anxious to continue where we are, because I am very loath to leave the party in its present menacing condition, without having first made every effort in our power to avert this public mischief'.[144]

Ever solicitous of Bright's totemic presence, Gladstone assured him that the Cabinet work lying ahead would not be severe. 'It is not by a multitude of small details however well handled they may be, that we can mend the position of affairs. It wants some one issue, clear, broad & straight.'[145] The Treasury was by now in a position to estimate that a surplus of £5 million would be available. Gladstone could look to a clear, broad, and straight path to eliminate the income tax and sugar duties and reduce rating incidence: but only if Goschen at the Admiralty and especially Cardwell at the War Office could yield substantial remissions. Increased death duties was an option, but it would be a sensitive issue for the Whigs, and not to be pressed. 'Have the Govt. & party any other mode of giving their friends fair play at the elections than by such a Budget as has been sketched?'[146]

It was a good question, to which there was no very ready answer. 'I am very far indeed from sanguine about the position of the party & the Government generally,' he told Argyll, '& I see no chance anywhere but in finance of mending the position, while in that department there are great difficulties for we are not I think so economical as we were at the outset of our ministerial career.'[147] Gladstone well understood that prospects of agreement with the War Office and Admiralty were 'for the present bad'.[148] He summoned Cardwell and Goschen, together with Granville and Bright, to conference on the 19th. But already Gladstone's mind had started working on an alternative tack. To Arthur Peel, the Chief Whip, he enquired whether, 'in search of topics of consolation', there was any statistical truth in the generally received notion that the Liberal party 'fares ill, even in good political times, at single elections as compared with General Elections'.[149]* It was on Sunday the 18th that Gladstone 'thought of dissolution'. 'Told Bright of it. In evening at dinner told Granville & Wolverton. All seemed to approve. My first thought of it was as escape from a difficulty. I soon saw on reflection that it was the best thing in itself.'[150]

It became Gladstone's justification that, having taken over the Exchequer in the summer of 1873 and entertaining the hope that it would be in the government's power to propose the abolition of the income tax, he thereupon found that while an 'immense surplus' would be available, there was no 'public authority' permitting the launch of 'what we thought would be the greatest and most beneficial propositions of finance to the country that it had ever been our lot, I may say, to submit'. Hence the necessity to dissolve Parliament and appeal to the country to provide that 'public authority'.[151] Gladstone here turns his statement of 10 January to Granville on its head. Then a big budget would be the means of restoring public authority to the government prior to a dissolution. Now a dissolution would provide the public authority needed to launch a big budget. Gladstone could, and did, later make the point that neither Wolverton nor Peel raised any objections on the grounds that the party's organization in the constituencies was defective and inadequate to the task.[152] Even in his paper of 10 January outlining the direness of the government's situation, Gladstone assumed that dissolution would result in a small majority, even if made up of Irish home rulers.

Of the motives which turned Gladstone's predispositions back to front that of the government's needing 'public authority' is the least plausible. More convincing were the fruits of his taking to his bed on 20 January after Cardwell and Goschen had refused to relent. There Gladstone reflected 'on our "crisis" '; there he drafted a long address to an unnamed constituency – 'almost a pamphlet' – setting out the case for an immediate appeal to the country. The material points bearing on Gladstone's thinking were, first: 'We gain time, & avoid for the moment a ministerial crisis.' This gain would put ministers in possession of better information about estimates and 'arrest the certain drain of the single elections', now

* No response from Peel appears to be extant in the Gladstone Papers.

a long series of defeats impairing the government's credit and taking the heart out of the Liberal party and damaging it for the final struggle. Then a further advantage would be that the 'formidable divisions in the party would be aborted or held in suspense if we have an *immediate* Dissolution upon a question of universal & commanding interest'. Every *week* of a pre-dissolution session would have its dangers in the present circumstances of division and dissension.[153] Godley, one of Gladstone's assistant private secretaries at the time, was in no doubt that another point bearing on Gladstone's decision was his embarrassment about the Greenwich seat. His status as an MP would undoubtedly be challenged in disagreeable debates at the opening of a new session.[154]*

All this added up, seemingly, to 'the best thing in itself'. January the 23rd was a 'very busy, stirring day, of incessant action'. At a cabinet Gladstone stated his motives for dissolution '& recommn to Dissolve on the grounds of general advantage. Granville concurred. All agreed.' The address was considered, with revisions and deletions of sensitive passages relating to ultramontanism likely to be offensive to Catholic Irish. Gladstone spoke of 'perseverance in economic efforts'.[156] There was talk of possible ministerial placements: after carrying his budget in redemption of election pledges Gladstone would hand over the Exchequer to Goschen, with Childers being brought back to replace Goschen at the Admiralty.[157]

It was, indeed, a stirring time. The news would be publicly sensational. Parliament, after all, was due to reassemble in a few days' time. Before the 23rd was far gone Godley reported, 'It is out!' The London correspondent of the *Manchester Guardian* knew of it. Soon so did Levy of the *Telegraph*. For all his later denials of 'theatrical motive'[158] it was very likely that Gladstone relished the element of political theatre involved. The precipitancy and abruptness of the event bore a dramatic charge bespeaking masterful urgency. Something of the élan and vitality of 1868 was now surely revived.

The 1868 Parliament was dissolved on 25 January, with a general election forthwith. The political world was stunned. The immediate impact seemed to ratify Gladstone's astonishingly bold stroke. Disraeli and his party were staggered and in disarray, uncertain whether to denounce the income-tax abolition as an unworthy bribe or to claim that they were intending exactly the same measure. Most Liberals agreed with Frederic Harrison that Gladstone had pulled off a 'dextrous party move'.[159] Derby was one of the few shrewd doubters: 'It is too early to judge, but on the whole I incline to think Gladstone has made a mistake.'[160]

It was not long before Gladstone himself had cause for doubts. He

---

* Selborne (Palmer) never doubted this as 'the determining cause'.[155]

spoke at Greenwich to a rain-sodden crowd on the 28th. 'An enthusiastic meeting. But the general prospects are far from clear.' That faltering of prospects made some colleagues nervous as to what Gladstone might say about the county franchise. If income-tax abolition was not, after all, attractive to the classes, might not Gladstone decide to turn then to the masses? As Cardwell put it, Gladstone was 'the turning point of the people's politics'.[161] Gladstone, however, was more inclined at this point to see the people's politics of Ireland as in need of prior attention. He had included in his Greenwich address friendly remarks about the desirability in Ireland of improvement in local and subordinate levels of government. Something with more bite was needed, he felt, to help save Liberal seats there. Gladstone selected Lord Fermoy as the recipient of a kind of Irish sub-manifesto. Fermoy was a nonentity whose only relationship hitherto with Gladstone was as an unsuccessful wheedler for a UK peerage. Now Fermoy learned from Gladstone, for the benefit of struggling Liberal 'home rulers', of the 'test' to be applied to the question. If home rule lightened the burdens of the Westminster Parliament but yet did nothing to damage the permanence and stability of the Union, it could be sympathetically, and with due caution, entertained. Gladstone pointed out that 'with respect to Home Rule I have not yet heard an authoritative or binding definition of the phrase which appears to have been used by different persons in different senses'.[162]

It was to be the case, indeed, that nothing in the way of an authoritative or binding definition of Home Rule was provided until Gladstone himself provided it in his Government of Ireland Bill in 1886. There were indignant defenders of the Union in Ireland and elsewhere in 1874 who began to get chilling glimpses of just that ultimate outcome; who began to wonder whether they were somewhat in the same position as were defenders of the 1832 franchise in 1864, or defenders of the Irish Church in 1865.

However, with the way the elections looked to be going, it was likely that Gladstone would cease to be an immediate, or probably a prospective, danger either on the home-rule side or the county-franchise side. By 3 February the Liberal chances, at first indifferent, started to look distinctly bad. The Liberal party was shedding seats everywhere, except in Ireland, where there were a few gains. Gladstone's own re-election in Greenwich, in second place 'after Boord the distiller', was 'more like a defeat than a victory'. By 5 February things were now 'irrevocably bad'. From Peel Gladstone requested explanatory information. Could it be confidentially determined from the constituency agents 'where the Elections have gone wrong or less favourably than had been hoped'? Was it 'Conservative reaction'? Was it the Licensed Victuallers? Dissentient Nonconformists? 'On the side of the Irish vote'? Or any other special causes?[163] In view of his own humiliating situation in Greenwich, it was understandable that Gladstone should give the Trade pride of place in villainy. 'We have been swept away, literally', he told Spencer, 'by a torrent of beer & gin.'[164]*

The Liberal party lost sixty-nine English seats, three Welsh, and twelve Scots. The Conservatives would have a majority of over fifty. It was the case, as Gladstone pointed out ruefully, that more seats were transferred from one party to the other than at any election since 1831–2.[165] He allowed it to be very much a 'national condemnation', 'emphatically enough pronounced'.[166] Granville was soothingly supportive. 'You go out as you came in a great minister, and we shall soon have a frightful clamour for you.' As to forming a new government hereafter, Granville could not be sure; 'but as an opposition, grace à vous, we go out unusually strong'.[167]

Gladstone's own mind was tending to thoughts of major changes in his life rather than continuities. He broached to Catherine selling up Carlton House Terrace: 'at first she was startled'.[168] ('Saw Mrs. Th. X. The last thus?') There was the matter of how best to leave office. Disraeli's precedent of 1868 suggested itself enticingly. It was a 'deviation from a sound general rule', but justified in the circumstances. Gladstone was inclined to think that the circumstances of his and his government's position in 1874 pointed to the conclusion that there would be no advantage to the public interest in meeting the new Parliament. The Queen was quite complaisant.[169] On the eve of going off to Windsor Gladstone gave a Cabinet dinner. 'It went well. I did something toward snapping the ties, and winding out the coil.' What he did was to disconcert his colleagues, much as he had done Catherine, with a statement about big changes in prospect. Aberdare recorded a 'startling announcement' that he 'would no longer retain the leadership of the liberal party, nor resume it, unless the party had settled its differences'. He would no longer expose himself to insults and outrages reminiscent of 1866–8, about which he still had a lively sense of bitterness. Although possessed of a keen awareness of having again been the victim of disloyalty over the past three years, Gladstone denied that his decision was dictated by temper or anger. The Liberal party would have to learn that all duties and responsibilities were not confined to leaders only but to followers as well. 'He wishes them', as Aberdare reported to Ripon, 'to enjoy the blessings of anarchy for a while in order that they may learn to appreciate the necessity of party obedience.'[170] Here was the true voice of Peelism.

---

* 'Next to this comes Education . . . with the Nonconformists & the Irish voters.'

[10]

At Windsor Gladstone had his audience of the Queen. Aberdare thought him 'evidently in a high-wrought state of sensitiveness'.[171] Victoria had already placed on record her offer to Gladstone at the previous audience 'of a mark of her recognition of his services – wh however he declines from motives wh she fully appreciates'.[172]* It soon became clear that Gladstone's announcement at the Cabinet dinner about withdrawing from the leadership was no mere evanescent whim, as in June 1867. After the Cabinet dinner he had 'walked on the flags up and down' with both Granville and Wolverton, resisting their objections to anarchy. He lay awake that night for three hours with an 'overwrought brain'. But he could see that all was good. 'That which is now come is the old aim of my wishes & my most unworthy prayers.' To Peel he wrote on 19 February: 'It is not my intention to assume the functions of Leader of the Parliamentary Opposition in the House of Commons to the new Government.' What was uppermost in his mind, as it had been in 1867, was the refractoriness of his party. He further informed Peel that he could even give his opinion 'if it were generally desired on the question' whether it be expedient that the leadership 'should be at present assumed by anyone else'. Gladstone denied motivation arising from 'any cause of complaint'. But he felt that public men who had given their best years were not bound 'in the absence of any strong and special cause' to spend their old age in service. After his labours since 1868 he was in need of rest; and the country had had sad experience of public careers unduly prolonged.[173] Gladstone was willing also to allow, at this 'hour of outward discomfiture', that his colleagues had had 'much to bear with and from me'.[174]

On 20 February Gladstone had final audience of the Queen at Windsor and kissed hands. 'H.M. was kind: the topics of conversation were of course rather limited.' There were resignation honours: Cardwell, his health shattered, was to retire to the Lords; Westminster was rewarded with a dukedom. Gladstone cleared his own room at Downing Street 'and bade it farewell, giving up my keys, except the Cabinet key'. By 3 March not an official box remained, though he still had the benefit of the daily visit of a 'kind Private Secretary'. That boon ceased on 5 March with Eddie Hamilton's final visit: 'tomorrow I encounter my own correspondence single-handed'.

It was to be material in relation to the legacy of ambiguity and uncertainty with which Gladstone endowed his party at this juncture that he

---

* This conventionally would have been an earldom.

should have declined the Queen's pressing offer of an earldom. He explained to his brother, Sir Thomas, head of the family. 'I do not see that I am wanted or should be of use in the House of Lords: and there would be some discrepancy between rank and fortune, which is a thing rather to be deprecated. On the other hand I know that the line I have marked out for myself in the House of Commons is one not altogether easy to hold: but I have every disposition to remain quiet there, and shall be very glad if I can do so.'[175]

So Gladstone would remain in the House of Commons in some, as yet, unclearly defined role. The precedents bearing more or less relevantly were those of Pitt in 1801 and Peel in 1846. Neither would have been grateful to Gladstone's colleagues in 1874. Ironically, Gladstone had been in 1846–50 Peel's keenest critic for unwillingness to fulfil in the Commons his appropriate and unavoidable function of leadership as the greatest man in politics.[176] Now, Gladstone's definitions of his role reeked of the ambiguities of conditional clauses: 'absence of any strong and special cause'; 'until the party had settled its differences'; remaining quiet if he could do so. Aberdare was quite clear that it was not a matter of permanent withdrawal from leadership; rather it was a matter of punishing the party for its refractoriness, and of the resumption of the leadership in due course when circumstances made an imperative call. Meanwhile Gladstone had the best of both worlds: the answer to 'the old aim' of his wishes and most unworthy prayers connected conditionally to resumption of high duty when the strong and special cause should call. This brilliant combination of personal advantages was in fact to be the leitmotiv of the rest of his career up to his 'enforced' retirement in 1894.

It was precisely from that basis of personal advantage that Gladstone's sense of entitlement to 'take counsel with himself' took the form of arrangements convenient for himself but grossly inconvenient for his colleagues and his party. But that, so to speak in Peelite terms, was entirely their problem, not his. He was unwilling to assume the conventional and tedious burdens of leadership of the Opposition. This took the form of looking 'to younger & fresher men to bear the burden of the day & the brunt of the battle'.[177] To Lady Elizabeth Pringle, Laura Thistlethwayte's great friend, he confided that 'old age is ill fitted for a course of high political strain & contention', and that he could not do 'any act which wd commit me for an indefinite time to responsibility for the conduct of a great party'.[178] Yet invariably he coupled such declarations with an escape clause: as having by no means renounced 'all hope either of witnessing or taking part in' the 'future triumphs of sound & active liberalism'.[179] Ostensibly, Gladstone's objection was that a 'minister who on his dismissal, in his sixty-fifth year, sets about reconstructing and conducting an Opposition' thus 'virtually enters into a re-engagement (supposing strength to continue) for the term of that opposition and for the term of that Power which may probably succeed it: in short for a time which may very well extend over seven or ten years & carry him, if he lives, far into old age'. Yet such objections must always be 'liable to be restrained and restricted' should there arise 'some great public cause for which to contend'.[180] Already there was a comprehensive category of such restraining and restricting formulae; added to which there was also Gladstone's conviction that 'the Conservative party will never arrive at a stable superiority while Disraeli is at their head'.[181]

Of all men, Granville was the least well equipped to contest 'manfully' Gladstone's contentions outright. All he could do was to 'suggest & consider the terms in which they are to be made known'. Peel, with equal ineffectualness, 'aided'. They were taken to Cardwell and Selborne for 'digestion'.

It says much for Gladstone's position of impermeable ambiguity that there was little that the keen minds of Cardwell and Selborne could do. They were all trapped in Gladstone's warmly enveloping web of subordinate clauses. It was not for him, as Gladstone elaborated on 7 March, to prejudge or indicate in any manner the course which the Liberal party might take. 'If they shall deem it their duty to arrange in the usual manner with some other person to discharge the functions hitherto entrusted to me,' such person, 'within the limits of action which circumstances at present impose on me, will have all the support which in an independent position I can give him.'[182] With a truly Peelite fortitude of mind Gladstone recorded that day discussing with various colleagues the question of the leadership. 'In my view clear & easy enough: but much otherwise by the wishes of others.' The following day there was 'much conv. on future course' with Halifax, Selborne, Granville, and Argyll. Peel arranged a meeting of all old colleagues on 9 March, where it was proposed that Gladstone should lead for two more sessions, until the end of 1875. Terms of a draft arrangement were prepared and provisionally accepted on 10 March but then 'readjusted with pain and difficulty, & the aid also of Wolverton & A. Peel' on the 11th, '*tant bien que mal*'. Gladstone would now only lead occasionally in 1874 and make a final decision at the beginning of 1875. The party meanwhile would be free to choose a 'provisional leader'.[183] Gladstone issued a circular to Liberal MPs on 12 March in the form of addressing explanations to Granville, as the leader in the House of Lords.[184]

Anything more inconvenient or unsatisfactory from the point of view of Gladstone's colleagues or the Liberal party could hardly be imagined. Goschen would later remark on a 'humiliating and *intolerable* position'.[185] The Liberal front bench in the Commons declined to take up the idea of a 'provisional' leader and adopted an informal arrangement of responsibilities. The leadership in the Commons, and in some vague sense the leadership of the party as a whole, was put into commission until such time as circumstances should dictate otherwise. Gladstone serenely explained himself to Döllinger: 'I have not recorded any vow on the subject of return to office; but I think it very unlikely that any adequate cause should arise to bring me back to my recent position.'[186] His colleagues meanwhile would have to make the best of this conditional state of being. Arthur Peel sufficiently indicated his own sense of the absurdity of the situation by resigning as Chief Whip.[187]* Harcourt, briefly in office as Solicitor-General, and never patient of Gladstone's imperial mode, informed Frank Hill of the *Daily News*: 'There is no whip, no office, no *nothing*. The thing is ridiculous & disgraceful. You will be safe in saying there is nothing decided, nothing arranged, nothing prepared. The fate of the Liberal Party depends on whether G. chooses to get out of the sulks.'[188]

When the 1874 session did get under way Gladstone found himself the object of long-accumulating resentments. In the Lords the Duke of Somerset attacked him for his letter to Lord Fermoy on Home Rule, which had caused dismay among Liberals. 'The Liberal party now see where his advice has brought them.' Gladstone's announcement that he would only lead if he had a united party to back him was attacked as arrogant. 'But who has prevented ours being a united party if it be not Mr. Gladstone himself?'[189] This provoked something of a scene, with Selborne coming to Gladstone's defence. Lord Grey was equally unforgiving, with acid remarks on the astonishing decision to dissolve Parliament in January, an 'act of political suicide', for which a coroner's verdict would have been 'temporary insanity'.[190] At this Granville protested. There were like resentments also among Liberals in the Commons about the abruptness of the dissolution. Gladstone attempted to head off trouble on this score by elaborately pre-emptive explanations, though not apologies ('For that advice we are responsible. We do not repent of having given it').[191] Perhaps a 'civil talk' a few days earlier with the new Prime Minister at Marlborough House[192]† did something to make Disraeli supportive when two MPs, a Conservative and a Liberal, moved a vote of censure against Gladstone for precipitately unconstitutional dissolution of the late Parliament. Their case was that Parliament had been summoned to meet and that no emergency had arisen. Gladstone defended himself on the grounds of justifying the abruptness of the decision 'by the peculiar circumstances out of which it sprang'. Disraeli

---

* He was replaced by the Scottish MP W. P. Adam.

† G, oddly enough, had been reading Disraeli's first satirical 'society' novel, *Vivian Grey* (1827) (he finished it on 20 March): 'The first quarter (*me jud.*) extremely clever, the rest trash.'

advised the resentful members to judge Gladstone at his best: 'I should remember the great victories which he had fought and won; I should remember his illustrious career, its continual success and splendour, not its accidental or even disastrous mistakes.'[193]

Gladstone did his best to counteract the effect of the Fermoy letter by reassuring his party as to his Unionist orthodoxy with a vigorous assault on Isaac Butt's 'ragged scheme' of Home Rule, which Gladstone trusted 'this House will never condescend to adopt':

that plan is this – that exclusively Irish affairs are to be judged in Ireland, and that then the Irish Members are to come to the Imperial Parliament and to judge as they may think fit on the general affairs of the Empire, and also affairs exclusively English and Scotch . . . I want to know in what portion of his plan are we guaranteed against the danger that our friends from Ireland who shall be invested with exclusive power over consideration of Irish affairs in Dublin may come here to meddle with matters exclusively English and Scotch?[194]

That question, ironically, was to be asked with equal pertinence of Gladstone's own schemes of Home Rule in 1886 and 1893.

Once these storms had subsided, Gladstone settled down to a leisurely and rather detached sessional leadership. His interventions were sparse, mostly formalities, or 'ecclesiastical evenings' on such things as Scottish Church patronage, endowed schools, and ritualism. 'Spoke in reply to Sir W. S. Maxwell,' he recorded on 19 March. 'I am tempted to say, I would it were the last.' There were occasional flashes of the old Gladstone, as when he roundly denounced the annexation of the Fiji Islands as wholly premature, predicting that there would be a repetition of the New Zealand case, which 'cost us many wars and many millions of money, and which made us responsible for much that has occurred in that Colony which we have great cause to regret'.[195] He was indignant also at 'that socialistic budget of Northcote's', giving special relief to the bottom end of income-tax payers.[196] But for the most part Gladstone was reticent and discreet. Indeed, at a reception for the visiting Emperor Alexander II of Russia (whom Gladstone assured of his 'profound interest in the transactions of his reign & the great benefits wh he had conferred upon his people'), Disraeli complained at Gladstone's absence from the Commons: 'said they cd not get on without me'.[197]*

Now there was much more space for personal and private concerns. Despite Catherine's dismay, Gladstone proceeded with the abandonment of 11 Carlton House Terrace. At Hawarden he reckoned up the state of

---

* The Emperor's daughter had been married in St Petersburg to the Queen's second son, the Duke of Edinburgh.

his finances and income. Under what Gladstone saw as Robertson's mismanagement, the Seaforth estate had ceased to be a beneficial concern. Gladstone's property was considerable if sold up, but what he had readily available in income, now that he was without official salary, was a mere £1,000 to cover annual expenditure. 'This speaks for itself.' He was 'afraid it will startle C.'.[198] The Hawarden estate itself was mending, and Sir Stephen moved back into the Castle, where the Gladstones, after staying with their son Stephen at the Rectory, joined him on 20 April. 'C. & I keep house till August, & S. is at once host & guest.' Sir Stephen was, as it happened, much in need of Gladstone's supportive presence at that time. The 'revolt of the labourers' touched Hawarden. There was dispute between the manager and the miners at the Aston Hall colliery. Depression in the trade led to a 15 per cent wage reduction. Gladstone put himself firmly behind the manager. Under threat of eviction the miners settled for a 10 per cent reduction. Gladstone certainly did not think that in this instance he was embarking against the labouring classes in a bad cause.

There was space too for literature. He '*touched* Homer', and soon found himself enchained in a translation of 'The Reply of Achilles to the Envoys of Agamemnon'.[199] There was much anxious correspondence with Döllinger on the state of Christian belief. Döllinger's excommunicated plight in Germany was material to Gladstone's attention to the beginnings of the *Kulturkampf* between the Reich and the Roman Catholic Church, and his expression of Britain's 'sympathy with Germany'.[200] 'Bismarck's ideas & methods are not ours,' he wrote to Odo Russell at Berlin. But he was clear that he was more with Bismarck than against him. 'I cannot but say that the present doctrines of the Roman Church destroy the title of her obedient members to the enjoyment of civil rights.' Gladstone would 'hate to say this publicly, for I want no more storms; but it may become necessary'.[201]

He was exercised also by the dangers of 'plutocracy', a 'great & threatening shoal if not rock' lying ahead, threatening to wreck the ship of state and its people.[202] That the new wealth and ease were sapping the nation's fibre was a theme common among dismayed Liberals at the time, at a loss otherwise to account for a Conservative election victory. For Gladstone it was a matter of recurring naturally and consistently to his denunciations of the 'metropolitan' ethos in his Whitby outburst in 1871. He was much gratified when Theodore Martin sent him the first volume of his *Life of the Prince Consort*, praising it for the 'rebuke & admonition' it gave to idle wealth and its dangers to the aristocracy.[203] (Gladstone was less gratified about the rather exiguous 'religious interior of the Prince'.) The copious religious interior of his 'Dear Spirit', Laura Thistlethwayte, on the other hand, was ever a matter of deep interest, if occasionally also of distress ('There can be *no* advantage however in any private conversation when words meant to be words of kindness prove to be words of deep offence').[204]* Possibly Gladstone shared Lady Elizabeth Pringle's misgivings about the reappearance on the London stage of 'the charming *Irish Heroine*'; but, as Lady Elizabeth pointed out, 'how can I answer when, she assured me she is *led to do that sort of thing* by *Divine Influence*'.[205]

The amenities of that Hawarden season were sadly compromised, however, by the sudden death, on 16 June, of Sir Stephen Glynne, while 'searching for antiquities in Shoreditch High Street'. With Catherine's two brothers now dead, the male line of the Glynnes of Hawarden became extinct. Under the arrangements of 1865[206] Catherine's eldest son Willy entered into his inheritance. Gladstone had always felt 'a strong repugnance to becoming the actual or the virtual master'.[207] After the funeral on 24 June 'came the interviews and explanations'. Willy – a notably reticent MP – 'expressed his perfect readiness to act as I recommended under the new arrangements'. The Gladstones were now the house guests of their son. Willy Gladstone stood now in Sir Stephen's place in the Castle as Stephen Gladstone stood in the Reverend Henry's place at the Rectory.

[11]

Quiet times in the Commons might well have continued had not Disraeli decided to put his government behind a bill which the Archbishop of Canterbury, Tait, had introduced in the Lords. The Public Worship Regulation Bill aimed at giving diocesan bishops powers to criminalize the 'ritualistic' practices of certain High Church or 'Anglo-Catholic' clergy deemed to savour of popery. Hitherto Gladstone had blocked Tait's efforts in this direction. Now all he could do was to make himself as much as he could of an obstacle to it in the House of Commons. Disraeli's and the government's official stance at the outset was one of neutrality. Salisbury managed to get the bill down to the Commons in a less ferocious form. Even so, Gladstone objected passionately to the Erastian nature of the measure. For him the 'thorny character of those paths which we are now invited to tread' evoked something of painful memories of the sad days of 1850. After all, what *was* 'Ritualism'? Some practices might be acceptable, but others not. The bill threatened to impose a wholly needless conformity, out of which many inconveniences

* See above, page 105.

were likely to arise. Parliament, warned Gladstone, was 'treading on the edge of a precipice'. Over that precipice might fall the Church as an Establishment of religion.[208] Gladstone could even discern in Tait's plan intimations of the 'claims of spiritual absolutism' currently disturbing Europe.[209] He counter-attacked with six furiously voluminous resolutions.

Disraeli had long been spoiling to strike at the 'Rits'. It would be popular in the country and in Parliament. The Queen egged him on. Now that Gladstone had committed himself so vehemently he seemed to have exposed himself in a position of extreme vulnerability in a Commons of decidedly 'Protestant' sentiment. Liberals of anti-sacerdotal leanings came out in support of the bill. Not a few of these were Gladstone's former colleagues: Forster, Lowe, Goschen, and especially Harcourt proved good enemies of priestcraft. Disraeli could not resist the temptation to put himself and his government behind the measure to suppress 'the Mass in masquerade'. This did damage to the Conservative party, but not as much damage as it did to the Liberal party. Gladstone and his resolutions were swept aside by the Protestant tide. There was a particularly bruising encounter with Harcourt, as Gladstone recounted eloquently to Granville:

instead of making any reparation to me, in defiance of all regularity, and without any practical issue before him, he spoke at me for above an hour (I believe): since even his slimy, fulsome, loathsome eulogies upon Dizzy were aimed at me, and I rather think the affair was got up between them, but in D. I have nothing to complain of. It was quite plain that he meant business, namely my political extinction, and thought that Ritualism offered a fine opportunity . . . However, I regret it *extremely*. It is a new scandal & a new difficulty for the party.

Disraeli had been in hopes in 1873 of securing Harcourt for the Conservative party;[210] and Gladstone now might well have assessed Harcourt shrewdly as 'thinking himself a Disraeli'. But what Harcourt did not perceive, in Gladstone's view, was that 'Dizzy himself, who is an extraordinary man and a genius, would not have been able to mount but for the most singular manner in which Derby & G. Bentinck played into his hands, the latter of the two first by his life, and then yet more by his death'.[211]

Tait and Disraeli got their Public Worship Regulation Act; but got little satisfaction from its working. It soon became discredited by a series of scandals caused by the ostentatious willingness of Anglo-Catholic clergymen to bear witness through the martyrdom of noisy trials and imprisonment. Heads were shaken at Gladstone's having yet again exhibited a propensity for excessive excitability and want of a sense of proportion. Selborne complained of him that Gladstone 'can hardly be brought to interest himself at all in matters (even when they are really great matters) in which he is not carried away by some too strong attraction'. When so carried away, 'he does not sympathise with, or take counsel with', those whose point of view was at all different from his own. 'This makes it hardly possible for him to be a Minister, except when it is the time for some "heroic" measures, for which he can excite public enthusiasm.'[212] Once the sessional reverberations had died away Gladstone retreated to Hawarden and Penmaenmawr to put his considered views on the problem of Ritualism in an article for the October *Contemporary Review*. But even as he prepared this defence of Catholic Anglicanism he was stunned at the news from Lady Ripon that Ripon was no longer able conscientiously to remain in the Anglican communion, and was preparing to submit to the Roman Church.[213] Gladstone's response – 'may he pause' – dwelt on the seeming strangeness of such an act 'at the time when the Roman Church has dealt itself such a blow in Germany'.[214]

It was to Germany as it happened that Gladstone was bound in September. His sister Helen was sequestered still in Cologne. Gladstone had not seen her for over six years. But it was to Munich and Döllinger that his mind as well as his heart was set. After luncheon at the Thistlethwaytes' and a post-dinner *soirée* with Laura Thistlethwayte, Gladstone set off on the 7th, accompanied by Willy and Helen (a daughter). He found his sister 'deeply to be felt for'. Her 'mind and soul are in great straits, but she is striving to battle for the truth and may she be blest'. Gladstone by no means abandoned hope that Helen's struggle for the truth would see her back to the Anglican Church. Then at Munich Robert Morier of the British Legation was indefatigable in his hospitality and attentions. He arranged that Gladstone's portrait should be painted by the eminent artist Lenbach. He was a mine of information about the dissident 'Old Catholics'. There was much intense talk with Döllinger; and an awkwardly embarrassing moment when in a Munich street Döllinger and Gladstone came upon Döllinger's excommunicator, Archbishop Gregor von Scherr. Perhaps it was the incitement of that encounter together with sad thoughts of the Ripons that caused Gladstone the following day to send off to Knowles of the *Contemporary* an insert for the Ritualism article asserting four propositions: that Rome had substituted 'for the proud boast of *semper eadem* a policy of violence and change of faith'; that Rome had furbished anew every rusty tool she was fondly believed to have disused; that 'no one can become her convert without renouncing his moral and mental freedom'; and that Rome had repudiated equally 'modern thought and ancient history'.[215] This converted a defence of unpopular Ritualism into an extremely popular attack on Romanism. Döllinger went off to his conference at Bonn of Old Catholics and Orthodox and Anglican observers. Gladstone and Willy and Helen set off for an exhilarating tour of the Bavarian Alps (including Berchtesgaden) and Salzburg.

After a farewell gathering with both Döllinger and Lenbach back in Munich on 20 September, the Gladstones proceeded via Nuremberg and Cologne (to see Helen once more), arriving in London on the 25th (dinner chez Thistlethwaytes). Gladstone returned to Hawarden the following day in a state of mental excitement. Something like the Neapolitan eruption of 1851 was building up. His experiences of late were accumulating into an emotionally explosive dynamic of resentments. There was the Roman Hierarchy in Ireland, and their part in killing his University Bill. There was his sister Helen's plight. There was the Public Worship Bill fracas. There was the Ripon bombshell. There was the *Kulturkampf*. There was the Ritualism article. There was Döllinger's brave fight against the proudly arrogant and aggressive Court of Rome. There was Gladstone's interest in the fortunes of the Cavourian ideal of a *libera chiesa in libero stato* in Italy in its struggle against the sinister forces of 'Vaticanism'.[216] Not least was Gladstone's conviction, as he later explained to Granville, that the ultramontane party in France was 'waiting, in one vast conspiracy, for an opportunity to direct European war to the reestablishment by force of the temporal power; or even to bring about such war for that purpose'.[217]

Before September was out Gladstone started work on what was to be published eventually in November as *The Vatican Decrees in Their Bearing on Civil Allegiance: A Political Expostulation*, a quarto, with appendices, of seventy-two pages. In substance this was an extension of the insert he had sent from Munich for his *Contemporary* article. He had told Odo Russell that he wanted no more storms, but that one might be necessary. That necessity he signalled in the October *Contemporary*. Roman Catholics were deeply offended. Lord Emly compared it to Russell's vituperative 'Durham Letter' of 1850; and pointed out to Gladstone that it was 'a serious thing . . . to declare war against the religion of the Irish people'.[218]* Gladstone insisted on the necessity of his expostulation. 'Had I been, when I wrote this passage, as I now am, addressing myself in considerable measure to my Roman Catholic fellow-countrymen, I should have striven to avoid the seeming roughness of some of these expressions; but as the question now is about their substance, from which I am not in any particular disposed to recede, any attempt to recast their general form

---

* William Morrell was an old friend and member of the 'Engagement' and a 'Limerick' convert to a cultivated lay ideal of Roman Catholicism. Former Postmaster-General.

would probably mislead.' Gladstone proceeded 'to deal with them on their merits'.[219] He proposed to justify his four propositions of October: that Rome had indeed substituted a policy of violence and change of faith for her old boast *semper eadem*; that Rome had indeed furbished and paraded every rusty tool she was fondly thought to have disused; that no one indeed could become her convert without renouncing moral and mental freedom; and that Rome had indeed repudiated equally modern thought and ancient history.

These principal indictments against 'Vaticanism' Gladstone laced with the pathos of the tragic case of Döllinger, taking his stand on conscience which the Church was now stifling: a species of 'moral murder'.[220] Gladstone gave his manuscript to three Hawarden guests to read, Arthur Gordon, Lord Acton, and Ambrose de Lisle. 'They all show me that I must act mainly for myself.'[221]* Acton was shocked by Gladstone's offensive tone. After six hours of argument with Acton on 30 September Gladstone sent the MS off to Murray's. The tempo was fast. After labour on proofs and revises Gladstone collapsed. 'Broke down from over work & hurry in afternoon from diarrhoea. In the night I rose & took castor oil.'[222]

The public impact of *The Vatican Decrees* was gratifyingly explosive. If Gladstone had been on the unpopular side of the Public Worship issue he more than redeemed himself now. Both Newman[223] and Manning[224] responded with rebukes on behalf of the British Roman Catholic subjects of the Queen. The Queen herself, for all her own Protestantism, was not amused. 'What an incomprehensible old man he is!' She reminded her daughter Victoria: 'Old Lord Palmerston was not wrong when he said to me; "he is a very dangerous man." '[225] While staying with Salisbury's nephew Arthur Balfour at Whittingehame in November Gladstone read up the arrears of letters and papers on the controversy, 'which swells and swells'.[226] (Of Balfour himself, who was thought to have matrimonial designs on Catherine's niece Mary ('May') Lyttelton, Gladstone observed: 'How eminently he is *del miglior luto*: how glad should we be to be nearer to him.') Murray reported 52,000 copies sold, and 20,500 more printed before the end of November. All Gladstone's time was now absorbed in correspondence and responses; but the subject he thought 'well worth the pains'. By December he had started work on a counterblast to his reprovers, 'into which I was carried with an impetus'.[227]

The detonations of Gladstone's irritated polemic reverberated also through Europe. There were illustrious admirers. Count Münster, the German Ambassador, conveyed from Chatsworth the thanks of the

---

* De Lisle was a Roman Catholic convert and one of the founders in 1857 of the Association for the Promotion of the Unity of Christendom.

Reich Chancellor. 'Prince Bismarck read it with the greatest interest and admired the manly courage and great lucidity with which you expose the false doctrines of Rome and treat a question that has such vivid interest for Germany at this moment.'[228] Gladstone's 'impetus' carried him on through a critique of Pius IX's speeches for the January 1875 *Quarterly* to *Vaticanism: An Answer to Replies and Reproofs*, which Murray's published in March, and beyond that to 'Italy and Her Church', an examination of the ways in which the Italian state and the Italian people might combine to resist and defeat the insolent sacerdotal ambitions of the Roman Curia, for the *Church Quarterly Review* in October 1875. After all, Gladstone's own ecclesiastical creation, the disestablished Church of Ireland, offered as good a specimen of a free church in a free state as might be had.[229] On receipt of *Vaticanism*, Bismarck responded directly to Gladstone: 'I anticipate some hours of instructive reading.' The Prince felt a 'deep and hopeful gratification to see the two nations, which in Europe are the champions of liberty of conscience encountering the same foe, stand henceforth shoulder on shoulder in defending the highest interests of the human race'.[230] Perhaps not entirely happy to be thus enrolled as a comrade in the *Kulturkampf* (Granville had warned against becoming implicated in 'injudiciously violent actions' of the German authorities),[231] Gladstone indeed conceded that 'a deep interest' in the ideal of freedom, 'inadequately represented by our Metropolitan Press, is felt by the nation'.[232]

That opposition between metropolis and nation was already a cliché of Gladstone's rhetoric. There were difficulties and anomalies in this case about who were 'the nation'. What was strikingly evident in the *Vatican Decrees* was precisely the absence of any confrontation by Gladstone to Romanism where it was a real power nearest home: in Ireland. Possibly Emly's point about its being a serious thing to declare war on the religion of the Irish people gave Gladstone pause. But it certainly distorted his argument.[233] As Gladstone put it in *Vatican Decrees*, noting that the Roman Catholic Church governed five million (or one sixth) of the population of the United Kingdom, it had ever been a 'favourite purpose' of his career 'not to conjure up, but to conjure down, public alarm'.[234] The fact that that incarnation of the ultramontane Curia, Cardinal Antonelli, had officially deprecated the insolent applause of the *Osservatore Romano* for the Irish priesthood's working for 'Irish autonomy' would hardly have reassured Gladstone. Nevertheless, he chose to evade the most immediately relevant instance of his general argument. There was therefore something of a curious gap between Gladstone's sense of the dangers of the threat and the continental distance at which he put it. He provoked a good deal of Irish Catholic indignation, but that too was distanced, centred in Rome mainly. There was also a curious emptiness in the congratulations Sir James Hudson, former Ambassador in Turin and Florence, offered to Gladstone for having given the newly elevated Cardinal Manning such a 'tremendous bastinata' in *Vaticanism*.[235] It was Cardinal Cullen whom Gladstone should have been bastinating.

[12]

'On this my 65th birthday I find myself in lieu of the mental repose I had hoped engaged in a controversy, which cannot be mild, & which presses upon both mind & body.' Nor was mental repose aided by Gladstone's reading of George Eliot's *Middlemarch*. That depiction of the wastes and futilities of lives and ambitions skewed and spoiled by muddled religion and misdirected science Gladstone found 'jarring'.[236] Even less was mental repose now aided by the prospect of the coming new session of Parliament. He defined three areas of difficulty: the first was the 'absence of any great positive aim (the late plan having failed) for which to co-operate'; second, the 'difficulty of establishing united & vigorous action in the Liberal party for purposes of economy'; and third, the 'unlikelihood of arriving at any present agreement respecting Education'. Gladstone's personal views on these two latter issues 'constitute at present serious difficulties in the way of union'.[237] Yet Gladstone was being badgered by such as Stansfeld that Forster's leadership in the Commons was out of the question because of the Education difficulty. 'Whatever your views of the next session may be, I believe that on such a subject as this you will not refuse to mediate in the interest of the reunion in spirit of the party of progress.'[238] While Gladstone was sure the 'party of progress' had been heartened by the *Vatican Decrees*, he could see 'no daylight' in 'general politics'. 'Nothing will rally the party but a cause: or such portentous blundering as is almost beyond hope or fear.'[239] He put it to Granville that there were great incompatibilities in the way of his resuming the leadership. There was the religious question generally, with the Church of England 'at the brink of a most serious crisis'. While this question remained unresolved, Gladstone felt that 'any *strapping* up' of the relations between himself and the party could only constitute a new danger, particularly when there was no public object on the pursuit of which the party was agreed.[240] Gladstone tried to appease Catherine. 'I am indeed sorry that you and I have not been able to take the same view of this important subject but you know ... that I have probed myself deeply and used all the means in my power to get at a right conclusion.'[241]

Granville did his best to hold Gladstone for the party. 'Even without a "cause",' he replied from Savona, 'I trust you will resume the place in earnest, in which *all* so much desire that you should be.' It appeared to Granville impossible that Gladstone should not do so.[242] But already Gladstone was drafting a memorandum of abdication to be read to his colleagues. Wolverton was called in to advise and consent. He sent on to Granville a draft of a letter from Gladstone, which Granville declared he would be sorry to receive. He told Gladstone: 'A great party should have a recognized leader in Parliament more especially the party favouring progress, but not unanimous as to the rate at which progress should be made.' Gladstone's intending to remain in the Commons would in itself create obvious practical difficulties.[243] Gladstone's prop-osition was that it would be 'for others rather than for me to take the lead in considering what arrangements may be requisite for the regular conduct of Parliamentary business for the convenience and advantage of the Liberal party'. It would be, concomitantly, his duty 'to conduct my own proceedings with the fullest regard to such arrangements'.[244] This notion of a kind of semi-detached relationship with the party in the Commons bristled with potential awkwardnesses. Granville nonetheless received Gladstone's letter, dated 13 January 1875, stating that he could see 'no public advantage' in his continuing to act as leader of the Liberal party; and that at the age of sixty-five, after forty-two years of laborious public life, he thought himself 'entitled to retire on the present opportu-nity'. 'This retirement is dictated to me by my personal views as to the best method of spending the closing years of my life.'[245]

The following day, 14 January, Gladstone's old colleagues, excepting Bright and Argyll, assembled at Granville's, where they listened to Gladstone's explanations and his memorandum. Leadership, he pointed out, could only be managed at present 'by broaching very few points, selected mainly with a view to avoid division & scandal'. Many things would have to be 'passed by'. It would not be easy for him as leader to pass these things by. 'It is easier for younger & less committed men.' His great object, Gladstone declared, was to 'labour for holding together the Church of England'. This would involve pleading for sufferance and be unpopular with the Liberal constituencies. He could expect no cooperation from the party. The same applied to any attempts on his part to deal with denominational education. 'In the present blank state of the horizon we must judge by probabilities & the question most likely to come to the front, most for the interest of the Tories to bring to the front, is that of denominational education.' He was 'out of harmony with the younger generation'; of the objects for which he had been accustomed to labour actively in public life he could see none which he could 'effectively promote as leader'.[246]

There was 'argument & expostulation & much kindness: but all was settled before four o'clock: & the terms of Granville's reply were agreed on'. Gladstone returned to Hawarden on the 15th, where he found Catherine 'rather low' as to what was happening. For himself, he seemed to feel 'as one who has passed through a death, but emerged into a better life'.[247]

Two things were not mentioned. Gladstone had denied 'any cause of complaint' at the time of his initial broaching of the question of the leadership in February 1874, though it was evident that he felt keenly the degree of disloyalty to him in the party, and that the element of punitiveness was still by no means absent from his mind. The other point was the 'conditional' aspect of a 'special call', or 'cause'. The nearest Gladstone came to this nub is in a memorandum probably misdated as 'Ab F12'.*

I shall not now resign my seat in Parliament; but after the labour of the last years I require rest particularly mental rest, and my attendance will only be occasional . . . I do not conceal my hope and expectation that this first step of retirement into the shade will be followed by others accomplishing the work . . . Deeming myself unable to hold [the party] together from my present position in a manner worthy of it I see how unlikely it is that I should hereafter be able to give any material aid in the adjustment of its difficulties. Yet if such aid should at any time be generally desired with a view to arresting some great evil or procuring for the nation some great good, my willingness to come into counsel for that occasion would follow from all I have said.[248]

The overwhelming testimony of the evidence available suggests that very few people who had any close personal knowledge of Gladstone believed that his retirement would stand the strain of many months, let alone years. Lord Blachford supposed that Gladstone would soon 'become désœuvré and take to prowling round the political pen, from which he has excluded himself and snuffing for an entrance'. And when he 'begins to snuff it will not be long before he makes a rush – an ugly one – at the door'.[249] Abraham Hayward concluded after a long talk with Gladstone that though he will quit the field for a time, he 'does not talk of permanent abdication'.[250] Mundella found it 'hard to believe that Gladstone has quite retired from politics'. He had seen Gladstone 'in his old place, full of health and brightness'. Soon Mundella concluded: 'Gladstone will assuredly return some day. He cannot resist the temptation of a good fight.'[251] Lord Strafford undoubtedly expressed a sentiment widespread among Liberals when he wrote to Gladstone of his letter of

* 'About February 12th.'

resignation to Granville: 'Mine is a sanguine temperament; & I cannot help indulging a hope that in those lines I do not "bow to him whose course is run"; but when the war trumpet of St Stephens utters a no uncertain sound, its blast may reach the groves of Hawarden, & recall Cincinnatus to rally, combine, & array our (now) fluttered Legions, under the only Leader who can inspire them with confidence.'[252] There were, as it happened, to be nineteen months elapsing before the war trumpet sounded.

Derby made the same point from a different angle. 'Politics are uncertain: but never since I entered Parliament, now 26 years ago, have I known a state of things such as exists now. The Liberals have lost their majority and their leader: are split up into discordant sections: and have alienated the Irish Catholics. I doubt if they could muster 250 votes on a critical division, against 340 or 350. Yet who will guarantee that this state of things shall last for 12 months?'[253] That state of things lasted somewhat longer than Derby allowed for. It was not until the general election of 1880 that the condition of the Liberal party in the House of Commons underwent any material improvement. But many other things had happened to it by then which made all conventional considerations of such matters entirely redundant.

Meanwhile, Gladstone's presence on and increasing interventions from the Opposition front bench exacerbated the Liberal party's problems. As Mundella observed, 'Gladstone attends the House very well and keeps a keen and watchful eye on all that is going on. His advent to power sooner or later is considered certain.' The very beginning of the new order was expressive of its embarrassed and provisional character. Gladstone was possessed of the curious presumption – an odd but characteristic and revealing imperial touch – that, by addressing his letter of abdication to Granville, he had somehow conferred upon the leader of the Liberal Lords the leadership of the Liberal party, as if it were an office in his gift.* Granville found this embarrassing,[254] and declined even as leader in the Lords to summon a general meeting of the party, leaving it to Peel's successor as Chief Whip, W. P. Adam, to arrange a meeting of Liberal members of the Commons. At this meeting, on 3 February, Forster having withdrawn his candidacy, the reluctant Lord Hartington was elected at the Reform Club to lead in the Commons. Bright presided; Villiers proposed; Samuel Morley seconded. Both Whig leaders were clear that in the extraordinary circumstances, an overall party leader was not electable: partly because of the fragmented condition of the party, but partly also because of Gladstone's awkward presence.

---

* See below, page 246, for G's taking it much amiss that in 1880 the Queen did not share this presumption.

The leadership of the party would be 'adjourned to the day when, a Liberal majority having been again constituted, the choice of the Sovereign created a Liberal Prime Minister'.[255]*

In the meantime Gladstone was free to speculate as to where in his irregular new capacity he might sit in the Commons when the new session commenced. His initial idea was to sit where the veteran Sir James Graham had sat, on the near corner of the front bench below the gangway; but Bright, having himself been brought to the front bench by Gladstone and having admitted Hartington to the leadership, felt that Gladstone would best be placed in comradely solidarity with them. Gladstone ought to have declined, but did not. It was Granville's belief that Hartington by no means shared Bright's rather naive sentiments; and felt much the oppressiveness of 'the anomaly of his (Hartington's) rising to speak for the party, with Gladstone sitting on the same bench'.[256]

The point never seems to have worried Gladstone. He was observed 'in high spirits, boasting of not having felt so well for many years, and cordially anxious to be of any use he can to Hartington and his late colleagues'.[257] A charmingly fitting envoi to official life had come from Lord John Manners, the new Postmaster-General. He assured Gladstone of the huge success of one of his last concerns, the ½d. post card ('The first million are all sold. Delarue cannot make them fast enough').[258] Gladstone could indulge himself with another outing to Newman Hall's Hampstead house, where he mended fences with the leading lights of Nonconformity.[259] By now he was much engaged in the intricacies of selling up the lease of 11 Carlton House Terrace. Sir Arthur Guinness, the Conservative Dublin County MP, took it on at £35,000 ('Sir A. G. has the chairs & sofa on which we sat when we resolved the disestablishment of the Irish Church in 1868').[260] There was much ado with arrangements for auctions of effects by Messrs Christie's and Messrs Sotheby's ('I am amazed at the accumulation of objects all of which have now, as by way of retribution, to be handled, & dispersed, or finally dismissed').[261]

Catherine was not at all pleased with the turn of events. She relished her share of the grand life in the grand house. She was never either assiduous or efficient as a political hostess whether in London or in Hawarden, but her devoted identification with her husband's fame and fortunes, and Gladstone's confidences to her about his great world of affairs, meant that in many ways his withdrawal would have greater consequences for her than for him. She could share very little of either his literary interests or his religious enthusiasms. 'We have rubbed a good deal about the contract of sale,' Gladstone recorded on 30 March,

---

* Disraeli had become leader of the Conservative party in 1868 on being appointed prime minister.

'wh she naturally regards with discomfort & reluctance.' Now she found Gladstone 'loath to contemplate a new *home*' in London as opposed to a new base merely of restricted operations. They took temporary refuge with the Frederick Cavendishes at 23 Carlton House Terrace and then at 4 Carlton Gardens, whence they departed to what Catherine must have thought the dismal purlieus of Harley Street. No. 73 had become vacant on the decease of the eminent geologist Sir Charles Lyell. To Gladstone this plain and modest house was appropriate to his sense of the restricted nature of his future and remaining part of life, to be devoted to the defence of Christian belief and of its purest witness, the Church of England. He remarked upon 'a departure from a *neighbourhood* where I have lived for forty years, & where I am the "oldest inhabitant". Truly one steps forward in life.'[262]

CHAPTER 5

'A VIRTUOUS PASSION': THE PEOPLE AND THE QUESTION OF THE EAST, 1875–7

[1]

For the most part Gladstone kept a loyally reticent stance in the 1875 session. He contributed nothing to the debates on the government's 'social' legislation, designed by Disraeli and Cross to be a reposeful political bromide to contrast with Gladstone's strenuous excitements. Gladstone was very willing, at the request of Hartington, to maul Northcote's budget, lamenting the passing of the epoch of a 'generous rivalry' between the two great parties of the state 'in matters of economy'; though he conceded that his 'ideas on the subject . . . may be antiquated and belong to a period of some 20, 30 or 40 years ago'.[1] There was a general consensus, in any case, that Northcote had held his ground to advantage. At Windsor the Queen was 'kind as usual', though not relaxing her attitude of reserve, which had become habitual, in spite of Gladstone's having sent her through Dean Wellesley his recent *Contemporary* article on 'The Life and Speeches of the Prince Consort'. There were other occasions of intervention by Gladstone, but Hartington on the whole had little cause for complaint, and in turn Gladstone could judge that 'Hartington does his work well; and he develops'. Gladstone's resignation from the Reform Club at the end of the year was taken to be an act of 'political significance', and 'engendered a somewhat bitter feeling in the Club' at being taken up at convenience and dropped without compunction.[2]*

The literary production which had been so marked a feature of 1874 continued apace in 1875. Much more time could now be spent in Hawarden rather than London. After the 'Italy and Her Church' piece, Homerology in various forms revived, culminating in 1876 in *Homeric Synchronism: An Enquiry into the Time and Place of Homer*, incorporating what Gladstone rather boldly interpreted as the implications of

---

* G agreed to soften the blow by becoming a trustee. He retained membership of the United Universities Club.

Schliemann's latest excavations. Gladstone played 'prophet' to Schliemann at the Society of Antiquaries on 25 June 1875. Professor F. Max Müller at Oxford was scandalized at Gladstone's twisting the evidence to make it fit his idiosyncratic purposes. 'So great a man, so imperfect a scholar!' To Max Müller Gladstone's abuse of the new findings was 'really painful, all the more so because it is cleverly done, and I believe bona fide'.[3]

There were personal and family distractions. Catherine's niece May Lyttelton, of whom there had been hopes as the intended of Arthur Balfour, died in March 1875: the only loss among George Lyttelton's numerous progeny; from which the depressive father never recovered. Later in the year Gladstone's enormous and eccentric brother Robertson died suddenly, leaving the family's business affairs in a state of confused dereliction. After the funeral at Knotty Ash Church on 28 September Sir Thomas remarked severely that Robertson's will was 'very faulty as to the relative positions of the brothers in particular'.* Robertson's death had the knock-on effect of leaving Harry's position in the firm a matter of dispute and uncertainty with the remaining partners. Gladstone set about remedying Harry's difficulties, costing him 'more care than any other of a temporal nature since the smash of 1847'.[5]† Happier was the case of Willy. In July he became engaged to be married to Miss Gertrude Stuart, daughter of Lord and the late Lady Blantyre. There was for Gladstone the gratification that Lady Blantyre, sister to the Duchess of Argyll, was a daughter of the lamented Harriet Sutherland. After Robertson's funeral Gladstone had the compensating pleasure of signing the deed constituting Willy absolute owner in law of the Hawarden estate; and the couple were married at St George's, Hanover Square, two days later.

It was gratifying also that Gladstone's relationship with Laura Thistlethwayte, subject to vicissitudes in 1874, was now on a steadier footing. He confided to her the details of Harry's problems.[6] There were visits to her at Oakley Park, Cirencester ('Oakley Park will be remembered by me, for itself, & for more than itself').[7]‡

What was of political note in the latter part of 1875 was the re-emergence of what, by long custom, was referred to as the 'Eastern question': the fate of the vast regions over which the decaying Ottoman Empire more or less held sway. Gladstone's last free initiative in this area had been his unsuccessful attempt in 1858 to persuade the Derby–

---

* As Catherine had earlier occasion to remark in Glynnese, 'Dear Uncle Tom cannot help being grubous and grim.'[4]
† From 1874 to 1889 Harry worked for the East India House of his grandfather and uncle, Gillanders, Arbuthnot & Co., Calcutta.
‡ The house was one of the properties of her admirer Lord Bathurst.

Disraeli government to repudiate Palmerston's 'Crimean system' and put itself in concert with the French and the Russians behind the cause of Romanian unity and freedom. The 'breasts of free men', he then contended, were a far better barrier to any ambitions the Russians might entertain than the decrepit and corrupt Ottoman Turks. From 1859 to 1866, as a colleague of Palmerston and Russell, he had been in the invidious position of having to toe the line of the Crimean system in public. As head of the party and head of his own administration from 1867 Gladstone had felt himself obliged not to offend Palmerstonian susceptibilities: their votes, however grudged, were precious. In any event, long and painful experience had taught Gladstone that, on foreign policy, the 'national' public was intransigent: and he still hurt from the bruises left after the Black Sea and *Alabama* affairs.

In his novel and irregular and anomalous situation in 1875, however, none of these inhibiting considerations any longer obtained, save the calculation that little political profit was in any event likely to be cashed from an issue of foreign policy, given the seeming solidity of 'Palmerston-ism' as a public tradition, and Disraeli's manifest intention to emulate its practice and benefit from its reputation and presumed popularity. Thus it was that, when in August 1875 Gladstone's attention was drawn to the atrociousness of Turkish attempts to suppress a Serb insurrection in Bosnia and the Herzegovina, he reacted in very much the same manner as with his refusals to concern himself with similar occurrences in Crete. His informant, J. Lewis Farley, formerly an apologist for the Turks and particularly the Ottoman Bank, professed now to realize the hopelessness of Turkish undertakings of reform and good government. The massive financial investment which had flowed in from France and Britain since the Crimean War had been wasted. Turkey was on the brink of financial collapse. And now 'the standard of the Cross is once more steeped in Christian blood'. What had been the atrocious case in Syria, Samos, and Crete was now to be repeated in Bosnia. Farley appealed to Gladstone: 'You, Sir, have before this raised your voice on behalf of freedom, and, at the sound of that voice, like the walls of Jericho before the trumpets of Joshua, the shackles fell from the limbs of Neapolitan captives. Will you not, Sir, say a word on behalf of the Christians of European Turkey, who are now fighting for their religion and their homes. Your voice will reach the Bosphorous, and the Sultan will listen.'[8] This evocation of the *Letter to the Earl of Aberdeen* could not divert Gladstone from his current obsession with inviting the Italians to take the disestablished Church of Ireland and the Free Kirk of Scotland as their models in the fight against Vaticanism, or displace his Homeric enthusiasms. Gladstone's voice did not reach the Bosporus.

His active interest in Near East matters of late had largely been confined to the 'curious question of the Bulgarian heresy', and the quarrel between the Greek Patriarchate in Constantinople and the Orthodox communion among the Bulgarians, who were demanding an autonomous Church government independent of the Greeks.[9]* This was linked to the sympathetic interest in Orthodoxy which he shared with Döllinger's 'Old Catholics' and their Anglican friends. When the Turkish financial crash came Gladstone thought it loomed 'very large' as 'one of the greatest political events'; but, as he remarked coolly to Granville early in November, he felt assured that Disraeli would handle it 'rationally'.[10]

From November onwards, however, this rather detached and cool response to events began to change. It was while Gladstone was staying with Hartington at Chatsworth that the news broke of Disraeli's startling coup of purchasing secretly the bankrupt Khedive of Egypt's 44 per cent holdings in the Paris-based Suez Canal Company, for £4 million. Gladstone's instinctive response to the 'amazing news' was entirely critical and negative: 'if not done in concert with Europe, I fear grave consequences: and am not in the least degree moved by the storm of approval which seems to be rising'.[11] That storm of approval – expressed most famously by the *Punch* cartoon of Disraeli as 'Moses in Egypt', holding the 'key to India' in his hand, and exchanging winks with the Sphinx – arose precisely because it was not done in concert with Europe. Disraeli's purpose was to assert Britain's international prowess in a manner not heard of since Palmerston's time. In his transactions with the Queen, he made of it a chapter of romantic *haute politique* from one of his own novels. The Queen applauded it particularly as a blow against Bismarck's 'insolent' pretensions that Britain had ceased to count as a European power.

When Gladstone wrote indignantly to Granville that, if done in concert with the other powers, it was 'an act of folly fraught with future embarrassment', and if done without such concert an 'act of folly fraught also with present danger', Granville could simply point to the public irrelevance of such objections. Since many senior Liberals, including not least Hartington, approved of Disraeli's stroke, Granville supposed that 'the quieter we keep about the Suez Canal at present the better'.[12] Colleagues of Disraeli such as Northcote and Derby, who echoed Gladstone's critique exactly,[13] had even more reason to take Granville's point. Disraeli himself was well primed as to the difficulties of his critics. He wrote to Lord Barrington: 'Your letters – amusing. I can see G's face & could have prophesied all he said.'[14]

Edward Levy of the *Telegraph*, possibly prompted from high quarters, was very concerned to protect Gladstone from himself. 'I hope to impress

---

* G disapproved the Bulgarian claim.

you with the necessity for not pronouncing yourself against the course the Government has adopted with regard to the Suez Canal – till you have thought "once, twice & even thrice" about the reasons, spoken and unspoken, which produced this wonderful unanimity in the public mind.' Levy could appreciate objections as to both method and motives – the way England was being dazzled by cleverness and flashiness and distracted from internal problems.

But, with all this in my mind, and with the deepest respect for sentiments which I share – will you permit me to suggest, with perfect frankness, that here is an occasion absolutely unique, where maxims too rigid may betray the best Liberal into an unprofitable alienation from the spirit of his country . . . The bargain would only be a bad one if it cost us the belief that you – my dear Mr Gladstone – and the Liberal Party did not warmly support what, I suppose, has for its inspiration, the safeguard of the Empire.[15]

Here Levy was prophetic both in the short term of the break between the *Telegraph* and Gladstone and in the longer term of an alienation between the Liberal party and the imperial spirit of the country in Gladstone's later years. For the moment, Levy struck with precision all the wrong notes. 'I rack my brains upon the great stroke of genius,' Gladstone wrote to Granville. 'And the manner in which it was received really makes me blush for my Countrymen and for their press. But I have always felt that while for domestic purposes our press is admirable we have no security whatever from it against even the most outrageous follies in matters of foreign policy.'[16]

In Gladstone's view Disraeli's government at least adopted what appeared to be a concerted policy with France and Italy in giving approval to the intervention of the 'Three Emperors' League' of Germany, Russia, and Austria–Hungary of December 1875, known in diplomatic parlance as the 'Andrassy Note'. The Austro-Hungarian foreign minister warned the Turks that if they failed to pacify Bosnia and the Herzegovina promptly, they would be confronted with a coercive intervention. Gladstone, at the time, was not to know that in fact Disraeli's Cabinet would have much preferred snubbing the note as an infringement of the stipulations protecting Turkish independence in the Treaty of Paris of 1856, and in order to challenge Bismarck's presumption to run Europe. The British Cabinet adhered to the note only at the request of the Turks themselves, glad to have a friend at court.

By the end of 1875, therefore, Gladstone could conduct his customary reflections undismayed by any sense that the Suez affair threatened to be the overture to any consistent policy of Palmerstonian Turcophile adventure. His mood was unusually serene. '*All* things are foreseen:

both the acts of free agents, and the performances of the unfree.'[17]* Neapolitan analogies of a special call were far from his mind. He was able to soothe himself with reflections that 'in the great business of unwinding the coil of life and in establishing my freedom' he had made some progress by resigning the leadership, selling his house, and 'declining public occasions'. But more had yet to be done. In defending his retirement from political life to Catherine, he had explained to her his conviction that the 'welfare of mankind' did not now depend on 'the state of the world of politics'. The 'real battle' was being fought in the 'world of thought', where a deadly attack was being made 'with great tenacity of purpose and over a wide field upon the greatest treasure of mankind, the belief in God and the Gospel of Christ'.[19] 'To minimise my presence in London is alike needful for growth, for any work, for the great duty & business of solemn recollection and preparation.' Gladstone hoped that his 'polemical period' was over. It had virtually occupied over a twelvemonth: 'but good has been done, especially in Italy'. 'May the next', he wrote at the year's end, 'be of purer & holier Retrospect.'

[2]

Hopes that the end of 1876 might afford a purer and holier retrospect than that of 1875 were by no means implausible as Disraeli's Parliament gathered for its third session in February. It was true that Gladstone continued to deplore the Suez shares coup as compromising the sense of European community and identity of interest with the other powers in the international waterway. It was true also that Gladstone held the Royal Titles Bill, by which the Queen was to assume the style 'Empress of India', to be of 'evil omen', giving rise to misgiving and mistrust in every circle of which Gladstone was conversant.[20] But, on the other hand, Gladstone had no compunction, from his anomalous place on the Opposition front bench, in cutting across Hartington's Palmerstonian faint praise for the government's Eastern policy in order to congratulate ministers for their recognizing, in complying with the Andrassy Note, the reality of the 'European conscience' embodied in the Treaty of Paris.[21]

Even when Disraeli revealed his true colours by vetoing the next initiative of the Three Emperors' League to coerce the Turks in the 'Berlin Memorandum' of May, and by ordering the Mediterranean fleet to Besika Bay outside the Dardanelles as a Palmerstonian riposte, reminiscent of

---

* G remarked to Laura Thistlethwayte about a book which had come into his hands 'by one of those accidents which I always interpret as being a purpose'.[18]

1849 and 1853, Gladstone's reaction was entirely lacking in severity. Nor was this restraint relaxed by the early reports of massacre by Turks of Bulgarians, attempting to emulate the Serb insurrection, also in the month of May. He was later profuse with apologies and explanations of what came to be seen as an extraordinary and astonishing insensibility. He had had in his possession, after all, every element proper to such a case ever since he laid the foundations of an alternative Eastern policy back in 1858, in the Romanian episode. All he needed to do now was to dust it off and apply it to the Bulgarians.

When in 1876 the Eastern question was forced forward by the disturbances in the Turkish Empire, and especially by the cruel outrages in Bulgaria, I shrank naturally but perhaps unduly from recognizing the claim they made on me; upon me individually. I hoped that the Ministers would recognise the moral obligations to the subject races in the East, which we had in honour contracted as parties in the Crimean war and to the Peace of Paris of 1856. I was slow to observe the real leanings of the Prime Minister, his strong sympathy with the Turk and his mastery over his own Cabinet.[22]

To which Gladstone might have added very reasonably a failure of prevision of an astonishing event; that the constituency he failed to raise in 1858 would come upon him unawares in 1876.[23]

    This restraint on Gladstone's part came partly from a sense of prudence in not taxing Hartington's patience too rudely, and partly from an awareness that, as with the Suez affair, the government's policy was decidedly popular, not least among the Palmerstonian Whigs and Liberals, who rejoiced that something of Britain's old proud standing in the world was restored. Gladstone was well aware of his invidious reputation on that score. And his sad experience over the decades had taught him that little political purchase was ever to be got from foreign affairs. Besides, he was now engrossed in his review of Trevelyan's biography of his uncle Macaulay (with regrets at the spiritual void at the centre). To Manning in April Gladstone remarked that 'great events' seemed to be 'drawing near in the East', but he remained rather blankly remote and detached.[24]

    Much of the Easter recess was consumed in domestic debate about establishing a house in Penmaenmawr and in holding Willy and Gertrude in the Hawarden orbit. Lord Blantyre was not happy with his daughter's situation amid the intensity of Gladstone family life. Willy's dual role as nominal master of the house and devotedly dutiful and obedient son was in its way even less grateful than Sir Stephen's had been. Blantyre pressed for Gertrude's moving from the atmosphere of familial adoration cultivated by Catherine in order to allow his daughter and son-in-law an independent domestic life. Gladstone and Catherine of course thought the idea quite improper, both as a dereliction in filial duty and as making Gladstone look all the more a great cuckoo in the Glynne nest. Meanwhile, however, they were distracted with their own preparations to move to 73 Harley Street.

Above all, there was the stunning news, early in May, of the death of George Lyttelton. At first, it appeared accidental: a fall over the staircase at 18 Park Crescent, Marylebone. But 'then it came before us that it was intended: intended not by him but by that which possessed him'. Lyttelton had fallen while 'running away from his attendant'. 'How deep are the mysteries of God. This is horrible. But let us trust, & adore.' Soon, however, Gladstone, after an inspection of the fatal site, was able to persuade himself of the notion he had previously entertained, 'of the *likelihood* that he never meant to throw himself over, but fell in a too rapid descent'.[25] It was God's will, as he told Granville, and doubtless for good.[26]

Thus it was that when, on 26 May, Lord Stratford de Redcliffe, disturbed by persistent reports of extraordinarily barbarous proceedings by the Turks on both sides of the Balkans, invited Gladstone to confer, Gladstone's response to 'a long conversation on Turkey and the East' was anything but urgent. Two days later he in turn conferred with Hartington and Forster, neither of whom was disposed to pick a quarrel with the government on an issue of foreign policy. Gladstone's main concern with Sir Henry Elliot, Ambassador at the Porte, was to plead for his good offices in aid of Schliemann's excavation projects. The Ottoman authorities announced that disturbances in Rumelia had indeed broken out, but they were hardly of the order of an insurrection, and that the Imperial government had in any case taken energetic and efficacious measures. Sir Henry Elliot's dispatches to Derby at the Foreign Office chimed in with Turkish and Turcophile assurances as to journalistic exaggeration and Russian propaganda. It was Forster, on the strength of an excited *Spectator* article of 3 June, who prodded Hartington to do something. Disraeli easily eluded Hartington's half-hearted effort to extract information; and the public success of the Besika Bay riposte to the Berlin Memorandum – 'popular now as a proof of vigour against Russia', as Granville pointed out to Gladstone[27] – seemed to put the matter beyond any likelihood of 'portentous blundering' which might be politically beneficial to the Liberal Opposition.

Soon, however, the pace of events quickened. Confirmation that extensive massacres had indeed occurred came from correspondents in the *Daily News* and *The Times*. Reliable estimates indicated some 25,000 killed, up to 100 towns and villages destroyed, 1,000 children sold as slaves, 10,000 imprisoned and undergoing torture. The principal perpetrators, it appeared, were those Circassians, known of old to Gladstone, who had fled from Russian oppression in 1864 to be planted among the Bulgarians.[28] They now largely composed the irregular bands of 'bashi-bazouks', whose name was to become notorious. At the Foreign Office Derby would later concede that Elliot might reasonably be criticized. He 'ought to have known more of what was passing, and known it sooner, than he appears to have done: and to this there is no quite satisfactory answer'.[29] Stratford, too, had received 'sad accounts' of 'Turkish atrocities in Bulgaria'. He would rejoice to be mistaken, he told Gladstone, 'but, to judge from present appearances, the cloud no bigger than a human hand appears to be spreading into a storm of infinite dimensions'.[30]

Not the least of the stormy indications was that the Serbian principality, reinforced by a stream of Russian volunteers, was preparing to declare war on its Ottoman suzerain. Gladstone relayed to Granville his and Stratford's findings: that the government had been quite wrong to exclude themselves from the Berlin initiative, that Derby's recent version of events in Rumelia as a 'civil war' was quite wrong, and that the dispatch of the fleet to Besika Bay sent an unwarrantably encouraging signal to the Turks.[31] Stormy indications were not lacking now in domestic public opinion. Bishop Fraser of Manchester denounced the government's apparent countenance of the Turkish proceedings. This lead was taken up by the Assembly of the Convocation of Canterbury, which petitioned to address a resolution to the Eastern Christian ecclesiastical leaders 'to free the Church of England from the scandal of appearing to look on unmoved at the atrocities'.[32] High Churchmen, still smarting from the iniquities of the Public Worship Regulation Act, were much to the fore. Stirrings of the 'Nonconformist conscience' were also evident. By 20 July an acute, perceptive, and suspicious observer like Fitzjames Stephen could discern 'the beginning of an outbreak of pseudo-Christian John Bullism about the Bulgarians'. The sceptical *Saturday Review* detected the same lamentable thing, and deplored the ebullience of a popular sentimental feeling of 'high Christian excitement' which might possibly and very unfortunately 'determine the future policy of the country'.[33]

For Gladstone all this remained, as yet, a matter of potential rather than actual consequence. He was but little attuned to it, not in any degree ready. Official and authoritative confirmation of allegations was lacking. Relevant blue books were not yet issued. Lewis Farley, who had founded in December 1875 a League in Aid of the Christians of Turkey, did not see Gladstone at this time as canvassable. Most of July, while public alarm mounted at what seemed Britain's virtual complicity in horrific transactions, Gladstone spent in desultory activities. A 'laborious but interesting day' was taken up with an expedition to the docks and warehouses of London's East End. 'I was greatly struck, returning

Holborn way, with the now really great beauty of the City, as well as its astounding stir.'[34] Fence-mending with the Nonconformists was ever a matter of intent concern. He attended a 'conclave' at Newman Hall's 'with much interest and advantage'.[35] This event took place the day after Gladstone had declined a requisition from a group of Liberal MPs, led by Mundella and Evelyn Ashley, generally dissatisfied with the government's response to the rising public agitation, who asked Gladstone to preside at a public meeting. He declined also opportunities to take part in deputations to Derby. Gladstone would reserve any pronouncement until after the production of official papers and after a ministerial statement about future Eastern policy.[36] It was arranged eventually that Shaftesbury should take Gladstone's place at a meeting held under the auspices of Farley's League on 27 July, at Willis's Rooms.[37]

By this time Gladstone was beginning to stir himself into a more receptive frame of mind. Random and seemingly contingent events began to assume an integrated, significant shape: Bosnia, Suez, the Indian title, Besika Bay, perhaps now Bulgaria. There were insistent pressures from his ecclesiastical friends such as Malcolm MacColl and H. P. Liddon that he 'speak on the Eastern question, and tear away the mask from the fanciful pictures of Turkey wh. the Government & a portion of the press have presented to the public'.[38] There would be a debate in the Commons on 31 July. A Conservative motion called, as Gladstone pointed out to Granville, 'upon us *inter alia* to vote approval of the proceedings of the Government. This I for one cannot do. I can hardly suppose you or H. will do it.' Gladstone was clear that a 'very grave question' had been raised. 'I must speak my mind.' Gladstone urged the moving of an amendment leaving out words of approval and lamenting the refusal of the government to adopt the principle of the concert.[39] By now, also, Gladstone could envisage the possibility that a Liberal motion 'involving blame' might be an occasion of break with the 'front bench'. 'What seems absolutely necessary', he urged Granville, 'is, early conference of your principal friends.'[40] This was the first of many jolts which Granville and Hartington were to receive from Gladstone in the following months.

[3]

Even so, for all Gladstone's talk of imputing blame and of breaking if necessary from the front bench, his speech of 31 July criticizing the government's policy was not at all the speech for which MacColl had pleaded, or for which Farley had pleaded, such as to reach the Bosporus and be listened to by the Sultan. Old Lord Russell, indeed, who hankered for a return to Canning's policy of Christian emancipation, dismissed it with contempt for timidity and 'want of earnest purpose'. Gladstone looked back, not forward. His speech on 31 July was the complement to the speech he had made on 8 February congratulating the government for its adherence to the Andrassy Note. He regretted now the disruption of the European concert by the government's veto on the Berlin Memorandum. He deplored the giving of undue encouragement to the Turks. He denounced unworthy distrust of the good faith of Emperor Alexander II. He spoke as the only remaining member of the House of Commons responsible for the Crimean War. On that ground he declared himself 'not ashamed' to insist on the principle of reconciling any notions of Christian autonomy with strict observance of Turkish territorial integrity. An independent Slav state would be too problematical to contemplate. He could but hope that the government might yet discover a solution giving 'consolatory assurance' that the Crimean War had not been fought in vain. He mentioned the rumours of extensive and atrocious repression of the Bulgarians only to declare that it was an aspect into which he did not propose to enter.[41]

MacColl and other leading figures in the public agitation, such as the historian E. A. Freeman and W. T. Stead, editor of the Darlington *Northern Echo*, welcomed Gladstone's 'noble speech' *faute de mieux*. Freeman 'trembled' when he read the speech, shocked at the emphasis on Turkish integrity.[42] On this score Bishop Fraser of Manchester did not hesitate to make his irritation public. To them and many others, asking for 'consolatory assurance' as to the 'wicked Treaty' of Paris was to miss the whole point of what was happening in the East. Gladstone was luckier than he deserved in having Disraeli respond with a rebuke which was later elevated into a cherished accolade: 'in that debate Mr. Disraeli had to describe my speech as the only one that had exhibited a real hostility to the Government'.[43] Disraeli did this, of course, simply to exhibit Gladstone's isolation from the general approval which the Commons accorded to his policy. To Gladstone it became the one precious item of evidence he could put forward to mitigate his otherwise consistent record of unknowingness. 'It was', he confessed, 'however at that time an opposition without hope.' Gladstone thereupon 'went into the country' and 'mentally postponed all further action to the opening of the next Session'.[44]

Hence it was that Gladstone was in snug retreat at Hawarden, immersed congenially in Homer and theology, through the last days of the session. These were the days in which the first sensational reports of the American journalist J. A. McGahan, describing in horrific detail the scenes of atrocity, exploded in the *Daily News*. These were the days when the Foreign Office grudgingly admitted that there were grounds for concern (Vice-Consul Dupuis of Adrianople put the figures of the massacred at 'below 15,000 (*sic*)'). These were the days when public outrage ignited in earnest, with even Delane of *The Times* jumping on the bandwagon of agitation. These were the days when two debates in the Commons were forced by Liberal backbenchers, in default of any lead by their front bench or even presence on the part of Gladstone. On the last day of the session, 11 August, Disraeli, brought to bay by Evelyn Ashley, put up a vigorous defence. Briefed by the Foreign Office as to exaggerations and with memories of his own of the hysteria over the Indian Mutiny, he continued in his earlier sceptical and deprecatory vein about 'coffee-house babble' and his 'alleged want of sympathy with the sufferers by imaginary atrocities'. Doubtless, he allowed, there had occurred deplorable excesses; but the government's duty remained none-theless to defend and uphold the 'empire of England'.[45]* Disraeli reflected ruefully that the session had come to an end not a day too soon. The awkward issue would drop out of sight during the recess. Frank Hill of the *Daily News* left for his vacation on 12 August, equally not foreseeing 'the clearing storm which was about to break'.[46]

Of all the lackers of foresight, it was Gladstone who lacked most unforeseeingly. He had even allowed Granville to dismiss Russell's call for a return to the tradition of Canning as mere senile raving.[47] Nor did he lack foresight for want of evidence. He described the official Turkish account of the affair, issued early in August, to Granville as shocking in its cynical effrontery, 'a sheer & gross mockery'.[48] Argyll, Gladstone's colleague of 1854, wrote 'in fury' to Granville after reading the blue book published on 10 August. This aroused from Gladstone a faint hope that the subject of the massacres might not 'slumber through the recess'; but it was a hope without faith.[49] Gladstone had already written to Granville, with a slight inkling of *esprit de l'escalier*, that there were 'two subjects on which I should have *dwelt* but for the belief that the debate must last and that others would handle them: the Bulgarian atrocities, and the pretended colonisation of European provinces with Circassians, one of the worst things the Turks have done'. Gladstone hoped, in a somewhat leaderish tone, that Granville would 'make sure before the prorogation that the results of the enquiry on Bulgaria will be published at once, not bottled up until February'. 'As a party question this affords no despicable material, but there are much higher interests involved.' There was 'some-thing horrid in reflecting that, while horrors were going on, our fleet was at Besika Bay within a few hours sail and not only was not there to arrest them but was believed by the perpetrators to be there for the

---

* Disraeli closed his career in the Commons on 11 August: it was announced the following day that he was to go to the Lords as Earl of Beaconsfield.

purpose of securing their impunity'. Gladstone had retreated to Hawarden 'in the hope of finality', but he remained available in case of need. He went so far as to hope that the subject of the charges against Turkey '*might* even come up in an amendment to the Address next February'.[50]

It was not that further incitements were lacking. Madame Olga Novikov, a Russian lady whose salon Gladstone occasionally frequented on the strength of mutual ecclesiastical interests,[51] wrote to Gladstone an impassioned account of the heroic death of her brother, a volunteer in the Serbian service. Gladstone told Döllinger on 11 August, apropos of the Vatican's strongly anti-Orthodox slant on the Eastern crisis: 'We have I fear played an unworthy part in the Eastern question. But not so bad, by a great deal, as the Pope's.' Bishop Fraser rebuked Gladstone at a big public meeting at Manchester on 9 August for his obsession with Turkish territorial integrity. H. P. Liddon, the eminent High Church divine, preached an electrifying sermon at St Paul's on 13 August, followed up by a letter to the *Daily News* calling on some public personage to 'meet the need of the moment'.[52] But the delights of theology held Gladstone in a powerful attraction. He was deep in the problem of eternal damnation, 'a chief and favourite point of attack', inadequately met, in his view, by the Early Fathers up to St Athanasius. Before Gladstone's mind became excited to a pitch necessary to permit a change of mental gears and a turn in the direction of the Eastern question, he had to be convinced that that question promised, for him, the chief elements of what he had come to miss in politics ever since the last spasm in 1870 of the spirit of 1868: a 'special call', a regaining of '*vital power*', 'some one issue, clear, broad and straight', a '*cause*'. Until such an awareness came upon him of the possibility of a rapport with a manifestation of moral excitement on a popular level and massive scale, Gladstone lacked the ultimate incitement. It had to be 'the nation, not the classes'.[53]

That ultimate incitement was not long in coming. The pivotal moment came on 18 August. Scanning that day's *Daily News*, Gladstone's eye fell on a news item announcing that a rally of working men was to be held in Hyde Park to condemn the government's Eastern policy and demand the recall of Sir Henry Elliot as an accessory to the crimes of the Turkish regime. As Gladstone put it later, in terms expurgated by the pudic Morley, it suddenly came upon him that 'the game was afoot and the question yet alive'.[54] Gladstone's imagery of inspired opportunism was equally as dramatic in his version of the crucial event to the trade-union leader and Liberal MP Henry Broadhurst: the issue, recounted Gladstone, he had thought 'for the moment dead', and he had '(mentally) postponed action on it', when 'tidings of an intended working men's meeting in Hyde Park altered my plan and made me at once perceive that the iron was hot and that the time to strike had arrived'.[55] Truly it was the nation, not the classes. 'So I at once wrote and published on the Bulgarian case.'[56]

These vivid images are *ex post facto* by twenty years, in the ample maturity of Gladstone's visions of the simple righteousness of the masses as contrasted with the selfishness of the 'metropolitan' classes. It was in fact not for a further ten days that Gladstone put aside his notes on 'Future Retribution' (docketing in pencil in 1879, 'From this I was called away to write on Bulgaria')[57] and 'worked on a beginning for a possible pamphlet on the Turkish question'. Gladstone's initial idea seems to have been a speech. His Greenwich constituency was ever eager for this. And already at Hawarden he was confronted by massive deputations of Liberal excursionists.[58] This would require squaring Granville and Hartington. He began softening Granville up on 20 August.

There is to be a meeting for the Bulgarians in Hyde Park. The letter which notifies it asks for subscriptions for the expenses. I have half a mind to send them a trifle. Do you object?

And altogether I feel more inclined to say something, during the recess, on the Turkish policy, than I have been for any such escapade during the last four years.[59]

Given Gladstone's habitual precision in such calculations, his reference to 1872 would appear to relate to his painful experience in the matter of the *Alabama* arbitration: an opportunity, in other words, to strike back at his critics with a major statement in the field of foreign policy, on grounds more advantageous to him than at any time since the high days of the Italian cause. Such an opportunity was offered by the Liberal candidate in the by-election in Buckinghamshire consequent on Disraeli's elevation to the Lords. But, as Gladstone explained to Granville, he declined the opportunity, not wanting to excite speculation 'on my position in the party, and thus possibly to produce distrust & division'. But he really hoped 'that on this Eastern matter the pot will be kept boiling'.[60]

Gladstone broke cover and emerged publicly with his own contribution to keeping the pot boiling in the form of a letter in response to some supposedly perplexed working men who asked his advice as to whether or not they should join in the public agitation. Gladstone duly conferred the desired benediction, declaring that Lord Beaconsfield's manner of dealing with the question was so 'inadequate and unsatisfactory' that he could not but think it 'well' that people should 'seek opportunities to speak for themselves' in order to 'assist' the government to judge the best course for future policy.[61]

Charles Wordsworth, Bishop of St Andrews, visiting Hawarden on 29 August, noted the striking impression Gladstone made of being a 'busy, restless-minded man, if ever there was one'.[62] Gladstone had started work on a possible pamphlet the previous day. The 29th was the day that his advice to the perplexed working men was read to a protest meeting at Hackney.[63] That was the day also on which the preliminary report of Eugene Schuyler, the American Consul-General at Constantinople, establishing officially the facts of the atrocities, was published in the *Daily News*. The 'possible pamphlet' could now take authentic and authoritatively verified shape. But the escapade needed some further preliminary manipulation of the duumvirate of Liberal leaders. The most important item of business for the restless-minded Gladstone on 29 August was composing a letter to Granville in which he made a point of applauding Granville's 'nursing' of the Bucks by-election.

I agree with the Spectator . . . that the existence of the Government should be challenged in this Election on the ground of the Bulgarian massacres – and of their conduct about them and what hangs on to them.

Good ends can rarely be attained in politics without passion: and there is now, the first time for a good many years, a virtuous passion.

I am much struck by the indications of feeling that the Post (as well as the newspapers) brings me daily.

The question of speech and subscription is gone by; but I am in half, perhaps a little more than half, a mind to write a pamphlet: mainly on the ground that Parliamentary action was all but ousted.

Does this shock you?[64]

Granville confessed to being 'a little startled'. While he felt he must veto a speech, he could not object to a pamphlet. His only specific pleas at this stage were for mercy to Elliot and for not dedicating it to Russell ('It is too late'). And if Granville's approval was grudging, Hartington's disapproval was decided. He saw no merit in the notion of a pamphlet; and was scathing about Gladstone's complaint that 'Parliamentary action' had been 'ousted'. It was Gladstone who had ousted himself from the debates.[65]

The striking reference to a politics of 'virtuous passion' was indeed startling. Gladstone was clearly getting into an excited condition: a reversal of the previous pattern in which it was Gladstone who excited public enthusiasm, but not the less portentous for that. Gladstone's colleagues were well versed in their analyses of his needing (in Kimberley's formula) to have 'a strong current of opinion in his favour', or (in Selborne's formula) needing to have an excited public enthusiasm behind his 'heroic' politics. Granville and Hartington had every reason to guess that there was more than a hint of Gladstone's seeing the people's 'virtuous passion' as the means of embodying all the subordinate conditional clauses with which he had invariably qualified his yearnings for retirement. Such a 'change or growth' of 'public feeling', as Gladstone remarked to Elliot on 3 September, 'has been witnessed as I have not known all my life, and the only question now is how far it will go'.[66] Did Gladstone himself have glimpses of its going as far as to provide him, as the exponent of the 'future triumphs of sound and active liberalism', with the means of 'arresting some great evil or for procuring the nation some great good'? As W. T. Stead put it, the Crusades were no longer an enigma. Gladstone's urgent images of hunting and forging (the 'game was afoot', 'the iron was hot, and the time to strike had arrived') are not wholly reliable witnesses in this matter as they were coined twenty years after the event. Perhaps more indicative was Gladstone's interest in the provenance of the 'quotation or proverb "Vox populi vox Dei"'. Nine references from *Notes and Queries* were extracted by Panizzi's assistant Fagan for Gladstone's solemn contemplation.[67]

That was done the day after the appearance of Gladstone's pamphlet, *Bulgarian Horrors and the Question of the East*, on 6 September.* Despite impediments of lumbago, which confined him at times to bed, Gladstone struck off his response to the virtuous passion of the people in fine frenzy. On 3 September – a Sunday, but respect for the sabbath could not stay so holy a work – he left for London to make checks and revises at the British Museum in a state of effervescence, exclaiming to Catherine, 'This is the most extraordinary moment of my recollection.' In London he revised and corrected the text, resisting objections from Granville against the principle of full autonomy for Christians with only titular suzerainty. He complied reluctantly with Granville's advice against attacking Disraeli 'individually'.[68] It was also for Gladstone an 'act of some self-denial' on his part to follow Granville's advice to 'abstain from all notice of the conduct of the Court of Rome' and its British and Irish manifestations.[69] 'Between ourselves,' as he later wrote to Bright, 'I may mention that G. who received my pamphlet in proof wished me to generalize the concluding part but I thought that with the purpose I had in view it was absolutely necessary to propose something that the country would understand.'[70] That 'demophilic' purpose was precisely why the duumvirate and the front bench sensed the imminence of a 'break' between them and Gladstone. By April 1877 Gladstone could reflect that he had not a single supporter in the '*Upper* official circle' of the Liberal party. 'But had I in the first days of September asked the same body

---

* There is no definite article at the beginning of the title, in spite of innumerable authoritative suppositions to the contrary.

whether I ought to write any pamphlet I believe the unanimous answer would have been no.'[71]

By 5 September, after a final consultation with Granville and Harting-ton, printed copies of *Bulgarian Horrors and the Question of the East*, dedicated to Stratford de Redcliffe, were delivered by Murray's. Copies were dispatched copiously among the higher echelons of the political world, including Lord Beaconsfield. In high good humour of intellectual and emotional release Gladstone went off to the Haymarket theatre to see a farce. A friend of Beaconsfield's witnessed the curious spectacle of three empty stalls in front of him being occupied successively by Gran-ville, Gladstone, and then, trailing disconsolately, Hartington. Gladstone 'laughed very much' at the performance; 'Harty Tarty' 'never even smiled'.[72]

[4]

So was born what was hailed, with pardonable misapprehension, as the 'well-timed pamphlet'. MacColl was enchanted at the prospect of the 'no less glorious fruit' it would bear than the pamphlet on the 'far less heinous' atrocities of the Neapolitan regime. Clayden of the *Daily News* also rejoiced to be able to announce its publication, 'as I see day by day', he told Gladstone, 'from the vast number of letters which come by every post how people are everywhere wishing for some statement from you'. George Anderson, a Glasgow Liberal MP, expressed no doubt the general judgement of the public 'movement': 'It was the one thing wanted to guide rightly the grand spontaneous outburst of national indignation.' Granville, despite his qualms, wished Gladstone 'joy of the receipt of *the* pamphlet'. Its 'receipt' became an instantaneous legend. After the first day of public sales Gladstone could report proudly to Granville that it was 'alive and kicking: four and twenty thousand copies now printed, and they think it is not at an end'. Within four days, 40,000 copies were sold: within a month 200,000.[73]

Bulgarian Horrors was a rehash of Schuyler, McGahan, the blue books, and Gladstone's speech of 31 July, laced with virulent invective against the Turks very much in the manner of his 1858 *Quarterly Review* piece on 'The Past and Present Administrations', excoriating Palmerston's Crimean policy. Nothing in the *Horrors* of 1876 surpassed the abuse Gladstone heaped on the Turks in 1858 (the Ottoman Empire simply 'a great savage incursion of brute force', 'like a deluge of blood rained from the windows of heaven'); and, in doing so, with extraordinary prescience and perspicacity, Gladstone then defined a post-Palmerstonian politics which would find its accredited formative exponent in himself.[74] Just as he had his case for the Bulgarians already formulated in the case for the Romanians in 1858,[75] so had he his case also against the Turks.

Bulgarian Horrors had no particular literary merit except perhaps for the famous 'bag and baggage' phrase in the rhetorical peroration. The provenance for this was Stratford de Redcliffe;[76] but in any case it confused the issue. It was not helpful in proposing 'something that the country would understand'. Rather, it proposed something the country misunderstood. Gladstone demanded merely the extinction of Turkish 'administrative action' in Bosnia, the Herzegovina, and 'Bulgaria' (strictly, a non-existent entity). The fame of the bag-and-baggage phrase led to the widespread misapprehension that he had called for the expulsion of the Turks from Europe.[77]*

This misapprehension, fostered deliberately or mistakenly, undoubtedly did the agitation more good than harm. It helped to conceal the fact that beneath the rhetoric the substance of Gladstone's case continued moderate. Turkish territorial integrity remained the foundation, though Gladstone did not, as on 31 July, go out of his way to assert that he was not ashamed to stipulate this. His main practical point was the necessity of coming to an understanding with Russia. Derby commented aptly: 'The conclusion … falls short of what might be expected from the premises … A tame conclusion for so vehement an invective!'[79] However apt, Derby's comment missed the point. The significance of *Bulgarian Horrors* lies in its character as a unique response to a series of stimuli which coloured its form and content and made it the supremely representative expression of a passionate moment of history. Had it been more original and informative it would have been correspondingly less effective. *Bulgarian Horrors* succeeded so completely because it concentrated into a single utterance a profoundly excited public mood struggling for articulation. The essential point is that it was far less a case of Gladstone exciting popular passion than of popular passion exciting Gladstone.

The alleged 'right-timing' of *Bulgarian Horrors*[80] was a consequence of opportunism, not of insight. Gladstone scrupulously did not list his dramatic intervention of 1876 among the grand occasions of providen-

---

* Beaconsfield: 'None of the howlers have [sic] any proposal, practical or precise. Gladstone, more absurd than any of them. He writes a fiery pamphlet to prove, for ethnological reasons, that the Turks, as a race, shd. be expelled from Europe, & then finding what a fool he had made of himself, even before his speech [at Blackheath, 9 September], the only point of wh. was to show how this was to be done – he writes a letter to the "Times" to say he did not mean the expulsion of the Turkish nation, only of the Turkish ministers. No doubt, he meant only the expulsion of the ministers, but I doubt whether they were Turks. His pamphlet is really a "Bulgarian atrocity".'[78]

tially inspired conviction of an appreciation of a general situation and its result, leading to his forming a public opinion. As he put it to P. W. Clayden of the *Daily News*, 'you have led the people of England; and I am about to walk as best I can in your steps'.[81] Buckle's highly coloured picture of the malignant Gladstone as the 'old hunter, once more sniffing the scent', stalking his noble quarry with cunning patience, waiting for the right moment to strike and pull down his 'too successful rival', does Gladstone far too much credit for perspicacity; although, ironically, echoing unknowingly Gladstone's own image of the game being afoot.[82] And only the blurred interpretation of events later received could allow Morley to get away with his wholly mythic presentation of Gladstone's breast being agitated by a 'mighty storm', lit by the 'lurid glare' of the atrocities. Morley suppressed Gladstone's honest phrase about the game being afoot and in effect substituted his own figment about Gladstone's heroic response to a Byronic trumpet call.[83]

Gladstone later said of the Bulgarian agitation: 'I admit to me it has been an unexpected movement. I have been astonished at its commencement and its progress.' It came, as Gladstone saw it, 'suddenly', at a time when the 'natural leaders of local parties' were dispersed. It commenced, survived, and expanded as an affair of the people, unaffected by and uninfluenced by sophisticated calculations of policy and party prospects.[84] This, in a way, was to Gladstone its supreme virtue. Awareness that he and a great movement of the virtuous public mind had come once more into rapport was more than a little intoxicating: the 'first time for a good many years'. That it thereby contradicted, in its autonomous nature, Gladstone's own grand formulae* about the essential nature of the political process did not at the time seem important. It seemed less important that 'the people' had arrived at their own conclusions – unexpected and astonishing as Gladstone found it – than that those conclusions happened to coincide with Gladstone's own predispositions. Gladstone's formulae had to do with 'the people' being the means to ends defined by himself. The great test would come when next Gladstone would define a great end and set about forming and directing the 'materials' of the public mind for attaining it.

That test would not come for another decade. For the moment, the crucial point is the logical link between Gladstone's astonishment at an unexpected movement and his lateness in perceiving it and tardiness in jumping on to it. 'Late it is true,' as one of the more excited 'atrocity-mongers' put it of *Bulgarian Horrors*, 'but still in time to do immense good.'[86] It is only the grandeur of unforeseeable events to come which gives this statement its grotesque and comically patronizing air. It was

---

* Of 1856 and 1896 (see above, page 4).[85]

perfectly natural and legitimate in its time. Gladstone's own testimony to his slowness of observation and his natural but perhaps undue shrinking from recognizing claims made on him rules out entirely such suppositions as that he must have 'waited for nearly two months in a mood of very dangerous calm'.[87] Gladstone was not waiting, and his mood of calm was indeed simple nonchalance, embarrassingly innocent.[88]

This nonchalance had its roots in the fact that the affair was one of foreign policy, an area hitherto politically intractable to Gladstone other than in the case of Italy: the one case in which his opinions conformed to those of Palmerston and Russell. Awareness of a public sea change contrary to the 'national' or Palmerstonian tradition would not have come easily or readily to Gladstone. Disraeli in 1854 had extolled the 'British' school of politics of Palmerston and Russell against the 'Russian' school of politics of Aberdeen.[89] When in 1867 Gladstone, Aberdeen's heir, succeeded Russell as leader of the Liberal party, the 'national' tradition, without being positively repudiated, was decidedly at a discount. With the Black Sea and *Alabama* affairs to prompt him, Disraeli in 1872 set about restoring to the disinherited national party of England the national policy discounted by Gladstone. It was a seemingly profitable manoeuvre, tricked out with Disraeli's plausible doctrine about the inherently 'national' qualities of Toryism as against the inherently 'cosmopolitan' qualities of Liberalism, and tricked out also with the new evocation of Empire. As the Suez affair indicated, Gladstone had no reason to suppose that Disraeli would not continue to have a profitable run along those lines. And indeed he did, until he was stopped in his tracks by the 'cyclone out of Bulgaria'.[90] Once Gladstone saw the game afoot and the iron hot for striking, he launched himself into action of undelimited possibility. 'From that time forward,' he later wrote, 'until the final consummation in 1879–80 I made the Eastern question the main business of my life. I acted under strong sense of individual duty without a thought of leadership: nevertheless it made me leader again whether I would or no.'[91] On the way to that consummation Gladstone formally equipped the Liberal party, at Midlothian in 1879, with his 'right' principles' of foreign policy to replace the remnants of the 'national' tradition.

[5]

There were to be many twists and turns on the way to 1879–80. Engaged to address his Greenwich constituents on 9 September, amid the furore created by *Bulgarian Horrors*, Gladstone found himself awkwardly placed in the dual role of abdicated leader and tribune of the oppressed. This made the speech he delivered to the great demonstration on Blackheath so curiously indecisive an event. In essence, it was a declaration by Gladstone that he still hoped for satisfaction from the government. His immediate object was to coax Granville into some kind of open endorsement of his attitude and action. He completed arrangements for the Blackheath meeting in Granville's dining room at Carlton House Terrace, which place he found more convenient to use as his field headquarters than his own house in Harley Street. He reported transactions to Granville with a subtly baited hook: 'The [Greenwich] people asked if you would go. I said I thought if you did you would like to have the option of going quietly.' Gladstone confided to his wife: 'Will Granville go I wonder.' If he did it would be 'a proof that his mind is working on and that he sees more ripeness in the time'. But Granville refused to be drawn. Not less than ten thousand people gathered under dripping umbrellas on Blackheath, but Granville was not among them, even 'quietly'.

Granville saw little 'ripeness' in the time. He had written to Hartington at the beginning of the month about the letters he received, as Hartington probably did also, 'reproaching the leaders of the party for remaining mute'. Granville had not answered them, and thought it 'very unlikely' that he would 'avail' himself of 'any opportunity to speak on the matter'. It was a question as to whether Hartington had 'better do so, or not'. It happened that Hartington was engaged to speak at the Sheffield Cutlers' dinner, and supposed he could not avoid saying something about the 'atrocities'. He consulted Granville on the best 'line' to take; and the outcome was that he treated the agitation and Gladstone very respectfully but yet made no outright condemnation of the government's Eastern policy.[92]

The scepticism of the Liberal leaders was powerfully reinforced by their Whig associates. Lord Halifax wrote to Granville in a state of disquiet. 'Of course you will see Gladstone before he appears on Blackheath & I hope that you will impress on him the wisdom of looking before he leaps.' The populace, it seemed to Halifax, were 'running a little wild on the Bulgarian atrocities'. Henry Reeve, editor of the *Edinburgh Review*, also wrote indignantly in the same vein. Harcourt, willing enough to attack the government but full of distaste for the possible return of Gladstone to a leading role, formed a link between the Whigs and those Radicals such as Dilke who also disliked the idea of Gladstone's return. Dilke wrote to Harcourt after the Sheffield Cutlers' dinner speech: 'Isn't Hartington doing his work splendidly.' However, Lord and Lady Sydney were pleased and proud to put their house at Frognal, Foots Cray, at Gladstone's disposal for the Blackheath meeting, and even tried to persuade Granville to attend. In the event, Sydney was able to report to

Granville that the demonstration was a 'great success'; the 'Assemblage was large & respectable. Not Rags but people in Cloth Coats & Top Hats . . .'[93]

Despite the respectability of the assemblage, the Blackheath demonstration had about it much of the character of a great revivalist rally.* In this respect it exhibited much of the inner nature of the atrocities agitation. W. T. Stead was an easily impressionable young man, but it still counts for something that to the end of his days he placed Blackheath among the most memorable scenes of his life. George Holyoake, who had witnessed Gladstone's first great reception at the hands of the masses at Newcastle in 1862, came down from Bedford to witness the 'mighty protest'.† Under the spell of enlightenment cast upon him by the *Daily News* report on 'Working Men and the War in the East', Gladstone made of the Blackheath demonstration a solemn affirmation of his conviction that the agitation sprang, pure and undefiled by party and political motives, from the very bedrock of morality and righteousness in public affairs, the simple, undesigning conscience of the masses.

But the almost religious intensity of the occasion tended, as in the case of *Bulgarian Horrors*, to obscure the moderation of its content. The real significance of the Blackheath speech, as far as Gladstone's personal relation to the agitation is concerned, lies in what he did not say, or refused to say. The cry 'We want a leader!' burst spontaneously from the crowd, ringing out again and again according to Stead's report.[96]‡ Gladstone evaded the demand by rejoining that when a nation had a good purpose in view a leader would always be found. These words, wrote Stead, were caught up eagerly by the crowd to mean that Gladstone was willing to take his place at their head,¶ whether or not he actually meant this. Gladstone remained silent in the face of continued importunities. Stead, to whom Gladstone's resignation from the leadership had been a 'personal sorrow, a grief akin to that of bereavement', consoled himself by reflecting that Gladstone at least did not directly repudiate the crowd's salute. He also realized that any decision by Gladstone ultimately to declare himself would depend mainly on the course taken by the government. Perhaps the clearest expression of the paradoxical

---

* An interesting example of this spirit is a long poem in Wordsworthian blank verse, presented to G: *Lines Written by a Young Man, (a London Clerk), One of the Multitude Which, on Saturday Last, Assembled on Blackheath, to See and to Hear Mr. Gladstone.*[94]

† 'It was a great & generous thing to come & speak to us in the rain, & mist, & wind. Voices in the streets speak only of gratitude and gladness. Horror-stricken, indignant, articulate, but aimless, the nation craved direction it could trust. It seems now as though the Humanity of the world had spoken in your voice.'[95]

‡ The *Daily Telegraph* report refers to the 'perfectly logical cry' of 'We will have you for our leader'.

¶ 'We will go back to you, Mr Gladstone.'[97]

nature of Gladstone's position in the speech is to be found in the mixture of surprise, relief, and bewilderment evident in the comments of the leading pro-government organs.

Gladstone continued to be importuned privately as well as in public. A workman of Hertford wrote to him on the theme that it was 'time we had a Leader': 'You told us we Must Be up and Doing and we must have our old Statesman for our Leader.' 'O Sir,' cried the Warden of Cavendish College, Cambridge (in his 'private capacity'), 'will you not hear in this great crisis the voice of God in the voice of the people?' There was indeed little likelihood of Gladstone's failing to do this sooner or later, if the interest he had evidently displayed in the *Notes and Queries* references to *Vox populi vox Dei* was any indication.

Embarrassed by these and many other importunities, Gladstone wrote to Adam, the Liberal Chief Whip: 'I am a follower & not a leader in the Liberal party and nothing will induce me to do an act indicative of a desire to change my position. Any such act would be a positive breach of faith on my part towards those whom I importuned as I may say to allow me to retire, and whom I left to undertake a difficult and invidious office.'[98] Gladstone's problem was, in short, that while the voice of the people was the voice of God, the official voice of the Liberal party remained the voice of the duumvirate, Lords Granville and Hartington. The embarrassment which Gladstone felt in his position in relation to the party leaders and to the party as a whole was now matched by a determination to see that the Bulgarian question should have full political justice done to it. This uneasy equilibrium of conflicting feelings, characteristic scruple and reluctance against equally characteristic tenacity and persistence, sets the theme of Gladstone's conduct as a 'follower & not a leader in the Liberal party' not merely for the period immediately after the *Horrors* and Blackheath, but for the years up to 1879–80 also. Nevertheless, though a long-drawn-out process to its final conclusion, the central issue of the problem was for all practical purposes worked out in the few weeks following 6 September.

Gladstone's difficulty in persuading Granville and Hartington into a more 'advanced' view of the Bulgarian question was much increased by the absence of a strong atrocity-conscious group in the upper levels of the party. The Duke of Argyll alone approached Gladstone in the warmth of his feelings. Lowe was also warm, but his personal hatred of Beaconsfield was so notorious and the decline of his reputation so complete as to make him a dubious asset at best. Bright's sympathies were strictly limited. Stafford Northcote, the Chancellor of the Exchequer, fell in with Bright on a railway journey in mid-September and reported to Beaconsfield: 'He was far from satisfied with Gladstone, though he did not like directly to abuse him; but he tried to impress on me that the true thing for England to do was to withdraw altogether . . . and let "natural forces" have full play.' Harcourt remained essentially Hartingtonian. Neither Childers nor Goschen looked with favour upon the agitation. Forster, on the strength of a visit to Constantinople, returned unimpressed with schemes of Christian liberation. The peers generally were apathetic.[99] As events were soon to prove, Gladstone overestimated greatly the amount of thoroughgoing support he could call on from the Commons rank and file. In that sense there was more than a whiff of 1866–7 and 1871–3 in the air. And the situation was complicated further by the fact that those at the head of the section of the party more or less aligned with Gladstone on the Eastern question were Radicals like Mundella, Fawcett, Anderson, and Chamberlain, men eager for Gladstone to supplant Granville and Hartington. Eventually, in 1877, Gladstone found himself obliged, for the sake of the Eastern question, to strike a bargain with the most important of them, Chamberlain;* and this was certainly not the least significant of the consequences implicit in the situation of September 1876.

Chamberlain himself had only very recently joined the Liberal party in the House of Commons, but with Birmingham solidly behind him and through his control of the Nonconformist-inclined Education League, which he was preparing to use as the nucleus of a national Liberal organization, he was already a major political force in his own right. In conjunction with John Morley of the *Fortnightly Review*, he was planning the coming Radical campaign on the basis of Church disestablishment and the county franchise. But the Bulgarian atrocities provided even better immediate grist to Chamberlain's mill.

Chamberlain calculated that Gladstone, if not exactly usable, could not fail to be useful. He wrote to Dilke: 'If he were to come back for a few years (he can't continue in public life for very much longer) he would probably do much for us, & pave the way for more.'[100] Chamberlain's confidences in this matter to Dilke were indiscreet, for Dilke took the Eastern question seriously for its own sake. Though willing to work with Chamberlain for the success of the Radical programme, he also took his Radicalism too seriously to imagine that Gladstone would be its unwitting agent. Dilke reported to Harcourt that Chamberlain wished Gladstone ' "formally to resume the reins" – and shows profound dislike of Hartington, founded on no reasons at all'. This confirmed Harcourt's suspicions that the 'extreme crew' were using the opportunity provided by the atrocities agitation to demand the deposition of Granville and Hartington and the recall of Gladstone; which consideration he passed on to Granville. Harcourt remained confident, however, that Gladstone was a spent force, and that there would be no 'return from Elba'.[101]

---

* See below, pages 202–3.

Harcourt's and Dilke's hopes of keeping Gladstone out were ruined by the intransigence of both the Whigs and the government, who thus cancelled each other out and let Chamberlain's thesis emerge victorious by default. As Gladstone tried to entice Granville into patronage of the Blackheath affair, so Carnarvon attempted to draw Beaconsfield back to a more conciliatory attitude. He was decisively rebuffed; as also was Salisbury, who urged unavailingly that the Palmerstonian tradition was played out, and that a completely new approach was required. Disdaining all 'quack' remedies, Beaconsfield prepared for a defiant counterattack in a forthcoming address at Aylesbury.

[6]

Beaconsfield's evident intransigence, seconded publicly by Derby, forced Gladstone back on the Bucks by-election. 'There is nothing for it but "the polls"', he told Granville; with the watchword 'Bucks Bucks Bucks'. He gave careful and fussy instructions to Granville as to how the campaign should be conducted. 'Pray continue', he added, on a curiously imperious note, as if once more issuing directives as leader, 'to give your mind to this.'[102]

Gladstone was looking also, however, beyond Bucks to 'polls' in a wider sense. He kept pressing and coaxing Granville with what must have been the rather irritating technique of assuming that Granville was really in substantial agreement with him. He also made efforts to carry Bright with him.

It may seem inconsistent in me to have been very active up to a certain point and then to speak of stopping short. This however is as I think my unavoidable position. My old Crimean responsibilities forced me forward: my position in the party as a leader who has abdicated holds me back. In my original pamphlet ... I did all in my power to keep off the ground of party, for if the matter is decided on that ground I have some fear of being dragged out of a retirement which though partial I had made real.

Gladstone desired therefore 'to leave the further prosecution of this great business', if he could, in the hands of 'others'. Bright's position, Gladstone pointed out, was 'far more free'. Bright had neither the 'old responsibility' to drive him forward, 'nor exactly the same limiting considerations' to hold him back. Bright, however, felt himself no less bowed down under a sense of limiting considerations; and clearly, as indeed he had already indicated to Gladstone, he was not to be lured into this 'great business'.[103]

For all his resistance to the mounting pressure of importunities to speak out more boldly than he had done at Blackheath and his reluctance to become the 'leader of the whole of England', Gladstone remained extremely restless and warm for action. Behind the reserve and the apology there was always present a sense of an impending breaking loose. He could not refrain from writing to *The Times* and *Daily News* of 16 September attacking Derby's 'mystifications' and backing Hartington's call for an autumn session, as a 'lever', as he explained to Granville.

Gladstone's next move was to embark on a series of private country-house visits in the north. He still adhered to his doctrine against 'over-activity'; and his motives in undertaking such a tour were undoubtedly more innocent than otherwise. But it did not require much perspicacity to predict – and Hartington so predicted – that a 'private' tour by Gladstone in the north in such circumstances had no chance of remaining private. Possibly Gladstone had half-consciously at the back of his mind a vague idea of testing the state of public feeling and perhaps helping to jog Granville a little into a less negative approach.[104]

The situation was getting too tense for Hartington's comfort. Delaying only to attend the Doncaster races, he departed for Constantinople via Vienna on the night of 14 September, 'with the Duchess of Manchester, accompanied by the Duke', as *The Times* chose to put it, to Chamberlain's rather malicious amusement. Gladstone apparently had no inkling of this escapade; he asked Granville whether by slip of the pen he had written 'Constantinople' instead of 'Kimbolton'. Harcourt commented to Granville: 'H. did (as he always does) the wisest thing he could in going away. But the situation is very uncomfortable.' Apart from the question of comfort, Hartington was also undoubtedly influenced by the example of Forster. By following him Hartington could trump Forster's trick.

Hartington saw Granville briefly before departing and expressed anxiety that Gladstone's going north would cause demonstrations that would 'put the rest of the country the wrong way'. Granville immediately passed this consideration on to Gladstone, though probably with little hope that it would deter him. Other Whigs were nervous about Gladstone's attitude and intentions. Lord Bessborough told Granville that Gladstone seemed to have 'gone wild'. No doubt the Turks were 'naughty'; but Lord Bessborough understood that the Christians were just as bad, so he could not 'quite go' with his party in the 'present crisis'. It must have been galling for Granville to see the 'party' thus naively identified with Gladstone's viewpoint rather than his own. Bessborough was pleased to see that Granville had declined to attend a Guildhall demonstration on the grounds that the non-partisan and spontaneous character of the agitation must not be compromised; but many Whigs failed to be reassured. The Rothschilds, resentful at the pressure put on them in Bucks, were practically in open revolt, and by the beginning of October had 'gone Tory altogether'.[105]

This gave the cue to the Jewish community in general to abstain from the agitation. Jewish experience of emancipated Christians made them appreciative of Ottoman tolerance. Gladstone felt he had cause to deplore deeply the 'manner in which what I may call Judaic sympathies, beyond as well as within the circle of professed Judaism, are now acting on the question of the East'.[106] The apostasy of the Levy-Lawsons of the *Daily Telegraph* was a painful case in point. Perhaps unavoidably, the issue of Beaconsfield's Jewish provenance obtruded. The agitation provoked by the Turkish atrocities in Bulgaria came to have quite a distinct anti-Semitic tinge to it. Freeman was particularly virulent. Gladstone himself confided to Argyll his 'strong suspicion that Dizzy's crypto-Judaism has had to do with his policy. The Jews of the East *bitterly* hate the Christians; who have not always used them well.'[107] Already critical of Manning's anti-Orthodox lead to the Roman Catholics, Gladstone would also have cause to deplore Irish Catholic unwillingness to see in the agitation anything beyond hypocritical English deployment of liberationist philanthropy at the square of the distance.

At Aylesbury on 20 September, the eve of the Bucks poll, in a speech of deliberate violence, Beaconsfield used the official Report of the Secretary of the Constantinople Embassy on the Bulgarian insurrection as a basis of an assertion to the effect that it was the work of the 'Secret Societies of Europe'. Disdaining to pretend that the Eastern policy of the government had for the time the support of the nation, Beaconsfield defied the agitation and denounced Gladstone's activities as 'worse than any of those Bulgarian atrocities which now occupy attention'.[108] After the speech (of which there were rumours of tipsiness) Beaconsfield told Colonel Napier Sturt: 'I think I have given that Greenwich Tartuffe his quietus.'[109]*

The Liberal figures in the Bucks election were creditable, but the Conservatives held the seat, much to the Queen's relief.† Granville pointed the moral to Gladstone that anti-Russian feeling was still strong and that, according to reports he had received, many Liberal votes had been given to the Conservative candidate. He pointed out that the Liberal party would probably face similar defections in a vote of censure in a

---

* In response to Stead's enquiries as to Beaconsfield's alleged tipsiness, G asked 'permission to be silent. I have been too much in personal conflict on political matters with Lord B. to be altogether a fair judge of incidents connected with his utterances.'[110]
† She was eloquent on 'that incomprehensible Mr Gladstone', and the 'disgraceful conduct of that mischief-maker and firebrand'.[111]

special autumn session, certainly more than from the Conservative side. Sydney wrote to Granville on 2 October that the Liberals were far from united. Some did not like to 'force the Executive in Foreign Policy'; others thought that the time had gone by for sensational meetings. Sydney himself agreed with the latter, and also objected to a 'Slavonic Empire'. 'I confess I do not see', he concluded, 'that we should do much good by an Autumn Session . . . I think that we are playing the Russian game too much & do not care for more meetings.' Harcourt was full of accounts of the restlessness of the 'Brooksites' and the 'Commercial men like Norwood Samuels & C. who find their pecuniary interests greatly damaged by the present state of things taking very adversely to the agitation'. And Hartington reported from Constantinople to his father the Duke that Christian autonomy was out of the question: the Christians were 'utterly unfit for public duties of any kind'.[112]

Aylesbury certainly diminished greatly Gladstone's lingering hopes for a change of heart on the part of the government. He was now convinced that a special autumn session would be necessary; only 'within the walls of Parliament by hook or by crook we can force them forward'. Gladstone insisted that he would 'very much rather they should come forward without it', for he was 'selfishly anxious' to avoid a 'ministerial crisis', though he could not say that it would in his judgement be a 'public evil'.[113]

Meanwhile, Gladstone's round of northern visits threatened to become a triumphal progress. He described to Frank Hill of the *Daily News* his impressions of the immensely strong popular feeling in the north and how he was having the 'utmost difficulty' in preventing his visits from changing into a 'tour of propagandism: which under the circumstances would be extremely objectionable'. He refused numerous invitations to appear or speak on the grounds of avoiding political 'notoriety', a consideration, he insisted, which applied 'in a peculiar manner' to himself. In particular, he declared that he would not let himself be provoked into public altercation by Beaconsfield's Aylesbury speech. In reply to a committee organizing a workmen's meeting in St James's Hall, he announced that, now that he had laid his views before his constituents and the public, the question ought to be left to the 'calm but resolute' consideration of the country. At Alnwick Castle he recorded: 'At every point on the road there were keen expressions of the public feeling, which it was impossible to escape. I never saw the like on any former occasion.'[114]

In fact Gladstone found it impossible to let Beaconsfield's provocation pass wholly without protest. At Staindrop station in South Durham, on the 23rd, he allowed himself to be 'carried away' into self-vindication by the frantic importunity of the crowd. His main theme clearly pointed a moral for Granville. He protested against Beaconsfield's demand, in effect, that the Liberals should efface themselves as a party on the Bulgarian question. If the Liberal party had been at fault, Gladstone asserted – and here he spoke with an only too full consciousness of his own fault – it had been in the direction of 'too great reluctance, too great reserve, too great tardiness'.[115]

Of the Staindrop indiscretion there were twinges of guilt: 'I shall soon seem a rogue and imposter.'[116] There were, more important, preliminary indications that something in the way of a mass popular adulation more portentous than the Tyneside and Merseyside episodes of the 1860s was in the making. The 'leadership of the nation' was being pressed upon him.

Staindrop was a premonitory indication that Gladstone's restraint was wearing thin. He wrote to Granville of his many refusals to address public meetings, but was careful to make allowance for prospective contingencies: at any time 'a local case might arise'; and 'a new question has come up, raised by Dizzy's declaration that he is not backed by the country conjoined with the fact that they are persevering in a disapproved policy without dissolving or consulting Parliament'. And Gladstone's particular desire was to hear what Granville was now thinking on the Bulgarian question and whether he had 'advanced' any further in considering the matter, 'that I may have regard to it even in charging my pocket pistol in the shape of short letters which I cannot altogether avoid writing & which sometimes struggle into notice'. It was clear that Gladstone's demand for 'decisive measures' would eventually force a more or less definite breach with Granville.

The Times was quick – ominously quick – to see the implications of Staindrop, and press them heavily upon Gladstone. 'To rouse the country against the Ministry without being prepared, if necessary, to accept the place and task of the Ministry would be unworthy of a serious politician.' Delane was beginning to trim again. He emphasized now the need to give the government time and freedom to implement its policy. He had already congratulated Granville for the 'safe-footed caution' which had kept Granville out of 'the pools into which others have stepped'. Staindrop was a small, but a very deep and splashy pool indeed. One of those spattered with mud was Lord Halifax. Alarmed, he wrote off to Granville full of misgiving that Gladstone would not 'do himself much good' by what he said. 'One outbreak of his feeling might have passed – but it has come now, to what quiet people even on our side may not unjustly characterise as an agitation.'[117]

Forster returned from Constantinople early in October as a further buttress to Granville's negative attitude. He impressed Granville with his conclusion that autonomy for Christians would be impossible to establish without a military occupation by the powers. In general he was pessimistic; and this coincided conclusively with the judgement agreed on by both Granville and Ailesbury that Gladstone was '*much too sanguine*' as to the readiness of the party as a whole to go ahead in a policy of emancipation in cooperation with Russia. In a speech at Bradford Forster administered a shock of disappointment to the agitation. In reply to Gladstone's request for a statement of the 'advance' of his outlook, Granville rejected the idea of pressing the government with a demand for a special session and suggested that Gladstone keep himself quiet: 'Your progress in the North has been an immense triumph, & the greater for the privacy which you have endeavoured to maintain. But if I were you, I should continue to avoid further utterances for the present moment, which appears critical.'[118]

This uncompromising negative forced Gladstone to declare himself. He remained extremely sensitive on the personal level. His 'repeated assurances', Ailesbury reported to Granville, 'that he looked upon you as the Leader of the Liberal party were quite touching to listen to'. But he realized that the logic of his opinions and his conscience made it essential for him to assert full freedom of action. He was not impressed by Forster's doubts. He resented Forster's Bradford speech: 'He should not have thrown me over *nominatum*.'[119]* 'Reflection', he told Granville, had already brought him to the conclusion that 'in all likelihood, after the practical emancipation of the three Turkish Provinces, a temporary military occupation on a small scale might be necessary, for purposes of police'. He had already been 'driven', he added, to the conclusion that he must make a further 'utterance' following the course of transactions. He decided to adhere to this conclusion notwithstanding Granville's opinion, to which he attached 'great weight'. He felt himself compelled to advise 'upon the career of that national movement' which he had 'tried hard to evoke and assisted in evoking'. Gladstone recognized Granville's special responsibility for the party, but asserted his own special responsibility as a maker of the Crimean War. He shared Ailesbury's regret that Granville had not been able to see his way to a 'more advanced and definite policy', but he was not at all inclined to recriminate. He abandoned all immediate hope that Granville would see a 'ripeness' in the time, though he could not help interpreting wishfully that Granville thus held himself in hand only for the purpose of holding his party in hand.

Nevertheless, whether willing or not to accept finally the painful fact that Granville really was in fundamental disagreement with him, Gladstone was quite ready to accept the consequences of it. He told

---

* i.e., by name.

Granville that he no longer felt under an obligation to attempt to keep in step with the party. He would be henceforth an 'outside workman', preparing 'materials' for Granville and the party to 'manipulate' and then to 'build into a structure'. For though he did not wish to 'shut the door' upon the government, he despaired of them, 'after so many invitations and so many refusals'. He was 'convinced that a virtual emancipation ought to take place', and he rather believed it would; and at any rate he felt himself 'bound to promote it as one of the public'. 'The distinction involved in these words may be fine,' he concluded, 'but I think I have only to observe it as well as I can.'

All was infinite gentleness. Few clashes of opinion on an important political issue have been so muted. It was nonetheless a real clash, and it involved a real break. Gladstone entered into what promised to be a distinctly new phase in his part in the atrocities agitation and the Eastern question.[120]

[7]

Meanwhile, however, the agitation of August and September was losing impetus. A 'reaction' had begun to manifest itself. The simple fact was that Gladstone had failed to fulfil the implicit promise given to the agitation in his pamphlet. The energy and impetus which in the nature of the case it was Gladstone's special function to contribute faded away in the weeks of futile effort to persuade Granville to accept the role of leadership which Gladstone at Blackheath had deliberately left vacant. Leaving the question to the 'calm but resolute' consideration of the country was not enough to sustain the agitation past the first week or so of October. Thus, at the very point where Gladstone came at last to the conclusion that he would have to go ahead without the active assistance of the leaders of the party, the atrocities agitation, the instrument he was to use, had exhausted its natural momentum.

Consequently the paradox emerged that Gladstone, the great leader of Progress, Freedom, and Humanity, as Newman Hall, on behalf of the Nonconformist community had hailed him,[121] continued for almost the whole of the remaining three months of the agitation period to be essentially a figure in the background. The saving element of the agitation was found in the idea of a national convention or conference, based on the precedents of the anti-slavery and anti-Corn Law agitations. This idea provided a far better alternative to the abortive scheme of a second full-scale series of protest meetings projected by Stead. It was much more practicable than either the project for a 'Bulgarian Sunday' or the proposal for a national petition which were being put forward. This latter was, as Bright objected, 'cumbersome', and moreover the very principle had been discredited by the Chartist fiasco. Anti-slavery and anti-Corn Laws, on the contrary, presented precedents of success to be in every way emulated. There were many natural connections, moral and personal, between the Bulgarian agitation and the anti-slavery and Corn Law movements; and nothing could be a more logical climax and culmination of a nationwide series of local meetings than a great central national demonstration. This concept had a further advantage: it would to a very great extent, if successful, compensate for the absence of Parliament, for the prospect of forcing the government's hand in this respect became increasingly recognized as doubtful. A national demonstration would, in effect, be a kind of out-of-doors, substitute parliament, all the better for not containing a majority hostile to the agitation and its programme, and a minority including many whose attitude was at best lukewarm.

Initial impediments to the conference plan – mainly from Chamberlain, who attempted to hijack it as a prototype of his own project for a national Liberal federation with Gladstone's patronage as its seal and symbol – left the 'agitation-mongers' for the time at a loss. 'What next?' enquired Stead on 16 October. Gladstone himself could hardly have been less perplexed than Stead. The logic of the situation did not point clearly, as it had done at the time of the *Horrors* and Blackheath, to a path of action. By 7 October Gladstone had made it clear to Granville that he would no longer consider himself bound by normal constraints of ordinary party membership; yet the period following 7 October was for Gladstone one of anticlimax. At the beginning of September his hesitation had been for want of will; now it was for want of 'adequate means'. He pottered about in a rather Micawberish way – arranging discussions between Samuel Morley and Frank Hill, receiving Bulgarian and Servian delegates, getting Liddon to have a treatise written on the evil influence of the Koran on the civil government of non-Muslims, supplying Stead with 'clews' for editorial policy, writing an article for the *Contemporary Review* defending Russian policy in Central Asia. This last made a rather bad impression.[122]* Then a government success in a by-election in South Shropshire came as a further discouragement; and Gladstone admitted to Granville that the great political reaction towards the Liberal party which he had hoped might arise out of the Eastern question clearly was not forthcoming. And

---

* Already the *Saturday Review* had invited G to contradict the 'scandalous report' that he had authorized a 'friend' to translate the *Horrors* into Russian (21 October 1876, 493). A Russian translation did in fact appear in 1876 under the auspices of the St Petersburg section of the Slavonic Committee. The translators were C. P. Pobedonostsev, a member of the Council of State and later famous as the Procurator of the Orthodox Holy Synod, and K. N. Bestuzhev-Ryumin.

little thanks Gladstone was getting from many sections of the party for his trouble. Lord Spencer, a Gladstonian Whig, complained to Hartington from Marleston, Northants, that he was 'amazed & horrified' at the tone of the Liberals thereabouts. 'They are simply mad agst. Gladstone & Russia.' A good indication of the general sense of anticlimax in the situation is John Morley's wistful half-complaint in the *Fortnightly* that if only Gladstone could be induced to place himself distinctly at the head of the movement for promoting the success of the agitation, it would gather strength and 'all indistinctness of aim would disappear'.

Far from placing himself at the head of the movement, Gladstone, to all appearances quite as much out of the running as he had been in mid-August, positively discouraged proposals put to him by Mundella and the Sheffield group to stage a rally of the agitation's forces. He had already forbidden Adam, the Liberal Whip, to entertain the project, mooted at Edinburgh, of a banquet in his honour, where much might have been done to revive flagging spirits. More clearly than ever, Gladstone depended utterly upon an agitation in being, owing nothing to his own efforts. Hartington, who arrived back in England shortly before 20 October, and who had complained to his father the Duke about Gladstone's 'exciting the agitation', now had the satisfaction of hearing from Gladstone himself that though he received 'much communication from parties anxious for further action', he deprecated such ideas.[123]

Hartington returned from Constantinople in much the same mind as Forster, with no faith in the feasibility of political autonomy for the Christians, and convinced that Derby's policy was sound. Tactfully, it was left to Hartington's brother and Gladstone's nephew-in-law and family favourite Frederick Cavendish to 'break' the news to Gladstone. This would hardly have come, as in the case of Forster, as a surprise and disappointment to Gladstone. Both he and Hartington took pains to keep some kind of bridge over the gap between them. Gladstone rather wishfully stressed that there was no fundamental difference in principle; and Hartington trusted that such disagreement as there was would not be made 'too evident'. Hartington's position was made more difficult by the sudden outburst of Lord Fitzwilliam, a Whig magnate, who took it upon himself to denounce Gladstone and the agitation in the name of the Whigs and the greater part of the leading elements of the Liberal party. Hartington succeeded in smoothing over party differences in a speech at Keighley early in November, by which he contrived to please not only Mundella, Argyll, Ailesbury, and T. B. Potter among the 'atrocity-mongers', but also Harcourt and Lord Grey on the anti-agitation wing. Compared to the shock administered by Forster, Hartington let the agitation down very lightly. But behind the confusing smokescreen of superficial amiability, Hartington remained as uncompromisingly negative as ever. Lord Spencer 'guessed' that Hartington was 'more anti-Russian than appeared'; and Acton later reported to Gladstone that Hartington was, in reality, less near agreeing with Gladstone than he had chosen to say.[124]

There was a comical interlude at Hawarden at the beginning of November, with a visit by Tennyson and his son Hallam. 'Tennyson read his *Harold*: it took nearly 2½ hours.' Willy Gladstone fell into a fit of barely repressed giggles, and Gladstone's daughters were excruciated by their fears that their father's struggles to stay awake might fail.[125] Tennyson had been rather a disappointment, declining Gladstone's urging that he emulate his Polish sonnets of the 1830s with something for the Bulgarians. Tennyson was too staunchly Russophobe. To escape Gladstone's pestering he eventually composed a sonnet on Montenegro. *Harold* was, however, quoted by Gladstone in the 'utterance' of which he had warned Granville on 7 October, 'The Hellenic Factor in the Eastern Problem', published in the December issue of the *Contemporary Review*. Gladstone's object was to establish a claim on behalf of the Greek provinces still under Ottoman rule to have an equal share in the emancipation movement being claimed by the Serbs and Bulgars. This was Gladstone's first full and mature formulation of his political philhellenism in a situation in which hitherto the Greeks had benefited ironically little from his somewhat misconceived philhellenic reputation. He cited the precedent of Britain's ceding the Ionian Islands to Greece in 1862 for all it was worth – 'or rather, for much more than it was worth'.[126]

A conference of the powers was now belatedly arranged to take place at Constantinople at the end of the year to persuade the Turks to accept a programme of reforms to be supervised by Europe. Lord Salisbury, the Secretary of State for India, was to be the British plenipotentiary. Gladstone's advice to Salisbury was that a British plenipotentiary on such an occasion should recall the spirit of Canning ('one of the most brilliant names in our political history' and 'one of the names dearest to the heart of Greece') and the spirit of Byron (a 'name which might yet supply a guiding light to some British statesman').[127] Salisbury's was a temperament utterly immune to such inspirations. On the other hand, he had a sound record of being anti-Palmerstonian; and, for all that Gladstone thought him 'not a very safe man', he accepted that his appointment was the best thing 'in spirit' Beaconsfield's government had so far done 'since the Eastern Question began to burn'.[128]

The Constantinople conference and Salisbury's being the British representative immediately stimulated the 'atrocitarians' to revive their project for a national conference. This assumed the function of being a supportive auxiliary to Salisbury's mission. The Sheffield Liberals now took the lead unhindered by Birmingham. A circular was issued on 6

November announcing a National Conference on the Eastern question at an early date. Its principal object, in Gladstone's words, was to cut Salisbury 'adrift' from Beaconsfield's latest truculent Turcophile pronouncement at the Guildhall on 9 November. Gladstone thought Beaconsfield's 'almost incredible provocation' to the Russians gave 'some new lights about his Judaic feeling in which he is both consistent and conscientious'. That speech certainly had the effect of galvanizing Gladstone into a much more positive outlook on affairs, indeed, of giving the agitation as a whole a much needed fillip. By 25 November Mundella could exult: 'I believe we shall have such a demonstration as England has not seen since the Anti-Corn law days.'[129] William Morris was treasurer. Illustrious names were signing on as 'convenors' (although Gladstone was shocked that Newman refused to do so, despite his evident inclination: in 1895 Gladstone instanced this as an outstanding example of the 'deadening and perverting influence of Rome upon the individual mind and conscience').[130]

Beaconsfield soon got wind of this 'organised attempt to revive agitation under the title of a Conference in London on Turkish affairs', which was (as he thought) to 'sit while the real Conference is holding its Session'; and expatiated to Salisbury on the insolence of this 'intolerable assembly'. He understood that several leading members of the Liberal party had declined to take part, 'but Lord Shaftesbury, who believes he is preparing a great career for Evelyn Ashley, is of course a leading member, & the Gladstone influence has prevailed on the Duke of Westminster to be President'. Gladstone could also, as the Queen observed severely, 'command' the Duke and Duchess of Argyll. Victoria, indeed, was wondering why the Attorney-General was not being set on these people.

Though Gladstone had begun to show great interest in the progress of the National Conference project, the most delicate part of Mundella's task was to make sure that he did not balk at the last moment from performing the function allotted to him as protagonist of the occasion. It was not until 2 December that he could write to its original Sheffield genius Robert Leader that he was 'pretty confident' that Gladstone would speak. In putting pressure on Gladstone, Mundella, with a sure instinct, stressed particularly the fact that the Liberal Whip, Adam, 'rejoiced' in the work, and especially in the prospect of Gladstone's joining in. Acton also truly reflected the bent in Gladstone's mind towards linking the Liberal party as advantageously as possible with the issues of the Eastern question when, in telling Gladstone that Hartington was less near agreeing with him than he had chosen to say, he added: 'But he can hardly fail to see the excellent position we are in, thanks to your initiative.'

In fact, Gladstone deserved no credit whatever for initiative. Nevertheless, as in the case of his pamphlet, he inevitably became in a sense

responsible for the situation created by the initiative of others. As Mundella pointed out, without Gladstone the National Conference would be
Hamlet without the Prince of Denmark. Gladstone could no longer even
pretend seriously to resist the force of the logic of the situation. He rejected
the argument of Granville and Hartington that he would embarrass
Salisbury at Constantinople by participating in the demonstration. He
asserted that, on the contrary, his main purpose would be to buttress
Salisbury's position. In this he represented with fidelity the efficient
intention of the National Conference.[131]

The fortune of the National Conference on the Eastern question held
in St James's Hall, Piccadilly, on Friday, 8 December 1876, was thus
linked intimately and inseparably to that of the conference of the powers
which commenced its preliminary sessions in Constantinople on 14
December. The convenors at St James's Hall, called by James Bryce and
his committee to the 'high and glorious mission' of vindicating the
'principles of humanity' and blotting out the legacy of the 'fatal Crimean
war', were invited to concern themselves with four general points: instant
reparation must be made by the Turks to the injured and despoiled
Bulgarians; the Muslim population must be disarmed; the Christians
must be accorded autonomous government; and British policy should
aim at fruitful cooperation with Russia.

The instructions issued by Derby to Salisbury avowing the desirability
of securing a minimum programme of concessions from the Turks constituted, as Gladstone later described it, 'a kind of point of junction', a 'sort
of union' between the agitation and the policy of the government. With
the Salisbury mission, Gladstone wrote to Granville, '& mainly by it, the
agitation was effectually suspended. In the St James's Hall meeting, we
frankly accepted it as a new point of departure.'[132]

The two weighty sessions at St James's Hall set the seal of a deep
sense of responsibility on the passionate movement of late August and
September; the National Conference reaffirmed solemnly and deliberately, after the heat of the initial reaction to the atrocities, the principles
and purposes of the autumn agitation. As a demonstration of 'Mind'
applied to politics it was of incomparable brilliance; so imposing, indeed,
as almost to conceal its shortcomings. Thomas Carlyle supportively
contributed his immortal phrase about the 'unspeakable Turk'. Ruskin
was his proxy for the occasion. Something of an intellectual fault-line
within the Liberal world was here becoming discernible. Browning,
Lecky, J. R. Green, Herbert Spencer, Darwin, and T. H. Green were
convenors; but Tennyson, Matthew Arnold, and J. F. Stephen were not.
The list of speakers included Trollope, the Bishop of Oxford, Henry
Richard, Bryce, Shaftesbury, Liddon, George Otto Trevelyan, Freeman,
Fawcett, and Gladstone. But the conference never quite succeeded in

establishing its claim to a character radically distinct from a Liberal demonstration: a Liberal demonstration moreover bereft, as Beaconsfield cheerfully calculated, of fully sixty names among the 'decided anti-Russian' section of the Liberals; while Derby could take comfort in the quite 'remarkable' 'absence & silence of the Whig chiefs'.[133]

Gladstone (escorting Madame Novikov) spoke 'I fear 1½ hours with some exertion, far from wholly to my satisfaction'. He thought the occasion 'great, notable, almost historical'.[134] His themes were to strike back at Beaconsfield (he had warned Granville that this was *'now wholly unavoidable'*) and to urge upon Salisbury the illustrious precedent of Canning, whose good understanding with Tsar Nicholas had unlocked the freedom of Greece. In spite of all Salisbury's efforts, and his good understanding with the Russian plenipotentiary Ignatiev, the Constantinople conference broke up in hopeless failure on 22 January 1877. The Turks, assured behind Salisbury's back of British support, defied Europe. With failure at Constantinople came failure at St James's Hall.

[8]

That failure Gladstone had no doubt of, though he insisted that the conference in itself had been a success. He allowed that the 'national' title was inappropriate, but it had been adopted in good faith as relating back to the precedents of Anti-Slavery and Anti-Corn Law conferences. To Lord Frederick Cavendish, a guest later that December at Hawarden, Gladstone was quite unapologetic on the matter of social disapproval. What good had society ever done? What the conference had revealed was that the popular feeling remained strong and decided, and would tell eventually on the House of Commons. For Gladstone, the conference had represented faithfully the initial character of the agitation of which it was the epilogue: the nation, not the classes. All this Lord Frederick reported back to his brother Hartington. Gladstone was 'of course' full of the Eastern question, 'but not so much excited as I have sometimes seen him'.[135]

Gladstone's unwontedly subdued mood related to the major implication of the possibility of the failure of the Constantinople conference: peace or war? Tsar Alexander, prior to the conference, had put what was calculated to be irresistible pressure on the Turks by undertaking that if they refused Europe's peaceful good offices, Russia would get satisfaction herself by war. To Frederick Cavendish Gladstone declared his confidence in the Emperor but his doubts about Russian policy and his regrets that all hope now depended on Russia. It was not to be wondered at that Gladstone's Christmas in 1876 he accounted the 'most solemn I have known for long: see that Eastern sky of storms, and of underlight!' For his birthday retrospect the same sombre theme prevailed: 'My desire for the shade, a true and earnest desire has been since August rudely baffled: retirement & recollection seem more remote than ever. But it is a noble cause, for the curtain rising in the East seems to open events that bear cardinally on our race.'

'Je me preoccupé incessement [*sic*] de la question de l'Orient,' he told a Greek correspondent in January 1877.[136] He was more suspicious than ever of the influence of Beaconsfield's 'Judaic feeling, the deepest and truest, now that his wife is gone, in his whole mind'.[137] He had no doubt that Beaconsfield and the hapless Derby, with Elliot their agent on the spot, were sabotaging Salisbury's efforts at Constantinople. Remoteness of recollection and retirement became ever more remote as Gladstone contemplated the consequences of Europe's failing to impose itself on the Turks. One consequence for him personally would be the need for firmer political footing than he had found in Greenwich. He would need a constituency much more ample in its public ambit and popular resonance. He confided to Granville and Adam that he would not contest Greenwich again, though for the time being this would be kept confidential; any announcement now would be 'premature'.[138] To Bryce he lamented that the Eastern question had 'hamstrung, for the time', his Homeric work. 'I look forward with longing to the day of redemption.'[139]

The coming of the new session would place Gladstone unavoidably in a position of much more anomalous prominence than in 1875 or 1876. Pre-sessional activity included a tour in Wiltshire and Somerset, centred on a gathering of Eastern sympathizers, including Liddon and Freeman, at Longleat, seat of one of the few notable Conservative supporters of the agitation, Lord Bath. Gladstone's presence caused a great local stir, with many pursuits through towns and at railway stations by enthusiastic crowds. Gladstone spoke at Frome and Taunton, making it clear that Parliament had not heard the last of the people and the question of the East. 'To my equal surprise & satisfaction', Gladstone informed James Bryce from his nephew's place at Bowden Park near Chippenham, 'I find the people of these rural & Tory counties in which I have lately been moving, as sound and as warm in the Eastern question as the men of the North & North East – where I visited in the Autumn.'[140] Gladstone assured the American Consul-General Schuyler (who had lately obliged him with the French translation of his report on the atrocities in Bulgaria): 'All that has been said about reaction in the national feeling here, is so much trash. The people do not repent of their outburst in August. The majority of London newspapers are governed by the sentiment of the Clubs of the West End.'[141] The 'nation is sound', he assured Madame Novikov.[142]

The most important pre-sessional work for Gladstone was to impress Granville and Hartington with the significance of his recent experiences in the West. He gave Granville a graphic account.

Now all this means simply *the Eastern question*. A life in the House of Commons as long as mine gives tolerably accurate means of gauging the public sentiment in its average condition towards one's self. The whole excess above the average is due to a speciality. I never while moving about as a private person have seen anything in the faintest degree resembling it. And my upshot is this: that, while my own course is in principle perfectly clear and plain, I think that you and Hartington will soon have to make up your mind on a great question, namely the attitude you are to assume with reference to this great popular conviction.[143]

This was as terse and to the point as Gladstone so far had come. The point had been reached when the leaders of the parliamentary Liberal party were being advised by the man hailed as the 'leader of the nation' to bow to a 'great popular conviction'. Granville, as ever, was gracefully evasive; Hartington had not abated his contempt for the National Conference and all it stood for, and his sense that the disgust of the 'Whigs and moderate Liberals in the House' would mean, if Gladstone went on much further, that *'nothing can prevent a break-up of the party'.*[144]

Gladstone outlined his plans for going on further to Madame Novikov. First the blue books would be published and digested. 'In a short time there may be serious debate.'

2. I cannot answer for the tone or the votes of the Parliament. In the House of Lords Turkish or anti-Bulgarian sentiment will have a blinding effect. In the House of Commons the Ministerial majority is remarkably compact; & the Irish Roman Catholics also have thus far behaved badly, in deference to the trumpet sounded from Rome. It may be three years before the Parliament is sent back to the Constituencies.

3. I consider that *we* (the agitators!) have gained two points, *a*: the re-establishment of the European Concert; *b*: extraction from a disgraceful position of virtual complicity with Turkey. So much I consider is *done*; but much remains to be done, all of it requiring careful consideration.

'Careful consideration' and 'serious debate' would centre on what Gladstone defined as the 'real issue': 'Is Russia to be left alone to execute the work and will of Europe?'[145]*

---

* He added a point of 'daring advice' as to the bad impression made by Russia's 'inopportune' annexation of Khiva.

At a meeting of the Liberal front benches at Granville's on 7 February Gladstone found the 'Tone rather good'. He lost no time once the session got going to resist the parliamentary mood and establish the credit of the 'great popular conviction'. Gladstone towered in the Commons as never before. Disraeli was gone, replaced by the rather recessive Stafford Northcote, who at one time had actually been Gladstone's private secretary at the Board of Trade. Gladstone vindicated the 'much despised "autumn agitation"'; he deplored the Concert of Europe's being most wantonly 'set at nought and repudiated'.[146] He vindicated also the St James's Hall National Conference, reminding derisive critics of the 'title assumed by another private association – the National Anti-Corn Law League' – equally derided in its time, but 'it proved its authenticity'. Above all, he defended his 'poor pamphlet'. 'I was simply an humble collaborateur with the English people in a work which they had taken into their own hands. In the matter of humanity and justice they required no instructor. It was the nation that led the classes and leaders, and not the classes and leaders who led the nation.'[147] Gladstone's laudations of the nation out of doors were by now familiar to the Commons; but not the more gratefully received for that.

At Gladstone's old favourite United Universities Club, on 14 February, A. J. Munby, 'at a writing table there, found myself vis-a-vis to Mr. Gladstone: old, eager, hurriedly writing: pen in mouth'.[148] The new blue books were out. Gladstone studied them assiduously between 10 and 19 February. They offered much in the way of means for 'going further'. Gladstone set out eagerly in his role as 'outside workman', preparing 'materials' for Granville and Hartington to 'manipulate' and then 'build into a structure'. His latest notion was, on the strength of what the blue books disclosed, the government might be vulnerable to a motion designed to 'attain some substantive result in the House: & that at all events a stroke would be struck in the country'.[149] The duumvirate were not amenable, especially to resonating in the country. Nor did they relish Gladstone's alternative proposition, that if his 'Bulgarian motion' did not '*smile*' to them, he must set to work again with his pen. This kept Gladstone busy over the Easter recess, which was otherwise enlivened by a visit to Sir John Lubbock, banker, scientist, and Liberal MP at Down in Kent. There he conversed with John Morley, Comtist editor of the freethinking *Fortnightly*, Professor Huxley, and Lyon Playfair. 'Called in & saw Mr Darwin, whose appearance is pleasing and remarkable.' It was an important moment when Gladstone recorded: 'I cannot help liking Mr. John Morley.'[150] Gladstone returned, enlivened, to his proofs. Thus came *Lessons in Massacre* in March, accusing the government of telling the Turks, in effect, '*Do it again.*'

Apart from that kind of polemic, *Lessons in Massacre* did explore issues raised in the blue books bearing on Britain's European role, and especially the problem of achieving an understanding with Russia.[151] At some recent time, very probably in 1876 and very probably inspired by the Suez shares purchase or by Salisbury's mission to Constantinople, Gladstone sketched out a formulation suggested immediately by a text of Grattan, but rather more reminiscent of the tradition of Lord Aberdeen, respecting Britain's special European office.

Because of its independence, and because it has less temptation than others to prosecute selfish interests in Europe or the Levant, there is for the most part a disposition in Continental States to confide in it more than in any of themselves, and to defer to it quite as much as it deserves.

Its influence is therefore assured by special causes, and can only be destroyed by particular errors of judgment, or by a disposition to domineer, or by an unwise self-seeking: whether these be the result of panic or pride.

If we can steadily refrain from wasting this influence by misuse; if we can discard all womanly fears of reproaches for abstention, which are never launched against us except with sinister motives; if we husband our moral strength by employing it in the interests of freedom peace and justice; it will be in our power not only to maintain the dignity and fame of England, but to increase it through succeeding generations, and then to hallow it with the unbought spontaneous gratitude of the civilized world.[152]

These words, steeped in Aberdeen and looking forward to Midlothian in 1879, exude a sense of release and emancipation from everything Gladstone associated with the name of Palmerston and the tradition of Palmerstonism. It was the tradition of Palmerston in which the blue books were steeped. The most notorious specimen of this tradition was the dispatch of Sir Henry Elliot to Lord Derby of 4 September 1876. Responding to Derby's anxieties about the manifestations of public outrage at Britain's seeming complicity in massacre, Elliot denied 'blind partisanship' on behalf of the Turks, affirming that his conduct had been guided by a 'firm determination to uphold the interests of Great Britain'; and that those interests were 'deeply engaged in preventing a disruption of the Turkish Empire' was a 'conviction' which he shared 'in common with the most eminent statesmen who have directed our foreign policy, but which appears now to be abandoned by shallow politicians or persons who have allowed their feelings of revolted humanity to make them forget the capital interests involved in the question'.

We may and must feel indignant at the needless and monstrous severity with which the Bulgarian insurrection was put down, but the necessity which exists for England to prevent changes from occurring here, which would be most detrimental to ourselves, is not affected by the question whether it was 10,000 or 20,000 persons who perished in the suppression. We have been upholding what we know to be a semi-civilized nation, liable under certain circumstances to be carried into fearful excesses; but the fact of this having just now been strikingly brought home to us all cannot be a sufficient reason for abandoning a policy which is the only one that can be followed with a due regard to our own interests.[153]

Elliot's words were described by MacColl as being of a 'repulsive selfish-ness' and 'cynical brutality'.[154] Quotation of them immediately became the centrepiece of all critiques of the government's late policy in particular and of denunciations of *raison d'état* or realpolitik in general. Gladstone quoted the offensive passage in *Lessons in Massacre*, with comments on the way the 'national' public had become 'case-hardened' in believing that the condition of the subject races of Turkey ought to be determined 'by whatever our estimate of British interest may require'. Again Glad-stone extolled the 'great example of Mr. Canning'; and insisted that a 'little faith in the ineradicable difference between right and wrong is worth a great deal of European diplomacy'.[155]

Lessons in Massacre was ready for the press by the beginning of March, but Gladstone restrained himself from setting it loose until he knew definitely that Granville and Hartington 'actually decline a parliamentary movement'. That would make Gladstone's 'duty clear'. The duumvirate declined decidedly a parliamentary movement on the grounds that the majority against Gladstone was rock solid. Granville's line was to 'let the enemy's wound fester, rather than probe it'. Hartington wanted to veto Gladstone's pamphlet. Gladstone promptly unleashed it, not without hope still that Granville would 'gradually incline' towards con-cluding that Gladstone had 'not been wholly irrational' in his estimate of 'the mind of the *nation*'.[156]

Lessons in Massacre achieved, understandably, little of the impact of *Bulgarian Horrors*. But it raised for Gladstone the issue about the clearness of his duty with respect to going further: which was first, on 23 March, a major statement in the Commons about the necessity of a Canningite policy of collaboration with Russia, and then the question of Elliot himself. Elliot was at this time back home on sick leave. He and Gladstone exchanged a stiff but civil correspondence on the merits of their respective cases, concluding with polite expressions of mutual esteem.[157] (Gladstone recorded dining with Elliot as guests of Willy's father-in-law Lord Blan-tyre on 22 February: 'animated conversation after dinner on Eastern matters. Sir H. Elliot & Lord B. about equally Turkish.') Peter Rylands and Forster raised the issue of Elliot's unfitness to return to represent Britain in Constantinople. Thus was there an affront to the decorum embedded in the establishments of politics, diplomacy, and society at large. Gladstone intervened decisively in support. 'Nothing can please me so much as to walk in the rear,' he assured Granville: 'but I ought to make known to you that my patience cannot stretch over this point & that if nobody else objects to Elliot I must.'[158] In his speech in the Commons on 27 March in support of Rylands and Forster Gladstone quoted the notorious extract from Elliot's dispatch of 4 September, without epithets. 'What is to be the consequence to civilization and humanity . . . if British interests are to be the rule of British agents all over the world, and are to be for them the measure of right or wrong?'[159]*

[9]

By now Gladstone was well launched in the mode of challenging, in the name of the nation, the leadership of his own party and the House of Commons at large, and in a sense Parliament at large. (At a levee on 12 March the Queen smiled 'but had not a word'.) Gladstone was inundated with assurances from the nation that he was their leader. Sir James Watson, former Lord Provost of Glasgow, was a representative specimen: 'Your friends here are as staunch to you as ever and their greatest wish is to see you again the Leader of the Opposition. I speak from a greatly extensive knowledge of the views of the Liberal party.'[160] Granville indeed, never convinced of the reality or efficacy of the abdication arrangements in 1875, had all but given up any pretence of leadership. The more Gladstone rather unctuously went through the forms of treating him as leader of the party, the more Granville deprecated the hollowness of the 'ephemeral honour'. 'Lord Grenville said', Granville told Gladstone on 27 May, 'that "the person who showed most sport would always be the real leader of the Opposition". If that person being an ex-Prime Minister is the ablest man in the House of Commons, who has during nearly fifty years accumulated an amount of experience, consideration, and hold upon the country, which no one else possesses, he cannot change by any disclaimer, however sincere, what appears to everyone to be the facts of the case, or avoid the responsibility which attaches to the position he has taken.'[161] Behind the smoothly bland words lay stings both at the head and the tail. The 'sport' was about Gladstone's next great exercise in going further. The 'responsibility' was about putting the Liberal party in the Commons under immense stress and making Hartington's position as leader there impossible.

* Elliot went on to Vienna, and was replaced at Constantinople by Austen Layard.

On 23 April, the eve of Russia's declaration of war on Turkey, Gladstone relentlessly asked Granville: 'Is not the moment now come for raising the rather stiff question whether a policy, or a substantive motion, is to be submitted to Parliament.' Gladstone enclosed a draft of a series of resolutions. Within two days he forwarded to Hartington a corrected draft. The resolutions aimed at preventing any British support for Turkey, at turning British policy in the direction of emancipation of the subject Turkish provinces, and at sustaining the European concert. 'It seems to me that the time presses a good deal: & those who like me have gone ahead at former stages begin to feel the extreme difficulty of silence. At the same time I need hardly say nothing will please me so much as to fall into the rear.'[162] Once more Gladstone received a negative response from his nominal leaders. On 27 April: 'This day I took my decision: a severe one, in face of my not having a single approver in the *Upper* official circle.' On the 30th he read out his resolutions to the Commons. They were greatly approved of by the Radical section led by Dilke and Chamberlain. There was a scurry in the upper official circle to limit the extensive damage to the Liberal party now likely to occur. On 5 May Granville and Wolverton 'opened the means of bridging over the chasm inadvertently made'. Gladstone agreed to modify his wording and to compress his line into one composite resolution. 'What they ask of me is really . . . little more than nominal. They have in truth been awakened as from slumber by the extraordinary demonstrations in the country.' ('3–4½ attended the Academy exhibition. 6½–10¼ at the dinner; spoke for literature! My reception surprised me, it was so good.')

The demonstrations in the country were indeed extraordinary. On 5 May Gladstone had near 140 letters in his post; 'they are most remarkable'. On 7 May his post carried reports of resolutions from about 100 meetings 'and say 200 letters or 250'. Gladstone no doubt saw in them yet another manifestation of that spontaneous moral instinct in the people which he delighted to recognize and celebrate. Matthew Arnold had other insights. 'They are in consternation at the Reform Club', he reported on 5 May, 'because, while most of the Liberal party want to go with Lubbock and Lord Hartington, the Liberal constituencies are pouring in letters and telegrams to their members desiring them to vote with Gladstone. *Chamberlain has organised the thing*, with the hope, no doubt, of winning over Gladstone for future purposes; and he is a great and successful organiser.'[163] As Gladstone prepared to give formal notice on 7 May he received a message from the Radical group of Walter James, Rylands, and Chamberlain: 'They say in the lobbies that you have "given in": most important that it should be made clear that this is not so.'[164]

Gladstone had the greatest difficulty in making this clear because his resolution was much impeded by procedural wrangles, and he was much hampered by having forgotten his eyeglass. He apologized for being obliged to stoop to 'rude irregular methods' in order to influence foreign policy, but insisted that was a recourse forced upon him by his party leaders, whose reluctance he could not understand. Of Lord Hartington: 'I really know not on what grounds he is not willing to accompany me on the whole of the Resolutions.'[165] Gladstone confronted a largely hostile House, with his own front bench 'virtually silent'. 'Such a sense of solitary struggle I never remember.' But eventually Gladstone struggled through the impediments to deliver one of his most brilliant orations. 'It was perhaps the greatest triumph of irrepressible moral and physical vitality over depressing conditions that was ever won in the House of Commons.'[166] A. J. Balfour cited it in his tribute after Gladstone's death in 1898 as a 'feat of parliamentary courage, parliamentary skill, parliamentary endurance, and parliamentary eloquence' which would, Balfour believed, always be unequalled.[167] Forster thought Gladstone an *'inspired man'* as he launched into a 'thrilling' peroration on the theme of 'other days when England was the hope of freedom'. But when after five nights debate closed on 14 May, the division revealed the government with a comfortable margin on top of its normal majority: 354 against 223. 'These numbers are not propitious,' observed Gladstone; 'but much good has been done, thank God.' Granville put the best face on it: 'the party voted pretty well'.[168] What the party had done, as far as Gladstone was concerned, was to revert to habits he had known too well of old, in 1866–7, 1871, 1872, and 1873. 'Only, would that God had instruments in plenty worthier of his purposes.'[169]

CHAPTER 6

'A GREAT AND HIGH ELECTION OF GOD': LEADERSHIP OF THE NATION REAFFIRMED, 1877–80

[1]

The first member to rise in Gladstone's support in the debate on his resolution was Joseph Chamberlain. He was, as Matthew Arnold remarked, a great and successful organizer, and he manifestly hoped to win Gladstone over for future purposes. He had organized a National Liberal Federation, which was due to be inaugurated at Birmingham on 31 May. Chamberlain wanted the grandeur of Gladstone's presence at the occasion to set the seal of his sanction on it and lend an auspicious aura to Chamberlain's ambitions. From Gladstone's point of view the logic of the matter was simple, urgent, and compelling. He, speaking for the nation, had been rebuffed by Parliament. He would return to the nation to recruit his strength, and send a great signal throughout the land. As he put it to 'Dear Spirit': 'But the people are one way and the Parliament another.'[1] There was no question about the sustained soundness of the people. His postbag every day now threatened to overwhelm Gladstone. 'Nothing but an office would give me real relief.'[2] From Herbert Spencer he was accorded gratitude for 'rousing public opinion' and saving the country from 'a war which would have been alike disastrous and disgraceful'.[3] Even the Miltonic sonnets he had failed to get from Tennyson he got from a young Magdalen man in Dublin, Oscar Wilde.[4]

Chamberlain invited Gladstone on 16 April to attend the inauguration of the National Liberal Federation at Birmingham. His letter was, as Granville remarked wryly, 'very well-written', and it dwelt on the claims which Birmingham had on Gladstone for its consistent Liberalism, and, above all, its leading role from the beginning in support of Gladstone's 'crusade' on the Eastern question. The dates are revealing: the debate on Gladstone's resolution closed on 14 May; on 16 May Chamberlain thanked Gladstone for accepting the invitation of 16 April. Gladstone asked for, and got, assurances that he would have full scope and full support on the Eastern question.

Granville had written to Gladstone: 'I presume you will not attend Chamberlain's meeting.' It was axiomatic in the upper official levels of the party that the enthusiasm of Chamberlain and the other 'malcontents' for Gladstone's resolution had behind it a desire for a final rupture in the party and riddance of the Whigs once and for all. Gladstone, who was certainly not under any illusion as to Chamberlain's far from disinterested part in the Eastern question, or any misconception as to his aim to promote the Radical cause at the expense of the Whigs, nevertheless thought a bargain with Chamberlain necessary. To Granville he defended his decision on the grounds that he could do good by 'minimising the difference which preceded the late debate', and also that it was essential to maintain continuous pressure on the government. 'From the Birmingham meeting there will be a ramification, through the Liberal Delegates assembled there, stretching all over the country, and I wish to warn them against giving ground for a renewal of the statement which obtained too much vogue before the last Debate that "the country" had repented.' Moreover, Gladstone's revived appreciation of the political virtues of the masses made him quite ready to accept a project for improved electoral organization 'from below'. He assured Granville that he would be careful to keep aloof from any suggestion that policy should be recast, but insisted that improved electoral organization would tend powerfully to promote unity of action, in which the party was still 'deficient' – a deficiency, Gladstone added delicately, 'now I think, after the party has been led with great judgment and caution for three years, to a degree even exceeding anything I can recollect since 1866'. The 'vital principle' of the Liberal party, like that of Greek art, he informed Granville, was *'action'*. And he was hopeful that the spread of the Birmingham principle of local party organization 'may prove a great stroke in the interests of the party'.[5]

The great demonstration at Bingley Hall, Birmingham, on 31 May, reflected a desire on the part of both Chamberlain and Gladstone to remake the party in their own terms. Gladstone was convinced that the Liberal party, 'as in so many other cases', was alone the 'instrument' by which a 'great work' was to be carried on.[6] If Granville and Hartington would not accept a policy of 'action' they rejected, in effect, what Gladstone conceived to be the essential function of the party over which they presided. 'What I of course regret is that the action of the party as a whole within the House does not come up to its action and feeling in the country at large.'[7]

Chamberlain made sure that Gladstone was received royally, with flags, bands, and crowds. Birmingham was to stand proxy for 'the country at large'. Staying with Chamberlain at Southbourne, Gladstone observed him closely. 'He is a man worth watching and studying: of strong self-consciousness under most pleasing manners and I should think of great tenacity of purpose: expecting to play an historical part, and probably destined to it.'[8] His speech on the Eastern question Gladstone found taxing. He did what he could to apply balm to the party's wounds by proclaiming Mill's doctrine that Liberalism was a political broad church. 'A most intelligent orderly appreciative audience: but they were 25000 and the building I think of no acoustic merits so that the strain was excessive.'[9]* Gladstone took solace in seizing the opportunity to call on Newman at the Oratory, in the somewhat incongruous company of the Unitarian Chamberlain. Gladstone hoped to allay a little the offence caused by the *Vatican Decrees*; but 'the wonderful pair were nervous and constrained, and each seemed a little relieved when, after twenty minutes of commonplace conversation, they rose to part'.[11]

'My earnest hope', Gladstone told Granville at the beginning of June, 'is that this Eastern Question is to reach a close or resting place during the summer and that then I shall be a free man again.'[12] But this was not to be. The Russians failed to pull off a quick victory and got bogged down in the Balkans. Before long Gladstone was deep in consultation with Granville, Hartington, and other colleagues 'on the disquieting rumours respecting the intentions of the Govt. to ask for money with a view to military contingencies'.[13] Frank Hill of the *Daily News* heard 'very positively' that the government were to ask for a credit of £5 million 'and that Lord Salisbury is to announce his resignation', together with Carnarvon and Cross; he was 'absolutely certain' about Salisbury.[14] Hartington, however, could not see that 'anyone seems prepared for a regular attack on the Govt., nor to recommend hostile measures against Turkey'. He agreed with the people who thought it 'rather ridiculous' that Gladstone 'should go on struggling as he does'.[15] Gladstone struggled on and loosed a letter for the *Daily News* on 3 July, denouncing the government's reputed intention and denying the relevance of his own request for a credit in 1870; the country would 'not on any terms, however plausible, consent to be either driven or cajoled'.[16] Gladstone detected similar intentions also in Egypt, where an Anglo-French dual control of the Khedive's revenues had been established in a Caisse de la Dette

---

* A notable feature of the Bingley Hall oration was G's citing the 'historical school of England' in his support: 'We are told that we are a school of sentiment. I ask how it happens, if we are a school of sentiment, that every historian in the country is strongly on our side? (Cheers) I ask how it is that men so widely differing in their accidents of character and opinion as Mr Freeman (loud applause), Mr Froude (renewed applause), and Mr Carlyle (cheers), and I believe I might add to them Mr Stubbs, Mr [J. R.] Green, and many more even of those gentlemen who represent the historical school of England, but those three in particular, how it is that those men share those opinions which have been expressed to us upon the platform tonight? (Cheers.)'[10]

Publique. Gladstone suspected that 'our first site in Egypt, be it by larceny or be it by emption, will be the almost certain egg of a North African empire'.[17]

A brief respite of sea-cruising along the south coast in July (a recourse Gladstone was to find increasingly congenial over the years) hardly interrupted the insistent pace of his activity. He was much embroiled in controversy about atrocities against Turks in the wake of the Russian campaign. He was aware of rising Russophobe emotions. He applied to the Russian Ambassador, Shuvalov, for assistance, given his knowledge 'which I think I have had the means of attaining in a more than usual degree, of the inflammable material which is at present rather abundant in portions of the public mind'.[18] Gladstone's fame as the tribune of the oppressed Bulgarians made him the object also of attentions from Greek patriots, eager to capitalize on his 'Hellenic Factor' initiative. Gladstone found himself having to walk warily between conflicting claims of Greek and Slav, and declined prudently to 'pronounce upon the merits of the controversy'.[19] (In the heat of it all he cooled his head with a walk on the evening of 21 July, and found himself at the Metropolitan Music Hall near Edgware Road station: 'The show was certainly not Athenian.')

Of the representations being made to Gladstone in 1877 by the delegates or spokesmen of oppressed peoples struggling rightly to be free, that of the Afrikaners of the Transvaal Republic was the most fraught, as being, in its way, nearer home. The Republic, bankrupt and threatened by Zulu invasion, had been annexed to the British Crown with a view to an eventual federation of South Africa. Gladstone prudently evaded the request of the Deputies of the Transvaal Republic, led by Paul Kruger, for an interview. They could understand his motives for feeling disabled from entering into the merits of their case against the British government. Yet, as Kruger enquired, what was going to happen in southern Africa if the 'wounded feelings' of the Afrikaner people were not assuaged by a 'policy of reconciliation'? What might be the 'evil fruits' that would 'grow up and overgrow any scheme of confederation in South Africa'? Would there be a 'revival of old antagonisms', of the 'deadly hatred between the Boers and the colonists of English extraction'?[20] These were shrewd questions. As with Gladstone's prophecy of Egypt's being the egg of a North African empire, the entanglements of historic irony and the law of unintended consequences would have a strange part to play in his future relationship with the question of South Africa.

The 1877 session passed without incident. The Russians remained stalled in front of the Turkish defensive lines at Plevna. The government made no outlandishly warlike gestures beyond dispatching the Mediterranean fleet to Besika Bay once more. Lord Salisbury had excellent cause to resign over the way he had been treated in Constantinople; but he held on for better times. Ministers had not the slightest intention of getting themselves involved in the Serbonian bogs of Egypt. Gladstone, nonetheless, still darkly suspected that 'Disraeli, or, not to defame him, Lord Beaconsfield', would like 'an occasion for action'. Gladstone declared himself to Frank Hill as having 'faith enough in the Prime Minister's patience & strength of will to be quite unable to put aside the contingencies of some *coup* during the recess'. He wanted Hill to urge 'those of the independent Liberals who have taken an active part in this matter' to 'hold themselves on the look out' in order to counterwork and resist such a coup. 'This could not well be done by the *ex officio* Liberals as a body or the "front bench".' Gladstone himself, of course, would be ready to come up from Hawarden if so called.[21] Gladstone had been trying to induce Salisbury to be a guest at Hawarden. Salisbury responded in August to the 'renewal' of Gladstone's 'kind invitation' with courteous evasion ('Office ties, both in the shape of Cabinets and India Councils, are likely to be somewhat exacting this autumn').[22] The old anti-Disraeli Hatfield axis was now quite extinct. The lesson Salisbury learned at Constantinople was not to spurn Beaconsfield but to get control of Beaconsfield's foreign policy. This was the end of Gladstone's very agreeable stays at Hatfield.

At Hawarden Gladstone reviewed his investments in the ever-disappointing Metropolitan and District Railway securities and in the much more lucrative Egyptian Tribute loan.[23]* He deplored Willy's and Gertrude's determination to migrate to Leeswood, near Mold. His work on his *Thesaurus Homerikos* was greatly impeded by the masses of Liberal excursionists who invaded the place to pay devotion to their leader and take renewed ardour from his presence, in the form probably of a chip from the great man's tree-felling. Hawarden was becoming a kind of political pilgrimage shrine and a cult-centre. Gladstone's prowess as an axe-man and woodman was taking on something of the same cult status as Lincoln's respected skills as a rail-log splitter. 'A party of 1400 came from Bolton! We were nearly killed with kindness.'[24] There were 2000 more from Bacup.[25] ('It is the *reporting* that makes the difficulty of these things.') 'A party stated at 600 came from Leigh and Rossendale. I submitted to the inevitable and turned the occasion to account by my references to Granville [Bradford speech] and by dealing pretty fully with the outrages now going on in a speech of perhaps 35 mins.'[26] These excursions, it seems, were not invariably spontaneously self-generated. A Liberal Association group of 2,000 from Salford came 'on the invitation' of Mr Gladstone, to be treated to a harangue on the deficiencies of Liberal organization in Lancashire and on the need to preserve a strict neutrality

---

* For G's Egyptian investments see below, page 303.

in the war between Russia and Turkey.[27] The last of the large excursionist parties left on 10 September, as Gladstone was glad to report to Laura Thistlethwayte; and he was 'relieved from further apprehension of what I have found an awkward and inconvenient necessity, which came upon me unawares'.[28] The central issue presented in this 'new invention in the way of public agitation'[29] was always Gladstone's intentions for the future. Much as he disclaimed with vehemence any hope or desire to lead again, the uncertainty could not be exorcized. Gladstone's own vehemence, for all its sincerity, was at bottom a function of an unresolved contradiction in his own mind. His embarrassment and guilt came out clearly in an apology to Granville on 5 September.

You must within these last 3 weeks have required a large fund of Christian charity not to give me up for a born fool.

I will not explain any more now about the repeated excursions, but only say I could not help myself; and have been obliged to be rather violent in defensive measures against ten more towns which wanted to 'go and do likewise.'[30]

By now, as the Russians began to push forward once more, the 'inflammable material' which Gladstone had discerned earlier as 'rather abundant in portions of the public mind' began to take fire. Gladstone became the main focus of a counter-agitation. There were many who blamed him, by the part he played in the autumn agitation of the previous year, for encouraging the Russians to suppose that they could deal with Turkey without any need to fear British intervention. His defence was not thought entirely convincing: 'What was I during these events? An insignificant private individual, having no official position.'[31] He informed Liddon that such was the 'furious condition of people's minds about me and my supposed co-operation with the Russians' that he would have to decline Liddon's invitation to subscribe to the Russian Sick and Wounded Fund.[32] There were forgeries in Gladstone's name being sent to the Russian authorities.[33] Forgeries were also circulating in Constantinople purporting to reveal Gladstone's project for a 'Slavo-Greek alliance' to go to war against the Turks.[34] Gladstone commented to Bryce: 'Every day makes more and more strange the present Tory, plutocratic, and rowdy feeling or rather fury against Russia, when contrasted with the perfect calmness with which they looked on as she perpetrated her real misdeeds in Poland.' He identified London as the 'great focus of mischief: through money, rowdyism, and the Daily Telegraph'.[35]

[2]

The twenty-seven days' visit Gladstone made to Ireland in October and November 1877 has, then and since, been seen as something rather odd and untoward, a waste of valuable time and opportunity.[36] There was speculation about his motives.[37] On the occasion of his being honoured with the freedom of Dublin, he stated that his purpose in coming to Ireland was 'a close and intimate social obligation'.[38] He explained to Granville that Catherine's great friend, Lady Meath, having been thirty-nine years in Ireland, had seen Catherine but once and Gladstone not at all. *'Hinc illud iter.'*[39] Possibly this was more a pretext than a reason. However that may have been, there is little reason to suppose other than that Gladstone's political motivation had to do with helping to repair the damage being done to Liberalism in Ireland by the Home Rulers in the context more especially now of Irish Catholicism's deliberate refusal of the moral claims Gladstone felt the Bulgarian cause exerted on Christian consciences generally. With the Bulgarian case he had mended his relationships with the Nonconformists of England and Wales, who now hailed him as the incarnation of principled political moralism, a witness for 'truth righteousness, & humanity'. 'He becomes more & more', as one Nonconformist put it to Newman Hall, 'a prophet of the most high God.'[40] Gladstone went to Ireland with a view to doing something towards putting the Irish right with him as much as putting himself right with the Irish.

Gladstone had been kept informed generally in 1876 of the feebleness of the Bulgarian agitation in Ireland.[41] The extent to which he would have been aware, however, that one of the commonest initial thrusts of Irish nationalist response to the atrocities was to equate the Turks and English as alien oppressors, and to identify with the Bulgarians as a people struggling for liberation,[42] is not clear. Gladstone would have been perfectly capable of taking the point, even if he thought the comparison with the Turks grossly inappropriate, and the general accusation, after his reforms of 1869 and 1870, in any case obsolete. That this is evident by implication, or omission, is suggested by some notes Gladstone made with reference to the Eastern question in 1877.

That no conquest can be legitimate unless it is marked by the introduction of superior laws, institutions, or manners among the conquered.

No conquest ever had been permanent unless followed by amalgamation.

[*Continued opposite*]

Saxons ⎫
Normans ⎰ in England

Franks   in France

Lombards   in Italy

The very least that can be expected is that the conquerors should be able to learn civilization from the conquered as the Romans from Greeks.[43]

The Turks in relation to the Bulgarians was what was foremost in Gladstone's mind; but his inability to cite the case of Ireland as a 'permanent' conquest would have been painful. For Ireland tended to occur instinctively to the English mind whenever this broad issue was raised. One potent reason for Disraeli's wishing to reject the Andrassy Note was that the agrarian and other reforms it urged on the Turks bore unpalatable analogies to Irish demands. 'Fancy autonomy for Bosnia with a mixed population: autonomy for Ireland wd. be less absurd, for there are more Turks in proportion to Xtians in Bosnia than Ulster v. the three other provinces.'[44] When Lord Houghton expatiated to Gladstone on the 'failure' of forty years of Greek independence he cited, as an argument against autonomy for Bosnia and Bulgaria, the absence of any basis for home rule or tenant right there. Gladstone was stung to defend the Greek record as a 'signal success' when compared with the state of affairs under the Turks, and insisted on the need for 'decisive measures' for Bosnia and Bulgaria. He could hardly have overlooked the logical implications for Ireland of their exchange. Dean Merivale, the historian, explained that he was pro-Turkish on the Bulgarian question, because all that Englishmen could say against the Turks 'the Irish have said, and still say, against us; and I don't want to set a precedent for a European Conference to extort Home Rule for Ireland, and the occupation of Ulster by the Russians, and Dublin by the Americans'.[45]

For Gladstone the sharp point of these considerations would have been blunted by his own grievances against Irish Catholicism. The official pressures of the Catholic hierarchy in Ireland deprecated responses to the Bulgarian case which identified the plight of the Bulgarians with the plight of the Irish. The special Catholic twist to the matter was to keep the Irish anti-English in the West but pro-Turkish in the East. The shifts observable in Parnell's views are in conformity with this twist.[46] Gladstone went to Ireland with his head full of the iniquities of the Irish bishops and of the iniquities of the Irish Home Rulers; not at all with thoughts of the iniquities of English rule. It is quite beside the point to lament that he failed to 'learn' anything there. He did not go to learn. He went to teach.

The event that in all probability triggered Gladstone's decision that he must go to Ireland* was a meeting at which he spoke in the Bristol Street Board School in Birmingham on 1 June, the day following his Bingley Hall speech. (It was characteristic of Gladstone's grudging attitude to a 'fine board school' to add: 'ay overfine?') In this rather exasperated address on 'Ireland and Irish Representation' Gladstone put his grievances. His legislation on Church and land had removed Ireland's most crying evils and had laid firm foundations for 'national contentment'. He thought the Home Rule party were making a 'great mistake' in parting from the Liberals of England. As far as the Eastern question was concerned, he could not carry the Irish with him in the recent great parliamentary struggle. He was forced to conclude that the Irish Catholic nationalists, demanding liberty for themselves, opposed the cause of liberty in the East.[48] It is quite likely that one of the reasons for the constraint of his conversation with Newman at the Oratory was that he raised this issue, and that he was rebuffed. That in itself might well have been enough to spur Gladstone to remedial action. He informed Granville a few days later that he was going to Ireland in the hope of doing good, in a quiet way, among the Irish members; also, characteristically, he wanted to sound opinion in the Irish Catholic hierarchy on general theological and ecclesiastical matters.[49] Liddon and MacColl made a tour through Ireland a few weeks before Gladstone arrived. MacColl reported to Gladstone that he was convinced that the Irish people were on the whole 'all right' in their individual attitudes to the Eastern question, which he and Liddon had made a special point of enquiring about; and he assured Gladstone of an enthusiastic reception.[50]

Gladstone invited Arthur Balfour to accompany him. Balfour politely declined, much as his uncle had done to Gladstone's invitation to Hawarden. Gladstone prepared himself on the Home Rule side of the expedition thus: 'I ask myself the question would O'Connell – perhaps the most vigorous, elastic and sagacious of all popular leaders known to history – have advised, or joined in, or given countenance to, the policy of the party of Home Rule in Parliament?'[51] Since O'Connell had wanted to repeal the Union, he might well have regarded schemes of 'home rule' within the Union as inadequate; but since also the answer of almost everyone at all conversant with O'Connell elasticity and sagacity would have been 'yes' on all counts, it was a curious question. It was far too late in the day to use O'Connell against the Home Rule party. In due course Gladstone would make a cult of him as the model for Parnell.† Equally unforthcoming were the Catholic bishops. Cardinal

---

* G cancelled plans for an autumn walking tour in Ireland in 1845.[47]
† See below, page 480.

Cullen explained to Gladstone that his reception might have been warmer but for the insults of *Vatican Decrees* and *Vaticanism*. There was going to be no mending of relations as there had been with the Nonconformists. As he made the rounds Gladstone found no reason to think any the better of the Church of Ireland; but on the other hand, there was every reason to think the worse of Cardinal Cullen's tyranny over his priests.

Thus it was that Gladstone got no 'enthusiastic reception'. It was not because he confined himself to the 'Pale' or to grand houses. Staying at the equivalent grand houses was habitual with him in every tour he had ever made in England. What was lacking was the will to set out among the Home Rulers and some kind of mediating political management to facilitate this. Gladstone seems not to have anticipated any need for such preparations. He declared himself at a loss: 'much perplexed with the number of kind invitations: the larger parts of my project gradually fade from view, and my movements must be in a small circle'. His comment after lunching with the Duke of Marlborough at Viceregal Lodge: 'But not enough of *Ireland*.'[52] That was not the Duke's fault, or Earl Fitzwilliam's, or Lord Powerscourt's, or the Duke of Leinster's, or Viscount De Vesci's, or Lord Annaly's, or (the ostensible purpose of it all) the Earl of Meath's. Gladstone was under no compulsion to accept invitations; but he had no experience of any other mode of operation. He expected that Ireland would be somehow presented to him as Merseyside or Tyneside or the West Country or Birmingham or the excursionists to Hawarden had been presented to him. It was Goldwin Smith's opinion that had Gladstone gone outside the Pale to see the 'real' Ireland he would have been much less enthusiastic later for Home Rule.[53] Gladstone expected also that the Eastern question would somehow be presented to him. He complained to Madame Novikov that the Duke of Marlborough was 'the *only man* who has spoken to me on the subject since I touched these shores!'[54]

The Irish visit of 1877 was untoward not because of Gladstone's failure to learn but because of his failure to teach. There was an additional ironic touch. The one thing Gladstone did apparently learn in Ireland was a thing he later consistently disowned. That was purchase by occupiers of tenancies. The 'Bright clauses' Gladstone had grudgingly allowed to be tacked on to his Irish Land Act in 1870 placed so many obstacles in the way of purchase that by 1877 only 900 tenants were taking over their tenancies under this provision. It was widely held that this was unsatisfactory. A parliamentary committee was set up in 1877 under the chairmanship of an advocate of tenant purchase as the way ahead in the Irish land question, G. J. Shaw-Lefevre. He looked to the example of the very successful system of secured loans to facilitate the sale of tenancies provided for Church lands under the Irish Church Disestablishment Act of 1869. Some 6,000 tenants on Church lands were purchasing their tenancies.[55]

In his Dublin speech of 17 November, after defending his Church Act and extolling his Land Act and proclaiming the need for far-ranging reform of local government to relieve the Westminster Parliament of unsustainable burdens, Gladstone declared his support for the principle of a more efficacious system of purchase of tenancies and applauded Shaw-Lefevre's notion of looking to the provision in the Church Disestablishment Act for that purpose. The landlord–tenant relationship, he declared, was natural in England, 'inseparable from our social state'. But there was a very different state of things in Ireland. Purchase of tenancies by occupiers in a 'good and appreciable number of instances' would be the best cure for the 'sharp division' between the interests of Irish landlords and Irish tenants. 'The creation of a class of small proprietors in Ireland' would give 'new views and new ideas' to the land problem. The object of making the same man both proprietor and cultivator was 'an object of great importance' for Ireland. Gladstone applauded Bright and looked forward to great improvements to his provisions.[56]

Formally, Gladstone spoke not as Liberal leader and head of a future Liberal government, but as the author of the Irish Land Act of 1870. But the impression he left was most decidedly that Liberal legislation on the Irish land question in the future would move in the direction he had deprecated in 1870. That is certainly what Shaw-Lefevre hoped and believed when his committee produced its report to that end in 1879. Gladstone's statement about the profound difference between landlordism in England and Ireland was in particular a quite revolutionary concession for him to make; and gave promise of a corresponding radical shift in Liberal thinking on the issue.

The Irish land question merely punctuated Gladstone's larger concern with the Eastern question. It was from Lord Powerscourt's seat at Enniskerry that Gladstone confided to Madame Novikov how the 'chapter of Polish accusations' had been answered and that the recent success of the Turks in repelling the Russians at Plevna and dragging out the war would not be a benefit to the Turks but a misfortune. He added: 'Our policy . . . has been ignoble. Look well to yours. I firmly hope your Emperor will not allow his eye to be diverted from that work of European liberation wh. he has undertaken. He has need of all human and more than human wisdom. May God give it him.'[57] These words took on premonitory power when the exasperated Russians succumbed to the temptations to impose upon the Turks in the early days of 1878 the Treaty of San Stefano.

For the time being Gladstone's efforts on returning from Ireland were concentrated on preserving British neutrality. It was cheering that his revived public stature should be marked by his victory over Northcote for the Lord Rectorship of Glasgow University. When dining with the Phillimores early in December he was observed as 'in very high spirits full of this visit to Ireland'. His high spirits took the form of trying to induce his own MP for Marylebone, Forsyth, a Conservative, to conspire against the Conservative government. Tension was rising again as the Russians broke through the Turkish defences and began driving down to the Thracian plain. Granville warned: 'The war clique of the Carlton are moving and sounding.'[58] Gladstone put it to Forsyth that it was 'in the power of a score or two of members on your side of the House to settle this question without noise or shock by making it known that they object to any alteration of our neutral course'.[59] Gladstone marked the close of 1877 as 'a year of tumultuous life': not the purer and holier air he had hoped for. But yet the 'part assigned to me in the Eastern question has been a part great and good far beyond my measure'. His keenest prayer remained 'through duty into rest'. There were other notions of the part assigned to Gladstone. Thorold Rogers wrote: 'I take it for granted that your comparative retirement from political or rather party life must be, whether you like it or not, temporary, and that you will have the advantage, when you are drawn back again to public business, of a new departure.'[60]

[3]

A 'new departure' in relation to party was indeed going to be of the advantageous essence of Gladstone's politics: a kind of comprehensive revenge for what he had suffered at the party's hands in those dreadful sessions of the sixties and seventies. 'You cannot doubt your power,' as Thorold Rogers put it to him in the new year, 'and you would not debate your duty.' The great requirement was a purging of Parliament: getting rid of plutocracy, 'society', and torpidity.[61] These themes would very likely have been aired at a new-year gathering at Hawarden: Argyll, Acton, Alfred Lyttelton, with Ruskin the lion of the party. There was 'much conversation, interesting of course, as it must always be with him'. Ruskin, so long the acolyte of the Gladstone-despising Thomas Carlyle, found himself deeply impressed. 'I have been greatly dismayed by the discovery to me of Mr Gladstone's real character, as I saw it at Hawarden: its intense simplicity and earnestness laying themselves open to every sort of mis-representation – being unbelievable unless one saw him.' Ruskin vowed immediately to cancel all attacks on Gladstone in his *Fors Clavigera* series of letters to the working men of England.[62]

To advocates of a new departure also in more boldly offensive manoeuvres against Lord Beaconsfield's assumably warlike plans Gladstone explained his reserved position.

I hang back and decline public action on the principle on which I have acted throughout. I cd not speak without more or less censuring the Govt; without censuring its head, more and not less. This I think from me a great evil & a bad precedent in foreign policy. I have done it in what seemed to me a case of necessity: & I am prepared to do it again if such a case arises. I wait therefore for positive indications of mischief . . . I am driven to suspect that Beaconsfield will despair of taking the country in front, & will try it in flank.

Gladstone speculated whether, for example, the purchase of the suzerainty of Egypt – in effect a war subsidy to the Turks – might be in view.[63] He warned Granville accordingly: if there were 'evil symptoms' he would probably, 'as a Bashi Bazouk on this question', 'join the agitation in the interval, which hitherto I have refused to do, while not discouraging local and spontaneous meetings'. 'Dizzy' was of course 'looking for the weak side of the English people', on which he had thrived so long; and 'he must feel greatly encouraged by the decided way in which they accepted his tomfoolery in the affair of the Suez Canal'. 'We are governed on Asian principles.'[64]

Beaconsfield summoned his 1878 session for what to Gladstone seemed the ominously early date of 17 January. What schemes were brewing as ministers contemplated the general collapse of Turkish resistance? The Russians were now surging on to Adrianople, which they would enter on 20 January. Soon Constantinople would be in their view. Ministers announced that they would be asking a vote of credit. On 23 January the fleet was ordered through the Dardanelles to stand off Constantinople itself. The order was rescinded at Turkish request: they were negotiating an armistice. Gladstone read in the resignation of Lord Carnarvon the most ominous implications. He was scandalized especially at the rumours of Beaconsfield's 'perfidy' in retailing to the Queen details of Cabinet infighting. Never had Gladstone mentioned to her the views, dissident or otherwise, of individual members of the Cabinet.[65] Gladstone fastened immediately on to Carnarvon's brother Auberon Herbert. Carnarvon and Gladstone dined at the Phillimores' on 26 January: 'long and interesting conversation with Carnarvon on Beaconsfield himself and the policy'. Phillimore observed that Gladstone was 'careful to restrain the expression of his private feelings'.[66]

Carnarvon's revelations about 'Beaconsfield himself and the policy' stimulated Gladstone exceedingly. He knew now that Derby had resigned and then withdrawn his resignation; and was on the brink.

Gladstone now also would have had a better estimation of Beaconsfield's genuinely disinterested view of Egypt (which Granville in any case appreciated quite accurately).[67] But this made Constantinople all the more something Beaconsfield was ready to go to war for. And from Carnarvon – known to Beaconsfield as 'Twitters' – Gladstone would have learned of the prime minister's masterful mien, with the Queen furiously in his support. At Oxford on 30 January Gladstone's private feelings got somewhat of an unrestrained airing. He was there under the auspices of Thorold Rogers and T. H. Green to speak first at the Corn Exchange to the Oxford Liberal Association. Amid denunciations as to Lord Beaconsfield's domineering over his colleagues, the abomination of the £6 million vote of credit, and the pity of the Irish party's selfish attitude (in hopes that 'those who have been struggling to free themselves will show respect and sympathy for the freedom of others' who had 'suffered oppression a hundredfold deeper and crimes a hundredfold blacker' than they), Gladstone let loose remarks deemed to be indiscreet to the point of scandal. 'To my great pain, and with infinite reluctance, but under the full and strong conviction, I may say, of my political old age, for the last 18 months I may be said to have played the part of an agitator.' 'My purpose, I will tell you fairly, has been with extremely inadequate means, and in a very mean and poor degree ("No, no"), but still to the best of my power for the last 18 months, day and night, week by week, month by month, to counteract as well as I could what I believe to be the purpose of Lord Beaconsfield.'[68]

That evening, at a dinner at the Randolph Hotel to inaugurate together with Cardwell the Palmerston Club, Gladstone 'said what was meant to do a little good'. Doubtless the 150 noblemen and gentlemen present (including Benjamin Jowett, Master of Balliol, and his prize pupil Alfred Milner, who presided) were buzzing with the shock of Gladstone's sensational Corn Exchange declaration. Gladstone commented on the oddity (to him) of the fact that the Tory Club at Oxford was named after Canning; for he believed 'that there were not two persons more nearly identical in their opinions than Mr Canning and Lord Palmerston'. Here Gladstone inaugurated a theme which was to become a centrepiece of his Midlothian rhetoric in the following year; the forced assimilation of Palmerston, so long his anti-hero, with Canning,* the first of his political hero-figures, and second only to Peel in that role during Gladstone's

---

* A. G. Stapleton, for long Canning's private secretary, responded indignantly to G's manipulation; Palmerston's policies were 'directly in defiance' of Canning's; Canning would *not* have approved of Mr Gladstone's ideas.[69] G had in fact taken his first step in expediently 'redeeming' Palmerston's reputation in 1876 from those who asserted that he would have consistently adopted an anti-Russian and pro-Turkish 'Crimean' policy in 1875–6.[70]

career. The particular twist in this calculated manipulation was that Aberdeen's reputation was consigned to limbo: the price Gladstone was willing to pay in order to prevent Beaconsfield's being accredited with the benefit of Palmerston's reputation. Gladstone rehearsed also another of his thematic standbys: 'Perhaps it was my fault, but I must admit that I did not learn when I was at Oxford that which I have learned since – namely, to set a due value in the imperishable and the inestimable principles of human liberty.'[71] Milner, in moving a vote of thanks, retorted 'with cool emphasis' that Gladstone had neglected a very important aspect of the Eastern question – 'the interests of the British Empire'. Jowett commented: 'Gladstone does not appear to me to have gained so much with the mob as he has lost with the upper and educated classes, who after all are still the greater part of politics.'[72]

There were many, like Phillimore, who judged Gladstone's Corn Exchange proceedings 'a mistake in point of judgment & taste. But for them the Govt. wd. have been in a great difficulty.'[73] Nor did Gladstone help his case by claiming in the Commons on 4 February in the debate on the £6 million supplementary estimate a 'consciousness that I have contributed what little in me lies towards the tranquil and concordant settlement of this great question. ["Oh, oh!"]'. 'Let bygones be bygones. [*Laughter*].' Gladstone explained his Corn Exchange words as being not in boast but in apology: it was a misfortune that a person serving the public and the Crown for such a length of time 'should have found himself driven to so much extra-Parliamentary action in such a time as this'. He denied motives of personal hostility; he had never made 'one imputation as to the motives of one single man'. His defence was that of precedents to opposition to official foreign policy, his own being in the cause of neutrality, peace, and the concert of Europe. 'I ask what is the brightest jewel in the fame of Fox? Undoubtedly, the resistance he offered to the Revolutionary War.' Canning, Peel, and Palmerston had all aroused animosity for their criticism of official foreign policy.[74]

Animosity certainly was what Gladstone now aroused, as the victorious Russians set about imposing armistice terms on the Turks. 'The temper of the majority is a thing hardly credible.'[75] Derby had the same opinion of the temper of his colleagues and of the Queen. (Gladstone had more confidential talk with Carnarvon on 14 February.) The public temper by now was marked by the vogue for 'Jingo' – 'the burden of a music-hall song', as Wilfred Lawson explained to the Commons, 'which had made much talk outside and had brought into politics a class-name which promised to live, and to be the first new descriptive party epithet since the days of "Whig" and "Tory"'.[76] On 24 February rowdy mobs gathered outside 73 Harley Street. 'Windows were broken and much hooting.' Mounted police intervened. 'There is strange work behind the curtain if one could but get at it.'

The Russians and Turks settled the terms of the armistice on 1 February. On 13 February the Mediterranean fleet was reordered through the Dardanelles to stand off Constantinople. On 3 March the Russians and Turks concluded the negotiations of the Treaty of San Stefano. 'Europe', it was to be hoped, had now been vindicated and redeemed from the humiliation at Constantinople in January 1877. 'Instinctively I feel a weight taken off my shoulders,' Gladstone recorded: 'but with this I suppose on the removal of tension, an increased sense of mental exhaustion.'[77] He was not too exhausted to contribute 'The Paths of Honour and of Shame' to Knowles's *Nineteenth Century* by way of preparing opinion in the forthcoming settlement of the Eastern question 'on the matter of equality, or rather proportion of treatment, as between Greek and Slav'. Once the Slav provinces were independent or autonomous (and 'neither the Balkans, on the one hand, nor the sea on the other, can be the true limit of the future Bulgaria'), Albania, Thessaly, and Macedonia could not remain under the old Ottoman administration. Gladstone warned particularly – and here the advice of Freeman and Bright and the testimony of Joseph Strossmayer, Catholic Bishop of Bosnia, Slavonia, and Sirmium* was evident – against reliance on cooperation with Metternichian Austria.[78]†

Close cooperation with Austria, however, was what the government decided was necessary when the details of what the Russians had imposed upon the Turks at San Stefano became clear. They virtually replaced Turkey-in-Europe with a Bulgarian satellite, sprawling across the Balkans from the Black Sea to the Aegean, and far into Macedonia in the west. This was not at all what had been envisaged at the Constantinople conference. It was not what Gladstone himself had envisaged in his 'The Peace to Come' in the March *Nineteenth Century*. To both Greeks and Serbs it was intolerable. More important, to the Austro-Hungarian monarchy it was unacceptable. It contradicted the agreement they had made with the Russians at Reichstadt which had enabled the Russians to undertake the war in the first place. Dangerous tension mounted between Austria and Russia. Austria insisted that the Treaty of San Stefano be brought before Europe for revision. Bismarck promptly stepped in to offer himself as an 'honest broker', and offered Berlin as host to a congress.

---

* Episcopal seat at Deakovar (Djakovo); Strossmayer corresponded with G from 1876.
† Knowles, having been ousted from the *Contemporary*, set up the *Nineteenth Century* in 1877 to fulfil Matthew Arnold's prescription for 'largeness of temper and lucidity of mind'. Between March 1877 and October 1896 G contributed to it on sixty-seven occasions.[79]

It was the obvious and logical policy for the British government to back the Austrian demand for revision. Tension in British opinion sharpened once more as preparations were set on foot to call out the reserves. Indian battalions passed through the Suez Canal to reinforce Malta in a very Beaconsfieldian-inspired touch. Beaconsfield's Cabinet debated occupying Cyprus or Alexandretta. The Jingo patriots were on the march once more. Gladstone's Harley Street house became again the target of mainly hostile crowds. The Gladstones found themselves beset as they walked towards Oxford Street, and had to take refuge in a house in Cavendish Square, from which they were rescued by a cab escorted by mounted constables.[80] On 11 March, at a levee, the Prince of Wales for the first time received Gladstone 'dryly'; the Duke of Cambridge, 'black as thunder, did not even hold out his hand'; and Prince Christian 'could not but follow suit. This is not very hard to bear.'

Amid all the turmoil there were for Gladstone the normal distractions of life. He attended demonstrations of the new telephone and phonograph inventions; he had observed trials at Tulse Hill of a new patent steam-saw for tree felling.[81]* There were some rescue cases ('But what a poor wretch I am').[83] Gladstone did not relax his attentions to the now largely reconciled Nonconformist body.[84] There were interstices of time for Homer ('Worked 6¼ hours on Homeric Primer. What a treat!').† There was much to lament on 4 April about Northcote's 'painful Budget'. Munby observed him speaking at the general meeting of the United Universities Club. 'It was interesting to watch, from so near, his eager mobile face, noble in feature and earnest in expression, and his easy apt flow of words.'[85]

But ever did the 'Sabbath dawning in the East' intrude itself. Phillimore recorded in his diary on 28 March: 'At 7pm Gladstone dashed into Arlington St with the news that Derby had resigned and that the Govt were going to call out the military reservists.' Gladstone asked Phillimore to look up the international law with respect to the preliminaries to a Congress of the Powers. 'The state of affairs is now painful,' he told Madame Novikov. It was a bitter disappointment 'to find the conclusion of one war, for which there was a weighty cause, followed by the threat

---

* The demonstration by Messrs Ransome of Chelsea was at the Roupell Park estate. G offered interesting remarks on woodmanship. Oak, though very hard, was not a bad tree to cut, for the grain broke off easily, and did not cling to the axe. Beech was far tougher, that and ash being the two most difficult to fell of our English trees, on account of their bending to the axe. Ash was subject to fracture in falling, and he had an ash splinter broken off in this way 2 ft 8 ins. in length. The pleasantest timber to cut was Spanish chestnut, because it came away so freely, the grain breaking easily. Yew was the most horrible thing to cut of all forest trees.[82]
† This produced 'The Iris of Homer: and the Relation of Genesis ix, 11–17' in the April *Contemporary Review*.

of another, for which there is no adequate cause at all'.[86] On 8 April Gladstone addressed the Commons on the theme that there was no 'great emergency' to justify the government's warlike measures and that there must be no notion of restoring the 'balance of power in the East' by building up again 'that fabric of iniquity – the Ottoman Empire'.[87] He gave ruthlessly short shrift to Granville's complaints. There was, Gladstone insisted, a 'higher duty than party allegiance'; and in any case he 'never made so great a sacrifice to party' as last year when he 'gave up bringing forward the Bulgarian question' in his resolutions, especially as he was 'convinced that the negative decision of you all was a mistake in the view of party'.[88] How refreshing was it for Gladstone to leave the plutocracy, 'society', and torpidity of his party and the Commons to address a gathering out of doors. 'To the Memorial hall for the remarkable meeting of Nonconformist Ministers, when I spoke for an hour . . . Never did I address a better audience.'[89]

It was not to be wondered at that in such circumstances of alienation from party and Parliament Gladstone should record on 18 June going to the Commons on three occasions: '*now* a rare event for me'. Other events impinged. He travelled to Lichfield on 16 April to attend the funeral of Bishop Selwyn ('His name must live: he is one of the band of great Bishops'). A few days later he was at Oxford for the official opening of Keble College, where, greeted with enthusiastic cheering, Gladstone controversially praised Newman 'as an academical name' as greater than Keble and Pusey.[90] He travelled on to Richmond and called at Pembroke Lodge for a last sight of Russell: 'a noble wreck'. Russell died on 28 May, a few days after Gladstone's friend Elizabeth Argyll, Harriet Sutherland's daughter, was taken by a seizure as she sat down next to Gladstone to dine at the Frederick Cavendishes'. Gladstone attended the funeral in Scotland (travelling by the new 'Pullman bed').[91] His omnivorous intellectual interest was attested at the Harvey tercentenary celebrations at the College of Physicians, where he spoke briefly ('Huxley's discourse on Harvey was remarkable: but he could not forbear a small touch at Belief').[92] Sittings for a portrait by Watts were interminable, especially in comparison with Lenbach's dispatch ('This length of time is really a national vice in English artists').[93] This was a portrait begun in 1874 and destined for Christ Church. It was not liked and returned to the artist. Watts eventually abandoned it. It was not until 1884 that Christ Church commissioned another (seated) version by Millais, whose handsome near full-length study was to be the Academy's centrepiece in 1879.[94]

[4]

A new departure pointed also to a new constituency to replace unsatisfactory Greenwich; one from which the implications of Gladstone's appeal to the 'nation' could assume an explicitly advantageous shape. If the Whig duumvirate were persistently unresponsive to Gladstone's offer to be an 'outside workman' preparing 'materials' for them to 'manipulate' and 'build into a structure', then so be it: Gladstone would have to take on the whole job. There were moves in Leeds to invite Gladstone to accept nomination in the populous environment of a great northern industrial centre. Its disadvantages were that Gladstone would be one of three candidates; and with Conservatives currently holding two of the three seats, there could be no certainty of Gladstone's topping the poll. Given his new public vocation, what Gladstone was in need of was a conspicuous single-member seat, preferably held by a conspicuous Conservative, who could be conspicuously challenged in an electoral tournament, a kind of proxy-battle on behalf of the masses against the classes; with prospects not too far short of guaranteed victory. On 16 May 1878 Gladstone recorded: 'Lord Rosebery *cum* Mr Adam.' The young Scottish peer and the Liberal Whip came to put the case for Midlothian (in effect Edinburghshire): a seat of fewer than 3,000 voters, and hence readily readable; held with a majority of 135 by the Earl of Dalkeith, heir to the great dukedom of Buccleuch. The following evening Gladstone dined with the Walter Jameses, and consulted on the 'Midlothian case'. It was tempting. There were the resonances of Sir Walter Scott. There were resonances of the origins of the Gladstones. Possibly a delegation of Scottish Presbyterian ministers offering Gladstone their wholehearted approval on the Eastern question was seen as auspicious.[95]

The Eastern question continued as tense and fraught as ever. Salisbury was now Foreign Secretary; but having gained his object by backing Beaconsfield against Derby, he was not well placed to make any immediate difference. Gladstone protested at the threat to constitutional liberties represented by shifting Indian contingents, untrammelled by the Mutiny Act, so near as Malta; evoking memories of the 'epoch of Charles I'.[96] The depths and inwardness of the question were further exposed in consultations with Carnarvon on 25 May disclosing more of the Queen's passionate involvement in Beaconsfield's policy. It was 'remarkable' 'how little at present within the royal precinct liberty is safe'. Cabinet ministers, it appeared, were being summoned to receive 'wiggings'; 'communications have from time to time been sent to the Cabinet warning it off from certain subjects and saying she could not agree to this & could not agree to that'. The Prince of Wales was alleged to have declared that when he came to the throne he would be his own Foreign Minister ('Why not learn the business first?'). As to the 'wiggings', Gladstone's thoughts recurred to James II and the Bill of Rights. To Carnarvon's opinion that it was 'their affair & fault if they allow to impair their independence',

I said that such an outrage as this was wholly new, totally unknown in any cabinet in which I had served; and that the corruption must be regarded as due to Lord Beaconsfield, which he [Carnarvon] entirely felt.

As to the second point I said that if it were realized the Prince made King would not only be his own Foreign Minister, but would probably find that he would have his Foreign Office in foreign parts.[97]

The obdurate unresponsiveness of the Commons provoked Gladstone to a blitz of publications out of doors. 'Liberty in East and West' in the *Nineteenth Century* castigated Beaconsfield and Salisbury at Bismarck's Congress in Berlin. 'The great champions of the anti-British tradition', the defenders to the utmost of their power to preserve continued servitude for the races subject to Turkey, 'were British plenipotentiaries'. Beaconsfield and Salisbury, the 'representatives of England',

fastened on their country the odious recollection that on this great occasion she had played the part of leading counsel for the cause of servitude and barbarism . . . Meantime the prophecy of Mr Canning that the forces and hopes of freedom would rally round England in an European convulsion have been completely reversed. A work of liberation, which is on the whole a great work, has been effected, but not by us nor with our good will: we have not had part or lot in the matter, except to cavil at it and to curtail it.[98]

Offence was taken in the Commons at Gladstone's publishing these denunciations while the Congress was deliberating; particularly his remarks on India's being exploited, and would Indians put up with it?[99] There would have been far greater offence given and taken had not Knowles, the *Nineteenth Century* editor, excised words from Gladstone's copy: a reference to Beaconsfield as '*that alien*', whose iniquitous purpose it was 'to annex England to his native East and make it the appendage of an Asiatic empire'.[100]

On 15 June Gladstone began work on 'a Morceau on the Popular Judgment in Politics for Mr Knowles' of the *Nineteenth Century*. Knowles invited a symposium of representative writers to offer pieces on the theme 'Is the popular judgment of politics more just than that of higher orders?' It is quite possible that Gladstone may have inspired the project; certainly in any case his frenetic public activities to call up the 'nation' invited rather imperatively some such consideration. In his contribution he updated in effect his doctrine of 1856 about the doings and intentions of leadership and the corresponding conviction wrought by them on the public mind. His stance then was of a high official personage at the heart of the governing order (albeit temporarily out of office); his stance now was that of an abdicated outsider, seeking ways to challenge effectively a governing order he saw as corrupted both by the general deleterious tendencies of the times and the particular evils of rule on 'Asiatic principles'. He drew three threads of his thinking together. One was the assembling of 'materials' of popular energy which could be 'manipulated' and 'built into a structure'. The second was the example of 1876. 'In the matter of humanity and justice they required no instructor. It was the nation that led the classes and leaders, and not the classes and leaders who led the nation.' The third was the implication for the future of the assimilation of the counties to the borough franchise, and the coming of something in the nature of political democracy.

In his contribution to Knowles's symposium Gladstone was in no doubt that in all the great controverted questions of the nineteenth century, with the sole exception of Catholic emancipation, the popular judgement was indeed more just than that of the higher orders. He expanded and refined his thinking in a controversy with Robert Lowe which took the form of an additional 'Postscriptum on the County Franchise'. In 'judging the great questions of policy' those classes excel, Gladstone concluded, who escape the 'subtle perils of the wealthy state'. It was in the 'moral sphere' that the causes of this superiority were to be looked for. Wealth and ease lead too often to egotism and selfishness. It was the unsophisticated mind, even the barbarian mind, that saw with simple clarity into the moral heart of matters.[101] Rather more implicitly, however, Gladstone was also making it clear that the political value of the masses was for morals and ethics and not for intellect. If they needed no instructor on matters of humanity and justice, they needed an instructor in the ways and means of attaining their ends, in deciding the when and the how. For Gladstone the spontaneity and autonomy of the 'nation's' lead in 1876 seemed the exception proving his rule. With Gladstone it was always a matter of reversion to the 1856 formula: the doings and intentions of the active 'minister' and the corresponding conviction wrought by them upon the passive public mind. To that formula he remained faithful all his life.

That faithfulness was a thing rather occult, not only because in its very nature it was not something to be publicly proclaimed, but also because, in Gladstone's mind, it was part of a much larger, and quite intensely private, area of his concerns where the inner and higher prescriptions of religion were applicable to the outer and lower world of affairs and politics. By the end of 1878 he would arrive at a culminating point where the slow accretions of religious conviction as to his assigned role in the lower world would constitute a critical mass.*

Until that point the lower world gave Gladstone more than enough cause for unremitting attention. On 8 July he was stunned by the government's 'astounding announcement' of the Convention with the Turks negotiated by Layard prior to the Berlin Congress whereby Britain would guarantee the integrity of Turkey in Asia in return for undertakings of reform and the occupation of Cyprus. Gladstone found this 'new Asiatic Empire' 'hard to take in at once'. Barrington reported to Beaconsfield in Berlin that 'Gladstone looks like a caged tiger with his bone taken from him'.[102] At Southwark Gladstone denounced the Convention as 'insane', an 'act of duplicity not surpassed and rarely equalled in the history of nations'.[103] Beaconsfield, returned triumphantly from Berlin with 'Peace with Honour', dismissed Gladstone as a 'sophistical rhetorician, inebriated with the exuberance of his own verbosity'.[104] In the Lords he complained of Gladstone's applying 'offensive epithets' – 'dangerous' and 'devilish' – to him.[105] Gladstone – as he invariably did in such cases – swiftly demanded chapter and verse, explaining that in any case his epithets applied to policy and never to character: an aspect of his 'aptness for making distinctions' which his opponents often found baffling.[106]

In the debates on the Treaty of Berlin Gladstone, on 30 July, almost exhausted his extensive repertoire of censure. He spoke for two and a half hours. 'I was in body much below par but put on steam perforce. It ought to have been *far* better.' It was frustratingly difficult to encapsulate nearly two years of tenacious, intransigent, and passionate crusade into one perfectly formed and articulated critique. Much of his speech rehearsed the themes of 'The Paths of Honour and Shame' and 'Liberty in the East and West'. The independence of Romania and Serbia was but poor reparation for the many delinquencies of the treaty. It was disgraceful that Turkey-in-Europe was re-established by reducing the San Stefano limits of Bulgaria to an autonomous principality north of the Balkans and a semi-autonomous province of Rumelia, the rest being returned to Turkish rule. The 'action of the English Government has not been directed to the extension of the work of liberation; but, on the contrary, to its contraction'. The Hellenes, relying on English patronage, had failed to obtain their claims in Thessaly, Epirus, and Crete. The 'selfish jealousy' of England's confederate Austria had deprived Montenegro of justice, and, by the Austrian occupation of Bosnia and the Herzegovina, had blocked the hopes of the Serbs. Huge wrongs had been done to the prerogatives of Parliament by the 'mad undertaking' of the Cyprus

* See below, page 228.

Convention.[107]* Gladstone found his consciousness of not having done justice to the case such that he supplemented his fulmination with 'England's Mission' in the August *Nineteenth Century*, the pith of which was that Beaconsfield's government had 'set up the principles of Metternich and put down the principles of Canning'.[108] Knowles was delighted with it: '*now* people will not be able to say that the Liberals have no clear chart to sail by in Foreign Policy'.[110] In that way it was an important step towards Midlothian.

By now the fact that Hartington conspicuously took an entirely different line in the Commons was not a matter of serious consequence to Gladstone. The real battle was being fought elsewhere. Gladstone was approached by a journalist, G. Barnett Smith, who judged there would be a thriving market for a celebratory biography. Gladstone was entirely willing to be cooperative, provided his name was kept out of the arrangements with Cassells. It might well make excellent electoral propaganda. The possibility of a general election was in the air. Beaconsfield's government had ended the 1878 session on a high note. There was speculation that he might take the opportunity to dissolve the Parliament and capitalize on 'Peace with Honour'. The 'forward policy' of his proconsuls in Afghanistan and South Africa seemed to be going well. At the Guildhall in November he was ebullient on the slogan of '*Imperium et Libertas*'.

A visit to the Isle of Man in October confirmed Gladstone's confidence in the buoyancy of his Eastern-question constituency. 'I look back with amazement at the notice given me during this little excursion, which was to be so private, & which has drawn out eight (longer or shorter) speeches. I am the first to recognize the cause: the deep hold taken by the Eastern Question & the prominence, into which I have been forced, in relation to that question. It will yet, I hope, all work well.' At Liverpool, on his way back to Hawarden, 'people even pursued me through the streets: and the galloping cabs I twice could not fully escape'.[111]† At Hawarden he pored over electoral statistics, especially those provided by by-elections. 'We have won *ten*', he pointed out to Granville, 'since the Eastern question has been before the public.'[113] His reading of the figures was that they augured well. 'The pot is beginning to boil,' he told Granville. 'I hope it will not boil too fast.' He was firmly of the belief that the Tory party was heading for a 'great smash', perhaps greater, and more enduring, than the Liberal smash of 1874.[114]

---

* There was bad blood with Layard, to whom G complained bitterly about comments published in parliamentary papers.[109] Their correspondence wrangled on through the autumn.

† William Morris, Secretary to the Society for the Protection of Ancient Buildings, rebuked G for supporting the restoration of the ruins of St Germain's church on the Isle of Man; G was 'dangerously influential'.[112]

The first shadows were in fact beginning to pass over Beaconsfield's fortunes. The economy stuck obstinately in depression. Gladstone could not understand 'Trade showing no gradual revival, with peace more or less established, and a fair harvest.'[115] Then the aggressive policies of Lytton in Afghanistan (trying to impose a 'scientific frontier') and Bartle Frere trying to make South Africa fit for a new white civilization both began to betray symptoms of overreach. A short session of Parliament had to be summoned in December 1878 to bail out the Afghan war financially. Gladstone took the opportunity to add Afghanistan to his long list of governmental delinquencies. 'I consider that this war is an unjust, a guilty, an unreasonable, and impolitic war – one of mischief for the fame of England – one of mischief to the future of India.'[116] Beaconsfield, observing Gladstone's oratorical progresses from Rhyl to Greenwich, asked Lord Barrington: 'Pray continue the correspondence during the "pilgrimage of passion" & keep me au fait to the effect produced.'[117]

[5]

Autumn in 1878 at Hawarden was enlivened by another visit by Ruskin: 'health better and no diminution of charm'; though Ruskin had before him the vexing legal altercation with the American artist Whistler, whose suit for libel and damages against Ruskin was scheduled for 25 November. Argyll was present also. 'Mr Ruskin at dinner developed his political opinions. They aim at the restoration of the Judaic system, & exhibit a mixture of virtuous absolutism, & Christian Socialism. All in his charming & modest manner.'[118] Years of grappling with Tennyson's ideas had attuned Gladstone to the ways of the great and simple sages. Ruskin, observing Gladstone's intercourse with the nation, accused him of being a 'leveller'. He was enchanted by Gladstone's response: 'Oh dear, no! I am nothing of the sort. I am a firm believer in the aristocratic principle – the rule of the best. I am out-and-out *inequalitarian*.'[119] The vexation at Hawarden was that the Willy Gladstones were still determined on setting up independently. Disappointed of earlier prospects near Mold they were now looking at a place near Hawarden village. Gladstone did his best to be discouraging: 'magnificent view but I suspect a bad soil'.[120]

Literature gained a little ground. Gladstone had been much delighted by an invitation from G. N. Curzon, Captain of Oppidans and President of the Literary Society at Eton, to address the society on Homer, on 4 July. The lecture went off very successfully (Curzon took pains to select and prepare suitable questioners). In December Gladstone could rejoice in the publication of his *Primer* on Homer. The philology of ancient Eastern languages and cuneiform inscriptions also gained much ground from Gladstone's leading role in 1878 in funding a place in Cambridge for the young scholar Wallis Budge. Gladstone had been rereading Tennyson's *Maud* of 1855, which he so disliked at the time, at the instance of his old Eton and Oxford friend Francis Hastings Doyle, lately Professor of Poetry at Oxford. Gladstone wrote to Tennyson 'a Note of Apology and partial retraction'. The Crimean War had 'dislocated my frame of mind'. Gladstone had to conclude that 'the fact is that I am wanting in that higher poetical sense, which distinguishes the true artist'.[121]* The higher moral sense was never wanting. He found a piece by Eliza Clarke in the June *Nineteenth Century* on Voltaire and Madame du Châtelet 'rather a loathsome article to be written by a woman'.[122] Oxford affairs were never far from Gladstone's mind. He lamented the decay of theological study there; he never intended his reform measures to produce that sad result.[123] 'Oxford today', he declared to a correspondent on the problem of Future Retribution, 'is indeed very far from the Oxford of my day. In some respects it is better, and much better. In others it is such that one is tempted to say the wild boar out of the forest doth root it up, and the wild beast of the field doth devour it! But yet I trust that the inner vitality will fight through it all.'[124]

A visit by Granville for Christmas disturbed Gladstone by indications of failing powers. 'I may be wrong but I do not think his [spa] water drinking has been favourable to his general mental force and especially his initiative. His nice tact and judgment remain.' What was sapping Granville's general mental force was mainly his despairing appreciation of the hollowness of his situation as *roi fainéant* to Gladstone's masterful mayor of the palace. Dealings with Gladstone, as the Queen would testify also, had about them an invariable consequence of being made to feel wanting, of not coming up to a mark set by him. There was with Gladstone never any lack of due forms of deference and respect. But there was always an awareness behind the forms of a relentless, overbearing obstinacy or tenacity of will. In December 1878 Victoria impressed Lord Cranbrook with the vividness still of her complaints about what Gladstone had put her through in the matter of the Prince of Wales and Ireland.[125]

Gladstone's own initiative was put to the test by Frank Hill on Christmas Eve. The editor of the *Daily News* had got wind of a project put by Frederick Greenwood of the *Pall Mall Gazette* to Beaconsfield of a national subscription in aid of the growing multitude of unemployed suffering distress from the depression of trade.[126]

---

* See page 531.

It is possible that as the distress in the country draws attention from foreign to domestic topics, the Government will step forward, in a theoretical and mischievous way, as the real friends of the poor. Lord Beaconsfield's writings are a perfect magazine of socialistic, or semi-socialistic ideas, only likely to be too attractive to the artizan population of this country even when it is not half-starving. Before long, we shall very likely hear of some ambitious project, seductive and economically false, for the relief of the existing distress. Would it not be desirable, on grounds much wider and deeper than those of party, that some authoritative voice should without delay summon the Government and the country to look at [the case?], and deal wisely and in time with the sufferings of the English poor? To allow Lord Beaconsfield to say the first word on the subject, and to relinquish to the Government the position of leading opinion and action, would be to give it an advantage which may help it to secure it a further term of power, and opportunities of mischief.

Hill's view was that 'a very few words' from Gladstone would suffice to pre-empt Beaconsfield and do a great service to the country and the Liberal party. But, if it were to be done, it must be done soon.[127]

Beaconsfield was indeed looking at Greenwood's plan, and was being strongly encouraged by such as Cairns and Salisbury among his heavy-weight colleagues that it was a very good idea, and what could he lose? It is one of the fascinating minor 'ifs' of history to consider what might have happened to the fortunes of Beaconsfield and the Conservative party had he not allowed the 'little busy bee' Northcote to argue him out of it. Salisbury tried manfully to counteract Northcote; but Beaconsfield, having failed to summon the nerve to dissolve Parliament in 1878, had relapsed into a passive fatalism, hoping against hope for a lucky turn of events. Hill got an equally negative response from Gladstone. 'I entirely enter into the justice of your proposal, but I think I am not the proper organ of giving it expression. It would be exerting prominence in a new line and one to which I have not any special relation. I would suggest Mr *Goschen*.'[128] Hill persisted, but Gladstone was proof against seduction. No doubt he recalled those dangerous times of the Lancashire cotton famine, when there was a grim possibility that sentimental opinion might force a tapping of public funds.[129] Were ministers to go ahead with 'measures aiming directly at the relief of distress', he informed Hill, 'they will fall into a blunder'. On the other hand Gladstone did not know 'what is open to us except economy and the liberation of industry'. 'But if you look to some counter-measures of a substantial kind, beyond what I have stated, I am afraid I have the greatest of all disqualifications for action in my ignorance of any such expedient.' That Lord Beaconsfield would 'bid eagerly for the English vote' Gladstone did not doubt, 'if he had the wherewithal to bid with'. He had already had 'some success' with the Irish.[130]

It was not a question of 'wherewithal', as Salisbury insisted in vain. All Greenwood was proposing was a government lead to private charitable subscription. The likelihood of little actual good being done was, as Salisbury again insisted in vain, beside the point. Northcote in this instance was being as true a Gladstonian as he had been in the Suez Canal shares affair. It was not that Gladstone was unaware of new trends in economic thinking. He heard Mundella make 'a most interesting statement and argument' about the dangers to Britain's manufacturing predominance at the Political Economy Club in December 1877.[131] He could see the possibility that the United States might become 'the primate nation in trade'. 'It may be soon: but that I think very unlikely. While she hugs Protectionism I think it nearly impossible.'[132] Extolling the 'creed of Cobden and Peel' was his guiding principle in communications with working men. To a group who approached him on the problems of 'Working Men and Free Trade' in December 1877, Gladstone grieved to observe the way people and consequently the House of Commons had 'almost ceased to think about restraining the great and growing expenditure of the country: and the fashion too much is, instead of this, for each class to consider how much, in its own separate interest, it can get out of the common purse'. He warned the working men against temptations to return to protectionism. 'All will suffer ultimately: but the working man will suffer most; and the landlords (of whom I am one) will have the cutting and carving pretty much their own way.'[133]

[6]

For all his conservative and Peelite reluctance to adventure in the economic sphere, Gladstone felt coming upon him in the last days of 1878 a new sense of adventure in his lifelong quest for the 'higher natural theology, which reads and applies to practice *design* in all the forms of incident that beset and accompany our daily course'.[134] Gladstone never doubted the profound truth of his conviction of 1832: 'Restrict the sphere of politics to earth, and it becomes a secondary science.'[135] Nor did he ever doubt his early assurance that he continued to 'read in the habitual occurrences of life the sure works of Providential care and love: I see all things great and small fitted into a discipline'.[136] No less than he was in 1840 was Gladstone in 1878 dependent ultimately on the 'details of Revealed truth' as the foundation of his political principles.[137] The two earlier great transmigrations of Gladstone's career – his change in 1845 from being a servant in politics of the Church to being a man of the Church in the service of the State, and in 1859 when as a Peelite he took on Liberal guise – made no diminution of the 'power exerted within Gladstone's political and public existence by commitment to a concept of spiritual mission, of moral redemption of the world, of great service to mankind by means of his devotion to Christ crucified and immanent within His Church Catholic'.[138] The applicability of the inner and higher prescriptions of religion to the outer and lower world of affairs and politics had arrived at the culminating point where the accumulated convictions of 'Providential care and love' as to his assigned role in the great design of the providential government of the world accreted into a critical mass which in turn constituted a kind of personal inspiration or revelation.

On the matter of divine inspiration Gladstone, as a Butlerian, had robustly untroubled opinions:

... it seems difficult to conceive why any intelligent mind should doubt the capacity of our Maker to choose, frame and regulate the modes of his communication with us.

No doubt some real impediments may be created by the injudicious claims of those who have not perceived that Inspiration is not necessarily uniform and may be adjusted by the Divine Wisdom to varieties of time, character and circumstances. Among its range of variety I take to be the degree in which it includes the company of elements not inspired. Again the inspiration of one who has received special commands, in the manner of describing the execution of those commands, may differ as to many points from the general inspiration accorded to those who have worked under the general laws of duty.

I lean to the belief that the comprehensive arguments of Butler are in no way tied down to the proposition he seeks to prove, and supply a master key to our obligations in respect to the problems associated with our relations to the Almighty.[139]

Gladstone for long had possessed that 'master key'. Now, on his sixty-ninth birthday, came the time to turn it. 'One year only from the limit of ordinary life prolonged to its natural goal!'

And now these three years last past, instead of unbinding and detaching me, have fetched me back from the larger room which I had laboriously reached and have immersed me almost more than at any time in cares which are certainly cares of this life.

And this retroactive motion has appeared & yet appears to me to carry the marks of the will of God. For when have I seen so strongly the relation between my public duties and the primary purposes for which God made and Christ redeemed the world? Seen it to be not real only but so close and immediate that the lines of the holy and the unholy were drawn as in fire before my eyes. And why has my health, my strength, been so peculiarly sustained?

For Gladstone – always as a rule very prompt to take to his bed at the first symptoms of even minor malady – not to have been confined to bed all the year past for more than a single day was indeed a cause for wonder. In the physical and mental effort of speaking, also, often to 'large auditories', he had been 'as it were upheld in an unusual manner and the free effectiveness of voice has been given me to my own astonishment'.

Was not all this for a purpose: & has it not all come in connection with a process to which I have given myself under clear but most reluctant associations. Most reluctant: for God knoweth how true it is that my heart's desire has been for that rest from conflict and from turmoil . . .

I am aware that language such as I have here used is often prompted by fanaticism. But not always. It is to be tried by tests. I have striven to apply them with all the sobriety I can: and with a full recollection that God sometimes sees fit to employ as his instruments for particular purposes of good those with whom notwithstanding He has yet a sore account to settle.

Gladstone declared himself still anxious for a 'lawful escape from an honourable struggle' which, 'but for the clearness of the evidence that it is honourable and pleasing to God', would make him 'wretched while it lasts'.[140]

[7]

All the indications as the new year of 1879 began to unfold were that the pot was indeed beginning to boil. Barnett Smith, thanking Gladstone for his assistance in the matter of the Cassells biography which 'will benefit the Liberal cause', remarked that it was 'possible we shall have cause to rejoice over a Liberal reaction within a shorter period than that you named to me in the brief interview I had the honour and pleasure of having with you in August last'.[141] The question of Midlothian was becoming urgent. Edinburgh itself would be a 'safe, easy, and certain seat'. The parties were more evenly balanced in the county. 'Still it is a seat to be won.'[142] Lord Rosebery was more positive. 'There is humanly speaking no doubt whatever of your return.'[143] Adam, the Liberal Whip, confirmed that the 'completed returns from all the different districts give results even better than I had anticipated'. After allowing all doubtful votes to the Conservatives, there remained a Liberal majority of about 200.[144]*

However, Gladstone thought it would be prudent to keep Leeds in play as well, in case Tory faggot voters 'garrotte the real constituency' in Midlothian. Gladstone declared himself to Adam 'much pleased with the signs of deliberation in the proceedings of the Midlothian Committee'. They had a 'right sense that the affair is a serious one. A defeat would be far greater as a calamity, than success as a gain.' The Conservatives could be counted on to fight frantically. 'This will enhance the notoriety of the contest. It may be necessary to make a pilgrimage in the County.' All this increased the 'value of the prize'.[145] To the Midlothian Committee chairman, Gladstone remarked that, after having been a member of eleven Parliaments, the conventional alternative would be 'either retirement, or at any rate the least conspicuous and most tranquil seat'. But the state of the finances, of expenditure, the arrears of legislation, and above all the fact that 'the faith and honour of the country have been gravely compromised in the foreign policy of the Ministry', together with the 'disturbance of confidence, and lately even of peace', which they have brought about, prolonging and aggravating the public distress, their augmentation of Russian power,† the unjust war they inflicted in India, their abridgement of parliamentary rights of treaty-making, all necessitated his decision to accept the invitation to contest Midlothian.[146]

Bright was at Hawarden that day, 30 January. 'We talked much on politics. On a crisis he said the entire Liberal party will require you to come forward: I gave him, besides the coward's reason, three strong reasons against it.' These were to do with the difficulties of a new government in relation to old colleagues and elements of trouble in the 'non-official portion of the Liberal party'. On the strength of these reasons Gladstone kept a low profile in the session. He was forward enough on the government's 'financial delusions', though even here he skipped the ex-Cabinet's deliberations on Northcote's budget. The disaster at Isandhlwana in January 1879 did not provoke him into hostile intervention in the Zulu War debate; nor did the sad unravelling of Lytton's campaign in Afghanistan exercise him unduly. He was resolute on the claims of Greece for 'rectifications' of frontier with Turkey under Protocol 13 of the Treaty of Berlin.[147]‡ He voted for Trevelyan's motion to assimilate the county and borough franchises on 4 March as an earnest of his faith in the judgement of the people. He did his best to help smooth things

---

* This estimate was very accurate. The poll in 1880 was 1,579 to 1,368.

† This was the burden of his 'The Friends and Foes of Russia', *Nineteenth Century*, January 1879.

‡ This issue became the fulcrum of foreign policy after G took office in 1880.

down after Chamberlain's savaging of Hartington over the issue of flogging in the Army.[148] When Shaw-Lefevre moved his resolution to increase the facilities for occupiers purchasing tenancies under the Irish Land Act of 1870, Gladstone declared his entire approval.[149] But by and large Gladstone now took little interest in the parliamentary dimension of his life. Over the session hung the likelihood of a dissolution and a general election. The 1879 session was the sixth of the 1874 Parliament: already an elderly Parliament.

As the Parliament dwindled away there were distractions enough. Laura Thistlethwayte became something of a problem again in 1878: 'My dear Mrs Th.' suddenly replaced 'Dear Broken Spirit' after August. Then in 1879 Gladstone was sorely embarrassed by ostentatious gifts; which in turn greatly offended Mrs Th. Mr Thistlethwayte was beset with suits at law for unpaid debts. ('Mrs Th. gave me intelligence which touched and moved me.')[150] Gladstone was served with a subpoena to appear as a witness before the Master of the Rolls; but fortunately the case did not come to court. Mrs Th. was not exactly a disreputable figure in society; but, for all the thronging of her salon by such as C. P. Villiers and Lord Bathurst, she was not exactly reputable either. Gladstone anyway was quite free and easy about the relationship. At Mentmore there was much conversation with Rosebery '*inter alia* on the Padwick–Thistlethwayte suit'.[151] There was also a good deal of theatre. Irving's *Hamlet* at the Lyceum deserved a second viewing. Sarah Bernhardt Gladstone found 'admirable' 'beyond my expectations' in a private performance during her first season in London in the Comédie-Française production of Racine's *Phèdre*.[152] Phillimore, an old Christ Church friend who could recall Gladstone's puritanical Evangelical days, had been amused in 1878 hearing Gladstone 'defend plays and the Theatre – on no subject have his opinions undergone a more complete revolution. Great favour was shown to painting and music – why not the drama?'[153]

There was a curious symmetry, expressive of the intellectual life of the time, in Gladstone's being at this juncture the recipient both of Balfour's exalting authority over reason in his *Defence of Philosophic Doubt* ('one with which you will be disposed to sympathise')[154] and Herbert Spencer's relentlessly positivistic *Data of Ethics*. Gladstone had started the year off by reading Seeley's *Stein* of 1878. This tribute to hard-headed Prussian statesmanship, rather like Bagehot's *Physics and Politics* of seven years earlier, would have been disagreeable in its implications as a critique of the politics of sentimental populism and 'loose talk about liberty' identified particularly with Gladstone. In his own quasi-theological production at this time, invoking Butler in 'Probability as the Guide to Conduct',[155] Gladstone suffered the mortification of being corrected for incompetent treatment of the Butler theme.[156] The sad case of the dying Panizzi was mortifying also ('I worked up my courage and asked him to let me say the Lord's Prayer').[157] It was distressing that in Louis Fagan's account of the last days there was no allusion to the consolations of religion.[158] A visit to Clumber, as a trustee of the embarrassed Clinton family estate, was also distressing enough. But staying at the Clinton Arms in Newark brought back happier memories of 'the scene of the Election toils and revels of 47 years ago'.[159]

At the Royal Academy dinner early in May Gladstone noted: 'Lord B. *not* warmly received by the general company.' It was gratifying that the Prince of Wales was 'just as of old: and other Royalties generally free and gracious'. For indeed Millais's near full-length portrait of Gladstone was the centrepiece of the Academy's exhibition. Cranbrook admired it: 'makes him look his best'.[160] What it made Gladstone look was prim, demure, and innocent. At tea at Lady Derby's on 21 May Gladstone found himself 'face to face with Lord Beaconsfield; and this put all right socially between us, to my great satisfaction'. Civil social relations, however, did not spare Lord Beaconsfield from Gladstone's post-sessional fulmination in 'The Country and the Government', in the August *Nineteenth Century*. Here Gladstone let rip on themes he had been recessive about during the session: especially the 'stain of blood' inflicted by the Cabinet on the nation in its unjust wars in Afghanistan and South Africa, adducing in support Mr Spurgeon's 'striking and powerful sermon' on the same painful subject at the Baptist Tabernacle. Gladstone was now the recipient of persistent representations from Pretoria about the shameful oppression of the Transvaal by British imperialism.[161]

Knowles of the *Nineteenth Century* enquired whether Gladstone approved of the article by the Nonconformist notable Guinness Rogers for that same August number, advocating Gladstone's resumption of the Liberal leadership: 'I replied decidedly not. I thought too that the appearance of such an article in his Review might raise a suspicion that I was concerned in it.'[162] Knowles duly excised mention of that point. But it was an issue that would not go away. Gladstone found Waddy, the Liberal MP for Barnstaple, 'under the tenacious conviction that I am the coming man'.[163] There were plans afoot both in Liverpool and London for a grand celebration at the end of the year to honour Gladstone on his seventieth birthday. A deputation would seek the patronage and blessing of Lords Granville and Hartington. The first impulse for the project of the 'great Liberal banquet' came from Liberal working men led by Thomas Burt, the mineworkers' MP for Morpeth.[164] Gladstone promptly took steps through George Howard and Granville to prohibit the plan. 'Apparently,' as one of its advocates disconsolately reported, 'the proposal is destined to fall to the ground.'[165]

A recuperative spell at Hawarden was enlivened by the now ritual address at the flower show on 'Garden cultivation which seems a subject for the times'. Of more moment was Gladstone's reviewing his letters written to the late Bishop Wilberforce, with a view to their inclusion in a forthcoming biography of the Bishop. Gladstone concluded that they were 'curiously illustrative of a peculiar and second-rate nature'.[166] But they raised a question which would impinge upon Gladstone increasingly as a survivor in a generation in which a cult of celebratory biography had taken shape as a feature of Victorian culture. As trustee of Aberdeen's literary estate Gladstone had already been in conflict with Arthur Gordon about what he considered Gordon's indiscreet propensities. The problem took two forms: one was the publication of material Gladstone deemed unwarrantably injurious to himself (this issue would arise soon with Theodore Martin's biography of the Prince Consort).* The second problem was that Gladstone could foresee his own life being published 'piecemeal'.† In any case Gladstone had his own 'piecemeal' version of his life in view with the preparation of a selection of his articles under the title *Gleanings of Past Years, 1843–1879*, which would be published in seven volumes in December. These had nothing about them of the crudely propagandist purpose of Barnett Smith's biography; but the cheapness of the edition together with its testimony to the almost superhuman scope of Gladstone's intellectual interests – classical and modern literature, theology, politics, history – did no harm whatever to Gladstone's repute with the nation.

The next adventure was an autumn tour on the continent, in company with Catherine, Mary, and Herbert. Gladstone rejoiced to leave behind him a mountain of intractable correspondence. The first step was a call on Helen at Cologne on 15 September; then on to Munich, where Acton was waiting to greet them at the railway station. Thence they proceeded to the Arco-Valley summer villa on the Tegernsee, high in the Bavarian Alps.‡ Döllinger, Madame Novikov, and Lenbach were of the party, accompanied by Lenbach's 'wonderful, unearthly picture of Bismarck'. The young Gladstones rowed their father and his friends across the lake. 'We dine at 6½. It does not suit me physically but the moral & social atmosphere are delightful.' Döllinger was now slightly deaf and less easy with his English, but 'the mind as heretofore free comprehensive and profound'. Gladstone delayed departure. But on the 25th the party (including the Actons) set off for Venice, drawn by the 'strong attraction of Lady Marian Alford'.[167]¶ 'The entry by moonlight in the gondola was nothing less than delicious.' Acton entertained the young Gladstones

---

* See below, page 469.
† See below, page 469.
‡ Acton's wife, Countess Marie, was of the family.
¶ Old friend of G and C G; widow (1851) of Lord Alford.

with an outline of his great plan for a history of liberty. When he 'turned the rays of his mind upon Gladstone's daughter Mary, she was enchained'.[168]

After two hours with Marco Minghetti, whose conservative Cavourian ministry had fallen in 1876 (and who was the intended beneficiary of Gladstone's 'Italy and Her Church' of 1875) on 5 October, the party returned to Munich (eating Venetian figs in their compartment). Gladstone sat to Lenbach and talked much again with Döllinger. At Paris on the way back Gladstone dined with the French statesman Waddington, who as Foreign Minister had represented France at the Berlin Congress. ('He did not open on the Eastern question and I thought it would be bad taste in me.') Gladstone was entranced again by Sarah Bernhardt, this time in *Hernani*. Madame Novikov, ever of service, arranged introductions, among them to Émile de Girardin, proprietor of *La France*. A reporter from *Le Gaulois* pressed Gladstone on the question of his returning to the Liberal leadership: 'your countrymen will force you to do so'.[169]

[8]

The Gladstones returned to a London humming with speculation about when Beaconsfield and his colleagues would take the electoral plunge. By 18 November Adam estimated, 'taking a very moderate calculation of our chances', that the Liberals would have a majority of twenty to thirty, independent of Home Rulers.[170] There were plans to slot Herbert Gladstone into a constituency. Adam was not sanguine about Aylesbury, as Nathan Rothschild preferred to 'keep matters quiet there'; but there was plenty of room for county candidates (Herbert would contest Middlesex). Gladstone's reading of the situation was that the Conservatives 'intended sailing on a quiet tack'. They wanted 'all the past proceedings to be in the main "stale fish" at the elections'. Therefore, as Gladstone put it to Granville, 'we should keep the old alive and warm'. That meant 'autumn work'. As Gladstone recounted to his son Harry in India, the odds were against a dissolution before February but in favour of its occurring before the budget. 'This is the meaning of my suggestion as to autumn work,' he explained to Granville, 'rather than that I expect a Dissolution.' It seemed to Gladstone 'a good policy to join on the proceedings of 1876–9 by a continuous process to the Dissolution'.[171]

He set out his plans to Rosebery, who was to be his impresario at Midlothian. Rosebery agreed that the old Lancashire technique would be best: 'to treat the different subjects in separate speeches'. Rosebery suggested suitable venues: county and Scottish issues at Dalkeith; general subjects at the Music Hall; what concerned the Liberal party at West Calder; and indictment of the government at the Corn Exchange.[172] As Gladstone prepared for his autumn work in Scotland there were efforts to revive the project of a public banquet for his seventieth birthday. Hollowell of the London Congregational Union insisted to Samuel Morley that it must go ahead.[173] Adam, however, was under instructions to discountenance all such schemes, making it known that there would be a strictly private celebration at Hawarden.

Gladstone set forth on 24 November; 'the journey from Liverpool was really more like a triumphal procession'. He delivered harangues in passing at Carlisle, Hawick, and Galashiels. At Edinburgh the 'scene even to the West end of the City was extraordinary, both from the numbers and the enthusiasm'. At Rosebery's seat, Dalmeny, there were torches and fireworks. 'I have never gone through a more extraordinary day.' The Music Hall on the 25th and the Corn Exchange on the 26th were ever more deliriously triumphant occasions. On the 27th he pressed on to West Calder. 'The enthusiasm, great along the road, was at the centre positively overwhelming.' 'All Scotland', noted his daughter Mary, 'is panting for a look at him.'[174] For the Midlothian crowds, Gladstone was being accorded the office of a 'charismatic "priest-king"',[175] prophet-protagonist of a popular theatre of politics,[176] oracular cult-figure of mass worship of redemptive leadership.[177]

For all the charisma, theatre, and *Schwärmerei* the pith of Gladstone's rhetoric was strictly, almost comically, conservative. It was 'a new method of Government' to which the country was being subjected. There had never been a government which had 'ventured upon so many measures not only mischievous, but new fangled' (here Gladstone was alluding to the social-reform legislation inspired by the 'quackery' of the 'New Social Alliance'). 'This Tory Government has undoubtedly created a greater number of innovations, broken away from a greater number of precedents, set a greater number of new-fangled examples to mislead and bewilder future generations.'[178] This self-adopted image of being a very old-fashioned elderly gentleman Gladstone dressed with studied deliberation in the habit of the 1840s. Nothing was more characteristic of him or revealing of his purpose than his conjuring of the spirit of Peel. 'Could his valuable life have been prolonged to this moment, could he have been called upon to take part, as we are now called upon to take part, in the great struggle which is commencing in this country, Sir Robert Peel would have been found contending along with you against the principles which now specially place you in determined opposition to the Government of today.'[179]

Much of what Gladstone said at Midlothian bore on purely local and Scottish questions, carefully rehearsed: land and liquor, tenant-right and the 'hypothec', the Kirk establishment. Most of what he said otherwise was a rehearsal of his invective against Beaconsfield's government since his return to the political fray in 1876. To the domestic iniquities of ministers and their 'most wanton' invasion of Afghanistan, which had broken that country into pieces and made it a 'miserable ruin', Gladstone added the case of the Transvaal, 'inhabited by a free, Christian, republican community', annexed against their clearly expressed will.[180] On two matters Gladstone broke new or newish ground. The first related to the problematic and ill-defined concept 'Home Rule', attached by now more or less indelibly to most Irish MPs. He repeated in essence his declaration at Dublin in 1877. 'If you ask me what I think of Home Rule, I must tell you that I will only answer you when you tell me how Home Rule is related to local government. I am friendly to local government. I am friendly to large local privileges and powers. I desire . . . to see Parliament relieved of some portion of its duties.' The only limit Gladstone would impose to such relief would be that nothing be done 'to weaken or compromise the authority of the Imperial Parliament'. Nothing which created doubt as to that supremacy could be tolerated by 'any intelligent and patriotic man'. Gladstone insisted that he was not going to be 'frightened out of a wise measure of that kind by being told that I am condescending to the prejudices of the Home Rulers'. He would 'condescend to no such prejudices'. He would 'consent to give Ireland no principle, nothing that is not upon equal terms offered to Scotland and to the different portions of the United Kingdom'.[181]

The second area of ground-breaking was in foreign policy. Here Gladstone continued on the line he had set out at Oxford and in 'England's Mission' in 1878. His purpose was to deny the 'new-fangled' Beaconsfield any claim to the Palmerstonian 'national' heritage by asserting assimilation with Canning by means of his own selective filiation to the genius of the 'Crimean system'. 'In the foreign policy of this country the name of Canning ever will be honoured. The name of Russell ever will be honoured. The name of Palmerston ever will be honoured by those who recollect the erection of the Kingdom of Belgium, and the union of the disjoined provinces of Italy.'[182]* This was unblushing humbug. The careful deliberation of the twist is indicated by Gladstone's making out extracts in 1879 of Disraeli's speech in March 1854 contrasting favourably the 'British opinions' of Palmerston and Russell with the 'Russian politics' of Aberdeen.[184] Privately, Gladstone was in no doubt that Palmerston and Disraeli were birds of a feather, though insisting that 'whatever was open to any degree of exception in Palmerston' had received a 'ten-fold

---

* It is noteworthy that the *Daily News* of 29 December 1879[183] made a great point of linking G with Palmerston.

development in Disraeli'.[185] As a further refinement in his juggling with reputations and filiations, Gladstone, having essayed to 'redeem' Palmerston, supplied Beaconsfield and the Conservatives in return with the name of Metternich's Tory colleague at the Congress of Vienna. On the testimony of Acton, Gladstone regarded Beaconsfield as 'the worst and most immoral minister since Castlereagh'.[186]

Yet if anyone was Gladstone's true mentor in foreign policy it was that disciple of Castlereagh, Aberdeen. Unlike Peel, Aberdeen was not mentioned by Gladstone at Midlothian as a name to be held in honour. In its way, it was curiously reminiscent of Gladstone's refusal to come to Aberdeen's aid when Aberdeen desperately needed support on 24 July 1854. It was a moment that Arthur Gordon never forgot, nor forgave. Gladstone excused himself feebly on the ground that he was 'commonly supposed to be tarred with the same stick'.[187] That stick then was 'Russian politics'. It was the same stick in 1879. Having been bold since 1876 on the need for a Canningite understanding with Russia, Gladstone in 1879 was more prudent. His latest tack was that it was the foes of Russia, Beaconsfield and his colleagues, who had augmented unwarrantably Russian power and influence.[188] That was his line also at Midlothian.[189] That way, he had it both ways. Still, when it came to the third big Midlothian speech at West Calder on 27 November and the formal definition of the 'right principles of foreign policy', the tone and savour of Aberdeen was there, even if his name was not.

It was of course of the very essence of the occasion that Gladstone should provide for the Liberal party a post-Palmerston doctrine on foreign policy. It had been long enough wanting. At Midlothian, and as an 'outside workman', Gladstone was at last free to discount the Whiggism and 'moderate' Liberalism in the parliamentary party which had impeded and harassed him in his time from 1867 to 1875 as leader, and which thus far since 1875 sustained Granville and Hartington in their resistance to his overtures and initiatives. 'I first give you, gentlemen, what I think the right principles of foreign policy.' The first is 'to foster the strength of the Empire by just legislation and economy at home, thereby producing two of the great elements of national power – namely, wealth, which is a physical element, and union and contentment, which are moral elements – and to reserve the strength of the Empire, to reserve the expenditure of that strength, for great and worthy occasions abroad'. 'My second principle of foreign policy is this – that its aim ought to be to preserve to the nations of the world – and especially, were it but for shame, when we recollect the sacred name we bear as Christians, especially to the Christian nations of the world – the blessings of peace.' 'In my opinion the third sound principle is this – to strive to cultivate and maintain, nay, to the very uttermost, what is called the concert of

Europe; to keep the Powers of Europe in union together. And why? Because by keeping all in union together you neutralize and fetter and bind up the selfish aims of each.'

Thus far the doctrine could be described as impeccably Aberdeenish. At this point Gladstone intruded an expediently Cobdenite note to qualify the doctrine sufficiently to avoid alienating Bright and his isolationist Manchester School people. 'My fourth principle is this – that you should avoid needless and entangling engagements.' This fitted not too uncomfortably with the first principle of reserving material and moral strength for great and worthy occasions only. Gladstone could then revert to the Aberdeen tone, with implications quite clearly in conformity to a Russophile predisposition. 'My fifth principle is this, gentlemen, to acknowledge the equal rights of all nations. You may sympathize with one nation more than another . . . But in point of right all are equal, and you have no right to set up a system under which one of them is to be placed under moral suspicion of espionage, and to be made the constant subject of invective.' Here Gladstone reverted to his passionate campaign in 1855 and after against Palmerston's 'Crimean system' and the Treaty of Paris, and the futile infliction of indignity upon Russia.[190] Gladstone's sixth and final principle, like his fourth, Cobdenite, principle, owed less to the Aberdeen heritage than to Gladstone's Italophilism and Austrophobia in the 1850s, and to his subsequent 'association' with the Liberal party after 1859. 'And that sixth is, that in my opinion foreign policy, subject to all the limitations that I have described, the foreign policy of England should always be inspired by the love of freedom.'[191]

After thus acquitting himself in keeping 'the old alive and warm', Gladstone proceeded triumphantly on to Edinburgh, where he addressed 20,000 at the Waverley Market. 'People were continually handed out over the heads who had fainted and were as if dead.' After an excursion up to Perth and Aberfeldy – 'enthusiasm everywhere marvellous' – he arrived at Glasgow. 'Fervid crowds at every station. The torch light procession at Glasgow was a subject for Turner.' Gladstone delivered his Rectorial Address at the University and two campaign speeches on 5 December. By 8 December he was back at Hawarden, calculating the grand total of his auditory at 86,930.[192] Lucy Cavendish found him for the first time 'a little *personally* elated'. The promise disclosed by the pivotal year of 1876 was evidently on the way to plenary fulfilment, if Midlothian was to any substantial degree proxy for the 'nation'. The 'party in the country' was, on that ground, his party. Was it not clearly the case that a grand design of things was beginning to reveal itself? The problem, however, was also beginning to reveal itself: how far, by now, was Gladstone, the 'outside worker', preparing popular 'materials', still simply an 'outside worker'? In certain respects he was back in the predicament he had been in over Maynooth, when he wished for a synodical decision to tell him to retire from public life;[193] or in the predicament over the Gorham case, when he wanted to believe two contradictory things.[194] At the close of the year Gladstone recorded his 'peculiar sense of the divine support both physical and moral' granted to him in Scotland. 'It could not have been without a purpose. To that purpose in its essence may I answer faithfully: yet as to the form I am permitted to hope *that** which seems to me most healthful, most urgently needful, for the soul.'[195]

At the Edinburgh Music Hall on 25 November Gladstone declared that he hoped that the verdict of the country in the coming general election 'will give to Lord Granville and Lord Hartington the responsible charge of its affairs'.[196] From the point of view of that duumvirate, Gladstone's decision to take so grand an initiative in the absence of any immediate likelihood of a dissolution took on unmistakably the character of de facto party leadership. This contingency had long been looming. Forster detected a 'coyness' in Gladstone's repudiation of any notion of his return to place and power.[197] Gladstone himself later insisted that it was well understood that a 'change in his position' was involved when he took up the Midlothian constituency.[198] Shortly after returning from his continental tour Gladstone made a special point of visiting Granville at Walmer bearing a copy of the *Gaulois* with its report of the interviewer's 'but your countrymen will force you to do so'. Granville related to Hartington Gladstone's repeating the eloquent gesture of response he had used in Paris: 'which looked like *Alors comme alors*'. Granville put the point to Hartington: 'I have sometimes asked myself the question whether, if I were you, I should press him *beforehand* to take your place. It would put you on velvet if he refused, as it is certain he would do.' But, as Granville reflected, the objection to that tactic was that 'it would be an illusory offer, and an offer to do what would not be for the good of the party'. Hartington was in fact all for taking up Granville's hypothetical suggestion and confronting Gladstone directly 'in such a way that he will not be able to refuse, or if he does, that the responsibility of leaving the party again without a leader will rest on him'.[199]

Hartington's impetuosity was deprecated by both Granville and Forster as injudicious. The thing was impossible. The parliamentary leaders went round in futile circles. Hartington was clear that there was not room for argument 'about the proposition that the man who leads the Liberal party out of doors ought to lead it in Parliament'.[200] The impasse was reminiscent of Clarendon's despair in 1867 at the insoluble conundrum that Gladstone would be impossible as leader but yet would

* *'that'* = retirement.

have to take the lead. Forster was in much the same mind; 'but worst of all that *he* should lead *without the responsibilities of leadership being brought home to him'.*[201]

There are no indications of any uneasiness in Gladstone's mind on the awkward issue. Granville's *'alors comme alors'* probably touched the point accurately. If Gladstone's 'nation' forced him to become their leader then so be it: certain consequences for the Liberal party would follow ineluctably. That would be their problem, not his. Gladstone was serenely playing a part assigned to him. It was no longer a question of his own personal wishes and intentions. He felt obliged to acknowledge that he was 'not very fit for composition after 5pm'. On the other hand, he mused on the theme of renewal, of *reculer pour mieux sauter.* 'Can it be that the decline of mind along with body – which reaches by analogy into the vegetable creation – signifies a rest of the powers as in a fallow – with a refreshed revival to follow?'[202] Gladstone mused inimitably on 28 December, his birthday eve: 'To die in church appears to be a great *euthanasia*: but not at a time to disturb worshippers.' However sublime, such thoughts were ephemeral. A day or two after his seventieth birthday his former private secretary Godley recorded Gladstone's saying to Catherine: 'It is a solemn thought that one has reached such an age; and yet, do what I will, I *cannot* feel myself to be an old man.'[203]

Quotidian matters on Gladstone's mind were such things as the 'terrible oppression' of the mail ('Yet the creation of an office would probably be worse').[204] The intensities of the year's end put things in correct perspective.

For the last 3½ years I have been passing through a political experience which I believe is without example in our Parliamentary history. I profess to believe it has been an occasion, when the battle to be fought was a battle of justice humanity freedom law, all in their first elements from the very root, and all on a gigantic scale. The word spoken was a word for millions, and for millions who themselves cannot speak. If I really believe this then I should regard my having been forced into this work as a great and high election of God. And certainly I cannot but believe that He has given me special gifts of strength, on the late occasion especially in Scotland . . . So then while I am bound to accept this election for the time, may I not be permitted to pray that the time shall be short?[205]

On New Year's Eve Gladstone pleaded: 'How long, O God? Thou only knowest. But it looks as if 1880 would find some solution for the question, and either give me my long wooed retirement or at worst place me on the ledge from whence I shall D.V. be carried into it by a single spring.'

[9]

The new year 1880 opened with another of those premonitory signals from South Africa. Jan Pretorius, one of the Transvaal Afrikaner notables, had been arrested. The insinuation of the Transvaal Deputies was that this was, in telegraphese, 'perhaps pretext for steps calculated exasperated people'.[206] The Transvaalers had every reason for counting on Gladstone as their man. Had he not roundly denounced the invasion and annexation of their land – 'the invasion of a free people' – in Glasgow?[207] Had he not, at Dalkeith, described the Transvaal as a country 'where we have chosen, most unwisely, I am tempted to say insanely, to place ourselves in the strange predicament of the free subjects of a monarchy going to coerce the free subjects of a republic, and to compel them to accept a citizenship which they decline and refuse'?[208]

Contemplation of the case of the Transvaalers struggling to be free was interrupted by alarming news of Helen in Cologne. The Gladstone brothers, Thomas and William, with Thomas's wife Lady Louisa, hastened there on 12 January; Helen died on the 16th. 'The last period was peace blessed peace. There was much that was beautiful before.' Gladstone examined the library of devotion. He concluded that she could not have submitted to the 1870 Infallibility dogma. He was then able to convince himself that her library disclosed that 'she died at one with us as before'.[209] It was distressing that the Episcopalian priest at Fasque lacked the necessary 'sympathetic spirit' in conducting the funeral on the 27th: the commendatory blessing was not given.

On the way up to Fasque Gladstone fell in for a stage in the rail journey with Hartington, alone, '& conversed on the situation'. That situation was transformed on 8 March, when it was announced that the Cabinet had decided to advise the dissolution of the 1874 Parliament on the 24th. Gladstone was summoned by Hartington's secretary Reginald Brett to confer at Devonshire House on the 10th. Gladstone was eagerness incarnate. Godley observed him in characteristic form on 12 March at the Newman Street Hall, off Oxford Street. 'A pale-faced, slim figure, with the head of age and a rapt, intense gaze', being shielded from the enthusiastic audience by Catherine – one of the earliest of political ladies to share her husband's platform. It was Catherine who yanked Gladstone up on to the platform and started pulling off his overcoat as he began to orate to the electors of 'Marrilbone', waving his arm just freed from the coat which Catherine – 'she exists only for him' – placidly folded, sitting behind him.[210]

Amid the turmoil Gladstone did not neglect to correct and dispatch the proofs for his latest *Nineteenth Century* piece, 'Religion, Achaian and

Semitic'. He hastened north to his field headquarters at Dalmeny. 'Was obliged to address the people at every point (5) before Edinburgh – At York there were I think 6,000: very quiet. At Edinburgh the wonderful scene of Nov. was exactly renewed.'[211] He launched into an exhilarating vortex of speechifying, 'enthusiasm everywhere the same'.[212]* The speeches also were much the same as in November, with certain explanatory and polemical revisions. Beaconsfield's election manifesto was in the form of a letter to the Viceroy of Ireland, the Duke of Marlborough. Beaconsfield pointed to the danger in Ireland of the attempt there to sever the constitutional tie uniting it to Great Britain. Gladstone denounced these 'baseless' and 'terrifying insinuations' as merely an artful dodge to divert attention from the government's failures and misdeeds. Gladstone was more concerned at the extent to which his doctrine on foreign policy was being confounded with that of the pacifist Cobdenite 'Manchester School'. He was at pains to correct that misapprehension. 'There is an allegation abroad that what is called the "Manchester School" is to rule the destinies of this country if the Liberals come to power.' No such thing, Gladstone assured his Edinburgh audience, would come to pass; 'no Government of this country could ever accede to the management and control of affairs without finding that dream of Paradise on earth was rudely dispelled by the shock of experience'.[214]

The polemical point touched on Gladstone's well-seasoned Austrophobic zest. On the strength of a newspaper report that the Emperor Francis Joseph had expressed to Sir Henry Elliot his best wishes for the government, Gladstone launched out, at the Music Hall on 17 March, on a vituperative indictment climaxed with the ringing assertion: 'there is not a spot upon the whole map where you can lay your finger and say: "There Austria did good." '[215] This insult was later to get Gladstone into an embarrassing difficulty. It was Edward Hamilton's belief that Gladstone's words were 'carefully weighed', designed as a rejoinder to Salisbury's greeting the Austro-German alliance of October 1879 as 'tidings of great joy'.[216]†

Voting in the elections began on 30 March. 'May God from heaven guide every one of them: and prosper and abuse and baffle us for His glory: lift us up, or trample us down, according as we are promoting or opposing what *He* knows to be the cause of Truth, Liberty, and Justice.' Within a day 'the doom of the Govt came into view'. On 1 April the

---

* Mountstuart Grant Duff later remarked to G: 'You must have gone through a tremendous strain.' 'Oh, no,' he replied, 'it was chiefly driving about in open carriages, and that is very healthy!'[213]
† Salisbury to Northcote, 20 March 1880: 'My impression is that the Emperor did say to Elliot something about wishing that we should succeed. I don't think he mentioned Gladstone's name.'[217]

Dalmeny party 'drove past the Buccleuch Gate which I last saw as a guest at Dalkeith thirty years ago. Such changes!' On 2 April Gladstone concluded the 'second series of the speeches in which I have hammered with all my little might at the fabric of the present Tory power'.

We cannot reckon on the wealth of the country, nor upon the rank of the country, nor upon the influence which rank and wealth usually bring … Above all these, and behind all these, there is something greater than these – there is the nation itself. This great trial is proceeding before the nation … A grander and more august spectacle than was ever exhibited either in Westminster Hall or in the House of Lords.[218]

At Dalmeny on 3 April Gladstone solemnly recorded: 'It seemed as if the arm of the Lord had bared itself for a work He has made his own.' The declaration of the Midlothian poll on the 5th gave Gladstone 1,579 votes to Dalkeith's 1,368. 'Wonderful, and nothing less, had been the disposing, guiding hand of God in all this matter.' Having already been elected for Leeds, Gladstone could now bestow that seat upon Herbert. He returned to Hawarden on the 6th. 'Travelled all night and had time to ruminate on the great hand of God so evidently displayed.' At Midlothian Gladstone had framed an indictment as he saw it not against a party or a government but against a 'whole system of Government' redolent of novel evils[219] which he summed up in the phrase 'Beaconsfieldism'. At Hawarden he observed raptly its parliamentary fabric disintegrate. 'The triumph grows & grows: to God be the praise.' To Rosebery he gratefully exclaimed: the 'romance of politics which befell my old age in Scotland, has spread over the whole land'. To Argyll: 'The downfall of Beaconsfieldism is like the vanishing of some vast magnificent castle in an Italian romance.'[220]

Wolverton arrived at Hawarden on 9 April. Gladstone spent the evening 'in full conversation with him. He threatens a request from Granville and Hartington. Again, I am stunned, but God will provide.' Wolverton also brought threatening news of plans for a triumphal reception of Gladstone in London. Gladstone's dependence on God's provision was apt, for he had himself none to offer beyond making it clear that he would not again take office other than as prime minister, and that any ministry headed by Granville and Hartington could depend on his full and cordial support. Wolverton departed to apprise the glum duumvirate of this – what it amounted to – ultimatum. By now the Liberal majority was of the order of forty over Conservatives and Home Rulers combined.* Gladstone meanwhile grappled with the proposal for a London triumph.

---

* The final figures were: 349 Liberals, 238 Conservatives, 65 Home Rulers.

He made it clear that he deprecated any rejoicing over the catastrophe of an administration and a political party.[221] He also jotted down some names for a new Cabinet, 'applicable to the occasion'. There was little doubt that Beaconsfield would resign, on the precedents of 1868 and 1874, rather than meet the new Parliament.

For the third successive time since the second Reform Act in 1867 a government had been decisively dismissed at a general election. The precise motives of the electorate on this occasion can only be a matter of speculation. It is possible that 'the romance of politics' in Scotland had indeed 'spread over the whole land'. On the other hand the government's defeat is probably more plausibly accounted for less by the iniquities of its foreign policy than by its helplessness in face of the distresses of the depression of trade. Gladstone's triumph in terms of parliamentary numbers masked some Liberal weaknesses in the patterns of voting. Many Liberal majorities were thin. The Conservative proportion of the vote actually increased in the big cities. And the Conservatives held sufficiently intact their strategic gains since 1868 in the Home Counties, London and Lancashire. It was easy for Liberals to delude themselves that the political process was back on the rails once more after the 'untoward' mishap of the Conservative success in 1874. Gladstone himself would make much in future years of Liberalism's prerogatived historical credentials as the habitual majority party of the country. The 1880 general election was ever Gladstone's benchmark of electoral success, greater even than 1868; it was a success he was never again to achieve, or to approach anywhere near to achieving. At the dizzying time of political 'romance' however, in these April days, a future in such terms was inconceivable.

The Queen was at the Villa Hohenlohe, Baden-Baden, in tears. She had long dismissed from her mind any notion of ever again recalling Gladstone to service. Beaconsfield suited her, personally and politically, absolutely. He excelled in the arts of managing her, both as Queen and woman; at which Gladstone had been hopeless – or, rather, for which he had never conceived either the propriety or the necessity. 'I never could take Mr Gladstone or Mr Lowe as my Minister again,' she declared in 1879, 'for I never COULD have the slightest *particle* of confidence in Mr Gladstone *after* his violent, mischievous, and dangerous conduct for the last three years.'[222] On 5 April she denounced to her daughter Gladstone's 'mad, unpatriotic ravings' at Midlothian.[223] As the horror came upon her that she might very well be confronted by him she told her secretary, General Ponsonby, that she would 'sooner *abdicate* than send for or have anything to do with that *half-mad firebrand* who would soon ruin anything, and be a *Dictator*'. She instructed Ponsonby to inform Granville and Hartington that Gladstone was entirely unacceptable to her. Ponsonby earnestly advised that such a declaration would be most injudicious; and hoped that Lord Beaconsfield would ease the problem by advising that she should summon Gladstone. Beaconsfield, however, did not do so.

It was not until 17 April that Victoria arrived back at Windsor from Germany. Gladstone on the 13th had put himself in a slightly more receptive position. Should Granville and Hartington 'see fit to apply to me, there is only one form and ground of application ... which could be seriously entertained by me, namely their conviction, that on the ground of public policy, all things considered it was best in the actual condition of affairs that I should come out'. He departed from Hawarden to Harley Street on the 19th. 'May He who has of late wonderfully guided, guide me still in the critical days about to come.' Beaconsfield tendered his resignation on 21 April, having advised Victoria that she send for Hartington, 'in his heart a Conservative, a gentleman, and very straightforward in his conduct'.[224] This was constitutionally perfectly correct. The Queen sent for Hartington on the 22nd and requested him to form a government. He demurred: from Wolverton he knew of Gladstone's ultimatum of all or nothing; and nothing would set the heather on fire all over the land. Victoria's request that he formally enquire of Gladstone whether he would accept office other than as prime minister Hartington could hardly refuse. Granville advised Hartington, as Ponsonby had advised the Queen, to make no statement to Gladstone indicative of any want of confidence in him from the sovereign. That would make Gladstone instantly withdraw his availability; and the fat would really be in the fire.

Gladstone recounted that Hartington 'enquired from me whether if he undertook the formation of a Government, I would form part of it. I at once declined. The work done had been my work: reluctantly and slowly undertaken in 1876–7, but, after it was once engaged in, persistently put forward.' The Queen, Gladstone allowed, had been quite right not to send for him, because he was not leader of the Opposition. Gladstone, in fact, was greatly put out that the Queen had sent for Hartington rather than Granville: 'it was to Granville that I had resigned my trust'; Granville was '*the* leader of the party'; the Queen 'seems to me wrongly to have passed by' Granville. This notion that the party leadership was somehow in his gift was more than a foible or a quirk. Partly it reflected Gladstone's old arrogance as a man of the high executive, and his correspondingly low view of party as the articulating hinge between the doings and intentions of the minister on the one side and the corresponding conviction wrought by them on the public mind on the other. There was more than a touch, also, it would be reasonable to deduce, of his quasi-messianic view of himself as God's instrument.[225] It was a view of himself in relation to his party that was not to be without importance in the years to come. For the moment, he was indulgent to Hartington in his predicament.

Nor do I say that Hartington was wrong in entertaining the proposal, or in making an overture to me but I conceive that I was plainly right in declining it for had I acted otherwise I should have placed the facts of the case in conflict with its rights, and with the just expectations of the country. Besides as the head of a previous ministry, and as still in full activity, I should have been strangely placed as the subordinate of one twenty years my junior and comparatively little tested in public life.[226]

Later, when animosities and recriminations attended on the political breach between Gladstone and Hartington, Gladstone raised doubts about Hartington's good faith as merely going through the motions at Harley Street. Gladstone somehow got it into his head that Hartington, '*to my certain knowledge*', tried to form a government. 'This statement is in all points beyond contradiction.'[227] Morley also expressed suspicions: 'As a matter of fact, I find no evidence that the two leaders ever did express a conviction that public policy required that he should stand forth as a pretender for the post of prime minister.'[228] Wolverton told Gladstone on 12 April that Granville and Hartington had not yet '*quite* realised the *position*' they were in[229] as mere train-bearers to Gladstone's majesty. There was no basis whatever for Gladstone's 'certain knowledge', 'at all points beyond contradiction'; for which he gives in any case no evidence. What neither Gladstone nor Wolverton (nor Morley) *quite* realized was the depth and the honesty of the Queen's detestation of Gladstone and the very real danger that this honesty might explode into the open. Granville and Hartington for at least a year had been under no illusions as to their prospects vis-à-vis Gladstone. Hartington in particular knew his position was entirely hopeless.[230] Granville and Hartington wanted to escape from their absurd situation as quickly as possible, but not so quickly as to create a risk of Gladstone's being told, from any quarter, that he was not welcome at Windsor.

Hartington duly returned to Windsor with empty hands. He and Granville succeeded in making the Queen realize she had no choice but to send for Gladstone. Gladstone expressed to them his 'sense of the high honour and patriotism with which they had acted'. He himself, he assured them in turn, had acted in good faith, and had only been drawn out of retirement by compulsion. 'They made no reply . . .'[231] Hartington's biographer remarks that Morley gives a 'very full and vivid account' of Gladstone's interviews with Hartington, Hartington and Granville, and the Queen; 'on each occasion Mr Gladstone evidently did almost all the talking, especially on the first'.[232] Gladstone was summoned to Windsor on 23 April.

CHAPTER 7

'THE ALMIGHTY HAS EMPLOYED ME . . .': EXORCIZING 'BEACONSFIELDISM', 1880–81

[1]

At Windsor on the evening of 23 April 1880 Gladstone accepted the Queen's commission to form a new government. Never was such a commission more reluctantly confided. Victoria had regained composure sufficiently to receive him with the 'perfect courtesy from which she never deviates'; but he was aware that she was being 'natural under effort', with a certain leavening of 'good-natured archness' on her part to cover the mutual embarrassment. Gladstone had recorded 20 April as a 'blank day', due he thought probably to the Queen's 'hesitation or reluctance, which the Ministers have to find means of covering'. It was due entirely to the Queen's attempt to get Hartington to deliver her refusal to have Gladstone back. Gladstone suspected darkly that the 'undoubted slight to Lord Granville' was at Beaconsfield's instigation. In his own kind of innocence, Gladstone did not know the half of it. Victoria found the fact of Gladstone's being once more her minister 'hardly possible to believe'. She told her daughter: 'I had felt so sure he could not return and it is a bitter trial for there is no more disagreeable Minister to have to deal with.'[1] The Queen's secretary, Ponsonby, was doing his tactful best to make things as smooth as possible, and the Prince of Wales also helped to ease the tension with a courtesy visit to Gladstone on the 24th ('in the main satisfactory').

In 1897 Gladstone set down his account of the event and some of its associations.

After going to Windsor upon acceptance I imbibed the idea that the Queen had conceived herself to be placed in sharp personal opposition to [me]: for she said to one of the Ladies that I had received her very kindly, as if she expected something different. I may take this opportunity of saying that though on the face of correspondence the waters may sometimes appear to be ruffled there never was any indication of this kind in the conversations between Her Majesty and myself. As she worked away farther and farther from me, she showed it negatively by talking on anything rather than public business at audiences which were supposed to be official.

She said to me on this occasion at Windsor, very fairly and frankly, that there were one or two things which I had said which had given offence. I intimated, but too faintly, my desire to know what they were, and to have an opportunity of explaining them, and excusing or admitting as the case might be. I have no conception what she meant. It was probably some new instance of her special identification with Beaconsfieldism.[2]

It was actually an instance of Granville's and Hartington's steering Victoria away from rejecting Gladstone by suggesting instead that she make stipulations about such things as the 'facts' created by the external policies of the previous government and apologies about such things as the insult to Austria. Karolyi, the Austrian Ambassador, had protested about the incident, denying that the Emperor had described Gladstone as a 'pestilential person', and assuring Gladstone that His Majesty had only, 'in an occasional conversation with Sir Henry, expressed his deep regret at your hostile dispositions towards us, and his hope that the cordial relations between England and Austria–Hungary would not be disturbed by them'. Karolyi trusted that a 'definitive conclusion' might be put to the furore. Gladstone made no difficulty over expressing prompt regret for the 'polemical language' he had 'used individually, when in a position of greater freedom and less responsibility'.[3]

In any case Gladstone had already taken advantage of what he thought was hesitation and reluctance. On the 21st there were consultations with ever ready Wolverton. He saw also a large number of his likely Cabinet. He consulted Algernon West, his former private secretary and now Commissioner of the Inland Revenue. The secretariat would be Godley as principal, assisted by Granville's nephew George Leveson Gower, Horace Seymour, Eddie Hamilton, with Herbert Gladstone as parliamentary private secretary. There was a precautionary visit to the dentist ('who operated a good deal'). Harley Street was proving inconvenient. Gladstone set up a field headquarters at Granville's house in familiar Carlton House Terrace.

Certain dispositions made themselves readily enough with the senior Whigs. Granville would go back to the Foreign Office and the Leadership of the Lords. Spencer took the Lord Presidency and Selborne returned to the Woolsack. Hartington would have a Secretaryship of State, which turned out to be India. Kimberley declined the Indian Viceroyalty and was accommodated at the Colonial Office. India went to Ripon, to cut down 'Lytton's swagger' (causing much offence among the Protestant sects). Argyll took the Privy Seal and Northbrook the Admiralty. The Whig lords having filled their Cabinet quota, Carlingford was offered the Irish Viceroyalty, which he declined, offended at not getting the Colonial Office. Cowper instead was to go to Ireland. Gladstone, to the general surprise, wanted the Exchequer for himself. Childers, despite royal opposition, was slotted into a great spending department, the War Office. Harcourt was well enough placed at the Home Office. After that, matters became more problematic. Cardwell was held to be out of the question for reasons of health. (To Gladstone's elaborately tactful demission Cardwell responded curtly and glacially: 'I do not want to leave your letter unanswered, lest it should seem to admit that I am in a state of health which I do not feel to be the case.')[4] Lowe also took demission badly. Gladstone had great problems with the Queen in securing Lowe a retirement viscountcy to save him from the ignominy of the ruck of official barons.

What to do with 'Gorilla' Forster, the man of iron and sinew? Gladstone held him suitable as Cowper's partner for Ireland, as yet seen as in the background of affairs. Forster would not return for the time being to the Cabinet. Whitbread steadfastly continued to decline office. Stansfeld preferred to devote himself to the moral cause of repealing the Contagious Diseases Acts. Goschen had effectively ruled himself out by his opposition to the extension of the county franchise, which, since Hartington's acceptance of it in 1877, had become Liberal party policy. He accepted Gladstone's proposal that he replace Layard at Constantinople as part of Gladstone's plan to dismantle the Eastern aspect of 'Beaconsfieldism'. Dodson, whom the Queen thought 'a respectable elderly man who looks like a shopkeeper',[5] went to the Local Government Board. Bright was persuaded to take the honorific Duchy of Lancaster, and to resume his role as totem. There remained the most awkward problem: what to do with the two most prominent of the younger generation of parliamentary Radicals, very forward in pressing claims in tandem, Chamberlain and Dilke? Gladstone was bound to temper somewhat the great preponderance in Cabinet of the official Whigs, but he found himself short of candidates in the older and more seasoned Radical generation. Fawcett's blindness ruled him out of Cabinet office. The Queen later complained to Carlingford that in 1880 she had been badly treated. 'Mr G. had told her that there would be no *Radicals* in his Cabinet, that things were on that footing for several days – then they were admitted.' Carlingford told her that he believed 'that when Mr G. began to form a Cabinet, he did not know that it would be necessary to admit Chamberlain and Dilke'.[6]

This was almost certainly correct. Dilke and Chamberlain had entered into a compact that one of them was to be in Cabinet: failing that, they would both prefer to act independently. Dilke's explanation of this put Gladstone in a difficulty. They would be more dangerous outside than in. Dilke was the senior of the pair, but getting the Queen's approval for an immediate Cabinet place would have involved a tremendous tussle which Gladstone preferred to avoid. As it was, placing Dilke as Under-Secretary at the Foreign Office was achieved only after he purged himself with elaborate explanations of and apologies for his erstwhile republicanism. Chamberlain was the extraordinary case: an MP merely since 1876 and without official experience, he entered directly into the holy of holies of government. Chamberlain was the archetypal *novus homo*: what Bright had been in 1868. A Nonconformist and a provincial (Birmingham screw-manufacturing), without any Oxbridge polish, his reputation was made entirely 'out of doors'. Gladstone expected that Chamberlain would temper sensibly political opinions 'which may on some points go rather beyond what I may call the general measure of the Government'.[7] Godley recalled seeing Chamberlain emerge 'radiant' from Gladstone's room with the offer of the Board of Trade.[8] Gladstone later told Morley that he should not have been sorry to have seen Chamberlain Secretary for Ireland *ab initio* in 1880. 'The appointment of Forster, which we thought a godsend, led to almost unmixed mischief.'[9] It was in fact a very great pity that Gladstone did not place Chamberlain at the Irish Office, either then or in 1882 when Forster resigned. What stood in the way in April 1880 was Gladstone's almost wilful unawareness that since 1879 Ireland was gripped by a quasi-revolutionary crisis. Gladstone's insistence that the Irish Office be not in the Cabinet in 1880 reflected his determination to believe that his legislation of 1869 and 1870 had set Ireland on the way to a 'national content'. Chamberlain's appointment was in any case agreeable to his sense of gratitude and esteem for the attitude throughout the Eastern question of the Nonconformist body. Gladstone and his colleagues proceeded to Windsor on the 28th when they were sworn in at a Council. 'Much popular feeling at all points of arrival and departure. Audience of H.M. 3–3½. I think H.M. was completely satisfied and relieved.'

So Gladstone persuaded himself. In fact the Queen shared the view of many Conservatives that the Liberal party in the Commons was an unstable coalition of Whigs and Radicals which would crack apart under pressure. Lady Salisbury reported to Beaconsfield: 'Depend upon it the Great Lady is right. It will not last long.'[10] The Court's discountenance was evident in the difficulties Gladstone had with the Household appointments. It took some doing to persuade the Duchess of Bedford to take on the Robes. There was much business to attend to other than appointments. Numbers 10 and 11 Downing Street were inspected on 30 April. At first No. 10 was designated for offices and secretariat and No. 11 for residence; but the Gladstones eventually moved into No. 10 on 12 May, no doubt to Catherine's gratification. (The lease on 73 Harley

Street was finally abandoned in 1882.) Far from seeing the Exchequer as a burden, Gladstone relished the prospect of demolishing in person the financial legacy of Beaconsfieldism. After a 'financial dinner' with the chief Treasury officers, Hamilton remarked that 'Finance seems quite a recreation to Mr G.'[11] He had plans for the malt duty by way of punishing the beer trade, and made of the intricacies of the probate-duty scale in relation to the legacy duty a congenial hobby.

Gladstone's 1897 account continues:

The views with which the Government was assumed by me on this occasion were not less definite, than in 1868. First and foremost stood the foreign policy of the country. I shall always think the Election of 1880 exhibits a noble example of the conduct of the people. By that election, they cashiered the subsisting administration because on behalf of the country it had exhibited not too little but too much self-assertion. With this fine national modesty was intermingled, doubtless, a strong sentiment of humanity and a lively recollection of Bulgaria. The first object of all was to change the tone of our diplomatic representation at Constantinople: and this, if I remember right, was effected when the Government was not many days old, if indeed it was at the time fully constituted.

In the rear, behind the foreign policy, stood the finance, which I personally had made the object of particular attack, holding as I did, on grounds set forth in my Midlothian speeches, that while Northcote had all the capacity and material for making the very best Chancellor of the Exchequer, he had in fact been one of the worst. I therefore felt it my duty to grapple personally with the existing situation, and I kissed hands at once as both First Lord and Chancellor of the Exchequer.[12]

As Gladstone later put it to Bright, he had accepted his 'mission' in April 1880 'as a special and temporary mission', which he hoped he might reasonably expect to 'get over', if not 'sooner than the autumn' of 1881, at least before the end of that year.[13] Such were still broadly Gladstone's assumptions as he made arrangements for his new Parliament to assemble without delay. Parliament would meet towards the end of April and start attending to serious business later in May. The mood once more was of Peelite strenuousness as cabinets commenced on 3 May.

Gladstone was now so overwhelmingly ascendant in the government and the country as to constitute a quite unprecedented phenomenon of popular politics. The greatest 'revenge' of which he had darkly spoken in 1865[14] was to be his revenge on his adopted party. There would be many kinds of difficulty confronting him in the ministry of 1880, but they would not include the old ignominies the Liberal party had so often inflicted on him. Palmerstonians who once had promising careers like

Knatchbull-Hugesson found themselves abruptly relegated to the limbo of the Lords. One veteran Liberal MP put the matter candidly in 1882: 'I know the right hon. Gentleman (Mr Gladstone) can do anything he likes. I do not think the country could have a better man at the head of affairs; but whatever he says, whether it be right or wrong, I believe will receive support from the country.'[15]* Harcourt later put it to Gladstone: 'Pray do not entertain the notion that you can say anything *personally* which does not commit and bind the party. *You are the Party* and your acts are its acts. It will never consent nor will the Nation consent to regard you as an individual . . .'[16] The Duke of Bedford spoke for many a despairing Whig lord when he confessed that 'there is no use standing up against Gladstone'.[17] The soubriquet of 'Grand Old Man', attributed to Henry Labouchere in April of 1881, captured the public imagination by its sheer appositeness: 'the name stuck'.[18] The GOM would indeed prove himself Cromwellianly formidable: intimidator of the Sultan and the Lords, liberator of Thessaly and Epirus, Afghanistan, and the Transvaal, master of the field of Irish Land, stern repressor of Irish anarchy, conqueror of Egypt, creator of manhood democracy.

One aspect of Gladstone's enormously enhanced stature was the corresponding eclipse of that of his colleagues. 'Puss' Granville in particular was now more than ever dependent on Gladstone's countenance. His grip on affairs at the Foreign Office, never very firm, loosened to the point when Gladstone complained of having to conduct foreign policy 'almost single-handed'.[19] At the India Office Hartington was exiled from the centre of things, especially after the Afghan war was wound down. Gladstone's taking the Exchequer underlined Hartington's shift to the margin. Increasingly Hartington came to depend on Gladstone for protection against the 'new men', Chamberlain and Dilke. Gladstone's social relations with his senior colleagues dwindled in these years. That Catherine had neither taste for nor competence in the arts of being a grand political hostess hardly mattered in this new dispensation. Gladstone's one new relationship of interest and possible importance was with Rosebery. This relationship was already beginning to betray signs of the temperamental moodiness which would increasingly distinguish Rosebery's career. On the strength of a 'self-denying ordinance' Rosebery had declined Gladstone's offer of subordinate office in 1880. Able, vain, ambitious, he wanted the palm without the dust: especially the dust of being seen to be in Gladstone's pocket.

There were others quite willing to slip into Gladstone's pocket. Acton by now was snugly installed, cultivating Gladstone's intellectually prone daughter Mary (who liked to think of herself as the 'Grey

* The MP was Sir Wilfrid Lawson.

Eminence')[20]* as an extra string to his courtier's bow. He could see John Morley as a coming rival for the GOM's interest in affairs of the mind. Morley was a 'new man' along with Chamberlain, planning, as man of thought and man of action, the transformation of the Liberal party into something much more intellectually uncompromising than the Whigs had so far allowed it to be. Morley was now editing the *Pall Mall Gazette* (with W. T. Stead as his assistant) in the Liberal interest. It was the only paper Gladstone could be bothered to look at – 'our faithful and able ally the Pall Mall Gazette'.[21] As Morley's political ambitions flowered – he became an MP in 1883 – he grew more congenial to Gladstone: an Oxonian, a *littérateur*, a classicist, in such respects so very different from Chamberlain. The other aspect of the drift of Gladstone's human intercourse away from the old political world was his growing easiness with a class of wealthy men of business, unproblematic and undemanding, who took pride in cultivating the great man by subsidizing his times of leisure and relaxation, especially on shipboard and at continental wintering resorts, in the coming years. Donald Currie, founder of the Castle shipping line, was one of these: it was his yacht on which Gladstone had cruised in the Channel in 1877.

[2]

It does not appear that Gladstone even went through the motions of trying to persuade the Queen to open the new Parliament in person. She declared herself 'not thinking fit to be personally present' when Lords and Commons assembled on 29 April. All that was achieved before adjournment was the initiation of the Bradlaugh scandal. The newly elected MP for Northampton, a professed freethinker, requested to be allowed to affirm rather than take the oath in the conventional religious form. Unluckily, Speaker Brand let slip the opportunity to take the trivial matter in hand at the outset and the issue got loose in a fractiously Christian Commons. The feeble Conservative leader, Northcote, out of his depth now that Hartington had been replaced by Gladstone, lost control of his party and was unable to respond to Gladstone's high-minded invitations that Bradlaugh (for all that Gladstone found his opinions 'loathsome and revolting')[22] be not made the victim of a religious test and that the House of Commons should not presume to supersede the law of the realm. Lord Randolph Churchill's cavalier Tory 'Fourth Party' exploited the problem to undermine the 'Old Gang' who ran the

* Mary G now became G's unofficial secretary for ecclesiastical preferment.

Conservative party in the Commons; for some Liberals it was their only way of baiting the 'Grand Old Man'. The matter was of no consequence other than of keeping the Commons in a chronic state of distraction and distemper, and occasionally uproar, throughout the whole period of the Parliament, sometimes getting in the way of serious and urgent business.

The serious and urgent business contemplated by Gladstone was, pre-eminently, an 'early and complete fulfilment of the Treaty of Berlin with respect to effectual reforms and equal laws in Turkey, as well as such territorial questions as have not yet been settled in conformity with the Provisions of the Treaty'.[23] Critical as he was of the treaty, it was part of the public law of Europe. Gladstone's strategy was to use the status quo as a fulcrum upon which the Turks might be levered into compliance, especially in the matter of frontier 'rectifications' in favour of Montenegro and Greece. Goschen was dispatched to Constantinople as Ambassador Extraordinary to manage the business together with Granville. Gladstone informed the Ottoman Ambassador, Musurus Pasha, that his 'union of opinion on Foreign Affairs with Lord Granville was such that whatever Lord G. said might be considered as coming from me'. He further assured Musurus that the idea that 'in the last resort the Ottoman Power is a British interest to be sustained by our arms does *not* form the basis or any part of our policy'.[24]

Rather more reluctantly, Gladstone accepted also that the status quo would have to apply to the Anglo-Turkish Convention respecting the British guarantee of Turkey-in-Asia and Britain's administering Cyprus. It was one of the *'facts'* stipulated for by the Queen. Gladstone's line was that 'we cannot measure our ideas of its force by the degree of approval which it met with among its promoters', but that equally it could not be treated as 'non-existent'.[25] Repudiating it was a temptation which would have to be resisted; even transferring the administration of Cyprus from the Foreign to the Colonial Office might compromise the strict respect for the Public Law upon which British policy now essayed to resuscitate a concert of the signatory Powers of the Treaty of Berlin. Peter Saburov, Russian Ambassador in Berlin, declared only half-mockingly in May 1880: 'Behold at long last, the realization of the philosophers' dream. The Concert of Europe is established.'[26]

In a wide range of domestic issues the status quo was not to be the rule. There were debts of morality and honour to be repaid, Liberal interests to be rewarded. The Nonconformists were to have attention paid to their grievances about burials in parish churchyards; and Gladstone was especially concerned to recognize their honourable part in the question of the East. The tenant farmers were to be assuaged in the matter of landlords' privileges as to ground game. The trade unions were to be mollified in the matter of employers' liability in industrial accidents. Dodson was to provide things for the Scots. The Irish also were to be placated by the non-renewal of the recent Conservative coercive Peace Preservation Act; and money would be available on loan from the Irish Church Temporalities Fund to relieve distress from agricultural depression; and there would be rectifications of the Irish borough franchise. Such were the times of innocence, still buoyant on the lulling waves of Midlothian.

In one important respect, however, Gladstone determined in his innocence that the status quo should prevail. Among the keenest observers of the fall of Beaconsfieldism were the Afrikaner 'Boers' of the annexed Transvaal and Orange Free State. They had been studious hitherto to keep their case for retrocession before Gladstone's eyes. They read eagerly his words at Midlothian lamenting their Beaconsfieldian captivity. Now that Gladstone had come triumphantly to power they were prompt to ask for deliverance at his hands. This their deputies Kruger and Joubert formally did on 10 May 1880.[27] After consulting Kimberley at the Colonial Office, Gladstone responded with regrets that so many of the settlers of Dutch origin in the annexed territories should want to repudiate the boons of government under the British Crown. 'We have to deal with a state of things which has existed for a considerable period, during which obligations have been contracted, especially, though not exclusively, towards the native population, which cannot be set aside.'

Apart from the annexation's being one of the 'facts' of the matter, Gladstone was impressed by Colonial Office arguments that there was a positive balance of benefits in going ahead with the existing scheme of South African confederation, and that Bartle Frere, Governor of the Cape and the proconsular strongman, should have his tenure extended to impose it, on the understanding that the Transvaal Boers would eventually be reconciled by its advantages. At the back of Gladstone's mind there was also the calculation that maintaining the imperial frontier in South Africa would be helpful with respect to his determination that the imperial *limes* set by Lytton and Beaconsfield in Afghanistan would not remain a 'fact'. To soften the blow to the Afrikaners, Gladstone assured them that 'consistently with the maintenance of that Sovereignty, we desire that the white inhabitants of the Transvaal should without prejudice to the rest of the population enjoy the fullest liberty to manage their local affairs'; which liberty would most easily and promptly be conceded 'to the Transvaal as a member of a South African confederation'.[28]

That seemed to be that. All that was now required was for Frere and the new Governor of Natal, Major-General Sir George Colley, the most brilliant member of Wolseley's 'African Ring', to coax or intimidate the Boers into compliance, however initially sullen. There was some sullenness among the Liberal ranks. There were those who wanted Frere – the original 'prancing proconsul' – to be sacked and the Transvaal abandoned forthwith; but they did not weigh heavily in Gladstone's calculations. In the meantime, as he chastised the Turk, Gladstone could reflect on deeper questions of the Liberal future, and particularly the legacy he might confer upon it. The most insistent and potentially fruitful component of Gladstone's thinking at this time was his sense of the need for something big and comprehensive in local government. Parliament was coming under pressures which threatened to choke its efficiency. Charges and spending where appropriate needed urgently to be shifted away from the centre and placed more in the hands of the localities which directly raised and expended the money. The case of Ireland presented itself with a special urgency: the more administrative and financial responsibilities were devolved from a Westminster to a local basis the better the Irish would be reconciled to the Union. Gladstone had already raised this theme of 'home rule' at Dublin and Midlothian. Yet it is the most puzzling and indeed poignant consideration of Gladstone's career after 1880 that, from a combination and entanglement of predispositions and circumstances, he would be directly responsible for no successful initiatives in local government either in Britain or Ireland, other than in the latter case to jump right over the local-government groundwork into the ambitious and overreaching constitutional complications of Home Rule; and would in effect leave it for the Conservatives and Unionists to produce the great measures of 1888 for England and Wales (and London), of 1889 for Scotland, and of 1898 – at least a decade too late – for Ireland.

Why this immense deficiency in the light of so much of awareness and conviction? Clues can be deduced at the outset from advice given to Gladstone by Rathbone, his former electoral manager at Liverpool, in the purest accents of the spirit of Midlothian. By far the greatest hope for the Liberal future, argued Rathbone, was 'the work of constructing an efficient system of local government for Ireland and Great Britain – which would not only satisfy all that is reasonable in the Home Rule demand but also regenerate local government in this country'. So far, so Gladstonian. With a view to this great undertaking, Rathbone went on to recommend Stansfeld for the Local Government Board, and for Samuel Whitbread to be made Irish Secretary with Shaw-Lefevre and the O'Conor Don as his Under-Secretaries.[29] This would indeed have been a brilliant array of talent. The difficulties were that neither Stansfeld nor Whitbread was available for office; and Gladstone seems not to have thought either Shaw-Lefevre or the O'Conor Don suitable appointments at the Irish Office.

It was well appreciated that behind the anterior question of Irish local government lurked the ulterior question of tenant purchase. Shaw-Lefevre was, notoriously, the great advocate in the Commons of tenant purchase as the way ahead in Irish land. Which is conceivably why Gladstone shunted him out of the way as First Commissioner of Works in 1880. The O'Conor Don, Liberal MP for Roscommon 1860–80, was an eminent Irish politician, and a member of the Bessborough Land Commission set up in 1880 to examine the Irish land question. He was notoriously a proponent of large-scale purchase and resale of Irish land by the state. This was the crucial moment of decision for Gladstone. He could hold fast to the opinions he proclaimed at Dublin in 1877 and in the Commons in 1879, which meant shifting the pivot of Irish land policy away from reconciling landlord and tenant towards buying out landlords by tenants.

The inhibitions which now came in on Gladstone were the inhibitions of the Treasury mind. Ironically, Gladstone went back to the Exchequer in 1880 to exorcize the evils of Beaconsfieldian finance. In doing so he was himself bewitched by Treasury animosity to any scheme whereby large sums of public money would be diverted to fund the relief of Irish landlords by means of the indebtedness of Irish tenants. Projects of unconventional notions of Irish land reform which looked well in the unattached days of independent opposition looked less well from a Treasury angle of view, which saw economies and retrenchments as the order of the day. It was another instance of greater freedom and less responsibility. Gladstone's mind began to turn back to the dead-end of propping up landlordism in the manner of 1870. Tenant purchase would become another of those deplorably 'new fangled' ideas adopted by the Tories, with the Ashbourne Act of 1885, funded with £5 million of taxpayers' money, as the pilot project. After a series of expansions, the purchase policy culminated in the epochal Wyndham Act of 1903, which converted Ireland to an overwhelmingly owner-occupier agrarian basis; and which 'solved' the Irish land problem twenty years too late.

None of this would have seemed in any case of pressing immediacy for Gladstone in a situation where his very continuing in politics beyond the confines of the 'mission' assigned to him out of the workings of the divine purpose since 1876 was in question. It was a matter of his being granted release. It was never a matter he would be entitled to decide for himself. For years to come he would be looking for 'signs' and 'tests' telling him that the door to freedom had been opened. That he was never to receive the order of his release was – given the rather critical and entangled nature of affairs in the 1880s – hardly surprising. Yet it was always a contingency hanging in the Cabinet air, inhibiting a settled capacity to look ahead, creating uncertainty, allowing Gladstone to indulge himself even more than had been his wont in matters congenial and to put off matters uncongenial. Kimberley recalled the difficulties of getting Gladstone to attend to any question 'where he thought the other way, or when he refused to take any interest at all'. Importuning him to attend 'was like bearding a lion in its den'.[30] Partly for Gladstone it was a matter of perspective and proportion. What were Kimberley's concerns to him? Partly it was a matter of the kind of freedom which comes from being an instrument of the Almighty. He recorded going down with Herbert to the Commons at the commencement of the business session on 20 May:

It almost overpowered me as I thought by what deep and hidden agencies I have been brought back into the vortex of political action and contention. It has not been in my power during these last six months to make notes as I could have wished of my own thoughts and observations from time to time: of the new access of strength which in some important respects has been administered to me in my old age: and of the remarkable manner in which Holy Scripture has been inwardly applied to me for admonition and comfort. Looking calmly over the course of experience I do believe that the Almighty has employed me for His purposes in a manner larger or more special than before, and has strengthened me and led me on accordingly, though I must not forget the admirable saying of Hooker that evil ministers of good things are like torches, a light to others, waste and destruction to themselves. In all good things, at all times, by all instruments and persons, may His will be done.

[3]

Gladstone's first major sessional operation, the budget which he introduced on 10 June, did nothing to compromise that deluded mood of exaltation. With a bravura flourish of expertise he abolished an old bugbear of the farming interest, the excise duty on malt, and he revenged himself on the Trade by a compensating increase in the duty raised on beer. But even as Gladstone deployed his old skills and his old cunning (Northcote observed at this time that it was 'a favourite habit of his to speak into the dinner hour, so that his opponent must speak either to empty benches or forego the advantage of replying on the instant'),[31] a new order of critical difficulties was beginning to take shape. Mutations were happening on the Irish benches which in turn were responses to intense pressures coming out of Ireland.

These pressures were generated by the impact of agricultural depression, notably since 1877. As agricultural returns declined, Irish landlords, themselves burdened with fixed debt repayments, lacked as a rule the margins often available in England for reducing or remitting rents. Incidence of eviction for non-payment of rent mounted horrendously. In October 1879 at Westport the Irish Land League was formed, inspired mainly by Michael Davitt, adopting a programme for the abolition of landlordism root and branch as alien to Irish custom, history, and nationhood. This was offered not only to tenants, but to the far greater numbers of landless labourers who, in the want of industrial jobs, faced the choice of the devil of worsening poverty or the deep sea of emigration. Present at Westport was the young MP (since 1875) for County Meath, Charles Stewart Parnell, a Protestant Wicklow gentleman of family who had made his name as destroyer of Isaac Butt's leadership of the Home Rule movement. Parnell was now sessional chairman of the thirty-five strong 'Mountain' or 'Jacobin' faction of Home Rule MPs, who elected to sit on the Opposition benches, by contrast with the thirty 'Girondins', led by William Shaw, on the Liberal side of the House. It was Parnell's genius to understand that something was now possible which hitherto had not been possible in Ireland: a union of middle-class, urban nationalism with organized agrarian agitation. The three essential elements of a great new Irish question were now in place: an extensive Irish grievance, Parnell's and Davitt's inspirational leadership, and Gladstone's presence at the head of a Liberal government.

If Gladstone had noticed Parnell at all before this time, it would have been as a deplorable example of Irish insensibility to the sufferings of the Bulgarians.* His 'real knowledge' of Parnell, as he told Parnell's biographer R. Barry O'Brien, began with the 1880 Parliament.[33] It was the 'Mountain' members such as O'Connor Power and Justin McCarthy who as yet made the Irish parliamentary running. What had been happening, below the surface configurations of politics, was the confluence of two streams of popular sentiment and emotion. The larger stream, in Britain, flowing strongest since Midlothian, was joined by an Irish stream, flowing strongly also since 1879, investing Gladstone with something akin to messianic status. Like the Afrikaners, the Irish could look for deliverance from their captivity. Just as in 1868 there had been a gathering swell of Irish expectations, hopes, even dreams, so by 1880 there was again such a swell. Justin McCarthy signalled its existence when he referred to the Irish people 'who usually look to a Liberal Government for relief of their grievances'; it was 'a habit with the Irish people always to look to a Liberal Government for measures of redress'. The new prime

---

* T. P. O'Connor claimed that Parnell was one of the crowd who looked on approvingly when G's windows were being smashed in Harley Street in 1878.[32]

minister, after all, 'was the first English Minister who had ever risked his reputation on the introduction of great and statesmanlike legislation for the benefit of Ireland'. Would not Gladstone, who had extolled the tradition of Fox, recognize Fox's doctrine that Ireland should be governed 'in accordance with Irish ideas'?[34] Gladstone at Dublin in 1877 had, seemingly, applied that doctrine quite decidedly to the question of landlordism.

That was in a time of greater freedom and less responsibility. Gladstone's initial response to Irish demands for new legislation on the land problem was precisely to have recourse to the status quo with which he had answered the Afrikaners. The Land Act of 1870 was his pole star, his alpha and omega. But by mid-June 1880 he sensed the disturbing power of the swell of Irish expectations, augmented by new styles of organized agitation. Forster's and Cowper's reports were dark with prognostications of great evil and civil tumult unless immediate measures were taken to stem the incidence of evictions. Gladstone was depressed by a dismaying awareness that there had been for long urgent cause for his enquiry about matters which did not come within the confines of his assigned mission.[35] That mission was 'special'; and its 'peculiarity' was that it mainly related to overseas questions, in no less than three of the quarters of the globe.[36]

Forster, backed by Chamberlain, proposed legislation to discourage or inhibit evictions for a temporary period in certain circumstances in restricted areas. This Compensation for Disturbance Bill raised a ruckus in Cabinet. Not only did it challenge 'English ideas'; it could be interpreted as bearing the character of a declaration of social war against the owners of property. Lady Salisbury reported eagerly to Beaconsfield: 'I saw Lord Hartington at Ascot. He said "You will soon be back again. I always thought it would be bad but it is much worse than I thought it would be. We have such a lot of cantankerous loons"!!!'[37] Gladstone had much ado persuading Argyll not to resign. But Hartington's Under-Secretary at the India Office, Lansdowne, would not accept Forster's claim that it was merely an extension of the principle of the 1870 Act; and forthwith did resign: the first pebble in what eventually would prove a Whig avalanche. Gladstone summoned Rosebery to fill the gap; and defended Forster's bill as being in the 'nature of a promise or engagement to the poorest part of the population of Ireland, now suffering heavily under a severe visitation of Providence'.[38]

Quite accurately, Gladstone defined much of the hostility to the Compensation Bill as 'a revival of the hostility, the smouldering hostility', to the 1870 Land Act, and denounced the 'heated language' of the Conservative Opposition as tending to 'cause the Irish people to regard it as a measure of vast magnitude, which is of itself a very dangerous misconception'.[39] In truth, it was more a case of Gladstone's own magnitude which magnified the bill for the Irish. Amid furious wrangling the Compensation Bill was forced through the Commons. Fifty Liberals abstained on the second reading, and twenty voted against. The manner in which Gladstone 'used the argument from terror' gave great offence.[40] It was promptly thrown out by the Lords on 3 August. Gladstone's memory of the affair retained a vivid touch of bitterness in 1897.

I was unhappily blind to the magnitude of the coming difficulties in Ireland; blind to them in part owing to the favourable picture which until recently the working of the Land Act of 1870 had presented, in part to the absorbing nature of the foreign questions in which I had been so long engaged, and with which I had to deal almost single-handed. Late in the Session came the decisive and disastrous rejection by the House of Lords of the Bill by means of which the Government had hoped to arrest the progress of disorder, and avert the necessity for measures in the direction of coercion. The rapid and vast extension of agrarian disturbance followed as was to be expected this wild excess of Landlordism: and the Irish Government proceeded to warn the Cabinet that coercive legislation would be necessary.[41]

Leo Maxse, the Conservative publicist, concluded in 1895 that the Lords made a 'grave moral and political mistake in throwing out Forster's Compensation for Disturbance Bill'. Gladstone should have resigned or dissolved.[42] An interpretation which takes the long perspective sees the logic plausibly thus: Gladstone is driven back on coercion; that makes the second Land Act of 1881 inevitable; that act, being a dead end, is doomed to failure; and that, in turn, gives the political game to Parnell and thus opens the question of a British response to his demand for a restored Irish parliament.

[4]

Even as Gladstone became aware of dismaying Irish revelations, it was borne in upon him that his assumptions about South Africa were also falling apart. Apologetic though he might have been to the Liberal party in the Commons ('Our views were in general discord, if I may say so, with the general tendencies of Sir Bartle Frere'),[43] he had persisted in being unapologetic to the Transvaalers. To Kruger and Joubert he repeated his earlier negative; looking to all the circumstances both of the Transvaal and the rest of South Africa, 'our judgment is that the Queen cannot be advised to relinquish her sovereignty over the Transvaal'.[44] This converted the swell of Boer anticipations of deliverance into a whirlpool of bitterness and exasperation. Disorders in South Africa began to take on what contemporaries could not fail to interpret as a sinister Irish analogy: British power was being challenged equally by Boers in the Bogs and Fenians on the Veldt. Before the end of June Kimberley advised Gladstone that the confederation policy had 'completely broken down'. The Cape government would not consent to negotiate with any but a liberated and independent Transvaal. There was no longer 'any good reason' for not recalling Frere.[45]

It was easy enough to sack Frere. He was on a special extended tenure at the Cape linked expressly to securing the goal of confederation. The fact that he was emblematically the last of the great proconsular exponents of the imperial idea after Layard's supersession at Constantinople by Goschen and Lytton's replacement in India by Ripon only made the mass of Liberals all the more impatient for his head to roll. The Queen did her best to defend him against 'bizarre' treatment at the hands of the Colonial Office.[46] The Palmerstonian Whigs, led by Hartington, still smarting from the Compensation for Disturbance affair, found it a sore point. But Gladstone, pressed on all sides, let Kimberley have his way. The Queen protested that 'Mr Gladstone *promised* . . . when he took office that there should be no reversal of *facts*'.[47] Great satisfaction was thus given to most Liberals and to the Transvaal Afrikaners. Logically this should have prepared the way for a resumption of the spirit of Midlothian, a swift about-turn of policy in South Africa, rescindment of the annexations of 1877, and the granting of generous 'home rule' to the Boers. This did not happen. Between August and December 1880 British South African policy lapsed into inertness. Partly this was because an entanglement of extraneous circumstances diverted attention. The 'new access of strength' which Gladstone had rejoiced at having been administered to him in his old age by the Almighty was suddenly withdrawn. There were obsessions with foreign policy. Then came the grapplings with the 'Irish revolution'. But mostly the inertness came about from a nonplussed awareness in the British official mind at the implications for Ireland of Home Rule for the Boers.

By the end of July Gladstone was reduced to a state of near collapse. He realized now that he had taken on the responsibilities of government in April in serious unawareness of what he would have to contend with. Beset in front with big questions of policy, he was being constantly harassed from the rear by the 'intrusion of irritating topics': Parnell's Irish 'Mountain' was fast perfecting the arts of parliamentary obstruction; and Randolph Churchill's 'Fourth Party' exploited the Bradlaugh and other issues at every opportunity to bait the two front benches. On 30 July Gladstone was seized with 'chill and nausea', and looked, Hamilton thought, 'wretchedly ill'. On the 31st, such was the state of his nerves and muscular system that he spent near an hour 'not shivering but shaking as a house is shaken by an earthquake'. He was confined to bed with 'strong and prolonged perspirations' and cabinet cancelled. By Sunday, 1 August, his case was diagnosed by his physician, Andrew Clark, as serious: lungs congested and temperature at 103°. Gladstone's condition gradually improved after that critical point, and by 3 August he was permitted to 'disburden' his mind by writing to Granville on the matter of the House of Lords and the Compensation for Disturbance Bill. But even with more favourable improvement and a relaxing visit to Dean Wellesley at Windsor Hamilton thought it 'hardly likely, however well he goes on, that he will be able to resume his place in the House this session'.[48]

The Queen, already sardonic about 'the People's William', observed rather hopefully in mid-September that 'Merry Pebble' was 'not what he was – he is *très baissé* and really a little crazy. He has not recovered from his illness yet and I doubt (and fervently hope) he won't be able to go through another session.'[49] There had been a stiff encounter over Gladstone's effort to pass on the late Stratford de Redcliffe's Garter to Lord Derby. The Queen simply would not have it. Even Hamilton thought it a false move on Gladstone's part. He covered his retreat with observations on the Queen's 'serious and unhappy change' of demeanour; 'now it is all grumbling and finding fault'. For the present, Gladstone managed to return to both Cabinet and Commons a few days before the prorogation of Parliament on 7 September. He spoke in the House on the Treaty of Berlin and his intention that the Turks would be compelled to bow to Europe's will in the matter of the Greek and Montenegrin frontiers. That would be his set piece for the autumn recess.

In the interval, he recruited his health and spirits with a cruise on Donald Currie's steamer *Grantully Castle*. Hamilton thought it wise to reject the Admiralty yacht *Enchantress*; but he found Currie, a shipping magnate and Liberal MP for Perthshire, a 'fawning and troublesome' man, and would much have preferred Thomas Brassey's offer of his *Sunbeam*.[50]* Currie seems to have suited Gladstone well enough. Together with Catherine, Helen, Willy, Stephen, and Herbert, the Godleys and Lacaita, Gladstone embarked at Gravesend and cruised westward, getting as far, in fact, as Dublin, where the party arrived 'in time to land suddenly and go to Christ Church. The congregation all agog. Out of doors an enthusiastic extempore reception.' (Gladstone read *David Copperfield* throughout the cruise: 'A most noteworthy book – it alters

---

* 'I presume Donald Currie aspires at least to a baronetcy.' He was knighted in 1881.

my estimation of Dickens.')* This occasion with Currie marks a further point when Gladstone began to look for undemandingly relaxing company otherwise than with his peers in the great world of affairs. The recuperative interludes of cruises and tours would come under the auspices of Currie and his like, unassuming rich businessmen such as George Armitstead or the cultivated but discreet armaments tycoon, Stuart Rendel, who were proud to be of service to the Grand Old Man and who took delight in picking up the bills.

Refreshed by his cruise, Gladstone, back at Hawarden, was gratified to be given reason to hope that, despite the 'recent short-sighted action of the House of Lords', and Parnell's incitement to Irish popular revenge for it, Ireland might yet compose itself into a healthier mood. Gladstone thanked Captain William O'Shea, late of the 18th Hussars and an MP for County Clare, for his thoughtful reports on the 'remarkable signs' of the 'warmth of Irish feeling' for Gladstone; which feeling exhibited the 'union of the people and their pastors in opposition to extreme and subversive schemes'.[52] Gladstone would not have been aware that O'Shea's wife Katharine (née Wood, niece of former Lord Chancellor Hatherley and sister of the future Field Marshal Sir Evelyn Wood) had become very intimate with Parnell: and in fact within a month of her husband's letter to Gladstone she and Parnell were lovers. That was as yet a purely private affair which, as it happened, bore immense public implications for the future. But an event with immense implications for the present was that a few days after O'Shea's letter the murdered body of Lord Mountmorres was found on his Galway estate.

[5]

What nonetheless was already exercising Gladstone's mind was the duty of redeeming the first and foremost of the pledges of his Midlothian mission. He admitted to Acton that he was as yet not quite sure of his capacity 'for a long and hard day's head work'.[53] But he could not afford to delay longer. Granville and Goschen had prepared the way as best they could, to the bemusement and wonder of the statesmen of Europe, who echoed Saburov's pronouncement, usually in somewhat more mocking tones. The Turks proved adept at procrastination and nimble in evasion. Gladstone fumed at the Sultan Abdul Hamid: 'the greatest of all liars on earth'; 'a bottomless pit of fraud and falsehood'.[54] He fed Hill of the *Daily News* with suggestions for public treatment. A scheme to

---

* Which had been low.[51]

intimidate the Turks was concocted whereby the powers would each contribute a warship to a squadron which would demonstrate Europe's menace off Dulcigno on the Albanian coast, for the ultimate benefit of Montenegro. In Gladstone's bitter words in 1895, this 'had no sooner been done than the demonstration was converted into a farce; Austria and Germany made it known that under no circumstances would they fire a shot'. The French were not much less pusillanimous. 'By this proceeding they made themselves sufficiently ridiculous, but with the consolation and inducement that, as we had taken the lead, they secured for us the chief peltings of the storm of ridicule.'[55]*

Bismarck in particular fumed at what he judged Gladstone's reckless irresponsibility. What was a merit in a comrade in the *Kulturkampf* was highly undesirable in the fragile state of post-Congress Europe. He thought Gladstone crazy – '*ein verrückter Professor*', unacceptably 'anti-monarchical, revolutionary, unpeaceful', with his amateurish 'adventures and complications'. Bismarck recalled Palmerston's prediction that Gladstone would die in a madhouse.[56] What incensed Bismarck was Gladstone's determination not to accept the Dulcigno farce as the end of the matter. Northcote relayed his fears to Beaconsfield of the danger of Gladstone's thinking a European war as 'a less evil than European ridicule', and that he would 'try to cut his way out of the mess by some insane exploit'.[57] Gladstone indeed was quite ready to take recourse in force; and he had a dramatic exploit in view.

It was carefully considered in what way coercion could be applied effectually with the smallest risk to peace. The port of Smyrna received regularly so considerable an amount of Customs Duties for the Porte as it could not afford to dispense with. All the military possibilities were carefully weighed, Sir Cowper Key appearing in Conference on behalf of the Admiralty as its professional organ, and I think Sir John Adye for the War Department. We satisfied ourselves that the operation was entirely and even easily practicable and no new provisions of force were required.[58]

Russian and Italian solidarity, together with a degree of encouragement from the French, was held to be a sufficiently European warrant for action; and when on 4 October the Turks refused the latest diplomatic application, it was determined that the Smyrnan operation would be set in motion should the Turks refuse further to budge. The Austrian and German negatives were not allowed as a veto, rather being the means whereby the Turks were made aware of the threat hanging over them.

---

* G drew up this memorandum in 1895 in relation to the currently analogous problem of Armenia.

On the 10th, 'with surprise equal to delight, Granville and I learned from Goschen that the Sultan had heard our proposal to the Powers', and determined to 'give way on both the territorial questions'.[59] Gladstone was in a high state of excitement. 'I do not recollect an instance in which the Providence of God has been more manifest.'[60] Gladstone's diary that day, however, recorded that a 'faint tinge of doubt remained!' There were fears that the Turks might have been re-emboldened by the attitude of Austria and Germany. Gladstone was in no doubt that 'one way or another, the Almighty will work it out'.[61] On Monday the 11th, 'Goschen's evening telegram was bad'. 'Granville and I met again on Tuesday, and "H" (I suppose Harcourt) was present. I was "under the circumstances prepared to proceed en trois" but my two colleagues "rather different"; of course it would have been for the Cabinet to decide. But "between eleven and twelve Granville came in with the news that the note had arrived all right".' The *threat of a threat* had worked.

In a separate memorandum of 24 July 1896 Gladstone gave 'an account of one of the most curious though unimportant incidents of my whole political life'. But it is Godley's version of Granville's delivery of the precious document which gives the episode its full value. Gladstone is sitting at his desk with Godley at his side. The door opens quietly and Granville enters on tiptoe with a paper in his hand. Gladstone, intent on his work, does not notice him.

Lord Granville then, brandishing the paper (which was a deciphered telegram) above his head, proceeded to execute a *pas de joie*, still silent and tip-toe, round the room; he danced it very gracefully, with wavings of his hands, and at last met Mr Gladstone's astonished gaze. Thereupon he stopped, and read out his telegram: the Turk had surrendered. Instantaneously Mr Gladstone exclaimed, with indescribable fervour: 'Thank God! Then I can go down by the 2.45'.[62]*

[6]

'Curious though unimportant' is an accurate assessment of the episode. In truth, the 'Europe' of October 1880 was but little less farcical than the 'Europe' of the Dulcigno squadron. But at least one pledge of Gladstone's mission had been honoured: the 'ideal of your life' in foreign policy, as Catherine loyally put it.[63] The Montenegrins were duly grateful to have

* In his own version, which does not mention any *pas de joie* by Granville, G records that he caught the 2.15.

an outlet on the Adriatic and the Greeks had cause to rejoice that Thessaly and Epirus were to be reunited to their homeland. Greek Cypriots took the cue to begin their own campaign to persuade the liberator of their brethren to countenance their *enosis* with Greece. Gladstone had little time in any case to savour his diplomatic success. The wearying realities of the domestic and Irish scenes soon imposed themselves as unforgivingly as ever. The irritating problem of parliamentary obstruction had to be faced. There were proposals to institute the French procedure of '*clôture*' of debate. Gladstone ruminated in a memorandum to Cabinet on ways of getting round the problem by means other than 'repression'. Quite apart from deliberately obstructive tactics the routine labours of Parliament had become 'unduly and almost intolerably severe'. There were the possibilities of developing the Grand Committee procedure; beyond that, projects might be envisaged under the heads of 'Local Government', 'Devolution', even 'Home Rule'.[64] But even were there a more forthcoming response in Cabinet – only Bright and Chamberlain gave much evidence of sympathy – the immediate and intense pressures of the deteriorating situation in Ireland forced themselves to the forefront.

At the time of his physical collapse Gladstone had left the Irish question at the point where, in the aftermath of the 'wild excess of Landlordism' in the Lords' rejection of the Compensation for Disturbance Bill on 3 August, Forster was proposing a stringent new bout of coercion. He wanted a special autumn session for this purpose. The shock of Mountmorres's murder sent forth ripples of panic. The shunning of Captain Boycott, Lord Erne's agent in County Mayo, soon added a new word to the language. Forster wanted for the Irish executive the power to suspend habeas corpus. Gladstone's later account of the matter was a sustained diatribe against Forster as a 'very impracticable man placed in a position of great responsibility'. Gladstone wrote in 1897 with not only the hindsight of time but the enlightenment of a convert to Home Rule. Forster had most of the Cabinet with him – even Bright and Chamberlain in the end. Gladstone 'finally acquiesced' to Forster's 'perverted ideas' of imprisonment without trial.

It may be asked why? My resistance would have broken up the Government or involved my own retirement. My reason for acquiescence was that I bore in mind the special mission under which the Government had taken office. It related to the foreign policy of the country: the whole spirit and effect of which we were to reconstruct. This work had not yet been fully accomplished, and it seemed to me that the effective prosecution of it was our first and highest duty. I therefore submitted: and became most reluctantly a co-operator in an odious task.[65]

That odious task took the form of the Protection of Life and Property (Ireland) Bill, which Forster set about preparing to ram through in the early stages of the 1881 session. Gladstone's insistence on a counter-weight remedial measure had Chamberlain's fervent backing. Gladstone told Forster: 'One of the forms of remedial proceeding will be giving greater facilities to the transaction of local and sectional, and therefore for Irish subjects.' Gladstone's intense anguish at the painful turn of events in Ireland took the form also of resort to the historical dimension of the case. This was a characteristic response. He had told his admirer, the historian J. R. Green, in 1877 that he could conceive no worthier subject for the new historical school in England than the struggle of the Montenegrins for freedom.[66] Within a few years, Gladstone's self-education in Irish history – albeit rather selective and partial – would become an integral element of his Irish policy. This is possibly the moment when he commenced that process. He further informed Forster: 'Do not suppose I dream of reviving the Irish Parliament; but I have been reading Union speeches & debates, & I am surprised at the narrowness of the case, upon which that Parliament was condemned. I think the unavowed motives must have been the main ones.'[67]*

'Local and sectional' and therefore Irish subjects never in fact got the legislative impetus Gladstone at that time seems to have envisaged. The reason why this was the case then, and remained so consistently through every session of the 1880 Parliament thereafter, is a matter of significance in relation to the way in which Gladstone decided ultimately, in 1885, that Ireland would have to be given back its Parliament. There were inhibitions enough in any case: Treasury inhibitions about money, par-ticularly in relation to 'Irish ideas' about land policy, Whig inhibitions about Irish County Councils in Irish democratic hands. None of these need have inhibited the man who rammed through the 1870 Land Act and who would shortly ram through the 1881 Land Act. It was true that Forster could reasonably ask for time for his repression to re-establish conditions of law and order. Nevertheless the fact remains that if Glad-stone had been seriously determined to get an Irish Local Government measure through between 1882 and 1885, whether in tandem with English and Scottish measures, or otherwise, he could have done so; and he could have got it pretty much intact through the Lords on the old, and good, argument of terror: that it was either this or Home Rule.

That Gladstone never reached that point in the 1880 Parliament is no doubt partly, or largely, explained by the fact that the big remedial measure he did decide to take up in 1880 was a Land Bill. His approach to this conclusion, and the scope of the details of it, were tortuously

---

* The 'Union speeches & debates' were those of 1799 and 1800.

pursued through the autumn and winter months of 1880 and 1881. He had a 'litter' of Royal Commission reports to guide him: the Richmond Commission, appointed by the late Conservative government to examine problems of agricultural depression, produced two reports. The Bessborough Commission would produce five, ranging from the ruthless political economy of Bonamy Price to the O'Conor Don's urging of state purchase. By 9 December Gladstone reached the conclusion that the 1870 Act would form a base for amendment and improvement rather than subversion, on the dubious ground that its record was 'one of general success, partial, and we may almost say, local, failure'. The thing to do was mark the causes and proceed accordingly.

Gladstone profoundly deluded himself. To Shaw-Lefevre, whose arguments yet again for tenant-purchase Gladstone found bristling with difficulties, the most regrettable aspect of Gladstone's procedure was his ignoring the Irish. The Bright purchase clauses would be amended, but Shaw-Lefevre failed to emancipate them from the Treasury mind. No attempt was made to obtain consent and support in Ireland. The bill was not promoted in Ireland. The Irish MPs were not consulted. Parnell himself was by no means 'impracticable' in the matter. The Irish party was almost forced into holding itself aloof.[68] The contamination of 'Irish ideas' Gladstone no doubt thought dangerous to his scheme in Westminster. But if 'Irish ideas' had argued him away from his 1870 fixation on enabling tenants to bargain freely with landlords on rents, and drawn him back to his 1877 Dublin position, some lasting good might have come out of the enormous labours he devoted to the question in preparing for the 1881 session.

In these circumstances, the Hawarden interludes at the back end of 1880 were but tenuously intervals of serene repose. There was much interruption for cabinets in London. Communication between the Castle and the Rectory was now facilitated by the installation of the new telephone invention in November ('most unearthly').[69] Gladstone reported glumly to Catherine that 'the Royal dinner table does not grow in liveliness I fear'.[70] There was time for lively concern with passing events. The marriage of the banking heiress Lady Angela Burdett-Coutts to the American William Ashmead Bartlett, almost forty years her junior, Gladstone condemned as 'disgusting', indeed 'loathsome'.[71] He confided to Laura Thistlethwayte that he had done his best to prevent it.[72] There was the endless problem of an honour for Tennyson; who now preferred that a baronetcy should be conferred on his son Hallam in the Laureate's lifetime.[73] Gladstone's habit of discourse, as observers noted, tended increasingly towards the 'long retrospect', with emphasis on the decadence of the present compared with the epoch prior to the Crimean War, with special regard to the 'lamentable change of feeling as regards economy'.[74] Gladstone's son Stephen wrote to Liddon of deeper thoughts.

What makes me more and more accept fully my Father's political views is the unmistakable way in which I can *see* his faith & goodness shining out *more & more* under the pressure of his political life. It is wonderful to see the solemnity with which he recognizes old age creeping over him; & all, that one could wish and dream of as desirable to come with old age, coming to him – & coming in spite of, and so through, all the tremendous worldly wear and tear he has gone through.[75]

That worldly wear and tear suddenly took on a much more wearing and tearing aspect in December when Kimberley broke the news to Gladstone – 'and he was hardly pleased' – that the Transvaal situation was deteriorating alarmingly. Colley telegraphed his uneasiness at the likelihood that Boer disaffection, incited by their celebrations of 'Dingaan's Day', 16 December, would fast become insurrection.[76] The Irish Office, itself in receipt of bad news about the arrest and indictment of Parnell and others for threatening violent resistance by the Land League to Forster's regime, had less reason than the Colonial Office to be 'stunned'. On Gladstone's seventy-first birthday Godley and Hamilton presented him with a 'Gladstone Bag', with which 'he seemed to be much pleased'.[77]* But for the first time in many years of office he was obliged to see the old year out and the new year in in London. A cabinet on the 30th left Gladstone 'too tired and distracted' to attend midnight service on the 31st. 'Is not that state a warning and judgment for our heavy sins as a nation: for broken faith, for the rights of others trampled down, for blood wantonly and largely shed. In our pride we have sinned, and in our pride especially are we punished.' Thus Gladstone saw out the old year, which had opened with such golden promise: 'in the hand of God I plunge forward into the New'.

[7]

That new year allowed but the briefest intervention before Parliament was summoned, on 6 January, 'a period earlier than usual', 'as some affairs of more than common urgency demand your attention'. The Boer revolt in the Transvaal (for that was the shape of things revealing themselves there) was in itself urgent enough. The Queen, indeed (after

---

* The *Shorter Oxford English Dictionary*: 'a light kind of travelling-bag, 1882'. A specimen displayed at the National Liberal Club is surprisingly small: 12 ins. by 3 ins. at the base.

having tried to prevent any reference to a withdrawal from Kandahar being included in the Speech) wanted ministers to put the restoration of imperial authority in the Transvaal at the head of their agenda. The advocates of withdrawal, such as Henry Richard, equally wanted an end 'to the miserable Transvaal war' to be the government's chief concern. Surely General Colley could afford to suspend hostilities? Surely the concessions intended by the government could be 'more definitely announced?'[78] Colley, however, was intent on crushing victory; and was uncontrollable by a distracted Cabinet and a bewildered Colonial Office.

Gladstone, and therefore his Cabinet, was transfixed by Ireland. There would be a 'further development of the principles of the 1870 Land Act' to meet the 'special needs of landlord and tenant', with provisions for giving to a larger proportion of the people by purchase a 'permanent proprietary interest in the soil'. Additionally, there would be a 'measure for County Government in Ireland, founded upon representative principles', calculated to form 'habits of local self-government' and 'popular control over expenditure'.[79] With a heroic legislative stroke in prospect, such as he had not delivered since 1870, Gladstone recurred to something of the desperate obduracy of that time. Beaconsfield found him very awkward to concert arrangements with. 'It was easy to settle affairs with Palmerston because he was a man of the world, & was, therefore, governed by the principle of honor: but when you have to deal with an earnest man, severely religious, and enthusiastic, every attempted arrangement ends in unintelligible correspondence and violated confidence.'[80]*

Forster rammed his coercion measure past protesting sticklers for the rule of law and frantic Irish. The House of Lords pushed it through with exemplary dispatch, and it was law by the beginning of March. Forster could point to its necessity after the failure of a Dublin jury on 25 January to convict Parnell and other Land Leaguers for conspiracy. Obstruction by the Irish reached such a pitch – 'crass infatuation', Gladstone called it – that they were cleared from the House on 3 February. Gladstone vainly invoked the memory of Daniel O'Connell to inculcate manners of better men and better times.[82] The great Baptist divine Spurgeon wrote words of solace: 'Now, honoured chief, may God bless you, and strengthen you, and spare you long to us all. Do not allow these Irish rowdies to ruffle the calm repose of your heart.'[83] 'The weary strain continues,' Gladstone recorded; 'it is the sameness of the tug which makes it tell on the brain.'[84]

Then, on 23 February, after dining at Marlborough House with the

* Beaconsfield was working on his unfinished novel *Falconet*, featuring an earnest, severely religious, enthusiastic anti-hero, Joseph Toplady Falconet. Augustus Toplady (1740–78), a divine, composed 'Rock of Ages'. G composed a Latin version of 'Toplady's Hymn'.[81]

Prince and Princess of Wales, Gladstone slipped on steps powdered with snow and struck his head violently, with profuse bleeding. This put him in bed for four days. On the day he was about to arise Gladstone was stunned by the news of the reckless General Colley's catastrophe at Majuba Hill on 26–27 February at the hands of the insurgent Boers. Colley was dead and all his force either killed or captured. Gladstone 'slumped back in bed'. Was it the 'Hand of Judgment'?

'The work and pressure of Parliament', Gladstone told a Liberal MP, 'have nearly reduced me to inanition.'[85] On the following day the background of events, already sombre enough, was now darkened by news of the assassination of the Emperor Alexander II of Russia. 'My day is drawing to a close', Gladstone confided to Ponsonby, 'and when a man gets worn out he gets gloomy.'[86] There was a 'tumultuary' cabinet on 22 March on the Transvaal over the Queen's objecting to the terms of the peace being arranged with the Boers by Sir Evelyn Wood. Gladstone could rejoice that demands for the vindication of British honour had been fended off; but there was no calm repose of heart in reflecting on the opportunities available to him since May 1880 to negotiate a peaceful disengagement in the Transvaal. It was a blessing that withdrawal from Afghanistan was taking place in the aftermath of a brilliant feat of arms by Sir Frederick Roberts; and it was gratifying that Herbert Gladstone should win his parliamentary spurs on 24 March with a spiritedly filial defence of his father's policy.

The dismal month of March 1881 culminated appropriately on the 31st with the resignation from the Cabinet of the Duke of Argyll. The Duke, a combative intellectual jack-of-all-trades, was not of much consequence politically either in Westminster or in Scotland; but he had been a Cabinet colleague of Gladstone's since Aberdeen's ministry in 1852 and he counted as a close personal friend.* Argyll resigned when the shape of the new Irish Land Bill became clear in Cabinet. He objected on three grounds. The first was that it had never been part of the 'programme' of 1880. The second was that remedial legislation should not be brought forward under threat of terror. The third, and most substantial, was that it was pointless to try to prop up Irish landlords as a native ruling class by depriving them of the last prerogatives of landed social authority and reducing them to mere collectors of shrunken rents. Gladstone, naturally, denied the validity of all three of these propositions; but the efficacy of his denials owed less to their own strength than they did to Argyll's political inconsequence. Gladstone was rather taken aback to find, from a 'stiff conversation', that Willy shared Argyll's misgivings.[88] Gladstone

---

* 'The Duke is the only man in the Cabinet to whom Mr G. subscribes himself as "affectly".'[87]

called Carlingford back to fill the slot, much to Rosebery's annoyance, and carried on regardless. After all, he now had the blessing (rather to his surprise) of the Bessborough Commission to opt for a radical imposition of the 'Three Fs' of Ulster custom: fixity of tenure, freedom of sale of tenure, and 'fair rent' for tenure. Clearing the Budget out of the way early in April was a simple matter. Gladstone had little left to say on budgets. 'I fully admit I have had no brilliant picture to present to the Committee. I have had no dazzling or bewitching proposals to make.'[89] He balanced a penny off the income tax with a surtax on foreign spirits and adjustments to the probate duty. Then, on the eve of the Easter recess, he introduced his great set piece of the session, the Land Law (Ireland) Bill.

It was a bravura performance in the old style, displaying, in Morley's words, 'unequalled mastery of legislative skill and power'.[90] There was much foreboding in the air about Gladstone's 'revenge' for losing the Compensation Bill. The measure took on all the appearances of heroism in terms both of the luridly dramatic backdrop of the 'revolution' in Ireland and of its extraordinary complexity and voluminousness as a masterwork of legislative construction. But it was hollow at the heart. To the embattled Conservatives and Whigs the Three Fs looked indeed like revenge. The assault on the principle of contract and the rights of property initiated by the 1870 Act would now be pressed home. Beaconsfield, who cultivated something of an obsession about Gladstone's 'vindictiveness' (endorsed by Manning), declared bravely that he did not mean to give an inch: 'we can but die like gentlemen'.[91] This too was hollow. There was no stomach for a fight to the finish among the Irish landlords. The Three Fs sounded terrifying but in practice would make little difference. They were much more important as a political slogan than as an agrarian reality. They represented the ultimate dead end of a pointless policy.

On 19 April Gladstone at Hawarden set aside the great matter of Irish Land to immerse himself congenially in considering some token that might be offered to the people of Montenegro in tribute to their inspiring defence of their freedom. He had already made his bow to the Nonconformists' 'invaluable service' during the 'Eastern controversy of recent years to the cause of liberty and justice'.[92] It was curiously apposite that at such a time of recalling the felicitous days of working for the downfall of Beaconsfieldism Gladstone should have news of Beaconsfield's death. It was not unexpected. Gladstone had been conscientious in his enquiries and calls at Curzon Street. 'It is a telling, touching event. There is no more extraordinary man surviving him in England, perhaps none in Europe. I must not say much, in presence as it were of his Urn.' Knowing the Queen's feelings (she had been sending the dying man cheering bouquets of primroses), Gladstone immediately 'sent to tender a public funeral. The event will entail upon me *one* great difficulty: but God who sends all, sends this also.' To the Queen he wrote that he would not seek, nor could he earn, 'Your Majesty's regard by dissembling the amount or character of the separation' between Lord Beaconsfield and himself. But that did not in any degree blind him to Beaconsfield's 'extraordinary powers' and 'remarkable qualities'.[93]

In reporting to Harry, Gladstone gathered his thoughts about the noble deceased, 'whose rival some call me, much against my will, for I am not and never was his rival, as far as it depended on my will or intention'. Always on good terms with Mary Anne, Gladstone felt there was 'something very touching' in Beaconsfield's 'determination to be buried by the side of his wife. His devoted and grateful attachment to her was I think the brightest spot in his whole life.' Gladstone held also that he had been 'most widely and sharply severed' from Beaconsfield 'by something totally different from personal hatred'; and he was 'bound to say' he did not think Beaconsfield 'felt any hatred' towards himself.[94] It was undoubtedly true that Gladstone's feelings were quite distinctly different from personal hatred, though it would take a student both of Gladstone's psychic energies of combativeness and his special kind of Butlerian Christianity to delineate quite that distinction. Beaconsfield, like Palmerston, was much more conventionally resentful at what, uncomprehendingly, they both felt to be a systematic persecution; in Beaconsfield's case, relentless.

Gladstone found it impossible through prior engagements to attend the funeral at Hughenden: Disraeli's executors had declined Gladstone's offer of a public funeral on the grounds of Beaconsfield's express desire to be buried next to his wife. Gladstone requested Sir Nathan Rothschild for permission 'on some *future* day, if it is not asking too much, to visit the spot in a private manner'.[95]* Possibly it was the widespread observation visited on Gladstone for not attending the funeral that provoked his much less generous remarks to Hamilton about Beaconsfield's 'pose' of simplicity in choosing the Hughenden parish graveyard. 'As he lived, so he died – all display, without reality or genuineness.' Beaconsfield's most striking characteristic, exacerbated by his Judaic feeling, Gladstone thought, was 'the utter absence of any love of liberty'.[96] For Gladstone it was seriously a 'great difficulty' as to how to compose a parliamentary *éloge* without dissembling. He left it to Lord Richard Grosvenor to move on the reassembly of Parliament that a national memorial be erected to Beaconsfield in Westminster Abbey. Godley noted how reluctantly Gladstone departed from Hawarden – 'like a

* It does not appear that he ever did so.

child'–to face the challenge.[97] In the end he pulled it off quite handsomely, choosing to enlarge on Beaconsfield's 'great parliamentary courage'; for which Gladstone could name but two statesmen in his experience as being Beaconsfield's equals.* The Queen expressed herself 'much gratified' by Gladstone's performance; which obviously came to him as a pleasant surprise.[98] Beaconsfield himself, after all, in his unfinished novel, had delineated the character of J. Toplady Falconet as having not only a disputatious temperament but also a 'flow of language which even as a child was ever at his command to express his arguments'.[99]

Perhaps it was Beaconsfield's passing, calling insistently to mind memories stretching back to the Parliament of 1837 in Lord Melbourne's day, which quickened Gladstone's 'brooding upon the desire, scarcely yet a hope', as he put it to Harry, of escaping from politics. 'But I do not know when or how God will open the door for me. Last year I used to say it would be this year, and this year I am beginning to say it will be next year.'[100] So begins the annual pattern which lasted until 1894. Gladstone never could discern an open door. Even in 1894 he had to be pushed through it. Hamilton later recorded Morley's opinion that Gladstone 'should have retired in 1881'.[101] Gladstone recorded on 17 May of that year: 'The fund of vital force is large for my time of life: but not large enough for the very heavy calls upon it. Nature murmurs and resents from time to time.' Heavy calls were indeed being made: Irish Land would distend the session to unprecedented length. Then the Transvaal matter would need attention. Still, Gladstone had done enough in Europe and Afghanistan, on finance, and would do enough on Ireland and South Africa, to have justified unarguably a title to retire on the terms he had proposed for himself in 1880; which were also the terms suggested by Morley. The mode of his not doing so is thus of considerable explanatory significance.

The tremendous difficulty Gladstone had in getting the Irish Land Bill through the 1881 session had nothing to do with its intrinsic merits or demerits, or its general importance. The Irish party regarded it as mainly an alien irrelevance as far as land was concerned and a possible danger as far as politics was concerned. The mass of the House had very little grip upon what Gladstone was at. Morley quotes the opinion that had Gladstone declared the *Koran* or the *Nautical Almanac* a land bill, he would have met no difficulty.[102] It became the object of obstruction by the Irish because it was Gladstone's great set piece and the Irish were bent on punishing him for coercion. It became the victim of obstruction at large because most of the Commons much preferred debating the

---

* The statesmen, implicitly, were Peel and Russell. Beaconsfield would have preferred Palmerston to Peel.

Bradlaugh case. To Rosebery, whose house near Epsom, The Durdans, was becoming something of a favourite retreat in these testing times, Gladstone complained of the 'squeeze and cram of business' which was 'worse this year than ever'.[103] Gladstone lamented accordingly that any hope of 'Local Government Boards' in Ireland had 'vanished into thin air'.[104] On the twenty-seventh night in committee Gladstone deplored the 'degradation' inflicted on this 'noble Assembly' by the systematic and 'unblushing openness' of persistent obstruction. Nevertheless by the thirty-second night – the longest process recorded for the committee stage of a bill since the first Reform Bill – Gladstone's 'mastery of detail', 'tact, judgment, good temper', 'outbursts of eloquence', and 'extraordinary physical power' saw the measure for 'breaking down the Land League' and 'pacifying Ireland' through. Hamilton had the great pleasure of quoting the *Daily Telegraph*'s tribute that whatever one's politics might be, the country must be proud of such a man.[105] Phillimore recorded Gladstone as 'radiant' on 5 July with his victorious progress. '"It is either the Government bill or the Land League now (he said to me). My bill is really a landlord's bill." G. wonderful, quite fresh and except in outward appearance quite young.'

The Irish Land Bill of 1881 was indeed a landlord's bill; but for a landlordism as an empty shell, gutted of all point and purpose. The provisions for purchase by tenants which advocates like Shaw-Lefevre hoped could be made into the practical and substantive core of the measure[106] were whittled down. Gladstone's driving the debates ensured that by the time he pushed it through the Commons and negotiated his way imperiously through the Lords' amendments, the purchase provisions (in the words of another advocate, Salisbury) had 'shrunk and shrunk in the emphasis and importance given to them' until they were 'nothing but a tribute to the personal position of Mr Bright'.[107]

This strategy became all the more evident in the 1882 and 1883 sessions, when Gladstone blocked and baffled all attempts to resuscitate and revitalize the purchase clauses of the 1881 Act. Ultimately, in 1883, insisting that the 1881 Act was 'in the main, a successful attempt', Gladstone contended with consummate deviousness that there was no point in revising the provision for tenant purchase 'except with the introduction of a local authority'.[108] The trick, of course, was first to get your Irish local authority. The more Gladstone proclaimed their urgent necessity in this Parliament the less he did actually to attain them. Gladstone was as unswervingly and immovably determined on having his way as ever he had been; and it seemed now there was no force in the Liberal party capable of challenging him.

The Lords could not quite see it as a 'landlord's bill'; but the new Conservative leader there, Salisbury, failed to rally enough troops to fight it to the end. Resistance crumbled. The House of Lords would not in the end resist any bill the Irish landlords were prepared to accept. The Irish landlords were in a state of funk. On 31 August Hamilton looked back over the session whose labours had exceeded that of any other legislature in the world, dominated by the 'Great Man', 'standing head and shoulders and likewise body, over everybody else'.[109] It was the simple truth. The contrast with the Gladstone at the end of his second session of his first ministry, in 1870, was equally telling. 'God grant modesty to me', Gladstone noted, 'and His blessings to the measure.'[110] To Catherine he wrote: 'We indeed have every reason to be gratified: and I in particular have been enormously overpraised. I do not remember such a case. I believe that many prayers from many hearts have upheld me: and I have been upheld by the hope that it would be my last labour of the kind.'[111] One of the many Irish hearts upholding Gladstone in those days was that of Oscar Wilde, who sent his latest collection of poems as 'a very small token of my deep admiration and loyalty to one who has always loved what is noble and beautiful and true in life and art, and is the mirror of the Greek ideal of the statesman'.[112]

CHAPTER 8

'AN AUTHOR OF UNBOUND INTELLIGENCE WHO WORKS TOWARDS JUSTICE TRUTH AND MERCY': TOWARDS AN UNBOUND FUTURE, 1881–2

[1]

The Irish Land Act of 1881 was effectively the finish of Gladstone's legislative concern with Irish land. As the mirror of the Greek ideal of statesmanship he was now freer to observe the actions of contemporary Greek statesmen. The Turks were making no difficulties about the second leg of the frontier rectifications, mainly in Thessaly. The citizens of Volo eventually were in a position to telegraph Gladstone with thanks for their liberation: the restoration of the Ionian Islands and now Thessaly was due to the leaders of English Liberalism, to whom they would look for aid in further reunions with their kinsmen.[1] Not quite so gratifying were the sentiments of the Cypriot Greeks in the same direction.[2] There was the embarrassment at having to authorize the governor of Cyprus to contradict reports that Britain had offered Cyprus to Greece.[3] Liberals in the Commons, led by Peter Rylands, were urging precisely that: the end of the 'insane' Anglo-Turkish Convention. The government, they insisted, must do in Cyprus the same wise and courageous thing it was doing in Kandahar and in the Transvaal. The way ahead would be to buy out Turkish interests and hand over to Greece. Gladstone's resistance – 'we are not called upon to give up possession of Cyprus' – was indeed all the more determined in view of expedient calculations that governments had best restrict the scope of wise and courageous concessions.[4]

Gladstone's two immediate concerns were to monitor the progress of the wise and courageous concession to the Irish embodied in the new Land Act and to negotiate a satisfactory settlement with the Transvaalers. On the latter front there was restive public sentiment which, linked to the retreat from Afghanistan, conjured up an imperial fervour not so readily applicable to Irish complexities. Demands for revenge for gallant Colley had about them a simple plausibility which did not attach to murdered Mountmorres. The Conservatives, having recoiled on Ireland, were all the readier to take the offensive over the Convention being negotiated with the Afrikaners at Pretoria. The Queen bombarded Gladstone with missives of her *'deep regret'* at Cabinet proceedings: 'an Exhibition of weakness' which would *'lead* to the *troubles* who *all* are *anxious* to *avoid'*.[5]* It was just as well that Gladstone stuck for retaining the Crown's 'suzerainty' over the newly liberated republics. His doing so was helpful to 'prestige', but his motives had much more to do with protection for the blacks: that was where 'we shall justly be subjected to the sharpest scrutiny' from Liberals.[7] A British Resident would represent the Crown, and there were to be certain restrictions on the powers of the new Boer governments. The Convention cobbled together at Pretoria in August 1881 has been aptly described as an 'illusionist's trick'.[8] The Boers were to be free, yet supervised in matters closest to their sense of *völkisch* identity and nationhood. Kruger would no more accept the Convention as an adequate or ultimate 'wise and courageous concession' than would Parnell so accept the Land Act.

At least the likelihood that the Convention would be ratified by the Volksraad, however sullenly and unwillingly, gave Gladstone plausible grounds for defence. 'Our case is summed up in this,' he told the Commons, ' – we have endeavoured to cast aside all considerations of false shame, and we have felt that we were strong enough to put aside these considerations of false shame without fear of entailing upon our country any sacrifice.' The government sought to recognize 'a higher ambition than that which looks for military triumph or territorial aggrandisement – an ambition which seeks to signalise itself by walking in the plain and simple ways of right and justice, and which desires never to build up empire except in the happiness of the governed'.[9]

Thus were the Liberal ranks steadied. More problematical was the relationship between empire and the happiness of the governed in Ireland. As the session drew to its end Gladstone began to manipulate opinion on the Irish case. He was eager to start releasing Forster's prisoners as a counter to the Land League's campaign to disparage, obstruct, and neutralize the Land Act. Parnell had embarked on a scheme to 'test' the judicial provisions for fair rents with the slogan 'No Rent'. 'We have now indeed come to a very critical moment,' Gladstone impressed upon Cowper, 'that of the real battle between the Land League and the Land Act'; with the release of prisoners to be 'looked upon exclusively with reference to its bearing on this tremendous competition'.[10] Gladstone further urged the point that clemency would 'tend

---

* She objected to Courtney for the Under-Secretaryship at the Home Office on grounds of his unsoundness on the Transvaal. G to Granville: 'I think this intolerable.'[6]

to counteract Parnell's desperate game, and it would remove barriers out of the way of those genial influences which ... I presume that we are more than ever justified from expecting from the Land Act'.[11] Gladstone could cite a successful Liberal defence of a Tyrone seat as auspicious: 'a great event as a defeat of Toryism in a strong hold but far greater as a defeat of Parnell';[12] and, as such, a good omen for a 'message of peace' to the Irish people.[13]

Forster, however, was much less inclined to send messages of peace. Far from releasing suspects, he argued for scooping up Parnell himself, and his chief lieutenants. He disconcerted Gladstone with intelligence of Parnell's preparations for a campaign of deliberate provocation. He wanted also a special session to legislate for the suppression of the Land League. Gladstone found 'much and disagreeable matter for reflection'. At Dublin on 25 September Parnell led a huge torchlight parade, halting outside the old Irish Parliament and pointing silently at it in a symbolic gesture rapturously applauded; and then proceeded to let loose on the 'hollowness' of the Land Act. At Cork on 2 October he declared that 'those who want to preserve even the golden link with the Crown must see to it that that shall be the only link connecting the two countries'. He then demanded a reduction of the Irish rental from £17 million to £2–£3 million per annum.[14] It happened that Gladstone was engaged to go soon to Leeds to give thanks for his election there in April 1880. Should he take this public opportunity to ban Parnell as an enemy of the Empire?

At Hawarden Gladstone contemplated a prospect rather bereft of genial influences. The 'indications in Ireland, and South Africa', he told Bright, were such 'as may develop into a very disagreeable state of things'.

I accepted my mission in April of last year as a special and temporary mission. I never hoped to get over it, so regarded, sooner than in the autumn of the present year ... Ireland, however, came upon us unawares, looming very large. This question, and the question of the Transvaal, still hang in the balance. From neither of them can I run away.[15]

The visit to Leeds loomed ever larger on the immediate horizon. There would be a cabinet on 12 October to decide whether to proceed against Parnell. It took the edge off the usual Hawarden recreations. Gladstone ruefully confessed that he was 'no longer equal to the true woodman's work'.[16]

Leeds put on a tremendous show. A torchlit procession of 250,000–300,000 was a good answer to Dublin – the 'most remarkable' that Gladstone had ever witnessed. Gladstone responded with his own tremendous show: 'Three speeches and four processions' on 7 October ('Lumbago just manageable'); on the 8th three more speeches and two processions. At the Cloth Hall the 'effort of voice' before 25,000 people 'for so long a time was the greatest I ever made: and I was completely exhausted'. Gladstone could hope that it had 'probably been my *last* serious effort of that kind'. The Queen telegraphed her hopes that Gladstone would be 'very cautious' ('surely such interference is not becoming in a constitutional Sovereign?' thought Hamilton).[17] Gladstone turned the cheek and gave assurances that he would indeed be cautious on the three themes presently occupying his attention: obstruction of business in the Commons, Parnell's campaign against the Land Act, and the appearances of 'Fair Trade' sentiment.[18] As to Parnell, Gladstone once more extolled O'Connell as the model of a loyal Irish agitator. He complained – very incautiously indeed – that a 'general cowardice' of opinion in Ireland was putting upon him the task of preserving the peace 'with no moral force behind it'. He concluded with the resonant threat that 'the resources of civilisation' were not yet exhausted.

The 'calculated insolence' of Parnell's riposte at Wexford, mocking Gladstone as a 'masquerading knight-errant, this pretending champion of the rights of every other nation except those of the Irish nation', and seizing on his admission about the absence of moral force – 'England's mission in Ireland has been a failure'[19] – ensured that the resources of civilization would take the form of the Cabinet's acceptance on 12 October of Forster's recommendation that Parnell be detained without trial under the new legislation for criminal incitement and intimidation. Gladstone took the occasion of the Lord Mayor's dinner at the Guildhall on 13 October to announce Parnell's arrest to 'loud and prolonged cheering, accompanied by waving of hats and handkerchiefs'. The Land League, 'an anarchical oppression exercised upon the people of Ireland', was to be suppressed. Lord Frederick Cavendish, returning from Ireland, reported to Gladstone that there the 'panic' was 'very great'; with general unanimity on the need to suspend habeas corpus.[20] With respect to that unanimity among the panicked, Shaw-Lefevre had some relevant thoughts, as relayed to his constituents at Reading on 27 October: 'Had they listened to the demand for Land Reform put forward by the Irish constituencies, the present crisis might have been averted, and the programme of the Land League defeated.'[21]

By the end of 1881 Forster had 800 suspects in his net. Gladstone was much exercised to establish the precedents set for this work as prepared by the previous administration. He was gratified particularly by a report on O'Connell's trial in 1844 which demonstrated that 'even at his worst he denounced this doctrine of *no rent* as criminal and likely to break up his (Repeal) Association'. Gladstone confided his hopes to Forster that by these drastic measures 'a more intelligent & less impassioned body of opinion' might be formed and extended in Ireland. For if that country remained divided between 'Orangemen & law-haters' 'our task is hopeless': 'for if we are at war with a nation we cannot win'.[22]

The resources of civilization were being expended elsewhere. Signs were gathering of the possibility of unwinnable wars with two other nations. The Transvaalers were demanding a renegotiation of the Pretoria Convention. And now the problem of Egypt was advancing to the fore. Under the strain of devoting most of the Egyptian revenue to servicing the debt as administered by the Anglo-French Control, the Khedival regime was starting to crack. As for the Transvaal case, Gladstone and Kimberley agreed that the best thing was to sit tight and wear the Boers down. Gladstone thought them 'a dirty lot', standing on 'L.s.d.'; he thought 'we need only hold our ground'.[23] On the Egyptian case Gladstone and Granville agreed that, with French and Turkish assistance, the status quo could be maintained. Wearing down the Irish with the genial influences calculated to flow from the Land Act was rather more problematic. Parnell's response to the imminent threat of incarceration was a grimly sardonic prediction ('looking through a glass of champagne which he had just raised to his lips', according to one possibly rather mythic version) that he would be replaced by 'Captain Moonlight'.[24] Throughout the winter of 1881–2 the incidence of 'outrages' and public disaffection escalated in west and south-west Ireland.

[2]

As everyone who observed Gladstone was aware, his capacity to throw off the cares of office when occasion and opportunity offered was remarkable. Once settled back at Hawarden after the Leeds and Guildhall exertions, Gladstone ('sadly bored by the police hanging about this house', as he complained to Forster) expanded genially. He was an exceptionally well-preserved septuagenarian. For all his dolefulness about no longer being equal to the woodman's work, he continued astonishingly active: the fund of 'vital force' was still in strength, large for his time of life. He revived very quickly after exceptional expenditures of energy. Although there were political problems enough, Gladstone was no longer oppressed by being a leader at odds with his own party. He combined a commanding new position as leader with plausible hopes of being soon able to divest himself, at convenience, of leadership. Granville complained apropos of Gladstone's incessant talk of retirement that he complicated the situation 'by insisting on discussing all Cabinet arrangements on the hypothesis that he might again shortly repeat the *coup de tête* of 1875'.[25]

In the autumn and winter of 1881 Gladstone combined the best of both his worlds: there were complaints at the 'indecency' of the lack of cabinets[26] while Gladstone canvassed colleagues on his imminent retirement ('subject to the condition that the calls to special exigency should cease').[27] Phillimore guessed that he would retire in May 1882. 'No idea of being Earl of Liverpool as the papers say.'[28] There were differences with Catherine on this score. 'I am more than she, desirous of keeping in view facilities for comparative retirement when going out of office.'[29] Catherine, entirely symbiotic with his public career, was appalled at the void that would face her should he achieve his desire that his 'next retirement from office may be an adieu not only to ministerial life but to general society'.[30] Hamilton, much in attendance at Hawarden that season, observed Gladstone's mind continuing to work on the 'question of disentangling himself from office'. Hamilton's own belief was that Gladstone might 'plan his future as much as he likes but that the matter will arrange itself – that is, he will be forced to remain at the head of affairs, as it is quite impossible for him to desert the helm so long as Ireland remains in this critical state'; and Ireland would take much longer to settle down than Gladstone, 'with too sanguine expectations, reckons'.[31]

Hamilton had another observation to offer, very material to the question of disentanglement: that Gladstone was beginning to establish himself as the sole cohesive power in the party.[32] Gladstone's immense, enveloping presence, redolent of the invulnerability conferred on him by his messianic repute in the country, curiously had the effect of allowing his colleagues in Cabinet the licence to loosen their own sense of obligation to cohere for the sake of the party. This especially was the case with Chamberlain, the more so when joined in Cabinet by Dilke at the end of 1882. Though they were more than willing to see the Whigs off, they could not afford to bear the blame in the country for breaking up the party. They needed Gladstone to cover for them. The Whigs, in turn, therefore needed Gladstone to defend them. And the longer Gladstone stayed on and the more, consequently, incoherent were his colleagues, the more he needed to stay on as the sole power of coherence. The incoherence in terms of relationships was exacerbated by uncertainty in terms of future arrangement of business. As he became inured to his situation, Gladstone increasingly resorted to the device of raising large questions in a hypothetical way, insisting that it was quite innocent in him to do so, as it was most unlikely that he personally would have anything to do with their ultimate resolution. It was rather like his woodmanship: the more he lamented its decline, the more zestfully he chopped. Hamilton recorded 'doing the proper thing for Hawarden' by joining Gladstone and Willy for a 'chop'. It was 'wonderful to behold the vigour with which the Great Man of nearly 72 sets to work, and the accuracy with which he accomplishes it'.[33]

What struck Hamilton most vividly, indeed, in those last months of 1881 was Gladstone's extraordinary animation and vivacity. 'I never saw him looking better or more cheery' (11 November). 'Mr G. is in wonderful force' (23 November). There was a Windsor to get through at the end of the month, but here too Gladstone was inuring himself ('much civility, but I am always outside an iron ring: without any desire, had I the power, to break it through'). The 'Great Man's' versatility in manifold interests and enthusiasms was endlessly impressive. 'The other day when he was writing to Forster on Ireland, to Lord Granville on public affairs generally, to Blennerhasset on Dr Döllinger and religion, he was also writing to some American professor on the cosmology of Homer and expressing a hope that the time would soon come when he would be able to test thoroughly the theories propounded by the Yankee.'[34]*
The Great Man was likewise animatedly opinionated on men and books. He had no doubt, apropos of the publication of Bishop Thirlwall's letters, that *the* letters of the nineteenth century would be Newman's. Lord Beaconsfield's ecclesiastical preferments were subjected to extensive critique. He 'harped' on the merits of J. H. Shorthouse's recently published historical romance *John Inglesant*.[35]† He was sure that the best recipe for a 'shaky liberal' was May's *Constitutional History*. Hamilton was surprised that he should have thought the biography of Bishop Wilberforce 'successful and satisfactory', since it included some 'grave indiscretions affecting Mr G. himself'. What Hamilton perhaps was not aware of was that Gladstone had supervised the availability of his own letters.‡ 'His avidity for books, especially theological, is simply extraordinary.'[36]

With Gladstone theology was ever the prime concern. He had earlier told MacColl that he wanted 'some solid and scientific work which shall set up historical or institutional Christianity to take its chance in the mêlée of systems dogmatic and undogmatic, revealed or unrevealed, particularist, pagan, secular, antitheistic or other, which marks the age'.[37] He professed himself a 'believer in the harmony between science and religion'; but he feared 'the effort to procure a greater ease in our position' would 'introduce a new element' destructive to religion's position. His response in these years to the 'strides in science' of Darwinism and

* Whether Homer conceived the earth as a plane or as a spherical or convex surface.
† 'The overrated *John Inglesant* was made a best seller by a photograph showing Gladstone holding a copy in his hands.'
‡ See above, page 234.

heredity was less defiant in tone than it once had been, more aware of the need to build defences. 'Broad and expansive as is his mind,' noted Hamilton of Gladstone, 'he shuns anything which seems to give an additional lustre to scientific discoveries that may run counter to the Bible and its teachings.'[38] He had assured a 'shaky liberal' like F. H. Doyle that he had 'no fears in this country from the progress of popular liberties'. He did not 'idolise the masses'; and was 'as far as possible from being an optimist in politics'. 'My fears are excited by the manner in which a large proportion of the educated community is wheedling itself out of the greatest and highest of all its possessions, the "jewel of great price".'[39] To Newman at the end of 1881 he declared his feeling that 'mankind is not now principally governed from within the walls of Cabinets & Parliaments – higher issues are broadly revived, & higher interests are in question, than those with which Ministers & Oppositions mainly deal'; and it was 'by subtler & less intrusive instruments that the Supreme wisdom acts upon them'.[40]

Hamilton set down the lineaments of Gladstone's weekday domestic routine at Hawarden.

His life is very regular. He rises a little before 8 o'clock and walks off to service at the parish church. On his return he opens his letter-bag and after giving it a glance reads the *Pall Mall Gazette*, the only paper he can now be got to look at. He then comes into breakfast, at which he is always especially agreeable, and which he does not hurry over. After breakfast he returns to his own room – the 'temple of Peace' as it is called – and gets to work. His letters with occasional dives into books occupy him till luncheon, when he again gives one the benefit of his conversation. He returns to his letters and books till about 3.30, when he goes out either for a walk or for a 'chop' in the woods, returning in time for 5 o'clock tea, which is a special fondness of his. Having devoted about half an hour in the drawing room to a cup of tea and a little chat, he once more goes back and alternates reading with his letters up till dressing time (which he makes a marvellously short business of). At dinner, though in a general way he perhaps hardly lays himself out so much for conversation as at breakfast, he is never silent and is always bright. The power of throwing off all his work and anxieties is among his chief wonders. If one fails to take into sufficient account this power, one might be tempted to think that the cares of government and responsibilities of office sit too light upon him, in an almost unbecoming manner. After dinner he soon resumes his book again which will occupy him till bedtime (11.30). I doubt if any public man ever read one tenth part of the amount he does. It is simply marvellous the amount of books he gets through, especially considering that he is not a rapid reader; on the contrary he reads everything, no matter what, with the greatest deliberation, as the pencil marks in the margin show; it is the amount of time he daily, hourly, and minutely devotes to books of every kind, from the 'tuppenny' tract to the stiff theological work, that enables him to get through the amount he does. His library at Hawarden is very large and very varied as may easily be imagined; and the arrangement, on which he prides himself, is all his own.[41]

Gladstone's parting words on Hamilton's departure from Hawarden on 25 November were about retirement – 'on which he is continually harping, and on which he harps too much'.

[3]

For all his harping, much of Gladstone's correspondence at this season was concerned with plans for the 1882 session. He did not bother much with preparatory cabinets. He had little direct, personal interest in legislative issues. His concern was to see how Ireland would go. He offered grandiloquent but empty phrases to Dodson on the theme of 'free and large decentralisation': local government in the three kingdoms, reform of local taxation and relief of occupiers by assistance from central funds, all with a view to alleviating the burdens on Parliament's time. These would stand 'in the very first rank when Parliament is enabled to resume the work of general legislation';[42] a 'grand decentralisation Bill' would be the set piece for 1882.[43] To Harcourt Gladstone doubted that dealing with the government of London would be feasible in 1882; though conceding that he had 'a certain amount of recollection' that Cabinet had agreed, 'at least provisionally', to doing something about 'creating a central body for the metropolis with subordinate organs for the parts'.

All he could offer in the end was to bless Harcourt's plan as well deserving of 'good fortune'.[44] In fact, nothing came in the way of good fortune for either Dodson or Harcourt. The Grand Old Man saw things now from an Olympian point of vantage. 'Next year', he wrote to Harry, 'will be the fiftieth of my public life: and beyond that very round figure I trust that, at all events in office, I shall not be called upon to go . . .'[45] On 29 December he recorded: 'never have I ever touched a birthday with such eagerness for a change of position, such a hope that my political work is all but done, such a dread of reaching the term of another of the very few years that can remain to me without being free of the great *fardel* now upon me'.

The greatest part of that great fardel was Ireland. Gladstone persuaded himself, as he put it to Acton, that 'the aspect of the speciality of Ireland somewhat improves: the reports and impressions of intelligent men become less unfavourable: the outrages tend to diminish: the Land League does not get its head lifted from the ground'.[46] It was highly gratifying that among the incidents of the new year was the tribute from O'Connell's daughter-in-law, 'in grateful appreciation of the generous way in which you have spoken of him on several recent occasions', of a bust of the 'Liberator'.[47] Nothing else at that moment seemed to be of urgent aspect. Gladstone assured W. S. Blunt, the Byronic adventurer who had set himself up as the tribune of Egyptian liberty, that he stood firmly by the doctrine of 'Aggression on Egypt and Freedom in the East' of 1877.[48] When it came to the Queen's Speech at the opening of the session on 7 February 'careful attention to the affairs of Egypt' was to the fore in the same tones as the announcement that there was 'no reason to qualify' anticipations of the 'advantageous working' of the Transvaal Convention, which the Pretoria Volksraad had at last ratified. The other point of significance was that legislation to confer new institutions of local self-government would now be confined to London and the English and Welsh counties. Having swallowed the bitter pill of the Irish Land Act, Hartington and his friends were reluctant about elected Irish country councils. Gladstone was content to humour them. It would be necessary to reserve the Irish case for 'separate consideration'.[49]

On the eve of the opening of the 1882 session Gladstone recorded the 'sad ungovernable nausea with which I return to the performance of the offices which this life of contention imposes on me as duties. It is not anything particular in the life, it is the life itself.'[50] On the first day the Bradlaugh farce irrupted yet again: 'Weary, weary!' Gladstone's insistence once more on asking the Commons to be high-minded and principled led to Northcote's being dragged haplessly by his party into being fractiously Christian. All Gladstone felt he could do was to protest at the loss of valuable time. 'Last night the H. of C. was dull and adverse: & I vaguely hoped they might say of me "he is done up".'[51]

Waiting on Ireland was beginning to have its own particular and peculiar consequences, especially as linked to the dropping of Irish Local Government even before the commencement of the session. Gladstone recorded a conversation with Herbert 'on "Home Rule" and my speech: for the subject has probably a future'. It certainly seemed clear that Irish Local Government did not. The statement Gladstone referred to was on 9 February, in response to one of the Nationalist Irish, P. J. Smyth, who had listed the familiar Home Rule citings of Deak's being the O'Connell of Austria-Hungary, the examples of Russia-Finland, Sweden-Norway, the self-governing Colonies, with the Union of 1801 being the *fons et origo* of the troubles.[52] Gladstone's response produced something of the same frisson as his 'pale of the constitution' declaration of 1864. He began by saying that he did not think exception need be taken to calls for 'an Irish Legislative Body to deal with Irish affairs', provided the integrity of the Empire was maintained and imperial questions continued to be dealt with in the Imperial Parliament. Gladstone would 'not undertake to say to what decision this House might arrive, provided a plan were before it, under which the local affairs of Ireland could be, by some clear and definite line separated from the Imperial affairs of Ireland'. Among the difficulties of the case was that 'neither Mr Butt before them, nor so far as I know Mr O'Connell before him, ever distinctly explained in an intelligible and practical form the manner in which the real knot of this question was to be untied'. By what authority was it to be determined that some matters were Irish and some Imperial in an Imperial Chamber in which Ireland was represented? Until the Irish Home Rulers laid before the House 'a plan in which they go to the very bottom of that subject, and give us to understand in what manner that division of jurisdiction is to be accomplished, the practical consideration of this subject cannot really be arrived at'.[53]

There was a buzz of astonishment, much as in 1864. Mitchell Henry, one of the Home Rulers, made the point that this was 'probably the first time a responsible Minister of the Crown – certainly the Prime Minister – had really shown a desire to grapple with the difficulties of the question of self-government for Ireland'.[54] Plunket, Conservative MP for Dublin University, observed that Gladstone's words could be interpreted only as 'an invitation to Irish Members . . . to re-open the question of Home Rule'; and wanted to know if this now was to be considered an 'open question'. It was clear to Plunket that 'whether the Prime Minister is or is not now more in favour of Home Rule than he was in the last Parliament, it is evident he has made a speech which has been interpreted in this House and in Ireland generally to mean that he is'.[55] Gladstone, again somewhat in the manner of 1864, responded with comments on his surprise at Plunket's 'sensitiveness'; and took refuge in explanations that his words might be construed as 'of a speculative character'. 'It is highly unlikely that I shall ever be called upon to take any practical part in any matter relating to these opinions'; but 'I have the strongest opinions upon matters in the nature of local government'.[56]

The Queen took alarm. She was anxious that Gladstone's words, however well meant, would undoubtedly encourage the Home Rule cause. The Irish would read into them meanings which Gladstone did not intend.[57] Gladstone did his best to offer reassurance. 'Nothing could be more improbable that Mr Gladstone should ever be called upon to advise Your Majesty as a Minister with reference to the subject known as Home Rule in Ireland.' But then Gladstone went on to expand his reassurance in a manner not at all reassuring. His sentiments about local government, Gladstone insisted, were 'part of a rooted creed', limited in application only in principle by the 'supremacy of the central authority'. He had, after all, expressed these sentiments on several previous occasions, including, of course, Midlothian. Rather more alarmingly he went on: lessons had been learned during the past half century. 'The self-government now practised in Canada, and generally viewed as safe if not wholly unexceptionable was regarded, in the first years of Mr Gladstone's Parliamentary life, as a thing fatal to the empire.' Then Gladstone continued even more alarmingly: 'There is a very real danger which may come above the horizon . . . That danger will have arisen, should a decisive majority of the representatives of Ireland unitedly demand on behalf of their country the adoption of some scheme of Home Rule, which Parliament should be compelled to refuse.' The great object of imperial policy would be to prevent the formation of such a majority. There had been a risk of it at the beginning of the 1880 session when sixty to seventy Home Rulers were returned. The government had done their best to break up this potential combination; 'and they have succeeded'. However, were the government to denounce in sweeping terms 'everything that may be comprised within the name "Home Rule", they would be paving the way for its reunion'.[58]

Gladstone concluded with three comments. The first was that there was general agreement that the Irish Nationalist contingent would be augmented at the next general election. In any case, however, Mr Gladstone's views 'must soon cease to be taken into account'. And he thought it prudent to make a final clarification: he did not mean to imply that the Canadian analogy could 'be safely or properly extended to Ireland'. The criterion would be what properly might (for example) be given to Scotland.[59] For like pacificatory purposes Gladstone attempted to clarify and defend his position in the Commons.

I believe that when the demand is made from Ireland for bringing purely Irish affairs more especially or more largely under Irish control outside the walls of Parliament, the wise way to meet that demand is . . . this – to require that before any such plan can be dealt with on its merits, we must ask those who propose it . . . What are the provisions which you propose to make for the supremacy of Parliament? That has been my course, and that is the course in which I intend to persevere.

Nothing could be given to Ireland which could not equally be given to Scotland, should Scotland so desire. Gladstone made a point of reminding the House of his former utterances on this theme, going back to Aberdeen in 1871; with references to his undeserved repute for 'formidable novelty' at Midlothian, 'scene of so many of my misdeeds'.[60]

What, exactly, was going on here? Was Gladstone simply, as he assured the Queen, engaging in tactical manoeuvre with strategic intent, a cunning spoiling manoeuvre to drag a red herring over the Irish trail? Or was there something deeper and of more moment involved? Was he preparing the way for an alternative Irish policy, 'manipulating opinion' in his old formula? Rathbone's plea of 1880 had been that by far the greatest hope for the Liberal future would be the 'work of constructing an efficient system of local government for Ireland and Great Britain – which would not only satisfy all that is reasonable in the Home Rule demand' but also regenerate local government in Britain.* What deductions might now be deduced from the fact that, in spite of claims that the cause of local government was 'part of a rooted creed', the sessions of Parliament from 1882 to 1885 were notable for the absence or abandonment of all local-government measures? Hartington and his friends were notoriously reluctant about the Irish dimension of local government, but that had never before stopped Gladstone from doing something he really wanted to do. Dodson and Harcourt, supposedly in charge of signal bills for England and Wales and London respectively, had every reason to suspect that Gladstone had merely wished them the best of parliamentary luck. Privately, Gladstone was informing everybody that impending retirement made the question entirely hypothetical anyway. Publicly, to confuse the issue yet more, he talked of the course in which he intended to persevere. Should indeed he persevere, what then? Were bills such as Dodson or Harcourt might manage through the Commons bills which he, Gladstone, need now devote his time and energy to? The Irish Land Act of 1881 set the style and the heroic dimension of things. Were there cause and purpose worthy of his denying himself the escape and freedom he longed for, surely such cause and purpose must reveal itself as something on an appropriately grand and insightful level, perhaps a 'juncture' comparable to the 1853 budget and the decision to go for Irish religious equality in 1868?

[4]

In the circumstances of the 1882 session such considerations were in any case entirely inappropriate and wholly premature. If there was to be a grand purpose in staying on, it was not going to be realized in 1882. Gladstone's last budget would hardly have mattered less ('this humble Financial statement raises but a single point of novelty' – the Carriage

* See above, page 257.

Licence Duty was to be augmented). He treasured a modest surplus and deplored an expenditure surpassing £84 million, with nostalgic references to the country and parties '40 or 50 years ago' ('my notions are too old-fashioned to allow me to view it with as much complacency as that in which it is viewed by others').[61]* The obstruction problem was at last resolutely attended to. 'A sustaining power seemed to come down upon me.'[62] New rules of procedure were proposed. The Speaker was to be armed with effective means of controlling debate. Necessary cooperation with the Conservatives would best be managed in a special autumn session.

To his son Harry, Gladstone wrote on 3 March: 'It will I hope be my last session as Prime Minister. I have now held that office for seven years. In the last century only three have held it longer: Lord Palmerston, Lord Liverpool, Mr Pitt.' He had 'good & growing hopes that the Land Act, in spite of Parnellites and Tories', would 'beat the Land League'. On the matter of the Tories, Gladstone took great exception to the Lords arranging a committee of enquiry into the working of the Irish Land Act. He displayed also intense and inveterate suspicion of the explorations in Ireland of Conservatives led by W. H. Smith with respect to tenant purchase, and to assistance given (most irregularly) in that matter by Welby and Frederick Cavendish at the Treasury.[63] He insisted to Forster that the first task in Irish land remained the rectification of the relations between landlord and tenant, and after that 'to relieve Great Britain from the enormous weight of the Government of Ireland unaided by the people, & from the hopeless contradiction in which we stand while we give a Parliamentary representation hardly effective for anything but mischief, without the local institutions of self-government which it pre-supposes, & on which alone it can have a sound & healthy basis'. Gladstone rebutted Forster's argument for waiting: 'It is liberty alone, which fits men for liberty.'[64] As to the hapless Dodson's ingenuous plans, Gladstone trusted that Local Government for England and Wales might be introduced before Easter 'should circumstances happily permit it'. Should they unhappily not permit, possibly it might be reintroduced in 1883.[65]

What Gladstone seemed much more interested and determined about was the introduction soon of the measure to extend the county franchise on a uniform basis throughout the United Kingdom.[66] This was another public declaration about a course in which he intended to persevere; and it was, for practical purposes, incompatible with private declarations about imminent retirement. It was inconceivable that Gladstone would,

---

* Gladstone, awestruck, contemplated the 'portentous scale' of the current expenditure of the French government of £120 million.

when it came to the point, leave the third Reform Bill to underlings – underlings like Hartington, who might well want to dilute its Irish application. It was one thing to let Hartington's reluctance about Irish local government impede progress on that aspect; in certain occult ways that might even be seen as a convenience. In due course Hartington might well find himself facing the prospect of swallowing a measure for Irish local government going far beyond Rathbonian notions of satisfying all that was reasonable in the Home Rule demand. But Hartington would certainly not be allowed to get in the way of Gladstone's plans for Reform.*

Early in March 1882 came worrying news of events in Egypt. The Khedival regime was threatened by a mutiny of its army. To Egyptian popular and national grievances against the Anglo-French Control was now added resentment at the French takeover of Tunis. Egypt, it seemed, was ceasing to be manageable on the comfortable old model of Mehemet Ali and Palmerston. Gladstone regarded 'a conflict between the "Control" and any sentiment truly national' with the 'utmost apprehension', and with 'a persuasion that one way or other we should come to grief in it'. As he had assured Wilfrid Blunt, Gladstone remained loyal to his values of 1877 and Midlothian. '"Egypt for the Egyptians" is the sentiment to which I should wish to give scope; and could it prevail it would I think be the best, the only good solution of the "Egyptian Question".'[68] But he was no longer up to the job of imposing such an eccentric opinion on his colleagues (16 March: 'my brain becomes a cloud: I have not sufficient force'). Gladstone and the Cabinet were prepared to be guided by Granville's advice that Colonel Arabi, leader of the mutinous Egyptian army, was by no means representative of 'a sentiment truly national'. ('I am afraid Blunt has been a good deal humbugged by Arabi Bey.')[69] The problem remained, however, of how to prop up the Khedive and the Control; and Granville, 'at his wits end',[70] could think only of military intervention: by the Turks alone, preferably (Arabi's nationalism was anti-Turkish and anti-Circassian as much as anti-Western); or, if unavoidable, assisted by generals provided by Britain and France. Gladstone inimitably deprecated adopting any such plan on the grounds that it seemed 'to suppose that there are producible reasons for apprehending a necessity of some kind for doing something precautionary'.[71]

Having persuaded himself of the absence of any kind of precautionary necessity, Gladstone was able to relax somewhat. He joined the Princess

---

* In February 1882 G put it to Bright that he 'did not think he was specially bound to continue through these great questions, though his zeal in regard to them had not slackened'.[67]

of Wales and Watts 'at Sir Frederick Leighton's to see his beautiful works'.[72] Two days later he examined the offerings at Herkomer's studio. Weekending at The Durdans with Rosebery he read '*the* chapter' in Froude's *Carlyle* on the marital deprivations of Mrs Carlyle at Craigen-puttock. ('Trash? Rosebery and I are quite agreed.')[73] Being introduced on 3 April to the 'Jersey Lily', the actress Mrs Langtry, was for Gladstone something of a puzzle. She seemed not to fit quite into any of the categories of *demi-mondaines* with which he was familiar. 'I hardly know what estimate to form of her. Her manners are very pleasing, and she has a working spirit in her.'

Gladstone was also freer now to resume close attention to Irish affairs. Changes in Ireland were in any case imminent. Cowper had signalled before the end of 1881 his desire to retire, and Spencer was already primed to take his place. Gladstone persisted in his plans to recruit Derby. But the Irish plot was already thickening in two highly intense respects. Morley in the *Pall Mall Gazette*, urged on by Chamberlain's 'leaking' Cabinet confidentialities, was running a campaign to get Parnell released from Kilmainham gaol, to clear arrears of tenants' debt, to end coercion, and to dump Forster and reform the Irish administration. (A 'counter-leakage' system run, as Hamilton suspected, by Forster through his adopted son and private secretary H. O. Arnold-Forster, was equally annoying to Gladstone.)[74] Then signals were received from Parnell via Captain O'Shea indicative of Parnell's willingness to come to terms. A cabinet on 22 April delegated Chamberlain (who had already been primed by O'Shea) to liaise with O'Shea; and, as Carlingford recorded, on the 25th 'Chamberlain gave us a most interesting and able report of his pourparlers with O'Shea' relating to the cessation of agitation against the Land Act in return for a measure dealing retrospectively with arrears of rent. 'Mr G. is willing to make the relief a gift.'[75] The Gladstones were guests for the Easter weekend of Francis Egerton at St George's Hill. Lady Frederick Cavendish recorded in her diary:

Uncle W. went this Saty. to St George's Hill . . . we heard afterwards that on Sunday he there received under cover from Mr Forster, a letter from Parnell to Mr O'Shea . . . to say, that if, as he understood was likely, Govt. meant to bring in a bill for dealing with arrears of rent by way of a gift, all possible excuse for outrage would be removed, & the Irish party would support law & order. [My Aunt Catherine] told me, that on getting this information, Uncle W. greatly rejoiced, saying it looked like a 'surrender' on Parnell's part 'all along the line' – release now justified.[76]

The most difficult part would be to square Forster. Gladstone, exhausted by the junketings of HRH the Duke of Albany's wedding ('the

explanation is simple: *anno aetatis suae* 73'), failed to argue Forster out
of his stipulating for a 'public declaration' by Parnell as the limit of
Forster's acquiescence to the paying of blackmail. Gladstone could not
impress him with the 'great sagacity' of Parnell nor with feelings of
indebtedness to O'Shea (whose assurance was 'the thing is done'). Not
that Gladstone could see the 'whole way smooth'. Parnell wanted a full
extension of the tenant purchase policy; as he put it on 22 April: 'The
Tories have now adopted my creed as to a peasant proprietary.'[77] Gladstone found this awkward. Forster in any event would not budge. At a
cabinet on 1 May Gladstone noted: 'There has been no negotiation. But
we have obtained information. The moment is golden.' Gladstone made
his ministerial statement to the House on 2 May.[78] Parnell and possibly
other imprisoned MPs were to be released from Kilmainham gaol.

The deal took Cowper 'by surprise'; and 'nothing but a series of
formidable objections' occurred to him.[79] But in any case Spencer was
available to be slotted in. But who to replace Forster? Chamberlain
thought it only too likely that Gladstone would see him as the obvious
man. A Liberal MP put the case to Gladstone: 'Many of the Irish Parliamentary party have spoken to me today about the Chief Secretary, and
amongst them Mr Sexton. They say that Mr Chamberlain is the only
man who is strong enough for the post. They would respect his determination.'[80] Chamberlain did not want the post, but would have felt obliged
to accept it if offered. He hoped it would be offered to Dilke.[81]* Gladstone
later told Morley that he never even knew of Chamberlain's willingness
to succeed Forster, however much others did. 'Would it have worked?'[83]
It is certainly odd that he never approached Chamberlain. Was he concerned that if it did 'work', Chamberlain's claims to Liberal leadership
in the future might be dangerously enhanced? In any case it is likely
that, the Irish Office now being at the heart of affairs in a way it was not
when Forster was appointed in April 1880, Gladstone preferred a Chief
Secretary who would be amenable to being closely supervised; and
accordingly selected his nephew-in-law and family favourite, Lord Frederick Cavendish, 'the son of his right hand'.[84] Cavendish had the utility
of being known not to be hostile to Parnell's desire for a tenancy-purchase
policy. (It was true also that Gladstone, as Hamilton complained,[85] was
too prone to 'jobs' for relations and personal friends: Lady Frederick's
brother Lyttelton's preferment as a Commissioner of Copyhold was one
recent case, as also was Herbert's following Willy among the Lords of
the Treasury.) For Gladstone the strain of the affair was immense. Lady
Frederick recorded her husband's returning home late on 3 May, 'saying
he had been greatly distressed about Uncle W. this evening – that for

---

* Dilke thought, incorrectly, that it was offered to Hartington.[82]

the first time he thought things were getting too much for him, & had advised him to give up the Exchequer'.[86]

Lord Frederick duly went off to acquaint himself with the Irish administration at Dublin Castle. Gladstone confided to Laura Thistlethwayte that in the Irish affair 'what is done, or what is left undone, is and must be very hazardous. But there are more and more genial days on the horizon than I have seen for a good while.' It was not possible at that time to 'make known all we know: a few weeks, say May and June, will probably make all clear, for or against us'.[87] Gladstone explained to the Commons on 4 May about the 'receipt of information' which had led ministers to deem it justified, in regard to the withdrawal of the 'no rent' manifesto, to order release of the Member for Cork City and others of his colleagues.

There is no arrangement between the hon. Gentleman . . . and ourselves . . . there is no bargain, no arrangement, no negotiations; for nothing has been asked, and nothing has been taken. By these words I abide in their strict sense . . . we have frankly availed ourselves of information tendered to us as to the views of men whose position in Ireland makes them, at any rate, sensible factors in the materials that go to determine the condition of that country . . .[88]

To Gladstone's indignation, the transaction quickly became known as the 'Kilmainham Treaty'. Forster's resignation statement repeated his objections to appeasement of terrorism and to the lack of public undertakings on Parnell's part; but what Gladstone ever after took to be evidence 'lowering to his intellect or his morale or both' was Forster's insistence that O'Shea read out omitted extracts in a letter from Parnell about cordial cooperation with the Liberal party in the future for forwarding Liberal principles and measures of general reform. 'This was a blow beneath the belt,' as Chamberlain saw it. 'Forster knew that Mr Gladstone had not accepted it, but could not resist the opportunity of making a point.'[89]

Forster's making that point came after the atrocity in Phoenix Park in Dublin on Saturday, 6 May. Cavendish, walking in the late afternoon sunshine in sight of the viceregal lodge in the company of Burke, the Under-Secretary at Dublin Castle, was knifed to death with his companion by members of a Fenian sect calling themselves 'The Invincibles'. The Gladstones that night were guests at the Austrian Embassy in Belgrave Square. Gladstone 'elected to walk home'[90] and Catherine went off to join Lady Frederick at a reception at the Admiralty. Gladstone was observed by a Conservative MP being accosted by a woman with whom, as the story was related in London dinner parties, he was actually arm in arm.[91] Both Gladstones arrived back at Downing Street almost at the same time to be told of the tragedy by Edward Hamilton. The shock broke them down completely but briefly; they recovered quickly to go at once to Lady Frederick at Carlton House Terrace. Lord Frederick's brother Hartington was present, but, being far from *homo loquax*, he seemed to Gladstone of little comfort. Gladstone himself, according to one version, 'went to Lady Frederick, knelt down by her side and offered a prayer, and then *went back to his work*. This is grand, but is *not* human.'[92]* Gladstone recorded: 'This grief lay heavy and stunning upon us but with much to do and think of as to Parliament, Ireland, and many things and persons.' Phillimore saw him on the 8th at Carlton House Terrace 'quite crushed'. That day, as he told Hartington, 'I was reluctant to go to the House for fear I should give way and make a scene: but it was thought requisite.' There Gladstone managed to get through 'the most painful task that ever devolved on me when standing at this Table'. Parnell declared his abhorrence of the foul deed and dissociated himself and his party from its perpetrators. On 10 May there was a 'stiff Cabinet of four hours on the Prevention of Crimes Bill – a good spirit on all sides has carried us through'. At the Chatsworth funeral on the 11th the crowds were near 30,000.

Harcourt introduced the further turn of the coercion screw, renewing the dispensing with habeas corpus and juries and enlarging powers of search and repression of intimidation and secret societies on 11 March, while Gladstone was at Chatsworth. Gladstone – the Queen saw him 'greatly shaken – and seemingly despondent and as if his energy was gone; very pale'[93] – introduced on 15 May the Arrears of Rent (Ireland) Bill. The Irish Church Surplus (£1½ million) would be brought to bear; claims were estimated not to exceed £2 million. Indignant sympathy with Forster's position and scandalized astonishment at the 'Kilmainham Treaty' were reactions natural among the Conservative Opposition. It was Arthur Balfour who most vividly and memorably articulated it: he did not believe that 'any such transaction could be quoted from the annals of our political and parliamentary history. It stood alone – he did not wish to use strong language, but he was going to say – it stood alone in its infamy.'[94] This wounded Gladstone sorely. He wrote to Helen, Vice-Principal at Newnham College, Cambridge, where Balfour's sister Eleanor Sidgwick was Principal, of his vexation, and of his being 'I might almost say cut to the heart' at Balfour's 'exhibition' – Balfour, whom he had coupled with the lamented Frederick Cavendish as 'the flower of rising manhood in the land'. He could not make light of it, even as the 'raving licence of an unbridled tongue'; and asked Helen to enquire of either Eleanor or her husband Henry Sidgwick so that he might 'at least know that it cannot possibly be insincere'.[95]

---

* The story was related by Lord Thring in 1894.

Dilke refused Gladstone's offer of the Irish Office without the Cabinet: a 'horrible mistake', in Gladstone's view.[96] Possibly also it was a 'horrible mistake' on Gladstone's part to pass over Chamberlain yet again and thrust the appointment on the dismayed and hopelessly unsuitable G. O. Trevelyan. And just as no one but Gladstone thought Trevelyan appointable to the Irish Office, no one but Gladstone thought that bringing back Derby would be of the slightest benefit to the government. Hamilton was quite scathing on the matter. Derby's refusal, Gladstone told Lady Derby (with whom he had a long conversation 'at the sacred hour of tea'),[97] was a 'horrid blow'; 'it takes away my last hope of sitting in Cabinet with your husband. My hour-glass is all but run out. He will reappear, when I disappear.' Gladstone had been exulting in the notion of divesting himself of the Exchequer, 'and thus becoming a little less unequal to the load on me'. But now any other mode of change would dislocate without advantage; 'and I must go straining and struggling'.[98] Goschen also declined again to assist, on the ground still of the county franchise.

As Arrears and Coercion bubbled away in the parliamentary pot, Egypt thrust itself inconveniently forward once more. By this time – late May – it was a question of sending ironclads to Alexandria and Port Said to menace the Egyptians and protect European lives and property, and, incidentally, to secure the 'Freedom of the Suez Canal'. On behalf of the Foreign Office Dilke gave assurances that the presence of the fleet at Alexandria, 'without the employment of force', would contribute to the 'maintenance of the status quo in Egypt, of the Sovereignty of the Sultan, of the position of the Khedive, and of the liberties of the Egyptian people'. Dilke added assurances also with respect to the debt: maintenance of the 'observance of the international engagements of Egypt'.[99] Gladstone calmed speculation as to intervention: 'not with the slightest belief in my mind that there is any probability of an occasion arising for the employment of force'. Nor was there any reason 'to suspect us of pursuing aggressive schemes, of immoderate doctrines, and notions of self-assertion, or of any other defect on that side of human weakness'. He much deprecated discussion of the matter for the mischief it might do to close and intimate concert with France.[100] The most apposite comment was made by Wilfrid Lawson: 'That I should live to see the day when a Liberal Ministry should come down to the House and declare that their policy is the maintenance of the independence and integrity of the Ottoman Empire!'[101]

[5]

These public signals of soothing reassurance on the Egyptian case were being complemented by private signals of soothing reassurance on the Irish case. Parnell's mistress, Katharine O'Shea (who was carrying his child when Parnell was in Kilmainham), approached Gladstone with what have been somewhat mockingly described as 'tearful appeals'[102] to convince Gladstone of the genuineness of Parnell's repudiation of the assassins of Lord Frederick. Hamilton disliked the business intensely. 'It would have been far better for Mr Gladstone to decline point blank to see her or communicate with her; but he does not take the view of the "man of the world" in such matters.'[103] She and Gladstone met on 2 June at her favourite hotel, Thomas's in Berkeley Square; the beginning of a lengthy relationship which curiously mixed certain components of his Thistlethwayte *amitié amoureuse* with something of the high seriousness of the late Duchess Harriet's discreet role. That she was Parnell's mistress – Granville made her reputation clear to Gladstone on 23 May,[104] and Hamilton also was quite *au fait* – would make her more, not less, of interest to Gladstone. In 1891 Gladstone admitted to Hamilton having been to see Mrs O'Shea twice at Thomas's Hotel in 1882, 'but had no clear recollection of the woman herself or of his conversation'. He claimed that almost all he remembered 'was saying to her that Parnell appeared to him to be an altered man after Kilmainham in which she concurred, and to show evident conservative proclivities which he (Mr G.) intended to do his utmost to encourage'. It was Lord Richard Grosvenor, Adam's successor as Whip, 'who was generally made the go-between in those days when communication with Mrs O'Shea was really necessary'.[105]

Mrs O'Shea's eager purpose was to arrange a meeting between Parnell and Gladstone. This Gladstone declined, for all her assurances of the utmost confidentiality – it would be disclosed 'not even to Captain O'Shea'. Gladstone did not object in principle, but thought such an encounter premature.[106] To Chamberlain, whose own good offices with Parnell and O'Shea he also counted on, Gladstone made clear that any 'covenant' on Irish policy with the Irish party was 'inadmissible' and would be prejudicial and counterproductive.[107] Forster's words had left their mark. Gladstone was acutely aware of rumblings of dissent from among his colleagues, expressed most plainly by Hartington. For the time being the priorities were to push through the Crimes and Arrears Bills (Gladstone sent Chamberlain to O'Shea to see if Parnell could be induced to support the Crimes Bill). There was much disaffection about Arrears; and it was likely to be contested sharply in the Lords. But to Gladstone these were all now matters at a secondary level of concern.

What really mattered was what he had said about Parnell to Mrs O'Shea: that Parnell was an 'altered man', and that there were encourageable 'proclivities' to be developed from that great fact. Before long there were reports of Gladstone's dinner-table conversation to the effect that the events of April and May 'had completely changed, as by religious conversion, the character and views of the Irish leader'.[108]

This faith that Parnell really had been converted into a second O'Connell remained until 1890 the prime bearing on Gladstone's Irish compass. It gave him hope that, whatever the obscurities and distortions incidental to the contours of the political terrain in the short view, in the long view his reading of the course and the direction was true. Thus in the aftermath of horrific tragedy Gladstone was not weighed down or despondent. He found time for an Eton excursion: an invitation from Edward Lyttelton to 'Aunty Pussy' to meet George Curzon and others among the Eton lights ('Such larks it would be!').[109] Then Ellen Terry, hearing from Henry Irving that the Gladstones were thinking of seeing his *Romeo and Juliet* production, pleaded that on next Saturday, 24 June, '*the* event of the season takes place! My "benefit" at the Lyceum.' It would make Miss Terry 'very happy' if Gladstone 'would come and beam on us, as you always do when you are at a theatre: I should feel prouder of your presence than of any other Englishman and would carefully secure you the most comfortable box in the house'.[110] Phillimore recorded Gladstone at dinner 'wonderfully vigorous and well'. Gladstone told him that 'his general health was stronger than it had been for years and he could only ascribe it to the prayers of his friends'. Sir Andrew Clark told Granville that Gladstone had the best chance of any he had known in his medical experience of living to be a centenarian: sound from head to foot and careful in his habits.[111] Gladstone divulged confidentially to Phillimore that there would have to be an autumn session to deal with the procedure and *clôture* question; 'having done wh. he will resign'. His eyesight was failing and deafness increasing slightly, otherwise he was stronger than two or three years ago.[112]

If there now was hope that Ireland would settle down once the current legislation was through, Egypt, it appeared, would be quite a different matter. Colonel Arabi, it seemed, was not a man who could be relied upon for conservative proclivities, not a man producible as another Parnell. The case was not responding to the treatment habitually applied hitherto to such cases. The more the western powers threatened the more defiant were the Egyptians. At the end of May the Khedive's coup to get rid of Arabi backfired. Arabi rebounded stronger than ever. There were many Liberals who saw him as Egypt's hope. Sir William Gregory told Gladstone: 'It seems hard to banish or bowstring such a man whom I believe to be the purest and noblest oriental I have ever met.' Diplomatists had conveyed false intelligence about Arabi, Gregory assured Gladstone, not intentionally but because of interests 'whose only wish is to convert Egypt into a coupon-paying machine directed by European Controllers and administered solely for European Employeés'.[113]* Gladstone (incidentally, a large holder of Egyptian bonds) was not impressed. He viewed with

satisfaction whatever there is in Egypt of real movement towards institutions & local self-government. But I am wholly at a loss to view Arabi's recent conduct as having any relation to them. He seems to me to represent at this time military violence and nothing else. I may of course be in error but it is not for want of taking impartial pains to inform myself by hearing all sides, and I have no reason in this case for self-mistrust beyond the measure in which a sober-minded man ought to carry it along with him in all questions and on all occasions.[114]

The riots and massacres in Alexandria on 11–12 June, in which some fifty Europeans were killed and much property destroyed, simply confirmed this view of Arabi.

The atmosphere at Westminster, meanwhile, bore certain, if remote, analogies to the Alexandrian convulsion. The vote in the Commons on 6 July for the Arrears Bill was disturbingly close: 'a seriously diminished majority'. The following day saw a defeat on the Crimes Bill 'through Whig defections & Irish abstentions'. Gladstone felt it 'a blow to me, very welcome if it displaced me; but from the nature of the case it will not'. There was talk of the ministry breaking up, and of Gladstone's resignation should the Lords throw Arrears out. 'Time too slips away,' he lamented to Mrs O'Shea. '"When is the Arrears bill to become law?" I ask myself in vain.'[115] Salisbury was making a great effort to embolden the Lords to challenge the government with a signal rebuff. There were 'stormy' cabinets. 'Mr Gladstone mixing Ireland and Egypt together, broke out in the House of Commons on July 7th, and afterwards privately told his colleagues that he intended to resign!'[116] Dilke observed 'Mr G's homeric rage – and – defeat'. Granville felt obliged to beg his colleagues 'to remember who Mr Gladstone was, and not to press him too hard in discussion'. In other words, as Dilke decoded, 'told them to remember they were dealing with a magnificent lunatic'. Gladstone's rage had much to do, Dilke felt sure, with the fact that he was being overborne by the merest subordinates: 'he looks upon us as clerks and boys – clerks like Northbrook and Childers, and naughty boys like Hartington, Chamberlain and myself'.[117] By 12 July Gladstone had waxed 'so

---

* Gregory, of Coole Park, Galway, was formerly an Irish MP and Governor of Ceylon.

belligerent' over Arrears that he threatened to prorogue, call another session, and pass the bill again, and dare the Lords to do its worst. For all Salisbury's invective against, in Granville's protesting words, 'a great statesman in "another place"', resistance in the Lords crumbled over Arrears as it had done the previous year over the Land Bill. Even if Gladstone's Commons majority was getting a little bedraggled, there was no chance of baiting him as in earlier Parliaments. And he was far too strong in the country for the Lords to adventure as yet a set-piece confrontation. By mid-August Gladstone, with reason, could look forward to a decisive diminution of Irish disaffection as autumn approached.

As he triumphed over the cowed Lords and wielded the coercive rod of Empire in Ireland, Gladstone had no particular reason to fear that the Egyptian affair posed any dangers to him. The French were rather too disposed to the idea of intervening, and some of the 'embarrassments' of the case, as he told Herbert, had been extreme. But a conference of the powers at Constantinople proposed by the French 'has gone to work and this is of itself a considerable fact; a bulwark against precipitate follies'.[118] *If* intervention became necessary, the Sultan would be required to save the Khedive from Arabi. Britain would concentrate on getting reparations for the Alexandrian outrages and damages. But the speed of events was now so accelerated that within a week Gladstone was looking into the abyss (or, more appropriately, Serbonian bog) of intervention. He put it to Granville on 1 July: 'In perspective there is a question that may be formidable – If neither Sultan, nor Conference, nor France, will act – and if the Khedive, really or ostensibly, settles his affairs with Arabi – and if we have no difficulty in dealing with the question of reparation – are we then, on our own sole account, to undertake a military intervention to put Arabi down?' For the moment Gladstone could step back from this hypothetical edge by assuring himself that the question, apart from its intrinsic absurdity, in any case had not yet 'arrived'.[119] Part of the problem was, however, that for Hartington it had arrived. He was now compensating for Irish humiliations with Palmerstonian insistence that if things were to come to intervention, it must indeed be intervention involving neither Sultan, nor Conference, nor France. That insistence was not without its consequences. Granville reported to Hartington on 8 July: 'Gladstone admitted to me yesterday for the first time that we were bound to protect the Suez Canal.'[120]

Yet still there were moments of scruple. 'The more I reflect,' confessed Gladstone to Granville, 'the more I feel unprepared to take any *measure* with regard to the Suez Canal single-handed, or in union with France, apart from any reference to the authority of Europe.'[121] A rally of non-interventionist forces offered Gladstone their best support. Frederic Harrison appealed fervently to him not to commit a great wrong in

Egypt 'of a kind which you have denounced with special force for the sake of the bondholders'.[122] The rather interesting fact here was that Gladstone's largest holding (one third) in his bond portfolio was precisely £19,400 of Egyptian Tribute Loan. He seems to have been quite impervious to any embarrassment in the matter. As he absolutely could not reproach himself with the slightest twinge of doubt that he had, or would, make any decision about Egypt with any thought of bondholding, his conscience was perfectly clear and no question of improper interest could possibly arise. That he should profit greatly in the way the transaction ultimately resolved itself was a contingency wholly remote and distinct from the decisions he made as responsible minister. Such, it must be presumed, were the rationalizations in Gladstone's own mind: assuming, of course, that he thought about the issue at all.* What was certainly clear was that there were crucial passages of time as the Egyptian question became critical when Gladstone was not thinking clearly about it. Hartington complained to Granville: 'I am afraid there is no chance of a Cabinet, or of getting Mr Gladstone to pay any attention to Egypt while the Arrears Bill is going on.'[124] Another part of the problem was that Granville was adrift, and so stumble and muddle could play its role. 'I am very sorry to have been so unbusinesslike,' he apologized to Gladstone on 12 July, 'and to have given you so much trouble.'[125]

At a cabinet on 9 July, amid the turmoil of its nearly breaking up on Ireland, a decision was taken on the question of Admiral Seymour's ultimatum to the Egyptians to cease strengthening the fortifications of Alexandria. 'The Prime Minister gave way to the forward party for the moment. "I do not feel the necessity but I am willing to defer to your decision and judgments." The old man, already at full stretch with the Irish Arrears Bill, for the moment had lost his grip on Egyptian policy.'[126] The order was signalled to Seymour on 11 July to reduce the fortifications by bombardment. Harcourt jested sardonically: 'At last we have done something popular.' Dilke observed Gladstone in the Commons on the 12th 'in a fighting humour'. 'He put our defence upon "the safety of the fleet" and "safety of Europeans throughout the East".' He was 'indignant', in reply to Gourley, 'about the bondholders, and, in reply to Lawson, about our "drifting into war"'. He asserted confidently that the 'international atrocity' of the Alexandrian massacres had been the work of Arabi, overruling the people.[127] The Arabists were, so to speak, the Land Leaguers of Egypt. And the Palmerstonian precedent, the Syrian

---

* The stock in question stood at 57 in the summer of 1882 and 82 after the invasion and occupation: 'so Gladstone had done well out of his investment, more than doubling its value in less than twenty years – a good performance for a government bond but a questionable one for a Prime Minister directly involved in the central act which increased its value'.[123]

intervention of 1860–61, was not, after all, that apocalyptically alarming.

All of which put Gladstone in a peevish and captious humour when Bright resigned on 12 July, declaring himself unable to accept any share of the responsibility for the 'acts of war' which had occurred at Alexandria. Gladstone defended his decision. 'I feel that in being party to this work, I have been a labourer in the cause of peace.'[128] Gladstone informed the Queen of his 'very deep concern' at Bright's resignation.

Mr Bright resigns exclusively on acct. of policy and proceedings in Egypt. He has been an energetic supporter of the Bills for Ireland . . . His present act may be open to criticisms, which it is not for Mr G. to anticipate . . . Mr G. is obliged to admit that he does not clearly comprehend Mr Bright's present view; and Mr Bright's letters & conversations have consisted very much more of references to his past career, & strong statements of feeling, than of any attempts to reason on the existing facts of the case with the obligations which they appear to entail.

After all, as Gladstone went on to point out, it was not the case that Bright disapproved of all wars under all circumstances. He was widely understood to have approved the war of the Northern States against the South in America in 1861–5.[129]

Dilke takes up the story in his diary:

A Cabinet was to have been held on July 20th to decide to send out an army corps; Mr Gladstone forgot to call it, and it had to be brought together suddenly (some members being absent), and agreed to the proposal of a vote of credit. Mr Gladstone informed his colleagues that he should not meet Parliament again in February, but should leave the House of Commons after the Autumn session, if not before it.[130]

On 29 July Freycinet's ministry fell in the French Chamber and with it any last chance of French partnership in intervention. The Italians declined to take part. The Turks were warned off. Britain alone would execute the will of Europe: in Gladstone's words, Egypt would be 'neutralised by European act'.[131] Sir Garnet Wolseley was appointed to command an expedition to rescue the Egyptians from Arabi and restore the legitimate authority of the Khedive. To Henry Richard's agonized protest on behalf of the Peace Society, Gladstone responded: 'I am not conscious of any change in my own standard of action, or in that of my colleagues, since the day when, after three military miscarriages, we tried severely the temper of this nation by declining to shed the blood of the Boers of the Transvaal, and afford them peace.'[132] There could be no doubt, as he put it to Ripon, that 'we are discharging single-handed an European duty'.[133]

In August 1882 Gladstone achieved his Arrears Act, to fulfil his bargain with Parnell, with the bonus of humiliating the House of Lords and Lord Salisbury. He went off for a cruise between Osborne and Dorset in Wolverton's yacht *Palatine*. Good news of Wolseley's progress began to come through; and then, on 13 September, Wolseley presented Gladstone with a splendid victory over Arabi's army at Tel-el-Kebir. The way was opened for a swift occupation of Cairo. Arabi was a prisoner. Gladstone was master of the Nile, the Canal, the crossroads of the world. It was something Beaconsfield deserved to have lived long enough to witness.

[6]

Though he did not realize it, Gladstone in fact inaugurated what an Austrian commentator at the time described aptly as a 'silent annexation à la Bosnia'.[134] A substantial British military presence would remain in Egypt until the time of Arabi's heir, Nasser, 1953. Such was the strength of the logic of the imperial argument which had been put forward from the 1870s about Britain's no longer being able to afford the Palmerstonian luxury of not taking direct control of Egypt. That logic had no bearing on Gladstone's actions or intentions, any more than did his bondholding. He acted throughout for Europe, within a European frame of assumptions and intentions. He applied the 'resources of civilisation' to Egypt as he applied them to Ireland. Once the Khedive's authority was restored, and that also of the Control, and things settled down, British forces would withdraw, having fulfilled their European vocation. 'Should the Khedive desire it,' Gladstone memorandized on 14 September, 'a small British force may remain in Egypt, at the charge of that country, until his authority is solidly established & placed beyond risk.'[135] Quite apart from the resistance of the Queen and the new imperial school to what they regarded as wholly premature ideas of withdrawal, it quickly became clear that the Khedival authority depended absolutely on Britain's continued military presence. Gladstone never was to square that circle. Europe became a fig leaf to cover the nakedness of Empire. There were moments even in 1882 when Gladstone seemed to sense, and relish, his proxy-role. 'Why should we promote the neutralisation of the Suez Canal,' he boldly enquired on the day after Wolseley's dazzling victory, 'if as the chief maritime Power we can probably seize it in case of need?'[136]

Much of the Liberal public of the Midlothian ethos was shocked and disillusioned. It was a characteristic Liberal of that anxiously idealist stamp who asked for reassurance from Gladstone that the Egyptian affair was not as bad as it looked. Surely the debt could have been compounded? The whole business looked dismally like a war of 'bondholders against the Egyptian peasants'.[137] What would have been his feelings, and the feelings of very many Liberals like him, had Gladstone's large holdings, and profits, in Egyptian bonds come to light? What was Gladstone thinking when he stipulated that 'the Khedive will continue to pay the Egyptian tribute as now' to his Ottoman suzerain?[138]

Yet perhaps what was most extraordinary about Gladstone's own responses to events at that juncture were his outbursts of eager triumphalism and vainglory, very reminiscent of his being 'stirred' in 1846 by victory over the Sikhs, 'for the battle was great and it was just'.[139] Much of this was, understandably, a natural emotional release after months of tension, relating as much to Ireland as to Egypt – and, for that matter, with more than a touch of Majuba and the Transvaal. Still, Gladstone's thirst for the trappings of triumph was inordinate. He wanted to know from Childers at the War Office why the guns were not fired in Hyde Park 'on Telelkibir'. 'Why should they not, still better, be fired tomorrow on that + Kafr Dowar + Cairo?' Gladstone reminisced nostalgically that he had had them fired '(as sham War Minister)' in 1846 for Indian victories; he hoped now that 'the guns will crash all the windows'; and took the trouble to congratulate Cardwell. There was much ado rallying the Church to a Day of Thanksgiving: the bells would be rung; as Canterbury was ill and London abroad, York would give the lead to the episcopate.[140] Honours were appropriately showered on the participants. A peerage for Wolseley, hitherto blocked by the Queen and the Duke of Cambridge, who found him more offensive even than Childers, could no longer be resisted. Gladstone tactfully commented that HRH the Duke of Connaught had proved himself an 'admirable general of Brigade'.[141]

To Madame Novikov Gladstone summed it all up.

We and the whole country are in a state of rejoicing, and I hope of thankfulness to God Almighty, who has prospered us in what I feel and know to be an honest undertaking ... we certainly ought to be in a good humour, for we are pleased with our army, our navy, our admirals, our generals, & our organisation. Matters were not so conducted in the days of the Crimea.[142]

In a general way, despite murmurings among the Midlothian faithful, it did Gladstone little harm to be laurelled with Egyptian victories. The Conservative Opposition, not quite knowing whether to hope for the best or the worst, conceded that ministers had done their duty to the national interest. Ireland now seemed to be settling down to something closer to 'normal' disaffection. Egypt looked to be definitively settled.

True, the Transvaal Boers were still restless. As Gladstone later put it to Ponsonby, the 1881 Convention was 'not a measure embodying a sound and perfect system of relations but an expedient, the best which the difficult circumstances permitted, and which was to be tried by its working and results'.[143] No doubt the Boers took a keen interest in what British military prowess had achieved at the other end of Africa. There seemed, in any case, to be no critical necessity for other than fuller trial by working and results for the time being. For Gladstone, these events towards the latter end of 1882 confirmed his confidence in the workings of a benign providential order within which his own inspired role took its assigned place. 'I too have my "Grammar of Assent",' he noted in allusion to Newman. 'The frame & constitution of things wherein we live teach me to believe in an Author of unbound intelligence who works towards justice truth and mercy.'[144]

Settling Egypt involved a lot of thinking about justice, truth, and mercy in which pious recognition of the European Concert dimension of the affair now mingled rather uneasily with newer notions about Europe's obligations in face of Britain's sacrifices. Piety about neutralization of the Suez Canal was now decidedly pushed aside. 'Why should *we* assume the responsibility of re-establishing on a permanent basis an arrangement in the interest of the bondholders?' Was this 'not a portion of the task which belongs properly to the European concert'? Perhaps provisional arrangements might be set in place convenient for Britain's immediate purposes?[145] Since Britain had no desire to assume 'definite responsibility for the internal government of Egypt', and had no desire to limit Egyptian self-government, and since the interests of all European powers with respect to Egypt were '*not* identical', because the 'object of the Control was the good of the country, an object not so strongly entertained by the other Powers', it followed therefore that Britain must guard against becoming dependent on the Powers in discharging its Egyptian responsibilities on their behalf.[146]

With Egypt thus marginalized and Ireland and the Transvaal mere simmering difficulties rather than critical problems, Gladstone was freer to look about him. On the face of things retirement now looked to be at optimum opportunity. It was Gladstone's political jubilee: what better time to go? Yet Gladstone's obsessive talk of it, like his talk about local government, rang curiously false. Once the autumn session cleared away the procedural reforms along the lines set out in February,[147] the anomalousness of Gladstone's position began to create a political problem of its own: a kind of 1874–80 in reverse. He proceeded in the autumn of 1882 on two divergent tracks: insisting on one track still on his determination to retire, but planning also on the other track for ambitious initiatives of policy for the 1883 session. A 'very long letter to

Spencer on the subject of my retirement' was the great event of 16 October; followed up by a declaration that, once the special autumn session should have disposed of the procedure question, he aimed to be out 'before the close of the year'. The tone of Gladstone's references to Granville suggest that he was now grooming Spencer as his successor.[148] A long conversation with Granville soon followed, 'much of it on my personal position and needs'. In a résumé on the 26th, however, Gladstone already began to shift the finishing line: 'I feel myself incapable of grappling with the hard constructive work that is now coming on. It will not, however, if I judge rightly, come on until after Easter 1883'; by which time, at least, he might have relinquished the Exchequer to Hartington or Childers.[149]

With Phillimore, himself at the point of retirement, 'we conversed on the two retirements. He encourages me.' To Chamberlain he discoursed on the 'monitor from within' which told him of 'some aspects being unequal to demands'. Gladstone felt therefore that he must 'keep in view an issue which cannot be evaded'.[150] But by this time it was December; and already in November Gladstone had marked out with Harcourt the lines of the 'hard constructive work' that was coming on. 'With regard to Devolution my own personal declarations are such as to leave me no power of receding. To postpone it would be either to abandon it or again to involve the business of the Session in hopeless confusion. It appears to me, on the merits, to be *the* battlefield which is immediately advantageous to us, and as thoroughly bad for the Conservatives.'[151] These were words of undelimited implication. And thus it was that plans would be announced in the Queen's Speech in February 1883 for comprehensive reform of local government 'in different parts of the United Kingdom', with the better government of the metropolis to the fore, and, 'if time should permit', followed by other measures. At the Irish Office Trevelyan was instructed to draw up a big Irish Local Government Bill, 'which would require not to be a timid one'. Gladstone had in view a new 'political system' for Ireland to be built on the foundations for social order provided by the Land Acts and answer the requirements of practical 'home rule'. The Irish much needed a sense that government was a thing of their own, 'not alien, not foreign'. 'I do not know', concluded Gladstone, 'whether such a Bill can be passed next Session, but in any case I hope it will be prepared, and pass it will if my convictions are shared by others.'[152]

That pretty well booked Gladstone up for the 1883 session at least. These shifting finishing lines became part of a comprehensive governmental and Cabinet reshuffle which forced the implications of non-delimitation even more decisively into being. The whole question of retirement, having become something of a comedy, now veered between tragedy and farce. It seemed somehow entirely appropriate that Gladstone, after dining with Granville, should go off to see *Iolanthe* at the Savoy theatre: 'a perfect piece of scenic representation – with much fun'.[153] Gladstone at last divested himself of the Exchequer, which he handed over to Childers. Hartington, his hopes dashed once more, was sent back to replace Childers at the War Office, which had been his first Cabinet post under Russell. Gladstone achieved at last his pointless ambition to entice Derby in, to the Colonial Office. The Queen, furiously indignant, declared candidly that he could not expect a 'cordial reception'.[154] She was equally indignant at Gladstone's bringing Dilke in to replace Dodson at the Local Government Board: again there had to be purging of republicanism. The great difficulty was Rosebery, still sore from being passed over for the Cabinet on Carlingford's replacing Argyll. Harcourt noted: 'Poor Gladstone has had a bad time of it this last fortnight, what between Windsor and the various claimants.'[155] Gladstone himself thought Rosebery a 'most singular case of strong self-delusion: a vein of foreign matter which runs across a clear and vigorous intellect, and a high-toned character'.[156] It was not long before Mrs Gladstone and Lady Rosebery had a 'sharp exchange' on the matter of Catherine's 'insolent' opinions on Rosebery's predilection for the Turf as well as his premature ambitions.[157]

What now possessed Gladstone was not the opportunity for retirement but the best opportunity he had known since 1868 for plenary engagement on his own terms. 'We took a slight survey of public affairs,' he noted of his negotiations with Derby. 'It was altogether hearty and satisfactory.'[158] Indeed it was – 'Beaconsfieldism' had been exorcized; all the critical problems following in its train had been confronted and mastered. Gladstone was poised so advantageously that the old formula of 'intense anxiety to escape' now became an important component of his advantages, especially as he was careful never to suggest that he would resign his seat in the Commons. He could wield a threat to 'bolt' as a ready weapon. As ever, the coherence he supplied from above was a licence to incoherence below. The fractiousness of the Cabinet, polarized between Hartington at one end and Chamberlain at the other, had become a positive prop and stay to his position. All factions preferred his staying on to the likely shape of things they calculated might ensue on his departure. Chamberlain needed more time to consolidate and prepare the way for what was to become in 1885 the Radical Programme. Hartington was clear that 'if any other leader should attempt to lead, I do not think that the tie – already strained – which unites the moderate section with the party would hold for a moment'.[159] The rest straggled between these two poles, trimming as occasion suggested. Gladstone's leadership was unchallenged, and for all practical and foreseeable purposes, unchallengeable. The Liberal party was at his beck and call to a degree unprecedented. The Almighty was telling him not that his time was fulfilled and the door of escape open to him, but rather that the great good times were yet to come. 'Another year of mercy and forebearance,' he recorded on his birthday. 'Why encumbereth it the ground?' Gladstone answered his own question the following day with yet another weighty missive to Trevelyan at the Irish Office, expressive of visions of vast and farborne harvestings. 'The subject of Local Government eclipses all the rest in importance.' Gladstone wanted Trevelyan to create 'responsible and weighty bodies' on the basis of the Four Irish provinces, not the counties. 'Such provincial bodies would I hope be capable of rendering far greater service than any weaker bodies could.'[160]

As 1882 drew to its close Gladstone could reflect on the compatibility of 'keeping in view' the prospect of retirement which could not, ultimately, be evaded; but could, for the promising time being, be legitimately postponed. He told Dilke on the last day of the year, 'I am afraid I differ from you on one point: your refusal to shorten my political future.' By this fiction of passing the decision to others Gladstone reconciled contradictions. The family 'court' was part of the same fiction. Catherine, Mary, and Herbert were now at the centre of what was becoming something of a pilgrimage cult. Willy and Gertrude had withdrawn. (Gladstone delighted to sign the deeds 'which divest me of my landed property and transfer it to Willy'.[161] That was another kind of fiction.) Helen was away in academic seclusion, as Agnes was in clerical matrimony. Stephen, Rector of Hawarden since 1872, was rather less happily placed. He felt himself 'too closely related to what might be called the "temporal power" or the ruling family of the place' – the 'Grand Old Couple', as William and Catherine were beginning to be called in slightly mocking terms by people who shared Lord Blantyre's opinion of the shrinish atmosphere. Stephen tried ineffectually to escape to an Oxford University Mission to Calcutta, where he would have had Harry's company. After talking to his father Stephen 'went off pliantly' to the Rectory.[162]

What is most remarkable about Gladstone's political jubilee at the end of 1882 – the King of the Hellenes and the Greek government were studious to convey their grateful felicitations[163] – is the absence of the agonized 'harpings' on retirement which had been such a feature at the end of 1881. In the hands of God he had plunged himself forward into 1882 at a time when both the obligations and the delimitations of the mission of 1880 could be reasonably held still to apply. Now, he plunged himself once more, into 1883, but on unbound terms of engagement.

CHAPTER 9

'WE HAVE THE INTERESTS OF JUSTICE, PEACE, AND FREEDOM IN OUR HANDS': IRELAND, EGYPT, REFORM, 1883–5

[1]

The early days of the new year of 1883 were disturbed by a sharp bout of illness. Gladstone, preparing for a pre-sessional visit to Midlothian, was ordered by Clark to abandon the plan and return to Hawarden for rest. 'In the Psalms this day,' he recorded on 5 January, 'as so often in the straiter passages of my life, God's love supplied me with a touching telling word. "Mine eyes are ever looking unto the Lord: for he shall pluck my feet out of the net." Can it be that he is backing, & thus taking, my side in the controversy about my early retirement? But what it may be, all Glory be His.' On the 16th he asked the Queen's leave to recuperate abroad at Wolverton's villa at Cannes until the opening of the session.

The prime minister's absence at this crucial preparatory time left his colleagues rather at a loss. They were inclined in any case to complain at the want of planning cabinets in November, when the only thing that Gladstone was taking much interest in was Irish local government. Harcourt thought that 'critical questions were shunted or evaded in the November Cabinets', to the detriment of his plans for reforming the government of London. Hartington lamented 'our unprepared condition' as the session approached.[1] Quite apart from his illness and his absence then, there were to be indications in the coming months that time was starting to catch up with Gladstone. Morley recalled Gladstone's confiding to him in 1883 that while speaking was no effort to him, 'the construction of measures' was now beyond him.[2] Herbert noticed of his father in April 1883 that he was 'rather disinclined to work and go *at* the difficult questions of the day'.[3] Gladstone remarked in the Commons when presenting his Representation of the People Bill in February 1884 that the 'faculty of authorship is getting very weak, I am afraid, in myself'.[4]

Longevity had its comforts as well as its distresses. Godley, by way of a 'Christmas card', and, as Hamilton remarked, 'knowing his former chief to the core',[5] had sent Gladstone a table of relative lengths of office-holding. Gladstone wanted to know if his Ionian service should properly be credited.[6] A year later Gladstone devoted a day and a night to 'reckonings of the line of Prime Ministers as such since the H of Hanover's succession. I have now touched 9 years & am the 7th of 31.'[7] By July 1884 Gladstone extracted from the *Pall Mall Gazette* a computation that he had been prime minister for nine years and 147 days: one day longer than Palmerston. The only others still in advance of Gladstone (the criterion being similarity of party politics over the past century) were Pitt (eighteen years and ten months) and Liverpool (fourteen years and ten months). Gladstone had been fifty-one years in Parliament, twenty-two years and ten months in office, twenty years and nine months in Cabinet. Granville alone among contemporaries surpassed him for office (twenty-eight years and one month) and Cabinet (twenty-one years and two months).[8] Such reckonings were an old hobby with Gladstone; they were an odd, if understandable, interest for a man ostensibly obsessed with a desire to retire.

'Construction of measures' still had to be set in train. From Cannes Gladstone pressed the merits of the big measure for Irish local government which he had been urging Trevelyan to prepare. Hartington might be resistant, but Forster was known to be favourable ('and his voice is an important one in the matter'). More than that: wintering at Cannes also was Argyll; who not only revealed sympathy with the Irish local-government initiative, 'but he even glanced quite spontaneously at the idea of some kind of Irish legislature as a thing which might have to be entertained'. From Argyll's son, Lorne, in Canada, came recommendations of 'a *large* allowance of local government to Ireland'. What Argyll and Lorne had in mind was upstaging Parnell and his party with a comprehensive pre-emption of Home Rule. Gladstone put the point to Granville that 'one of the most vitally important objects we have attained since we took office has been splitting the Home Rule party and reducing it for all practical purposes from (say) 65 to 40'. What would the Shawite section now aligned with the Liberals say to a Hartingtonian negative from the government? Gladstone admitted that the government's undertakings had touched county government only, and that his own leaning now to provincial assemblies was an 'ulterior development'. 'I am told that that was Lord Russell's plan. I can readily believe it, for, regarding the scheme as Conservative, I incline to consider this form of it the most Conservative.'[9]

A 'Hartingtonian negative', however, was what Gladstone's colleagues mostly preferred. But then they mostly would have preferred Gladstone's not coming up with his Irish Land Bill in 1881. Harcourt wanted space for his London Bill. Chamberlain and Dilke wanted less attention to

Ireland and more work on English domestic concerns. Gladstone could not fight effectively at such a distance. Perhaps he lacked the will. Perhaps he took the view that if his colleagues persisted in playing Parnell's game, then so be it. He did not stint himself his time on the Riviera. Was there a plot among his colleagues to encourage him to stay there until Easter so as to keep him out of political harm's way? Or did he stay on deliberately in an attempt to demonstrate his indispensability? Mary Gladstone was amused at the fuss. 'It is too funny the way people imagine he is panting to return and that it is we who are restraining him by main force. It is exactly the contrary. Mama and Spencer [Lyttelton] are simply dying to get home. They are both bored to death.'[10]* Assurances from Granville were amiably but cautiously responded to amid the Cannes Carnival season ('a strange, fantastic, but wondrous sight'). Protected by a wire mask, Gladstone was 'pelted largely'. Also at Cannes was Cardwell, in hopeless quest for health: 'a sad spectacle, admonitory of our lot'.[11]

In fact, Gladstone's colleagues had no need of a plot to neutralize his legislative aspirations. The debate on the Address had been allowed to fall into the grasp of the Fourth Party and the Irish. Gladstone discussed with Harcourt whether it might be best to postpone arrival to avoid any 'tendency to stir up the embers'. He expounded indignantly to Spencer on the 'wanton' consumption of time in 'retrospective debate', materially cutting into the session and 'abridging our means of action' and giving force to the 'dilatory argument on every difficult measure'.[12] In truth, what was most lacking was redressive vigour on Gladstone's part. He no longer possessed the awe-inspiring energy for routine government as in his days at the Board of Trade or at the Exchequer. Now that he had finally given up the Exchequer he lacked the promptings that finance even yet might have offered. Most of all, he lacked the stimulus of great critical issues either initiated by himself, as in 1881, or impressed upon him by circumstances, as in 1882. He had in immediate view no 'doings or intentions' calculated to incite a 'corresponding conviction' on the public mind. Even were his proposals for Irish local government to go ahead they would hardly fill that demanding role. The 'dilatory arguments' of 1883 were met by nothing of that psychic stamina. In its absence Gladstone could only lament to Lorne (who had been supplying relevant Canadian data for Irish devolutionary proposals) 'the block of business still continuing in the House of Commons, even after the mitigations of the new rules', smiting with paralysis 'a multitude of good wishes and intentions'.[13]

By 7 April Trevelyan was informed that the Irish Elective Councils

---

* Lyttelton was one of G's private secretaries.

Bill was not to be proceeded with. The 'Right' had 'got the upper hand', as Gladstone explained to Ripon; though the new 'Grand Committee' procedures were working thoroughly well, which might turn out to be of 'vast importance'. On 5 May Cabinet decided to abandon the London Municipal Bill (Harcourt's jealousy of releasing the Home Office's grip on the Metropolitan Police being allowed to be sufficient cause). Gladstone protested that the Liberal party 'as a rule draws its vital breath from great Liberal measures'. It was therefore a serious matter to drop out the 'central piece', especially as it would be difficult to secure room for it in any future sessions of the 1880 Parliament.[14] Gladstone spoke almost as a spectator rather than a participating leader of government. It was a matter not only of wanting stimulus and the energies generated by stimulus; it was a matter also of his anomalous situation as semi-abdicated leader and the incoherences this permitted. These incoherences developed into quarrels. Gladstone took on the role of peacemaker, having no energizing dynamism to offer. Derby thought him too patient, too willing to allow himself to be contradicted. Soon Gladstone preferred not calling cabinets, leaving important decisions to be made in extra-Cabinet 'Cabals'.[15]*

There were protests in the party which told of a deeper Liberal dismay than mere circumstantial disappointment. Rathbone, oppressed more than ever with the loss of Ireland's most precious time, forwarded to Gladstone a memorandum he had earlier drawn up for Forster, demonstrating how local government 'could be safely extended to Ireland'.

I do not see how we can settle Ireland without Local Govt reform & yet how to do this I do not see except by passing a Bill for England which . . . the Irish would ask to be extended to Ireland.

Now fortunately the Bill which Wright & Ilbert† drew for Whitbread & myself would apply even more easily to Ireland than England & no party there would venture to oppose a measure which would give much relief.

Rathbone pleaded that Gladstone ensure the carrying of such a bill in the 1884 session.[16] In the same spirit, Firth, one of the London MPs, pleaded in vain for the London Government Bill. Popular opinion favoured it. The time was opportune. Squabbles about police should not

---

* T. A. Jenkins makes the valuable point that the reputation of this Liberal government for quarrelsomeness is misconceived: it was allowed by Gladstone's situation to become quarrelsome.

† Courtenay Ilbert, a parliamentary draftsman, went on to be law member of the Governor-General's Council in India, 1882–6.

be allowed to hinder. 'No police better than no Bill.' It was 'a noble conception nobly worked out'. The feeling in the party in the Commons was that 'it should be made the test of the legislative power of the party'.[17]

Rathbone duly drew for Gladstone the moral of the tale about testing the legislative power of the party. 'But what I would ask you kindly to consider is whether this is not the time when, if the Party is vigorously pulled together, this Parliament may yet be led to accomplish what is reasonably expected from it and the fearful danger be avoided of a bitter sense of want of confidence in the House of Commons becoming rooted in the mind of the thinking part of all classes.' Either, urged Rathbone, 'the Party should go to their leaders, or the leaders should appeal to the party publicly to declare that it is not safe any longer to allow the labour of the House of Commons to be so barren of results'. The government seemed incapable of carrying 'even the non-party administrative measures that the country wants'. MPs like Whitbread wanted the party called together soon to secure a 'reasonable amount of legislation', including Corrupt Practices in Elections – 'a diminished programme'. Rathbone quite understood that Gladstone had been under 'tremendous strain'. So why not let Hartington take over while Gladstone recruits his strength and keeps his 'leadership of the nation'? The 'Liberal Party would be on honour to work all the more loyally and better for fear lest any failure on their part should bring you back from your needed repose'.[18]

This was cutting very close to Gladstone's bone. In a way Rathbone had divined the essence of Gladstone's politics since 1875. In another way he was putting forward a devastatingly accurate critique of how Gladstone's 'leadership of the nation' made him a wrecker of the Liberal parliamentary party. And if there was one lesson which his experiences over the years as leader of the Liberal party had taught Gladstone, it was to have as few meetings of the party as possible. His leadership in the years to come would testify most tellingly to that lesson. In any case it does not appear that Rathbone's or Firth's pleadings did more than help the cause of the Abolition of Corrupt Practices in Elections measure. This proved quite effective in suppressing electoral corruption; but it had the unintended consequence of stimulating the extremely successful system of unpaid election activism on behalf of the Conservative party in the guise of the Primrose League. Gladstone could, of course, point out that the county-franchise issue remained in reserve for a future session. It was simply not possible in any event for Gladstone to ask Granville and Hartington to resume their postures of leadership as of 1875 in the understanding that 'the leader of the nation' might at any time decide to emerge from his repose once more in the manner of 1880.

What it would have been possible for Gladstone to have done in that situation in 1883 was to have interpreted Rathbone and Firth as in effect opening the door for his exit to freedom. Theirs were really rather more plausible cues than that of Psalm xxv, 14.*

Instead, Gladstone continued in desultory fashion, leaving the session to look after itself. He was careful to condole with the Queen on the death of her faithful friend, the gillie John Brown – 'attached, respected, and intelligent domestic' – although the last word would not have struck quite the right chord.[19] He had to fend off royal complaints about Chamberlain's provocatively Radical speeches, setting class against class.[20] He gently reprimanded Chamberlain with acknowledgements of the difficulties of those 'markedly in advance or in arrears' of colleagues 'on subjects of high politics'.[21] He humbugged his way through the abolition of the Contagious Diseases Acts, professing to recall nothing of his own part in their origin.[22] At least that would release Stansfeld for possible future employment. Gladstone was in dispute with the Queen also in the matter of Church patronage. The Queen thought his preferments 'all on the side of the High Church'; which Gladstone denied, calculating that of the thirty of his important appointments only eleven could be deemed 'High', though he admitted that of the 'non-High' ('repugnant' terms, and used only as unavoidable currency) too many had been 'Broad' rather than 'Low', which Her Majesty preferred.[23] There was a great occasion on 1 May when Gladstone dined with Dean Bradley of Westminster to hear Tennyson recite *Tiresias* and talk of the projected Channel tunnel (the Gladstones had *not* liked Tennyson's Lincolnshire-dialect melodrama *The Promise of May*, in 1882). He decided that dinners at Windsor wanted 'enlivening & it is necessary to start subjects & not merely give replies'.[24] Gladstone could remark to Spencer without a trace of irony at the end of June: 'The atmosphere of the House of Commons is now calm, & the horizon for the time clear.' When it came to the end of the session in August Gladstone was quite prickly and defensive and unconvincing in his defence of its work.[25]

[2]

One of Gladstone's colleagues who did in his own way comment brusquely on the government's abdication of its powers was Rosebery. To Gladstone's 'bewildered' and 'stunned' surprise, the Under-Secretary at the Home Office abruptly announced his resignation and his intention

---

* See above, page 311.

to undertake a world tour, with a view especially, as a great admirer of Professor Seeley's newly published *Expansion of England*, to examining the potential prospects of empire. Could not Australia wait 'for some unencumbered interval of your life'? pleaded Gladstone. What was to become of Scottish affairs? And, more than that, of the office of Secretary of State for Scotland, 'which Parliament is evidently about to create'? Undeterred, Rosebery set off for Australia via America on 1 September. His ambition (to use Seeleyan terms) was to be the Stein of the British Empire. The last thing he wanted was to be typecast as the Liberal manager for Scotland. This set Gladstone off on the trail of making Cabinet room for a peer at Carlingford's expense in the context of releasing Trevelyan from his Irish burden, and of plans to convert honorific sinecure posts to either non-salaried or actively executive status. Dufferin's succeeding Ripon in India left the Constantinople Embassy vacant. But Gladstone found Carlingford unobligingly limpet-like after exchanging the sinecure Privy Seal for the sinecure Lord Presidency.

The usual problems were much abated. It was becoming tediously clear that the Transvaal Boers were determined on a renegotiation of the Pretoria Convention. They insisted on coming to London, the better to get at Derby. Renegotiations extended wearily from July 1883 to February 1884. For Ireland Gladstone could see hope. Though Parnell was a 'Sphinx', 'the most probable reading of him', as Gladstone told Spencer, 'is that he works for & with the law as far as he dare'. Gladstone could 'even doubt that he hates the Government'. And he was persuaded that there was a 'good deal of underground gratitude in the mind of the Irish people'.[26] This was the message he was getting from both O'Sheas. With Katharine, Parnell was settling into a kind of domestic bliss. Captain O'Shea, busily promoting himself to Chamberlain as Parnell's spokesman, declared that the Irish Tribune was 'getting sick of agitation'. Incidence of agrarian outrage dropped notably. Chamberlain discussed notions of Irish local government in which O'Shea misled him into believing Parnell took a keen interest. Parnell in fact was much keener on flirtations with the Conservatives, tenant-purchase policy being the link. Bright denounced an Irish–Tory conspiracy vitriolically at his jubilee celebrations in Birmingham in June 1883. One of Gladstone's few interventions of note in the session was to condemn a Conservative attempt to amend the 1881 Land Act to encourage purchase by tenants. Gladstone insisted that 'substantial justice has been done in Ireland'. He believed that 'we have got to the root of the matter, and have established relations, substantially just, between the landlord and the tenant'; and that, therefore, he was 'not ready to admit that the Land Question is unsettled'; and he considered the proposed amendments 'dangerous and impolitic' in the way they made the state creditor for loans, especially in the absence of responsible local authorities.[27]

The biggest problem at the time was Egypt. It was proving much harder to get out than it had been to get in. Gladstone enquired anxiously of Dufferin on 3 August of 'our degree of advancement as respects the most important particulars of preparation for leaving Egypt'.[28] That was the day before the *Pall Mall Gazette* listed the ministerial statements promising prompt withdrawal: three citations from Granville (including his Circular Despatch to the Powers of 3 January 1883), two from Harting-ton, two from Chamberlain, one each from Derby and Northbrook, and no fewer than five from Gladstone – three in the Commons in 1882, one at the Mansion House in 1882, and most recently in the Commons on 5 March 1883.[29] The great Liberal public was getting impatient. Granville, attempting to appease it, found Evelyn Baring, the Consul-General and Resident, adamant that reform of the Egyptian system of government would be impossible without a strong British military presence. He had the vehement support of Lord Wolseley. This, as Baring put it, 'might not commend itself to public opinion in England', but it was nonetheless the prevailing fact of the matter. All Granville could get were 'softening alterations' in Baring's report.[30] It was not until November that Gladstone could claim that by withdrawing from Cairo 'we have narrowed the scope of the Egyptian problem'. But it remained serious: 'how to plant solidly western & beneficent institutions in the soil of a Mohamedan community?'[31] One difficulty was the Egyptian government's itself widening the scope of the problem by persisting in holding on to its Sudanese empire centred at Khartoum, on the upper Nile.

[3]

The great post-sessional event in 1883 was the cruise in one of Donald Currie's steamers, *Pembroke Castle*. This started out as a week's excursion among the West Highland islands early in September, with the lions of the party being Tennyson and Gladstone. However, at what appears to be Tennyson's instigation, cruising scope was expanded grandly: as far as Norway and Denmark. This shift put Gladstone in the difficulty of having to make a hasty apology to the Queen for not having been granted permission to go abroad. Hallam Tennyson described Gladstone and Tennyson as 'jovial as boys', but taking 'good care to keep off politics'. 'What struck me most in Gladstone's expression of his thoughts was his eagerness and mastery of words, coupled with self-control and gentle persuasiveness; and a certain persistence in dwelling on those topics which he had himself started for discussion.'[32] Gladstone recorded there being one long conversation with Tennyson on the 'state & prospects of belief, another on Homer'. Tennyson, patient under persuasive persistence, found himself very pleasantly surprised to be offered a peerage by Gladstone. Hitherto, Tennyson had been difficult about honours, not finding a baronetcy acceptable. It is quite possible that the Queen herself had prompted the idea of a peerage.[33] It was in any case a happy thought on Gladstone's part to enliven an agreeable occasion with an exceedingly agreeable gesture.

At Christiansand Gladstone found a 'most courteous, & apparently happy, people'; which gave him pause for thought on the apparent benefits of the Sweden–Norway relationship, much extolled by the Irish Home Rulers. Then on to Copenhagen. The Queen was to express herself *'very much surprised'* at hearing Gladstone's account of his reception at the hospitable Danish Court, and the junketings of the *Pembroke Castle* party with the King and Queen of Denmark, and their imperial and royal relations, the Emperor and Empress of Russia, the King and Queen of the Hellenes, and numerous other royalties, adult and juvenile. Gladstone (who resented deeply the Queen's reference to his *'escapade'*) attempted to mollify Victoria with an elaborate account of the 'singularly domestic character' of this remarkable assemblage, and the 'affectionate intimacy', 'so kindly and so simple', of its personages. He recorded for himself: 'As a domestic scene it was of wonderful interest; there was no etiquette: the sovereign personages vied with one another in their simple & kindly manners.' The Emperor and Empress* of Russia congratulated Gladstone on his Balkan policy in favour of Bulgaria. 'The Emperor and the King of D both observed the old custom and drank wine with me.' Currie was in ecstasy when the royalties in turn were received on *Pembroke Castle*. The Emperor Alexander toasted the Queen; Gladstone proposed the health of the King and Queen of Denmark, the Emperor and Empress of Russia, and the King and Queen of the Hellenes. The King of Denmark toasted Gladstone. The genial bearing of the Emperor much impressed Gladstone. *Pembroke Castle* sailed off on 18 September, 'with unusual accompaniment of bands playing & the rigging manned as we passed the great Russian Yacht & a Danish ship of war'. The Gladstones were back in London on the 21st with 'rather triumphal landing at Gravesend with special train provided (*free*)'.

Gladstone formally recommended Tennyson's barony to the Queen on 20 September (citing the precedent of the peerage offered to, though declined by, Grote as being in cultural point). Gladstone was able to

* Dagmar, daughter of the King of Denmark, sister to the Princess of Wales and to the King of Greece.

assure Hallam in December that the matter was consummated, and would be made public in the new year. Tennyson himself wrote to Gladstone of his being touched that he should be 'the first *thus* publicly to proclaim the position which Literature ought to hold in the world's work'.[34]* Gladstone had occasion to thank Hallam for sending on his father's behalf a copy of Seeley's *Expansion of England*. Possibly Gladstone was already aware of Rosebery's addiction to it; and perhaps it figured in some of the shipboard conversation. Gladstone was gracious, though he may well by now have regretted his preferment of Seeley to the Cambridge chair in 1869. He thought 'the Professor gets on slippery ground when he undertakes to deal with politics more practical than historical or scientific, yet it is certainly most desirable that English folk should consider well their position, present and prospective, in the world'.[36]†

Tennyson's peerage marked a historic moment in the recognition by the British state of the claims on it of the worlds of letters, the arts, and science. Gladstone had already in 1883 offered a pension to Matthew Arnold 'as a public recognition of the high place you have taken in the poetry and literature of England'[37] (though he blocked Arnold from a Charity Commissionership on the grounds that it would give 'considerable offence among Nonconformists').[38] Gladstone both knighted and boosted the pension of the naturalist Richard Owen in 1884, on the grounds (as Owen put it) of 'approval of the performance and tendencies of my official and scientific career' – which tendencies being decidedly anti-Darwinist.[39] A 'political' angle was rarely absent from such patronage. For all that Tennyson would sit on the cross-benches in the Lords – party being to him 'too much of a god in these days'[40] – Gladstone expected him to vote as a Liberal peer: Liberal peers becoming something of a rarity 'in these days'.

Tennyson's gift to Gladstone of a copy of Seeley's *Expansion of England* was, in its own way, a historic gesture 'in these days', reflecting an important shift in the pattern developed in Britain through the Victorian era of the public relationship between intellect and politics. When Gladstone appointed Seeley to the Cambridge History chair in 1869 Seeley was a Liberal in the sense that intellect was habitually Liberal at that time – the time of Mill's famous dubbing of the Conservative party as 'the stupid party'. By the mid-1880s Seeley was much more ambiguous in his Liberalism and quite unambiguous in his dislike of the 'loose talk about liberty' which he thought infected Gladstone's politics. This was

* The world of literature included some satirists of 'Baron Alfred Vere de Vere': 'The Senior Wrangler of our bards / Is now the Wooden Spoon of lords.'[35]
† Gladstone read the *Expansion*, starting on 27 December 1883 and finishing on 5 May 1884.

a view shared by a great many of Seeley's peers in the broad world of the higher Victorian culture, including both Tennyson and Arnold. It was precisely symptomatic of their cultural-political shift that the Conservatives should have launched the *National Review* in October 1883 in an attempt to divest themselves of their 'stupid' reputation. Carnarvon on its behalf claimed that 'three-fourths of the literary power of the country and four-fifths of the intellectual ability' were now on the Conservative side.[41] This claim was extravagant; but there was enough legitimacy in it to make it entirely arguable. The balance of intellectual power in politics was shifting. This was another way in which Gladstone was becoming 'old-fashioned'. 'Conservative rethinking of Conservatism in the later nineteenth century was much less important to Conservatism than was Liberal rethinking of Liberalism.'[42]

This thinning of Liberalism's cultural-political dimension was not unobserved or unregretted by Gladstone – both Acton and Morley were acutely aware of it – but he found no reason to sympathize with the predicament of Liberals whom he could identify as choosing to share the values of the 'classes' and the metropolis in distrust of the values of the 'nation'. Gladstone's riposte to Seeley's *Expansion* was to reward Stubbs, the Regius Professor of Modern History at Oxford, a faithful Puseyite and Liddonian, with the bishopric of Chester; and to prefer in his place the faithful Turcophobe democrat, E. A. Freeman. In the very fact of meeting the Emperor Alexander at Copenhagen Gladstone was reminded of the days when he had saluted the Emperor's father as liberator of the Bulgarians, while deep in the turmoil of leading the 'nation' against the metropolis and the 'classes' in the Eastern question.

It happened, unfortunately, that the latest stirrings in the Balkans would soon cause quite critical problems in Anglo-Russian relations. The question of the union of the two Bulgarias created at Berlin in 1878 was now coming up. Gladstone was in the gratifying position of being able to point out to the Queen that his speech in 1858 on the union of the Danubian Principalities and the making of independent Romania was material to the case: his words then were aptly applicable to the Bulgarian question now; and the principle of self-determination involved in either case was one of vital consequence. It is very probable that such matters were much in Gladstone's mind when he and Catherine visited the Derbys at Knowsley early in October. Ostensibly, Gladstone was catching up on the Transvaal negotiations. Derby noted Gladstone's liking for 'long, casual conversations when paying business visits'. Gladstone confessed that he now found 'much work impossible' at his age. Of 'serious desk work' 'three hours were his usual limit, in case of necessity he could go up to five hours, but anything more exhausted him'. Kruger and the Boers did not long detain him. He was avid for 'long

& interesting conversation with Lady D[erby]. on Lord B[eaconsfield]., H[er]. M[ajesty]., D[erby]'s resignation, & other matters'.[43] In due course Gladstone would cite precedents in the Balkans as being material in the case of Ireland.[44]

[4]

It did not seem at all necessary to Gladstone to arrange a systematic series of autumn planning cabinets for the coming 1884 session. The pattern of 1882 was repeated, in the teeth of protests from the activist wing of the parliamentary party in the persons of Rathbone, Caine, and Melly. It appeared to them that 'we are in danger of destroying the improved position of the Liberal party if as some seem to advocate we go to the country with no more practical legislation than we have yet passed'. There 'must be some substantial good work next session or we shall see a return to the bad state of things of last Easter'. It would be 'necessary to satisfy the great practical mass of the Liberal party who will certainly not be satisfied with nothing but County Franchise'. 'What I should wish', pleaded Rathbone, 'is Local Govt. not only as the most important thing in itself but because I do not see how we County Members are to face our constituents after relief of local taxation has been a second time promised.'[45] To such pleas Gladstone was impervious. The 'practical' interest he had in local government was an Irish interest. That, it seemed, was barred to him. In any case he no longer had the strength for a session full of 'practical legislation' for the 'great mass'.[46] Bills for Local Government and London Government could be introduced for ritual purposes, and just as ritually withdrawn. On the other hand, he had a great interest in extending the electoral power of the 'great mass'. Once the 'nation' was fully armed politically, great things might become possible. The Liberal party would have to be satisfied willy-nilly with 'nothing but County Franchise'.

It was a question now ripe for legislating. The difficulty about it was the way it got entangled with Ireland. Extending the borough franchise of 1867 to the counties was a measure generally much approved of in the Liberal party, not least because of calculations of the damage likely to be done to the traditional Conservative ascendancy in the agricultural counties when for the first heady time the rural and mining working classes marked their secret ballots. It was the application to Ireland that gave pause. Gladstone had pledged himself absolutely to a uniform United Kingdom basis for the legislation. It would be a Reform Bill entirely different from those of 1832 and 1867 in that it merely extended existing franchises laterally rather than creating deeper new franchises; and it would not be a matter of supplementary Scottish and Irish bills following on the English–Welsh primary model. There would be no opportunity, in other words, to differentiate between Reform in Britain and Reform in Ireland. Conservatives in Britain did not like the county franchise, but they prudently kept publicly quiet about it. Ireland was another matter. Reform in the Irish boroughs in 1868 had made little impact in thinly urbanized Ireland. What would happen in Ireland when the mass of cottiers and labourers cast their votes was a matter of lively speculation. Debate about Reform therefore tended to be debate about the comprehensive Redistribution of seats, which it was generally admitted was unavoidable in a situation where, because of anomalies of constituency electorates, something like three quarters of MPs were elected by one quarter of the voters. So immense a shift in the constituencies towards uniformity in the value of votes, and the details of how they would be reallocated in new constituencies, would have consequences difficult to calculate.

There was need for Gladstone to move circumspectly in bringing on the county franchise question in November and December 1883. He had painful memories of the way Redistribution had been used as a weapon against Reform in 1866. Gladstone was in an incomparably stronger position vis-à-vis the parliamentary Liberal party now than he had been then. On the other hand, it would be important to carry Hartington with him in Cabinet, where his grip was loose. And another aspect that did not arise either in 1866 or 1867 was the House of Lords, and what it might do at Salisbury's behest. What is most immediately remarkable about Gladstone's approach to the county franchise was his evident determination that the 'Right' was not to get the upper hand. He requested Spencer to supply statistical information on the likely impact of such a measure on Ireland; and Spencer was deputed also to prepare the way with Hartington, with a view to softening him up. The advice Gladstone got from the Irish Attorney-General was bleak enough: in Ulster the Liberal party would lose all, or nearly all, its seats. The Catholic vote would be given solidly against Liberals. In the rest of Ireland an extended franchise would strengthen the party opposed to the English connection.[47] Since Gladstone had to have a bill and had to have a bill in which Ireland was treated equally with Britain, there was nothing to be done about that advice except hope it was wrong and trust to possible mitigations in Redistribution. Gladstone chose to take the view that the new labourer vote in Ireland was '*quite* as likely to establish a dual current in the constituencies, as to increase the volume of that single force which now carries all before it'.[48]

There were the temptations, much canvassed by Hartington and his friends, to abandon the initial idea of simple assimilation of the borough franchise, and create a new uniform county franchise at some point on the rental scale above mere occupancy. The advice of the Irish experts, however, was that 'there would be no advantage, were it open to us, in attempting to hold the £4 line'.[49] Hartington also attempted to block the plan for a 'single-barrelled' bill including Redistribution as well as Reform. He was defeated in a Cabinet fracas on 22 November. The looseness of Gladstone's grip on his Cabinet was well exposed by the furious locking of horns by Hartington and Chamberlain. Salisbury was astonished. 'Chamberlain & Hartington are adopting an attitude to each other to which the history of past Cabinets offers no parallel whatsoever. Has Chamberlain made up his mind to split up the Cabinet – or is this his way of putting his spurs into Hartington?'[50] Gladstone tried to pacify Hartington by sugaring all proposals with hypotheticality and by enticing Hartington with the prospect of Gladstone's definitive abdication ('which would enable me – in my 75th year – at least to begin the session with my colleagues . . .').[51] He assured Hartington that 'the effect of the altered franchise in augmenting the power of Parnellism' was greatly over-estimated. To refuse equality to Ireland *would* be a blow to the Union and the Empire.[52] And to Hartington's threats of resignation Gladstone responded with a counter-threat: the government would fall, Hartington would have to form another, with Reform postponed, and with Gladstone forced into alliance with the Radicals, with a dissolution in the offing, and the Liberal party split into two camps.[53]

Gladstone was equally soothing on the Redistribution side of the case. Hartington and the 'Whigs and moderates' feared the effect of mere 'numbers' or 'population' swamping the constituencies at the expense of property and educated political leadership. Gladstone's own views on the matter were in fact quite conservative. He explained to Harcourt that his faith was in 'the nation', and he could not say it would be shaken whatever way the country was 'district-ed'. But he was against 'all changes which distract or disturb, and which are not called for by any motives of necessity'.[54] He thought Hartington the victim of 'prepossessions (more than reasoning)'; he mocked Hartington's fears: 'one of the phantoms which has been scaring Hartington's usually manly mind, is that of Electoral districts; and he probably suspects me of looking to a plan on this basis'.[55] In fact Gladstone was ready to postpone Redistribution, though wanting to settle it within the frame of the 1880 Parliament if possible.

Franchise and Redistribution were left by the opening of 1884 in a state of simmering volatility. There was a tense two-and-a-half-hour interview with Hartington on Gladstone's return to London on 31 December in which Gladstone dilated on 'ruin to the party' and the 'fearful evil of branding Ireland with political inequality'. As was now his wont, Gladstone could conveniently brush awkward questions under the carpet of his ever-impending retirement. 'I am glad', he told Harcourt, 'the time has not yet come when new points of departure in Irish legislation have to be considered, and that good old Time, who carries me kindly on his back, will probably plant me before that day comes outside "the range of practical politics".'[56] But not quite yet. 'My position is a strange one,' Gladstone recorded in bidding farewell to 1883. 'A strong man in me wrestles for retirement: a stronger one stands at the gate of exit, and forbids.'

[5]

Back in October 1883 Gladstone had remarked to Catherine on the 'one smooth even forward current of opinion & feeling' shown in Cabinet. 'In fact I should say matters in general look tranquil and rather comfortable – is this a sign of *coming* storms?'[57] Something of a squall had come with Hartington. But Gladstone could console himself by another of his assertions that it was 'certainly impulse more than reasoning, which has moved Hartington in the wrong direction'.[58] By 3 January Gladstone could declare that 'our little crisis' was 'virtually over': 'a great mercy, though in one sense I have to pay the piper by an extended engagement'. A 'very harmonious and satisfactory' cabinet agreed to go ahead with the Franchise Bill without linkage to Redistribution. That would be settled later but within the present Parliament. Local Government and London Government would make their ritual appearances. Irish Local Government was, of course, no longer heard of. Gladstone applied balm to Hartington's wounds. He asked Grosvenor to find 'any *convenient* occasion' of letting Hartington know 'in a quiet way' the negative view that Parnell was said to take on the 'effect of the extended franchise on the interests of his party'. But Grosvenor was not to let Hartington suspect that he had been 'coquetting with these worthies'.[59] Hartington had enough reasoning to suspect shrewdly that Parnell was feeding Gladstone and the Liberal Chief Whip with the kind of agreeable misinformation it suited them to believe.

It suited Gladstone also to let Derby go ahead and appease Kruger and his Transvaal delegates by dispensing with the British 'suzerainty' established at the Pretoria Convention in 1881. The argument was to stick to the substance of a British veto over the Transvaal Republic's relations with foreign countries rather than to quibble over terminology. 'We have abstained from using the word,' explained Derby, 'because it is not capable of legal definition, and because it seemed to be a word which was likely to lead to misconception and misunderstanding.'[60] Derby was on the run from Boer 'ferocity'. Gladstone knew perfectly well that the fundamental problem remained unresolved. 'Derby has not got the key to the S. African question,' he told Granville: 'but who has?'[61] What Gladstone lacked here was the resource of easy high-mindedness provided by the ideal of the European Concert. The Egyptians had the blessings of that. Appeasement of the Boers was the easier option in a situation fraught with critical problems about Reform and Egypt. Kruger had got 'Home Rule' for the South African Republic and the British government thought it had retained imperial supremacy. Thus was created 'the framework of politics and policies which ultimately resulted in the Anglo-Boer War'.[62]

That was not to come in Gladstone's time. But signals for coming storms in north Africa had already been raised. The Egyptian campaign to restore the authority of Cairo in the Sudan, then being overrun by the forces of a Muslim messiah, or 'Mahdi', came abruptly to a catastrophic end with the massacre of an army commanded by a British officer, Colonel Hicks, early in November 1883. To Baring it was clear that Khartoum could not be held and that the whole bloated apparatus of Egyptian empire would have to be dismantled and withdrawn. Gladstone sensed the possibility of trouble. 'Late incidents & especially the Sudan disaster', he warned Grosvenor, 'have very much ruffled the aspect of foreign affairs & Egypt again looks as if it might work out into a serious difficulty.'[63] The Cabinet agreed on 22 November that the Egyptians should be pressed into making an 'honourable withdrawal' from their empire on the upper Nile. The problem was that the Egyptians, sullen under British military occupation, were in a mixed state of inability and unwillingness to do this; and it could be done, from a practical viewpoint, only under the direct supervision of British administrative direction and British military power. The prospect of having to ask the Liberal party and public opinion to agree to what would amount to a serious campaign on the Nile was a daunting one.

How to square the circle of getting Egypt out of the Sudan without getting Britain in? A solution presented itself with what at the time seemed to ministers of providential cogency. Major-General Charles Gordon, of Chinese fame and Sudanese experience, was on the point of accepting an offer from King Leopold of the Belgians to manage the King's plans to open up the Congo basin to beneficent commerce and industry. Gordon's earlier exploits had made him a public hero. Ever since the end of his last official employment in Mauritius in 1882 his name had been suggested to ministers as one eminently available and suitable for enterprises requiring energy and panache. Sir Harry Verney, MP for

Buckingham, several times pressed on Gladstone the case for Gordon's employment on the Indian frontier or with the Boers and natives of the Transvaal. 'He has a wonderful, an unique power of influencing & taming untameable tribes.' Verney rejected the objection that Gordon was 'half mad'. 'He is not at all mad – but he is, above all things, a man of religion.' Miss Florence Nightingale, a great admirer, quite agreed.[64]

When the Sudan problem came up in 1883 Gordon's name again came to notice. It was in December 1883 that Granville first enquired if Gordon could be employed in the Sudan. Despite Egyptian protests and Baring's opposition, the idea took on a vivid life of its own. W. T. Stead, now Morley's successor as editor of the *Pall Mall Gazette*, made Gordon's humanitarian and Christian mission into a sensational stunt of the 'new journalism'. As Granville put it eventually, Gordon's mission 'would be popular at home'. The 1884 session was at hand. The Cabinet, including Gladstone, followed the thrust of events with haphazard flaccidity, obsessed with the Reform crisis. Having got the sessional programme agreed Gladstone returned to Hawarden to rest. It was from Hawarden, much to Hamilton's doubts as to putting trust in a 'half-cracked fatalist', that Gladstone telegraphed acquiescence to the decision of four ministers who happened to be in London – Granville, Hartington, Northbrook, and Dilke – to divert Gordon from the Congo to the Nile.

It was unfortunate that Kimberley was not present, for he had had experience of Gordon's services in South Africa: 'knew him well', and would certainly have put a stop to further employment. As it was, Granville said to Hartington the following day: 'We were proud of ourselves yesterday. Are you sure that we did not commit a gigantic folly?'[65] Hamilton protested that nothing was settled as to what Gordon was being instructed precisely to do. Was his mission executive or advisory? On to Baring was put the task of translating suggestions into instructions. Gordon in any case ignored them. As Gladstone was soon to discover, Gordon 'takes very little notice indeed of any general questions we put to him'.[66]

Ministers were led to believe, as Gladstone later plaintively recalled, on no evidence whatever, 'that Gordon had at his back a large faithful population'. In all his long career, Gladstone found a match only in Gordon for sublime and inspired confidence in being an instrument of the Almighty. In due and painful course, Gladstone reviewed the origins of the tragical farce of the Gordon mission. 'I have from the first regarded the rising of the Sudanese against Egypt as a justifiable and honourable revolt. The Cabinet have I think never taken an opposite view . . . We sent Gordon on a mission of peace and liberation.' Gladstone 'never understood how it was that Gordon's mission of peace became one of war'.[67]

In the innocent days at the beginning of 1884 such deep puzzles lay inscrutably in the future. Liberal opinion was for the time appeased. 'The Egyptian business has been sadly entangled & is now the most perplexing of our cases,' reported Gladstone to Ripon. 'Now we are making much progress in South African affairs. But the tone of the public mind is healthy & the Government shows no sign of decrepitude.'[68] It was indeed an entirely novel experience for Gladstone as prime minister to go into the fourth year of a ministry not manifestly in a state of deliquescence. There was a moment of unwonted agreeableness from the Queen when she allowed Gladstone the privilege of a pre-publication reading of her *More Leaves from the Journal of a Life in the Highlands* ('to show how wrong *Truth* is'). 'It is innocence itself,' was Gladstone's private comment.[69]* But, by the time the published presentation copy arrived, as Hamilton sourly noted, there was not even a 'lukewarm' inscription ('to Mr Gladstone from the Queen').[70]

Already the Sudanese problem was starting to unravel out of control. Disasters struck on the Red Sea coast. The first questions were being asked whether the government did not think it advisable to 'send any material aid' to Gordon at Khartoum. Gladstone assured the fretful Queen that her ministers were very sensible of their responsibility with respect to General Gordon, 'which, in the case of any miscarriage, will in all likelihood be promptly visited upon them'.[71] Motions of censure soon had to be confronted. Gladstone noted on 11 February: 'The times are stiff & try the mettle of men. What should *we* have done, with the Mutiny at the Nore?'† Hamilton commented glumly that certainly there never was a government whose steps were so dogged with ill luck. The Queen, 'clearly inspired by the Horseguards',‡ was demanding immediate military intervention. Gladstone found it 'a sore time combining difficulties in Council constantly renewed with effort for & in the House. But God sent to me His words: "when thou passest through the waters, I will be with thee; through the rivers, they shall not overthrow thee." So I have been in his sight: praise be to His great Name.'[72]

On 13 February the Cabinet decided, rather against Gladstone's judgement,[73]¶ to send a 'limited relief expedition' to the Red Sea as a sop to the unreasonable and jingoistic and sentimental public agitation. This, together with what Hamilton judged to be Gladstone's 'crushingly suc-

---

* The weekly *Truth*, founded by the Radical MP Henry Labouchere in 1876, was consistently critical of the level of royal expenditure.

† Naval mutiny in 1797 at a critical moment in the war against France.

‡ The Whitehall office of the Commander-in-Chief, the Duke of Cambridge.

¶ An extract from the *Pall Mall Gazette* of a leaked report of the Cabinet decision shows Northbrook, Hartington, Dilke, and Chamberlain for vigorous action, Gladstone, Derby, Granville, and Childers against.

cessful' response to the recent censure motion, stemmed for the moment the public cry. Gladstone resented being hustled. He resented what he felt was the Queen's harassment. He told Hamilton 'that he was often minded to write to the Queen to say that, as he seemed to differ with Her in every political respect, he had better ask to be relieved of his service under Her'.[74] Unfortunately for Gladstone, there was need to save Gordon, in the sense of saving Gordon from himself. Gordon was in the habit of issuing contradictory statements, 'and never seemed to feel that there was any need for explanation'. Ministers in London were left floundering in the effort to make sense of 'fluctuation and inconsistency'. What it took long to get a clear sense of was the gradual and astonished realization that Gordon had, without informing the government, 'changed the character of the mission', and 'worked in a considerable degree against our intentions & instructions'. Having sent some 2,500 Egyptian civilians back down the Nile, Gordon set himself up in Khartoum to defy the Mahdi and save the Sudan for Egypt. By the middle of March Khartoum was effectively under siege. To Gladstone it was infinitely strange that 'one who bore in his hands a charter of liberation should be besieged and threatened'.[75]

[6]

Gordon thus made of himself in the most dramatic conceivable manner the heroic epitome of knightly valour and Christian devotion. Hamilton concluded that 'the man must be mad'.[76] Gladstone could see that 'Gordon will be the death of us (the Government) now, before we have done with him'.[77] Gordon bolstered his position with the Sudanese by proclaiming the legality of slavery. He wished further to bolster his position by enlisting the aid of Zobeir Pasha, undoubtedly the strongest man in Egypt, but in bad odour in the West as 'favourable to slave-hunting'. Gladstone was willing to sanction Zobeir's being sent since Gordon obviously set much store by him. But Selborne and Chamberlain, representing the Anglican and Nonconformist consciences respectively, turned abruptly away from their former leanings to intervention. Some stormy cabinets ensued. 'The position is getting too much like a dance on a tight rope,' Gladstone remarked to Northbrook. Had Gladstone the strength, he might have forced the issue. But, under the extra burden now of having introduced the Representation of the People Bill into the House of Commons, Gladstone collapsed on 10 March. 'From the 10th onwards until 30th I was forbidden to attend Cabinets.'[78] Gladstone recuperated at Coombe Warren, Wimbledon, the guest of Sir Donald

Currie. Hartington, the Cabinet's envoy to the sickbed, was said to have reported back to his colleagues on the Zobeir issue: 'He thinks that he himself might carry the proposal through the Commons, but that we can't, so we had better not try.'[79]

The Reform Bill exacerbated the problem. The Conservatives, terrified by the county franchise and horrified at the prospect in store for Ireland, found the Gordon issue a convenient means of getting at Gladstone by the displacement method: they could not attack Reform directly, because that would mean insulting and alienating the new voters; but they could direct their displaced energies into the government's embarrassments in the Sudan. In 1885 John Morley, analysing the origins of the Gordon 'catastrophe', argued that if there was 'one cause more than another' that conduced to it, it was the attitude of the government's critics – including especially W. E. Forster – incessantly importuning ministers with questions, and bringing so tremendous a pressure to bear on them 'that they dare not – and I blame them for it – that they did not dare to comply with General Gordon's own constantly repeated petition to send Zebehr Pasha to Khartoum'.[80] In a vote of censure debate on 3 April Gladstone bitterly denounced the Opposition's tactics in pressing the government to a wholly unreasonable degree with irresponsible harassment over the last seventeen sittings in the House; those seventeen nights 'will be looked upon by the future student of parliamentary history as a perfect curiosity of politics'.[81]

Unfortunately for Gladstone's prediction, the greater part of that harassment bore upon the question of whether ministers were taking steps either to reinforce or to rescue Gordon; and Gladstone's responses were uniformly scornful and defiant ('one might suppose that Egypt lay in Yorkshire, and that the Sudan was in Caithness or Sutherlandshire'). The excitement being raised in the Commons was 'out of all proportion to the pressure and urgency of the question', he insisted.[82] To the Queen, Gladstone (convalescing still at Coombe Warren) was quite candid on what he saw as the problems created for his government by Gordon: 'the number and rapidity of his various declarations, in some instances from their want of consistency, & from his too free communication with persons who act as correspondents of public journals'. Baring's advice that an expedition should be sent to Khartoum Gladstone dismissed as Baring's going 'awry'. It amounted to 'a reversal of policy: he overrides the most serious military difficulties'. Baring 'proposes to provide for danger to General Gordon, of the existence of which at the present moment Y. M.'s Govt. do not posses evidence: & he does this in ignorance of what are at the time General Gordon's circumstances, opinions, & desires'.[83]

In the same spirit of stiff unwillingness to be hustled and overborne,

Gladstone consistently deprecated in the Commons any suggestion that Gordon was in danger. He assured the House on 21 April that the 'general effect' of the intelligence reaching the government was that, 'according to the expression used', Gordon was 'hemmed in' at Khartoum; 'that is to say, that there are bodies of hostile troops in the neighbourhood forming more or less a chain around it'. Gladstone went on to 'draw a distinction between that and the town being surrounded, which would bear technically a very different meaning'. Supplies at Khartoum were abundant, and there was no apprehension at all of danger.[84] In the light of the tragic outcome of the Gordon mission, these words came to take on the appearance of a classic specimen of Gladstone's finessing with words.[85] As he himself once ruefully admitted, it could be said that he was too apt at drawing distinctions.[86] In fact, Gladstone was quoting Gordon's own description of his situation.[87] But Gladstone should have taken warning from his own awareness that 'recent telegrams from Gordon appear confused and contradictory'.

Thus, the correct response to Gordon's latest rambling demand – that a Turkish force should be sent to 'smash up the Mahdi' – was not to respond with a pained official negative, but to interpret Gordon's verbal escapade as a cry for help. Gladstone's telegram to Baring of 16 April later became the centrepiece of the censure debate in February 1885. On publication in the blue book of 5 May 1884 it caused, in Northcote's words, 'a very great sensation in the country, and not unnaturally'.[88] Gordon had used the phrase 'indelible disgrace' to describe the consequences of his not being succoured by military relief and his being refused Zobeir. He held himself 'free to act according to circumstances'. He would hold on as long as he could and attempt to suppress the 'rebellion'. If he could not achieve this Gordon would retire to the Equatorial province, leaving the government with the certainty that, if it wished 'to retain peace in Egypt', it would 'eventually be compelled to smash up the Mahdi under great difficulties'.[89] Gordon's phrase was certainly a jolt to the Cabinet. Dilke noted on 21 April that 'a majority now begin to see that an October expedition is certain'.[90]

That majority, however, did not include Gladstone. He made sure in the coming months that all discussion of relief expeditions remained strictly contingent and hypothetical. He was irritated by Archbishop Benson's proposal to offer public prayer for Gordon. 'But Gordon according to his own (I believe true) account is not (what is called) in danger.'[91] Given his prepossessions about Gordon ('a man who is not wholly sane and who perpetually contradicts himself', 'who has disobeyed his instructions and changed his plan of action'),[92] it was a failing in Gladstone to allow himself to become too personally resentful at the pertinacious offensiveness of the most 'jingo' of his harassers, Ellis Ashmead Bartlett.

It got to the point of Gladstone's refusing to reply to simple and direct questions as well as baiting questions.[93] A famous diatribe by Forster in the censure debate on 13 May on Gladstone's stubbornly proud unwillingness to concede the danger to Khartoum and Gordon achieved the notoriety of being quoted by Bartlett in February 1885:

I believe everyone but the Prime Minister is already convinced of that danger. I do not say that he is aware of the danger himself; I think he would act very differently if he were; and I attribute his not being convinced to his wonderful powers of persuasion. He can persuade most people of most things, and, above all, he can persuade himself of almost anything.[94]

Gladstone rode out the censure debate of 13 May with a majority of twenty-eight. 'Spoke for one hour on the Gordon question: the best I could, though far from good: but I declare, in the eye of God, with an active & absolute desire to speak according to truth & justice, & as I shall answer to Him for it in the great day.' He accused his critics of trying to saddle England with the task of reconquest: 'a war of conquest against a people struggling to be free, ["No! No!"] Yes; these are people struggling to be free, and they are struggling rightly to be free.'[95] He got into a furious altercation with Hicks Beach, who flung the 'indelible disgrace' phrase at him ('what does he mean by pointing to me – what does he mean by pointing to me to dishonour me in the eyes of my country – [*Cheers and counter-cheers*]'). Gladstone's substantial point was the need to harmonize and reconcile obligations both to the nation and to Gordon. 'We must consider the treasure of the nation, the blood of the nation, and the honour of the nation.' On the question of intervention he was reluctant to go beyond recognizing a possible contingency. 'It may be our duty to plant a British force in that terrible country.'[96]

The vote on 13 May marked a critical point. Parliamentary pressures thereafter eased over the summer. Contact with Gordon himself had been for the time lost, and with that a loss of inciting fuel for public anxiety and political agitation. Gladstone was soon in a position to endorse a counter-agitation: such things as Labouchere's accusations of Gordon's making himself 'a sort of Egyptian Jingo'; and Healy's question (expressive of an Irish view about a people struggling to be free) as to 'whether difficulties have not arisen through General Gordon's asking for assistance to put down the insurrection and smash the Mahdi'. Gladstone was gratified to be able to answer that Healy was 'perfectly justified in his reference'.[97] Gladstone was also able to fend off the Queen with an undertaking that 'Ministers, while anxiously awaiting news from General Gordon himself, and finding little occasion for present anxiety, have been & are very seriously engaged in examining the various routes and methods by which in case of need aid could be supplied; a question of great complexity, in which however much progress has been made.'[98]

Much more congenial to Gladstone was playing his favourite gambit about Britain's occupation of Egypt as service to an authority, 'the highest in the civilised world', the European Concert. The French were trying to strike a bargain whereby a British withdrawal from Egypt within five years would be matched by a French undertaking of non-entry. Gladstone found this kind of bilateral dealing distasteful. He much preferred the alternative of subjecting any extension of British occupation beyond 1889 to the 'concurrence of the Great Powers of Europe'.[99] Prudence, however, made him decide not to put that proposal to the Queen; it was cancelled as 'too argumentative'. He consoled himself, to Baring's dismay, by being argumentative with the French, rebuking them for their selfishness on the financial side and their want of sympathy for the plight of the *fellahin*. Gladstone's Cabinet was tending to split between two poles on the Egyptian question, neither of which would be in the least acceptable to the French or agreeable to Gladstone. One pole, represented by Harcourt and Chamberlain, wanted to lift the financial burden off Egypt's back by simply declaring its bankruptcy, and then 'scuttling'. The other pole, with Hartington as spokesman, wanted to guarantee Egypt's service of its debt within the framework of a British protectorate.

Gladstone's parliamentary ascendancy made it possible for him to fill in the cracks with compelling but indeterminate rhetoric. 'I was much oppressed beforehand', he recorded on 23 June, 'with the responsibility of my statement about Egypt: but pleased with the reception of it & the subsequent course of the debate. God is good: & I feel strong in the belief that we have the interests of justice, peace, & freedom in our hands.' Of more immediate consequence was Hartington's request for a short cabinet as he really felt that he did not 'know the mind or intention of the Govt. in respect to the relief of Gen. Gordon'.[100] Certain 'preparatory measures' which did not assume an expedition but that would save time were one found necessary, had been discussed (10 June); but within the frame of Gladstone's opinion (as he put it to Childers) that 'as to the real case for an expedition, I think the odds are seriously against its occurring, though no doubt it may occur'.[101] Gladstone was anxious not to disturb the year's financial dispositions. He attempted to evade Hartington by suggesting a circular letter. 'Our Cabinets this year have been (of necessity) beyond all precedent in frequency, & this makes me desire to avoid a meeting where this can be done without inconvenience.' Hartington, however, had his way on 5 July. But all he achieved was Gladstone's commentary on the discussion of a rescue expedition: 'Much difficulty felt.'

[7]

Gladstone's political skills for the while neutralized the Egyptian problem and relegated the Gordon problem, as Chamberlain put it, to 'five minutes at the fag end of business'.[102] He was aided in doing this partly because the Reform question was now presenting itself as the great matter for attention. Local Government and London Government were once more thrown to the winds. There was an early squall on the issue of women's suffrage, and Dilke, Fawcett, and Courtney were ready to resign rather than accept Gladstone's line that including it would give the Lords too good an excuse to 'postpone' the measure.[103] In the end they acceded to Gladstone's request 'to do us the favour to retain their respective offices'.[104] What, however, gave the Lords an even better motive for postponement was the by now frantic insistence by the Conservatives that a fair and comprehensive measure of Redistribution must proceed in tandem with Reform. Once it was clear that Gladstone would not entertain either Ireland's being separately treated, or any new uniform county franchise unassimilated to the existing borough franchise, there was no great question of principle or contest involved in the Reform issue. But Conservatives, led resolutely by Salisbury, were coming to the view that their party's hopes of surviving the county franchise even as a strong opposition depended crucially on gaining some compensating benefits from a radical restructuring of the constituencies on the basis of equal population and single-member seats.

Liberals (their expert being Dilke) could not be averse to this in principle. Gladstone agreed with Chamberlain that any scheme of 'just redistribution' must *ipso facto* be beneficial to the party of the 'nation'. In any case Liberals looked upon Redistribution as a supplementary tidying up after the great and decisive Reform measure was passed. They were shocked when Salisbury, on behalf of the Conservative party, announced that the Lords would block the Reform Bill until they got satisfactory assurances that an equitable Redistribution Bill would be processed concurrently. The Conservatives knew they could not keep a grip on Redistribution unless they kept a grip on Reform. This could not be done in the House of Commons, so it had to be done in the Lords. Salisbury's message was that if the government refused a reasonable request to link an agreed Redistribution to Reform, the Lords would be entitled to throw out the Reform Bill and invite the government to dissolve and put its case to the electorate.

What was most shocking to Liberals was this notion of the House of Lords assuming a 'referendal' function in the constitution.[105] Liberals, including the indignant Gladstone, saw it as a wholly illegitimate species of political blackmail. By the beginning of July it was evident that Salisbury was quite intent on putting the question to the test. Having suffered a painful series of humiliations at Gladstone's hands since he became Conservative leader in the Lords in 1881, Salisbury saw his chance to deploy the Lords in a constructive role by challenging Gladstone either to negotiate or to dissolve on the old registers. Gladstone appealed to Archbishop Benson to use his influence with Salisbury. The embarrassment disclosed itself that Tennyson, Gladstone's brilliant new peer, was much of a mind with Salisbury. Gladstone wrote to Lionel Tennyson trusting that his father could be counted on. The best Tennyson could promise was: 'I cannot vote with you & I will not vote *against* you.' Gladstone passed this on to Granville with three marginal exclamation marks.[106] He was astonished that Tennyson should be 'the *only* Peer, so far as I know, associated with Liberal ideas or the Liberal party, who hesitates to vote against Lord Salisbury'.[107] Gladstone wrote also to Lady Tennyson to keep her husband straight lest the House of Lords 'plays pranks'. Tennyson obdurately insisted that it must be taken for granted that 'both Houses are equally anxious to do justice for all'. He felt it would be 'base abdication' for the Lords to forgo their right and duty calmly to 'reconsider on all important questions'. He was quite clear that Redistribution must be promised; and if so promised he would come up to vote for the Franchise Bill 'notwithstanding gout'.[108]

Notwithstanding Tennyson, Liberals felt strongly that it would be beneath the dignity of the House of Commons to submit to blatant menaces. An honourable assurance to the Conservatives that Redistribution would be attended to before the next general election was quite as much as they should expect. Gladstone took pains to canvass all the bishops he had mitred. The episcopate, he told them, should trust the people. Gladstone could hardly believe that Salisbury would go through with his utterly reckless gamble. He attended at the Lords on 8 July to witness the astonishing spectacle: 'What a suicidal act of the Lords!' They threw out the Representation of the People Bill by 205 not-contents to 146 contents (of whom, in the end, Tennyson was meekly one). The ball was very much now in the government's court. The great trouble was that, either way, they were in difficulties. Dodson put it to Gladstone in a note at cabinet on 9 July: 'To allow Lords to force a dissolution would be precedent against liberty worse than anything since beginning of reign of George III.' There was in any case a sense of the absurdity of dissolving on the old registers on the eve of the creation of a new democracy. And, if it came to that, would the electorate necessarily agree that a stipulation by the Lords that they were perfectly willing to pass the Franchise Bill if an equitable and satisfactory Redistribution Bill were linked to it was so obviously, as Gladstone put it to the Queen, 'a gross and deplorable error'?[109]

The greater part of Gladstone's sense of the grossness and deplorability of the Lords' so stipulating was that, by challenging a Liberal government, they were *ipso facto* challenging 'the nation'. Gladstone further put it to the Queen that he knew, 'like the rest of the world, how formidable an opponent the House of Lords has habitually been, and especially for the last 30 years, to the Liberal party, which has had the nearly uniform assent of the nation'.[110] This view of Liberalism's natural hegemonic status in politics Gladstone complemented by a view of the decadence of the old Conservative party which he had known. He thought the new 'tone' of Conservatism was set by what he called 'the Beaconsfield influence',[111] of which Lord Randolph Churchill was the most egregiously demagogic and exemplary specimen. 'Conservatism so-called,' he observed in 1885, 'in its daily practice, now depends largely on influencing public passion, and thereby has lost the main element which made it really Conservative, and qualified it to resist excessive & dangerous innovation.'[112] In 1882 Gladstone drew up a list of 'Causes tending to help the Conservative party & give it at least an occasional preponderance though a minority of the nation'. Mostly these rehearsed the indictment he had made at Whitby in 1871 against the influence of wealth, land, and the professional classes maintained by 'privilege or by artfully constructed monopoly', and the concentration of these 'higher and social influences' in the metropolis and the legislature. Being a minority, the Conservatives had to be the more disciplined and unified party. But above all, while *'class* never slumbers', it was difficult on the Liberal side to keep the public's mind 'lively and intent upon great national interests'.[113]

The difficulty now would be to rally the public mind into being 'lively and intent' on this scandalous case of the challenge of hereditary privilege to the representative principle. Beneath the ground of Gladstone's notion here of renewing and restating the claims of Liberalism's habitual hegemony there were, however, forces which were shifting and displacing the foundations of the mid-nineteenth-century social and political order. Gladstone was unaware that the epoch he took to be habitual in its assent to the Liberal party was coming to its end; and that, with the emergence of a new social and political order, the redistribution of constituencies as eventually agreed by the negotiations stipulated for by the House of Lords would prove to be diagnostically symptomatic and of crucial explanatory power. The Conservatives, equally, had little inkling of quite how decisively the terms of political trade were about to turn in their favour. Salisbury made himself an expert in the field of redistribution precisely because he accepted the validity of Liberal predictions as to the desperate plight of the Conservative party. It was Salisbury's highest hope to get politics back to the healthy pre-1868 dispensation, with blurred party lines, collusive front benches, and with governments deprived of the dangerous privilege of having Gladstonian means to Gladstonian ends. He thought Conservatism was in its optimum situation as a strong minority in the House of Commons, facing a weak Liberal government, and having the House of Lords in reserve. In 1897, in the wake of the Conservative triumph of 1895, Salisbury bemusedly declared that 'the history of recent times, as it will be written, is a very strange history'.[114] The best he was hoping for in 1884 was that he could pick up some advantage out of the demolition of the hostile electoral structure of 1880.

A tense and bad-tempered confrontation clouded the next three and a half months. Gladstone would not, on principle, dissolve the Parliament at the behest of the Lords. The Lords would not give way without definite assurances as to an agreed Redistribution. Gladstone warned that the Lords had opened up a vista of organic constitutional change which would prove ultimately much to their disadvantage. Liberal activists, encouraged by Chamberlain, began to get up a 'peers versus people' and 'mend them or end them' campaign against the Lords in the country. Conservatives mounted a counter-agitation in defence of the Lords' perfectly reasonable and constitutional case. (A notorious riot at Aston, when a Conservative meeting was invaded by a chair-throwing Liberal mob, was dubbed by the Tory wit James Lowther as the model 'redistribution of seats'.) The Queen, anxious at the public unrest and concerned to fend off a serious contest between the two Houses of Parliament, offered her mediation. Gladstone's line was that, while the Lords had wantonly exposed themselves to severely punitive action from the people, he would himself do all he could to temper the popular wrath. He valued the hereditary principle, and would like to help the House of Lords to save it from itself. 'I am . . . an absolute worshipper of the hereditary principle,' as he put it in 1886 ' – hereditary titles and possessions; but would that it were not so often abused as it is in certain hands!'[115]

For the Queen's guidance in providing her good offices Gladstone gave her the benefit of his thoughts on the link between the political and constitutional components of the present crisis. His point of departure was the proposition that once the Liberal party incorporated into its creed a fixed conclusion on a great political or constitutional question, that question must ultimately be resolved in the Liberal sense. That was 'the lesson taught by history'.

During the last half century, the whole course of our legislation in great matters, has been directed by the Liberal party . . . any great question, once adopted into its creed, has marched onwards, with real & effectual, if not always uniform progress, to a triumphant consummation . . .

It seems difficult . . . to deny that we seem to have hold of something like a political axiom when we say that the adoption of a legislative project into the Creed of the Liberal party at large is a sure prelude to its accomplishment.

Defiance by the Lords of this 'political axiom' could have but one consequence: it would provoke from the Liberal party a demand for 'organic change' in the constitution. And once this demand is incorporated into the Liberal creed its accomplishment becomes certain. Gladstone's view was that that incorporation had not as yet taken place. The demand for organic change was not 'deeply rooted' and had not 'assumed permanent form'. There was much 'tall talk' on both sides of the question. So there was time still for the Conservatives and the Lords to extricate themselves from a dangerously exposed position. Once the Reform Bill was passed the current agitation against the Lords would die away; but only if the bill were allowed to pass. If not, the government would come under intense pressure and there would be a great conflict on the issue 'whether hereditary or representative majority is to prevail'.[116]

The better to add a touch of terror to this menacing lesson of history, Gladstone further pointed to certain implications arising possibly from the current flirtations between the Conservatives and the Parnellites in relation to a dissolution forced by the Lords.

It is believed on all hands that the so-called National Party in Ireland will on a dissolution be increased. It is supposed that the increase will be from a little over forty to near eighty; that the principal part of this increase would be obtained by taking (say) twenty-five seats from the Liberal party; and that, if the Liberal Ministry were then still in power, these eighty votes, added to the votes of the Tories, would promptly displace it.

It was not necessary to enquire, Gladstone continued, whether the position thus obtained by the Conservatives would be a stable one; or whether they would be able to 'keep down not only the Liberal opposition, but any of that united action between the regular opposition and the Irish Nationalists, which has been so common in the present Parliament, and to which they would probably have owed their obtaining the reins of government'. But what it was necessary to realize, argued Gladstone, was that the Liberals would be then a 'disappointed and incensed minority', who would see the House of Lords as the author of their misfortunes; the Lords would be targeted and 'organic change' adopted into the Liberal creed. All this would have incalculable consequences, compromising to the 'foundations even of the throne'.[117]

No doubt the Queen took all these points with the best grace she could muster. Gladstone struck back at the Lords by announcing that there would be an autumn session in October. He observed gravely to the Queen that he much feared riots and disorder if the Lords rejected the Reform Bill a second time. For her part Victoria felt she had cause to complain of Gladstone's 'constant speeches' at railway stations, doing nothing to help for mediation. She was *'utterly* disgusted' especially at his *'stump* oratory' in Scotland, 'almost under her very nose' at Balmoral. Gladstone, on the line from Haddo to Brechin, found the whole journey 'a tempest of demonstrations, addresses, and replies'. (He was dismayed to observe 'alack! six obelisks', on John Brown's grave.)[118]

[8]

The Reform Bill was reintroduced in the House of Commons on 24 October. Conservative efforts to get guarantees as to Redistribution failed yet again. Tension mounted as the bill passed up to the Lords where it was due for its crucial second reading on 20 November. Eager brokers of mediation pressed forward, including Argyll. Tennyson offered advice in irritatingly sententious verse.* In the background persisted distant thunders out of Egypt. When Granville shifted the second reading forward to 18 November Salisbury exclaimed: 'Mark my words, Khartoum has fallen.'[120] The Sudanese problem had gradually been working its way back into distracting prominence. As early as 16 July Gladstone recorded his disappointment at the Cabinet's leanings towards an expedition 'for or towards Khartoum'. His errant colleagues included 'even Granville a little'. Gladstone fenced and parried indefatigably. As he put it to Selborne (now 'headlong' for an expedition), Gordon appeared merely to *'enquire'* about an expedition. 'I do not know on what ground you can as yet say he expects one.' There was still no evidence of present danger. 'It is not a question of condemning him for adopting this policy: but are we to adopt it and to be responsible for it, and its consequences?'[121] In the end Gladstone agreed to move for a precautionary vote of credit.

By 2 August Gladstone noted: 'This day for the first time in my

---

* 'Steersman, be not precipitate in thine act
   of steering, for the river here, my friend
   parts in two channels moving to one end
This goes straight forward to the cataract –
   That streams about the bend:
But though the cataract seem the nearer way,
Whate'er the crowd on either bank may say,
Take thou the "bend", 'twill save thee many a day.'
   – 'To Miss Gladstone', 5 November 1884[119]

recollection there were three *crises* for us all running high tide at once: Egypt, Gordon, & franchise.' By September Gladstone's resistance to the idea of an expedition had weakened to the point 'at which I cannot dispute the propriety of putting Wolseley in a condition to proceed if necessary'.[122] Rumours that Colonel Stewart and his party had been massacred in attempting to get down the Nile from Khartoum came on 8 October.

This black hint of even greater tragedy enormously raised the temperature of the Sudan fever. Gladstone began overtures to lower the temperature of the franchise/redistribution fever. Already he had told Dilke that he was willing to move further on details of Redistribution 'if we could thereby effectually promote peace & get the Franchise Bill passed'. This was on the day (29 September) on which he read Salisbury's article in the *National Review* on 'The Value of Redistribution: a Note on Electoral Statistics'. Those details had to do with what Dilke wonderingly described as the 'revolutionary criticism of Lord Salisbury', who seemed to be moving towards a ruthless willingness to throw overboard all notions of mechanisms to protect minority interests and to accept that an equitably straightforward system based on simple numbers would produce a perfectly adequate fortuitous proportionality as between the electorate and the representation of party in the House of Commons. Both Dilke and Gladstone were astonished at Salisbury's radical readiness to go for single-member and equal-population electoral districts. It was another case of Conservatism's propensities for newfangled innovation. Gladstone did not regard proportionality as between population and representation as a thing necessarily to be aimed for, especially as regards the metropolis. He complained that they were not dealing with a *'tabula rasa'*; he was tender towards 'long usages and tradition'; he was 'inclined to respect individuality'.[123] But it occurred to neither Gladstone nor Dilke that it would be detrimental to the Liberal party if Salisbury were humoured in these directions.

Salisbury managed with difficulty to hold the Conservative party outwardly steady on the eve of the critical Lords vote. Had Gladstone held out longer the Conservative nerve might well have cracked. On the other hand, the Liberal campaign in the country against the Lords had not provided anything like overwhelming assurance that the 'nation' saw the matter as a simple conflict between hereditary and representative principles. The offers of mediation by the Queen and others willing to provide good offices tended to undermine Gladstone's bluff just as much as Salisbury's counter-bluff. Gladstone certainly had reason to want to clear the question out of the way in case the Egypt and Gordon problems went from bad to worse. With infinite reluctance he unleashed Wolseley to take command of the expedition to relieve Khartoum which had been prepared in Egypt. Wolseley arrived in Cairo on 9 September. Pragmatically, giving Hartington the Sudan expedition made it easier to get him to swallow the franchise and redistribution pills. Granville was near collapse: Egyptian anxieties had 'laid him on his back'; and the Queen thought him 'absolutely *passé* and *baissé*'; 'weak and sweet as *eau de rose*'.[124]

On 7 November Gladstone canvassed with Derby the expediency, 'with a view to an early settlement', of accepting 'the Salisbury–Beach radical scheme', whereby, to Gladstone's shocked conservative dismay, the 'principle of population' was to be adopted absolutely, and traditional arrangements were 'to be ripped asunder everywhere & to the uttermost'.*

Gladstone took occasion at a reception at the Algernon Wests' to approach Northcote 'in an air of curiously midnight conspiracy'. Northcote reported to Salisbury on 13 November that as a consequence of an interview 'held in shrouds of deepest mystery', it could be concluded: 'I think our friend was eager for a settlement.'[126] Gladstone placed in Northcote's hand the question: 'What assurances will you require about the character of our Redistribution Bill, as a condition of engaging that, if we produce it before the Franchise Bill reaches the Committee in the Lords, and make it a vital question, the Franchise Bill shall then be put forward without difficulty or delay?'[127]

That was enough to break the deadlock. On 17 November Gladstone in the Commons and Granville in the Lords announced that if the Franchise Bill were allowed to pass in the Lords the Redistribution Bill would be made the subject of friendly communication with the Opposition leaders. Last-minute hitches were smoothed over on the 18th by Gladstone's 'conciliatory & satisfactory explanation'.[128] Gladstone brushed aside complaints from Radicals that the House of Commons had been 'as good as extinguished' and 'humiliated'.[129] By 19 November Salisbury and Northcote were received at Downing Street: 'all was courteous & free, & rather hopeful'. The efficient negotiators among the map-strewn tables and sofas and carpets were Dilke and Salisbury. Gladstone observed Northcote sitting by Salisbury 'like a chicken protected by the wings of a mother hen'.[130] Granville was withdrawn after a decent interval. Hartington invariably found the maps the wrong way up. Gladstone was gratified to be back on terms with Salisbury, finding it a pleasure to deal with so 'acute' a mind. So inherently strong did Gladstone and Dilke assume Liberalism would be in consequence of the

---

* Even Dilke's redistribution scheme, as G sorrowfully informed the Queen, involved 'more extensive changes than Mr. Gladstone would have thought necessary or desirable'.[125]

county franchise that they made no resistance to Salisbury's radicalism. On the one point where Salisbury held out for tradition, the university seats, Gladstone overruled Dilke in support. Neither party made any difficulty over the rather gross Irish over-representation. Gladstone needed to keep Parnell in humour and in play, and the Conservatives were conducting their coquettings with the Irish as two parties who shared a common interest in mitigating the coming Liberal majority. '*Ils five-o-clockèrent chez moi*', Gladstone recorded, until 26 November, when negotiations were concluded to general satisfaction.

Gladstone introduced the agreed Redistribution Bill to a puzzled and fretful Commons on 1 December. 'All prospects rosy.' The two front benches colluded in imposing the settlement on their followers. Northcote told his party: 'swallow your medicine'.[131] There was no serious resistance. The principles were evidently equitable; their consequences were too intricate to be readily comprehended. The upshot was that 170 seats were abolished and 182 seats created. Hardly any constituency was unaffected. The second reading passed without a division on 4 December. The third reading of the Reform Bill was passed by the Lords on 5 December, and received the royal assent on 6 December. Nearly two million new voters were to be added to the existing register of three million. Something like 60 per cent of adult males were now eligible to vote: two out of three in England and Wales, three out of five in Scotland, and one out of two in Ireland.

The new electorate which Gladstone was responsible for creating in 1884 was portentous in its evocation of 'mass'. Something like a 'democracy' could be said to have come into being. Yet in certain ways the popular energies embodied in the new constituencies were constrained. There were vested electoral interests which the Conservatives and Whigs had every interest in conserving, and which Gladstone felt, conservatively, no compelling call to disturb. In the first place the criteria for possessing the franchise remained complex, with a sizeable admixture of multiple votes. A vote remained very much a privilege rather than a right. Secondly, the registration system remained intact in the hands of party registration agents, registration solicitors, and revising barristers. This fact was to become of crucial importance in a situation which involved not only millions of newly eligible voters but millions of existing voters transferred to new registers. The curious paradox obtained that although Gladstone was now the re-accredited leader of the nation in its new 'mass' age – 'Gladstone for the million' was already a familiar slogan – in fact it was to be an age alien to him in certain important and ultimately decisive respects.

Gladstone's motive for moving for the great enfranchisement of 1884 remained rooted in his experiences between 1876 and 1880. The Represen-

1. *Gladstone's Cabinet, 1868*, by Lowes Cato Dickinson. Standing (*left to right*): Hartington, Fortescue, Cardwell, Childers; seated (*left to right*): Lowe, Bright, Argyll, Clarendon, Bruce, Hatherley, Ripon, Gladstone, Granville, Kimberley, Goschen *'This Cabinet is the most laborious as a whole I have ever seen'*

2. *Punch* lampoons the introduction of the Ballot Bill, 1 July 1871. Gladstone's helpers with the ballot box are (*left to right*) Robert Lowe, H. A. Bruce, and W. E. Forster. Disraeli looks on derisively (*far left*). Of 'Dizzy himself', Gladstone allowed that he was *'an extra-ordinary man and a genius . . . whose rival some call me, much against my will, for I am not and never was his rival, as far as it depended on my will or intention'*

THE STRONG GOVERNMENT.

BEN (*to rude boy*). *"Now, then, all together! — and be very careful as you don't overdo yerselves!"*

3. (*Above left*) Gladstone with Catherine '*At no period of my life have I been guilty of the act which is known as that of infidelity to the marriage bed*'
4. (*Above right*) Laura Thistlethwayte, a mid-nineteeenth-century engraving by Frank Holl '*The extraordinary history, the confiding appeal, the singular arousal*'

5. A family gathering at Hawarden, *c* 1868. Standing (*left to right*): Mary Gladstone, William Ewart Gladstone, Sir Stephen Glynne, Agnes Gladstone (at the window), Lady Cavendish; seated (*left to right*): Jack Gladstone, Helen Gladstone, Willy Gladstone, Catherine Gladstone, Herbert Gladstone, Henry Gladstone, Lord Frederick Cavendish '*I have a large scheme in prospect . . . an institution for religion and learning, but under the care of the family; such is the blessing of being able absolutely to trust my children*'

6. A contrived picture of Gladstone's Cabinet, 1883. Standing (*left to right*): Hartington, Derby, Gladstone, Dilke, Northbrook; seated (left to right): Dodson, Kimberley, Harcourt, Granville, Selborne, Carlingford, Childers, Chamberlain, Spencer *'My position is a strange one. A strong man in me wrestles for retirement: a stronger one stands at the gate of the exit, and forbids'*

7. Gladstone with his secretariat, *c* 1883. Left to right: Horace Seymour, Spencer Lyttelton, George Leveson Gower, and Edward Walter Hamilton *'Your services have been simply indescribable'*

8. (*Above left*) Joseph Chamberlain *'With other notable gifts, a good deal of repulsive power'*
9. (*Above right*) John Poyntz, fifth Earl Spencer *'The wonder is ... how you compass your immense work without ever losing balance. May your strength continue'*
10. (*Below left*) Spencer Cavendish, Lord Hartington, later eighth Duke of Devonshire *'After the election of 1880 ... he,* to my certain knowledge, *tried to form a Government ... This statement is in all points beyond contradicton'*
11. (*Below right*) John Morley *'I cannot help liking Mr John Morley'*

12. (*Above left*) Alfred, Lord Tennyson '*Singularly mixed true greatness, genuine simplicity, and some eccentricity*'

13. (*Above right*) Lord Rosebery, fifth Earl '*A most singular case of strong self-delusion: a vein of foreign matter which runs across a clear and vigorous intellect, and a high-toned character*'

14. (*Below left*) Lord Granville, second Earl '*The most intimate of them all*'

15. (*Below right*) Gladstone with Ignaz von Döllinger, September 1886, an unfinished portrait by Franz von Lenbach '*The mind as heretofore free, comprehensive and profound*'

16. (*Above left*) Gladstone and Catherine at Midlothian, 1880 '*Scene of so many of my misdeeds*'
17. (*Above right*) Gladstone introduces the Home Rule Bill, 1886 '*This is one of the golden moments of our history – one of those opportunities which may come and may go, but which rarely return*'

Pair of cartoons by Tom Merry showing Charles Stewart Parnell with Gladstone, as Dr Jekyll the Patriot (*left*), and as Mr Hyde the Moonlighter

18. '*He is certainly one of the very best people to deal with that I have ever known*'

19. '*I had no idea of the depths of disgrace . . . to which he would descend*'

20. Gladstone and Catherine at a picnic near Blackcraig Castle, September 1893. Among the party (*rear, left to right*): Lord Acton, George Armitstead, *'old shoe, and tame cat'*, and Reverend Stephen Gladstone

21. Gladstone addressing a fête at Hawarden, September 1894 *'Numbers are put at 54,000: it strained me a bit'*

22. Gladstone with Stuart Rendel *'a real warming and cheering influence on my public as well as private life'* A note by Maud Gladstone on the reverse of this photograph states that it depicts Gladstone's last long walk, taken during his stay in Biarritz, 1894

23. The Prince and Princess of Wales with the Gladstones, Hawarden, 1897 *'They do so much towards us from a sense of the Queen's deficiencies'*

tation of the People Act of 1884 was his acknowledgement to the 'nation' that it, as he put it to Argyll, had remained 'strong & sound'.[132] Gladstone's outlook was essentially backward-looking. It was fixed in the Peelite ethos. Gladstone deplored most deeply and genuinely the 'dissolution of the connection between the Liberal Party & the heads of the great Whig families'. It made for a 'serious change', as he told the Duke of Bedford, 'in the composition & the tone of the Liberal party itself, & places a gap between it & its older tradition & practice, for the introduction of which I at least do not wish to be in any way responsible'. Gladstone here spoke of the Aberdeen Cabinet as 'the first Liberal Cabinet to which I belonged'.[133] It was from this spacious perspective that he assumed that the future would be very much of the same. His great worry about it was in the divorce between actual Christian religion and trained human reason, and the consequent declining morality of the upper classes of society. This is what made him speculate to Newman that 'we have lived through a quiet period; the next half-century may be quieter still: I think it looks more alarming'.[134]

Still, such alarm was tempered by his assumption that the mighty popular energies extractable and manipulable from the 1884 enfranchisement would be bigger and better but essentially the same as the energies he had extracted and manipulated from the 1867 enfranchisement: bigger and better if only in making the 'reaction' of 1874 inherently improbable in the future. He assumed wholly that the 'nation' had given, and would continue to give, its habitual assent to Liberalism; and that it would continue to be an 'axiom of politics' that once a great question had been adopted by the Liberal party its ultimate triumph was certain. This 'great lesson' of the history of the time would obtain in the future with an enhanced potency. Gladstone had no conception of the nature of the magnitude of the electoral logic he unwittingly set loose by the Redistribution Bill, which went up to the Lords on 15 May 1885 and which received the royal assent on 25 June – two days after he ceased to be prime minister.

That logic had at its core the immense fact that for the first time the urban population was given due weight in the electoral process; which meant for effective purposes that the great conurbations were broken up into multiple divisions ringed with swathes of outer suburban constituencies. The modern geography of British politics had been set in being. The shape of future politics would be determined by the loyalties of this new civic and suburban electoral order. Metropolitan London now comprised no fewer than sixty-four of these single-member divisions: 'Megalopolis.' A great industrial county like Lancashire comprised twenty-three divisions; Yorkshire West Riding nineteen. Manchester-Salford and Liverpool each had nine divisions. The Lancashire manufacturing boroughs which survived intact accounted for fourteen further divisions. Industrial West Riding added twenty-one further divisions. A party that could dominate the metropolis and at least one of the two great northern industrial regions would have an English majority already half in its grip. It was a world quite remote from Gladstone's experience. It was a world equally remote from the previous habits of the old electorate.

[9]

As 1884 moved to its close Gladstone had cleared the political decks of the lumber and tackle of Reform and Redistribution. Apart from lively disputes with the French over Egypt there was little to attend to that was immediately urgent. Wolseley had launched his expedition up the Nile, which at least tided that problem over for the time being. Gladstone had managed at least a partial reconstruction of the administration. Dodson was removed rather abruptly[135]* and replaced at the Duchy by Trevelyan, who in turn was replaced at the Irish Office by Henry Campbell-Bannerman. All efforts to dislodge Carlingford to make room for Rosebery, however, failed. Gladstone was amazed at the 'tenacity of a man who finds that it is thought that his room is better than his company'.[136] To Carlingford tenacity was the revenge of talent over genius. Rosebery would have to wait yet longer for his coveted Cabinet place.

One of the uncomfortable consequences of falling out with the French over Egypt was the eruption of a 'navy scare' instigated by H. O. Arnold-Forster and Captain John Fisher, RN, who put W. T. Stead up to making a sensational stunt of it in the *Pall Mall Gazette*. The 'Jeune École' of French navalists, inspired by the example of the *Alabama*, were promoting the idea that a '*guerre de course*' against Britain's merchant marine would be much the most effective mode of waging war against a power which depended utterly on its importing and exporting over the sea routes of the world. The matter was mainly of consequence as the first step towards the Naval Defence Act of 1889. It happened that at this time Gladstone (in common with large numbers of his contemporaries in fashionable and intellectual society) was going through one of his periodic spiritualist phases,[137] and was in the habit of attending seances promoted by Mrs Emma Hartmann and Lady Sandhurst. At one of the latter's seances, the entranced medium (a Mrs Duncan) conveyed to Gladstone that he was promised 'repeatedly help; & said I had been

* He took a peerage as Lord Monk Bretton.

helped. Especially by my sister (no doubt Helen) who was now quite happy & was aware that she need not have made her religious change.' For good measure the entranced Mrs Duncan then added the message that 'the Navy ought to be looked after'. Gladstone was willing to concede that 'good advice is to be remembered come how it may'.[138]*

He did not long remain so patient and tractable with an agitation which he could identify as a case of Conservatism's propensity for 'inflaming public passion'. He and Northbrook stood stoutly by their declarations that the government could be trusted to take all necessary measures to maintain Britain's naval supremacy. The special irritation of this Navy scare for Gladstone was that, just as it came out of the quarrel with France over the settlement of Egypt, so it fed back into the quarrels in his own Cabinet between the 'bankruptcy and scuttle' school and the 'guarantee and protectorate' school. Within the quarrels between those schools over Egypt lay implications for naval policy in relation to the security of the Mediterranean sea route, the Straits, and the Suez Canal. The highlighting of the question of the adequacy of Britain's Navy unavoidably added yet another entanglement in the way of being able to afford the luxury of not occupying Egypt.

The year's end at Hawarden found Gladstone suffering from disturbed nights and dismally aware that the pressure on him was 'too much for the requisite recollection'. 'It is indeed a time of *sturm und drang*.' What with the confusion of affairs and the disturbance of daily life he could not 'think in calm', but could 'only trust & pray to Him who heareth the prayer'. At cabinet on 2 January Carlingford observed Gladstone looking 'unwell and weak and said with some emotion that he had lost his sleep, and did not know what A. Clark might order'.[141] The pattern of 1883 seemed to repeat itself. With apologies to the Queen Gladstone retreated back to Hawarden to rest and recuperate. Granville, presiding in Gladstone's absence, was no improvement ('so difficult to know whether he heard what was said and intended to act according to decisions come to'. 'Evidently hates tackling Bismarck in any way').[142] There was a new sense among Gladstone's colleagues that the 1880 government had reached its assigned limit. Both Hartington and Northbrook contemplated resigning over Egypt. Northbrook was particularly scathing about Granville. 'He spoke of Granville as responsible for a great deal of our mistakes – having no policy of his own – making no use as against Gladstone of his position as Foreign Minister, but being entirely ruled by Gladstone etc.'[143]

* 'Help' presumably was through the efficaciousness of prayer. At around this time Gladstone also recorded notes of a seance with a Mrs Hart – 'who was reluctant to divulge the name of the winner of the Cesarewitch'.[139] Gladstone was elected an honorary member of the Society for Psychical Research in 1885.[140]

The air of Liberal politics was now thick with rumours that this was the end for Gladstone. On the morning of 5 January Harcourt informed Dilke that 'Mr Gladstone intended to resign, and that Lord Granville would follow Mr Gladstone, in which case Hartington intended to make him, Harcourt, Chancellor, to move Lord Derby and Childers, to put in Rosebery, to offer Chamberlain the Chancellorship of the Exchequer, and me the Secretaryship of State for Foreign Affairs'. Dilke, however, was clear that neither he nor Chamberlain could accept, 'great as were the offices proposed', if Mr Gladstone had 'gone out notoriously dissatisfied'. If he were to resign on health alone, it would have been another matter.[144] Rosebery, according to Dilke, tried to 'force us to dismiss Lord Granville and Lord Derby'.[145] Chamberlain's view was that Gladstone's retirement was 'possible, and might be necessary'; that 'Hartington and Harcourt could bring it about'; but that he and Dilke must be careful not to allow them to say that 'we had been engaged in an intrigue with them against Mr Gladstone'. After cabinet in Gladstone's absence on 5 January Dilke, Chamberlain, and Trevelyan met at the Local Government Board 'to deliver the terms on which we would join a Hartington administration', finding Egypt the only real difficulty. Harcourt informed them that 'our Egyptian policy made the formation of a Government impossible, as Hartington would not consent to accept office on our Egyptian policy'.[146]

In the uncertainties of the situation it seemed to Chamberlain the time to start piling on the pressure. At Birmingham he added to manhood suffrage and payment of MPs his notorious doctrine about the 'ransom' which private property would need to pay for its security. There were many who agreed with Lord Cranbrook that 'all this comes from the Irish measures for wh. Mr. Gladstone is responsible'.[147] There were outraged demands on Gladstone from the Queen and the Whigs for Chamberlain's dismissal. A. D. Elliot pointed out that if Chamberlain's statement did not represent the views of the Cabinet, he was being 'false to his colleagues'.[148] (Elliot was later the biographer of Goschen.) Chamberlain detected a 'dead set at him' and Dilke also diagnosed a Whig plot to force Gladstone to break Chamberlain 'in place of his breaking Hartington after Mr G. is gone'.[149]

Gladstone knew that breaking Chamberlain would involve also breaking Dilke; which would be too much to sustain. Dilke's argument was that the object of the Whigs was to force the Radicals into a war with Gladstone, 'who is strong', and not with Hartington, 'against whom the Radicals would hold winning cards'.[150] Gladstone returned from Hawarden more needed than ever as the point of coherence but less competent than ever to direct a coherent policy. On Egyptian finance he 'grew very impatient, lost his temper, and put the question in a very perverse way'.[151] Derby wondered at the 'careless, slipshod way in which Cabinet business is done', with questions taken up but no decisions made. 'I can scarcely think that in his best days he would have let things slide as he does now.'[152] There was hopeless disappointment about Egypt and bitter squabbles about leaks to the press. 'It would have been a *breach of trust* to my colleagues', Gladstone angrily declared, 'had I written such an account to the Queen.'[153]* And always, as Derby observed, there was the 'peculiar position of the Premier, who is always declaring himself to be on the point of retiring', and who thus 'increases the difficulty, for he is very unwilling to do anything that may bind him to stay longer in office, and we cannot act without him'.[154]

All this tended to make the logic of Gladstone's 'peculiar position' all the more peculiar in one direction but, through its very absurdity, it tended also to open up the possibility that something big might yet be made of it. It was impossible for Gladstone, as 'leader of the nation', to struggle on absurdly as merely the mediator in quarrels which his own 'peculiar position' had in any case done so much to foment. It was difficult, though not impossible, in the circumstances of the beginning of 1885 to contemplate 'running away' from the government's problems on grounds of health. But it was less difficult to contemplate the possibilities latent in a wider view of a situation fraught with great shapings of great events in a not too distant future, far worthier, it might reasonably be assumed, of the attention of the leader of the nation. A general election would be held probably before the end of 1885. Once the new registers were drawn up and once the new constituency boundaries were fixed, it would be hard to hold it off for long. The Liberal party, by general consent, would emerge with a resoundingly emphatic assent of the nation. What then? What if it should happen that Gladstone's prognostications about Parnell's confronting Parliament as the undoubtedly accredited leader of the Irish nation's demand to be free were actually to come to pass?†

That deeply fraught question was in all likelihood not at the forefront of Gladstone's mind when he and Catherine went up to stay with Hartington at Holker early in February, as the guests of the Duke of Devonshire. Something plausible had to be concocted for the reopening of the 1884–5 session on the 19th. Hartington had to be pacified about Chamberlain and about Egypt if there was going to be any chance of his taking over the leadership from Gladstone. 'After 11 AM,' Gladstone recorded of 5 February, 'I heard the sad news of the fall or betrayal of Khartoum.' Wolseley had arrived two days too late. It appeared that

* The press lobby was set up at Westminster in 1884 to mitigate the problem.
† See above, pages 290 and 338.

Gordon judged his situation hopeless on 14 December, and was over-whelmed by assault on 26 January, after a siege of 317 days. The Gladstones and Hartington hastened to London and reached Downing Street soon after 8.15. 'The circumstances are sad & trying: it is one of the least points about them, that they may put an end to this Govt.'[155] The Queen made her feelings plain by the extraordinary mode of telegraphing *en clair*: 'These news from Khartoum are frightful and to think that all this might have been prevented and many precious lives saved by earlier action is too fearful.'[156] Offended and resentful, Gladstone found himself 'compelled' to respond voluminously and quite stiffly, rehearsing his familiar litany of the difficulties confronting ministers and the intracta-bility of the terrain, adding very specifically what was to become the central theme of his defence: that Khartoum fell not for want of defensi-bility, but by treachery from within.*

Hero Gordon was now Martyr Gordon. Public outrage naturally cast Gladstone as the chief villain of the case. As the Queen put it succinctly to her daughter, 'He will be for ever branded with the blood of Gordon that heroic man.' Not the least of her resentments against the 'old sinner' was that she, as 'head of the nation', would have to 'bear the humili-ation'.[158] Gladstone's greatest difficulty was that a cogently reasoned public defence of his and his colleagues' position could hardly avoid bearing on Gordon's manifold defects and eccentricities as an amateur proconsul. The hysteria of the moment, and for long after, made that impossible. The 'gloom and rage of London knew no bounds', as Hamil-ton recorded.[159] Old friendships were broken off. Schliemann, it appears, consigned Gladstone's autographed photograph to the lavatory.[160] It so happened that new arrangements for the Cabinet involving Rosebery's promotion could be made public on the 9th, giving a much-needed impression of solidarity. Gladstone proceeded immediately to neutralize this slight advantage by going to the Criterion theatre after dining with the Dalhousies on 10 February ('"The Candidate": capitally acted'). It was not mere thoughtlessness. Gladstone felt perfectly justified in that the reports had not as yet been formally confirmed. But at no point in his career did he allow his love for the theatre to lead him so foolishly astray. The Queen enquired of Carlingford: 'Does he not feel it at all?'[161] Hamilton was appalled. 'I told Mr G. in the morning that it was foolish; I ought to have written to Lady Dalhousie to give up the idea of the

---

* An oddity of the case, given Gladstone's recent attendance at spiritualist seances, was the message of one J. F. Hunt of Biggleswade ('a frequent correspondent') to G, 7 February 1885,[157] with news supplied 'by spirit informants': Gordon was killed in an assault on 26 January; his body had received decent burial; there had been no treachery; Khartoum had been stormed by overwhelming force, in which the Mahdi lost greatly in men.

theatre under the circumstances; but it was thought it would fuss Mr G.'

Mr G. is singularly devoid of misgivings or anything approaching to remorse. He has no qualms. He does not think 'If only I had done this, or only had done that.' He has a clear conscience. He acted for the best, and must abide by the results of his judgment. But he feels the responsibility acutely; and though we may marvel at his coolness, one ought to be thankful that in national troubles he should be able to keep his head, and that he does not take to heart too much everything that goes wrong.[162]

Gladstone took to his bed on 12 February. 'He continues to retain perfect calmness.' He denounced the Queen as 'one of the greatest Jingoes alive'. There was much ill-natured talk and many abusive letters on the play-going incident. It was a mistake no doubt, Hamilton remarked, 'but the practice of questioning the private actions of public men is an entirely novel growth'.[163]*

On the eve of the reopening of the parliamentary session Hamilton still marvelled at Gladstone's retaining his equanimity. Mainly, Hamilton thought, this was attributable to Gladstone's sense of good conscience, but in part also to Gladstone's hope that the inevitable vote of censure would release him from office. Already Gladstone had countered Acton's argument that the coming of democracy and the crisis in the state that it would involve forbade Gladstone's retirement. Gladstone insisted that there would be no 'crisis in the history of the Constitution, growing out of the extension of the franchise'. There would be no question of Gladstone's being needed to 'steer the ship through the boiling waters of this crisis'. Gladstone allowed that there existed a 'slow modification and development' mainly in directions which he 'viewed with misgiving'. He had in mind the demagogic attributes of 'Tory Democracy' and the rise both of the evil principle of class interest and of the ideas of collectivist state action which he dubbed 'Construction'; all of which were detrimental to the 'pacific, law-abiding, economic elements'. But even so, Gladstone felt assured that the sense of justice still abided tenaciously in 'the masses', who would ever repudiate the 'Fiend of

* Mrs Bradley, wife of Dean Bradley of Westminster, later related an account of a curious and pathetic incident at the memorial service at the Abbey on 13 February, as Archbishop Benson was about to speak: 'Just as they were going in to the service a rumour arose that he [Gordon] was not dead so the Archbishop had to give notice of this from the pulpit & preach another sermon. The real & particular interest of her story was the effect this had upon Mr Gladstone, who sat with them. Mrs Bradley said she did not know whether she & Mrs Gladstone would be able to get him out of the Abbey without his making a scene.'[164]

jingoism'. All this, he was sure, would mitigate the chronic distemper; and Gladstone had not the smallest fear that it would bring about an 'acute or convulsive action'.[165]

In the short term, however, he had to confront the acute and convulsive actions of the Houses of Parliament. 'At present every day', he told Catherine, 'only opens more and more to view the extraordinary difficulties of the situation.'[166] Gladstone made a ministerial statement in the Commons on 19 February, shortly after Northcote gave notice of a motion of censure. The pith of Gladstone's statement was that there had 'now been shown to be, betrayal' at Khartoum. He announced also (he had really no option) that military operations against the Mahdi would continue.[167] When it came to Northcote's motion on 23 February, Gladstone pressed his line that Gordon – 'a hero among heroes' – was a victim of betrayal; betrayal, moreover, *because* the relief force had come so near; and that he would have been betrayed *whenever* the relief force arrived; so that the question of the time of its setting out was irrelevant.[168] The difficulty with this characteristically excellent debating point was that it depended, as Gladstone confessed to himself amid ruminations on the 'mystery' which 'still hangs in many respects over the state of Khartoum both now and at the period of its fall', not on 'official information', but rather a matter of 'opinion or speculation'. Gladstone placed strong reliance on the report of the *Daily News* correspondent, which, in Gladstone's view, 'distinctly confirmed the evidence as to plot for betrayal when the English Army came near'.[169] 'The Almighty bore me through amidst all my weakness.' John Morley also helped to bear him through by muddying the waters with an amendment to Northcote's censure deploring the decision to continue military operations in the Sudan. On the 24th Gladstone had a 'serious conversation with the Speaker on the possible resignation'. After four nights of debate in which Northcote failed to give a convincingly hostile lead the government scraped home by a majority of fourteen. The majority against Morley was 343. 'The final division in my mind turned the scale, so nicely was it balanced.'*

Also nicely balanced was the Cabinet the following day on the issue Gladstone put to them: 'I prefer all circs. consd. the alternative of resignation.' In favour were Granville, Derby, Hartington, Selborne, Spencer, Northbrook, and Childers. Against were Kimberley, Lefevre, Trevelyan, Harcourt, Dilke, Chamberlain, and Carlingford, with Gladstone giving a deciding vote against. (*'Rosebery would not vote!'*)[171] Gladstone's argu-

---

* An analysis of the division on Northcote's motion supplied G with the information that of those who voted against him, 232 were Conservatives, 13 were English Liberals, 2 were Irish Liberals, and 41 were Irish Nationalists. Among the Liberal defaulters were Joseph Cowen, Forster, Goschen, and Albert Grey.[170] Salisbury's censure motion in the Lords was carried overwhelmingly.

ments for staying on were want of precedent, astonishment in the party, the likelihood of a clearer opportunity, 'our position false', and issues of the finances. Gladstone contemplated carrying on sessional business with Conservative support for the time being. The Redistribution Bill still had to be seen through; there were matters of foreign policy ('Bismarck's insolent threat') to be attended to.[172]

It is clear also that Gladstone wanted to keep policy in the Sudan in his grasp: 'broader grounds of policy and justice' which included *not* making Wolseley Governor-General.[173] Fallout from the Gordon tragedy included also the awkward problems of his diaries and their proposed publication, involving delicate negotiations between Gordon's family and the War Office about 'certain names & imaginary conversations'.[174] Hamilton remarked on Gordon's intimating 'abominable charges'.[175] He wrote to Hartington on the embarrassments likely to be caused by 'poisoned stuff'.[176] The falsity of the government's position was underlined by the felicitations it received from the Ambassador of the Porte, Fehmi Pasha. 'His visit was an extreme case of the irony of Fortune,' noted Gladstone. 'He came in pursuance of a telegram from the Sultan expressly to congratulate the Govt. & me personally on the defeat of the Opposition & on our continuance in office.'[177]

[10]

Continuance in office meant immediately for Gladstone a series of complex manoeuvres by which he attempted to secure Cabinet agreement about how to deal with the French primarily and 'Europe' secondarily over Egypt, what further to do in the Sudan (when Childers outlined the cost, 'Gladstone groaned'),[178] how to balance coercion and conciliation in Ireland, and how to deal with the budget deficit (Chamberlain and Dilke were awkward about indirect taxation 'on the working classes'). The larger question remained as to why Gladstone continued still in office. That there were rationally adducible reasons and motives hardly dispersed the general effect of the 'irony of Fortune' which overlay the circumstance that Gladstone had declined yet again to see a door opened for him. That the Queen was disappointed was, perhaps, immaterial to the point. More to the point was Granville's disappointment and annoyance: 'said he had understood from Mr G. that he would resign'. Spencer also went back to Ireland equally disappointed. 'The Ministers who wanted to escape were those who have the greatest difficulties.' At dinner after the censure division Granville was 'very sulky', while 'Mr G. talked a good deal' about George Eliot and her companion G. H.

Lewes ('seemed incapable of doing her justice') and Bishop Stubbs and his successor at Oxford, E. A. Freeman.[179]

The clue to Gladstone's bland insouciance is perhaps offered by remarks made by Dilke and recorded by Carlingford before the censure debate in the Commons. Dilke, who expected defeat, observed 'that Mr G. wishes to be beaten – that he had given up the idea of retiring and reckoned on coming back to office in November!?'[180] Carlingford's combination of exclamation and query was an understandable reaction to what on the face of it was a highly paradoxical statement. But behind the paradox it is perhaps possible to discern certain explanatory considerations. November was the month by now generally assumed to be most likely for the next general election. Gladstone's remarks to Dilke indicated that his line of thought was recurring probably to the 'lesson of history' applicable to the precedent of 1868: a big new electorate in prospect, with a big new majority to be had from it, and a big new opportunity to wield the beneficent powers of government on the strength of some great new 'axiom of politics'. On balance, Gladstone preferred to stay on in February 1885, on the ground that there were other and better opportunities for getting out, and because he had particular motives of damage limitation. But the larger prospect of being once more 'terrible on the rebound' was beginning to present itself with allurements irresistible to the 'leader of the nation'. When would such a leader ever have such spacious opportunities offered to him? And, as has been aptly observed, the 'fall of Khartoum did wonders for Gladstone's health'.[181]

In the meantime, playing out his absurd role as ringmaster in the Cabinet circus, it was all quite hard going. The Queen complained to her daughter that Gladstone 'writes such confused reports – so contradictory'.[182] It was also rather hard going weekending with Rosebery. Hartington and Professor Seeley were two other guests. Seeley reported to his wife: 'I had a good deal of talk with Gladstone, about Mark Pattison's memoirs and George Eliot. He has a curious difficulty in understanding G. Eliot, but listened with great docility to my exposition.'[183]* Then, it seems quite suddenly, almost casually, there was one epiphanal moment, early in March, which was to have a decisive bearing on Gladstone's formulation of his new 'axiom of politics'. He read the report of a speech by the Irish MP William O'Brien, at Phoenix Park in Dublin, on 1 March. This was the precise moment, as he later related, when Gladstone realized he was a Home Ruler.[185]

Increasingly, however, through March and April, events in Central

---

* There were large elements of Positivist thinking in Seeley's quest for a science of politics. Gladstone evidently declined to nominate Seeley for a KCMG in 1884. Rosebery repaired the omission in 1894.[184]

Asia began to overshadow both squabble-bound ministers and literary diversions as well as disturbingly epiphanal Irish insights. The Russians and Afghans had differences over frontier delimitations. By early March it seemed the Russians were 'very threatening and aggressive', and that the 'passive attitude' which Britain had obliged the Afghans to adopt could not be maintained. By 12 March ministers found it necessary to examine the 'somewhat menacing state of the questions connected with the frontier of Afghanistan, and especially the considerable advances of Russian troops'.[186] Gladstone recorded on the 16th: 'The pressure of affairs, especially Sudan, Egypt, & Afghan, is now from day to day extreme.' By 24 March it was agreed that the Russians should be warned that their penetrating as far as Herat would be considered a *casus belli*.

At this juncture Gladstone commented to Sir Henry Taylor, an old friend of Colonial Office days, that the 'surface of life' in the country was 'much troubled'. 'It strikes me that we are at this moment more subject to thrills of panic & were hungry for excitement than any other people, more also than England was when you & I were young.'[187] Possibly Gladstone was forgetting the Crimean case. But 'thrills of panic' could be turned to advantage. Gladstone could well see that 'an Imperial duty of so high an order' in Central Asia 'might conceivably at this juncture come to overrule the present intentions as to the Soudan', and that it would 'consequently be imprudent to do anything which would functionally extend our obligations in that quarter, as it is the entanglement of the British forces in Sudanese operations which would most powerfully tempt Russia to adopt aggressive measures'.[188] To that the Queen had no answer; and indeed by 26 March was remarking to Carlingford that 'Mr G. was sound about the Russian question and "better" about the Soudan'.[189]

A cabinet on 4 April found Gladstone in a very high mood. The Russians, he felt, were treating Britain 'as though Russia were a superior dealing with an inferior'. Granville was deputed to confront the Russian Ambassador, de Staal. Harcourt stood out alone for scuttle. Even Chamberlain felt it necessary to request Harcourt not to 'think it necessary to address us as if we were a bunch of Jingoes'.[190] There had been a serious collision between Russians and Afghans (including some British officers) at Penjdeh on 30 March. The Queen wished to express 'her satisfaction to Mr Gladstone at the firm and proper tone held by the Govt to the Russian ambassador, which she cannot help hoping may have some effect as she thinks the Russians expected the Govt would swallow everything, especially as, whether wrongly or rightly, it is believed that Mr G's views lean towards Russia'.[191] To Catherine, Gladstone reported on 8 April: 'a troubled and painful day of successive telegrams each one more grave than its predecessor'. The upshot was that the Russians had 'impudently & perfidiously attacked the Afghans in Penjdeh'. It looked *'very bad'*. Reginald Brett, Hartington's secretary, reported de Staal as 'considerably alarmed' at the 'probable set of opinion in this country'.[192] On this occasion Gladstone was very careful to do nothing to quell alarms. In his communications to Hartington at the War Office Gladstone made a point of being deliberately bellicose: the contingency of war could not be wholly shut out of view; the best military advice would be wanted. Could not 'some secret agent' report on Black Sea defences? Could not Odessa be a point of 'retaliation' should Russia meddle with British colonies?[193]

On the face of it this was astonishing language for Gladstone. In its breathtakingly deliberate evocation of the Sebastopol-raid policy of 1854 it was quite Palmerstonian or 'Crimean' in tone. But the underlying motive was patent. Gladstone telegraphed the Queen on 13 April that, given the state of imperial and foreign affairs generally, it might be the duty of her confidential servants to 'recommend abandonment of Sudanese operations & evacuation of country'.[194] This was too much for Victoria, and another angry bout of recriminations intervened. By 20 April both parties got to the point of agreeing that things were getting out of hand ('with regard to Y.M.'s gracious declaration as to the absence of reserve in these difficult & trying communications Mr G. is sensible of the great advantages derivable from Y.M.'s unfailing frankness. On his own part he has striven to act on a similar rule . . .').[195] All this meant that the manoeuvre was working well. Finding himself a solitary presence at the parliamentary dining club, Grillion's, Gladstone had no compunction in disposing of a bottle of champagne on his own account, appending in the record the Miltonic quotations: 'Among the faithless, faithful only he', and 'The mind in its own place, and in itself / Can make a heaven of hell, a hell of heaven.'[196] No wonder that in the cabinet on 14 April when the 'idea of abandoning the Khartoum expedition' had 'ripened' rapidly under the pressure of a very possible Russian war, Gladstone was observed as exhibiting a novel aspect, 'a kind of senile cheerfulness'.[197]

On 20 April Gladstone recorded that he had never known 'political anxieties or more crowded, or more complicated. I feel as though I could never have strength for the day. But "when thou goest through the waters". And our rule is plain: in each and all to strive to do what the Lord Christ would have done . . .' This meant public declarations of unbending severity. The Russian action at Penjdeh 'bears', he informed the Commons, 'the appearance of unprovoked aggression'; it was a 'very painful matter'; it created 'critical circumstances'.[198] The 'grave nature of the case' was exacerbated by the French choosing the opportunity to make themselves excessively disagreeable over Egypt. Gladstone gave notice of a vote of credit 'to hold the military resources of the Empire

... available for service wherever they may be required'. In the debate on the vote Gladstone described his labours for an honourable settlement in the light of the 'sad contingency of an outbreak of war'. 'We will strive to conduct ourselves to the end of this diplomatic controversy in such a way as that, if, unhappily, it is to end in violence and rupture, we may at least be able to challenge the verdict of civilised mankind . . . to say whether we have . . . done all that men could do by every just and honourable effort to prevent the plunging of two such countries . . . into bloodshed and strife . . .'[199] Unfortunately, Gladstone rather compromised the full impact of this unaccustomed rhetoric by an excessively violent attempt to justify his behaviour at the time of Beaconsfield's vote of credit in 1878. He was obliged to make a personal statement of regret and correction.[200]*

There is no ground for assuming here that Gladstone was merely playing games, overcompensating for the Gordon fiasco. It was far too blatant for that. As Acton remarked to Dilke after observing closely Gladstone's shifts and adjustments in the Gordon affair: 'Cannot make up my mind whether he is not wholly unconscious when working himself up to a change of position. After watching him do it, I think that he is so. He lives completely in what for the moment he chooses to believe.'[201] On 2 May Granville brought to Gladstone at the Royal Academy dinner the 'glad tidings of the Russian answer, which humanly speaking means peace. God be praised for His merciful and gracious work.' What had been 'a ray of light yesterday', as he put it to Catherine, 'is a flood today', and the 'great Russian question' was amicably settled. 'Say this very quietly at Hawarden and in less flaming terms.' Parliament was to be informed on Monday; by which time the papers would probably have the story. 'How is it possible to be sufficiently thankful?'[202] On 4 May Gladstone announced in the Commons that both the Afghan and Russian governments had agreed to provide means for a settlement and to refer if necessary any outstanding issue to mediation.[203] For Gladstone there was the relief of a blessed deliverance which came with the ripening of spring.

> Troubled memories, trooping by,
> Ancient quarrels, let them lie;
> Let them lie and let them rust
> Let them gather clouds of dust
> Let them not this peace impair,
> Mar this pleasant nimble air
> Clog the liberated breath
> Hale the living back to death.   May 3, 85.[204]

* For the 1878 occasion, see above, page 215.

[11]

The 'great event' of the quarrel and the settlement with the Russians – for Gladstone had no doubt that such it was – had for the while upstaged the stock familiar players. Childers brought in his budget on 30 April, with the task of finding £11 million for the vote of credit and £4 million to cover the estimated deficit for 1885–6. Gladstone was effusive in his gratitude to Dilke and Chamberlain for their forbearance in the matter of indirect taxation. The credit for general imperial purposes notwithstanding, Gladstone could fairly hope that the Sudan problem was neutralized. The dispute with the French over Egypt also had settled itself for the time into a not too uncomfortable impasse. Gladstone could discern 'reasonable likelihoods' of a 'general winding up of this Parliament & Government such as to be beyond all my most sanguine anticipations'. What stood out as the big difficulty was Ireland. At the very least, and possibly as a point of departure, there was the question of the 1882 Prevention of Crimes Act, due for renewal at the end of 1885. But on Ireland Gladstone could now see his way 'with tolerable clearness'.[205] Here too was a new hope of ancient quarrels being let to rest, of the liberated breath unclogged.

How so? It was now two months since Gladstone had read William O'Brien's Phoenix Park speech. Those two months had crowded out any deeper consideration of the impression it had made on Gladstone at that time.* Now, with the winding up of the 1880 Parliament in view and the general election on the new franchise in prospect, Gladstone's thinking recurred to the import and implications of the impact O'Brien's speech had made on him. Five years later, when on a tour in Norfolk,† Gladstone met H. Lee Warner, of Swaffham, the son of an old Eton and Oxford contemporary, and talked with him. Lee Warner recalled the occasion.

I remember in the year 1890 asking Mr Gladstone whether he could identify in his mind the crucial moment at which he determined to adopt the policy which made him plunge like Curtius into the gulf that yawned in our British forum. I can see him now as he paused and thought and then replied, 'Yes, I had been reading a speech by Mr William O'Brien, and I put it down and I said to myself, "What is there in this speech which I must get to realise before I throw it aside?" And I saw then that there was and never could be any moral obligation to the Irish nation in the Act of Union.'[206]

---

* See above, page 352.
† Gladstone was in Norfolk for several days in May 1890.

Gladstone's response to the O'Brien speech told much more about Glad-stone at that critical moment than it did about O'Brien. The speech in fact was a rant, rabid even by O'Brien's standards, occasioned by Speaker Peel's having ejected him from the Commons chamber for unparliamen-tary behaviour. It did not touch Gladstone by any largeness of outlook or distinction of mind. It happened to hit Gladstone at a time when Gladstone was looking to the spacious opportunities assumably available to the leader of the Liberal party in and after November. Once that profound insight had come upon him, Gladstone could see his way with 'tolerable clearness' as to the subject concerned and the object to be attained. The problem was that, as he later explained, it was a question of 'subjects ripe for action'.[207] In the context of the analogy with the 1868 situation, Gladstone then was much better placed than he was now. Gladstone had declared himself publicly, in principle, three years before the subject of the Irish Church became ripe for action in 1868. The case of Irish Home Rule was utterly different. In due course Gladstone would be defending himself, resentfully, from accusations of concealment and precipitancy.

The revolution in Gladstone's thinking on Ireland between March and May 1885 constituted a node in which two strands of development in the Irish question intersected. The first strand was the history of Gladstone's own opinions on the subject of Irish Home Rule, commencing with his declaration at Aberdeen in September of 1871. The pith of that declaration was that there was 'nothing that Ireland has asked and which this country and this Parliament have refused'.* The next thread in this strand was Gladstone's declaration at the beginning of the 1882 session, the pith of which was his question to the Home Rulers: 'What are the provisions which you propose to make for the supremacy of Parliament?' Pithy also was his supplementary point that it 'passed the wit of man' to devise a solution to the 'real knot of the question', that is, how the Irish were to have both autonomy in Dublin and representation at Westminster.† The last thread of this strand was Gladstone's confidential memorandum to the Queen on the theme of the critical danger to the state that would arise in the circumstances of a 'decisive majority of the representatives of Ireland' unitedly demanding on behalf of their country 'the adoption of some scheme of Home Rule, which Parliament should be compelled to refuse'.‡

Between the end of 1882 and late 1884 the Irish problem was relatively quiescent. It was stirred into life once more by the implications for Ireland

* See above, page 101.
† See above, page 289.
‡ See above, page 290.

of the settlement of the Reform and Redistribution questions. The county franchise would impact far more powerfully in Ireland even than in Britain. And Redistribution would leave unreduced the 103 Irish representatives at Westminster, fixed by the Act of Union at a time when Ireland was one of the most densely populated countries in the world. The second strand of development intersecting with the nodal area of Gladstone's becoming a Home Ruler commenced in November 1884 when Chamberlain, having been encouraged by Gladstone since 1882 to keep fences mended with Parnell, concluded that the time was ripe for a big initiative on Irish local government. Hitherto this had been a matter of much rhetoric on Gladstone's part but little purposeful action. For Chamberlain, the Reform Act of 1884 meant that 'a peaceful revolution had been accomplished and the reign of democracy was about to begin'.[208] He too, like Gladstone, looked forward to the end of the 1880 Parliament, the coming general election, and the bright promise of a new epoch of Liberal politics. He was preparing the way with what was to become the *Radical Programme*, parts of which were to become the 'Unauthorised Programme' at the time of the elections. His interest in the Irish question was to clear it out of the way of this bright prospect and to have eighty or more Irish votes at his disposal in the new Parliament. He was encouraged by Captain O'Shea, Parnell's emissary, to suppose that 'some *modus vivendi*' might be found which would 'enable the Irish nationalist party to work with the Government and offer the chance of the settlement of the Irish difficulty'.[209]

This '*modus vivendi*' took the form of a deal with Parnell whereby the Prevention of Crimes Act was to be much softened on re-enactment, and possibly re-enacted for one year only, in return for which Parnell would countenance a comprehensive local government measure for Ireland comprising elected County Councils and an Administrative Central Board, 'altogether independent of English government influence', with powers of taxation for strictly Irish purposes. Chamberlain and Parnell, however, were at cross purposes, greatly aided in being so by O'Shea's duplicity. Parnell was willing to countenance comprehensive local government reform provided it did not become a pre-emptive obstacle to Home Rule. That was precisely how Chamberlain saw it: a 'solution' which would be 'sufficient to satisfy the Irish people'. Chamberlain was surprised that Parnell's draft scheme was much less bold – in matters of control of police, for example – than his own. But, misinformed by O'Shea, he persisted in this quest for a substitute for Home Rule; and reported accordingly to Gladstone in January 1885. Gladstone also received, with Katharine O'Shea as intermediary, Parnell's scheme. Gladstone commended Chamberlain's efforts and requested him to continue the communications.[210]

'During the whole of this time', Chamberlain innocently recorded, 'I was in frequent communication with Mr Gladstone and others of my colleagues in reference to the whole subject, endeavouring to bring them to accept something in the nature of Mr Parnell's proposals and at the same time to consent to some modification of the Crimes Act.'[211] Gladstone could see that Chamberlain was at cross purposes to Parnell. When Gladstone decided early in March that O'Brien's speech was good enough to convert him to Home Rule, he then placed himself also at cross purposes to Chamberlain. Gladstone had shifted the base of his nodal area in such a way that the Chamberlain strand intersected but glancingly. When at the beginning of May Gladstone communed with himself as to seeing his way 'with tolerable clearness', it was at the moment when Chamberlain was pressing his case to the Cabinet for his Central Board scheme, together with a Land Purchase scheme. Gladstone had already gone far beyond the former, and was no less hostile to the latter, though prepared for a 'judiciously constructed' version of it to be helpful.[212] It was something, after all, that Parnell had always wanted. Gladstone presented himself to Chamberlain in his guise as one on the brink of retirement, for whom such matters would personally have no application: an 'amicus curiae' as he put it.[213]

Chamberlain pressed his scheme on the Cabinet as 'the only way of avoiding Home Rule'. To most of his sceptical colleagues, his plan for elective councils and a Central Board in Dublin was simply Parnell's version of 'Grattan's Parliament' under another name. Carlingford was 'filled with astonishment that any serious politician could take it up'. He and his colleagues had every reason to believe that Chamberlain had 'received the scheme from Parnell', and that Cardinal Manning had come to Chamberlain to support it. 'It is a most serious state of things.'[214] Hartington, Harcourt and all the peers except Granville opposed it. Childers, Trevelyan, Shaw-Lefevre, and Dilke were supportive. Spencer saw it as a '*Convention* sitting in Dublin'. At the final discussion on 9 May Carlingford was shocked at Gladstone's support for Chamberlain: 'Mr G. was *with* him – "only hope for Ireland" etc but would not go into the argument – "quite useless" – . . .'[215] This was an occasion when Gladstone had neither desire nor intention to turn his colleagues around. Gladstone ended the discussion by pronouncing Chamberlain's proposal 'dead as mutton'; but he added, 'for the present only'. It would 'quickly rise again, & as I think perhaps in larger dimensions'.[216]

Once Chamberlain's project was safely dead as mutton, Gladstone could afford to be solicitously sympathetic and to drop hints expansively while standing outside the Cabinet room on the first-floor landing at Downing Street. Chamberlain recalled his declaring, 'These men have rejected this scheme, but if God spares their lives for five years more they will be glad to accept something infinitely stronger.' Chamberlain at the time judged Gladstone's remark as 'uttered in a fit of temporary irritation'.[217] Dilke's version was: 'Within six years, if it pleases God to spare their lives, they will be repenting in ashes.'[218] It was certainly not a matter of temporary irritation. It was rather Gladstone's way of beginning his emergence from the covert or reserved position he had been in for the past two months. He wrote to Hartington almost gleefully on 30 May that Chamberlain and Dilke held the 'winning position' on Irish local government. 'You will all, I am convinced, have to give what they recommend; at the least what they recommend.' Gladstone was prepared, indeed, to go 'rather further than they do'. A local-government matrix not only for Ireland, but for Scotland as well, would be good for 'the country, and the empire'.[219] Later, he put the matter of Irish local government even more cheerfully to Richard Grosvenor: 'That question is now happily disposed of and the field is open for the consideration of future measures.'[220]

To the Queen, on 23 May, Gladstone was rather more restrained, and in his mode once more of one on the verge of retirement. That letter, as he glossed it to Ponsonby, was to be understood by HM not as a 'proposal'. 'It is rather, if I may so speak without impropriety, a post-humous bequest. Nothing is to be decided or done upon [it], so far as my knowledge or intention goes, & I do not expect anything to be raised upon it after this recess. Lord Granville has seen it and it will probably go to Lord Hartington.'[221] This explanation arose out of the Queen's puzzlement about it. When she showed it to Carlingford, he thought it was meant as a 'political legacy'. It was a general review of options relating to Irish policy, with particular emphasis on the Central Board proposal and the differences in Cabinet relating to it. Its implication was that, as he had earlier put it, the 'winning position' was with those who were proponents of some big measure uprooting the Dublin Castle system of imposing government upon Ireland from outside, and giving local self-government to the Irish people. Gladstone indicated further that if some such timely concession were not made, he was in fear of a future dishonourable surrender to Irish demands. 'Mr Gladstone has troubled Your Majesty ... because he believes that Your Majesty will hear of the subject again. He earnestly hopes that it may be dealt with in time.' Dealing with it 'would have the effect of making the Government of Ireland Irish, in the same sense that the Government of England is English, and the Government of Scotland, Scotch'.[222]

Carlingford thought it 'a most remarkable and important statement of views upon Ireland'. It did not reveal 'whether or not the writer expects or intends to take part himself in giving effect to them' – hence his view of it as probably a 'legacy'; which Gladstone clarified as a 'posthumous bequest'.[223]* What is perhaps most interesting about it was that Gladstone made no mention of the point he had earlier made much of to the Queen: the situation that might obtain if the new Parliament were confronted by a united demand from the vast majority of the representatives of Ireland for self-government.

The problem of 'ripeness', or by analogy on the theological usage of the doctrine of 'reservation' – how and when to disclose, if circumstance and occasion should beckon – Gladstone for the time being covered with his now familiar device of insinuative manipulation of imminent departure. To Spencer he put the case:

You ask me where I shall be. I shall be neither with the enacting party nor with the resisting party, but shall avail myself, before the tempest bursts, of my title to retire on the simple ground that my engagements are fulfilled. No one has the right to ask me my opinion on a question which has not actually risen, though it may be about to arise. Policy often determines duty: and it is my present impression that there will be no call on me to take part in the fray which I desire and seem entitled to avoid.[224]

'Present impression' still seemingly obtained when Gladstone walked at Hawarden with Stephen, speaking 'of my retirement and its grounds'.[225] But by the end of May a drive and a walk and 'much conversation' with Wolverton 'opened rather a new view as to my retirement'. That 'new view', it may reasonably be supposed, related to 'subjects ripe for action', which Gladstone had 'mentally considered', though as yet neither adopted nor rejected;† which Wolverton a little later defined to Gladstone as 'your proposed Irish policy'.[226]

[12]

For Gladstone now, possessed of a deep insight and a 'new view', there hardly seemed much purpose in straining any longer to play the absurd ringmaster role. (May the 16th: 'Very fair Cabinet today – only three resignations.') There was more than a little of the mood of 1874–5 in Gladstone's comments on 'whether I am to work any more or not': 'I can neither meddle with a party which is simply a party, nor with a party which is in schism against itself.'[227] A high Peelite view of the

* In October 1885 the Queen showed the letter to Hicks Beach (then Irish Chief Secretary), who sent it to Salisbury.
† These are phrases used later by Gladstone in his explanatory and justificatory *The Irish Question* (1886), denying concealment or precipitancy.

instrumentality of party for the purposes of strong government would require another 1868 or another 1880 to supervene. There was certainly little enough on the legislative front at the tag end of the 1880 Parliament to warrant valiant efforts to reanimate the government. That Parliament had manifestly done all the good that it was capable of doing. The Redistribution Bill was within days of completing its course. Childers's budget was working its way; though Rosebery recorded in his diary Gladstone's opening the cabinet on 8 June 'by saying that there was some chance of our being beaten on budget tonight'. The Conservative–Irish entente which had almost upset Gladstone over the Gordon affair in February was now preparing for attack. The Irish had plausible fiscal grievances; and they were eager to punish a coercive government. The Conservatives, nervous enough of flirtations with Parnell, were nonetheless ready to brave the contingency of undertaking the government. There were many Liberals equally ready to let them have the opportunity – perhaps their last. In the division on 8 June there were many Liberals mysteriously unpaired. Gladstone was beaten 264 : 252. 'Adjourned the House. This is a considerable event.'

Gladstone telegraphed the Queen at Balmoral submitting the government's resignation. There was no question of a dissolution: as in 1868, the registers were not yet prepared. His feeling was that, as in 1873, he ought not to release a conspiratorial combination from the 'responsibility of victory' illicitly contrived.[228] Summoned to Balmoral, Salisbury could hardly do other than accept the Queen's pressing request that he rid her of Gladstone. There was delay and a little confusion as Salisbury bargained with Gladstone as to the new minority government's not being harassed or upset by the Liberal majority while it completed necessary public business before the dissolution. Balfour, Salisbury's emissary, found Gladstone sticky and awkward, and there were moments when his retaining or resuming office seemed possible. However, the Queen contrived to extract a formula from Gladstone which she presented to Salisbury as adequate security; and Gladstone's resignation became definitive.

On 26 June Gladstone circulated a memorandum to his late colleagues stating with carefully strict accuracy that he did not 'perceive, or confidently anticipate, any state of facts which ought to alter my long-cherished, and I believe wellknown desire and purpose to withdraw, with the expiration of this Parliament, from active participation in politics'. He proposed, in the meantime, when the new government was formed and the session resumed, to take his seat 'in the usual manner on the front Opposition Bench'. He would desist from speaking to restore throat and voice; but any absence would be 'a bodily not a moral absence'.[229] He said nothing specifically about retiring from Parliament by not standing at the coming general election. Wolverton's comment was that of one who could read the oracle: 'your proposed Irish policy should produce the "state of facts" which would at least give you some grounds for the further consideration, before the close of the Parliament, of the position'.[230] The 'state of the facts' was inseparable from the 'ripeness of the time'. To Spencer Gladstone opened up a little the new vista of possibilities: 'Nothing can withhold or suspend my retirement except the presentation of some great and critical problem in the national life, and the hope, *if* such a hope shall be, of making some special contribution towards a solution of it.'[231]

The 22nd of June was 'a day of much stir & vicissitude till 7 P.M.'. The 23rd was 'chaotic': 'Saw Granville who was much moved.' 'My room peopled with visits & returns.' He was scrupulous to render thanks to his secretariat. 'Your services to me', he told Hamilton, 'have been simply indescribable.'[232] There were resignation honours to consider. Gladstone was anxious to press for 'Arts Baronetcies' to become accepted: there had been nothing of the kind since the time of Sir Godfrey Kneller. Gladstone rehearsed the claims of Watts for the 'ideal school' and of Millais for the 'realistic school'. Landseer alas was suffering from a mental calamity; and Leighton could perhaps be postponed for the while. Leighton, on behalf of the Royal Academy, saluted Gladstone's offer of baronetcies to Millais and Watts as making him the 'first among English Prime Ministers' to honour artists as an outward token of the store which the state should set on their labours as an element of the country's higher life.[233]* Gladstone would like to have done something for his old love, the stage. He considered a knighthood for Squire Bancroft, pressed by Labouchere: Bancroft had done a great deal to 'raise the stage in public repute', and his fortune would allow him not to act on the stage again.[234]† This was thought to be premature. There were peerages for Lingen (testifying to Gladstone's partiality for civil-service peerages), Evelyn Baring, and – at last – Nathan Rothschild. Gladstone was studious to establish for the Queen's benefit that he was asking for less than Beaconsfield had got in 1880.[235]

At Windsor on 18 June the Queen was 'most gracious & I thought most reasonable'. She quite appreciated Gladstone's motives for declining once more the earldom she offered him. He explained to his brother Sir Thomas that his fortune was not adequate to sustain so great an honour and that he was in any case anxious to retire and going to the Lords would keep him 'until my dying day chained to the oar of a life of conflict & contention': subject only to the qualification that nothing would

---

* Watts declined the honour.
† Irving and Bancroft were knighted in 1895 and 1897 respectively.

prevent his retiring 'unless there should appear to be something in which there may be a prospect of my doing what could not be as well done without me'.[236] Now houseless, the Gladstones on their return from Windsor were guests of the Bertram Curries at Richmond Terrace until they could move to lodgings provided by the Aberdeens at Dollis Hill in Willesden. Gladstone was sure 'we shall fall readily into our displacement'. Catherine possibly was less sure. He cleared his rooms at Downing Street on 25 June (asking his successor as First Lord, Northcote, for a room to store things for a few days more) '& had a moment to fall down and give thanks for the labours done & the strength vouchsafed to me there: and to pray for the Christlike mind'. There was an 'extraordinary scene' at an Edgware Road bookshop on 30 June when Gladstone was mobbed enthusiastically by a crowd of some 3,000, making escape to Dollis Hill difficult. On that day he recorded: 'Much thought on the situation, actual & prospective.'

CHAPTER 10

'SUCH A SUPREME MOMENT': PEELITE HEROISM IN SHOCK-TACTIC FORM, 1885–6

[1]

The letter to the Queen of 23 May – Gladstone's 'posthumous bequest' – set out to all appearances quite clearly his sense of what he referred to as 'some great and critical problem in the national life' which would justify his withholding or suspending his retirement in the hope of his making some special contribution towards a solution of it. It would be a big measure of Irish local government. Chamberlain's proposals to the Cabinet in May 1885 set the going rate. Indeed, in the minds of many people Chamberlain's Central Board scheme retained the reputation through all the vicissitudes lying ahead as the most practicable scheme available, balancing nearest the point at which Westminster might fairly be induced to offer and Ireland fairly induced to accept. In March 1893, as Gladstone confronted certain defeat in his second attempt to push through the radical measure of Home Rule with which he had supplanted the 1885 scheme, Rosebery concluded that the ultimate solution to the Irish difficulty might possibly be 'the establishment of 4 Provincial Councils as projected in 1885 by Chamberlain'.[1]

The Queen would have known through Carlingford the general lines of what was afoot. Like Carlingford she would have found certain things acceptable and certain others unacceptable. As far at least as the viceroyalty was concerned, she was anxious to dispel any misapprehension that she disapproved of its abolition. On the contrary, she thought a kind of devolution or 'amalgamation' on the recent Scottish model, with a Secretary of State, 'would be for the best'.[2] Chamberlain set the scene publicly with a speech at Holloway on 17 June in which he stated boldly that 'the pacification of Ireland at this moment depends, I believe, on the concession to Ireland of the right to govern itself in the matter of purely domestic business'. What was the alternative? To govern as Austria had governed Venice? Dublin Castle was an absurd and irritating anachronism. This was the work to which the new Parliament would be called.[3]

Carlingford grumbled that this was quite the kind of speech Parnell or Healy might have made. He could even envisage a new Gladstone ministry with a renewed majority behind it dispensing with or coercing the opponents in the late Cabinet of Chamberlain's scheme. But this would not have been because of the eager pressure of Parnell or Healy or their friends. Parnell made impressively vague declarations about Ireland's demands to be 'independent'; but what he most eagerly wanted was an expansive land-purchase policy and what he least eagerly wanted was some scheme such as Chamberlain advocated which would pre-empt 'Home Rule' and become a huge obstacle to its ultimate attainment. What is most notable about the Irish party at this juncture is their very relaxed attitude to the question of how Home Rule was to be defined and legislated for. None of them had essayed to answer Gladstone's question of 1882: how do you propose to resolve the conundrum of the relationship between an imperial and a subordinate Parliament? They very seriously and intelligently could see that any measure that would satisfy them would startle the British and make them bolt.

T. M. Healy put the case to Labouchere in December 1885: 'Is it not plain that if we plunge into Home Rule plans just now before your intelligent public apply their enlightened minds to it that we shall get far less than what we should get by waiting and worrying you for a few years?' Davitt was very certain that the land question should take priority over hypothetical constitutional conjectures.[4] Parnell, Healy, and Davitt knew perfectly well that a governing Liberal party left to its own devices would take some time to reconcile itself to the notion of Ireland's governing itself. What no one quite envisaged or predicted was the way 'an old man in a hurry'* would cut across this comfortable assumption about waiting and worrying for a few years and would proceed heroically to coerce the Liberal party into doing something very radical very promptly which, left to itself, it would never have done at all. How could Healy have dreamed that in just over three months from the time of his letter to Labouchere Gladstone would launch his first Home Rule Bill?

Many among the Irish leadership were in fact beginning to think that, at least in the short term, the Conservative–Irish combination which had brought Gladstone down might well be the germ of a more profitable bargain. Salisbury's 'Caretaker' government made a great point of not renewing the 1882 Crimes Act. The 'coming man' of Conservatism, Lord Randolph Churchill, former private secretary to his viceregal father at Dublin in the 1870s, ostentatiously meshed into his 'Tory Democratic' doctrine a line about liberality and generosity to Ireland – stopping far

---

* See below, page 444.

short, however, of Home Rule in anything like a Gladstonian version of it. The Conservatives, after all, had an invaluable asset in control of the House of Lords. In the coming months there would be much comradely toing and froing between Churchill and Parnell. Churchill and Beach ostentatiously colluded with the Irish in a dead set against Spencer's handling of the affair of murders in the west of Ireland: Liberals could plausibly take revenge for 'Kilmainham' with accusations of a 'Maamtrasna Treaty'. Parnell made a point of snubbing Chamberlain when the latter proposed a tour of reconnaissance with Dilke in Ireland to solidify the Central Board scheme. Above all, in the new Viceroy, Lord Carnarvon, the Conservative government had a convinced believer in some kind of devolved Irish autonomy; a conviction shared by Robert Hamilton, Burke's successor at the head of the Dublin Castle administration.

July at Hawarden opened with a visit from Acton: '2 to 3 hours of conversation which included Ireland & the situation'. John Morley later told Acton that he, Morley, had 'no share' in bringing Gladstone 'over to Home Rule'; and that Acton therefore remained the 'decisive author of the policy'.[5] Morley, Acton's chief rival for the intellectual affections of the Grand Old Man, was possibly being mischievous in his flattery. Yet Acton, for all that he was duly flattered, was also a connoisseur of Gladstone's capacity to live completely in what he chose to believe. Gladstone's being 'brought over' to Home Rule was in fact owing, if anyone, to William O'Brien and was by now of five months' standing. The problems were to define what 'Home Rule' specifically meant and then to discern when the radical version of it eventually disclosed by Gladstone early in the opening session of the new Parliament in April 1886 formed itself in Gladstone's mind. Lord Iddesleigh (the erstwhile Stafford Northcote), urging on the Conservative party a policy of meeting the wants and conciliating the feelings of the Irish people, pointed out that 'Home Rule' was a slippery 'undistributed middle term', interpretable equally as separation or local self-government.[6] Until Gladstone revealed himself differently, the political world would remain assured that something of the nature of Chamberlain's local-government scheme remained the measure of any intentions he might have occasion to declare as Liberal policy: intentions which might well be interpreted as conformable with the reservations stipulated for by Iddesleigh as to integrity of empire, security of property, and preservation of law and order.

In public Gladstone kept himself prudently reserved about his being 'brought over', but, as John Morley remarked, he was quite free in conversation and correspondence, and it was evident to his interlocutors and correspondents 'in what direction the main current of his thought must have been settling'.[7] Thus Goschen was favoured on 10 July with Gladstone's views on 'the policy with regard to the establishment of separate central national councils for the different parts of the United Kingdom, which have been distinctly foreshadowed by Mr Chamberlain'. This view was coloured largely by the contribution to the June *Contemporary Review* of the Rev. Dr Dale, the foremost Nonconformist divine in Chamberlain's Birmingham apparat, on 'Home Rule all round'. But by 17 July, to Derby, Gladstone's thinking had taken a decided tilt in directions going far beyond Chamberlain. The fulcrum of the tilt was Gladstone's reading of what was going on between Parnell and the Conservative ministers. That reading was that Lord Salisbury was 'nursing the idea of the same experiment'.[8] Gladstone would later be reported as declaring that 'he happened to *know* as a fact that Lord Randolph, Lord Ashbourne* and Lord Carnarvon had prepared a scheme of home rule'.[9] Gladstone could not possibly have *'known'* any such thing as a 'fact'. He constructed a fact out of garbled rumours and Parnell's tendentious misinformation. Thus it was that to Derby he opened up a much ampler prospect of things:

I am not fully informed but what I know looks as if the Irish party . . . excited by the high biddings of Lord Randolph, has changed what was undoubtedly Parnell's ground until within a short time back. It is now said that a Central Board will not suffice, and that there must be a Parliament. This I suppose may mean the repeal of the Act of Union or may mean an Austro-Hungarian scheme or may mean that Ireland is to be like a great Colony such as Canada. Of all or any of these schemes I will only now say that of course they constitute an entirely new point of departure and raise questions totally different to any that are involved in a Central Board appointed for local purposes.[10]

What they constituted as far as Gladstone was concerned, it seems, was a willingness on his part to transfer the question of what might best be accorded to Ireland in the matter of self-government from a calculation as to what might be extracted from the 'English', or Westminster, end to a quest to discover what the Irish themselves wanted. That he should use the alleged 'high biddings' of Churchill to account for the Irish departure from the vicinity of the Central Board scheme is one thing; but why Gladstone should then conclude that this necessitated an 'entirely new point of departure' from the same vicinity on his own part is an interesting question. Did he have a particular motive in wishing to upstage and sideline Chamberlain? Was his *'knowing'* for a 'fact' about 'high biddings' an instance of Acton's diagnosis of Gladstone's ability to live completely in what he chose to believe? When, after fruitless efforts to get information through Grosvenor of Parnell's intentions,

* Irish Lord Chancellor; author of the 'Ashbourne' Land Purchase Act of 1885.

Gladstone applied directly to Mrs O'Shea on 4 August (much to Hamilton's disapproval)* to confirm or deny whether Parnell's position was as it had been at the beginning of the year, she replied that Parnell had now gone far beyond county councils; and Gladstone then accepted that in so doing Parnell had 'for a limited prospect' substituted 'a field almost without bounds'.[11] What he learned further from Mrs O'Shea was that Parnell was now thinking in terms of 'a constitution of a similar nature to that of one of the larger Colonies with such modifications as may be necessary to secure practically certain guarantees firstly for the maintenance of the supremacy and authority of the Crown, secondly for the equitable treatment of [the] landowning interest, and thirdly for the security of conscience and fair treatment of the minority by the majority'.[12]

In thus looping out far beyond Chamberlain, Gladstone was not competing with Lord Randolph in 'biddings'; he was preparing to hand over to Parnell the very procedure of bids. This was partly because he had convinced himself since 1882 that Parnell was a trustworthy person with whom he could collaborate in good faith. But it can be suggested also that Gladstone needed something much bigger than a Central Board to deal with as 'leader of the nation'. A Central Board was the sort of thing that Hartington could be left to fight out with Chamberlain. But for Gladstone to justify continuing in political life and taking control of the new Liberal government in circumstances of optimism and golden prospect for yet another heroic exercise in wielding Liberalism as the means to the end of validating his 'axiom of politics', Gladstone required an object worthy and appropriate. He also required, correspondingly, that Parnell wield Irish Nationalism worthily and appropriately. To Spencer he stressed the likely fact that the 'greatest incidence of the coming election is to be the Parnell or Nationalist majority' in Ireland. 'And such a majority will be a very great fact indeed.' It would 'at once shift the centre of gravity in the relations between the two countries'. How was it, and its probable proposals, to be met? 'If the heads of the Liberal party shall be prepared to unite in rendering an *adequate* answer to this question, and if they unitedly desire me to keep my present place for the purpose of giving to that answer legislative effect, such a state of things may impose upon me a formidable obligation for the time of the crisis.' On the other hand, of course, there was always the chance that the Conservatives would take up the challenge, and 'solve all these questions for me, & for us all'.[13]

One of the difficulties Gladstone was to have with this notion of an *'adequate'* answer, ironically and in a sense comically, was getting and

---

* Though no longer in official connection with G, Hamilton counted as a family friend and confidant.

keeping the Irish up to it. Walsh, Cullen's successor as Archbishop of Dublin, was susceptible to Dale's 'Home Rule all round' idea. 'It seems to me to get rid of many difficulties.'[14] This was at a time, in 1887, when Walsh was suggesting that Gladstone might climb down a little from the imposing and ambitious heights of his 1886 Home Rule Bill. Gladstone, nonplussed, could only respond that 'if Ireland shall consider a smaller measure or a different measure of Home Rule satisfactory, (no injustice at the same time being due to Great Britain or the Empire) I shall wish it all success'. But Gladstone hoped to 'deal with Ireland as an integer'. But by all means let Walsh communicate with his friends 'so that we may be able to say to ourselves, this & no less or more than this is what Ireland wants & is willing to accept'.[15] (The parenthesis is a treasure of Gladstonese.) Another insight is gained retrospectively into the matter from Parnell himself, who was in 1890 reported (somewhat loosened from his usual taciturnity after a banquet in Liverpool) to have stated that he was much impressed by his visit to Gladstone at Hawarden and by Gladstone's cordiality, 'but more than that with the thoroughness' of Gladstone's 'proposals in regard to Ireland which went really farther than he could have expected from any great English statesman & that they meant a most satisfactory solution'.[16] It was a case not only of Healy's being overtaken by Gladstone's promptitude, but also of Parnell's being overtaken by Gladstone's generosity.

All still depended on how the elections would go, in Ireland as much as Britain. But much also still depended on Gladstone's being sure of his ground. Parnell's presenting the criterion of 'one of the larger Colonies' (the reference was invariably taken to be Canada) might have been expected to alert Gladstone to the precarious and indeed rather fictional status of the prerogatives of the British Crown in the self-governing colonies. He had wrestled tenaciously but unsuccessfully against the claims to fiscal independence asserted during his first ministry by the Australian colonies and New Zealand as well as Canada. It might be thought that his sad experiences of the '*reductio ad absurdum* of colonial connection' in 1871 would have cured him of his hankerings after clear-cut distinctions between questions of a local as opposed to an imperial character, implying in turn the necessary supremacy of the metropolitan centre over colonial dependencies.* On the contrary, throughout the Home Rule controversy to come, Gladstone would cite the self-governing colonies as material to the case, and as entirely endorsing his view of it.

In other respects also Gladstone appears extraordinarily willing to take cues offered by Parnell. One of them was to dangle before Gladstone the alleged 'biddings' of the Conservatives; which had, as his mouthpiece,

---

* See above, page 103.

Mrs O'Shea, conveyed, made the approach to a 'Central Legislative Authority for Ireland' no longer the great difficulty it used to be because of 'recent events', and the 'attitude of both the great English political parties towards Ireland'. What Parnell alluded to was his confidential interview with Lord Carnarvon on 1 August. Carnarvon, a rather naively idealistic character, preened himself as the reconciler of the Quebecois with Canada and of Boer with Briton in South Africa within the matrix of a future imperial federation. He hoped now to convert the Conservative party to a reconciled and self-governing Ireland within that imperial-federation matrix. His guide and inspiration were the writings and conversations of the former Irish-Australian statesman, Charles Gavan Duffy. The cause was hopeless; but Salisbury rather recklessly humoured Carnarvon's request to be allowed to sound Parnell, stipulating, however, that Lord Ashbourne must be present to prevent the possibility of Carnarvon's becoming hostage to Parnell's fortunes. Somehow Carnarvon slipped Ashbourne and, assuming Parnell to be a man of honour, conducted his interview solo (in the spectral ambience of the vacant Mayfair house of the late Lady Chesterfield, erstwhile *amie amoureuse* of Lord Beaconsfield). In this 'excellent parody of a historically significant fact',[17] Parnell carefully said nothing to alarm Carnarvon about the Act of Union or protective Irish tariffs; and Carnarvon duly reported to a sceptical Salisbury that the 'singularly moderate' Parnell could be worked with.[18] Matters got no further than that as far as the rather embarrassed Conservative government was concerned. But Gladstone almost eagerly swallowed the bait: the old situation, he agreed, had indeed changed, not least because of the 'altered attitude of the Tory party, and I presume its heightened biddings'.[19]

Hamilton talked to Catherine on 4 August. 'She said Mr G. had been talking to her about the future.' He was never more 'embarrassed as to what to do; and he cannot even now make up his mind. He is still pondering.' Catherine thought – but Hamilton guessed that 'the wish may be father to the thought' – that Gladstone 'may really be counted on to face another fight. If he could only succeed in leading his party to victory, it would be a fitting climax to a great career . . .'[20] Catherine was almost certainly on the right track as far as Gladstone's combative instincts were concerned, more so as to victory and a fitting climax to a great career. Hamilton rather glumly contemplated what was coming into view: Gladstone's accepting that Parnell had thrown over the Central Board plan, and Gladstone's leaping over any Conservative 'biddings' by a willingness to give back to the Irish their 'Parliament on College Green'. In such circumstances Gladstone's finger-wagging warning to Mrs O'Shea that 'into any counter-bidding of any sort against Lord R. Churchill I for one cannot enter' was entirely superfluous. Quite apart from the fact that Churchill, a convinced and consistent Unionist (shocked later to learn of Carnarvon's indiscretion), had made no 'biddings', 'heightened' or otherwise, Gladstone had transcended that level of operation. He requested Mrs O'Shea to forward on Parnell's part 'such a paper as you describe, and appear to tender, as one of very great public interest', setting out Parnell's ideas about an Irish constitution based on that of 'one of the larger colonies'.[21]

Hamilton's glumness had much to do with a civil servant's view of the difficulties of the conundrum of having a colonial constitution somehow tacked on to Westminster. 'If the proposal were admissible and safe in principle, the difficulties of working out such a scheme would probably be prodigious.' He added some extremely perceptive analysis of the question.

My own present belief is that public opinion is not yet ripe for so large a scheme of Local Government, for Home Rule, or for whatever you like to call it. Accordingly, if Mr G. made up his mind to embark on it, he would inevitably shipwreck his party. In short, the country is not prepared for it. The public must first have a taste of a Parliament in which the Irish party holds the balance and brings Parliamentary Government to a standstill. Here, then, according to present appearances, we have a dilemma. It looks as if Mr G. must either retire or take in hand a piece of work which will bring his party to pieces.[22]

[2]

Gladstone lost no time in setting out to form and direct the materials of his public opinion. He alerted James Knowles of the *Nineteenth Century* with 'private and confidential' prompts ('if I were in your place'). 'The chapter of competent administrative development' in Ireland was 'the one which remains to be treated'. 'I can only indicate two sections of the question: a searching and impartial article on the history of the Union; and a careful account of the novel and critical Austro-Hungarian experiment, its terms and actual working.' As to his own plans, Gladstone informed Knowles, he could say nothing. Probably at this moment the Irish national party did not know their own plan. 'But it strikes me that to collect and present to the world solid and relevant *materials* of judgment on what may be, three or four months hence, a most important & most urgent question, would be a *point* for your review.'[23]

Knowles duly obliged with a few pieces on the Union[24] and on a variety of European instances.[25] It was an extraordinary illustration of Gladstone's incautious and uncritical readiness to take up cues proffered by the Irish. The instances of Hungary, Norway, and Finland were commonplaces in the Nationalist repertoire. It is not clear whether Gladstone was ever aware that the Austro-Hungarian and Swedish–Norwegian cases were dualistic in character: that both parties were on a footing of absolute constitutional equality in relation to one another. The Hungarians had their own army (which they were agitating to get equipped with artillery). Gladstone appears to have shielded himself in his excursion to Norway in August from any awareness of how acrimonious and unstable the Sweden–Norway relationship was (it was dissolved with recriminations in 1904). The story of the Austro-Hungarian monarchy was of how the Hungarian tail wagged the Austrian dog with a vengeance. A better constitutional analogy for Gladstone's purposes would in fact have been the Hungary–Croatia relationship; but its acrimoniousness and instability surpassed even the Sweden–Norway case. The Russians eventually suppressed Finland's 'Home Rule'. Pragmatically, the best working devolutionary arrangement was that of Galicia to Vienna. But that was founded on a Polish aristocratic 'Grattan's Parliament' type of monopoly rendering allegiance to the Austrian Crown in return for a free hand to run Galicia in its own interests and to the detriment of economic development and of the Ukrainians in its eastern half. The trouble with Galician devolution from Gladstone's point of view was that it mirrored only too painfully the kind of consequences pointed to by opponents of Irish Home Rule as likely to ensue in a Clerical-Nationalist Irish state.

Having given Knowles his prompts, and on the eve of departure for a sea cruise, Gladstone drew up a memorandum designed for Hartington's edification. He outlined to his heir-apparent a series of policies for the party to consider in relation to the coming polls; hardly troubling to conceal his own indifference to them ('for such as they please: & *as* they please'). It was Ireland that really mattered.

An epoch: possibly a crisis . . . Considerable changes may be desired; & may be desirable if effected with a due regard to the unity of the Empire. I cannot treat the people of Ireland as foes or aliens, or advise that less should be done for them than would in like circumstances be done for the inhabitants of any other portion of the UK. Those are my opinions. What to say publicly must be very carefully considered on my return. Had the party been agreed, & other circumstances favourable, on the Central Board Scheme, I should have been ready to offer myself at the Dissolution on that basis . . . But of this little chance.

If so no ground remains for me *unless it be* on the verdict of the country by the recent change in the Representation of the People & on those who have made it.

In my case, if I should stand again, I must make it clear that my age does not permit me to overlook the difference, for me, between 1880 & 1886; or to expect in the coming Parliament the work of the last one.[26]

Perhaps Hartington wondered whether 'such as they please, & *as* they please' would be applied to the Irish case. And he might well puzzle at precisely what lay behind the gnomic remark about the 'verdict of the country' under a new franchise as being Gladstone's likely ground of action. Hartington passed on his puzzles to Granville. 'I never can understand Mr Gladstone in conversation, and I thought him unusually unintelligible yesterday.' Hartington thought 'Mr Gladstone's state of mind about Ireland is extremely alarming'. The collapse of the Central Board plan seemed to have left in Gladstone's mind only the possibility of 'some kind of separate legislature'; and equal treatment with England and Scotland 'he does not seem to consider a practical policy'. Hartington innocently supposed that 'as a united party under such conditions is an impossibility, he will not go on'. That Hartington should 'not much regret, but he will probably say something before he retires which will greatly strengthen the Irish demands'.[27]

The wheels of manipulation having thus been set in motion, the Gladstones departed from Dollis Hill on 7 August to join a party for a cruise along the fjords of Norway on Thomas Brassey's yacht *Sunbeam*. This time there were no tiresome problems about getting the Queen's permission. (He had earlier declined a social invitation to Osborne because of throat and voice problems: 'a festive and august occasion' would find him 'as a statue among living people'.)[28] Gladstone found the cruise more relaxing than the previous one. He did not have the leonine presence of Tennyson to contend with. There were no grand junketings. Rustic Norway was quite a different matter from courtly Copenhagen. He was fascinated by the quaint old wooden churches. Professor Lorange of the Bergen Museum later wrote to Gladstone: 'My countrymen and I are proud of the favourable impression you have received of Norway and very grateful for the kind words, by which you have honoured the Norwegian people.'[29] Gladstone recorded that 'nothing could be more touching than my reception by (I may truly say) the people of Norway'.[30] The Sweden–Norway constitutional connection inevitably was a matter of keen interest, if only because Irish Nationalists cited it so often as a case in point. The seascapes and landscapes of the fjords were entertaining enough but for Gladstone they needed the 'dress' of 'atmosphere'. 'Only the most finished forms can dispense with it. For the mass it makes all the difference between beautiful and (so to speak) beautiless.'[31] Gladstone began to draft his election address for Midlothian. As he contemplated at the end of August return to the broils of politics Gladstone mused: 'How cold I am & how far from God'; 'how terrible is, at its acmé, the calling which I have pursued for 53 years: last, & least, & lowest, among the sinful children of God'.[32]

Notwithstanding which, throat and voice repaired, Gladstone returned among the sinful children of God refreshed and ready for the fray. Chamberlain rejoiced that his chief's health was so far re-established that he could contemplate continued leadership of the Liberal party.[33] Gladstone, in fact, had never made other than purely ritual incantations about retirement since his resignation. His conviction as to what needed to be done was now quite clear and quite steady. The old formula of 1856 was as apt and serviceable as ever. It was to generate in the public mind a conviction corresponding to his doings and intentions. The problem for the time being was that he could not make those intentions public as in the manner of 1865. But that he did not see as an insuperable problem. Equally, as a start, getting his former Cabinet colleagues to swallow Parnell's pill when most of them had already gagged on Chamberlain's would be difficult but not insuperable. He had predicted openly that they would eventually be glad to settle for something far more radical than the Central Board scheme of May 1885. He cajoled Hartington: 'your views and declarations on Ireland will carry with them the great mass of British opinion'.[34] The great logic of the matter was that as leader of the Liberal party in the general election of 1885, Gladstone would surely return as 'leader of the nation' in the style of 1880 but to a degree immensely enhanced and with a prerogative and a power to move opinion unprecedented in the popular politics of his time.

That Gladstone should list 'the proposal of Home Rule for Ireland in 1886' in his 'General Retrospect' as third in a series after the 1853 budget and the Irish Church disestablishment of 1868[35] was of the essence of the case. It would be a matter of bringing the people over to Home Rule, as he himself had been brought over, by their being made aware, as he had been made aware, that the Act of Union, in itself, provided no answer to the claim of the Irish nation to have its Parliament restored. As far as can be determined that insight came gradually upon Gladstone during the Irish turmoils of 1882, was repressed by the onset of the Egyptian and Sudanese issues, revived with the emergence of the franchise and redistribution measures of 1884, and crystallized at a moment he came to identify early in March 1885. Behind Gladstone's confidence that the thing could be done was his inspired 'appreciation of the general situation and its result' derived from an 'insight into the facts of particular eras, and their relations one to another', generating in his mind a 'conviction that the materials existed for forming a public opinion, and for directing it to a particular end'. And there was also his supreme assurance about 'the lesson taught by history', that the adoption of a legislative project into the Liberal creed meant that 'that question must be resolved ultimately in the Liberal sense'; that it was 'something like a political axiom' that 'when the Liberal party comes to a final conclusion on a great political or constitutional question', that question 'has marched onwards, with real and effectual, if not uniform, progress, to a triumphant consummation'.* Gladstone's confidence now was more than a supreme assurance of Peelite cast: it was imperial, inspired. The Liberal party was at no point going to be consulted as to whether it wished to undertake this particular great political or constitutional question.

[3]

What Gladstone found most saliently on his return from the *Sunbeam* cruise at the beginning of September was that Parnell had proclaimed in Dublin on 24 August 'a platform with one plank only and that one the plank of national independence'; which was to be attained by the 'concession of a constitution similar to that which is enjoyed by each and all of the larger colonies and that is practically what we are asking for'.[36] To the public world at large in Britain this came as a 'jolt'. Gladstone could take it rather more in his stride. He had, after all, privately requested Parnell's views as to a constitution for Ireland based on that of 'one of the larger Colonies'. That Parnell had chosen to make a public declaration instead was not perhaps the most courteous mode of response. Harting-ton duly responded to Parnell with an instinctively decisive negative.

Gladstone deplored this. He had returned to terra firma, he assured Hartington, 'extremely well in general health, & with a better throat: in full expectation of having to consider anxious & doubtful matters, & now finding them rather more anxious & doubtful than I had anticipated'. As yet he was 'free to take a share or not in the coming political issues, & must weigh many things before finally surrendering that freedom'. Gladstone owned his own regret that Hartington had found it necessary 'at this very early period to join issue in so pointed a manner with Parnell & his party'. No doubt Parnell's speech was 'as bad as bad can be' in its 'monstrous promises' to 'all & sundry' in Ireland. But Gladstone's regret was 'not connected with any doubts as to the "legislative independence" of Ireland'. It related to the facts that it was the duty of the government, not those opposed to it, to lead in this matter; that 'premature or early declarations from us supply a new point of departure for R. Churchill & his party in their tricks'; that the whole question of the position which Ireland will assume after the general election was 'so new, so difficult,

---

* See above, page 337.

& as yet I think so little understood', that it seemed 'most important to reserve until the proper time all possible liberty of examining it'. Gladstone had hoped there were good prospects of 'effecting a disintegration' of the Irish party as in 1880; but that now seemed unlikely, especially with the 'new attitude of the Tory party' shifting 'the poles of the problem'.

Gladstone's intention seems to have been to coax and cajole Hartington along a path of grudging and grumbling compliance by stressing a distinction between 'more or less of opinions and ideas' which did not, nevertheless, constitute 'intentions or negotiations'.[37] Hartington had special weight in the party and in the country. And, after all, his irrational fears, as Gladstone held them, had been overcome in the cases of Reform and Redistribution. Gladstone was in effect applying paradigmatically to Hartington primarily, to the upper Liberal echelon secondarily, and to the 'nation' ultimately a political version of the theological doctrine of 'reserve'. Possibly Gladstone here took example from that master of the 'principle of economy', Newman. The 'economical method' was 'an accommodation to the feelings and prejudices of the hearer, in leading him to the acceptance of a novel or unacceptable doctrine'. It might involve 'apparent inconsistencies or mysteries', with substantial issues 'kept in the background', to be 'brought forward at a time when, reason being proportionately developed', 'its presence becomes necessary'. 'Those who are strangers to the tone of thought and principles of the speaker, cannot at once be initiated into his system . . . because they must begin with imperfect views.' Newman's *Disciplina Arcani* was specifically a method of 'withholding the truth', with 'the tenderness or the reserve with which we are accustomed to address those who do not sympathise with us, or whom we fear to mislead or to prejudice against the truth, by precipitate disclosures of its details'.[38]

Hartington, playing Kingsley to Gladstone's Newman,* responded with increasing puzzlement. He was clear that the readiest way to keep the Liberal party united was under Gladstone's leadership, and he urged Gladstone to come to a decision as to the part he intended to play at the coming election and to announce that decision as soon as possible. 'I do not say that under your leadership unity in the party could be certainly secured.' Hartington especially did not know enough of Gladstone's 'ideas with regard to Ireland to say whether it would be possible for me to accept them'. There was Chamberlain also to consider. Hartington, innocently as ever, thought that Gladstone might perhaps 'consider it desirable' to have some meeting and discussion with members of the late Cabinet on these points at an early date. 'If this is not done, I

---

* Newman's *Apologia pro Vita Sua* of 1864 was a response to Charles Kingsley's accusations that Newman did not consider truth a necessary virtue.

apprehend that the differences among us are likely before long to become quite irreconcilable.'[39] The last thing Gladstone wanted was meeting and discussion. He told Hartington he was 'strongly in favour of waiting'. And, given Hartington's views on the leadership, Gladstone could fairly conclude that his late colleagues would wish him 'to take a share in the election'. Accordingly, he would prepare an Address for Midlothian in pamphlet form. Gladstone concluded in headmasterly style by hoping earnestly that Hartington and his friends 'will give the Irish case a really historical consideration'. The 'general development of popular principles' and the 'prolonged experience of Norway' and the 'altogether new experience of Austro-Hungary' required the 'reconsideration of the whole position'.[40]

Mary Gladstone, in her loyal familial way, was over-impressed by her father's oft-proclaimed doubts as to 'surrendering' his freedom not to take a share in the coming political battle. 'These few days', she recorded of 12–15 September, 'have really been, if people knew, the crisis of the leadership of the Lib. Party.'[41] Gladstone had every motive for engendering a crisis-laden atmosphere about the leadership which would enhance his powers of control and manipulation. But his leadership itself was never a seriously critical matter of uncertainty. How could he contemplate handing over the magnificent prospects and heroic responsibilities of the coming Liberal government to the clerks and the boys?

With his honest puzzlement now enhanced, Hartington could not understand how 'the policy of the party' could be agreed on without a meeting of the party. 'I consider that you are the leader of the party,' he told Gladstone, 'and that you are the only person who can declare the policy of the party.' The object of a meeting would be, Hartington thought, 'to ascertain whether . . . the various sections of the party can acquiesce in the policy you propose to adopt'. For all Gladstone's insistence on the unity of the Empire, Hartington found his exotic references to Norway and Austria–Hungary, on top of Parnell's declarations, giving him 'the greatest uneasiness', and leading him 'to fear that the return to power of the Liberal party, whether pledged or not beforehand, would involve the adoption of an Irish policy for which I at least am not prepared'. Hartington stressed once more the reasonable expectations of the party: was 'agreement possible before the party is committed'?[42]

The short answer to that was, and remained, No. Gladstone's position, in the last analysis, was simply as Harcourt had put it to him: '*you are the Party* and your acts are its acts'.[43]

The long answer was, and long remained, an exercise in filigreed 'reserve' in the mode of the *Disciplina Arcani*. Hartington's 'apprehensions' arose solely, Gladstone soothingly responded, from the fact that he was looking to the footing on which a new Liberal government should hereafter be formed; whereas Gladstone looked to what footing – 'far more free & open' – the Liberal party should now go to the election on. The former of these was quite 'premature'. 'Nothing can be more unlikely according to *present* appearances', he assured Hartington, 'than any effective or great legislative action for Ireland.'[44] Gladstone continued sinuously to evade Hartington's request for party consultation and discussion to attempt to arrive at a common understanding. Rather pathetically, Hartington eventually conceded that the only suggestion he could offer was that 'perhaps, as the intended issue of the Address has been made known to a few, it should be communicated to some others of the late Government'.[45] Gladstone's ultimate formulation was that the 'protest' which Hartington registered signified that Hartington was 'not willing to be bound to the *extent* to which I bind myself in regard to Ireland', but that Hartington did not 'on that account withdraw from the general opinion that under all the circumstances' it was desirable that 'I should issue an Address, directed in my view to the election, and so framed as by no means to imply that I hold the party ripe for action'.[46]

Behind Gladstone's insistence that he had at present 'no other purpose than that of promoting, what I think dangerously deficient in many quarters, an historical & therefore a comprehensive view of the Irish question',[47] lay the presumption that what he later described as a 'healthful slow fermentation in many minds, working towards the final product'[48] would eventually release him from his position of 'reserve'. As with earlier occasions, he was unwilling to accord Hartington's alarms as being other than manifestations of irrational morbidity. Hartington's studied reference to himself as having 'no unexpressed personal object' stung Gladstone by its obvious implication that the same might not be said of him. This was explicable to Gladstone only as evidence that Hartington, following a visit to his mistress the Duchess of Manchester at Kimbolton, must have been in 'a jealous frame of mind'.[49] It was something of an embarrassment that Willy Gladstone revealed himself as sharing much of Hartington's opinion, and declared that he would not contest a seat for the new Parliament. The ostensible motive, which Gladstone quickly promulgated, was Willy's desire to take 'better care of the estate'; and indeed Willy had never made much of a fist of his twenty years as an MP. Gladstone later put 'considerable pressure' unavailingly on Willy to stand for Shipley.[50]

A 'historical and therefore a comprehensive view of the Irish question' was something in which Gladstone had felt himself dangerously deficient. He set about repairing that deficiency with an intensive course of self-instruction. The autumn weeks at Hawarden were occupied in convincing himself that the historical literature supplied testimony over-whelmingly in favour of restoring a parliament in Dublin. In this respect his conclusion was almost certainly correct. What he also convinced himself of, however, was that the passing of the Act of Union in 1800 was a transaction of unexampled baseness and depravity; and that indeed the whole history of the English tutelage of Ireland with particular reference to the post-Reformation Ascendancy was an unmixed story of historical horror.

This episode is a signal illustration of Acton's diagnosis of Gladstone's faculty for living completely in what he chose to believe. He had dipped into the 'Union speeches and debates' at the time of Forster's Coercion Bill in 1880 ('pray do not suppose I dream of reviving the Irish Parlia-ment'), and was 'surprised' then at the 'narrowness of the case, upon which that Parliament was condemned'. Even more surprising, perhaps, was the simplicity of Gladstone's suspicion that 'the unavowed motives must have been the main ones'.* That simplicity erupted in a moral explosion when it became the catalyst of Gladstone's tendentiously selective reading in the modern nationalist school of interpreting Irish history. The effects have been described as 'cataclysmic'. 'He had Gavan Duffy's word for it that Carew's campaign in sixteenth-century Munster was the closest historical parallel to the Bulgarian atrocities.' Gladstone's reading 'dazzled' him with somewhat misconceived notions of Grattan's Parliament of 1782 – 'the respectable face of Irish nationalism'.[51] 'I have long suspected the Union of 1800,' Gladstone recorded on 19 September. 'There was a case for doing something: but this was like Pitt's Revolution-ary War, a gigantic though excusable mistake.' In due course, with his expertise, Gladstone was to find Parnell strangely deficient. He remarked of Parnell to R. Barry O'Brien: 'His knowledge seemed small. I never saw a sign of his knowing Irish History.'[52] With the passionate zeal of the newly converted, Gladstone sought above all else to 'know Irish History' in order to confer moral and intellectual credentials upon his Home Rule policy. No doubt the most sublime aspect of his simplicity in this respect was his hope and expectation that his colleagues and the nation at large would also want 'to know' Irish history the better to understand and accept the Irish claim to Home Rule. The intellectual recklessness of Gladstone's mode of applying Irish history to Irish politics repelled the greatest contemporary figure in Irish historical scholarship, W. E. H. Lecky, whose authentic credentials as an Irish patriot and a critic of Pitt's Act of Union were as impeccable as was his later critique of the tendentiousness of Gladstone's historical underpinnings of his Home Rule policy.

* See above, page 269.

[4]

The proofs of Gladstone's Address to the Electors of Midlothian were ready to be circulated by 18 September. As far as its Irish aspect was concerned it bore the marks of his historical reading bout ('long ages for which on the whole we blush') but it also confined itself within the reservations of the *Disciplina Arcani*. As a whole, Rosebery well described it as a capacious 'umbrella'. The *Times* thought it 'dispiriting'.[53] It satisfied Hartington well enough and displeased Chamberlain ('A slap in the face'); which was no doubt Gladstone's exact intention. Although confined within the *Disciplina* Gladstone said enough about Ireland to raise the question as to why it was the lack of other things that caused most comment. Gladstone repeated the criteria for limitations he would place on 'enlarged powers' of Irish self-government he had stipulated in 1882: maintenance of the supremacy of the Crown, the unity of the Empire, and the authority of Parliament. Irish self-government, he insisted, would not be a source of danger but the means of averting it by providing a better guarantee for increased cohesion, happiness, and strength. What was new was Gladstone's projection of a sense of critical urgency with a touch of menace. 'My personal answer to the question is that history and posterity will consign to disgrace the name and memory of every man, be he who he may, and on whatever side of the Channel he may dwell, that, having the power to aid in an equitable settlement between Ireland and Great Britain, shall use that power not to aid but to prevent or to retard it.'[54] Carlingford noted: 'He offers himself for election, but leaves it doubtful whether he would form another administration. The address is moderate, not exciting or inspiring.' On closer examination, Carlingford had to admit Gladstone's skill in keeping the party together. 'What power he has! What influence over public opinion and action! – generally well-used.'[55]

For all this tone of urgency, the worlds of politics and opinion remained undisturbed and unalerted by Gladstone's hints. The general presumption remained innocently that of Hartington's in the previous month: that as the unity of the Liberal party would be an impossibility should Gladstone venture anything really radical in the way of Irish self-government, then quite clearly he would not try it on. This was certainly Chamberlain's presumption when Gladstone turned his attention to the genius of the newly published *Radical Programme*, with its heady mix of Church disestablishment, graduated taxation, free elementary education, compulsory powers of land purchase by local authorities, taxation of urban land values, and so forth. Chamberlain had lately earned goodwill by adopting a 'self-denying ordinance' as to stipulating terms for his joining a new Liberal administration. It was pointless to challenge the Grand Old Man with that kind of political pea-shooter. But for Gladstone's purposes, Chamberlain, like Hartington, was worth coaxing and cajoling. Gladstone agreed with Chamberlain in 'assuming' a Liberal majority. But: 'Supposing Parnell to come back 80 to 90 strong, to keep them together, and bring forward a plan which shall contain in your opinion adequate securities for the Union of the Empire, & to press this plan under whatever name as having claims to precedence . . . Do you not think you do well to reserve allowance for a case like this?'[56]

Chamberlain's reply was that he had not contemplated the contingency outlined by Gladstone. 'I had supposed that the first work of a Liberal Ministry would be Local Government, & I thought it probable that Bills for the three countries would be brought in together.' Given Parnell's 'change of front' to impossibly spacious demands, Chamberlain also supposed that 'these Bills would not go beyond County Councils, & that any further proposal could be left over to a more favourable time'.[57] All that Gladstone's further probings revealed ('Mr Chamberlain – three hours of stiff conversation')[58] was a fixation on a good domestic reform programme, which Goschen was soon to dub famously as the 'Unauthorised Programme' of the Liberal party. Given the current controversy over giving local authorities powers of compulsory purchase to provide allotments, Chamberlain was amused to discover its advocacy in Gladstone's election address at Newark in 1832: 'curious, in relation to recent discussions'. Gladstone had to confess to his 'little bit of Socialism'.[59]* This fond recollection of his youth did not hinder Gladstone from brushing aside Chamberlain's attempt to insert free education into the frame of discussion. 'An instinct blindly impresses me', he informed Chamberlain, 'with the likelihood that Ireland may shoulder aside everything else.'[61]

This at least jolted Chamberlain into feeling 'uneasy'.[62] His reply reflected a new awareness; and he added some very pointed comments to Gladstone about the scope of possibilities.

I cannot see my way at all about Ireland. Parnell has shown that he is not to be depended upon. He will not stick to any 'minimum' – even if he could be induced to formulate another. After his recent public utterances he must go for a separate independent Parliament. For myself I would rather let Ireland go altogether than accept the responsibility of a nominal union. But I think that a great number of Liberals – probably a majority – are not willing to give

---

* 'I remember it well: & the old Duke of Newcastle (a high Tory) but a great gentleman, smelt a rat, & asked me in 1832 what I meant. I do not recollect my reply. Probably rather lame.'[60]

more than English Local Government – National Councils would have tried them very severely – & beyond that I do not believe they can possibly be pressed at present.[63]

These were judgements Derby certainly would have endorsed. After a visit by Gladstone to Knowsley and 'an hour's good conversation', Derby found himself bemused. 'Gladstone discoursed for full half an hour, with scarcely any interruption from me . . . I listened with some surprise, for though I knew that he favoured Irish claims, I was not prepared for what is in fact a declaration in favour of Home Rule.'[64]

By now Gladstone was using Herbert at Hawarden as a conduit for disseminating, as he put it to Granville on 22 October, his belief that there would be 'great advantage in a constructive measure (which might be subject to change or recall) as compared with the Repeal of the Union'.[65] Thus had the '*present* appearances' he had put to Hartington on 11 September, that 'effective or great legislative action for Ireland' was unlikely, changed quite dramatically. That Gladstone should now cite Repeal as the alternative to the 'constructive measure' he had in view was indicative of the radical trend of his thinking. The line Herbert was relaying as his father's surrogate was that the Irish and the Conservative government should be encouraged to work together to produce their own 'constructive measure'. Failing that, 'nothing but a sheer and clear majority in Parliament could enable Liberals in Government to carry a plan'. Gladstone assured Herbert that he shook himself 'free of any other idea'.[66] To Laura Thistlethwayte Gladstone declared it a 'sad disappointment' for him 'not *now* to make a total, and final retirement' after his '53 years of labour'. 'All our people expect a large Liberal majority. The other side limit themselves to a hope that by steady aid from the Parnellites they possibly may have strength enough to get in.' Gladstone thought that, for the Conservatives, this was 'not a very honourable prospect'.[67]

Meanwhile Gladstone 'read & ruminated on Ireland, & wrote important stuff'. The kind of important stuff he was writing in these autumn weeks was memoranda sketching the main outlines of a measure 'to establish a legislative House or Chamber for the conduct and controul of Irish, as distinct from Imperial affairs'. One of the provisions he sketched at this time was that Irish representation in either House at Westminster 'be continued without change, so that Ireland may possess her just influence thereby on Imperial matters, reserved from the jurisdiction of the Irish House or Chamber'.[68] A critical step had been taken beyond the level of dropping broad hints in correspondence or conversation towards emergence from the *Disciplina Arcani*. Gladstone scrupulously covered this with a gnomic statement to Hartington on 10

November. 'Either directly or through Granville you know all my mind down to a certain date.'[69]

What was vexing to Gladstone was Chamberlain's tiresome persistence in thinking that the really important thing was that the people were about to take power in the land and that the reign of democracy would soon begin, with the *Radical Programme* as the guiding text for the new epoch. Henry Maine produced his *Popular Government* to join issue with the *Radical Programme*. Maine's was a signal text, following on from Seeley's *Expansion of England*, of the dissident Liberalism of the time, much approved of, like *Expansion*, by Tennyson 'as an exposition of the views of moderate men in England'.[70] Chamberlain was certainly aiming to take centre stage on the political boards amid this grand contention about the future of Britain.* This did not suit Gladstone, it may fairly be presumed, at all. As the unfolding of events later would make plain, he did not care for Chamberlain as a person (so very different from Chamberlain's erstwhile companion in arms, Morley) and even less as a politician. Gladstone saw politics in 1885 as a continuum; he was not at all attuned to the idea that an old order was about to be replaced by a new. Since he first became leader of the Liberal party in 1867, Gladstone had never suffered even an approximation to a rival pretender to his throne. Even at his worst times with the party there was never the shadow of a doubt as to his prerogative. He displaced Granville and Hartington with a crook of his finger. He was never stronger as leader than when pleading his desire to retire. Now Chamberlain was the first serious contender to stake a claim. Gladstone had perfectly good reasons for wishing to see Chamberlain off quite apart from any affront he may have endured to his pride or sense of possession.

In the first place, Chamberlain was agitating for disestablishment of the Kirk in Scotland as a preparation for disestablishment in England, giving the Conservatives an excellent handle for a 'Church in danger' cry. Gladstone had to ward off this diversion. 'Much harm' had been done '*among the best men*', he rebuked Chamberlain, 'by the plan propounded in "the Radical Programme" – which, between you & me, I conceive to be outrageously unjust.' Already the Bishop of Oxford, on behalf of those who had 'trusted, and looked up to' Gladstone 'for these 40 years and more', 'very earnestly' asked for some words from Gladstone 'disavowing the strange threatenings of the "Radical Programme" against the Church'.[71] In the second place, much more consequential than these irritations, was Chamberlain's obstinacy in not seeing that it was the future of Ireland, not the future of Britain, that was presently to be at

---

* Dilke by now was in the toils of the Crawford divorce action, which broke his official career.

centre stage. 'Will Ireland be the first & overriding business?' Gladstone asked Chamberlain. 'The chances of it increase.'[72]

Much harm was indeed being done among the moderate men. Acton wrote to Mary Gladstone that it was 'not the popular movement, but the travelling of the minds of men who sit in the seat of Adam Smith' that was 'really serious and worthy of all attention'. Maine's *Popular Government*, 'a Manual of unacknowledged Conservatism', was selling well. 'It is no doubt meant to help the enemy's cause, and more hostile to us than the author cares to appear.'[73] Gladstone was quite sharp with some of those who ventured to explain themselves. 'It is thought, & probably with justice,' he admonished Lord Southesk, 'that Radicalism is rampant & forward at the present juncture; and I believe the causes to be mainly two: first the adoption of Tory democracy into the creed and policy of the Government; secondly the defection piecemeal of persons high in station and in influence from the Liberal party.'[74] This convenient twist of converting the consequence into the cause was to be the gravamen of Gladstone's later critique of Hartington. Hartington himself was warning Gladstone that his own friends were 'losing confidence and slipping away from us'. Albert Grey and Selborne were two names cited by Acton. Hartington urged that the only possibility of keeping the moderate men in the Liberal party seemed to be in Gladstone's taking a 'strong and decided line against the Radicals', and making it clear that he would come back at the head of the party and as prime minister of the new Liberal government. 'Thousands of votes will be given under the impression that you will come back as Prime Minister, which would not be given if it were known that after the election the Liberal party would fall into the state of disruption which it inevitably will on your retirement.' After all, if Gladstone were determined not to return to office, 'it seems hardly fair to allow this to be kept secret'.[75]

This was on the eve of Gladstone's progress to Midlothian on 9 November. As he proceeded on his 'animated journey' to Edinburgh, delivering at 'four or five places conversation-speeches to the head or heads who with the reporter were within our carriage', Gladstone could ruminate on the very mixed elements in the political scene. The unity of the Liberal party and the stability of a new Liberal government – the addiction now appeared hopeless – depended upon his leadership. Yet Gladstone had no interest whatever in the party simply as a party, nor in the objects which that party might devise for itself, whether in the movement line pushed by Chamberlain or in the resistant line of Hartington, or in any likely compromise between them. For Chamberlain, Gladstone's leadership was a convenience, a means of transition from the old politics to the new. For Hartington, Gladstone's leadership had become a stark necessity. They both agreed with Granville's dictum that if there was to be a Liberal majority in the new Parliament, they would have to keep Gladstone as leader.[76] In terms of personal preferences about the style and manners of future Liberalism Gladstone was in no doubt that the 'gradual disintegration of the Liberal aristocracy'[77] was far more to be deplored than was Radical frustration at the slow pace of movement. And as for the great question immediately at hand, Gladstone had to consider not only the stability of the Liberal party, but equally the stability of the Conservative-Parnellite entente. But yet, ultimately, what was the greatest element in politics, its most potent and precious component? 'What power Gladstone had! What influence over public opinion and action!'

[5]

Gladstone's 'last counsels in England were his first words in Scotland, for immediately on his arrival in Edinburgh he insisted strongly on the necessity for the Liberal party to hold together, not only for purposes of party, but in order that they might be in such a majority as would be sufficient to maintain the independence of the House of Commons as a whole in dealing with the Irish question'. It would be the duty of that Parliament to give Ireland, 'with a generous hand, all means of local self-government' consistent with preserving the unity of the Empire.[78] To Carlingford this seemed to 'contain an intention to give Home Rule'.[79] Parnell certainly declared Gladstone's words as 'the most important for Ireland ever uttered by an Englishman'.[80] Their careful construction, however, allayed alarms among those whom Gladstone was accustomed to address, and whom he feared to mislead or to prejudice against the truth, by precipitate disclosures of its details. The term 'local self-government' was familiar and seemingly innocuous. The statement was interpretable, and was meant to be interpretable, as applying just as much to the present Conservative government as to any future Liberal government. The precise purport and context of Gladstone's words got lost amid the grandeur of his presence in the great Midlothian show, amid the roar of the streets and the throngs in the halls. What came across was the majestic fact of the Grand Old Man's imperially demanding a clear majority in Parliament from the country, without needing to tell the country quite why he wanted it. If the Liberal party remained united 'it cannot fail to be returned to the House of Commons in a majority such that it may deal independently with the Irish or any other question'. 'This is a matter of absolute necessity.'[81]

At Brooks's Club, in December 1887, Henry James, Gladstone's

Attorney-General in the 1880–85 government, told Hamilton that he 'never could forgive Mr G. for so misleading him and others in the electoral campaign of 1885'. Granted that Gladstone 'had made up his mind about Home Rule before the election' and had 'scruples about doing anything which had the appearance of a mere bid' for Irish votes, 'why should Mr G. have gone out of his way' to call on the electors 'to give him a clear majority over the Tories and Parnellites in order that there might be no temptation to truckle to the Nationalists?'[82] James's question might seem utterly obtuse were it not an accurate reflection of the horror in which Parnell and his party were held by the generality of his peers and expressive of their interpretation of Gladstone's motives in 1886 in going ahead with his Home Rule policy in the absence of such a majority. Gladstone, as Carlingford could perfectly well see, wanted a clear majority precisely in order to ensure that granting Home Rule would not be and would be seen not to be a matter of truckling to the Nationalists. Gladstone explicitly stated in Edinburgh on 9 November – the point bears reiteration – that it would not be 'safe' to enter into an organic constitutional issue on the strength of a majority provided by the Irish only. It was on the grounds of this 'obviousness' that Gladstone later defended himself against accusations from such as Bright of concealment.[83]*

Privately, at Dalmeny, Gladstone put the case to Rosebery that the 'idea of constituting a legislature for Ireland, whenever seriously and responsibly proposed', would cause 'a mighty heave in the body politic'. It would be 'as difficult to carry the Liberal party and two British nations in favour of a legislature for Ireland, as it was easy to carry them in the cause of Irish disestablishment'. It would require 'full usage of a great leverage'. That leverage could 'only be found in their equitable and mature consideration of what is due to the fixed desire of a nation, clearly and constitutionally expressed'. Liberal prepossessions would not be altogether favourable; 'and they cannot in this matter be bullied'. Gladstone had therefore endeavoured to lay the ground by 'stating largely the possibility and the gravity, even the solemnity, of that demand'. He was convinced that 'this is the only path which can lead to success'. At present there was all the more reason, then, for circumspection and reserve, for keeping the party united.[84] To Hartington Gladstone stressed the receptiveness Lord Salisbury was showing in his recent statements about the advantage of a 'large central authority' in Irish local government.[85] By 14 November, at Dalmeny, Gladstone had his draft outline of a measure for constituting a legislature in Ireland substantially in shape. He qualified the notion he had in October of maintaining Irish

* This was cited against G in 1892. See below, page 524.

representation in both Houses unchanged by stipulating 'for Imperial subjects only'.[86]

With the 'three great speeches' at Midlothian in November 1885 Gladstone hoped to rekindle the enthusiasm of the Liberal party and to heal its breaches. His campaign evoked the precedents of 1868 and 1880. But it lacked a central focus such as both those precedents possessed. Gladstone had to project himself as a kind of substitute for the missing big question. No one else could have come anywhere near doing it. It did well enough at Midlothian, but the question was how far and wide beyond would the rekindling spread. Apart from being oracular about Irish local government and imperial about demanding a good majority, Gladstone had nothing to offer. He asked the Scots to be patient about disestablishment of the Kirk. He denounced the 'quackery' of Fair Trade. He dismissed as spurious the Conservative cry about the 'Church in danger'. He had kind but indeterminate words about free schools. Wherefrom 'a mighty heave in the body politic'? Whereto 'full usage of a great leverage'? There were observers at the time who failed entirely to understand not only what Gladstone was at, but also that he was 'at' anything at all. They envisaged him back at Hawarden as 'Archimedes in his garden at Syracuse', revelling in powers of mental abstraction, not caring 'so very much which way the elections go' and having no burning ambition for a return to the office. 'He must, too, feel pretty certain that his demand for an overwhelming Liberal majority will not be realised, & that whatever party holds office next year will only be able to carry on permanently by the help of the Irish vote.'[87]

This was a good reading of the election but a bad reading of Gladstone. He had a burning ambition to see, one way or another, a legislature established in Dublin. The Conservatives could not be relied upon to do their duty as in 1829 or 1846. For those reasons he cared very much about having an overwhelming Liberal majority, and had good reason to suppose that he would have at the least a clear working majority. He conferred with Lord Richard Grosvenor on 18 November, five days before the polls were to commence. In September Grosvenor and the party agent, Schnadhorst, had estimated conservatively a Liberal return of between 370 and 380, with the Irish at 80–90 and the Conservatives at 210.[88] There were many Liberals who did not rate the Conservatives as getting as many as 200 seats. 'Let us hope for an utterly overwhelming victory,' Acton wrote on 11 November, 'in spite of some perceptible progress on the part of the Tories.'[89] Grosvenor and Schnadhorst revised their estimates: 298 Liberal seats in England and Wales, 57 in Scotland, three in Ireland, 'giving us 46 as a good working majority over all other factions'.[90] That was before T. P. O'Connor in Liverpool, at Parnell's behest, pronounced that Irish voters in Britain would be best advised to vote against the candidates representing the party who 'coerced Ireland, deluged Egypt with blood, menace religious liberty in schools, and promise to the country generally a repetition of the crimes and follies of the last Liberal Administration'.[91]

This was brutal work. Like the Conservatives, the Irish had an obvious motive in trying to keep the Liberal majority at an optimally low level. Gladstone could only interpret it as confirmation of Conservative–Irish connivance. Even so, there still seemed little doubt that the future Liberal government would have a majority, if not 'sheer and clear', at least adequate to its needs. Contingent preparations were set afoot. Gladstone began deliberately but delicately to remove the veils of his reserve for Hartington's nonplussed benefit. His technique was to draw Hartington in by cajolingly assuming that Hartington was already half in agreement with him.

The main questions are, does Irish Nationalism contemplate a fair division of Imperial burdens, and will it agree to just provisions for the protection of landlords. I do not think that, on the other hand, sufficient allowance has been made for the *enormous* advantage we derive from the change in the form of the Nationalist demand from Repeal of the Union (which would reinstate Parliament having *original* authority) to the form of a Bill for a derivative Chamber acting under imperial authority. The whole basis of the proceeding is thereby changed.[92]

From Hartington's very uncajoled point of view there was nothing for practical purposes to choose between originality and derivation. The Irish certainly would make no distinction. But more dismayingly, Gladstone appeared to Hartington as beginning to express a hitherto unexpressed personal object: 'putting forward an Irish policy for which he has obtained nobody's assent'.[93]

[6]

The elections turned out to be a great puzzle. By the third day of polling fifty-six Conservatives had been returned as against fifty-four Liberals; on the fourth day twenty-eight Conservatives were returned to twenty-five Liberals. These were mainly in borough constituencies. Liberals began to pick up well in the counties, where the traditionally ascendant Conservatives were mauled by the new occupier voters and came out catastrophically with a mere ninety-eight of 231 English county divisions. They had made the mistake of mocking proposals for smallholding allotments as 'Three acres and a Cow'; their mockery was very effectively turned against them. But this spectacular success, even combined with the usual solid Scottish and Welsh returns, could not reimburse the Liberal party for its strange failure in the English boroughs, where the Conservatives won a small but historically unprecedented majority. By the last day of polling, on 18 December, the return of 335 Liberals was matched exactly by 249 Conservatives and eighty-six Irish Parnellites. For Parnell it was manifestly a triumph: his party had nearly doubled its number by clearing away all the surviving Liberals in Ireland and all the Liberal-leaning Home Rulers who had sat on the Liberal benches. Only eighteen Ulster Conservatives remained to dispute the Irish representation with him. Gladstone diagnosed the failure to Grosvenor: 'Fair Trade + Parnell + Church + Chamberlain have damaged us a good deal in the boroughs . . . I place the *causae damnae* in what I think their order of importance.'[94]

The great fact was that there would be no overall Liberal majority when the Parliament met in the new year. Outside Midlothian itself, parts of Scotland and the North of England, there was little of the spirit of 1868 or 1880. Gladstone returned somewhat crestfallen to Hawarden on 28 November. He admitted the point to Hartington on 1 December: 'we cannot now hope to *beat* Tories + Nationalists'. His list of damnable causes was rational enough. Anti-Free Trade sentiment was strong in places such as Sheffield, which returned three Conservatives to two Liberals. As to the 'Church in danger', Gladstone always allowed that the 'common ruck of the Clergy' would always be a 'Tory Corps d'Armée'.[95] Chamberlain had certainly frightened off many fearful moderate men. The Liberal managers offered Parnell as their best excuse. Schnadhorst held the Irish vote to be worth twenty-five seats to the Conservatives in eighty constituencies. Close investigation casts doubt on this claim. Gladstone was willing to settle for fifteen purloined seats. No convincing corroboration either way can be demonstrated.

But in any case a much more cogent explanation of the Liberal failure in 1885 is simply the effect of the maturing of fundamental social and demographic trends which had been apparent to perceptive Liberals in 1868 and 1874. Analysis of the vote in the great conurbations in 1880 revealed that it was there that the Conservative vote was expanding fastest. The effect of Redistribution was to optimize the urban and suburban vote, which accelerated this expansion. Liberalism, underpinned by the free trade and fiscal policies of Peel and the younger Gladstone himself, was in effect subverting itself by working its way through and out of its central Peelite-Gladstonian vocation of reconciling the mass of the people to government as a beneficial agency. As the social analyst W. H. Mallock observed, the most significant social fact of the 1880s was the recruitment of large segments of the working classes into the newly definable category of the lower middle class. And as the extraordinary success of the Disraeli-inspired Primrose League suggests, there was a sizeable 'Tory Democratic' working class also in being. Thus a purposed political achievement of Peelite-Liberalism was being transmuted into a blind social trend, of which the Conservative party, largely undesignedly and certainly unmeritoriously, had become the beneficiary. As time disclosed, the 1885 election was 'already setting the pattern of the future'.[96]

One of the most telling of the indications of this deep mutation of the times was the move at the beginning of 1886 on the board of the *Daily News* to drop the veteran editor Frank Hill. *Daily News* circulation was not rising, whereas that of the *Standard* and the *Telegraph* was. Pleading for Gladstone's support, Hill argued that it was not his fault: it was simply that 'in virtue of the character impressed on it a generation ago', the *Daily News* was 'out of relations with the predominant opinion of the classes which read daily newspapers in the district in which it is published'. Moreover, the metropolitan Conservative papers had a large provincial circulation, because none of the best provincial papers was Conservative.[97] Yet it was a typical provincial Liberal MP, Channing of Northamptonshire, who candidly made the point to Gladstone that 'instead of the sweeping victory expected in the counties, we have but staggered through – by the help of the Franchise cry – to a qualified & unstable success'. There was a danger that the Liberal position in the counties might melt away if the Conservatives offered local-government reform and allotments, and possibly free education and more 'working man' legislation. That meant there should be no delay in putting a Liberal government in place. Channing wanted a party meeting soon. 'Such a meeting would not only declare but produce unity, & it might by a decisive pronouncement of the party wh. has the majority & therefore the constitutional duty, remove or modify the difficulties of the Irish situation.'[98]

Given the startling nature of the sketches at Dalmeny of the outlines of a Home Rule bill a month previously, the last thing Gladstone could contemplate with equanimity was a prompt party meeting designed to engender unity in order to remove or modify the difficulties of the Irish situation. Such a meeting might conceivably make something of Chamberlain's Central Board scheme; it would certainly not, at that time, go further. Doubtless what Channing envisaged, like the great majority of his Liberal parliamentary colleagues, was some measure of more or less generous local-government reform, with elective councils, such as had been urged ever since the early days of the previous Parliament by such as Rathbone and Whitbread. Parnell would have to like it or lump it. For Gladstone it was, as he put it to Granville, 'a case of between the devil and the deep sea'. But, being Gladstone, he was in a position to avoid both. There would be no party meeting. What there would be, Gladstone trusted, was 'a healthful slow fermentation in many minds, working towards the final product'.[99] That 'final product' he felt he had defined sufficiently, for present purposes, at Midlothian.

To Spencer at the beginning of December Gladstone confessed that he had 'Ireland on the brain', and felt he 'may be bound to take my turn at such a supreme moment'. Lady Cowper encountered something of this obsessed temper when she paid a call at Hawarden while staying with the Westminsters at Eaton. She talked alone with Gladstone about Ireland. She discovered that he was not aware of the extent to which rents, even judicially settled rents, were not being paid.

He got so excited when he talked about Ireland, it was quite frightening. He ended the conversation by saying 'Well it has come to this, we must give them a *great deal* or *nothing*.' And I answered with some warmth 'then *nothing*'. Upon which he pushed back his chair with his eyes glaring at me like a cat's, he called to his wife that it was time to go out . . . I saw his table covered with MS of an answer to Huxley upon some religious subject.[100]

Something of a healthful slow fermentation was observable in the mind of a Liberal MP such as James Bryce. He was useful to Gladstone as an expert informant about Ulster. But Gladstone paid little attention to his advice. Although Bryce concluded that 'things cannot go on in their present state', he was convinced by Michael Davitt that a Dublin Parliament was not the first object to aim for. The land question needed prior attention: a land-hungry Irish Parliament would have to be pre-empted with a big extension of tenant purchase.[101] The Chief Whip, Lord Richard Grosvenor, was perhaps rather less healthfully fermenting. He was much relieved to learn from Wolverton that Gladstone had assured his colleagues that there would be no negotiations with the Irish party. 'Hardly a Liberal comes to see me here', he reported to Gladstone from Liberal Central Office in Parliament Street, 'who does not say before leaving "Now mind *no* coquetting with Parnell", nothing would do the Liberal party more harm just now than any underground communications with the Irish party, such a course would prevent any measures being satisfactorily carried by the Liberal party, *but* I do hope that the Tory party will be forced to deal with the Irish question.'[102]

That hope, though from a different angle of approach, was now very much Gladstone's official leitmotiv, together with a new urgency as to time. 'For long I have been mourning over the slowness with which the pupil of the political eye in many enlarges itself to take the light.' 'Immediate action' was, too, his conviction. He declared himself 'amazed when I hear people talk of waiting games. Time is indeed most precious.'

But I am of opinion that it is the *Government* who ought to act: first because they are the Govt. & none but the Govt. of the day can act with effect or hope. Secondly because they are a Tory Government.

For my part, if they will not trifle with the subject but bring in a measure adequate & safe, I shall use them as I have used them about Afghanistan and about Bulgaria. If they flinch, then it is a different affair.[103]

At this point Frank Hill of the *Daily News* chimed in most appositely with misinformation ('I do not know whether I am indiscreet or intrusive in telling you') that 'a leading member of the Cabinet, especially concerned with Ireland, had by arrangement an interview with a prominent Home Rule member', having 'expressed his desire, and, as I understand, Lord Salisbury's, to come to an understanding with Mr Parnell'. Lord Salisbury and Lord Carnarvon, so Hill understood, 'believed they could concede all that was essential in his demands; but feared that they would not be able to carry their point in the Cabinet; and if they did a secession in the party'. The matter, so Hill also understood, was to come before the Cabinet that day (14 December).[104]

The Conservative government had flirted with Parnell in the summer of 1885 on the principle that a drowning man will grasp at a serpent. Apart from Carnarvon's noble but naive initiative, the Conservative ministers involved (others, who knew nothing at the time about the intrigues, like Cranbrook, were unutterably shocked by the whole discreditable affair) were engaged in the honest chicanery of an alliance of convenience. Salisbury killed Carnarvon's initiative dead as mutton in September. But he kept the policy of Irish local-government reform afloat. Gladstone read rather too much into this, as he read far too much into Hill's flyblown misinformation. 'The last four days', Gladstone replied, 'have certainly witnessed some astonishing disclosures.'

The public are slowly opening their eyes to what it has long been easy to anticipate – the bigness, and the urgency, of the question of Irish Government. If Nationalism is reasonable, it must be dealt with. It can only be dealt with by a Government. It can probably best be dealt with by a Tory Government. It cannot be delayed without mischief.

And the singular announcement that the Ministers mean to ask a vote of confidence seems to have *that* element of good in it that it recognises delay as a thing inadmissible.[105]

Gladstone's obsessive excitement was becoming a thing in itself formidable. In sober fact, Salisbury's haste had to do wholly with a wish to extricate himself from office as quickly as possible. Deploring in principle the series of immediate dissolutions since 1868, he wanted to restore the conventional practice of meeting a new Parliament; a proceeding utterly pointless without a confidence vote. Gladstone was living completely in what he chose to believe. 'So far as I can learn', he informed Hartington, 'Salisbury & Carnarvon are rather with Randolph, but are afraid of their colleagues & their party.' (What Salisbury was afraid of from his party was indignation at his having let the indiscreet Carnarvon loose, unsupervised.) There could be no doubt, Gladstone was sure, 'that the urgency & bigness of the Irish question are opening to men's minds from day to day'.[106] On 15 December Gladstone walked across from Hawarden to Eaton Hall to attend the 'beautiful morning service' in the Duke of Westminster's chapel. 'Saw the Duke – the Duchess – Lady M. Alford: and A. Balfour to whom I said what he will probably repeat in London.'

Balfour, lately promoted by his uncle Salisbury to the Local Government Board, was astonished amid the party at Eaton to be confronted by the intense figure of Gladstone – at one time his prospective uncle-in-law. Balfour could not be sure whether Gladstone's 'primary object in calling was to use me as a connecting link with Lord Salisbury, or whether this was a happy thought which occurred to him when he found me among the guests'. For an hour Balfour was the bemused recipient of Gladstone's grim assurances as to the supreme urgency of the government's need to respond to the Irish crisis, given Parnell's sweep of the Irish constituencies. Lord Salisbury's government could be assured of Gladstone's full support and of the benefits of his good offices with the Liberal party. What most struck Balfour was Gladstone's claiming to have 'information of an authentic kind, but not from Mr Parnell, which caused him to believe that there was a power behind Mr Parnell which, if not shortly satisfied by some substantial concession to the demands of the Irish Parliamentary Party, would take the matter into its own hands, and resort to violence and outrage for the purpose of enforcing its demands'. Balfour's effort at a satirical riposte – 'In other words, we are to be blown up and stabbed if we do not grant Home Rule by the end of next Session' – fell flat. Gladstone replied gravely: 'I understand that the time is shorter than that.'[107]

The 'information of an authentic kind' cited by Gladstone probably explains his reference in his letter to Hill about 'astonishing disclosures' in recent days. The matter has always been something of a puzzle. The demeanour of the Irish party generally was on the side, quite sensibly, of giving the British public time to digest the elements of the new situation. In January 1886 Gladstone became convinced that there was a plan by the Irish party of a 'withdrawal *en bloc*' from Westminster and setting up an Assembly in Dublin: 'by far the most formidable thing that can happen'; 'which brings into view very violent alternatives'.[108] There appears to be no evidence that such a plan was ever envisaged.[109] There had long been rumours of Ireland's being 'full' of Irish Americans and American money 'organised for violent action (assassination?)' and stories that, in return for a suspension of violence, Parnell would be given a year to succeed by parliamentary means.[110] But again there is nothing in the records of any subsequent critical degree of violent action. What is possible is that Robert Hamilton at the Irish Office in Dublin, who was hand in glove with Carnarvon and Gavan Duffy in pushing for a Conservative initiative, could now see that the only chance was to hope that Gladstone and the Liberals would take it on; and that Gladstone might need a touch of stimulus to spur him into movement. If so, Hamilton was carrying coals to Newcastle. What seems in any case most likely is that Gladstone, having boxed himself in at Edinburgh with his stipulation for the 'absolute necessity' of a clear Liberal majority, now chose to believe and live for the moment completely in a self-induced conviction which would justify his unboxing himself.

A few days after his Eaton excursion, Gladstone followed up with a letter to Balfour.

On reflection I think that what I said to you in our conversation at Eaton may have amounted to the conveyance of a hope that the Government would take a strong and early decision on the Irish question. For I spoke of the stir in men's minds, and of the urgency of the matter, to both of which every day's post brings me more testimony.

This being so I wish, under the very peculiar circumstances of the case to go a step further and say that I think it will be a public calamity if this great subject should fall into the lines of party conflict. I feel sure the question can only be dealt with by a Government, and I desire especially on grounds of public policy that it should be dealt with by the present Government. If therefore they bring in a proposal for settling the whole question of the future Government of Ireland, my desire will be reserving of course necessary freedom to treat it in the same spirit, in which I have endeavoured to proceed with respect to Afghanistan and with respect to the Balkan peninsula.

You are at liberty if you think it desirable to mention this to Lord Salisbury ... I am writing for myself and without consultation.[111]

Salisbury received this message amid the turmoil over the public revelation of Gladstone's opinions known as the 'Hawarden Kite'.* He exploded with a mixture of outrage and guilty embarrassment at this

---

* See below, page 397.

unlooked-for outcome of his clutching at the Irish serpent. The Conservative–Irish entente had been conducted from Salisbury's point of view as a damage-limitation exercise within a political world shaped by Liberalism's natural hegemony: a hegemony, moreover, which he took to be monumentally a guarantee of the Union. His lodestar as Conservative leader was to ensure that the grisly series of 'betrayals' of 1829, 1846, and 1867 would never again be repeated. He responded to Gladstone purely in that spirit: Gladstone the manipulative hypocrite, inviting the Conservative party yet again to sacrifice itself for a higher good defined by Gladstone. Balfour replied to Gladstone with politely evasive phrases about the difficulties of keeping such an issue out of party lines. Ireland was a part of the United Kingdom, not a remote region like Afghanistan or Rumelia. Gladstone came back with further assurances that so long as there was hope of the government's acting he would 'entirely decline all communication' of his own views 'beyond the circle of private confidence, and only allow to be freely known my great anxiety that the Government should decide and act in this matter'.[112]

The blank negative with which Salisbury finally responded to this was written when Gladstone's views had dramatically ceased to be within 'the circle of private confidence' and had become public property. In due course Gladstone would be eloquent on the moral delinquency of the Conservative party's failure to rise to the occasion. It was possible, Gladstone later told the Commons,

that they might have made one of those Party sacrifices which seem now to have gone out of fashion, but which in other days – the days of Sir Robert Peel and the Duke of Wellington – were deemed the highest honour – namely, when they saw the opportunity to serve their country, to cast to the winds every consideration of the effect upon the Party, and to secure to the nation the benefits which they alone . . . were capable of securing.[113]

Liberals, as they heard this, could envisage, with a variety of sinking feelings, the doom of a Peelite sacrificial future which lay before their own party, which would be given no choice but the highest honour of serving their country.

[7]

All this now put Gladstone in a dilemma. His line hitherto was that as the Conservatives and the Irish amounted to half the House of Commons it would '*warrant* the adoption of a waiting policy by the Liberals'. But '*if* Tories & Nationalists part company, what then?'[114] Now that the Conservatives had in effect given notice of intent to make an honest Unionist party of themselves, the logic implicit in this situation would inexorably wind itself forward that if anything were to be done as a matter of urgency, it would have to be done by the alternative Liberal–Nationalist combination. This would be a far more complex undertaking than the classic exercises of Peel and Wellington in serving their country by ordering the Tory party to turn about. Hartington was all the more anxious. He pleaded on 11 December that Gladstone give him 'any information' on the development of Gladstone's views on the Irish question. He had heard of the possibility of 'some considerable concessions of local government'. There were persistent rumours of plans and communications with Parnell and others. Hartington was 'entirely ignorant of what may be going on'.[115]

Lord Richard Grosvenor's 'hope that the Tory party will be forced to deal with the Irish question' was but the necessary corollary of his warning to Gladstone that nothing would do the Liberal party more harm than 'underground communications with the Irish party'. In fact, as things turned out, Lord Richard had no particular personal desire in any case that the Liberal party should shoulder the burden of sacrifice from which the Conservative party had unworthily unburdened itself. And in this respect he was by no means an unusual kind of Liberal. Gladstone, however, as Hamilton glumly observed, 'has Ireland on the brain: and thinks himself bound to make an effort, heedless of consequences, to effect a settlement'.[116] Gladstone now started on a new tack of working up to 'what seems to me the plain duty of the *party* in the event of a severance between Nationalists and Tories'.[117] That duty was so plain that consulting the party about it would be entirely superfluous.

Now Gladstone was stuck with a 'waiting policy' in new circumstances to complicate further his exercises in the *Disciplina Arcani*. There were now but a few weeks before the commencement of the new Parliament. The trouble with 'healthful slow fermentation in many minds' was that it was slow. 'How the fermentation is going on,' he rejoiced to Hamilton on 16 December; but that had to do with Gladstone's embarrassed attempts to put a positive spin on the irruption of the affair known as the 'Hawarden Kite', which certainly gave an impetus to the process but of a doubtfully healthful kind. Herbert had been assisting his father in various ways to further the healthful fermentation. One of the ways was keeping the Liberal press on the right track. The great problem, of course, was to discern whether there was a track in the first place. Herbert set off from Hawarden to talk to Dawson Rogers at the National Press Agency, 'to guide him and his editors and prevent them from being absolutely at sea'. Herbert himself was a dutifully filial Home Ruler and could see the time for educating opinion closing apace. It is possible that Herbert's initiative was provoked by an 'escapade' of Dilke's, urging precedence to English local-government reform and postponement of an Irish settlement. Herbert pointed to the 'inevitable effect' of Parnell's overwhelming victory on his father's position as defined by the 'Address speech of '82'.[118] That was enough. The immediate embarrassment in December 1885 was caused by the Press Agency's material coming mysteriously into the hands not only of the Liberal *Leeds Mercury* but of the Conservative *Standard*, which made of it a sensational exposé on 17 December of a stealthy conspiracy to foist 'Mr Gladstone's Plan for Ireland' on to the unsuspecting British public. The worst of it was that to those many who had overlooked or failed to construe Gladstone's oracular utterances up to his Midlothian address, the impression was given that Gladstone, ambitious for power, was opportunistically tailoring his opinions to fit the shape of the new House of Commons.

Gladstone could not disapprove Herbert's 'giving, when he thinks it advisable, what he thinks I think'. Hamilton was quite clear that Herbert would not have moved in the first place unless his father had 'tipped him the wink'. Herbert's thoughts accurately rendered Gladstone's thoughts. Herbert accounted for the 'explosion' of public excitement from 'the tension of the public mind'. 'Given the wish to create a sensation and a convenient opportunity for such creation, a little padding and much *a priori* argument pretty nearly account for all that happened.'[119] From Hawarden Gladstone did his best to stem the tide of scandalized speculation. He was glad to have W. T. Stead's *Pall Mall Gazette* steadfast (for all that he much disapproved of Stead's recent stunt sensationalism about 'The Maiden Tribute of Modern Babylon').[120] He repudiated the *Standard*'s 'irresponsible speculations' about his intentions. He would remember his responsibilities to his political friends, 'who may safely understand that I am bound to none of the ideas announced in my name'. He felt himself excused from replying 'in the present state of facts to any further enquiries, rumours, or allegations'. The National Press Agency, embarrassed at the leak, announced that, after all, 'in that statement nothing was said to indicate any settled plan or scheme'. It was still Mr Gladstone's wish that the Conservatives would take up the issue and legislate in a liberal spirit. 'As to certain rumours which have found currency of negotiations between Mr Parnell and Mr Gladstone, there have been no such negotiations, either direct or indirect.'[121]

Eddie Hamilton found himself mobbed at Brooks's Club by dismayed Liberal MPs. 'Mr G. has given by telegraph a guarded disclaimer. The assertions are certainly not authentic; but representing as they do with certain inaccuracies the bent of Mr G.'s mind, they do not admit of flat contradiction.' Hamilton found Gladstone's repudiation distasteful. 'It does with some reason give grounds for the everlasting charges brought against Mr G. as to his prevaricating, his disclaiming this and disclaiming that in terms savouring of an origin from Jesuitical dictionaries and his thirsting for power.'[122] There was much talk in the Carlton Club of a Whig and moderate Liberal secession and a coalition with 'Tory Democratic' Conservatism. Randolph Churchill asked Labouchere to convey to Gladstone that if Gladstone went for Home Rule, he, Churchill, would not hesitate to 'agitate Ulster even to resistance beyond constitutional limits'.[123]

Gladstone's political friends were not much reassured by his declaration that he was not 'bound' to the ideas announced in his name. Derby sent immediately to Granville for a contradiction of the report that Gladstone planned to give large powers to an Irish Parliament subject only to a veto by the Imperial Parliament. It was, Derby urged, impracticable, it would split the party, and in any case the party ought not to be committed without previous discussion.[124] Hartington was prompt to inform his constituency that he knew nothing of any policy to be adopted by the Liberal party as to Irish Home Rule; on which his own opinions remained unchanged.

Gladstone was also quick to get back to Hartington in an effort to repair damage. 'Now considering that I have thought people astonishingly blind to the approach of a gigantic question, & have thought it our absolute duty to try to prepare them for it, I think I have laboured hard to avoid committing anyone, & have succeeded as far as possible.' He had, after all, been advocating the cause of local self-government for fourteen years; and for good measure reminded Hartington of his statements on the Irish aspect of it in February 1882.[125] He advised Chamberlain: 'Be *very incredulous* as to any statements about my views and opinions. Rest assured I have done & said *nothing* which in any way points to negotiation or separate action.'[126] He slammed on the brakes as to urgency. Almost all men, he now complained to Granville, 'seem to me to be in too great a hurry as to defining what is to be done a month hence at the opening of the Session'. Gladstone could not doubt that his explanations would make Derby see that 'in the main, I am entirely with him'.[127]

In his now customary style of unwillingness to allow Hartington a rational opinion awkward for Gladstone's purposes, Gladstone could only conclude that Hartington must be 'in a state of morbid sensibility'.[128] For his part, Hartington concluded that Gladstone appeared to be acting in a very extraordinary manner 'and I should think will utterly smash up the party' by imposing upon it an Irish policy without consultation or consent.[129] Hartington was unwilling further to allow Gladstone to shelter behind the sophistry that, since he was not 'bound' to 'any settled plan or scheme', there was no justification for public alarm or concern. 'My chief difficulty is this,' he told Gladstone: 'how to reconcile the advice which you give that we should not commit ourselves with the position that has been created by the rumours of which you complain, which, though perhaps inaccurate, appear to be not very far from the truth.' It was 'very difficult' for those who, like Hartington, were 'unable to share your opinions' to 'refrain from committing ourselves while this most vital question is being discussed with the knowledge, not indeed of the details of the Home Rule scheme which you think should be given, but that a scheme of Home Rule should be prepared by this or some other Government'.[130]

To Granville Hartington was blunter. It was impossible to reconcile the advice Gladstone was giving with the position which had been created. 'He has allowed it to be known publicly, not that he has settled the details of a Home Rule plan, but that he is of opinion that the time has come when that demand for Home Rule must within certain limits be conceded.' This could not be contradicted, and in Hartington's opinion constituted 'action of the most important and decisive character'. Hartington was unwilling to allow that Gladstone had 'as he seems to imagine, done nothing'.[131] Hartington brushed aside impatiently Granville's efforts at mollification.

Mr Gladstone may say as much as he likes about our not committing ourselves; but he has committed himself up to his chin. He may not have formed a complete scheme; but he allowed it to be known that in his opinion Home Rule, including an Irish Parliament, must be granted ... This has not been denied and cannot be denied. Is it possible to conceive anything more absurd than that he should allow these opinions of his to be made known, constituting as they do a most important element in the discussion, and then ask us not to be in haste as to any decision?[132]

Chamberlain's position, like that of Grosvenor, was that he would like to be able to give Gladstone the fullest possible support 'in any proposals you may ultimately see your way to make'; but he was much relieved to find that Gladstone agreed with him in thinking that it was the duty of the government to negotiate with Parnell and his friends and to take the appropriate initiative. Chamberlain offered some comments which later events revealed to be prescient.

If there were a dissolution on this question, & the Liberal party or its leader were thought to be pledged to a separate Parliament in Dublin, it is my belief that we should sustain a tremendous defeat. The English working classes, for various reasons, are distinctly hostile to Home Rule carried to this extent, and

I do not think it would be possible to convert them before a General Election.

I fear that with the expectations now raised in Ireland, it will not be possible to satisfy the Irish party with any proposals that are likely to receive the general support of English Liberals.

If I am right, we must wait until Parnell has broken with the Tories, when [there] will be pressure upon him to come to terms with us, & he may perhaps moderate his demands. I confess, however, that I cannot feel sanguine of any satisfactory agreement.[133]

[8]

Implicit in these exchanges was the break-up of the Liberal party which occurred six months later. Having failed to draw Gladstone as to intentions, Chamberlain joined with Hartington, Harcourt, and Dilke to 'resolve on some way of bringing Mr Gladstone to book'.[134] Gladstone meanwhile had his own plans to bring his former colleagues and his party to book. On 26 December he drafted proposals which looked to the hypothetical contingency that the Conservative party and the Irish party might part company; that the Liberal half of the Commons would be obliged to vote for an amendment to the Address praying Her Majesty to choose ministers possessed of the confidence of the House. 'Which under the circumstances should I think have the sanction of a previous meeting of the party.'[135]

This was the first moment since the emergence of the Home Rule issue that Gladstone contemplated summoning a party meeting. But his purpose precisely was to keep the party out of the Home Rule issue. 'An attempt would probably be made to traverse this proceeding by drawing me on the Irish question.' But Gladstone had a disclaimer to hand: 'It is impossible to justify the contention that, *as a condition previous* to asserting the right and duty of a Parliamentary majority, the party or the leaders should commit themselves on a measure, about which they can form no final judgment, until by becoming the Govt. they can hold all the necessary communications.' But on second thoughts even Gladstone had to admit that this demand for a blank cheque signed by the party as a condition previous to *his* willingness to lead it in government might excite something of what he had already ascribed to Hartington as 'morbid sensibility'. His formula in this instance was 'jealousy': 'in all likelihood jealousy will be stronger than logic and to obviate such jealousy, it might be right for me to [go] to the very farthest allowable point'.

The case Gladstone supposed was: 'the motion made – carried –

Ministers resign – Queen sends for me – might I go so far as to say, at the first meeting, that, in the case supposed, I should only accept the trust if assured of the adequate, that is of the general support of the party to a plan of duly guarded Home Rule?' Were that support withheld, Gladstone would see it as his duty to 'stand aside'; and while with him the Irish question would remain paramount, he much preferred the prospect of a Liberal government 'without an adequate Irish measure to a Tory Government similarly lacking'. And such a Liberal government 'would be entitled to the best general support I could give it'.[136]

Not a blank cheque then; but a menace of abdication. Gladstone's late colleagues could envisage only too well the likely circumstances attending Gladstone's threatened second abdication of the Liberal leadership. They could see Gladstone as 'leader of the nation', with his own idiosyncratic notions of what his 'best general support' would consist of, mounting yet another grand *coup de tête* against the parliamentary party as in the days of 1876–80. Harcourt summed up his own view of the matter at the sad end of Gladstone's career: 'He does not care a rush for the party. So long as the party suits his purpose, he uses it.'[137] It was Harcourt who asked Hamilton to represent to Gladstone on 31 December 1885 'what his colleagues felt at the Home Rule balloon, sent up by Herbert G., without any intimation or warning to his colleagues'. Gladstone recorded that the 'contents of Hamilton's letter read today, I confess, made me indignant for a while'.[138]* Gladstone's view of the matter was that he had gone to 'unusual lengths in the way of consulting beforehand, not only leading men but the party, or undertaking some special obligation to be assured of their concurrence generally, before undertaking new responsibilities'. Gladstone in any case dismissed out of hand the notion that a *'late cabinet'* could exist out of office.[139]

The resistant group of Gladstone's colleagues met at Devonshire House on 1 January 1886. Granville had apprised them of Gladstone's desire for a blank cheque or alternatively his grudging willingness to humour a weakness for jealousy as against logic and to go to the very farthest allowable point of requesting a general support in return for disclosing that he had indeed 'a plan of duly guarded Home Rule'. Granville does not seem to have informed them of Gladstone's threat to 'stand aside', beyond telling Hartington that 'Gladstone may leave us, in which case I particularly wish that it should not appear that you are the cause of his doing so'.[140] None of the resisters was willing even to join Gladstone on a simple motion that a government in so marked a minority could

---

* 'J. M[orley] has come to the conclusion, he says, that the machinations of December 1885 strike him more and more as "the most absolutely indefensible thing in Mr G.'s career". They drive him wild. "There were", he adds, "only two honest men in the whole affair – namely Hartington and Parnell."' (31 July 1902)

not possess confidence, 'without knowing what is to follow'.[141] Hartington put it to Gladstone on their behalf that it was of great importance
that as early an opportunity as possible should be given, in the first place
to the leaders, and subsequently to the party itself, 'of hearing what are
your views and intentions on this subject, and what course is to be taken
on the meeting of Parliament'.

Gladstone's riposte to this was to let it be known through Granville,
'the great feud-composer', that he did not intend to leave Hawarden
until the very opening of the session on 12 January, holding that the
interval between electing the Speaker and the commencement of business
would be perfectly adequate for the necessary consultations. Hartington,
his patience wearing thin, stressed that the fragility of the Conservative
government's position might lead to Gladstone's being called on to form
a ministry at any moment.

The possibility of your doing so would depend mainly on Irish policy. If,
instead of a possible, you were the actual Prime Minister, and had this great
difficulty to deal with, your main proposals would have been placed before
your colleagues in November. At all events, they would not have been called
upon to decide upon them in a week, or in the hurried interval which would
elapse between the resignation of the present Government and your own
acceptance or refusal of office.

The responsibility incurred by a design to eject the government on
the earliest occasion 'without some knowledge of what would follow',
seemed to Hartington to strengthen the 'necessity for the fullest previous
consultation that the circumstances admit of'.[142]

To this Gladstone countered by declining to admit that the Conservative–Irish alliance was defunct: the duty of waiting for the government to
disclose its Irish 'plan' was far too valuable an evasionary and justificatory
device for Gladstone to discard. But in any case Gladstone's ideas were
'but floating ideas only'. So he was 'totally unable to submit any proposals
for consideration; and desirous of gaining whatever lights intervening
time may possibly afford'. A meeting of the party would be 'a serious
matter, but may be found requisite'. Gladstone's most wounding point
was to assert his standing of moral superiority in the most headmasterly
terms. 'I am indeed doing what little the pressure of correspondence
permits to prepare myself by study and reflection. My object was to
facilitate study by you and others – I cannot say it was wholly gained.'[143]
To Spencer Gladstone let it be known that he felt himself strong in more
material respects. From 'the nature of the case' Gladstone must hold the
Irish question 'paramount to every interest of party'. But he knew also
that 'a part, to speak within bounds, of the Liberal party will follow me

in this respect'. And, given this, could the Irish long refrain, 'or possibly even refrain at all', '*dare* they long refrain', from coming to terms?[144]

To the compliant Granville, Gladstone was more insinuatingly disarming. The 'complications of the situation, due to the existence of *two* other parties', greatly 'aggravated by the premature action of Hartington and Dilke', rendered particularly difficult the 'time and mode of communication with leading men of the party', a question in which Gladstone felt his 'own personal responsibility to be deeply involved'. The desire for meeting together, Gladstone thought, was really 'prompted by an apprehension that my mind is either made up to make, or tends towards making, some decisive motion on the Address'. But since Gladstone could see the likelihood of 'no palpable split between the Tories and the Nationalists', he was perfectly prepared to 'fall in' with what seemed to be the 'prevailing disposition among leading men', and let the Address pass as far as he was concerned without any such motion: 'only waiting the *prompt* production of the Irish plans of the Govt., and reserving a right to obtain from them satisfactory declarations on that head'.[145]

To the 'leading men' this was all utter make-believe. Far from having any Irish 'plans' of their own, the fixed determination of the Conservative ministers was to force Gladstone to come out from cover, and reveal himself for the appeaser of Parnell that he was. It was also utterly beside the real point, which was that, to all appearances, Gladstone was prepared to concede Home Rule to Parnell and was aiming to foist that policy upon the Liberal party willy-nilly, a policy which the Liberal party of itself would never adopt, by avoiding consultation and discussion, and – it might readily be deduced – by threats of abdication if his intention be thwarted. Something of the intensity of the emotional and psychological pressures upon Gladstone at this juncture emerges in a most curious assertion to Granville: that he had 'done nothing, and shall do nothing, of myself, except what I firmly believe that those whom I speak of not only ought to, but in principle would assent to and even desire'.[146] What Gladstone seems to be saying here is something relevant to the *Disciplina Arcani*: the objectors would be believers, though they did not yet know it. It related also to his headmasterly rebuke about study and reflection. It was not possible that the objectors *could* study and reflect, without coming to the same conclusion as Gladstone.

To Hartington, very much in his Kingsley role, the whole thing was baffling. He enquired of Granville: 'It is useless to expect him to be intelligible; but to whom do you understand him to refer as "those of whom he speaks" who "not only ought but in principle would assent to and even desire" – "what he will do of himself"?'[147] What Gladstone would do of himself was to keep the whole business firmly in his own single grasp. He would allow the possibility of a '*first*, limited but collective consultation' with colleagues within bounds demarcated by himself. One side of these bounds was Gladstone's declaration of 31 December that there could be no undertaking by Liberalism of the responsibilities of a parliamentary majority 'unless I am able to lay it down, as an understood rule of future Liberal policy, that, in the event of the accession of the party to power, there will not be proposed under any circumstances any measure of what is termed coercion for Ireland'.[148] The other side of the bounds was Gladstone's asserting his prerogative to meditate otherwise than the demand for prompt production of the government's Irish plans. Should he do so, he undertook, as he assured Granville, that the 'leading man' should not be 'taken by surprise'. 'I think you will deem it not unreasonable that beyond this, and inclusively as to time (but not in any case beyond the 12th) I should retain my liberty: acting under a responsibility perhaps the heaviest ever laid upon me, and one of which I feel that no other person can relieve me.'[149]

To which Hartington could only despairingly enquire of Granville: 'Did any leader ever treat a party in such a way as he has done?'[150]

CHAPTER 11

'HOLD THOU UP MY GOINGS IN THY PATHS': THE SLIPPERY PATHS OF HOME RULE, 1886

[1]

'Go then old year with thy work undone: and O may the time come for doing it, and come quickly.' Thus Gladstone's farewell to 1885. He proposed to appear chez Lady Frederick Cavendish, 21 Carlton House Terrace, on the morning of 12 January 'to gather & consult some of the late Cabinet'. It was not very easy to choose, as he confided to Grosvenor; 'it would not do to summon all. Perhaps about six to begin with.' Granville, Spencer, Hartington, Harcourt, and Chamberlain would provide him, he thought, with a preponderantly sympathetic grouping. In fact, in spite of Harcourt's notion of a 'posse comitatus', Gladstone eventually arranged separate interviews. As Harcourt put it to Hamilton, 'it is the Headmaster going to see his naughty boys singly'.[1] Hartington appealed to Granville, as the only one of them who had any influence with Gladstone, 'not to allow these interviews to exclude a more general collective consultation'.[2] That is precisely what Gladstone did exclude, with masterful ease.

Nor was Gladstone willing to give the traditional pre-Address dinner to his former ministerial colleagues. For this, he told Grosvenor, one reason 'above all others' governed him, which Grosvenor 'could perhaps guess'. Gladstone had 'talked the matter over with Granville' at Hawarden.[3] It was not in fact difficult for the Chief Whip to guess that the leader of the party wished to avoid all occasions of discussion and consultation in which 'the party which is simply a party' might find a voice. Grosvenor's own unhappiness with the way things were going led to his resignation at the end of January and his replacement by Arnold Morley. Meanwhile, as Gladstone put it to Harcourt, the question of the Irish government 'as it stands before us, & whichever way we lean, is I think the biggest of our time: & my own share of the responsibility is, in my own view, the largest I have ever had'.[4] Gladstone prepared himself with copious readings of Burke on America. On 4 January: 'Read Annual Register on Ireland 1782, 98, 99.'

What Gladstone had in mind was to recommend the Liberal party to follow his example and wait to hear what the government had to say, give it a dispassionate consideration, keep its own counsel, turn over the subject from all points of view, and reserve its freedom of action until an occasion might arise when there might be a hope of acting usefully.[5] With this doctrine of reserve Gladstone seemed to be keeping the situation under control. Selborne declared his defection, but that could be interpreted as a harmless replay of 1868. On 15 January John Morley called at Carlton House Terrace to report about Hill's being sacked at the *Daily News*. Morley 'asked if there was likely to be a basis of cooperation in the party: he said on the whole he felt that there was: that after talking with his colleagues he thought practical union was not impossible'. Gladstone referred to his manifesto of September 1885 and said he stuck to it. He had 'expressed opinion, but not plans or intention'.

We must advance by stages: consider each stage as it arises: next stage is the Address. Told me his preferred course . . . Said he felt the importance of not taking a false step which might produce repetition of George 3 & Lord North. I thought, as I have often done before, that he regards Parnell far too much as if he were like a serious & responsible party leader of ordinary English style. This vitiates his idealism, I fear.[6]

Hartington was nearing the point of open rebellion at what he saw as Gladstone's brazen intention to hijack the Liberal party in a step-by-step strategy. 'The question of Home Rule may not be in a parliamentary sense before the House. But it is now in a quite distinct manner before the country, and I fail to see how any political party can avoid expressing its opinions upon it.'[7] Hartington had in mind a forthright declaration of his determination to maintain the legislative union. Gladstone reacted very stiffly to this notion of an 'absolute resistance without examination to the demand made by Ireland through five-sixths of her members'. As he put it to Granville, appealing for his intervention, Hartington would 'play the Tory game with a vengeance', produce an 'explosion' which would reduce the Liberal party to chaos and make Gladstone's position impossible. 'I do not see how I could as leader survive a gratuitous declaration of opposition to me such as Hartington appears to meditate.' Gladstone suddenly became quite solicitous for the party. If Hartington still meditated his stroke, 'ought not the party to be previously informed?'[8]

By now stirrings in the country were impinging. Gladstone had already been made aware through Herbert and Eddie Hamilton of Sir Robert Hamilton's warnings from Dublin Castle of the new rising tide of expectation in Ireland.

We are indeed approaching a crisis here of no ordinary kind. Unless the dreadful policy of *drift* is superseded by some statesman taking a bold line the difficulties all round will become intolerable. We are in the throes of a revolution. There is no use in blinking the fact, and the press is a poor guide in such a case unless directed. Public opinion in England moves slowly when it has to hammer out its own policy, but I am not sure the movement is so slow, when the issue is clearly before it. We are now face to face with the serious alternative either of letting Ireland govern itself with all the dangers attending this course, or of ruling her with a rod of iron involving disfranchisement in one shape or another, & coercive legislation.[9]

It is noteworthy that Hamilton mentioned nothing commensurate with the terrors with which Gladstone startled Balfour at Eaton a month previously. However, Gladstone was in a good position to impress upon Hartington that Home Rule might well be thrust aside for the time by the 'social state of Ireland'.[10] Resolutions from the Belfast and Ballymena Liberals declared that the establishment of an Irish Parliament would be 'inconsistent with the maintenance of the Union and fraught with danger to the Empire'.[11] Gladstone declined to receive a Belfast deputation on the ground that it was to see Lord Salisbury, and he could not appear to be in competition with the prime minister. From Edinburgh there was a demand that British opinion as well as Irish opinion should be consulted. In Edinburgh, opinion, 'commercial and professional, shop-keeping and artisan', while ready to support devolution to some degree, was hostile to an Irish legislature.[12] There were stirrings also at the highest level: Derby recorded Ponsonby's touting, no doubt at the instance of the Queen, the notion of a Hartington–Salisbury ministry.[13] Goschen was known to be eager in this direction.

The Queen, quite willing to be seen candidly offering countenance to her Conservative ministers, opened personally the working session of the new Parliament on 21 January. Having headed off Hartington's impetuous initiative, Gladstone, in a 'morning of much oppression', met his colleagues chez Granville. 'Only Hartington stiff.' He could mark Granville, Kimberley, Spencer, and Chamberlain as conformable, with Rosebery and Trevelyan probables, and Derby, Northbrook, Harcourt, and Dilke uncertain. It was agreed to challenge the government on the Address with a motion as far removed from Ireland as possible. Jesse Collings, Chamberlain's henchman, would be deputed to put an amendment on the allotments for smallholders question. This manoeuvre disconcerted the Conservative ministers, who were planning to flush Gladstone out from cover by offering a defence of the Union as a 'fundamental law' of the constitution.

Thus Gladstone was able to be expansive yet coy, 'occupying the place of the Leader of the Opposition'. He explained to the Commons that his main reason for not 'yielding to long-cherished intention of repose' was 'a slight, but yet a real hope that it might be possible – I hardly think it probable – that I might be able to make some peaceful contribution towards dealing with the legislative case as well as the social condition of Ireland'. A 'new situation' had arisen. Gladstone quoted from his Midlothian address on the theme of giving the Irish people 'enlarged powers for the management of their own affairs' within the limits of the supremacy of the Crown, the unity of the Empire, and the authority of Parliament. He pointed out that no one had made any comment or remark at the time. Lord Salisbury was, in his speeches at the time, 'not very far from being of the same opinion'. It would be a calamity if this question were to become an issue of 'Party conflict'. The government alone could act and should act. Gladstone defended himself about a 'certain amount of misapprehension which has gone abroad'. He did not challenge the unity and integrity of the Empire, but he did challenge the unconstitutional notion of the Union as a 'fundamental law'. It was the duty of Parliament to accord 'freely a patient, a respectful, and a candid hearing' to the representations of five sixths of the Irish MPs. Something more was requisite than preserving the status quo established by the Union of 1801. Gladstone addressed the very high proportion of debutant MPs in the 1885 Commons:

I may avail myself of the privilege of old age to offer a recommendation. I would tell them of my intention to keep my counsel, and reserve my own freedom, until I see the moment and the occasion when there may be a prospect of public benefit in endeavouring to make a movement forward ... and I will venture to recommend them, as an old Parliamentary hand, to do the same.[14]

It was an inspired move on Gladstone's part to make a good joke out of the *Disciplina Arcani*.

Gladstone was master of the field. He had, as one admirer put it, with 'perfect all-round sympathy & masterly skill', 'conserved the fullest possibilities of party' while 'keeping the way open for wholesome and enterprising future action'.[15] Mrs O'Shea transmitted the message that Parnell was now willing to help in ousting the government if given a 'reasonable assurance' that Gladstone would be sent for and would form a government. But if all that was on offer was a 'Hartington–Chamberlain ministry – which he had already been invited by Mr C[hamberlain]. to help in' – he would be obliged to support the Conservative government.[16] Parnell still hoped to stimulate a little bidding. Hitherto, Gladstone had declined to offer advice to Mrs O'Shea, since advice was equivalent to negotiation. Now his response was oblique and implicit but not negative.[17] Catherine was reported to be looking forward eagerly to returning to Downing Street. The Collings amendment duly went forward to a division on the early morning of 27 February, foiling desperate efforts by ministers to head it off. 'Three acres and a cow' now added insult to injury. Harcourt deplored the haste. If Gladstone had only waited for the government to produce their Coercion Bill, 'Mr G. might have made a much milder proposal in the direction of Home Rule, which the Irishmen would have accepted'.[18] But Gladstone had no interest in a 'much milder' proposal. Gladstone slipped through. 'We beat the Government, I think wisely, by 329:250 so the crisis is come . . .' The initial fact of the crisis was that Gladstone was short of about 100 Liberal MPs; and his majority was provided by the Irish.

This was ominous. It confirmed Hamilton in the doubts he had from the beginning. Hamilton had called at Carlton House Terrace on the morning of the 21st, and there found 'confidence still prevailing that all will come round to Mr G.'.

Mrs G. is clearly under the impression that he will surmount all the difficulties and expects to see him once more in Downing St. This is very natural: and so wonderful is his power of masking difficulties, however great they may be, that anyone is rash to assert that this is not a possible issue. But, though the party may be careful not to commit themselves to a decided line on the Irish question, and though some, even many, may in their hearts think that in the doctrine of Home Rule lies the solution of it, yet I still hold that for the moment the mind of the country is resolutely made up. This being the case, I can see nothing for it but that Mr G. should stand aside. Moreover I think this ought to be the consequence. He has over and over again declared that the only further political work to which he will set his hand is Ireland; his plank for Ireland is practically Home Rule or the equivalent of it; that plank will not at present hold water; therefore to attempt to form a Government without being able to take in hand that specific work would be an act of inconsistency on his part – would indeed almost have the appearance of a greed for power which I believe is not in him . . .[19]

Gladstone, however, had no intention of being inconsistent. He had no doubt, from the interviews he had had with his colleagues and from their collective gathering later in the morning of the 21st, that he could form a government. Selborne was out and Hartington would probably be out, which would be damaging but not necessarily ruinous to its prospects. Whether the plank would hold water or not would depend, ultimately, on deep and hidden agencies in the providential efficacy of which Gladstone could not but have the most profound faith and confidence. As Michael Davitt put it, 'there is only one man alive who can successfully grapple with this question'.[20]

[2]

To his surprise, Gladstone was not immediately summoned to Osborne. The Queen was naturally distressed at the turn of events. After the cruel deferment of so many fervent hopes that she might at last be rid of Gladstone it was the cruellest cut of all now to be confronted with the author of the 'posthumous bequest' rising from his grave. There was much talk at Osborne of some Conservative–Liberal Unionist combination to block Gladstone's Liberal–Irish combination. After all, there were near a hundred Liberal MPs floating somewhere in political limbo. The necessary linchpin of any such combination, Hartington, well realized however that his influence with his Liberal following both in the House and the country would be fatally compromised by a too close proximity at this stage to Lord Salisbury. Meanwhile Gladstone conferred about jobs and appointments, entertained and was entertained. Hamilton saw him 'much bowed down' by the difficulties of ministerial construction, 'but he still maintains his pluck'.[21] Everyone observed his high spirits. There was something of a festive family atmosphere as Catherine prepared to set up house again. Mary had become engaged to Stephen's senior curate at Hawarden, Harry Drew, at Gladstone's birthday celebrations on 29 December. From Catherine's point of view the match was not entirely desirable. Mary had 'bolted' to get engaged to a man much younger than herself, which would mean moreover leaving an awkward gap at the centre of the domestic management of the lives and comforts of the 'Grand Old Couple'. However, there it was and the wedding would have to be looked forward to.

It was now possible for Gladstone to assure Parnell through Mrs O'Shea that very soon he would no longer be confined to making his views known to Parnell through his public declarations only. 'Full interchange of ideas with Ireland, through her members, & with them through their leader, is in my opinion an indispensable condition of any examination of the subject which has been called "autonomy" undertaken by a responsible Minister.'[22] There was fear in Ireland of Gladstone's 'precipitate action'. Davitt thought that this danger could 'be averted by setting to work at once to get the *land* question out of the way'. He and Parnell were in agreement about how to remove 'hobgoblin fears' of confiscation and separation.[23] Gladstone was at ease on the question of separation. 'It is much debated whether the Irish people are in favour of separation. I lean to the opinion that they are not. After all we must not presume them to be political madmen.'[24] He was ready now to take the Irish cue on the matter of tenant purchase. But he was in no doubt that he wanted to get on with Home Rule as a matter of urgency. He asked Eddie Hamilton to take charge of his secretariat. Hamilton called in Rosebery's brother Henry Primrose to assist. Gladstone prepared himself for the summons to Osborne by drawing up a memorandum of intent for the Queen's benefit:

I propose to examine whether it is or is not practicable to comply with the desire, widely prevalent in Ireland, and justified by the return of eighty-five out of her one hundred and three representatives,* for the establishment by Statute of a Legislative Body, to sit in Dublin, and to deal with Irish as distinct from Imperial affairs; in such a manner as would be just to each of the Three Kingdoms, equitable with reference to every class of the people of Ireland, conducive to the social order and harmony of that country, and calculated to support and consolidate the unity of the Empire on the continued basis of Imperial authority and mutual attachment.[25]

The infinitely reluctant summons to Osborne came on the morning of 1 February. Hamilton found Gladstone that day 'in the most charming of humours and in good spirits'.[26] 'I kissed hands,' Gladstone recorded, '& am thereby Prime Minister for the third time. But as I trust, for a brief tenure only. Slept well, D.G.' The Queen had already made clear that she would not have Granville back at the Foreign Office nor Childers in either of the service departments. Dilke, tainted in the divorce court, she would not have in any office. All projects of immediate coalition had been dropped. Goschen's advice was cogent: Gladstone must be given the chance to try and fail. Any attempt to block would create sympathy for him. 'A dissolution *now*', Goschen urged, 'would not favour the Constitutional sections of the House of Commons.' Better to wait until the end of the session.[27] Victoria noted that Gladstone 'looked very pale, when he first came in, and there was a momentary pause, and he sighed deeply. I remarked that he had undertaken a great deal, to which he replied he had, and felt the seriousness of it.' She thought him throughout 'dreadfully agitated and nervous'. He did his best to be tactful about Home Rule: 'he might fail, it was 49 to 1, that he would, but he intended to try'.

In a second audience, after lunch, Gladstone was 'intensely in earnest, almost fanatically so, in his belief that he is almost sacrificing himself

* The eighty-sixth Irish Home Rule MP was T. P. O'Connor, in the Liverpool Scotland division.

for Ireland'. Gladstone explained that Hartington, Derby, Selborne, Northbrook and Carlingford would not join him; and that there was a general consensus that Granville was impossible for the Foreign Office, which would go to Rosebery. Chamberlain, though convinced of the advisability of his own Central Board scheme for Irish local government, was willing to join on the ground of being ready to give 'an unprejudiced examination to any more extensive proposals that may be made' with an 'anxious desire that the result may be more favourable' than he was then 'able to anticipate'.[28] Chamberlain was unhappy that Dilke was barred, and that Morley should step into the Irish Office while he, Chamberlain, was blocked from the Colonial Office, and obliged to accept the Local Government Board. When Chamberlain mentioned the Colonial Office Gladstone reacted with a withering comment about unseemly ambitions for a Secretaryship of State. Chamberlain disdained the Admiralty as a mockery. The Colonial Office in the end went to Granville, extremely disgruntled at his demotion. Efforts to get him to accept the dignified precedence of the Lord Presidency failed: he desperately needed the salary attaching to a senior working department.

Wolverton indeed had proposed to Gladstone that both the Queen's and Granville's sensitivities might be assuaged if Granville took the First Lordship and Gladstone the Exchequer.[29] Gladstone instead coaxed Harcourt to take the Exchequer (he much preferred the Lord Chancellorship): 'It is for me in forming a Govt. to propose the terms on which I ask others to join with me: unquestionably they commit no one to the advocacy of a separate Parliament.'[30] Childers went to the Home Office (much to Hamilton's disgust: Mr G. 'will never harden his heart sufficiently' when it came to forming a government. 'He can never "see through" people; and his inability to gauge character has been a great drawback to him.')[31] The faithful Whig lords, Ripon, Kimberley and Spencer, took the Admiralty, India, and the Lord Presidency respectively. Campbell-Bannerman was promoted to the War Office and Mundella went to the Board of Trade. Trevelyan was shunted to the Scottish Office outside the Cabinet and, likewise, Aberdeen took on the Irish viceroyalty. Gladstone was 'very indignant' that Kimberley's cousin, Edmond Wodehouse, should take it upon himself to reject offers of posts at the Colonial and Foreign Offices on grounds of principled objection to Home Rule when there were as yet no principles to object to.[32] Gladstone failed to entice Henry James to take the Lord Chancellorship, which went to Farrer Herschell, former Solicitor-General. One of his more imaginative appointments was that of the 'Labour' MP, Henry Broadhurst, who went to the Home Office as Under-Secretary. Wolverton got the Post Office and Herbert Gladstone went to the War Office as Financial Secretary. Harcourt summed up the feelings of most of his official colleagues in relation to Chamberlain's rather tentative and conditional acceptance of office.

But we are all in the same boat. We none of us believe in Mr G's plan; but we have no alternative policy to suggest. It is just as if Mr G. declared that he had a scheme for moving traffic by balloons. Some of us, like Hartington and H. James don't believe, and have publicly declared our disbelief, in balloons . . . Others like Chamberlain and myself recognise the existence of balloons; and though we do not believe that they can be turned to account as motive power, we feel bound to approach the consideration of Mr G's boasted invention and to see if it can be worked out practically. If the invention prove, as we expect, to be unworkable or unsafe, we must then give it up and take our own line.[33]

John Morley as Chief Secretary was conspicuously the *novus homo* in Cabinet. Gladstone's liking for him personally was of long standing.* Gladstone was grateful for Morley's warmly supportive speeches recently at Newcastle. Gladstone wanted an Irish Office team he could be at ease with. In Aberdeen he replaced Spencer with an agreeable nonentity. Morley was an agreeable substitute for Dilke, with none of Chamberlain's angularities. It was unfortunate that Gladstone felt himself obliged to dock the salary of Chamberlain's lieutenant Jesse Collings at the Local Government Office. This caused more bad blood. As Morley moved to the centre of things Chamberlain was marginalized. Gladstone prepared Morley for his new responsibilities on 2 February.

It would be too much to say I have a desire to propose an Irish legislative body: for I do not sufficiently see my way as to what it would be reasonable to recommend to the Cabinet, the Queen, & Parliament. But what I propose is an examination of the whole subject . . . On the removal total or partial of the Irish members my mind is quite open . . . About land, I think it has a logical priority, but that practically it is one with the other great members of the Trilogy, social order and autonomy.

It was on this day that Gladstone played his part at his daughter Mary's wedding at St Margaret's, Westminster. It was an occasion highly inconvenient amid the pressures of ministry-building; but Gladstone 'looked as if he had nothing in the world to do but give away a daughter'.[34]

On 5 February a letter from the Queen made Gladstone 'anxious'. He called for Granville to advise him how best to cope. Dean Wellesley's death in 1882 had deprived Gladstone of his most valued source of wisdom in times of strained dealings with Victoria. The defection of the

* See above, page 196.

Bedfords meant that the Mistressship of the Robes had to be left vacant for the while: indicative again of the sparseness of figures at the more exalted levels of the Court at all sympathetic with Gladstone. The Prince of Wales had taken an agreeably supportive view of the formation of the government; but this was of less moment than the turn against Gladstone over the Home Rule issue of the Queen's Private Secretary, Ponsonby. What the letter that made Gladstone anxious required was that he should '*state explicitly what* his "examination" would lead to – for it wd not be right that the Country shld be led step by step ... to approve a measure, which Mr Gladstone *knows* the Queen cannot approve – & wh had deterred 4 highly respected & influential Cabinet Ministers from joining his Govt'.[35] Gladstone's reply blandly disclaimed 'the idea of leading on the country step by step to a given conclusion, as he has no such conclusion before his own mind to which to lead them'. He enclosed a copy of his 1885 address: 'the whole ground, which forms the basis of union in the present Cabinet', and which 'will bind him before the world'.[36]

Vague intimations at Edinburgh about Irish local government indeed bound Gladstone to no given conclusion. That was the work he resumed now on the basis of his earlier Dalmeny outlines. At Holy Communion on Sunday 7 February there were 'most solemn thoughts for Ireland'. On the 8th Gladstone 'worked for some hours in drawing my ideas on Ireland into the form of a plan'. Gladstone had extended the range of his observations of suggestive mechanisms of autonomy from Europe to the United States. He was much interested in Argyll's notions of how the relationship between the powers of the federal union and the states might be applicable to the Irish case particularly or a federal British Isles generally.[37] What he came up with in his 'Rough sketch of proposed Constitution for Ireland' made no great advance on his November draft. There would be an elective Chamber of 300 members sitting for three years to legislate for purely Irish matters. The lord-lieutenancy would be abolished. The Dublin government would contribute £1 million annually to the Imperial Treasury in lieu of taxes. The Imperial Parliament would have the right to legislate in Irish domestic concerns 'for weighty and urgent cause'. There would be no Irish volunteer force without the consent of the Crown or enactment by the Imperial Parliament. Irish representation in the Imperial Parliament 'might be retained or might be given up'.[38] In November Gladstone had included 'Provisions for securing to minority a proportionate representation'. There was no mention of that now. Morley meanwhile grappled with the question of a Land Bill – 'some settlement of the Land question which would prevent the tenants from confiscating the property of the landlords'.[39] Gladstone in turn applied to Harcourt to exert '*to the uttermost*' the financial strength of the country to enable it to sustain the burden of credit on behalf of Ireland to fund an adequate tenant-purchase measure; without which 'we cannot either establish social order, or face the question of Irish Government'.[40]

[3]

Other diversions were rather briskly disposed of. The riots of the unemployed which held the West End in terror held no terrors for Gladstone. He deprecated the Court's anxieties about them, very much in the same tone he had used at the time of the Lancashire cotton famine in the 1860s and to the abortive project for a national subscription to ease the distress of depression at the end of 1878.* State aid, he assured Ponsonby, was 'dangerous in principle'. Public works were a slow and cumbrous remedy. The existing law gave local authorities in any case ample means of finding work. The mass of the working class were 'not ill but well off, through the cheapness of commodities, especially provisions'.[41] It was for Gladstone of much more moment that the politic Archbishop Walsh of Dublin should convey the views of the Roman Catholic hierarchy in Ireland on the matter of Home Rule. It was particularly gratifying to Gladstone that they considered that a scheme for Irish self-government 'not incompatible with the conditions defined in your Address to Midlothian of September' 'alone will be effective'. They did not see the need for a big Land Purchase measure. They favoured indeed the rigorously economical views of Mr Robert Giffen: 'nothing like confiscation sought for'. But they did enjoin suspending the right of eviction.[42] To Gladstone this was the one point of difficulty in 'an important document' otherwise 'moderate & conciliatory in tone'.

To all appearances, indeed, as Gladstone's government prepared to meet the prorogued Parliament on 18 February, he was 'a political master player exultantly in command of the political stage'.[43] He was observed in sparkling form at the Roseberys', reminiscing on the earlier parliamentary scene, with vivid anecdotal details of Lord Palmerston's sleeping habits on the front bench. In a ministerial statement Gladstone announced his intention to 'introduce measures of a positive and substantive character' in relation to Ireland, in which he would undertake 'the most difficult and arduous of all the questions which in 53 years of political life I have had to deal with'. Beyond that Gladstone declined to elaborate. Instead, he denounced the Conservatives for not having the nerve to brace

* See above, page 226.

themselves to make sacrifices and for having nothing to offer Ireland other than another bout of coercion. He also later made sarcastic comments on the marked tendency for Conservative politicians to make 'pilgrimages to the North of Ireland'.[44]

The 'North of Ireland' was indeed beginning to obtrude notably. The Irish Nationalists had early set a tone of mockery and contempt for any notions of Ulster Protestant resistance. Healy assured the Commons that 'subtract from the Orange organisation the landlord party and it would fall like a house of cards, and great would be the fall thereof'. Once the land question was settled and the landlords had the money for their estates in their pockets 'they will care very little more about the Irish people'.[45] This Irish cue was in fact the cue Gladstone would take consistently about Protestant Ulster. It was not for want of contrary indications from his own party. Colonel Salis-Schwabe, one of the Lancashire members, informed Gladstone that his election pledges would not allow him to vote for an all-Ireland legislature; a separate Assembly for Ulster in Belfast 'would make all the difference'.[46] (Salis-Schwabe had supported Gladstone in the crucial division of 27 January. He did not support him at the supreme moment in June.) The Liberals of Cambridge University likewise urged on Gladstone a modified form of Home Rule, leaving Ulster separate as a kind of Swiss canton.[47] James Bryce advised Gladstone copiously of the determination of the 'Liberal Presbyterians' to resist Dublin rule. Their links were rather with Liverpool and Glasgow.[48]*

What most Liberal MPs were mainly interested in, in any event, emerged on 9 March when Lewis Llewelyn Dillwyn, veteran of 1865,[49] introduced his Welsh Disestablishment motion. It failed by only twelve votes. Gladstone cautiously abstained, as he did a few days later on a motion for Scottish disestablishment. These, 'together with allotments for smallholders and free schools', were precisely the issues which had been of most interest to most Liberals in the election campaign. There was a susurrus of resentment in the party that Gladstone had so imperiously sidelined its interests in order to impose his own interest. Even were Gladstone fully apprised of these seethings, there could be no concession to them, no deviation from the path set for him, not by him. In the certitude of this faith was a kind of freedom. In this freedom Gladstone exuded an extraordinary confidence and self-sufficiency. He was seen in March 'more full of life and energy than ever', in truly magnificent form, insisting to the solicitous Spencer and Rosebery that 'fog did him no harm';[50] to all appearances 'a sane, balanced, good-humoured but old-fashioned old gentleman', dining out almost continually, 'almost always in capital form' at the dinner table.[51]

* Bryce was then Under-Secretary at the Foreign Office.

Still, the physical toll on an old gentleman was exacting. Gladstone kept the Home Rule measure 'entirely in his own hands'. Apart from occasional references to Spencer and Morley, and consultations with the chief legal officers, he had 'the monopoly of it; and he seems to monopolise the whole interest in it'.[52] Hamilton, deputed to pass the Home Rule draft for the consideration of the Treasury Secretary, Welby, was surprised and impressed by the sheer ingenuity of Gladstone's legislative contrivance. The papers 'certainly show no symptom of any failure of ability on his part to construct. They are indeed masterly.'[53] It was after very stiff work with Thring, the Treasury draftsman, on the Irish Land Sale and Purchase Bill, that Gladstone collapsed. He missed church on Clark's orders on 10 March. 'Whatever energies I possess are drawn off by the inexorable demands of my political vocation.' He was 'much better' when Bright dined on the 12th. Gladstone was now clear in his mind that the only way out of the conundrum of Irish representation at Westminster was simply to abolish it. Bright much approved:[54] for many Liberal MPs it was the one thing that recommended Home Rule to them. On the other hand, it would raise the principle of taxation without representation; and it had unwelcome separatist implications.

The following day, 13 March, was the critical moment of Gladstone's introducing the draft Land Bill into Cabinet. This provided for putting up £50 million of credit in order 'to afford to the Irish landlord refuge & defence from a possible mode of Government in Ireland which he regards as fatal to him'.[55] Apart from objections to the plan of 'wholesale purchase on a falling market' being 'necessarily unjust either to landlord or tenant', such as James Caird had put forward,[56*] there was the consideration that with a Dublin Parliament there would be no security for the money. The scheme was generally unpopular with the British public, for whom neither the notion of bailing out the Irish Ascendancy nor being made aware of the assumably larcenous character of an Irish legislature was attractive. These were the issues seized upon by Chamberlain, who linked the implications of Land Purchase to the implications of Home Rule, and flushed Gladstone out into the open by demanding an exposition of what specifically would be involved in conceding to the Irish people 'large local powers of self-government'. In this Chamberlain was supported by 'Kimberley & others ditto'. After hearing Gladstone's exposition, Chamberlain declared that what Gladstone proposed would be 'disastrous': 'an unstable & temporary Government which would be a source of perpetual irritation & agitation'. Chamberlain disliked the exclusion of Irish MPs from Westminster as an invitation to separation.

---

* Caird advised G to extend the purchase provisions of the 1881 Act and the 1885 Ashbourne Act from time to time as might be judicious.

He was sure that the enormous expenditure contemplated would not secure 'closer & more effective union of the Three Kingdoms', but would merely 'purchase the repeal of the Union & the practical separation of Ireland from England & Scotland'.

For the first time since the Irish question emerged in its new phase in 1885, Gladstone, having to abandon the *Disciplina* and put up a practical case, had run into a serious obstacle. Chamberlain requested Gladstone on 15 March to offer his resignation to the Queen. Gladstone's 'surprised' response was entirely consistent with his *modus operandi* hitherto. Chamberlain knew 'little but shreds and patches' of his ideas on Ireland; and could one resign *'on ideas'*? In any case it would be entirely premature. It was Chamberlain's duty to stay on and see what emerged. All Gladstone asked was a 'needed minimum of time to make ready my proposals for the Cabinet'. 'It has been absolutely beyond my powers,' he told Chamberlain with a touch of pathos, 'though I have worked as hard as my age permits, to fashion a plan of Irish Government.' All that Chamberlain had glimpsed were but 'bricks & rafters which are prepared for a house'; they were not in themselves a house.[57] Morley found Gladstone 'Vy vehement on the "childish lawlessness" of resigning merely because disclosure had bn made at last Cabinet of "an idea in the mind of the P.M.".'[58] Chamberlain agreed to postpone his resignation for two weeks. Bright was in no doubt that Chamberlain's view was 'in the main correct'.[59] Tennyson chimed in with a quotation from Pindar's Fourth Pythian Ode on the theme that it was easy to shake a city but difficult to set it back in place again.[60]

Indomitable, Gladstone was observed on 16 March by Morley working on the Land Bill, 'figuring up the sums of his Irish arithmetic just like a boy at school, his grandchildren making a hideous noise on the piano in the neighbouring room, but himself all serene and cheerful'. A few days later, though 'drowned in business', Gladstone could not resist reading a paper on Chaldean astronomy, finding 'the passage from Diodorus extremely valuable'.[61] Gladstone tried hard, in a two-hour interview ('historical in character'), to win over John Bright. Bright objected to the Land Bill as unnecessary. He thought a Dublin Parliament 'would work with constant friction, and would press against every barrier' Gladstone might create 'to keep up the unity of the 3 Kingdoms'. Bright moreover thought Gladstone far too trusting in the leaders of the 'Rebel Party'. His conversation, Bright allowed, was 'free and open', 'cheerful and earnest'. He cited against Bright the authority of Bessborough, Monk, Spencer, and Robert Hamilton. He was 'resolved to go on'. Bright concluded that the solution could be found 'only through the energy and resolution of a Minister in whom the nation has learned to place a confidence quite unusual between a political party and its leader'.[62] Morley found Gladstone again on the 23rd 'Vy confidt.'. He was sure that the Land Bill's providing a 'fair option of escape from a false position, tendered once for all to the Landlords of Ireland, might very greatly ease the passing of the entire political settlement'.[63] Confidence in March 1886 could hardly go higher than that.

By now Morley was the go-between with the Irish. As Cabinet braced itself for a full view of the Home Rule Bill Gladstone conveyed that he was 'perfectly ready to give Ireland the right to impose protective duties on British goods'. But British prejudice had to be taken into account; and the main thing was to 'pass our measures'. Therefore the wisest plan would be a reciprocal arrangement whereby 'either country, raising the Customs Duty on the produce of the other, should impose a corresponding duty of Excise'. And as to foreign policy, Gladstone was much taken by the way the 'foreign affairs of that United Kingdom', Sweden–Norway, were conducted by 'delegations'.[64] This rather startling notion presumably was quietly strangled at birth by Morley. After cabinet on 23 March Gladstone was 'strong' for Bright and Whitbread to be brought into office; 'but none of us sanguine'. Gladstone became 'irritable, fidgety'.[65] He was to present his Home Rule Bill to the Cabinet on the 26th. There might well be vacancies to fill in consequence.

On viewing the 'bricks and rafters' now constructed into a house, Chamberlain definitively resigned. Trevelyan followed suit. Gladstone indefatigably 'went to work immediately to supply their places' with Stansfeld (last in Cabinet in 1874) and Dalhousie. The Government of Ireland Bill provided for an Irish executive and legislature of indefinite powers for the peace, order, and good government of Ireland, subject to a series of exceptions and a series of restrictions to those powers, comprising such matters as the Crown, foreign policy, military and naval forces, trade and navigation, coinage, establishment or endowment of religion, religious disability, and setting of customs and excise duties. Ireland would contribute a proportion of Imperial financial charges. The Lord-Lieutenancy was to be continued. The Dublin Metropolitan Police and the Royal Irish Constabulary would remain under the control of the Lord-Lieutenant. An Irish Legislature of two 'orders' would have the power to create county and borough police forces. Irish representation at Westminster would cease. The Crown, in the person of the Lord-Lieutenant, would have the prerogative to 'give or withhold the assent of Her Majesty to Bills passed by the Irish Legislative Body'. Gladstone had dropped his earlier notions of the Westminster Parliament's retaining the right to legislate for Ireland for weighty and urgent cause and of provision for proportionate representation of minorities.

As one of its most formidable and influential critics at the time allowed, Gladstone's Government of Ireland Bill of 1886 was 'a most ingenious attempt to solve the problem of giving to Ireland a legislature which shall be at once practically independent, and theoretically dependent, upon the Parliament of Great Britain; which shall have full power to make laws and appoint an Executive for Ireland, and yet shall not use that power in a way opposed to English interests and sense of justice'.[66] This 'Gladstonian Constitution' combined federal and colonial elements. It raised deep juristic questions as to whether under its provisions the Parliament of Great Britain at Westminster continued to retain the sovereignty of the existing Parliament of the United Kingdom. But the more practical issues about which most of the debate on it turned were, first, that in the absence of Irish representation at Westminster, Ireland, though a component of the Empire, would have no voice in Imperial policy. The second point was about the viceregal veto. The Crown had not vetoed a bill at Westminster since the days of Queen Anne. Would the Crown's representative in Ireland dare otherwise? A third point of controversy lay in the practicability of extracting Ireland's financial contribution, or 'suzerain tribute' as it was immediately dubbed. Another area of controversy was the absence of any specific securities against executive and legislative oppression; which shaded into the wider issue of Ulster Protestant objection in principle to be governed by such a legislature in Dublin. Ulster Protestants were a quarter of the Irish population, concentrated in the north-eastern corner of the island.

All these issues and problems were aired in the Liberal Cabinet and the Liberal party. Gladstone's greatest advantage, and the crucial advantage of his bill, apart from its intrinsic merits of ingenuity in attempting to fit the square peg of Ireland free into the round hole of Ireland bound, was the absence of a ready alternative. It was within Gladstone's power to push Chamberlain and his Central Board scheme off the table, and keep them there. As Harcourt had implied in his balloon analogy, the only alternative was the status quo, which meant in effect a renewal of British coercion of the greater part of Ireland. The greater part of the Liberal party had no stomach for that. Gladstone set about exploiting this advantage to the hilt. He was now in a condition of intense and exalted excitement. He continued confident that if the landlords accepted his Land Sale and Purchase policy there was 'no doubt of his being strong enough to carry it off'.[67] And if he carried that off, he would have the 'entire political settlement' in the bag. Morley, on going to Downing Street to settle matters with Thring about the Land Bill, found Gladstone 'in something very like an altercation' with Spencer. 'S. very plaintive: G. vehement and masterful beyond belief.'[68]

Harcourt was unhappy at Chamberlain's departure, and the mode of it. He put it to Gladstone:

I cannot too strongly express an opinion that you should *see him personally* as a matter of *feeling* as well as policy. His attitude is not at all personally hostile but he says with some truth that you have never really discussed the question with him. A good deal in the future will I think depend on how he is personally handled. I do not mean by this that I [think] his determination to retire will be altered. I refer rather to his post-resignation attitude.[69]

As things turned, this was prescient advice. Gladstone made a mistake in alienating Chamberlain: evidently in quite a deliberate manner. When Chamberlain departed, Morley whispered to Hamilton the following day at a Cabinet committee, 'Joe might have been kept.' But Hamilton knew that 'Mr G. is not in a humour to make a compromise for Chamberlain. He has been forced too long and too hard by Chamberlain.'[70] Among other things Gladstone had never forgiven the 'leaks' which he thought discredited his Cabinet of 1880–85. Catherine may well have played her own part in this respect. Hamilton observed her keenness to get Gladstone back in office again. 'She is not a little jealous of Chamberlain and the increased position he has lately made for himself.'[71] Chamberlain was a man who made an excellent enemy. Doubtless Gladstone's distaste for him (which emerged clearly in later exchanges) was bound up in the character traits thus observable in the 'first gentleman of Birmingham'. What Disraeli was to Peel, Chamberlain in due course would be to Gladstone.

At the end of March Gladstone was deep in J. A. Froude's *The English in Ireland in the Eighteenth Century* (from which he was to quote extensively when he introduced the Sale and Purchase of Land measure on 16 April). 'The burden on mind & nerve becomes exceedingly heavy: heavier than I ever felt it. May God sustain his poor failing & unworthy instrument.' The Cabinet met hurriedly on the 29th and agreed that Gladstone should introduce his Home Rule measure on 8 April. There was agreement to exclude Irish representation, but the door was left open for modification on that point. Control of Irish customs and excise was a lively point of controversy. Gladstone's position was that if the Irish were not allowed control of the collection, Irish members would have to be retained at Westminster. 'Mr G. sees endless difficulties in retention.'[72] He had defined this in February 1882 as 'the real knot of the question'.[73] Some special treatment for Ulster was also kept on the agenda. Stansfeld, Chamberlain's replacement, was not that far removed from Chamberlain's sceptical position on these matters, as well as landlords and tariffs. And behind Stansfeld were many Liberals of the rank and file, increasingly anxious at the trend of events: offended at the way Gladstone had treated the party; bewildered at the hurtling pace he was driving; fearful for damage and possible disaster to the party in the constituencies.

Heneage, Chancellor of the Duchy, was one such. He wrote to Gladstone as spokesman for a variety of Liberal notables outside the ministry. He warned Gladstone candidly that the existence of the government would be assailed for certain and *'with success'* as soon as Gladstone proposed a statutory Parliament in Dublin, irrespective of the land-purchase scheme. The grounds of Heneage's opinion were, firstly, that 'the Country will not hear of Home Rule, as you propose', and secondly, that the government as constituted had not the confidence of any party.[74] It is not clear whether Heneage was alluding to the nature of the vote of confidence division two months previously, or whether he was making a prediction about a second-reading division in the future. As events were to demonstrate, they came in either case to the same thing. Such disaffected Liberals were beginning to look to John Bright as their totem. Bright much feared 'that Mr Gladstone has led himself and his Party into a difficulty which cannot be measured'.[75] Harcourt, fulminatingly but not very effectively, was their representative in Cabinet. He made furious scenes early in April over the financial provisions. Parnell was willing to accept that he could have no tariffs, but wanted to trade customs and excise for a more favourable level of contribution to the Treasury.[76] Gladstone felt 'sorely tried' by Harcourt. 'Angry with myself for not bearing it better.'[77] Harcourt was sorely tried at seeing the Liberal party on the brink of being torn apart. Spencer dissuaded Harcourt from resigning. Herschell was getting cold feet. He had joined the government, he explained, on the strength of 'enquiry' into the issue; and had not envisaged things going so far. He feared that an Irish Executive would mean victimization of 'all who have been loyal & order loving & peaceable throughout Ireland'.[78]

Bright, aware of 'great anxiety' on the Irish question 'in the House and thro' the Party', had another interview with Gladstone on 3 April. 'He seems weary and not so brisk and eager as when I saw him a fortnight since. He insisted on it that there was no Cabinet difficulty, only the ordinary difficulties as to details. This I know not to be accurate.' Gladstone seemed 'obstinately determined to go on with it'. Bright was embarrassed by Gladstone's pressing invitation that he dine: it was awkward to 'oppose a Minister on a critical question and to associate with him and frequent his table'. Bright felt in Gladstone 'a certain wilfulness in all this not usual with him, and it does not promise any good'.[79] Possibly Gladstone's wilfulness derived from messages from his spiritualist friend Lady Sandhurst; who certainly understood shrewdly the best way to his heart. She reported that one of her spirits had informed her, 'Daughter, there is a message from Sir Robert Peel to Mr Gladstone – it is this "Tell him to hold fast to his intentions on the Irish question. Never mind if he stands alone. Let him carry out his intention".'[80]

Certainly Mrs O'Shea's messages now at last bore their fruit. Morley arranged a conference at his room at Westminster between Gladstone and Parnell to settle contentious matters of financial arrangement. Hamilton was in hopes that once the customs and excise problems were out of the way much opposition would be disarmed and much alarm quietened. The difficulty was that Parnell was not satisfied with the reduction of the Irish contribution to the Imperial Exchequer. Gladstone had reduced it from one fourteenth to one fifteenth of the overall revenue; Parnell insisted it should not be above one twentieth. Morley recorded the occasion: Gladstone 'shook hands cordially with Mr Parnell and sat down between him and me'. It struck Morley that Parnell was sitting on the sofa 'where poor old Forster had laid his weary head many a night – he died today'. Parnell was 'very close, tenacious, & clever'. Too tenacious for Gladstone, who announced at midnight: 'I fear I must go: I can't sit late as I used to.' As Morley ushered him out, Gladstone remarked of Parnell: 'very clever, very clever'.[81] Parnell himself, astonished at how far and how fast Gladstone was driving, adjusted his demands to keep Irish acquiescence tantalizingly out of Gladstone's reach. He found Gladstone himself an astonishing sight, as he reported to William O'Brien. 'I never saw him so closely before. He is such an old, old man! . . . Once, when he yawned, I really thought he was dying, but he flared up again.' Later, when asked how the Home Rule Bill was going, Parnell replied: 'Badly, and going to be worse.' He did not get his twentieth. The great moment was in most respects 'anti-climactic'.[82] Justin McCarthy found him 'less optimistic than I have seen him yet during this chapter of our history. He is afraid Gladstone may be led to make concessions to English partners which might make it difficult for us to accept his scheme.'[83]

[4]

Messages in any case were coming to Gladstone from quarters more exalted than Lady Sandhurst or Mrs O'Shea. On the fateful 8 April, at his habitual Bible-reading in his dressing room, 'The Message came to me this morning: "Hold thou up my goings in thy paths: that my footsteps slip not".'[84] That afternoon Gladstone appeared in the Commons to introduce his Government of Ireland Bill. 'Extraordinary scenes outside the House & in. My speech, which I sometimes have thought would never end, lasted nearly 3½ hours. Voice & strength & freedom were granted to me in a degree beyond what I could have hoped. But many a prayer had gone up for me & not I believe in vain.' Now was the time to initiate publicly that 'mighty heave in the body politic' which Gladstone alone was capable of exerting. Now was the test of the 'full usage of a great leverage' that would tilt on the fulcrum of politics the ultimate great purpose of his life. Gladstone had never yet failed in the mighty heaves and great leverages of his career. He was God's instrument, and he knew that it was in the 'precinct of Christendom' that was found 'the actual mastery of the world', where all that exists existed 'in the main by its permission, or under its control'.[85]

'Actual mastery of the world' is – making necessary allowances for time and place – an accurate description of Gladstone's own sense of his political role in 1886. He possessed the insight telling him that 'the great question of autonomy for Ireland had been brought to a state of ripeness for practical legislation'. His 'promptitude' – misconceived as he later insisted by opponents as 'precipitancy' – he recommended in 'doctor's mandate' terms: it could be as disagreeable in politics as in medicine or surgery; but it was often indispensable for health. He had no doubt that the requisite popular materials were there to be formed and directed to the end he had divined.[86]

There was a sense also – Bright had felt it – that Gladstone's wilfulness in a way welcomed grimly the recalcitrance of the party and the obstacle of the Lords. He had dealt faithfully with the party before. He had also dealt faithfully with the Lords, from whom he had had little gratitude for his mercy to them – as he held – in 1884. There is no reason to think that Gladstone would not have relished a collision in 1886 and an ultimate settling of accounts. That he would conjure a majority in the Commons in 1886, however reluctant in many ways and degrees, however bewildered or even resentful, he did not seriously doubt. His line consistently was that, on the analogy of Catholic Emancipation, a Commons majority was the key thing. Intimidating the Lords could come later. There were many tactical manoeuvres available in the course of debate and committee to give him ample play in the parliamentary struggle to come. It was J. L. Hammond's sorrowful conclusion that 'a man with gifts far inferior to his could have obtained a second reading for his Bill once that Bill had reached the position the Home Rule Bill reached in April 1886'.[87] It took someone of Gladstone's overweening confidence and wilfulness to create the conditions of failure.

'Yesterday', as Hamilton recorded on 9 April, 'was indeed a notable day – the most notable day in the annals of the present Houses of Parliament. It was moreover a great day in a great career.' Hamilton could see that 'the stake played for by Mr G. was as stupendous as the risk attaching to the gamble – a risk to which his eyes were wide open'. There was 'never anything like the excitement'. Every seat in the Chamber was bespoken hours before. There was a 'storm of applause' at Gladstone's entry. Hamilton's view of the 'gamble' was that of a cautious Treasury civil servant. He knew far too much about the technical difficulties to be able to share a layman's optimism. His analyses of the overall prospects had invariably been acute and pessimistic. His prediction now was, on first impressions, 'from a sort of pulse-feeling of the House', that 'the Bill may be and probably will be read a second time; it will be scotched and killed in Committee or undergo most radical amendment'.[88]

Behind the magnificence of Gladstone's rhetoric and the heroism of his purpose lay much muddled thinking. Labouchere reported to Chamberlain of Herbert Gladstone's comment: 'H.G. says that the real *bona fide* difficulty of father is that he cannot devise a scheme.'[89] Gladstone had romantically misconceived notions about ancient Irish Parliaments for 500 years and about 'Grattan's Parliament' of 1782. He denied that his bill was a bill to repeal the Union. The Union was to be preserved, which was why the Dublin Parliament he proposed would not be a restoration of Grattan's Parliament. Gladstone held Grattan's Parliament to be in all respects equal to and coordinate with the then Westminster Parliament of Great Britain. There would be no return to 'co-ordinate Parliaments', and therefore it would not be necessary to discuss national independence, legislative independence, or 'Federal arrangements'.[90] Gladstone then invoked the precedents of Sweden–Norway and Austria–Hungary;[91] yet those were instances precisely of 'co-ordinate' Parliaments. And by ruling out federation, Gladstone had to confront the 'formidable dilemma' of the 'practicability of the distinction' between Irish domestic and imperial concerns. And if Irish peers and MPs were not to sit at Westminster, on what ground of representation was Ireland to be taxed? 'There is the dilemma.' Hence the expedient of preserving fiscal unity by leaving Irish customs and excise in the hands of Westminster.

The hole concealed at the time in Gladstone's Government of Ireland Bill in 1886 was that the problem he had pointed to in 1882 as 'passing the wit of man' still obtained. The Irish would suffer both taxation without representation and debarment from a share in imperial policy, or Britain would suffer, with Irish representation at Westminster, Irish privilege in enjoying both self-government and a share in the government of others. And this latter case invited the awkward expedient of restricting certain MPs to 'imperial' as opposed to 'British' concerns. 'Dualism', or coordinate Parliaments, was logical and intelligible; so was federalism. Imperial authority over self-governing colonies was a pious fiction, theoretically existing to the extent it was patent that it would never be exercised. Gladstone's Home Rule Ireland was a muddled mix of these. The best practical models had to be ruled out. Polish Galicia was a corrupt reality of a 'Grattan's Parliament'. The Diet at Zagreb exemplified every variety of the friction and ill will in its relations with its sovereign legislature in Budapest predicted by critics for the working of a Dublin Parliament. And then there was the Ulster question. The essence of this question was that if Ireland had a claim against a united British Isles, did not Ulster have a claim against a united Ireland? Gladstone was on this point candidly dismissive. He could not allow that a Protestant minority was 'to rule the question at large for Ireland'. There was no justification for removing Ulster or parts of Ulster from the operation of the bill. 'That is what I have to say on the subject of Ulster.'[92]*

Yet for all these muddles and difficulties, Gladstone's Home Rule Bill would stand or fall not on abstruse considerations of coordinate parliaments or divisions of power. The issues that practically mattered to the mass of Liberals were guarantees against separation and securities for the Protestant minority. Debate focused on the question of Irish representation at Westminster and on Ulster's claims respectively. The initial impact of the Grand Old Man's splendid performance generated a positive impetus behind the measure. Bright observed Gladstone a few days later 'very cheerful and well'. Hamilton noted him 'in excellent heart, full of confidence and determination'. Gladstone recorded on 13 April as being '"astonied" as Holy Writ says at the strength given me in voice & tongue, after a day in which I felt to the uttermost the sum of weakness isolation & dependence'. But after the initial reception of dazzled wonder the doubts, misgivings, and bewilderment in general passed steadily on to complaints and criticisms in particular. The initial deficit of nearly a hundred Liberal MPs hung ever more ominously over the Commons scene. When Bright dined on 12 April there was a strained atmosphere. Bright was 'querulous' and Gladstone very short with him.

Heneage's resignation from the Duchy of Lancaster and Lord Morley's from the Board of Works set off a chain reaction. Gladstone held a 'conclave' on 9 April 'on vacancies which thicken'. Resignations poured in, he told Rosebery; but his *'mot d'ordre'* was 'to close the ranks at once'.[94] Gladstone admonished one ex-Lord in Waiting for the prematureness of his resigning before the production of the Land Bill, for it was an integral and indispensable component of the great Home Rule policy.

All this I represented to [Lord] Morley, but in vain. He set the ball rolling. At my age, being on the eve of political extinction, I view with the deepest concern the rapid disintegration of the Liberal party among the Peers. Few causes, so far as I can see, will more effectually contribute to the advance of democracy, or will more seriously endanger the continuance of that moderate & stable character which had hitherto marked the course of British legislation.[95]

---

* The Nationalists in 1885 won a narrow majority of the Ulster seats: a point much observed upon by Gladstone. See the comments of Lyons[93] on 'dangerous delusions'.

To Lord Sydney Gladstone fulminated on the ludicrousness of the 'daily splutterings of resignations'. But there were splutterings closer to home. John Morley recorded of a cabinet on 14 April: 'Preceded by a curious scene of violence agst Mr G.' inflicted by Harcourt on Spencer and himself. 'Repetition in Cabt – not much less direct. Mr G. said he held exactly my opinions abt. exclusion of Irish members – namely that no feasible alternative cd. be invented.' Gladstone noted sardonically: 'only two resignations *in this* Cabinet today, happily both withdrawn'.[96]

The Sale and Purchase of Land (Ireland) Bill came next. It was trumpeted as a vitally essential concomitant of Home Rule. It would create the conditions of social peace. In introducing it on 16 April Gladstone once again had cause to be 'thankful for much support' from on high. But his bill fell flat. Designed to provide massive credit to fund purchase of tenancies, it failed to inspire confidence. Gladstone, after all, apart from the curious episode in Dublin and after, 1877–9,* had been a consistent and indeed relentless opponent and saboteur of all previous legislative exercises in this genre, up to and including Lord Ashbourne's Act of 1885. Labouchere had warned Herbert Gladstone of resistant sentiment. There was much reluctance among Liberals to undertake, as taxpayers, a big risk to bail out the Irish landlords.[97] Gladstone was hoist on his own petard. The Irish Nationalists denounced it as a 'transparent sham'. They were offended especially by the provision that a British Receiver-General would ensure that none of the flow of funding would leak away in Ireland. Its intended beneficiaries, the landlords, had but small reserves of gratitude for the author of the Land Acts of 1870 and 1881. A general verdict emerged that the bill's most obvious outcome was 'a decided weakening of the Ministry'.[98] Gladstone himself, who had the highest hopes of it as buoying up and floating Home Rule through, now could see it as an 'albatross around its neck'. He allowed it to fade quietly out of sight and out of mind.

With this fiasco Gladstone's position slumped. Harcourt was inspired to make a brilliant fighting speech on behalf of the Government of Ireland Bill only because he was convinced it was 'dead as mutton'. Gladstone took some sardonic amusement at Harcourt's embarrassment.[99] The point pressed by Harcourt about the expediency of keeping Chamberlain in some degree conformable took on a new cogency. The sticking point for Chamberlain was the exclusion of Irish members from Westminster and the separatist implications he saw in this. Was there not scope to ease his disquiet on this point? Proposals that a reduced contingent of Irish MPs might remain, in proportion to Ireland's financial contribution, were, after all, being much canvassed. So urged Arnold Morley, the

---

* See above, page 211.

Whip, anxious to negotiate terms for Chamberlain's re-entry to the Cabinet. Convinced that he had made an impression in debate, Chamberlain was heard to declare at the Athenaeum that nonetheless 'his feelings of admiration and wonder for the power of the G.O.M. over the minds of men was greater than ever'.[100]

Gladstone, with John Morley fervently in support, made great difficulties about it. Experience with Chamberlain had shown 'that such concession is treated mainly as an acknowledgment of his superior greatness & wisdom, & as a fresh point of departure accordingly'. Gladstone declined to write 'Kootooing letters to Chamberlain & I doubt as to their effect'; Chamberlain had in him, Gladstone remarked to Morley, 'with other notable gifts, a good deal of repulsive power'.[101] Chamberlain quickly reverted to antagonism. Dining on 28 April with a party including Edwin Arnold,* Courtney,† and Hutton of the *Spectator*, he acknowledged grimly Gladstone's power over the minds of men. 'I don't know what I *can* do. I don't see what I am to do.' He added 'with a very savage expression', 'What can be done with a madman as leader? . . . Why, he is going to destroy Ireland and we are helpless. It is all very well saying prevent this and prevent that. The mischief is already done. The evil has taken root.'[102]

[5]

Resistance to Gladstone was starting to take shape and substance. A meeting of peers at Derby House on 15 April comprised forty-eight attenders and sixteen sending letters of support. Hartington was present, as also, to Hartington's irritation, quite irregularly, Randolph Churchill. Selborne distinguished himself in virulence against Gladstone. A Liberal Unionist office was established at Spring Gardens to cater for dissident MPs on 22 April. But it was the peers who attracted Gladstone's attention. He was now preparing himself, if and when occasion suggested, to be virulent against the representatives of class privilege and class selfishness. To Argyll, one of those present at Derby House, Gladstone wrote with oracular menace: 'I have not spoken, & may not speak, at all freely.'[103] What Gladstone had in mind, and no doubt what Argyll could guess he had in mind, was the theme he had opened to Arnold Morley that day, 20 April. 'It is the *people*, & in the main the people only, to whom we have to look.'

---

* Poet and *Daily Telegraph* journalist.
† Liberal MP, former Secretary of the Treasury, Deputy Speaker of the Commons.

Gladstone was now in retreat at Hawarden for the Easter recess. Godley cheered him on his arrival there with another of his computations of office-holding. 'Pelham was Prime Minister for 10 years and 7 months (less one day). You have today been Prime Minister for 10 years, 6 months and 20 days. If therefore you can keep your grasp of power until the end of the recess, you will have beaten him and will have started in pursuit of Lord North (12 years and 2 months).'[104]

Another rather less welcome message received at that time was yet another offering from Tennyson, resolute as ever for Gladstone's enlightenment from the latest luminaries of the science of politics. This time it was a copy of Maine's *Popular Government*. His previous offering had been an extract from the November issue of *Macmillan's Magazine* ('with our love') containing his poem, 'Vastness', with its reference to 'raving politics' ('lies upon this side, lies upon that side, truthless violence mourn'd by the Wise'). Gladstone might perhaps have taken it for a comment on his Midlothian tour, were it not that Tennyson had added a footnote: 'This of course does not refer to the sane statesman – only to the unscrupulous politicians.'[105] On this later occasion Gladstone's riposte was brilliant: alluding to their earlier acquaintance, when rivalry for the memory of Arthur Hallam came between them, Gladstone asserted, on behalf of the Home Rule cause, 'a strong assurance that the subject of *In Memoriam* would have been with us, & I cannot surrender hope of the author'. Gladstone assured Tennyson that he would not, in his seventy-sixth year, have thrown himself into struggle 'midst of these tempestuous billows' without a 'clear conviction' and 'a strong sense of personal call'. 'For 42 years at least of the 54 of my public life, Ireland has had a rather dominant influence over it. Which is those of my opponents that has had occasion to study it as resolutely & for the same time?'[106]

Leaving Tennyson to chew on that, Gladstone brooded about Ireland and the people. The signal event that season at Hawarden had been a manifestation of the people. At Easter Hawarden church was beset by large crowds eager to see him at prayer. On Easter Saturday 3,500 enthusiastic pilgrims paid their respects at the Hawarden shrine. Gladstone deputed Herbert to address them. Gladstone tried to keep the field clear of routine governmental distractions. He was reluctant to share Rosebery's concerns with Greek problems. 'Many tactical lessons are to be learned from Peel's conduct, and I recollect that in 1846, with the repeal of the Corn Law in view, he went very great lengths, perhaps even too great, in order to avoid side issues.'[107]* What Gladstone was

---

* Gladstone was in some embarrassment over Greek applications to him with respect to the recent aggrandizement of Bulgaria.[108]

immediately intent on was drawing up an address to the Midlothian electors both as a call to battle at the renewal of the parliamentary session on 3 May and as a manifesto aimed at the Conference of the National Liberal Federation at Birmingham on 5 May. It was the aim of the Liberal managers to wrest control of the organization of the Liberal party in the country from Chamberlain's caucus.

In his address/manifesto Gladstone made a great point of asserting his leadership of the nation, by implication, against Parliament. He deplored the way the House of Commons occupied itself with the petty details of the Government of Ireland Bill instead of attending to the high and historical principle of Irish self-government which it embodied and which was what really mattered. He held out to the Scots and the Welsh the prospect of Liberalism's solicitude for their own versions of autonomy, without committing himself to Scotland's version of Church disestablishment. But the main burden of Gladstone's message was to accuse his opponents of representing the 'spirit and power of class'. Here he would fulfil his discreet menace to Argyll and speak out freely. In the great struggle to confer the boon of Home Rule in Ireland the 'adverse host', he alleged, consisted of 'class and the dependants of class'. Gladstone here reverted to the doctrine of his *Nineteenth Century* piece in July 1878 on the moral superiority of the popular judgement to that of the higher orders.* The mood and tone was now that of 1878, and all which that holy time portended. The 'formidable army' of class was the same that had fought 'in every one of the great battles of the last sixty years', and had been defeated by the just judgement of the masses. 'The classes have fought uniformly on the wrong side, and have uniformly been beaten, by a power more difficult to marshal, but resistless when marshalled, by the upright sense of the nation.'[109]

Herbert Gladstone's spokesmanship for his father at Hawarden reflected more precisely calculations about the marshalling of the upright sense of the nation in the contingency of class resistance blocking Home Rule on its second reading. Labouchere had long been pressing on Herbert that the two things necessary were to get rid of the albatross around the neck of the Home Rule Bill, the Land Bill, and to neutralize Chamberlain's hostility. 'For Home Rule', declared Labouchere, 'there is a majority, if not in the House of Commons, in the country.' Gladstone's great weapon would be a dissolution of the Parliament and an appeal to the nation.

Mr G. can, I am sure, carry anything in the latter, that does not involve the idea of monetary sacrifice. The country cares no more who his colleagues are,

* See above, page 221.

than who his footmen are. Parnell declares that he can turn at least 40 seats, that are now held by Conservatives through the Irish vote. If this be so, the combined opposition would have to win above 100 seats. The only possibility of their doing so is the Radicals being weakened through the effect of a purchase scheme.

If Gladstone would keep Land Purchase clear of Home Rule, until either Home Rule has passed the House of Lords or a general election has been called, it was 'as certain that he will win, as anything can be certain in politics'. 'Do pray point out to your father', urged Labouchere, 'that he ought to realise his own strength in the country.' Labouchere reported that Parnell had asked him to tell Chamberlain 'that, if he stands in the way, the Irish will make it a sine quâ non of any support of a Liberal Ministry for the next twenty years, that Chamberlain is not in it'.[110]

Labouchere was attempting also to steer Chamberlain away from that role and that fate. A cabinet on 4 May, on Gladstone's return to London, having ruled out the feasibility of a party meeting to reconcile the Liberal dissidents, discussed possibilities of expedient concessions including reduced Irish representation at Westminster. Labouchere hoped that this might be the germ of a formula for holding Chamberlain to Home Rule. Arnold Morley reported to Gladstone that a 'considerable number' of Liberal dissidents 'outside the 65 whom I consider to be certain to vote against, would be satisfied with the recognition of the principle of Irish Representation and possibly some 2 or 3 of the 65, but there are others whose action would more or less depend on C's vote, and I still think it all important to secure his support'. Labouchere was 'evidently under the impression that great pressure was being brought to bear on C. to pledge himself against us, and the less delay before he is convinced that some such change is proposed, the better'. Labouchere thought that an interview the following morning with some such general assurance would bring him in.[111]

Gladstone and John Morley, however, even as their ranks thinned, remained adamant against any 'Kootooing'. Chamberlain 'wants us to go down on our knees', as John Morley put it, 'and this cannot be done for the money'.[112] On 5 May the Gladstonian forces wrested control of the Council of the National Liberal Federation from Chamberlain. 'Though Chamberlain is rather in the dust,' Gladstone told Rosebery, 'Hartingtonism is on its high horse, & I am sorry to say that though things are said to be moving in the right direction, & I have much faith in the country, the Parliamentary outlook at this moment is very far indeed from clear.'[113] There was a rally of Liberal notables offering good offices to redeem the situation. Stansfeld held against an absolute extrusion of Irish MPs, 'to which I, in common with Childers, I believe, am opposed'. Stansfeld's notion was to leave the issue *'not quite closed'* on the second reading; and he offered his own plan of 'Federation', bringing in a simplified version of Grand Committees extendable to England, Scotland, and Wales severally, with powers similar to those of an Irish legislature.[114] Stansfeld criticized accurately Gladstone's memorandum to the Cabinet on the handling of the second reading as 'expedients not founded on any clear principle carried to a logical conclusion'. They would 'not recommend themselves to the popular mind in or out of the House; & that as evidences of weakness, & as insufficient in their character as concessions, they would damage the chances of passing the 2nd reading of the Bill'. Either let the Irish 'depart in peace' *or* have 'indubitable unity'. 'The true solution, & I think the most popularly acceptable one, is the principle of Federation practically & simply applied.' Stansfeld did not anticipate the possibility of carrying the present measure without an appeal to the country.[115]

This was brutal good sense and good logic, but for those very reasons inapplicable to Gladstone's wilful purposes. It was also too much like Chamberlain's argument for comfort. Gladstone would stick to his Home Rule Bill as he had stuck to his Reform Bill in 1866. He opened the second-reading debate on 10 May: 'The reception decidedly inferior to that of the Introduction.' Gladstone offered his concessions in 'one of his famous "porridge" speeches, the substance of which escaped even acute observers'.[116] The import seemed to suggest that any concessions would be subject to Parnell's approval. Gladstone took away with one hand what he offered in the other. The Liberal backbenches were left dismayed and seething. The atmosphere was now charged with Randolph Churchill's notorious pronouncement that 'Ulster will fight and Ulster will be right'.*[117]

From the backbenches Whitbread, coached by Bright, urged that prospects for the second reading would be materially advanced if it were made known that the government would allow time after the vote for consideration of objections which had been raised on what was, after all, 'a subject newly presented to Parliament'. The government 'would then stand better before the Country when an appeal to the Constituencies has to be made if they can show that they had no desire to force this question on with haste'. Many voters now doubtful, Whitbread was sure, 'would be brought in by this course'.[118] Alfred Illingworth chaired a meeting of fifty Liberal MPs anxious to carry the second reading but 'painfully aware that there is a considerable number of earnest Liberals who are hesitating as to their course'. Illingworth conveyed a plea to Gladstone to summon a 'private meeting of the party if you could see

---

* He formulated this jingle in a public letter to a Unionist Liberal on 7 May 1886.

your way to convene it at a very early date'.[119] Gladstone was most unreceptive. He had offered all that could reasonably be expected in a spirit of goodwill for the removal of difficulties felt by 'sincere friends of the principle of the Bill'. It was 'dangerous at this late stage for the Govt. to produce appendices to their own suggestions'.[120]

John Bright's vote in the second reading would be crucially influential. Gladstone hoped that he would abstain, and lead a large following of like-minded Liberals with him. In his eloquent representations of 13 May to Gladstone Bright indeed left open that possibility. He made a last plea that 'more time should be given for the consideration of the Irish question. Parliament is not ready for it.' A policy of such gravity 'cannot and ought not to be thrust through the House by force of a small majority'. It was quite a different matter from Reform Bills, the Irish Church Bill, and the Land Bills.[121] Sir Joseph Pease, the heavyweight Tyneside notable, put the matter even more candidly than Stansfeld. The bill would not pass its second reading. The break-up of the party would be deplorable and it would not be healed by a general election. The only thing to do was to withdraw the measure and prepare a new one for an autumn session such as 'would satisfy the reasonable wants of Ireland and have the support of the *entire Liberal* Party', and become law in 1887. Pease aimed for both the 'good of Ireland and to prevent the disintegration of the Liberal Party'.[122]

These pleas were not entirely without their effect. On 14 May Gladstone put before his colleagues five possible expedients as to withdrawal or holding on. 'Can there be truth in the statement', he asked Arnold Morley, '. . . that Hartingtondom, let alone Chamberlaindom, is ready to vote a Resolution in favour of Home Rule on the withdrawal of the Bill?'[123] There had indeed been suggestions that a resolution on the principle of Home Rule in lieu of a second reading might be a mode of avoiding a confrontation of Liberal against Liberal. For John Morley it was 'rather distressing to see the desperate sort of tenacity with wh. he clings to his place'. It was in the spirit of desperate tenacity, and with his habitual assumption that the moral agenda was set by him, that Gladstone responded to Pease. 'I must observe that the whole force of the dissentients *has not yet availed to tender to us a single suggestion in a practicable shape.*' What Parliament was sadly defective in would be remedied by the people. 'Meanwhile the body of the nation, so far as we can judge, has hailed our imperfect efforts with enthusiasm, & so has the great British race throughout the world.'[124]

At this juncture came Salisbury's most notorious 'blazing indiscretion' at St James's Hall, a fitting companion-piece to Churchill's Ulster indiscretion. Salisbury, dabbling indiscreetly in amateur anthropology, implied the relevance to Ireland of consideration of the eligibility of

Hottentots for self-government. The Irish, as racist as anyone else in those racist times, were rabid with offence; particularly as Salisbury barged on to advocate Irish emigration to Manitoba as preferable to expensive schemes of tenant purchase, and to proclaim that what Ireland needed was not Home Rule but twenty years of resolute government.[125] Gladstone was shocked. 'Salisbury's speech!!' This stiffened Gladstone wonderfully. He brushed aside Heneage's insistence that, with the Land Bill dead, it was necessary to withdraw the Government Bill; and that in the gap thus created some of the useful measures promulgated in the Midlothian campaign might be proceeded with. Gladstone conferred on the 18th with John Morley and Parnell – 'who is very noteworthy in conversation'. 'Most satisfactory man,' he remarked to Morley as Parnell departed. What appears to have been most satisfactory about Parnell was that he would have no truck with concessions to the bill's candid friends. The upshot was that Gladstone would 'stick to his guns' and neither withdraw, postpone, or proceed by resolution on the principle. Morley recorded: 'Mr G. has not been well all day – and P. told me afterwards that he had not realised how old Mr G. was: the light came full strength on his face from the large window, but his eye was undimmed.'[126]

With undimmed eye Gladstone crushed the persistent Pease, who had reiterated his feeling as to the *'intense'* desire of a great many Liberal MPs to avoid 'an entire break-up of the party' ('the disintegration would be as terrible as it would be complete') and who presumed to dispute the view hinted at by Gladstone that an appeal to the country would be successful.[127] 'A Government', Gladstone admonished Pease, 'cannot afford to degrade itself by the confession of errors it has not committed.' Were ministers to 'turn tail', they would suffer Disraeli's fate in the deplorable case of the India Bill of 1858, 'laughed & mocked out of court'. As to the coming in of the Tories, 'that would be the certain & early triumph of the policy'. If the bill was essentially bad, and the government could not see this, it was not fit to frame a good one; if its bill was essentially good, but defective in some particulars, the place for amendment was in the committee stage. Gladstone was at his most crushing in his dismissal of Pease's doubts about the healing powers of a general election. 'As regards the country, you will excuse me if (without pretending anything like certainty) I in contemplating my *fourteenth* Dissolution – if that is to be the issue – am more confident than I should be.'[128]

Arnold Morley and Schnadhorst ('reputed arch-wirepuller') had in fact consulted with Gladstone on 19 May on the question of a possible dissolution. Schnadhorst did not doubt the preferability of an immediate appeal if the second reading were lost. Though not without risk, it would be preferable to 'showing the white feather'. Gladstone cordially concurred. It appealed, as Hamilton observed, to his 'natural pluck' and partiality to a 'bold front'. The managers calculated that the Irish vote would affect some thirty or even possibly forty seats. Schnadhorst believed in Gladstone's 'ability to carry the country with him'.[129] Gladstone was full of analogies with the defeat of the Reform Bill in 1866, and of the mistake then made of not boldly taking the question to the country. 'Herein lies the root of the position he has taken up,' noted Hamilton. 'It is for him to settle the Irish difficulty or to put it in train for being settled, he has not time at all to lose. This is how the question has come to have been so "rushed".' To Hamilton's arguments about the dangers of a dissolution Gladstone demurred. His next resignation must be more than a resignation from office. 'The hour that has next to strike for me is not the first but the last upon the dial.'[130]

Nor, with such a dissolution in prospect, was Gladstone at all apologetic to those Liberals, like Hutton of the *Spectator*, who deplored Gladstone's recourse in his manifesto of 1 May to the rhetoric of class. Gladstone rejoined in characteristic mode.

I *do* think the common ruck of your 'Unionists' from Dukes downwards are warped by the spirit of class, but that few comparatively are aware of it, & a few consequently compromise their integrity. So, among the opponents of Peel in 1846, there were some of the best men I ever knew. And the average were men worthy of respect. Am I warped by the spirit of anti-class? Perhaps – I cannot tell. My dislike of class feeling gets slowly more & more accentuated: & my case is particularly hard & irksome, because I am a thoroughgoing inequalitarian.[131]

It was on that day that Sir Donald Currie informed Gladstone regretfully that he could not agree with the Home Rule policy. And it was on that day also that Gladstone's other provider of seaborne relaxation, Sir Thomas Brassey, associated with Whitbread, Maguire, Pease and others, made a supreme effort to convince Gladstone of his party's 'one universal and anxious desire to avoid defeat on the second reading'. Hartington, timing his stroke well, had made a great impression with his assault on the Home Rule and Land Bills on 18 May. Brassey pleaded that with Gladstone 'things may be done which would be impossible for any other statesman'. Would it not be best for the promotion of the cause in the longer term to drop the Home Rule Bill, and replace it with an Irish Local Government measure acceptable to the party? 'Could it not be done by you without discredit?'[132]

[6]

Pressures were now too insistent even for Gladstone to resist longer the expedient – for him, truly desperate – of a party meeting. It was summoned for 27 May at the spacious Foreign Office. Invitations were confined to those Liberal MPs sympathetic to the principle of the Home Rule Bill; among whom specifically not included was Chamberlain. On the 26th Gladstone 'prepared materials for a statement of importance & of extreme delicacy tomorrow'. The Cabinet's view was now that the bill could not be proceeded with without an autumn session and 'necessary amendments' once the second reading was passed. A meeting of the Liberal party was looked upon by Parnell as much as by Gladstone as a dangerous recourse. Gladstone's procedure thus far, first of a prudent 'reserve', then of a 'mighty heave' and leverage of heroic statesmanship with the Liberal party as instrumental fulcrum, was not at all what Parnell would initially have advised. He and his party were now in fact vindicated in their deprecation of risky haste. But still, he had to take things as he found them. If Gladstone could pull it off, all would be well that ended well. But Parnell was not pleased at the possibility of being asked to settle for less than what Gladstone had initially and generously offered.

Parnell's refractoriness disconcerted Gladstone. 'That is a nice morsel you have brought me,' he grumbled to John Morley. Parnell now was talking loudly of not voting for the second reading. If anything, this cheered Gladstone's party. The Foreign Office gathering was attended by some 260 Liberal MPs. Gladstone's line was to refuse a vote there and then on the principle of a legislative body in Dublin for the conduct of Irish affairs, but to agree that the second reading would be treated as a vote on the principle with particulars such as Irish representation to be attended to later. Members would not be bound to support the Land Purchase Bill, which in effect was consigned to oblivion. The main issue was whether to keep the Home Rule Bill alive after passing the second reading and proceed with it in the autumn, or wind up the session and summon Parliament for a new session when the bill could be reintroduced with necessary amendments. Gladstone preferred the latter course, which was agreed to.[133]

'The meeting went off well enough,' Gladstone recorded ' – but I don't believe in these tactics.' He immediately set about making distinctions, which a later commentator at All Souls College, Oxford, attempted to unravel.

Mr Gladstone afterwards contended that his proposal was not in the nature of an abstract resolution, because those who voted for the second reading would be committed – not only to the 'principle' as previously defined, but to the general outline of the plan. But he was precluded from using this argument by his own declaration.

In the first place, Mr Gladstone had made a concession which involved (as Lord Hartington pointed out) not a mere change of detail but a complete recasting of the Bill. There was therefore, no plan, or even outline of a plan, before the House.

In the second place, Mr Gladstone had undertaken to withdraw the Bill if it passed the second reading. When a Bill is withdrawn, it is plain that nobody stands committed either to its principles or to its details. In the passage at arms between Lord R. Churchill and Mr Gladstone (reported 3 Hans, cccvi, 336) it seems to me that Lord Randolph, for once, had much the best of it . . . It is the business of party leaders to capture votes if they can. I know . . . Mr Gladstone honestly believed in his plan, and in the possibility of modifying without destroying it. He took his stand on an abstract formula, not intentionally, but instinctively, because he felt that it was the best ground to fight on. And so it is.[134]

The Foreign Office rally of sympathizers was answered by a meeting of dissentients on 31 May, summoned by Chamberlain to Committee Room 15 in the Palace of Westminster.* Chamberlain's position was much strengthened by Gladstone's denial in the Commons on the 29th that he had undertaken to remodel the bill: 'Never, never, never,' he exclaimed to the delighted Hicks Beach. This greatly disconcerted many attenders at the Foreign Office, who had understood Gladstone to allow precisely for that. More than ever, Gladstone's indefatigable twists and turns to avoid departing from his own text were reminiscent of the distressing sessions of 1866 and 1867. 'Great dismay in our camp', Gladstone recorded, 'on the report of Chamberlain's meeting.' Fifty-two representatives of Hartingtondom and Chamberlaindom attended, though not Hartington personally. Trevelyan spoke trenchantly to the effect that if Gladstone's Home Rule Bill were not positively opposed 'we should stand before the world as the most dishonest and cowardly party in the House of Commons by voting for a Bill of which we disapproved'. The dramatic climax to the occasion was Chamberlain's reading a letter from Bright at Rochdale announcing his intention of voting against the second reading, 'if Mr Gladstone is unwise enough to venture on it'. Bright was willing enough for dissentients to abstain if this would result in a small majority for Gladstone. That would be '*almost*' as good as defeat, and it might have the advantage of avoiding

* G. M. Trevelyan remarked on the room as 'a place of evil omen for the unity of parties'.[135]

a dissolution, instead of compelling one.[136] Thirteen votes only were for abstention, and thirty-one for voting against the second reading. Three only favoured voting for the second reading. On the main question there were forty-five votes for positively voting against the second reading.

Bright's letter was, in John Morley's phrase, the 'death warrant' of Gladstone's Home Rule Bill. Gladstone took a certain relish in what was to come imminently as a prelude to what he would bring about by way of retribution in the fullness of time. 'I think with great comfort', he said to Rosebery, 'of the fact that in all human probability all connection between Chamberlain and myself is over for ever.'[137] Throughout the critical debates of April and May Gladstone had kept up his sprightly touch in public, presenting an assured conviviality as his *métier*: 'full of talk', 'very pleasant', 'full of Eton and flogging', 'never saw him more at his ease', 'in high glee'. Gladstone was always known as one who demarcated strictly between his public and private lives.[138] Early in June, a few days before the fateful division, Hamilton observed him 'in great form and spirits, notwithstanding all his anxieties and troubles. Nothing seems to weigh him down.'[139] On the 4th Gladstone admitted to Childers that the '*odds* are still I imagine in favour of the rejection of the Bill – In that case our *main* subject of discussion will of course be a Dissolution or a resignation – though it is just possible there may be other alternatives.' Possibly Gladstone envisaged a further vote of confidence on some understanding of substantial concession. On the morning of the division, 7 June, a letter from Lecky was published in *The Times* calling attention to Gladstone's remoteness from public opinion over Home Rule. 'It is, I believe, perfectly notorious that if it had not been proposed by Mr Gladstone there are not fifty English members of Parliament who would vote for it.'

'At last came the Old Man's speech, as vigorous as ever and in beautiful voice, but it was a losing speech.'[140] For the first time in public Gladstone burst out with his denunciation of the 'dreadful story of the Union' of 1800, 'unfolded in all its hideous features', which so offended Lecky's patriotic but scholarly historical conscience. Gladstone's appeal to the House was that the vote to be taken was to be on the 'principle of the Bill as distinguished from the particulars of the Bill'. He insisted characteristically that there was a great distinction between promising that a bill was not to be reconstructed and not promising that it would be reconstructed. He condemned Chamberlain for resigning before ever seeing the whole bill.

His more effective eloquence was to assert that 'this is one of the golden moments of our history – one of those opportunities which may come and may go, but which rarely return, or, if they do, return at long intervals, and under circumstances which no man can forecast'. He digressed on what he saw as Ireland's previous golden moment, the abortive mission of Lord Fitzwilliam in 1795, when the cup of emancipation and reform was dashed from Ireland's lips. 'The long periodic time has at last run out, and the star has again mounted into the heavens. What Ireland was doing for herself in 1795 we at length have done.' The forces opposed to this golden endeavour were the forces of 'class and its dependants; and that as a general description – as a slight and rude outline of a description – is, I believe, perfectly true'. 'You have power, you have wealth, you have rank, you have station, you have organization. What have we? We think we have the people's heart; we believe and we know we have the promise of the future.' On behalf of the people, Gladstone and his friends hailed Ireland's demand 'for what I call a blessed oblivion of the past. She asks also a boon for the future, and that boon . . . will be borne to us in respect of honour, no less than a boon to her in respect of happiness, prosperity, and peace. Such, Sir, is her prayer. Think, I beseech you, think well, think wisely, think, not for the moment, but for the years to come, before you reject this Bill.'[141]

The magic did not work. There were many, especially perhaps among the Irish, who felt that if a golden moment was being missed, it was being missed because of the combination of Gladstone's wilful haste and imperial style. The fateful legacy of the 1885 elections hung over the Commons in the last days of the Parliament then created. If Gladstone had only got the commanding majority he had asked for at Midlothian, he need not have concocted the drama of violent Irish revolution to justify his going ahead regardless of having failed to get the majority he had stipulated for as 'a matter of absolute necessity'.*

The Government of Ireland Bill was defeated on its second reading by 341 to 311 votes: the largest division thus far recorded in the lobbies. Only thirteen MPs (including, curiously, Captain O'Shea) were absent. The missing Liberal votes of 27 January had now reappeared, with devastating impact on Gladstone's fortunes. 'We are heavily beaten on the 2nd Reading . . . a scene of some excitement . . . one or two Irishmen† lost their balance.' Gladstone put the best face he could on the matter. 'Upon the whole we have more ground to be satisfied with the progress made, than to be disappointed at the failure. But it is a serious mischief. Spoke very long: my poor voice came in a wonderful manner.' The Dowager Lady Russell, relict of an illustrious name in the making of Liberalism, consoled Gladstone with the thought that 'some defeats are grander than victories'.[142]

A cabinet on 8 June decided on a dissolution *nem. con.* Wolverton and

---

* See above, page 386.
† Notably Healy and O'Connor.

Schnadhorst both recommended it decidedly. Gladstone was 'entirely composed though pallid'. He thought 'dissolution is formidable, but resignation would mean for the present juncture abandonment of the cause'.[143] Gladstone had doubts about an immediate dissolution, believing there would be problems about arrangements and candidates, given the split in the party. But Schnadhorst's 'unhesitatingly' preferring an election the sooner the better swayed opinion and Gladstone did not resist. Great hopes were confided in the Irish voters who assumably could give the Liberal party back its lost majority of 1885. Gladstone was perfectly assured that there was no question of 'apathy' among the people which had been raised in 1866 to justify resignation. Gladstone, 'excellently well and full of go', proceeded thereupon to advise the Queen to proclaim what he was later to describe as a 'people's dissolution' for a 'people's election'.

CHAPTER 12

'NOW BEGINS THE GREAT STRUGGLE': APPEAL AGAINST THE VERDICT, 1886–90

[1]

At Downing Street Gladstone prepared to make his progress to Edinburgh. The mood was revivalist: revival of the spirit of 1880, revival of the positive cause of 1868. It had been want of that latter which had stultified the promise of 1885. Now all the elements were in place. The power of the people would, Gladstone trusted, give him the means of repairing the omissions and derelictions of Parliament. Thus far they, and he, had come since his first, tentative, essay in the genre of summoning the nation against its recalcitrant representatives back in the Easter recess of 1866, in Liverpool.*

Taking the whole perspective of Gladstone's career, this has the best claims to figure as the supreme moment. 'I am now arrived at the last of the series', as Gladstone put it; for more than twenty years he had been possessed of the idea that the 'object of the highest prize' was to 'complete the list'.[1] Ireland alone remained on that list. 'The first two were the Church and the colonies. Freedom of trade the third. The discussion upon finance, the fourth. Then came the emancipation of the subject races the fifth.'[2] 'Series' was ever one of Gladstone's keywords. He defined his 'vocation' in 1863 as a 'series of efforts'.[3] Well-defined traits of consistency, characteristic and recurring features, an inner logic, a sense of structural pattern: these emerge as the salient decipherments of what Gladstone called the 'argument of *design*'. 'Design' is another fundamental Gladstonian keyword. It linked two crucial points: Gladstone's awareness of what he called his own 'proper and peculiar exercise' in correctly decoding that higher natural theology 'which reads and applies to practice *design* in all forms of incident that beset and accompany our daily course', with his sense of a reciprocal design in the natural theology of the political world, as set forth for him by Bishop Butler's doctrine of deducing a moral politics within a Christian providential

---

* See above, page 17.

scheme, 'an argument for religion at large, drawn from the course of natural government at large'.[4]

At that moment in June 1886 nothing would have been more evident to Gladstone than that the series and the design were culminatingly interlocked. 'In the battle of good and evil, Providence, though it may seem to be fighting in disguise, chooses its side and makes known its choice.'[5] Gladstone was utterly imbued with the conviction that no one could or ought to be more deeply penetrated than he with consciousness that there is a Providence shaping our ends, rough-hew them how we may. 'The whole of my public and esoteric life has been shaped as to its ends for me, scarcely rough-hewn by me.'[6] In 1887 he pronounced, apropos of rough-hewing, that history, 'complex and diversified as it is, and presenting to our view many a ganglion of unpenetrated and perhaps impenetrable enigmas, is not a mere congeries of disjointed occurrences, but is the evolution of a purpose steadfastly maintained, and advancing towards some consummation', the consummation of the 'Christian scheme'.[7] And it was in the 'precinct of Christendom' that the 'actual mastery of the world' was to be found, where all existed 'in the main by its permission, or under its control'.*

In summoning the nation to his aid Gladstone, masterful within the precinct of Christianity, would put to the proof his conviction that, just as his determination to implement Home Rule – as Catherine herself put it, 'a duty owed by man to God'[8] – so the people, uncontaminated by the derogations of class, must 'feel the issue of the moment as part of the eternal duel between good and evil', and take their stand accordingly in that 'conflict between virtue and vice, which incessantly prevails in the world'.[9] Gladstone called the Queen's attention to one of the 'new elements' in the case, 'the popular enthusiasm of the liberal masses which he had never seen equalled'. Against that enthusiasm would be arrayed anti-Irish prejudice, the power of rank, station, and wealth, and the influence of the established clergy.[10] Gladstone tactfully refrained, as one having no skill in such matters, from any forecast of the likely result of the contest between these forces. Chamberlain himself was shaken by the seeming 'universality and completeness' both of the passionate devotion of the British democracy to the prime minister and of the sentiment 'out of doors', 'which, I dare say, has taken many of us by surprise, in favour of some sort of home rule to Ireland'.[11] This was the supreme moment of Max Weber's insight about Gladstone's 'completely personal charisma' challenging the 'everyday power of the party as a continuing enterprise'.[12]

---

* See above, page 425.

[2]

On the eve of departure for the great struggle came a word of cheer from the daughter of one of the Scottish Liberal members, Sir Charles Tennant. 'I wish you à Dieu & well through the time that lies in weariness & complication before you,' wrote Margot Tennant. 'Monday night was a noble effort only heightened by the majority against you.'[13] In truth, the majority against her father at Peebles and Selkirk in a few weeks' time would put an end to his political career, and help to usher in a time of weariness and complication for Gladstone unimagined as he set out from St Pancras station, accompanied by Catherine and Willy, on the now familiar way to Dalmeny, on 15 June. The 1885 Parliament was dissolved on the 26th, and elections were to get under way from 1 July.

Through England and Scotland there were 'wonderful demonstrations all along the road' and 'many little speeches' that 'could not be helped'. At Edinburgh on 18 June Gladstone proclaimed his 'doings and intentions'. He put to the test Salisbury's recent pronouncement on Ireland's great present need being not self-government but imperial government applied resolutely for twenty years to make Ireland fit for self-government. 'Again God gave me a voice according to the need.' At the Music Hall Gladstone declared the case to be that of a 'people's dissolution' and a 'people's election'. It was to be, like Inkerman in the Crimea, a soldiers' battle. The officer class of politics had failed in their duty to give the right lead. Thus was the logic of the Liverpool incitement of April 1866 fulfilled. As to Lord Salisbury in particular, Gladstone invited his audience to 'reflect in the name of Almighty God in the sanctuary of the chamber, in the sanctuary of your heart and Soul', what it was, in that year of 1886, after nearly a century of continual coercion, to propose such a remedy 'as an alternative to the policy of local government for Ireland!' He invited the people to join him 'in that happy, I may almost say that Holy, effort'.[14]

There were protests against the blasphemy of public invocation of the Almighty for partisan purposes. One of the protesters, Lord Randolph Churchill, added to denunciation of 'audacious profanity' the notorious comment about Gladstone's frenetic proceedings: 'an old man in a hurry'.[15] As he was fêted at Midlothian the indomitable old man was at the centre of 'a crush which was trying & might have been dangerous': quite in the spirit and manner of 1880, the 'whole scene a triumph'. As in 1880, the Nonconformists were, it could be assumed, as a body, sound. Gladstone had Guinness Rogers's word for it that in spite of Spurgeon's going the wrong way, 'happily his political influence is in reverse ratio to his spiritual & religious force'.[16] On 22 June Gladstone (unopposed for Midlothian) departed for Hawarden, via Glasgow, Manchester, and Liverpool. Already the Queen was 'expostulating' about his being a 'universal agitator'. As Gladstone was unapologetic about invoking God, so he was unapologetic for his invocation of the masses. To Sir Thomas Acland, who had remonstrated, Gladstone responded: 'I am not ready to say *peccavi* about Class, and to say the truth I do not quite understand your objection.'[17] To Hengler's Circus in Liverpool, on the 28th, Gladstone 'went in bitterness, in the heat of the spirit: but the hand of the Lord was strong on me'. That hand had Gladstone declare: 'All the world over, I will back the masses against the classes.'*

'Now begins the great struggle,' Gladstone supplicated as polling began on 1 July. 'Govern it O most High.' At Hawarden Gladstone had a great many 'grave letters & messages to write'. Mary's new independent matrimonial status left her father at a loss for secretarial assistance (his official secretariat of course could not be involved in party political matters). Helen was summoned from Cambridge, conveniently in vacation. She proved 'a capital worker'. ('Indeed I have tried almost all my children, & never met with a failure.') Helen's misfortune was that it was precisely at this juncture that the call came to take up the principalship of Holloway College in London. She found the prospect of taking over from Mary 'rather grim'. She wanted to be a dutiful daughter, but not at the cost of exchanging the freedom of the academic world for 'home duties'. She got no support from Catherine, who had always rather disapproved of female intellectual ambitions at places such as Newnham. Gladstone reported to Catherine that Helen was being 'intensely sensible about Holloway College': that is to say, accepting the higher call of her obligations to the 'Grand Old Couple' in conformity with the patriarchal manners of the time.[18]† It was Willy, rather, who was the domestic problem. He remained firm in his opinion 'that Home Rule was not the thing Ireland required & was not necessary for clearing the honour of England'. Gladstone still hoped that Willy might be induced to stand again to save appearances, but ruled out the moral coercion applicable to daughters ('we do not try to force'; he 'could only have been forced, and this I will never do').[20]

In her personal misfortune Helen entered into a dire inheritance of her father's misfortunes. The elections soon revealed themselves as a

---

* This saying, like Churchill's, made its way into the *Oxford Dictionary of Quotations*.
† A Newnham contemporary on Helen: 'One could not be ten minutes in her company without knowing that he *was* her father. Indeed I think one of the things that kept her such an "unmarried" person was her ingrained attitude as daughter.' Crosby draws attention to the fact that the Gladstone sons were all late or latish marriers: Willy at thirty-five, Harry at thirty-eight, Stephen at forty-one, and Herbert (after his father's death) at forty-seven.[19]

disaster. A great many constituencies (217) were uncontested, unsurprisingly, given that the 1885 elections were hardly more than six months since. Something of the order of 1,700,000 fewer votes were cast in 1886 compared with 1885. Conservatives and Liberal Unionists struck a bargain to avoid splitting the Unionist vote. Gladstone enquired of Arnold Morley his 'present anticipations – in what direction they move – & what does Schnadhorst say?'[21] The managers were nonplussed by the English electorate, where the Conservative and Unionist Liberals enjoyed the benefits of the larger number of non-contested returns. And, as Gladstone himself observed, the agricultural-labourer vote, which had done such execution against the Conservatives in the counties in 1885, found the Irish case rather baffling. 'Poor Hodge, another of our allies, I fear may lose heart.'[22] Many Liberal candidates had no answer to the accusation that 'after accepting office in 1886 on Mr Jesse Collings's amendment . . . Mr Gladstone threw aside the interests of the English agricultural labourer and insisted on forcing Irish affairs to the front'.[23] Still, the 'experts', as Gladstone called them, 'while admitting the difficulties of the case, were all of opinion that we should at least sensibly mend our position'.[24] But Henry Primrose reported Schnadhorst as taking a 'gloomy view' of the polls as early as 2 July. Clearly he had overestimated the benefits to be had from the Parnellite vote in Britain; and 'holding our own' and 'avoiding defeat looked the best to be hoped'.[25]

The most damaging blow struck at Gladstone was by Bright, who up until the opening of polling had been silent in public. Bright had told Whitbread that if Gladstone dissolved the Parliament, he 'would be responsible for the greatest wound the Party has received since it was a Party'.[26] Every word in his unforgiving Birmingham speech, in John Morley's phrase, 'seemed to weigh a pound'.[27] The gravamen of his accusation was that Gladstone had deceived the electorate in 1885 by concealing his conversion to Home Rule. To this imputation that he had disguised his wolfish intentions in the sheep-like garb of 'local government' Gladstone reacted with a vigour tinged with bitterness at what he felt was a foul blow.[28] In the first place, as was made clear in his Edinburgh speech of 18 June, he deliberately used the 'policy for local government for Ireland' as synonymous with 'Home Rule for Ireland'. But this was open to attack as weasel usage: if the shoe fitted, by all means wear it. Gladstone's substantial defence was that, ever since 1871 in Aberdeen, he had stipulated precisely the restrictions and limitations to be applied to Irish self-government with respect to the sovereignty of the Crown, the integrity of the Empire, and the supremacy of the Westminster Parliament, which he was stipulating still. This did not get around the weaknesses of his case: the *Disciplina Arcani*, his specific assurances at Edinburgh in 1885 on the absolute necessity of an overall Liberal majority and then, nonetheless, the startling emergence of an Irish legislature which would replace Irish representation at Westminster. No amount of pointing even to the undoubted fact that his Edinburgh speech of 9 November 1885 was positively dripping with heavy hints about an Irish definition of Home Rule availed; nor even his assurance that it was 'the will of Providence that these islands should be united together in a United Kingdom'.[29] The paths of Home Rule were proving very slippery indeed.

Bright's blow struck a responsive chord in the British public mind. The general election of 1886 was a most intensely and unforgivingly fought contest. Anti-Catholic prejudice, stimulated by the very effective 'Home Rule means Rome Rule' jingle, flared up. The 'slumbering genius of Empire' also was awoken. Memories of Gordon at Khartoum mingled with Ulster's war-cry of 'No Surrender'. Thorold Rogers explained his defeat in Bermondsey as due to 'abstentions'. Between 500 and 1,000 of his old supporters stood aloof. The Tory vote was no stronger than 1885. This aloofness was due to two causes. 'First the electors cannot as yet understand what they deem is an entire change of front.' Secondly, 'the silent vote of Bright and much more his speech uttered when it could not authoritatively be answered were most damaging'. 'People said how can a scheme be sound which this radical of radicals and lifelong tribune of the people denounces as unsound, dangerous and uncertain.'[30] As the days passed, evidences accumulated analogous to Bermondsey. On 3 July eighty-eight Conservatives were returned as against twenty-seven Gladstonian Liberals. Gladstone wrote to Catherine that day that he thought the chances 'slightly against us'. By the 4th, 'the storm is upon us'. By the 6th: 'The Elections perturb me somewhat: but One ever sitteth above.'

Perturbation provoked much wild flailing of telegrams showering forth from Hawarden which Helen was powerless to stem. 'If Warwickshire does not wish Dukes & Earls to overrule the nation & wreck its fortunes,' he informed the Liberals of Rugby in a typical specimen, 'she will return the Liberal candidate not Tories nor seceders who are working with & for the Tories.'[31] H. P. Cobb, a champion of the 'cause of justice peace & true union with Ireland', duly defeated his Liberal Unionist opponent. Not so was the case of George Leveson Gower for his Staffordshire division; which incited Gladstone into protestations of amazement 'at the deadness of vulgar opinion to the blackguardism and baseness (no words are strong enough) which befoul the whole history of the Union'. If the folly lasted, Gladstone feared it might well 'in the end contribute to Repeal'. He advised Leveson Gower 'to take resolutely to the study of Irish history.'[32] By this stage Primrose and Herbert had studied the returns and glumly prognosticated a House in which 197 Gladstonians and eighty-five Irish would be confronted by no less than

315 Conservatives and seventy-two Unionist Liberals.[33]* Pease had been right: the break-up of the Liberal party would not be healed by a general election.

Holmes Ivory, the Edinburgh Liberal Chairman, desponded that the reports from the English boroughs and counties were 'heartrending'. It was a case of 'Scotland, Wales & Ireland against the prejudices & slow power of understanding political truth & justice of England & above all of London'.[34] More prosaically, the Conservatives were holding their borough gains in England of 1885, and recovering the counties with the collapse of the agricultural labour vote. Beneath and behind Liberal voter bewilderment at Gladstone's seeming 'entire change of front' and Liberal party resentment at being relegated to a merely instrumental function, the consequences of the new pattern of social influences on politics which the electoral revolution of 1883, 1884, and 1885 had institutionalized continued blindly and steadily to realize themselves. It was less a matter of failing to understand political truth and justice than it was the end of the era in which Gladstone had flourished as the manipulator of opinion engendered by his doings and intentions, and in which, accordingly, the Liberal party had ceased to be the recipient of the nation's 'habitual assent'.

'The defeat is a smash,' Gladstone recorded on 8 July. The supreme moment had metamorphosed into a grotesque parody. 'I accept the will of God for my poor country or the English part of it. To me personally it is a great relief: including the cessation of my painful relations with the Queen, who will have a like feeling.' The remedy was obvious. 'The people do not know the case.' The 'whole iniquities of the Union', he insisted to Bryce, must be 'laid bare and become common property'. After all, as Gladstone had it, Corn Law repeal 'was neither (generally) cared about or understood till Cobden illuminated it with his admirable intellect, Bright putting in the passion'.[35] To Kitson, the Leeds notable, Gladstone put on a brave front.

We have Scotland, Wales, Ireland, Yorkshire & I hope the North: & we have with us the civilized world.†[36] From this cause it is probable that our cause will visibly move upwards. It has indeed enormously moved upwards within

---

* The final figures were: 193 Gladstonian Liberals, 76 Liberal Unionists, 316 Conservatives, 85 Irish Nationalists.

† There was indeed massive evidence of support for Gladstone from the self-governing colonies and the USA. It was something of an embarrassment that Döllinger and his fellow German anti-ultramontanes were unwilling to countenance Irish Home Rule because of their dislike of the temper of Irish Roman Catholicism. Ironically, much of the Liberal Catholic opinion in Italy which Gladstone had celebrated in his 'Italy and Her Church' piece was of the same opinion.

the last twelve months. Its final triumph is certain. The only question is how much there will be of unhappiness for Ireland, of difficulty & delay, of pain & shame for England before the consummation will be reached.[37]

To John Morley he put the case that 'the more complete our smash now, the more bitter the humiliation England, & England alone of the four, will have to go through'.[38]

The shock of the catastrophe left its mark on Gladstone. He found it difficult quite to reconcile himself to the enormity of what had happened. 'Everybody will be puzzled,' he insisted to John Morley, 'no one happy.'[39] If he was puzzled and unhappy at the manner in which the Most High had governed the affair, how could others feel differently? In this querulous mood he was prone to grasp at consoling rumours, such as Thorold Rogers's account of a 'secret but carefully planned conspiracy' by which Chamberlain in collusion with Randolph Churchill had for the past year aimed at displacing Gladstone from the leadership.[40] There were more urgent problems. Should the government resign at once? Should they meet the new Parliament? Would Morley kindly 'ascertain from Parnell what he has to suggest'? Even now Gladstone was reluctant to loosen his grip on the levers. There was the conceivability of remaining on until an autumn session. The National Liberal Federation people wanted this as a means of forcing the 'so-called Liberal Unionists' to 'define their position'.[41] Gladstone was tempted. 'If this last be within the compass of possibility I am inclined ... to say the best mode of proceeding *then* wd be by resolution.'[42]

Perhaps this was merely an evanescently desperate mood. In any case Gladstone's colleagues steered him gently back towards the inevitability of summary resignation. It was proper that the opponents of Home Rule should be obliged to undertake the responsibility of governing Ireland as soon as possible. It was not until near the end of July that the final official returns came in. The Queen was awkward about resignation honours so soon after the 1885 batch ('She has different measures, I fear, for different parties'). Granville in any case declined a proffered marquessate. Victoria found Gladstone 'pale and nervous' at his closing audience on 30 July. He found the Queen in good spirits; 'her manner altogether pleasant. She made me sit at once.' Her single remark about him personally was that he would require some rest. She carefully avoided all political and controversial matters. 'On the following day she wrote a letter, making it evident, so far as Ireland was concerned, she could not trust herself to say what she wanted to say.'[43]*

---

* She had said to her granddaughter, Princess Victoria of Hesse, 'I really think he is cracked.'[44]

One of Eddie Hamilton's last services before his official relationship with Gladstone ended was to combine with Malcolm MacColl and W. T. Stead to warn Gladstone that his reputation for 'nocturnal activities' had had a 'baneful effect' in the London constituencies, and that a plot was afoot to blacken his character. There had been an incident during the 1885 elections when Lady Sheffield, wife of Sir Robert Sheffield, Bt, of Normanby, accused Gladstone of being a 'common whoremonger'.[45] Hamilton begged Gladstone to consider the risks; and Gladstone promised to restrict his interest to a couple of cases he wanted to pursue further.[46]* Hamilton commented that 'if proof were wanted of his innocence, it would be found in the candour of his note'. Somehow, in the stress of it all, it seemed to Gladstone appropriate that he should see out his third ministry with a visit to Mrs Thistlethwayte. 'I told her how glad I should be if I could be able to feel that I had been of the smallest use to her in any particular.'[47]

[3]

Aside from the exigencies of extricating himself from office, two things occupied Gladstone's mind. One was the prospective question of rebuilding the Liberal party's unity. Now that a Conservative administration with a robustly coercive policy for Ireland had come to office, it might reasonably be assumed that many Liberals who could not stomach Home Rule would now find it equally difficult to stomach 'resolute government'. But for Gladstone this prospect had dangers as well as benefits. It was clear that many Liberal dissentients had in view the replacing of the 1886 Home Rule measure with something much more akin to Chamberlain's scheme. Gladstone would have none of it. As James Knowles of the *Nineteenth Century* remarked of Gladstone, 'While he was personally so absolutely modest and diffident, he was "officially" entirely the reverse. No pope, indeed, was ever more infallibly certain and immovable than Mr Gladstone when once he had become convinced that such or such a course was right and true. It was then "borne in upon him" as a duty.'[49] On 12 July he drew up his opinion. 'Could we hope to remodel our measure, this might be ground for an endeavour to make up a majority through a union of Liberals, Seceders, & Nationalists. I, however, though I might suggest some amendments, do not at all see

---

* Gladstone would not have much cared for Stead's part in the matter. By now he detested him: 'That man has done more harm to Journalism than any other individual ever known.'[48]

my way to remodelling the Bill, or presenting a new Bill.'[50] In due course, Gladstone would go so far as to lay it down that 'to propose any measure, except such as Ireland could approve on the lines already laid down, would be fatuity as regards myself, and treachery to the Irish nation'.[51]

This rather menacing note had immediate implications for the leadership; which was the second matter on Gladstone's mind. If Gladstone wished to continue, the party would have to accept his leadership and the 1886 Home Rule Bill en bloc. Gladstone did wish to continue. He was not the man to fade away in the discredit of defeat. His life thus far was as a fighter and a winner. But he would continue on his own terms. As Hamilton remarked: 'What are Land Laws and County Government to him?'[52] Gladstone put the matter to Herbert, his general disseminator and soundboard.

Another turn of the wheel has placed us on the underside; but the turning has not ended, only begun. We, the promoters of Home Rule, continue in the certitude of our belief that the measure will and must pass. But I cannot find on the part of the opponents any corresponding certitude that it will not. They are waiting upon Providence, or upon what people take to be synonymous, the chapter of accidents; living from hand to mouth, united in objecting to what we propose, and united in nothing else . . . The general outlook is of an uncertain, uneasy, changeful time, until a settlement of the Irish question is reached; and that settlement can only be real by Home Rule, or partial and temporary by some strong coercion, which it will be difficult perhaps impossible to pass, and quite impossible to maintain for any length of time.

As to myself personally, the element of old age renders all these matters extremely perplexing. What I think possible is that, if such an arrangement be cordially accepted by my friends and colleagues, I should obtain a dispensation from ordinary and habitual attendance in parliament, but should not lay down the leadership so as to force them to choose another leader, and would take an active part when occasion seemed to require it, especially on the Irish question. The proper policy for the Liberals, put out of the government, will be to promote freely and actively Liberal legislation generally in cooperation with the Dissentients, so as to allow the party to re-form itself.[53]

A cabinet on 20 July accepted these terms ('if so deemed advisable'). It was a case of between the devil and the deep sea, with no way out; the ultimately absurdly logical irresolution, in its way blackly comic, of the innocent notions of 1880 and 1881; and 'all applauded'.

Salisbury's minority Conservative ministry presented itself in August to a short session of the new Parliament in order to complete necessary public business. Hartington raised the issue as to seating arrangements for his Unionist section. Gladstone declared that, for his own part, he 'earnestly' desired, subject to the paramount exigencies of the Irish question, 'to promote in every way the reunion of the Liberal party'.[54] Long before, he had urged Hartington 'not to encourage talk of a coalition with the Conservatives'. Coalitions were always unpopular, and seldom lasted long, and 'union with the Conservatives must mean extinction for the Whig party'.[55] The Liberal Unionists sat together with their Gladstonian confrères on the Opposition benches, much in the manner of the Peelites consorting with Disraeli during Russell's Whig ministry of 1846–52.* To Harcourt, who led the way among his colleagues for moves to reunion, Gladstone was studious to establish that his definition of what 'Ireland' involved took priority; which pill he sugared with the old threatening promise that, after all, he could always retire from the lead. 'As in the case of Ireland, so in the matter of reunion, I am above all things determined not to be personally an obstacle in the way of what is good.'[56]

As for the session itself, Gladstone made a point of endorsing Salisbury's foreign policy, with special reference to the unity and freedom of the Bulgarian people, envisaging even 'something like a continuity in the foreign policy of the country'.[57]† But on Ireland he gave unapologetic notice that Home Rule as he had defined it remained entire and intact. Nothing that had happened 'had produced the slightest change in my convictions with regard to the basis of that policy'; he could not afford 'the slightest encouragement or the smallest ground' for any suppositions to the contrary. All that had happened, 'instead of weakening, has confirmed me in my strong belief that we did not err in the main principles of the measures we recommended to this House'. Gladstone denied that the late election result had about it anything of an 'irrevocable' verdict of the country.[58]

What Gladstone did do, however, by way of quasi-apology, was to issue, on that day, 19 August, an elaborate pamphlet, *The Irish Question. I, The History of an Idea. II, Lessons of the Election.* He declared this as having the same explanatory motive as *A Chapter of Autobiography* in 1868; though, of course, the explanations were of rather different sorts. In the case of the Irish Church it was a matter of explaining a change of opinion which had already been publicly professed. In the case of Irish Home Rule, it was a matter of explaining away what to many seemed to be a change of opinion not publicly professed but covertly sprung. Gladstone's line was to deny that any change of opinion was involved. 'On the present occasion, I have no change to vindicate; but only to point out the mode in which my language and conduct, governed by uniformity

---

* The Liberal Unionists did not in fact share benches with the Conservatives until 1895.
† Salisbury himself used the word 'continuity' with respect to Rosebery's policy. Gladstone was not so happy when Rosebery returned the compliment when he replaced Salisbury in 1892.

of principle, have simply followed the several stages, by which the great question of autonomy for Ireland has been brought to a state of ripeness for practical legislation.' He denied either precipitancy or concealment. The principles which had guided his conduct had been made clear in several public declarations. What he was asserting in effect, and quite accurately, was that his progress to Home Rule had been publicly observable to the observant who were willing to follow his tracks, take the hints, and decipher the not too oracular pronouncements. He quietly passed over, however, his undertakings that a clear Liberal majority would be absolutely essential for any action. He did not address the 'Hawarden Kite' furore. As for the former charge, 'What antagonists call precipitancy I call promptitude.'

The 'lessons of the election' were that 'Toryism' could not by its own resources win a majority 'unless and until the temper of the British nation shall have undergone some novel and considerable change'. The pattern of the nineteenth century would once more be repeated: Dissenter and Roman Catholic Emancipation 1828–9; Corn Law abolition 1846; the Franchise in 1866–7. Toryism would resist and then retreat. When reunited, Liberalism 'must again become predominant in Parliament', for it spoke for the nation against the 'classes'. Four fifths of employers, alleged Gladstone, were hostile to Home Rule, as were five sixths of Liberal peers. These could not and would not prevail against the fact that only one twentieth at most of Liberal working men were against Home Rule. A close reading of the election figures revealed the thinness and instability of the Conservative and dissentient Liberal vote. Home Rule in 1886 was in the same position as Corn Law abolition was in after the 1841 election. The people would come to realize how 'unspeakably criminal' had been the means of attaining the Union of 1800. Likewise they would see through the 'gigantic bribe' of the Ashbourne Land Purchase Act of 1885, a bad and dangerous scheme which his own Land Bill would replace.

Other features of *The Irish Question* are noteworthy. Ulster was not mentioned. The role allowed to Parnell in assisting to displace Chamberlain's scheme by interpreting how Gladstone's stipulation as to the 'unequivocal and rooted desire of Ireland expressed through the constitutional medium of her representatives' should take legislative form in Gladstone's Home Rule Bill was likewise not mentioned. Gladstone was indignant at the susurrus of rumour and speculation about his dealings with Parnell and his friends. 'There was no communication of any kind', he later asserted, 'between the Nationalists and myself before the fall of the Salisbury Government.'[59]* To the connoisseur, that was a defining

---

* The Salisbury government in question fell in February 1886. Rendel carefully observed this passage with Pressensé.[60]

specimen of Gladstone's aptness for 'making distinctions'. But the most significant feature in many ways was his certitude in the unchanging substance of the electoral materials he saw himself forming and directing. All his assumptions about the nature of politics remained fixed and rooted in the high Victorian epoch of his own prime. It was within the reassuring frame of these assumptions that Gladstone could assert that, looking at the Irish question 'which way we will', the 'cause of Irish self-government lives and moves, and can hardly fail to receive more life, and more propulsion', from the unwitting hands of the new government. 'It will arise, as a wounded warrior sometimes arises on the field of battle, and stabs to the heart some soldier of the victorious army, who has been exulting over him.'[61]

[4]

Having loosed this Parthian shot, Gladstone prepared on 25 August in the company of Acton for yet another tour to the Tegernsee, via Brussels, Cologne, and Frankfurt. George Leveson Gower came upon Gladstone at Tegernsee in high spirits, singing Negro melodies including 'Camptown Races' and 'Dinah Doh!' with 'great relish'.[62] He saw Lenbach, his portraitist, again; but, as ever, the great object was to talk with Döllinger; from whom he reluctantly parted on 10 September ('most kind & affectionate'). This was to be Gladstone's last visit to Germany* and his last sight of Döllinger, now in his eighty-seventh year. Munich, Gmunden ('its banks the resort of Count Chambord & other great folks'), and Ischl, the Emperor Francis Joseph's summer retreat, were notable stations on his return to London on the 19th. 'My short excursion to Germany', he reported to Laura Thistlethwayte, 'was of great use.' It broke the 'flood of correspondence, and it took me for a time entirely out of the atmosphere of contention and suspicion, for which I got in exchange free & harmonious conversation with friends on subjects of deep interest'.[63]

Back at Hawarden the flood of correspondence did not slacken. There was a wrangling and skirmishing bout of it both with Hartington ('to whom I told my mind') and Chamberlain. Otherwise that Hawarden autumn was most notable for deputations from Ireland bearing thanks to Gladstone for his exertions in the cause of Irish liberty: Clonmel, Waterford, Limerick; with the presentation of the freedom of Cork early in October. It was these Irish tributes which spurred Gladstone to an addendum for a new edition of his *Irish Question* in October, expanding

* Other than a cruise which took him to Kiel in 1895.

his historical critique of the 'horror' of the years 1795–1800 in Ireland. Having exposed the delinquency of the governments of Naples and Turkey, he explained, he was morally bound to expose the like delinquencies of his own country. 'Our opponents' – for example, Bright – 'do not seem to understand why these historical arguments require to be opened up.' They required to be opened up, Gladstone insisted, because they exposed the 'moral invalidity' of the Union. Gladstone could only admit to the irony of the fact that 'the only two persons . . . of real historical eminence, who are against us in this' – Lecky and Goldwin Smith – 'are two men who, as historians, have said the very things which form a main foundation of our bill'.[64]

By this time Gladstone was deep in polemical controversy with others of his historical enemies. Lord Brabourne, the former Edward Knatchbull-Hugesson,* accused Gladstone of gross distortions in his interpretation of Irish history by confining his studies 'to the writings of a particular school of Irish politicians'. The Union Parliament of 1801, Brabourne argued, even allowing for the unfortunate delay in Catholic Emancipation, was the first decent Parliament the Irish people, as opposed to racketeering ascendancies, whether medieval or modern, ever had.† Gladstone was unconvinced. The 'relations of England to Ireland have as a whole perhaps been more profoundly disgraced by cruelty and fraud, than those between any other nations in the entire history of Christendom'.[65] To Professor Dicey, author of the widely admired (even in some degree by Gladstone) *England's Case against Home Rule*, he explained the need for his 'contention as regards the historical argument'. When he first introduced the Home Rule policy, 'acting in all things on the remote hope of an early accommodation', Gladstone 'scarcely touched' on its historical bearings in the early stages. '*Now* we must go forward with it: we cannot dispense with any of our resources, and the historical argument has the most judicial bearings on our argument as to the Act of Union.'[66]‡

There were opportunities otherwise that season to escape the atmosphere of contention and suspicion. October the 6th was a red-letter day. 'Got my first tolerably clear forenoon on Homer.' By early November Gladstone recorded his having finished the *Iliad* 'say 35th or 30th time? & every time richer and more glorious than before'. There was a 'strange American proposal' from the Curator of the Buffalo Library for one of Gladstone's 'literary mss'. After consulting Herbert, Gladstone dispatched 'Russia and England' of 1880. There were consequences following

---

* See above, page 252–3.
† Brabourne's 'Facts and Fictions in Irish History' came out in October and November 1886 in *Blackwood's Magazine*.
‡ Bright praised Dicey.[67]

Hamilton's earlier initiative in the matter of rescue cases. Gladstone burned old letters 'which might in parts have suggested doubt & uneasiness'. Two cases especially, those of Dale and Davidson, struck him as being 'of great interest, in qualities as well as attractions, certainly belonging to the flower of their sex. I am concerned to have lost sight of them.'[68] That other flower of her sex, Laura Thistlethwayte, complained at the offensiveness of Madame Novikov. Gladstone was 'astonished' to learn that Novikov had accused Laura of being 'an enemy to my wife', to whom, as Gladstone acknowledged, Laura had always been 'particularly kind'. Gladstone explained that he had known Olga Novikov as a woman said to be 'handsome and fascinating or both' – 'I am not conscious of her being either' – but, having seen her perhaps a score of times, Gladstone could not have supposed her capable of such rudeness.[69]* Otherwise, also, there were occasions for reflection. 'Bed strictly kept all day . . . There is a disposition to grudge as wasted these days. But they afford great opportunities of review. Especially as to politics and my politics are now summed up in the word Ireland, for probing inwardly the intention, to see whether all is truly given over to the Divine will.'[71]

The turn towards the end of the year put Gladstone increasingly in the way of preparation for the 1887 session. He was under pressures to modify his stance on the Home Rule question to reassure what Kay-Shuttleworth described to him as 'influential Liberals of various classes' in the constituencies 'who hold aloof from us & follow Lord Hartington'.† These Liberals wanted efficient guarantees against the likely 'excesses & acts of injustice' of an Irish legislature, for the supremacy of Parliament, and for a settlement of the land question before the setting up of a Dublin legislature. There were pressures also from Ireland about the virtues of hastening slowly: a 'hearty friend of Home Rule' suggested that 'it might be an advantage to Ireland that Home Rule should come rather more gradually than it would have done if we had passed the Bill this year or next'.[72]

Such moves made no discernible impression. Gladstone's constant rule henceforth was to admit the conceivability of any amount of modification, but subject to the approval and acquiescence of the Irish party; which approval and acquiescence was most unlikely to be forthcoming. Rather, Gladstone's attention was directed to what he described to Campbell-Bannerman as the 'deplorable change in the state of Ireland since the cup of hope was dashed away from the lips of the people': the beginnings of what in 1887 would emerge as the 'Plan of Campaign', a systematic refusal of rent payments in certain circumstances. Gladstone meanwhile

---

* Catherine did not meet Mrs Thistlethwayte, it appears, until 1887.[70]
† Kay-Shuttleworth had been Chancellor of the Duchy of Lancaster in the late ministry.

declared himself to Gavan Duffy's daughter as 'far from discouraged' in his bid to 'complete the list' with the 'last of the series' of his life's campaigns.

I am deeply thankful for the great progress the cause has made during twelve months at home; for the wide & warm sympathies of other lands, including markedly the Colonies; & for having enjoyed the support & co-operation of a body of colleagues than whom none are more experienced in affairs of State, or stand higher in public estimation.

But you do well to remind me . . . that there is One above us & them who rules & overrules our poor counsels, & to whom we may fearlessly commit a cause alike beneficial to all the countries concerned in it, & to all sects & classes of the people.[73]

[5]

It was that day, 11 December, that Gladstone was jolted by Tennyson's proffering yet another literary gift – this time his *Locksley Hall Sixty Years After*. Exploiting the dramatic monologue form of his original *Locksley Hall* of 1838, Tennyson had the grimly covert pleasure of giving Gladstone and his Liberalism a severely Carlylean trouncing. It was a kind of revenge on Gladstone for all those years of having to fit in with Gladstone's fussing political supervision, of having to swallow the 1884 Reform Bill, the Gordon tragedy, the failure to keep the Fleet, and, now, truckling to Parnell and his fellow rebels. It was little less than a hysterical scream of rage at the decadence of the times, with choice abuse of politicians unnamed but clearly of a Gladstonian typology: 'leaders of realm-ruining party', 'tonguesters' leading astray the simple goodness of the people. 'When was age so crammed with menace, written, spoken lies?'

To Gladstone this was more mutinously dangerous than any amount of Lord Brabournes or Professor Diceys. Here was the revered Poet Laureate, the 'pre-eminent Victorian', declaring – no one took seriously the pretext of the Narrator – that the society of the time was rotten with greed and misery and that the politics of the time was a pit of hypocrisy and demagogy. For Gladstone the danger lurked in the circumstance that the Narrator of the old *Locksley Hall* had been a fitting partner with Gladstone himself in setting out on the 'march of mind'. Just as the young Gladstone renounced the narrow vocation of political service of the Church and stepped forward into the ampler role of Christian service of the state, so Tennyson's young Narrator renounced the temptations to flee the obligations of being 'the heir of all the ages, in the foremost files of time', and declared his commitment to the 'wondrous mother-age' and his solidarity with 'men the workers' building 'all the wonders that would be'. Gladstone had spent considerable amounts of time and energy over the years in keeping Tennyson steady in the yoke Gladstone had devised of a literary-political, Arthurian-Peelite partnership which would betoken the coming of a better age. Tennyson had never been comfortable in this Gladstonian yoke; but Gladstone proved relentless in his consistency. He soothed Tennyson's social tantrums;[74] he humoured Tennyson in his distempers; he ignored Tennyson's overt hostility to Home Rule. But he could not ignore a literary explosion which (despite some of the worst lines in English poesy) bore so directly and invidiously before so large a public on the merits of the Peelite and Liberal record over the past sixty years.

James Knowles of the *Nineteenth Century* proposed to Gladstone that he should review the new *Locksley Hall* with a view to a critique taking a 'hopeful rather than a hopeless view'.[75] The *Nineteenth Century*, after all, had been founded precisely to celebrate the coming of better times, the achievement of the Peelite-Liberal world. Gladstone jumped at the opportunity. Within days he began work on a riposte. 'Reperused the Two Locksley Halls – & made a slight attempt at a beginning.' Two days later: the 'wheels driving heavily'. Gladstone's polemical method was to insist that the Narrator's voice must not be mistaken for Tennyson's voice and then to rebuke Tennyson for the impropriety of commencing the Queen's Jubilee year of 1887 with so dark and pessimistic an effusion. The burden of '*Locksley Hall* and the Jubilee', published in the January *Nineteenth Century*, was to rebut Tennyson's speaking rantingly through the mask of the 'Old Prophet' and to prove that in fact the times had not betrayed the hopes of the Young Prophet. Gladstone's method was to deploy every possible statistic to demonstrate the immense betterment of the lives of the people under the wise and beneficent guidance of Peelism and Liberalism. There were new dangers of plutocracy and luxury; and Home Rule for Ireland remained the great political task remaining to be fulfilled. Yet: 'If fifty years ago censure was appeased and hopefulness encouraged, is there any reason now why hope should be extinguished and censure should hold all the ground?' The Queen's Jubilee should not be marred by 'tragic tones'.

Tennyson, in telegraphed felicitations for the new year, played his part in the charade of 'old comradeship' by offering 'best thanks' for the 'kindly eloquent Locksley article'.[76]

[6]

But even the Tennyson affair was pushed to the margin just before Christmas by astonishing news of the resignation of the Chancellor of the Exchequer and Leader of the House of Commons, Lord Randolph Churchill. 'It will, I think,' recorded Gladstone, 'have varied & far-reaching consequences.' Any shock to the status quo could only be interpreted as unfailingly beneficial to the Home Rule cause. One possible far-reaching consequence might have been the break-up of Salisbury's rickety government. Salisbury once more, as in July, offered to serve in a Unionist coalition under Hartington; but Hartington knew that he could not hold his Liberal Unionist section in being within the Tory fold. Chamberlain was at a loss. A species of entente with Churchill, as the joint representatives of the younger generation against their respective 'Old Gangs', had been an important feature of his recent occupations in political exile. Chamberlain was indeed very prompt in declaring at Birmingham that the time was ripe for Liberals to come together. They agreed, after all, on nine points out of ten, and Chamberlain could not doubt that a 'few representative men meeting round a table' would agree on a programme for a reunited Liberalism. An Irish land policy would be the best point of junction.[77] Here was the germ of what later would be dubbed the 'Round Table Conference'. Gladstone assured John Morley that 'everything honourable should be done to conciliate and soothe' Chamberlain. 'On the whole I rejoice to think that, come what may, this affair will really effect progress in the Irish question.'[78]

There would always remain the difficulty that Gladstone's definition of what was 'honourable' in effecting 'progress in the Irish question' was not easily reconcilable with the hopes and expectations of many Liberals anxious for reconciliation and union. One such was Reginald Brett, Hartington's former private secretary. 'At such a moment,' he appealed to Gladstone, 'the efforts of all Liberals must be directed towards re-establishing their great party in its proper position. You have always shown yourself ready to meet half-way all those desirous at arriving at a common understanding on grave political issues.' Chamberlain had made 'a large concession in spirit as well as in substance'. The decision 'remains with you'.[79] That old Nonconformist symbol of 1880, Guinness Rogers, chimed in. Chamberlain's initiative opened the way to negotiation; Rogers had reason to know he had parted from Gladstone 'on principle & with pain'. 'Subject only to a feeling of loyalty to you, there is a general longing for reconciliation.'[80] Of the Liberal chiefs, Harcourt made the promptest and most eager acknowledgement of Chamberlain's overture. Chamberlain responded once more on the theme of '3 Liberals round a table'. Harcourt insisted to Gladstone that there was a 'solid basis for union'.[81]

Surer than ever of the strength of his position and his prospects, Gladstone imperturbably brushed aside these eager brokers of unity. He stressed that Churchill's fall could only be 'in favour of the cause'. Chamberlain, he could see, preferred the Conservative government plus Churchill to Gladstone; but preferred Gladstone to the government without Churchill. Yet care must be taken not to give Chamberlain too much scope. It was, as Gladstone observed to Labouchere, 'a besetting sin in the Liberal party, to measure, each for himself, the power of doing good by the power of doing mischief'. Gladstone thought that the 'average politician (which Mr C. is not) can do ten times as much mischief as he can with equal effort do good'. Especially was this true of 'evil & good in the House of Commons'. Gladstone did not wish the 'forward steps' which Chamberlain had taken on his own responsibility to be 'thrown away'; but he thought 'very great caution, & a very great regard for others', was to be observed, especially by himself, at this moment. 'The tendency of the late exciting events is to stir men's minds from their moorings; & we must be on our guard.'[82] Gladstone agreed with Harcourt that Chamberlain's Birmingham declaration was an important event. But he was adamant on the theme of 'very great concern for others'. There could be no abandonment of Home Rule and replacement by a land policy and alternative schemes of local government unless such a course were acceptable not only to the Liberal majority as well as the Liberal dissentients, but equally to the representatives of Ireland.[83]

Gladstone parted from 1886 as a year of 'shock and strain'. He had not, he felt, a chance given him 'of escaping from this whirlpool, for I cannot abandon a cause which is so evidently that of my fellowmen *and* in which a particular part seems to be assigned to me'.[84] January 1887 was marked by a wide distribution of his '*Locksley Hall* and the Jubilee' piece and by friendly accommodation to Mandell Creighton's request for countenance to the rather precarious project to put the English historical school on a substantial footing with an *English Historical Review* ('Lord Acton warned me that the primary duty of an editor was to make himself a bore'). There was a very pleasant Sandringham party where the Prince and Princess of Wales were immensely amiable to the Glad-stones. (In 1885 Gladstone had been instrumental in making arrangements agreed with the Queen whereby the Prince was allowed access to matters being treated in Cabinet.)[85] Back in Dollis Hill for sessional preparations, there was a poignant moment on 17 February when Gladstone came across Bright in Piccadilly, with constrained acknowl-edgements.

Constraint was also the keynote in conversation with Chamberlain shortly after, set up by Malcolm MacColl by way of smoothing the path to the 'Round Table'. A 'friendly conversation' with Trevelyan was encouraging. The 'Round Table' negotiators were Harcourt, John Morley and Herschell for the Gladstonians and Chamberlain and Trevelyan for the dissentients.[86] The talks commenced at Harcourt's house in Grafton Street, actually at a round table, organized by Harcourt's son Lewis ('Loulou'), beginning on 13 January. 'Bouts one and two' were completed by the end of the month. Chamberlain contended for the standard requirements: recognition of Ulster's special claims, for guarantees of the supremacy of Parliament, for Irish representation in that Parliament, and for a big new land-purchase policy. At a distance, through Morley, Gladstone kept him in play, avoiding giving Chamberlain any pretext for accusations of bad faith. A third bout in February chez Trevelyan was judged by Chamberlain to be 'satisfactory'.[87] By the end of February Gladstonian Liberals were fretting that reconciliation would result in sacrifices of principle, as evidenced, so ten of them memorialized Gladstone, by the 'recent actions and utterances of prominent Liberal dissentients'.[88]

They need not have fretted. Gladstone's consciousness of the part 'assigned' to him would always be proof against any weakness for conciliation. Gladstone saw the negotiations as a means of allowing heretics to rehabilitate themselves and abjure their heresy. Time, he was convinced, was on his side. Chamberlain no longer could call on the Liberal Federation for help. He was isolated, in the open. Soon the Conservatives and Hartingtonians would start cracking down on the Irish, exposing his position even more invidiously. Goschen, as Hartington's alter ego, had gone over to Salisbury as Churchill's replacement at the Exchequer. Where could Chamberlain go? A by-election success at Burnley on 19 February for the Gladstonians in recapturing a Liberal Unionist seat looked very much like the turn of the tide. Hamilton found Gladstone 'quite up in his stirrups' on the strength of it.[89] Possibly it contributed to Chamberlain's being 'very friendly' at a dinner on the 21st at the Devonshire Club.

This did not deter Gladstone from explaining to Liberals who wanted their own legislation, and particularly Nonconformists who wanted to get Welsh Disestablishment under way, that their wishes were being blocked by intransigent Liberal Unionists. This provoked Chamberlain into replying that, on the contrary, 'poor little Wales' was being made to wait 'until Mr Parnell is satisfied and Mr Gladstone's policy adopted'. They were not waiting alone, Chamberlain added. 'The crofters of Scotland and the agricultural labourers of England will keep them company. Thirty-two millions of people must go without much-needed legislation because three million are disloyal.'[90] Gladstone hit back with a letter to the *Baptist*, whose editor had complained that law-abiding Wales was neglected, while Ireland gets her way through agitation. 'I have been telling the country on every occasion I could find, that no great political matter of any kind ... could be practically dealt with, until the Irish question which blocks the way is settled and put out of the way.' Therefore, he who wishes to have 'a great Welsh question' attended to must see that 'his own aim is to clear the road'.[91] This was an instance of the distorting effect on the Liberal party of Gladstone's imposition upon it of the highly restrictive terms of his leadership. Gladstone sufficiently advertised the obduracy of his stand in 'Notes and Queries on the Irish Demand' in the February *Nineteenth Century*.

By now recriminations between the two Liberal sects had got to the point of mutual blackballings at Brooks's Club. The Duke of Westminster, in what could be interpreted as an ungracious (and ungrateful) expression of the 'political animus' of the 'classes', put Millais's portrait of Gladstone up for sale. Sir Charles Tennant loyally redeemed it.[92]* It was still possible by the middle of March for Gladstone to have an 'easy *general* conversation' with Chamberlain on neutral dinner-party ground. But by this time the Round Table negotiations had dwindled into inanity.

[7]

There was plenty of reason for Gladstone to remain 'up in his stirrups' as the lengthy and fraught session of 1887 wore on. Hamilton observed a change in him from 1886. 'He is no longer the "old man in a hurry". He recognises time as the essential element of a settlement. He is full of confidence in the strength of his cause and in its eventual consummation; but he will be content to have initiated it.' Dining at Dollis Hill with Welby and Primrose on 19 March, Hamilton observed Gladstone 'in great form – in high spirits and buoyant mentally and physically. The suburban retreat evidently agrees with him thoroughly. He does not mind the going to and fro; and enjoys the immunity from continued interruption.' Gladstone was especially vivacious on 'one of his favourite topics', Sir Robert Peel – the greatest man he 'ever knew or could conceive of'. Peel was indeed 'a perfect God with Mr G'.[93]

Salisbury's government, although shored up by Hartington, looked anything but convincing. Gladstone could patronize from on high Goschen's 'hum drum budget' ('those who are in their second half-century will appreciate my position in the circumstances').[94] Confronted with

* It is now in the National Portrait Gallery.

the task of subjecting Ireland to 'resolute government', Salisbury was in difficulties. Beach's health could not stand the strain. Salisbury took a deliberate risk and replaced him with Balfour. This could plausibly be interpreted as an act of despair by a collapsing ministry. So Chamberlain at the time was disposed to think. The Criminal Law Amendment (Ireland) Bill which Balfour took charge of was a comprehensively swingeing measure to replace temporary coercive arrangements in a systematic counter-attack on terrorism and intimidation. It would be rammed through by an unapologetically abrupt use of the new 'Closure' provisions to restrict debate. Gladstone denounced it as 'a Bill aimed at the Irish people', 'a Bill aimed at the nation'.[95] Chamberlain and his friends were in an agony of doubt between Gladstone and Parnell on the one side and Balfour and Hartington on the other. A trickle of dissentients came across back to Gladstone, including Trevelyan. Gladstone deftly exploited some civil words exchanged between Catherine and Chamberlain to arrange for Chamberlain's being received at Dollis Hill on 5 April. 'The general impression left on my mind by the interview', Chamberlain recorded, 'was that Mr G. confidently counts on the unpopularity of coercion to bring about an early appeal to the country and to secure a decision in his favour and that under these circumstances he does not desire to proceed further in the direction of conciliation and does not believe that the party will allow him to do so.'[96] Gladstone commented: 'ambiguous result but some ground made'.

Time was to show, however, that Gladstone's confidence was misplaced. Ministers stubbornly fought their ground and held their line. Salisbury's gamble in putting Balfour in the van of battle proved a brilliant success. Hartington very effectively soothed Liberal Unionist consciences about collaborating with Tory reaction. Coercion of the Irish did not, by and large, prove unpopular with the English nation. Chamberlain held his nerve. The trickle of Liberal seceders abjuring their heresy dried up. All this was much assisted by *The Times*'s publishing, on 18 April, the day of the introduction of the Criminal Law Bill, a sensational item in a special format, first in a projected series called 'Parnellism and Crime', designed to expose the intimate collusion of Parnell and his party with criminal terrorism. Most sensational of all were facsimiles of letters allegedly signed by Parnell, one of which stated that while the death of Lord Frederick Cavendish was regrettable, Under-Secretary Burke had got no more than his deserts; and that in the circumstances of the case, Parnell had no choice but to denounce the event as atrocious and distance himself and his party from it. Parnell immediately declared the letters to be rank and impudent forgeries, and requested a parliamentary committee of enquiry. Salisbury, however, sensing that he had Parnell by the throat, decided on a full-scale judicial commission designed to expose Irish Nationalism as a vast criminal conspiracy. To Gladstone the affair was a painful jolt. 'Without doubt,' he wrote on Sunday, 24 April, 'words of Scripture carry their communication. Today it was "I shall find trouble & heaviness, but I will call upon the name of the Lord: O Lord I beseech thee deliver my soul. Amen." '[97]

Trouble and heaviness for Parnell was indeed trouble and heaviness for Gladstone. One of the forms it took was a resurgence among Liberals of demands for rethinking the policy of 1886, and for a convincing repudiation of Churchill's charge that Gladstone was 'Leader of the Repeal of the Union'. For all Gladstone's indignant insistence that there was 'the broadest distinction between what I propose and the repeal of the Union',[98] the Liberal rank and file remained uneasy. They observed that the Irish people and Professor Dicey were agreed otherwise. The issue of Irish representation at Westminster simply would not go away. There was disaffection at the remoteness and partiality of Gladstone's leadership. Kay-Shuttleworth pleaded for attention to the Lancashire members: a social meeting 'with some of your truest supporters might be politically useful'.[99] Certainly there was a feeling that the garden parties offered by Catherine at inconvenient Willesden did not quite meet the need to connect Gladstone with his following. Samuel Whitbread, ever one of the more candid of those trying to help Gladstone to help himself, called Gladstone's attention to a recent utterance by Trevelyan, which was calculated to make the public 'wonder what it is that keeps the party from reuniting'. He warned Gladstone: 'the enemy will not be slow to assert that it is because you will not consider any alternative to the plan of last year'.[100] Gladstone's dismissive marginal comment was: 'The Irish!' To John Morley he was prompt to stress that any discussion of the question of continued Irish representation at Westminster must not be made 'a ground for impairing the gift of real and effective autonomy to Ireland in Irish concerns'.[101]

If Kay-Shuttleworth's Lancashire Liberals were not to benefit from Gladstone's social radiance, there were arguments that big things might beneficially be done in Wales in the Whitsun recess. The arguments put forward by the *Baptist* were not to be disdained. Gladstone knew his Scotland and felt his position there secure. It would be a mistake to risk Welsh disaffection for the want of a touch of cultivation. Gladstone took Scottish disestablishment seriously. He estimated highly the Free Kirk. He thought Scottish ecclesiastical affairs to be of high moment. He was not solicitous for Welsh disestablishment. He considered it a new, shallow, derivative movement without bottom, a matter of crude sectarian agitation. But still, there it was. The thing to do was hold it at bay while bringing Welsh opinion around to understanding that the primary duty of 'the most Protestant nation in Europe' must be to help bring about a Roman Catholic government in Dublin. A stroke in arousing a mass response in Wales in the Midlothian manner would be a way of hitting back at the coercive Tories. By swaying the Welsh he could at the same time deflect the pesterings he suffered from in England about the 1886 policy as well as the pesterings about Welsh disestablishment. Swansea would be preferable to Cardiff: more Western, more Welsh. Thus it was that Hussey Vivian, one of the Swansea members, suddenly found Gladstone accepting the invitation to Swansea he had been unsuccessfully pressing for many years.

The imminent descent among them of one whom they held in awe as 'some Grand Llama of Thibet or Vested Prophet of Khorassan'[102] had the Welsh in some turmoil. There was jealousy in north Wales, expressed particularly by Stuart Rendel, MP for Montgomeryshire, that Sir Hussey Vivian (who had voted against the Home Rule Bill in 1886) should be allowed to conspire with Gladstone to push disestablishment and land questions into the background. For that certainly was Gladstone's strategic intention.[103]

The manner and method of Gladstone's triumphant progress, accompanied by Catherine and the Rev. Stephen, from Hawarden to Swansea at the beginning of June 1887 recalled the grand precedents of populist excursions in Tyneside and Merseyside and Midlothian: the 'charismatic priest-king' in plenary splendour. The Welsh crowds who besieged his train as it passed through Llanidloes, Newtown, Builth and Merthyr and the Swansea throngs who tried to storm the High Street station were converting their chapel, radical, and national emotions into a hero-worshipping response to the first major British statesman who had, in turn, responded sympathetically and encouragingly to Welsh grievances and aspirations. But it was Gladstone's purpose to convert those Welsh energies into tractive power for the movement of Irish nationalism and Irish grievance. At Hussey Vivian's seat, Singleton Abbey, Gladstone addressed the Welsh Liberal elite evasively on disestablishment ('I am going to be very stilted and jejune indeed on this subject with you'; 'I have a great horror of premature decisions'). In his diary he recorded: 'Got through a most difficult business as well as I could expect.'[104]* He had skated very skilfully on thin ice. His real message was 'the cause of Ireland is the cause of Wales'.

That was his unspoken evangel to the great mass demonstration at Singleton on 4 June when 50,000 marchers paraded before Gladstone as he took the salute, a large leek on his lapel, surrounded by the flower

---

* Gladstone stayed at Singleton Abbey on this occasion, not at Park Wern as is stated in D (see page 593), 2 June 1887.

of Welsh Liberalism. Refreshing claret was provided thoughtfully in teacups. The politicos clustered around him were recharging the batteries of their prestige by public proximity to the most powerful source of political dynamism. Gladstone on his part was recharging his own batteries by immersion in the invigorating dynamic of the 'people'. The Swansea episode buttressed and confirmed his confidence as a populist wielder of power, a harnesser of public energy, a manipulator of great issues.

There were, perhaps inevitably, problems about the small print. Apart from evasive coquetting with disestablishment, there was the question as to what he had said, if anything, about the vexed issue of Irish representation at Westminster. It had been widely assumed that Gladstone was going to use the Swansea occasion to make a revisionist move. Advocates of this revision scanned anxiously the reported texts, both at Swansea and at Cardiff on his way back to London. Gladstone was construed as mentioning oracularly a renewal of his Irish policy in a 'modified form';[105] but, as with his declaration about 'home rule' at Edinburgh in November 1885, it was difficult quite to decipher the utterances of the oracle. To a seeker of such enlightenment in later days, Gladstone insisted that at Singleton Abbey, in a 'reported and published speech', he had declared that the public sense appeared to be in favour of retention and reduction of Irish members, and that, this being so, he was perfectly prepared to accede to this alteration. However, it seemed that the specific statement was only to be had in a special 'authorized version' of the speech.[106]

Gladstone returned to London well pleased that he had got the better of the implicit bargain with Welsh Liberalism. As he opened another volume of his diary on 12 June he noted: 'Yet have I more to say, which I have thought upon; for I am filled as the moon at the full.'[107] It was cheering that Andrew Carnegie, one of Gladstone's most influential American admirers, was shaping promisingly in the way of channelling funds to the by now cash-depleted Liberal party.[108]* Less cheering was a 'grave conversation' with Morley and Harcourt. Gladstone found Harcourt 'a most uneasy travelling companion for a political journey along rough roads'. Harcourt's version of the same occasion was that 'Gladstone and John Morley will not come up to scratch about conciliating Hartington because they cannot get hold of Parnell and dare not move without his consent'.[109]

* G himself provided £700.

[8]

By now it was the Queen's Golden Jubilee season. Gladstone thought the Abbey service on 21 June 'too courtly'. 'Courtly' certainly was not the word appropriate for his presence at the garden party at the palace on 29 June. 'Disposed of eleven royalties. Saw Abp of Canterbury – and the Pope's Nuncio.' How briskly Gladstone disposed of the greatest royalty was most entertainingly recorded by a lady-in-waiting from the testimony of the Queen's cousin, the Duke of Cambridge.

That brute Gladstone stood in the forefront of the circle outside her tent while she had her tea, bang opposite her, hat in hand; she said to the Duke: 'Do you see Gladstone? There he has been standing hat in hand, straight opposite me this Half-hour, determined to force me to speak with him! But I am as determined *not* to speak with him!' So he continued to stand the *whole* time! But when she came out of the tent, instead of coming out in the centre, upon him, she went out at the end, and went along the line to the right, then made a circuit and took the other line to the left and most skilfully avoided him so that she neither spoke to him nor gave him her hand. But alas! the Duke heard afterwards, which is too *exasperating*, when she had so successfully and markedly avoided him, the brute contrived to get round to *inside* the house and placed himself so, that when she passed through the house to go away, at the last moment she came all suddenly *upon* him, round the corner, and was forced to give him her hand!!! Too provoking.[110]

Otherwise, before the recommencement of political battle, there were grateful diversions. It was a pleasure to look over the new building of the National Liberal Club in Whitehall Place, of which Gladstone was president, designed for the provincial elites deemed ineligible for the Reform. Soon renewed political conflict centred on the great fight over Balfour's driving of the Crimes Bill, which Gladstone denounced as marking the onset of a new and disastrous era: it was 'an alternative to the policy of what is termed Home Rule or self-government for Ireland', aimed not at crime but at association. Seven hundred years of English mastery had resulted in a discredit, misery and shame more indefensible than Austria in Italy and Russia in Poland. 'You know', he taunted the Unionist benches, 'that the literature of the world is against you.'[111] In the bitter end Balfour got his bill by grace of Hartington and Bright; but in the course of it Gladstone could observe Chamberlain's twists and turns with a certain sardonic satisfaction. 'J. Morley came at 4,' Gladstone recorded back at Hawarden. 'Conversation of 3 hours on the last Chamberlain overture. We are agreed. Every time I see him I admire him more, especially the *morale*.'[112] Another splendid by-election success in recapturing the Nantwich division of Cheshire from the House of Grosvenor put Gladstone more than ever up in his stirrups. He interpreted it as making 'considerable addition to the evidence, now somewhat rapidly approaching to a demonstrative character, that the people of England intend to do full justice to the people of Ireland'.[113]

Spurred on by the Nantwich triumph, Gladstone got down to 'Electoral Facts of 1887', which came out in the September issue of Knowles's *Nineteenth Century*. It was an updated version of the psephological analysis in *The Irish Question* as to the assured and imminent electoral success of the Home Rule cause, repairing the anomalous false step of 1886 and restoring Liberalism's historic and natural hegemony. More than ever was the analogy of Home Rule in 1886 with Corn Law abolition in 1841 potently cogent. Then the dramatic denouement of the government's resolute Irish policy, Balfour's proclamation under the Crimes Act of the Irish National League, became strangely entangled with the last and most torrid crisis of the Thistlethwaytes. On 7 August Gladstone received news of the 'sad calamity' of Mr Thistlethwayte's death, apparently by suicidal gunshot wound. (He reputedly was in the habit of summoning servants by firing into the ceiling.) On 24 August Gladstone dined with Mrs Thistlethwayte, 'who related to me the very sad story of her husband's death'. Promptly, as in the case of Lyttelton, Gladstone convinced himself, as he reported to Catherine on the 25th, that he was 'now really persuaded the death was by accident'.

Thus it was, in the aftermath of the sad calamity of the widowed Laura Thistlethwayte and the sad calamity of the Irish people's having Balfour's 'sword of Damocles' hanging over their heads,[114] that the 'horror' of Mitchelstown came upon Gladstone.[115] An affray in which the Royal Irish Constabulary defended themselves against what was termed the 'Blackthorn Brigade' on the occasion of the first prosecution under the Crimes Act of William O'Brien, genius of the 'Plan of Campaign', in County Cork, left many police grievously injured and one demonstrator dead and two mortally wounded. One of the Irish administration's new 'strong men', Edward Carson, was present, and ever after praised Balfour for his unflinching support of the beleaguered forces of law and order. Irish Nationalists made a great set at 'Bloody Balfour'; and it was a cause of considerable scandal that Gladstone should, as he later unapologetically related the case, have telegraphed 'to some correspondent the words, "Remember Mitchelstown", and that I had in a speech at Nottingham developed my meaning in using that phrase and gave whatever force I could to the meaning of my words'. The phrase immediately became a watchword. Gladstone asserted that he had not used the words 'inconsiderately'; and indeed insisted that never in his life had he uttered words which he 'more rejoiced to have used'.[116] The words he used at the end of the 1887 session, never forgiven by Carson and others who were present at the incident, were that the actions of the Constabulary evidenced a 'degree of stupidity and negligence which it is hardly possible to conceive'.[117] By 1889 Gladstone was citing it as one with Peterloo.[118]

[9]

Hawarden that autumn was much taken up with plans for the 'intended muniment room' to house the Gladstone archive. By the middle 1880s Hamilton calculated that Gladstone was in receipt of something like 20,000 letters a year,[119] and by 1888 had retained near to 50,000 of them.[120] It was essential that something be done to house them and relieve the pressure on space available in the Castle interior. Gladstone took a great interest in the project, as one who ever preened himself on his skill in the efficient arrangement of shelving. The question of an archival depository was apropos of materials relating to biographical projects then either completed or in prospect. There were lucrative proposals to Gladstone himself at this time about autobiographical writing.[121] But what most concerned him was that his survival and consequent seniority among the great public figures of the time exposed increasingly his vulnerability to the modern tendency to biographize. Theodore Martin's *Life of the Prince Consort* had offended him in 1880;* Edwin Hodder's *Life of Shaftesbury* in 1887 came as a vexatiously disagreeable shock. Hodder admitted that material from Shaftesbury's journals animadverting on Gladstone was of a 'profoundly painful character', but defended its inclusion on the grounds of its being part of the historical record. Gladstone was much concerned that it would cause public mischief and be turned to account by Tory reviewers.[122] Then came, a little later, the memoirs of F. Hastings Doyle, whom Gladstone assumed to be an old and loyal friend. His response this time was brusque: 'the silly parts might be cut out'.[123]

Gladstone consequently was much on his guard in the matter of biographical materials. He at first refused permission to let his letters be published in the biography of Manning planned by E. S. Purcell. It would be absurd, as Hamilton approvingly remarked, to 'allow his biography to be written piecemeal'.[124]† However, once it became clear to Gladstone

---

* See above, page 234.
† Gladstone refused permission for Andrew Lang's biography of Stafford Northcote (Iddesleigh).

that Purcell had in mind something rather subversive to the ultramontane party and was amenable to a degree of direction in return for access to materials, Gladstone was prepared to be quite helpful.[125] Wemyss Reid's biography of Forster, in 1888, was another matter. 'I find matters which do not lend themselves to a treatment satisfactory to myself,' Gladstone admonished Reid, '& on which I must [resort?] to my normal expedient, a suspension of final judgment.'[126] Gladstone's review of the book in the September 1888 *Nineteenth Century* well exemplified a remark he made to Lady Rothschild at that time: 'I never write a review without some object beyond the review.'[127]

As lone surviving trustee of Aberdeen's literary estate (after Graham's death in 1861) Gladstone was in a good position to protect his interest and his estimation of the interests of Aberdeen from what he felt were the superfluous literary ambitions of Aberdeen's deplorable younger son, Arthur Gordon. After having made himself objectionable during the Ionian mission,[128] Gordon went on to make a career out of colonial governorships. Gladstone twice vetoed Gordon's plans to publish Aberdeen's papers on the grounds that they were indiscreet about Aberdeen's private life. Gladstone later made difficulties about Gordon's biography of his father and about Sidney Herbert's widow's biography of her late husband.[129] But Gladstone found himself the biter bit when, in pursuing his polemic against Forster, he was refused permission by the Queen to publish extracts from his letters and memoranda to her on the matter of Parnell's release from Kilmainham in 1882. He considered her prohibition 'insulting' and 'absurd'.[130]

His polemic against the Irish Union of 1800 Gladstone kept in good repair. He contributed 'Lessons on Irish History in the Eighteenth Century' to James Bryce's *A Handbook of Home Rule* in 1887. He dealt unsparingly with Professor T. D. Ingram's *A History of the Legislative Union of Great Britain and Ireland* in the October *Nineteenth Century*; which was to begin another polemical controversy, especially lively after Knowles allowed Ingram to use the word 'unveracity' in his reply to Gladstone.[131] His already extensive repertoire of polemical weaponry Gladstone augmented with skills in the art of 'political meteorology'. Analysis of the by-election results revealed quite conclusively, he asserted, that the general election of 1886 'indicated not the conviction, but the perplexity of the country'. The 'rational Tory, and still more any Dissentient', might well ask themselves, '*Where is all this to end?*'[132] There was time also for Frances Hodgson Burnett's '*delightful* "Little Lord Fauntleroy"'.[133] Hamilton noted that Gladstone's frisky exertions in tree-felling were such that the entourage took alarm and appealed to Andrew Clark's decrees about the risks involved and the need to take all necessary precautions.[134]

The new year of 1888 was to be celebrated in Florence. The Gladstone party (Catherine and Helen in attendance) departed for Paris on 28 December ('a luxurious journey all provided by the S.E. Co.'). Gladstone entered his seventy-ninth year amid the bustle of travel. 'When can I find a moment of sufficient withdrawal to *think*, or when even to say what I have thought.' There was an interview with the newly elected President Sadi-Carnot ('a frank straightforward courteous gentleman') before departure with all the best attentions of Messrs Cook's (whom Gladstone had extolled in his '*Locksley Hall* and the Jubilee' piece as a signal indicator of the better times). The passage into Italy at Modane evoked memories of fifty-six years before. At Florence the Gladstones were lodged chez Sir J. P. Lacaita, Viale Principe Amadeo. There was no stint of society ('entrapped into a tea party at Miss Dickson's'). Harry stopped by en route from India. Gladstone was much pleased to meet the American authoress of *Little Lord Fauntleroy*, Mrs Burnett. The book, he felt, would tend to good relations with the United States. There was sightseeing: Bellosguardo (where he planted a tree), Fiesole, Castagnole, Villa Palmieri. Gladstone was shocked to learn the weight of income tax bearing upon Italians: 13 per cent, equalling '2/8 in £!'[135] There was time for literature: Homeric proofs were corrected and dispatched; his defence of Christianity against the American agnostic, Colonel Ingersoll, was prepared for the *North American Review*. The Gladstones departed early in February, being 'most kindly received by the Actons' at Cannes en route. 'So I am planted once more in London', Gladstone recorded on 9 February, 'for a life of contention: how hateful, but how deserved.'

The new headquarters for the life of contention was in James St, Buckingham Gate – 'the first hired house as Mrs G. said they had ever lived in'. Hamilton was much disapproving of Gladstone's refusal to give dinners for the party. Gladstone never dined at the House of Commons when its Leader;[136] Hamilton feared that Gladstone's invulnerability to the parliamentary party was making him inexpediently aloof and unconciliatory.[137] Gladstone imperturbably knew where his necessary support came from. At The Durdans, staying with the Roseberys, Hamilton and Rosebery left the Sunday-morning church service early to allow the Gladstones a clear way to proceed back. 'That is just what she likes. She can see the salutations of the congregation, and overhear the remarks of the crowd; just as if she were new to such demonstrations in his honour. There is nothing certainly more touching to be seen in married life than her adoration of him.'[138]

Contention was at depths of bitterness unusual even in Gladstone's experience. Salisbury declared in the Lords, in his blazingly indiscreet manner, without expressing regret after protests by Granville and

Kimberley, that most Conservatives would prefer to avoid social inter-course with Gladstone.[139] What was felt to be Gladstone's ambivalent attitude to the 'Plan of Campaign' gave at this time particular offence. It was admitted that there had been 'no want of care or caution' in Glad-stone's public language. 'But the construction likely to be placed on your reservations by ignorant men will, it is to be feared, lend by implication the sanction of your authority to means that in themselves are bad.'[140] Gladstone's unabashed defence of his 'Remember Mitchels-town' watchword exacerbated these fears; as did his constant harping on the theme of the illegitimate and ultimately self-defeating deployment, 'systematically and boldly', of the power of wealth and high station against his policy.[141] He also gave offence by giving unreserved public credence to Parnell's version of the Carnarvon interview,[142] on the strength purely of his willingness to accord implicit trust in the Irish leader. This appalled Hamilton, who had ever been convinced of the 'absolute untrustworthiness' of Parnell. 'He is as slippery as an eel and cunning as a serpent. Mr G. has always pinned his faith too much to Parnell.'[143]

Ever in the background of events were the stirrings of the 'Parnellism and Crime' issue and the setting up of the Special Commission. With difficulty Gladstone was restrained from direct assault on what he held to be a most unsavoury transaction, 'so unjust to Parnell and so disgrace-ful to the government and to parliament'.[144] Gladstone insisted that the allegedly forged letters were the 'head and front of the matter'. Everything else was 'in comparison ancient history; everything else passed the ordeal of our debates from 1880 to 1885; passed the ordeal of the Dissolution of 1885; passed the ordeal of the Tory policy of that memorable Autumn which history will never forget; passed the ordeal of the General Election'.[145]

With Parnell in March 1888 Gladstone conferred in the first review of the post-1886 Home Rule policy. Gladstone discerned that Parnell's 'coolness of head appeared at every turn'; and that the 'whole of his tone' was undoubtedly 'very conservative'.[146] Parnell was willing, it seemed, to consider some mechanism whereby 'parliamentary inter-vention to stop extreme and violent proceedings' in a Dublin legislature might be instituted. He had never regarded Irish representation at West-minster a matter of much moment either way. All he had to do was sit tight and observe Gladstone's self-imprisonment in the formula that any revision of the 1886 Bill would have to be approved by the Irish party. Gladstone's 'chief point' in these conversations was whether 'the idea of the American Union' afforded 'a practical point of departure'. This – a notion much touted to Gladstone by Carnegie – was an astonishing relapse into unsurveyed constitutional territory, reminiscent of Gladstone's earlier hapless meanderings amid the *terra incognita* of Austro-Hungarian and Swedish–Norwegian dualism; especially as Gladstone volunteered lamely that he 'had not been able to obtain sufficient information'.[147]

One reason why Gladstone was unable to obtain sufficient information was his devoting time to immersing himself in current literature. He began reading on 16 March Mrs Humphry Ward's *Robert Elsmere*, dedicated to the memories of the Oxford philosopher of the politics of social conscience, T. H. Green, and of Laura Lyttelton, who had died tragically in 1886, sister of Margot Tennant. George Russell, a fellow guest of the Rothschilds at Aston Clinton over Easter, reported Gladstone's fascination with the novel: 'he talked of it incessantly, and said he thought he should review it for Knowles'.[148] Gladstone was intensely anxious at the trend of religious life at Oxford toward transference into a secular struggle against social evils. He then went off to stay with Warden Talbot at Keble College, Oxford. It happened that Mrs Ward (niece of Matthew Arnold) was also at Oxford at that time; for Gladstone the feasibility of a meeting made it a necessity.

There ensued an hour on the night of 8 April and an hour and a half on the morning of the 9th of 'strenuous argument'. Gladstone 'fidgeted greatly' in a small, uncomfortable chair on the first occasion; on the following morning, as Mrs Ward recounted to her husband, 'the great man got quite white sometimes & tremulous with interest & excitement' in a 'battle royal' over the treatment in *Robert Elsmere* of 'Christian evidence'.

He was *very* charming personally, though at times he looked stern & angry & white to a degree, so that I wondered sometimes how I had the courage to go on – the drawn brows were formidable. There was a moment when he talked of 'trumpery objections' in his most House of Commons manner. It was as I thought, – the new lines of criticism are not familiar to him, & they really press him hard. He meets them out of Bishop Butler & things analogous but there is a sense I think that the question & answer don't fit, & a vast development of interest & sometimes irritation produced by it.

'I don't believe in any new systems,' he insisted. 'I cling to the old.' The 'great traditions' were what attracted him. 'I believe in the degeneracy of man, in the Fall, – in *sin* – in the entirety and virulence of sin, & sin is the great fact in the world to me.' Gladstone would not accept that moral evil was connected with physical and social and hence removable conditions. He denied that an individual life such as T. H. Green's could give any confidence in that direction. The 'great difficulties' about religious belief 'all lay in the way of Theism'. As to miracles: 'granted a

God it is absurd to limit the scope & range of the *will* of such a being'. ' "The difficulty is", he said slowly, "if you sweep away miracles you sweep away the Resurrection!" '

There were many reminiscences: Oxford in the days of Newman ('How Oxford had been torn & rent, what a "long agony of thought" she had gone through. How different from Cambridge!'). He rehearsed some of the themes of his recent critique of Tennyson. 'It has been a *wonderful* half-century'; though, during the latter part of it, marred by a moral 'recession, & retrogression in the highest class of all'. Mrs Ward got him to admit that in spite of all drawbacks, there had been a gradual growth of and diffusion of 'earnestness, of the social passion': 'with the decline of the Church & State spirit, with the slackening of State religion, there had unquestionably come about, a quickening of State conscience, of the *Social* conscience – I will not say what inference should be drawn'. Withdrawing promptly from this dangerous precinct of socialism and 'constructionism', Gladstone insisted that there were 'still two things left for me to do! . . . One is to carry Home Rule; the other is to prove the intimate connection between the Hebrew and Olympian revelations!'

His *Robert Elsmere* piece was ready for the May *Nineteenth Century*, putting the novel at the centre of public interest much as in the case of *John Inglesant* (a precedent of which Mrs Ward was very aware) and stimulating sales enormously. Gladstone set himself to grapple with the 'new lines of criticism' in a memorandum on Christianity in relationship to government and the 'modern movement of political ideas and forces'.[149] He took trouble to peruse other literary manifestations of those ideas and forces. Émile Zola's naturalistic depictions of the realities of the human condition he found especially offensive. He condemned *La Terre*: 'the most loathsome of all books in the picture it presents'.[150]* It did not seem to him that he needed to concede anything of substance to the modern lines of criticism in his own prepossessions as to either Christianity or political ideas and forces. He conversed with Mary on that 'saddest & most sickening of subjects', birth control. He corresponded with Dr Pomeroy of Boston, appalled at the scene which Pomeroy opened up in *The Ethics of Marriage* on the divorce rate in the United States, 'which filled me with alarm'. 'What then is to be done? What are priests, clergymen, pastors, about?'[151] 'The longer I live', he confided to Laura Thistlethwayte, 'the more I am impressed with the idea that shallow & deficient *sense of sin* is the greatest danger of our time; it prevails of course in all ages among the careless and obstinate; it is the great snare, so far as I can see, of the sceptics of the present age:

---

* A bookseller, Vizetelly, was imprisoned later in 1888 for selling translations of Zola's novels.

but it prevails also among believing people and those who believe themselves to be endowed with high spiritual privilege.'[152]

Politics, on the other hand, was going well. By the end of the 1886 Parliament the Unionists would lose a net twenty seats. Guinness Rogers congratulated Gladstone on the 'many signs that the flowing tide is with us', and that he would before long 'see the complete triumph of your noble struggle'.[153] Carrying Home Rule at this time meant mainly holding the line against revisionists. The particular danger of the pressure to reinstate Irish representatives at Westminster was that it might be a wedge opening the way for much more radical revision. This question took on a new urgency with the publication of correspondence between Parnell and the South African empire-builder Cecil Rhodes, who visited Britain in April. Rhodes wanted to mesh Irish Home Rule into a grand scheme of imperial federation, and offered £10,000 to the Irish party if it pledged itself to retaining members at Westminster. This was eagerly seized upon by revisionists who wanted to capitalize on the continued flow of by-election successes. 'Nothing will spread such dismay in the Tory Unionist camp here', urged Holmes Ivory on Gladstone, 'as a declaration from you favourable to the retention of the Irish Members.'[154] It did not escape Gladstone that many such revisionists were also persistent advocates of upgrading Scottish and Welsh disestablishment and also persistent defenders of the existing Conservative land-purchase policy in Ireland. A member of the Irish Land Commission begged Gladstone to 'kindly reconsider your opposition to a further grant under the Land Purchase Act', which opposition 'blighted the hopes of thousands of Irish tenants'.[155] Once again, Archbishop Walsh proved disturbingly prone to heresy on this matter ('I hope there is nothing inconvenient in what I say about Lord Ashbourne's Act');[156] as did some of the younger Liberals such as R. B. Haldane and Edward Grey.[157]

Very gingerly, Gladstone did begin to move in the direction of conceding the point that retaining Irish MPs at Westminster might become a matter for consideration. 'The change in Mr Gladstone is wonderful,' as one observer prematurely noted. 'Two years ago he believed that it would "pass the wit of man" to devise a scheme for the retention of Irish members. Now he says – "As to the practicability of making such a plan, there is no question at all about it".'[158] Ivory assured Gladstone: 'Your latest statements with regard to the retention of the Irish Members in the Imperial Parliament have been received in Scotland with practically unanimous approval.'[159] On which the distinction was yet to be made that the 'practicability' of any given proposition was not at all the same thing as commitment to making it practicable.

[10]

Gladstone was an old man, getting more and more to be seen as an old man, with appropriate foibles remarked upon. Hamilton observed that 'Mr G. is difficult to move from London, as he is from Hawarden once he is down there'.[160] He felled his last tree, it seems, in December 1891. His discourses in the Commons and anecdotes in society ranged amply over a field of reference taking in the times of Grey, Melbourne, and Wellington as well as the unsurpassable Peel. He was a great Burkean denouncer of all procedural innovation. ('I have the greatest objection to these wholesale departures from those ancient traditions of Parliament which were the practical result of long experience continued through centuries, but which have been thrown overboard during the past four or five years . . .')[161] In private Hamilton noticed that 'he is apt to monopolise the conversation more than formerly; and to expect more attention from those sitting within hearing distance'.[162] Rosebery feared that Gladstone was outliving his political time. He observed what seemed to him Gladstone's losing a sense of proportion: small details occupied his mind as much as great principles; he became obsessed with footling issues.* 'However, Mr G. may do what he likes – his closing years may comparatively be a fiasco – but he can't change the position he must occupy in the history of this country.' Where he was to blame, Rosebery thought, was in his being 'wholly engrossed in one subject', thinking that at his time of life he need trouble himself about no other. He 'forgets that he is . . . the Leader of one of the great parties of the State'.[165]

The precious time at Hawarden in the recess between the two sessions of 1888 was devoted mainly to settling the site for the muniment or archival depository – the 'Octagon', as it eventually took shape – near the north-west corner of the Castle, close by the 'Temple of Peace'. The 'formidable business' of arranging papers was begun in August. Gladstone had good grounds for claiming that he conducted 'probably the largest correspondence that any human being had ever had'.[166] Harry recorded Gladstone's estimating his 'select letters' at 60,000, including 5,000 from the Queen. Once that project was under way, Gladstone began discussing with Catherine the 'subject of the meditated institute'.[167] As he explained in a letter to Harry: 'I have a large scheme in prospect, a building meant to be the nucleus of an institution for religion and

---

* A good example of this was G's amiable obsession later in 1890 about the puzzling fact that he was unable to wear hats he had worn in his younger days. He 'declared he had never heard of a similar case' of expansion of head size.[163] The eminent physician Sir Morell Mackenzie informed G that Henry Irving's head had increased in size with age.[164]

learning, but under the care of the family; such is the blessing of being able absolutely to trust my children.' Its 'higher purpose' would be for the furthering of 'Divine learning and worship', and its 'secondary and possible' purposes would be as a home for retired clergy, a centre for occasional instruction, and as an aid to the parish church.[168] Liverpool's 'inhospitable atmosphere' ruled it out as the site; and 'St Deiniol's', as Gladstone began to refer to the foundation in September, came to be established outside the Castle gate in Hawarden village.* It was a concept quite characteristic of and conformable to Gladstone's long-held prepossessions, but the immediate stimulus was the implications for Christian belief he saw dangerously present in such things as *Robert Elsmere*, the 'new lines of criticism' pressing hard, and needing to be resisted. Gladstone invited the Humphry Wards to Hawarden in September to witness, so to speak, Gladstone's preparations for his bastion of defence against them.

The big occasion on the eve of the reassembling of Parliament for its autumn session in 1888 was Gladstone's speech to the National Liberal Federation Conference at Birmingham, under Chamberlain's nose, on 5 November. He had already upstaged Chamberlain earlier in the 1888 session by urging on the Commons the equitable principle of raising death duties on landed property to equalize those on personalty. As events later in 1894 indicated, this was little more on Gladstone's part than an expedient gesture; but it helped to set the Birmingham scene with an appropriately Radical flourish. At the Town Hall he 'spoke 1h. 40m. with a voice *lent* me, as heretofore, for the occasion'. Then, at Bingley Hall on the 7th he addressed a vast audience of near 20,000: 'strength & voice were given me'; 'I am baculus in manu ambulantis: sed Ille magnus est qui ambulat.'[169]† His chosen themes were Ireland and Liberal Unionism. He kept the door to Irish representation at Westminster ajar without further opening it. Themes pressed upon him by deputations of Liberals wanting measures 'parallel' with Ireland were one-man-one-vote, payment of MPs, and labour representation. Gladstone countered with his standard point about the need to clear away the Irish obstacle. He had hoped to take the opportunity offered by the Birmingham occasion by paying his respects to Newman at the Oratory. His previous visit, in the rather incongruous company of Chamberlain in 1877, had been a sad affair which he would have wished to efface. But Newman by now was no longer up to it. 'It is a great kindness and compliment your wishing to see me. I have known and admired you so long. But I cannot write

---

* St Deiniol (Daniel), d. *c*584, founder of two monasteries at Bangor and reputedly the first Bishop of Bangor.
† 'I am a stick in the hand of him who walks: but it is He who walks that is great.'

nor talk nor walk and hope you will take [my] blessing, which I give from my heart.'[170]

Gladstone's awareness of his 'assigned' role as 'baculus' within the unfolding scheme of the divinely ordered providential government mingled with memories of his recent bout with Mrs Humphry Ward's exposition of the 'new lines of criticism'. After a speaking foray outside Birmingham Gladstone stayed with the Philip Stanhopes at Wodehouse, Wombourne, 8–9 November.*

I woke without a voice: and in the pouring rain, after *four* days of fair weather while we needed them. How He maketh all things in measure & number. I think there have been since 1879 not less than fifty of these fair days: and not *one* has failed us. And I am asked to believe there is no Providence, or He is not 'Knowable'.[171]

This curious vision of the Most High attending to the state of Gladstone's vocal chords and to the microclimate of the West Midlands for the ulterior benefit of the cause of Irish Home Rule is a striking specimen of the sheer cosmic faith in his assignment which sustained and energized Gladstone.

Back in the Commons Gladstone felt sustained by that knowability ('Poor broken reed. But the word sent me was "Arm yourselves therefore with the same mind"').[172]

There was more than a little of it in the liveliness of his denunciations of Balfour's insidiously tyrannical government of Ireland.† No doubt not the least detestable thing about it was that Balfour seemed to be making ground. The Unionist alliance was working well. The Conservatives were willing to pay Chamberlain a high price for his support in getting their big Local Government measure for England and Wales through: something the Liberals had promised since 1880 but consistently failed to achieve. For many Liberals it was an indelible disgrace that it had been left to the Tories to create an elective London County Council. Gladstone was unsure of his footing in relation to manifestations of the 'modern movement of political ideas and forces'. A deputation of colliers, headed by Keir Hardie, addressed him on the eight hours question. The whole of Gladstone's reply 'centred round the need for maintaining the liberty of the collier'.[174] A deputation of representatives of the

---

* Stanhope was Liberal MP for Wednesbury, 1886.
† This was an occasion notable for the target's refusal to accept Gladstone's distinction between denouncing the policy but not the man. Balfour: 'that is one of the distinctions the right hon. Gentleman is fond of drawing, but in which my slower mind has difficulty in following him. When he describes the system I am administering as insidious and tyrannical, he in effect describes me as an insidious tyrant . . .'[173]

unemployed put their case to Gladstone at the House of Commons. 'You are good enough to observe', he replied, 'that in the case of Naples and in the case of Bulgaria I raised my voice on behalf of suffering humanity.' But the distinction to be drawn, he pointed out, was that in those instances he had acted only on receipt of adequate and carefully considered information; which in this case he did not possess; and in the want of such, all he could do was to recall to their minds the great achievements of Liberalism and to recommend faith in the 'efforts of enlightened personal benevolence'.[175]

Given the terms which Gladstone had laid down in July 1886 for the conduct of his leadership, with a dispensation for 'ordinary and habitual attendance' and taking an active part only when occasion seemed to require it, especially on the Irish question, he was under no very heavy sessional pressure in these years. He lived a full social life. 'I dined with Mr Knowles & afterwards witnessed the astonishing performance of Mr Eddison's [sic] phonograph, and by desire made a brief address to him which is to pass vocally across the Atlantic.'[176] He much enjoyed the 'refined' and 'bounteous' hospitality of the Stuart Rendels. A wealthy member of the Armstrong engineering and armaments concern, Rendel cultivated Gladstone assiduously in these latter years. Gladstone found him agreeable; though his 'kindness' was 'possibly more remarkable than his aptitudes'.[177] A sub-plot in their relationship was that Harry Gladstone was soon to be engaged to marry Rendel's daughter Maud. It was as Rendel's guests that the Gladstone entourage proceeded in December to see the old year out and the new year in at the Villa Rocca Bella, Naples. Hamilton disapproved. 'I am sorry that Mr and Mrs G. should go abroad in this fashion. It gives the unkind world such ground for charging them with always *sponging* upon others: though I admit that having been done so often before it does not greatly matter if it is done once more.'[178]*

On his birthday, after a week in Naples and its environs, Gladstone recorded as he entered into his eightieth year: 'All I can see is that I am kept in my present life of contention because I have not in the sight of God earned my dismissal.' Amid 'scenery and weather almost heavenly' Gladstone renewed more memories of fifty-six years before. It was in these Neapolitan evenings that he became addicted to the game of backgammon as a stimulating diversion. He was as ever tempted by the idea of a trip to Rome; but reflected that he could not pay calls on King Humbert or Prime Minister Crispi 'without speaking out plainly' against the alliance with Bismarck which Italy had recently entered.[180] The tone

---

* It must also be recalled, however, that Gladstone's 'Expenditure for Charity and Religion' 1886–90 was £18,407.[179]

of Gladstone's piece for the *Nineteenth Century* in May 1889, 'Italy in 1888–89', was in some degree aggrieved: almost as if the Italian state had followed the Italian Church in letting him down in his hopes that free Italy would prove itself Europe's noblest moral achievement. 'It is in truth my affection for Italy which makes me in my inner mind deplore her tremendous expenditure and her entangling alliances . . .'[181]

[11]

True to his instinct for ripeness of time, Gladstone did not contemplate at the opening of the 1889 session any signal departures in policy. His aim was to stall eager Liberal promoters of a legislative programme to replace Chamberlain's. 'I shall be delighted to open the way to practical measures,' he assured the impatient Labouchere, 'but I do not venture yet to do more than hope for it.' Although the stream of political indicators 'may be flowing in the right direction, I cannot yet say I am convinced the time has come for an active policy on our part'. A Home Rule Bill would be brought in at the right time, by the proper person; but the walls of resistance would need to start more visibly to crumble before the rightness of the time became more evident. 'It would be most unwise of me to press into a forward position.'[182] Gladstone had no stomach for big and contentious issues such as Scottish or Welsh disestablishment. He had no taste for any variety of the currently urged 'progressive' measures in the line of 'temperance' or the miners' eight-hour day. And any attempt either to define Home Rule as being strictly a replay of the 1886 bill or to open up the question at large of redefining it for the next Parliament would invite dissension on principle and dispute over detail in place of the existing pragmatic willingness to let sleeping dogs lie. His extolling O'Connell in the January 1889 *Nineteenth Century* was in effect his comment upon Parnell as a worthy successor to the 'Liberator'.*

It was Parnell's being pressed into a more forward position, however, which rather pulled Gladstone along with him. By the middle of February 1889 the Special Commission investigating 'Parnellism and Crime' had, after fifty days of sittings, arrived at examining the letters allegedly signed by Parnell which *The Times* had published in 1887. On 21 February Sir Charles Russell's cross-examination of the Irish journalist Piggott exposed Piggott's forgeries. Gladstone recorded at dinner on 24 February:

---

* O'Connell's daughter, in her acknowledgements, was a little tactless in trusting that Gladstone would be spared to carry out the 'dream' of her father's life, 'the Repeal of the Union'.[183]

'An animated evening party.' Piggott's confession was posted from Paris on 26 February; whence he departed to Madrid and suicide. Parnell appeared in triumph in the House of Commons on 1 March, with Gladstone giving the lead in a standing ovation. (Hamilton thought it 'an unprecedented kind of ovation, which rather overstepped the bounds of decorum'.)[184] Gladstone spoke: 'A poor scannel pipe indeed unless He play on it.' His theme was a mocking attack on the government's endless postponements of its Irish Local Government measure. There was a 'conclave on the Parnell explosion 12–2' on 2 March; where plans were mooted for some public recognition of Parnell as Liberal hero of the hour. Gladstone duly proposed to Parnell a public dinner, 'which he readily accepted'. It took place eventually, privately but publicized, on 2 April.

But behind the dramatic scenes of incrimination and vindication Gladstone was confronted with his own sad domestic drama. *The Times*, possibly motivated by an element of revengeful malice, fastened on the fact that Willy Gladstone, in managing the Hawarden estate, had executed distraints of rent accompanied by notices to quit on certain tenants. The *Liverpool Daily Post* among others raised the hunt on the theme of 'evictions' and hypocrisy; which *The Times* promptly joined. 'Lord Clanricarde himself might shelter behind the defence which Mr. W. H. Gladstone sets up for the management of the Hawarden estate. The dignified surprise, the restrained indignation, and the delicious simplicity with which the defence is put forth make it quite the funniest thing that ever issued from Hawarden.' Gladstone's letter angrily denouncing 'misstatements' and 'inaccuracies' and a 'trumped-up sensation' was published in *The Times* on 25 February; accompanied by editorial comment on the 'extremely droll parallelism' with Irish cases much held up to execration by Gladstone, and by concern that it seemed 'quite possible that Mr Gladstone does not see the joke'. In any case, the joke went sour when, on 2 March, Willy Gladstone suffered a severe stroke; news of which was kept from his father in the midst of the Parnell affair. Then a 'relieving' telegram from Hawarden crossed an 'anxious' one from Fasque, where Gladstone's unforgivingly Tory eldest brother Sir Thomas was dying. Gladstone and Stephen went up to Fasque for the funeral of the second baronet on the 26th: 'abundant tokens of respect'. At Fasque the following day Gladstone learned of Bright's death. He travelled back overnight to learn that there was little relief in Willy's case. His stroke turned out to be evidence of a brain tumour from which he was never to recover. 'A cloud hangs over our dear Son,' Gladstone recorded on 23 June: 'may God be pleased to disperse it.'

Gladstone did not long delay resuming his place in the Commons. He could not resist the occasion offered in April by a debate on Home Rule for Scotland to point to the contrast between the Unions of 1707 and 1800: the latter characterized by 'a combination of fraud and force, and tyranny and cruelty' on the part of the English Executive, 'hardly to be equalled in the pages of any Christian history ["Oh!"]'.[185] Gladstone lamented his return to 'slavery' at the end of the Easter recess; but in truth, after the 'Parnell explosion', he exploited fully the terms of his leadership: to the extent indeed of choosing not to give a lead to the party on the question of the Naval Defence Bill, which set up a rolling financial programme over five years to pay for a 'two-power standard' of naval supremacy, whereby the British Navy would be capable of defeating the combined forces of the next two naval powers in Europe (understood to be France and Russia). While critical of the unprecedented mode of financing the building programme ('wants of the year should be provided out of the revenues for the year'), Gladstone steered clear of attacking directly the policy embodied in the measure; which, considering his passionate objection in 1893–4 to the second phase of the programme, is curious. The Naval Defence Act of 1889 was quite candidly a British contribution to what was becoming identified as Europe's 'arms race'. The explanation of Gladstone's act of omission at this moment is probably quite simple. To distress at Willy's case was added a general failure of energy. Tennyson commiserated: 'We do not wonder at your feeling of exhaustion just now.'[186]*

There was time even so for convivial occasions. Gladstone dined with 'Mr Lucy and the Punch camp', offering commentary on political cartoons.[187]† After dinner a little later with Lucy Cavendish he was knocked down by a cab and 'badly shaken'; but not so badly as to be unable to apprehend the errant cab driver and consign him to the police. A cruise in Mrs Elliot Yorke's yacht *Garland* early in June, touching at most places on the south coast between Portland and Plymouth, provided welcome respite. On return there was dinner with the Carnegies. 'A large American party: pleasant, effusive, courteous: manners generally different from ours.'[189] To Gladstone Carnegie was ever the embodiment of that 'enlightened personal benevolence' he put so much store in as a counter-manifestation to the modern movement of political ideas and forces.

Gladstone's interest in current literature as an element in the great debate about the 'modern movement' of social and political ideas and forces persisted. The novels of Marie Corelli (née Mary Mackay) excited his attention as exemplars of the uplifting power of fiction to 'move the

---

* 'The companionship of former years is, I need not say, a grateful memory to us.'
† Sir Charles Oman (*Memories of Victorian Oxford* (1941), 141) remarked on the chivalry of the cartoonists in ignoring the maimed finger on Gladstone's left hand.[188]

masses and sway the thoughts of the people'. (Zola's *Nana*, on the other side of the debate, he thought 'a dreadful & revolting delineation', which he cast away from him.)[190] Observing in the case of Mrs Ward how helpful Gladstone could be as a public 'befriender' of books, she had sent him a copy of *A Romance of Two Worlds*, 'as dealing with the scientific and religious questions which agitate the minds of many in the present century'.[191] He called at Miss Corelli's Earls Court house unavailingly. She wrote immediately to the 'most profound thinker and sage of the century' of the privilege she had missed and sent a copy of her latest, *Ardath, the Story of a Dead Self*. Gladstone called again the following day, and stayed talking for two hours while Catherine drove up and down Longridge Road in the victoria.[192]* Corelli attempted to entice Gladstone into reviewing both the *Romance* and *Ardath* with promises to reveal 'the faith practised by a certain few, whose devotion to Christianity cannot be doubted', which made her 'whole life one of gratitude to God and happiness'.[194] Gladstone, however, when it came to faith practised by a certain few, preferred the delicate spirit, 'so profound in its insights',[195] of Marie Bashkirtseff.[196]

With July the Irish question once more began to come to the front. (At a reception for the Shah of Persia on 4 July 'Selborne was something between ice & ink'.) A Durdans visit and 'much conversation' with Rosebery a few days later revealed that Rosebery persisted with the notion he had raised earlier of a 'Cabinet Committee' to revise the Home Rule Bill of 1886. Behind Rosebery were half the ex-Cabinet, eager to ditch the Home Rule policy altogether. It was Hamilton who first suggested to Rosebery the tactic of getting Parnell to formulate proposals in the Commons which he would request be referred to a Select Committee of both Houses. Rosebery adapted the idea to the appointment of a small committee – possibly Harcourt, Morley, and Herschell – to go carefully through the 1886 bill and submit recommendations to Gladstone.[197] Gladstone at The Durdans was unresponsive.[198] 'Mr G. however won't *see* it,' as Rosebery had to conclude in exasperation.[199] Gladstone would keep the matter entirely in his own hands, as it had been from the beginning. If there was going to be revision, it would be done by negotiations directly with Parnell. For this purpose Gladstone drew up a preparatory 'Prime Points of Difficulty' on 8 August.

For the moment all such cares and concerns had to be set aside for the celebrations in July of the Gladstones' golden wedding. Gladstone was much gratified by the presentation of a 'silver inkstand of the old official type' by Algernon West, Reginald Welby, and Eddie Hamilton, to mark the fifty-fifth anniversary of his official life as well as his wedding. The

---

* Gladstone recorded 'an hour with Miss Corelli'.[193]

family celebrations were on 25 July, with an album designed by Walter Crane. The Gladstones came down from Dollis Hill to Carlton House Terrace. 'For me it should have been a day of retreat & recollection, of mingled thankfulness & shame. But was one . . . of incessant calls outwards of every kind.' Gladstone felt 'overwhelmed with undeserved kindnesses' of 'most loving visits, greetings, gifts', together with 'correspondence, business in its inevitable increasing round so that I am whirling round & round instead of being deeply still'. At Hawarden early in August the estate and the village contributed their felicitations. A commodious new entrance porch on the north side of the Castle (convenient for the storage of Gladstone's collection of axes) was provided by the children. The village marked the occasion with a handsome drinking fountain. Behind all the loving visits, greetings, and gifts lay the sad figure of stricken Willy.

Much of August at Hawarden was taken up with inspecting with Harry and Stuart Rendel sites for the St Deiniol's project. It was decided to build temporary structures of corrugated iron, and a start was to be made in September. There was the problem also of what to do about Parnell. The Gladstones were due to be in Paris early in September as guests of Sir E. W. Watkin, Chairman of the South Eastern Metropolitan Railway, and promoter of the Channel Tunnel, at the International Exposition. He wanted before then to fix a date for a visit by Parnell to Hawarden to discuss the shape of a new Home Rule Bill. He inserted a note of caution by way of alluding to problems about such things as the Roman Catholic University issue. 'The back-bone of the Liberal party lies in the Nonconformists of England and Wales, and the Presbyterians of Scotland. These men have a higher level and a stiffer rule of action than the Tory party.'[200] There was the problem also that the question of retention of Irish MPs at Westminster was now causing open dissension in the Liberal ranks. Professor Freeman was unhappy at the indications that the Irish would stay on at Westminster, which 'seems to be taken for granted. This seems to be wholly inconsistent with the nature of Home Rule. If it means anything, it can only be a step towards Federation. By itself, it would practically be making Great Britain dependent on Ireland. Now I would like to know what it is that we are now to struggle for.' Freeman (an expert in the field) was not prepared for federation; and to continue with Irish members at Westminster without federation seemed to him neither one thing nor the other. 'Federation is surely in place when it takes the form of union, not when it takes the form of disunion.'[201]

Freeman was a professional pedant in such matters; but it was material for Gladstone to be aware of doubts. Gladstone pacified Freeman for the time with denials that he was committed to Irish retention. Freeman, relieved, rejoiced at what he trusted was an authoritative clarification. 'The federal idea for Great Britain startles and almost shocks me; but I am ready to think it over if it is put forward plainly as a scheme for something quite different from Irish Home Rule, for something which ought to be discussed separately on its own merits or demerits.'[202] But what was now becoming clear was that the question might well slip out of Gladstone's grip and get out of control. Gladstone wanted to keep as the best ground for keeping control what another observer at this time recalled as the 'abstract principle' Gladstone had formulated at the Foreign Office meeting of his party on 27 May 1886.

At present the Home Rulers are winning, because they have a creed so loosely expressed that it satisfies the Nationalists, properly so called, on the one hand, and the people who talk about 'reform of local government' on the other. Some members of the party (Asquith e.g. and Stead) are federalists; others (Morley e.g. and Freeman) are obstinately anti-federalist. What could hold all together except a 'principle' as flexible as the principle declared at the Foreign Office in '86? Whether the party is strong enough to keep them all together if they have to frame an actual measure of Home Rule – this is a question only to be solved by experiment.[203]

Parnell was not too elusive to be tracked down for an exploratory interview before Gladstone left for Paris. (The Irish leader's roving life, flitting between his mistress and his party, and between Britain and Ireland, was indeed a fugitive and complicated affair.) As ever, Gladstone found Parnell's opinions 'loyal and satisfactory'.[204] It was arranged that Parnell would visit Hawarden in December. Paris, meanwhile, was a whirl of activity in which Gladstone's international stature, even out of office, was sufficiently advertised. The Hôtel Bristol was the base. When the Gladstones appeared at the Hippodrome the performance was arrested and 'God Save the Queen' struck up. At the Opera they were lodged in the presidential box ('C. was overdone'). September the 7th was their visit to the Exposition. Gladstone, his 'poor weak head' for once 'hardly disturbed', braved the ascent of the sensational new Eiffel Tower and delivered a brief speech at its summit ('C. unhappily prevented by indisposition'). At the banquet of the Paris Society of Political Economy 'after doubting to the last moment I attempted & made my speech (15 min?) in French: *all* its faults were drowned in kindness'.

Hawarden that autumn, however, was not quite the happy retreat of old. There had been something of a sour note when the Queen, visiting nearby in Wales, declined an invitation to Hawarden on the ground of pressure of engagements.[205] Apart from the distressing case of Willy, which puzzled the medical consultants, Gladstone found himself on returning from Paris at odds with the younger female generation. 'Mary, no doubt from a sense of duty, made a conversation which much distressed me, but may do me good.'[206] There was a further fraught conversation 'on the subject' with Lucy Cavendish that evening. The 'subject' remains mysterious.[207] Possibly it related to the question of Gladstone's 'rescue work', as relayed by Hamilton. It is more likely that it related to the side of Gladstone's life veiled from his family: the 'entwined lives' of the late Newcastle, Lady Susan Opdebeck (formerly Lady Lincoln), and Laura Thistlethwayte, with Gladstone's.[208] Gladstone's letters to Laura Thistlethwayte 'could not but astonish those who read them and dismay members of his family'.[209] A few days later there was a further conversation with Lucy 'on detachment, & my own case which I could not make good to her satisfaction'.[210]

[12]

The reopening of the serious political year in late 1889 confronted Gladstone with yet more indications that the question of the shape of the Home Rule Bill might get dangerously out of control. Partly this was quite rational trouble-stirring by Conservatives, who carefully drew attention to such things as the *Pall Mall Gazette*'s denunciation of Professor Freeman's version of what he thought Gladstone's letter of 20 August authorized him to say. Might he take it, wrote the current Conservative candidate for the North Bucks by-election,

that your present attitude is to be regarded as *favourable* to the retention of Irish Members at Westminster in any future scheme of Home Rule? And if this be so, may I venture to point out, that there is evidently widespread misconception in the country on the point, which is of the greatest public interest. It cannot be doubted that your letter on the occasion of the Enfield Election in March last, stating that the scheme of 1886 was still before the country, was generally interpreted as signifying your adherence to the plan then proposed of excluding the Irish members, and that this is the view still taken by some of your most prominent supporters.

No doubt, he concluded, 'Professor Freeman will be equally grateful with myself for your direct pronunciation on the subject'.[211] Freeman was not in a position to be thus grateful, since Gladstone avoided any such 'pronunciation'. All that the baffled Freeman could observe was that he hoped the country would 'change its mind' about keeping the

Irish on. 'Surely everybody is not led astray by the "imperial" and "federal" ravings of the Pall Mall Gazette.'[212]

Such squabbles set off ripples and caused disturbance in the party. Channing, one of the promising new men of 1885, put the point to Gladstone.

The rank & file of the party have few opportunities of making known to their leaders exactly what they feel as to party policy . . .

You are being daily pressed by correspondents and by some speakers on one side, to define more fully the lines of the next Home Rule Bill.

Much as I admire Mr Asquith's brilliant powers, I think he is wholly wrong – at any rate as to the proper time for such a step.

This is a point I have repeatedly discussed with other members and heard discussed again and again during the past two years, and I am convinced that the vast majority of the party in the House have perfect confidence, unmodified by the course of events, in the wisdom of the attitude adopted for the time of the Singleton Priory [sic] speech. It is the broad idea of justice to Ireland embodied in Home Rule and contrasted with Coercion which has visibly consolidated our party in the country, and is surely and increasingly concentrating popular opinion in one irresistible current, straight and strong as a mill stream. If public discussion is diverted into questions of details, this great current will lose half its volume in back eddies, and the crotchety, hair-splitting politicians will do much harm.

By fighting on the widest issue alone can we get the maximum popular impulse in the right direction. If that impulse is strong enough the details will take care of themselves as they usually do.

So far, from Gladstone's angle of view, so good. But what Channing then went on to deduce was ominously dissonant.

Another point surely is this. The great feature of the bye-elections has clearly been the growth of the proper conviction that English & Scotch reforms will only get full working out from a Liberal Govt. In this you are getting stronger & stronger a second wave of popular feeling. Is it not clear that the maximum of strength at the next General Election will be attained if English reforms run abreast of Irish reforms, and the conviction spreads among Irishmen as well as Englishmen that the two go together and must be fought for and won together. But if political controversy is concentrated, as it inevitably would be, on the numberless theoretical difficulties and objections ingenious opponents will raise to any detailed proposals, however sound, our whole time will be taken up in these sterile contests, instead of being given to working up the growing impulse to get English reforms by helping the Liberal party.[213]

The great problem here for Gladstone was that it was much more difficult for him to generate the energies of 'doings and intentions' to which this 'second wave of popular feeling' could reciprocate in the old style. But in any case Gladstone had never been much interested in what the Liberal party in itself wanted to do. That had been at the bottom of his problems with it in the first phase of his leadership, to 1875. In the second phase, since 1880, he had been able to keep the party in hand, until he judged the time ripe to manoeuvre it into executing the last of his requirements of the 'series'. This was not compatible with any notions of 'running abreast' or of Irish reform in tandem with English or Scotch (or Welsh) reforms; or any notions of what was now canvassed as the 'complementary' or 'parallel' programmes of reform.

Channing undoubtedly spoke for the larger segment of opinion in the party. That was precisely why the rank and file were given few if any opportunities of making known to the leadership what they felt as to party policy. To Gladstone this was a problem to be manoeuvred around. Channing was demanding something Gladstone had no intention of conceding: that he act as leader of the Liberal party rather than as leader of the Home Rule policy. When he characterized audiences at pre-sessional speeches at Didsbury and Manchester as 'satisfactory: but Radical',[214] that was what he meant. For manoeuvre he still had potently in reserve his imminent departure from the scene. As he soon had occasion to write apropos of pressures for Welsh disestablishment: 'The words used by Sir W. Harcourt, or reported as used, were without doubt the expression of his own opinion as to the contents of the next Liberal programme with which it is perhaps unlikely that I shall have much to do.'[215]

Compared with Channing and what he represented, dealing with Parnell would seem to Gladstone a matter of ease and repose. There was a slight twinge of anxiety on account of the declared intention of Captain O'Shea to initiate legal proceedings, citing Parnell as co-respondent in a petition for divorce. Gladstone asked for all the information that Parnell could 'properly' give. 'I hope that the actions will in no case have the effect of losing another Parliamentary campaign.'[216] He had feared that a 'thundercloud is to burst over Parnell's head'.[217] Parnell assured Morley, who assured Gladstone, that O'Shea's action would fall dead. Parnell himself assured Gladstone: 'We expect to get the action tried before the end of the year, or early in the next. It cannot take more than a few days & should certainly be disposed of before the commencement of the Session.'[218] Once that detail was out of the way, Gladstone could survey a generally promising political scene. The municipal elections under the new local government arrangements in England and Wales produced good results, which could be translated into parliamentary terms as indicating that while all the county losses in 1886 might not be retrieved, there would be big gains in the boroughs.[219] Holmes Ivory in Edinburgh was equally cheering: 'everything is going as well as possible, the tide is running strongly in our favour in Scotland'. He informed Gladstone that, after Home Rule, 'the two questions which excite the greatest interest in Scotland . . . are, Scottish Disestablishment and Scottish Home Rule or Local Rule'.[220]

Parnell was to be accorded the distinction of the entrée to Hawarden for 19 December. Gladstone prepared copious memoranda. He had nominated the issues needing to be discussed: possible changes in the 1886 Home Rule plan; the land-purchase question; and Parnell's own position in relation to the findings of the Special Commission (which did indeed unearth a great deal of evidence of criminality in the activities of the National League and otherwise). A preparatory select gathering of conformable ex-colleagues was arranged at Hawarden for 18–20 October: Ripon, Granville, Morley. There was reluctant agreement that there had to be retention of Irish MPs at Westminster. Morley argued for a reduced number; and for a necessarily more restricted Dublin legislative body. Gladstone was more for restricting the competence of the Irish members to imperial matters only. Granville conveyed the candid opinions of Spencer and Harcourt that Irish representation should be undiminished both in numbers and in scope: the party 'shall want them for a Liberal majority'.[221]

Then came the great encounter in December. Parnell arrived at 5.30 on the 18th; 'and we had 2 hours of satisfactory conversation but he put off the *gros* of it'. There were two hours more on the 19th. 'He is certainly one of the very best people to deal with that I have ever known.' Gladstone showed Parnell around the estate and the old castle. 'He seems to notice and appreciate everything.' Gladstone was able to report on the meeting to all his ex-colleagues still attached to him, as well as Arnold Morley, with the encouraging news that Parnell was without crotchets, full of good sense, and in all respects satisfactory.

From what can be pieced together from his later recriminations with Parnell, it appears that the essence of this conjunction was a kind of nullity. Gladstone was shackled by his own pledges that it would be impossible for him to propose any measure except such as Ireland could approve on the lines already laid down. All he could do was talk around various possibilities and convince himself that Parnell's encouraging nods and impeccably satisfactory sentiments of loyalty and conservatism constituted some sort of working understanding. Gladstone put on record later that:

1. Not a single 'proposal' was made at Hawarden: i.e., no proposition was mentioned to which a binding assent was asked.

2. Mr Parnell had acted as a warm friend of the Bill of 1886, & had in 1889
   the confidence of 85 Irish members. Reciprocally I named to him various
   suggestions, in order to improve my knowledge of the field within which
   the ex-ministers might confer without having reason to fear Irish dissent.

Neither constabulary nor magistracy was mentioned.[222] Parnell reported
to representatives of his party at Liverpool immediately after the interview his entire satisfaction with what Gladstone had had to say.

From Gladstone's point of view the event was a nullity, but a creative
nullity. The important thing was that to no suggestion mentioned by
Gladstone did Parnell offer 'serious objection'. Gladstone remained
uncommitted and as free as Parnell. That meant he kept the matter of
Home Rule entirely in his own hands and could continue his manoeuvres
unimpeded by acceptance or commitment on either side.

Nothing could have been more gratifying to Gladstone, in the warm
afterglow of this most satisfactory visit by the Tribune of Ireland, than
an invitation from the Warden of All Souls that Gladstone avail himself
of his privileges as an Honorary Fellow of the College. Warden Anson
was in fact responding to a heavy hint dropped by Gladstone indicating
that he 'would like to return for a while to College life'. That being so,
a comfortable set would be readily available during the University
vacation, and there would be no problem in Gladstone's bringing his
own servant with him.[223] The arrangement was that Gladstone would
be in residence from 31 January to 8 February. Before departing from
Hawarden, Gladstone recorded in his birthday retrospect something of
the spirit of puzzlement which had been evident in the stunning aftermath of the 1886 'smash'. 'O for . . . insight into the true measure of my
relations to Him who has done such wonders for me, and yet Who
mysteriously holds me on in a life of suspicion and contention, at a time
when Nature which is the voice of God calls & sighs & yearns for repose.'
Of the physical signs of age Gladstone could identify a decline in sight,
hearing, and locomotion; with memory not quite consistent. 'But the
trunk of the body is in all its vital operations . . . what it was ten years
back: it seems to be sustained & upheld for the accomplishment of a
work.'[224]

[13]

The eight days of retreat in All Souls College were for Gladstone something of an escape into an almost irresponsibly juvenile mode of life.
Catherine, of course, and the domestic world she embodied, were

excluded (a matter which was possibly something of an irritation to her). He had never forgotten the splendours of his representation of the University in the House of Commons; Oxford, for its part, could not deny his stature, on any computation, as one of its greatest sons. Every effort was made, on both sides, to avoid issues of contention. 'During his brief retreat at All Souls, party strife was hushed, and a sort of Truce of God prevailed through University and Town.'[225] There were many invitations. The President of the Union (a Peel) hoped Gladstone would consent to speak there, 'the voice of the most distinguished President we have produced'.[226] President Warren of Magdalen volunteered eagerly to entertain. Canon Fremantle offered breakfast at Balliol (there was no invitation, notably, from the Master, Dr Jowett). Freeman, abroad, recommended the historian York Powell to Gladstone's attention as 'one of the first men now in the University'. There were invitations also from Christ Church, Oriel, and 'the Club'. Gladstone in turn deployed all the charm of his 'patronage' style – the gracefully distinctive word to fit every case – to flatter the All Souls Fellows: no difficult task, it appeared. 'I have been reading the Lessons,' he informed Catherine gleefully, 'and all sorts of things – such pranks.'[227] A Fellow of Magdalen, late of All Souls, C. R. L. Fletcher, made a point of observing Gladstone closely. 'He has "le grand air bourbonien" and his manners are very perfect. Quite without affectation, he has the views and habits of an earlier age.' (Gladstone's *ipse dixits* on music: No great musical composer for fifty years. Donizetti, Rossini, and Bellini the last. 'La Donna è Mobile' the last air that has been written. Women's voices are not what they were. Now there's L[aura]. T[histlethwayte]. 'She has a nice voice, but absolutely no style.') 'All his portraits make him look too fierce. There is a great mobility and play of face, as well as of gesture of the hands, which he is fond of bringing down plump on the table to emphasise a point . . .' At a breakfast party at Magdalen Gladstone tactfully discoursed in strong condemnation of Welsh disestablishment.

To Charles Oman it seemed that 'in many ways he was an old-fashioned Conservative'. A modern slackness in codes of dress offended him: members of the University smoking while in cap and gown; he was shocked at the 'scanty costume' of the sporting men, of the 'laxity' of undergraduates perambulating the streets in 'shorts'. He protested also: 'There are too many ladies in Oxford.' Oman observed how, in the interests of avoiding party strife, all Gladstone's anecdotes bore on the earlier part of his career. There was nothing after 1866. Disraeli was not mentioned.[228]

An auspicious occasion on the eve of departing for Oxford was attendance at the marriage, on 30 January, of Harry to Maud Rendel, at St Margaret's, Westminster. Stephen officiated with Dean Farrar and

Warden Talbot of Keble in support. Then, back in London for the new session, the Gladstones abandoned inconvenient Dollis Hill and took a lease on Lord Tollemache's house at 10 St James's Square: 'a large but very gloomy-looking mansion'. Hamilton thought Gladstone looked 'wonderfully well, but complained of his growing deafness, which however is not very apparent'. Hamilton suspected that it was 'an infirmity which Mr G. makes light of when he is bent on doing anything, and makes the most of when he wants to make an excuse for not doing something': such as not giving a pre-sessional dinner to his colleagues. Hamilton was vexed at Gladstone's neglect of his obligations to the party in this and other respects. He tried later to persuade Acton to talk candidly to Gladstone.

He can say things to Mr G. which hardly anybody else can say. I told him that what I thought ought to be impressed upon Mr G. was the expediency of holding more frequent communication with his ex-Cabinet colleagues and occasionally with his party, and of not putting off *sine die* the consideration of some Home Rule measure, so that the difficult points might be met beforehand. Lord Acton thought Mr G. somewhat age-ing, and that want of proportion and perspective was growing upon him.[229]

When Gladstone appeared direct from All Souls on 8 February to report verbally to his colleagues on the Parnell interview he made it very clear that he was not letting the Home Rule measure out of his control for any such consideration of 'difficulties'. 'Sir W. H[arcourt]. ran restive: but alone.' Morley's diary provides another angle of view on the occasion: 'of course P[arnell] wd make no difficulties until he had to'; Harcourt wanted only a 'big county council' for Ireland; and, as to that, half the ex-Cabinet were for shelving Home Rule and being done with it. He thought Gladstone looked 'old and weary', 'rather deaf and a little confused'. 'He does not see that we are less and less able to force a strong scheme, as the years go on.' Morley afterwards felt 'a mort dans l'âme' at the spectacle he had witnessed.[230] Gladstone intimately at ease with an ex-secretary for whom he was a revered father-figure was evidently a very different Gladstone from the leader of the Home Rule policy stubbornly protecting his precious burden from the attentions of resentful and exasperated representatives of the Liberal party. Harcourt and Gladstone could at least agree in launching off the session with a joint assault in the Commons on the government's discreditable and discredited handling of the 'Parnellism and Crime' affair; Gladstone fulminating on the 'cruel, as well as unusual' treatment of Parnell.[231]

That, together with deploring efforts to latch Scottish Home Rule on to Irish Home Rule (there was need to wait for 'further light and for further maturity of this question in the minds of the people of Scotland'),[232] and opposing Balfour's Purchase of Land and Congested Districts (Ireland) Bill as yet another improper extension of Treasury credit, was practically the sum of Gladstone's sessional contribution. Energetic and coherent opposition in the 1890 session might well have driven Salisbury's government to resignation. As it was, its legislative programme collapsed in a shambles as resentful Conservatives reacted against their party's being held in thrall to the Liberal Unionists. There were restless Liberals who resented their party's being held in thrall to the Irish. It happened that the one area in which Gladstone took any consistently serious interest, Ireland, was the one area of conspicuous Conservative success, as Balfour broke the Plan of Campaign and faced down the National League. He was in a position to 'unproclaim' the greater part of Ireland at the beginning of the 1890 session. This left Gladstone somewhat at a loss. He still worried about Parnell and the O'Shea suit. He was afraid that, 'from his not having asserted himself much lately', Parnell might be feeling vulnerable, and might have to withdraw from public life. Gladstone told Hamilton that if Parnell had to go, Davitt was the man the Irish should look to.[233]

Gladstone conspicuously did not assert himself on issues of foreign policy. Freeman had failed in 1889 to persuade him into a 'Bulgarian'-style intervention on behalf of the Cretans struggling against Ottoman rule.[234] Now, in 1890, it took Schwann, one of the Manchester MPs, a considerable effort to elicit from Gladstone a rather perfunctory statement about Turkish outrages in Armenia.[235] There were further efforts to try to interest Gladstone in his rank and file. Stuart Rendel made a point of dining him to meet the Welsh MPs, including the newly elected member for the Carnarvon Boroughs, David Lloyd George, who 'had a long talk with the old gentleman, mostly about compensation'.[236]*

The 'old gentleman' otherwise lived a quite relaxed, rather enjoyable life. There was, of course, theatre. It happened that the startling news of Bismarck's dismissal reached Gladstone as he was being escorted at the Garrick theatre by Eddie Hamilton. Gladstone talked about Bismarck at dinner. 'There were certainly never two men', as Hamilton commented, ' – the two most conspicuous men alive – who had so little in common.'[237] What is most notable about them thus considered is that whereas Bismarck had a lot to say about, and against, Gladstone, Gladstone had very little to say about Bismarck. W. B. Richmond, the artist, had a story about returning to England after having painted a portrait of Bismarck with a message from Bismarck to Gladstone that, while Gladstone was chopping trees down, he, Bismarck, was planting them. Richmond's

---

* The compensation was for publicans deprived of their licences.

message fell quite flat. Gladstone received it with a complete blankness of response. It was rather as if Gladstone was determined that Bismarck was not to have the benefit of any lapse of formality in their intercourse. Probably what stuck most painfully in Gladstone's craw was his recent memory of Italy, infected and depraved by the plague of alliances and war preparations. 'In old times, looking forward to the union of Italy,' he reminisced, 'I had the feeling, and I believe made the prophecy, "She will and must be a conservative power": the Alps will be in the main for her what the channel is for us. Since then I admit there has been a new *Elan* of many Powers.' Gladstone wanted 'neither triple alliance, nor *duple* alliances; the inner mind and meaning of such alliances is not favourable to peace'. He feared that 'the future of Europe is dark, though the calm, please God, may last yet awhile'.[238]

Such sombre thoughts were not the rule, however, in the 1890 session. There was never any want of society. A. E. Elmslie's painting, *Dinner Party at the Earl of Aberdeen's*, with Gladstone prominent among the guests, shown at the New Gallery in April 1890, was an agreeable image of Gladstone's general social agreeableness at this time.[239] Tennyson he found 'well, but as C.G. observed, undoubtedly "gruff"'.[240] Lady Monkswell, wife of one of his former legal officers, observed the 'wicked old man' dining at the Lefevres', marvelling at his 'wonderful old face, & occasionally hear his deep voice booming'. Later, at the Kay-Shuttleworths, she noted Catherine looking '*dreadfully tired*', with the GOM concealed behind a mass of red peonies: the 'prophetic voice arising from out of the flowers'. After dinner the company arranged themselves in a circle around him, '& heard him hold forth on the highly uninteresting subject of *compensation to publicans*'.[241] There were further sessions with the phonograph, with a message to Lord Carrington at Government House, Sydney.[242] There was a tragicomical encounter with the explorer H. M. Stanley, who hoped by means of a map of Africa to enlist Gladstone's support for his plans against the slave trade. Stanley found himself helplessly diverted into unequal and utterly irrelevant conflict with Gladstone on abstruse questions of Herodotan topography.[243] There was much ado helping to arrange a guarantee from Carnegie to save the near-bankrupt Acton from having to sell his library at Aldenham.[244] He attended at Rosebery's triumph, inaugurating, as chairman, the London County Council. 'Many Councillors retain a vivid memory of the venerable figure seated in the recess of the dais.'[245]

While lunching with the Roseberys and Gladstones at The Durdans, Hamilton noted Gladstone 'harping' on the dreadful prospect of Acton's having to sell up his library, leading him into the 'delightful bathos' of suggesting that Acton might write a memoir of Madame Dubarry instead of *not* writing a dozen volumes on Liberty.[246] Certainly Gladstone could not be accused of any relenting in his own literary production. He disapproved of Stead's new venture, the *Review of Reviews* ('a great hit, of doubtful morality');[247] but Stead did have the merit of choosing to republish most of Gladstone's 'Impregnable Rock of Holy Scripture' series from *Good Words*, a counterblast to the 'new lines of criticism'. Gladstone's recent encounters with deputations of miners and the unemployed spurred him to set out his views (thoughtfully conservative) on 'The Rights and Responsibilities of Labour' for *Lloyds Weekly Newspaper*.[248] On the literary front, Gladstone turned his attention now to the uplifting fiction of Hall Caine, with an encouraging letter to the publishers of *The Bondsman* enquiring about connections between Scandinavia and the Isle of Man.[249]

As the first, hectic, session in 1890 wound itself down, Gladstone's general recessiveness, for all that it was fully in accordance with the stipulations he had made in 1886 about the restrictions on the time and scope of his parliamentary obligations to the party, yet did raise the question of his fitness to continue even in relaxed harness. Catherine, normally resolute in encouraging Gladstone's fighting instincts, was beginning to have doubts. She was gradually, Hamilton thought, 'better recognising facts, and to be conscious that resumption of power is not at all a certainty, and possibly not desirable, for Mr G.'.

'Yes', she said, 'I always remember now that you told me we should have to wait. It has been a very happy wait, and if political events had marched differently, they might have marched much worse'. She evidently looks to Spencer to succeed Mr G. in the lead. 'Rosebery can well afford to wait.'[250]

Nothing of these doubts appeared to have impinged on Gladstone amid the gentle routines of Hawarden life. Catherine handed out the prizes at the Hawarden flower show (which had replaced the Horticultural Society, dissolved in 1887 on the issue of Catherine's wanting some of its proceeds to be diverted to support the parochial school).[251] Gladstone discoursed on the dignity of 'hand labour', and the too great fondness in these modern times of young people wanting to promote themselves out of it up to 'head labour', and become clerks.[252] There was always uneasy awareness of the cloud hanging over Willy. The doctors were as baffled as ever about his 'slowness' towards recovery.[253] It was cheering that the St Deiniol's project was going from strength to strength. Gladstone had grave doubts about alterations to the approach road and the yard ('all this troubles my Conservatism'). By 6 October bookcases were prepared for between 22,000 and 24,000 volumes; with a full 12,000 already shelved. Gladstone had long before set forth his *modus operandi* for this laborious undertaking.[254]* Social life was about as intense as in London ('Dinner party every day this week!')[256] Adelina Patti's singing gave Gladstone great pleasure. He diverted himself with 'a little wood craft' from time to time. He read William Booth's exposé of the life of the city slums, *Darkest England and the Way Out*. He read also Froude's *Beaconsfield* and Andrew Lang's *Iddesleigh* (the latter 'ill done'). He made no comment on *Beaconsfield*. The situation seemed well in hand.

> Fret not, haste not, droop not, fear not!
> When the siren warbles fear not.
>
> Fear not, fret not, haste not, droop not
> Climb the heights of faith and stoop not.
>
> Droop not, fear not, fret not, haste not
> Heed thy store of time, and waste not.
>
> Waste not, droop not, fear not, fret not
> I have taught thee; thou, forget not.[257]

[14]

A late autumn session to try to mend the government's earlier sessional collapse was due to commence on 25 November. Gladstone had completed his preparations with an excursion to Edinburgh to receive the freedom of the city and bear testimony on Ireland ('voice came as usual, dropping as it were from the skies'; and Madame Patti provided a 'beautiful little box with her lozenges').[258] The National Liberal Federation began assembling at Sheffield for its conference on 19–20 November. But already siren warbles were heard in the land. Gladstone alerted Laura Thistlethwayte on 16 November: 'It is dreadful news which you will read in the papers tomorrow about Mr Parnell.'[259] The long-delayed O'Shea divorce suit exploded into public notoriety. Parnell, it was revealed, had no defence. He was exposed as a furtive adulterer, 'mean, & tricky, & ignoble', in the words of Malcolm MacColl's report to Gladstone. MacColl asked the question natural to any Liberal advocate of Home Rule: 'Cannot Parnell be prevailed upon privately to disappear from the political arena for the present?' And no doubt Gladstone agreed with MacColl's opinion that it would be 'a fatal error in tactics for the Irish to retort with the case of Lord Hartington': Lord Hartington was

---

* Archbishop Walsh reorganized his Dublin library on Gladstone's principles.[255]

not mean, or tricky, or ignoble, and above all had not got himself 'publicly convicted' in the courts.[260]*

The caution which Gladstone had offered Parnell back in August 1889 – the 'backbone of the Liberal party lies in the Nonconformists of England and Wales, and the Presbyterians of Scotland' – now came home. Channing wrote to Gladstone from the Reform Club: 'I am profoundly convinced that among earnestly religious Nonconformists such as I represent, & who are the backbone of the party, in every constituency, our position will be indefinitely weakened if the very natural desire of the National League to brazen it out & keep their leader at all hazards is persisted in.'[261] Stead informed Gladstone that he had interviewed John Morley, Cardinal Manning, Michael Davitt, the Nonconformist notable Dr Clifford, Reginald Brett, and Lady Ripon; and the 'net result' was that 'unless Mr Parnell resigns his leadership of the Irish party', Stead would be – most unwillingly – 'compelled to undertake a vigorous campaign in press and platform agst having this convicted liar and thoroughfaced scoundrel foisted upon us by virtue of our Home Rule Alliance'. If the Irish stick to this man of 'systematic deceit', of 'disguises and firescapes', then 'farewell to Home Rule'.[262] Promptly, the following day, Stead announced that, Parnell's resignation not having been offered, Stead's campaign would begin. 'I know my Nonconformists well, and no power on earth will induce them to follow that man to the poll, or you either, if you are arm and arm in him.'[263] Gladstone's advice to Harcourt and Morley at the Liberal Federation Conference at Sheffield was that it should be left to the Irish while the Liberal party waited and watched. But he concluded with the 'delphic utterance', 'It'll na dee.'[264]

Promptly also the Nonconformist chiefs proclaimed their anathemas: Dr Clifford at the Liberal Federation Conference on behalf of the Baptists; Hugh Price Hughes for the Wesleyans ('what is morally wrong cannot be politically right'); then Joseph Parker for the Congregationalists. The Irish Catholic hierarchy had long been resentful of the National party's forgetfulness of what it owed to Mother Church; and anathemas would soon enough, but more deliberately, be issuing thence. Manning was only too ready to follow suit in England.† Gladstone was shocked by the sordidness of the systematic deceit. 'Remember this has been a revelation to me,' he told Labouchere. 'I had no idea of the depths of disgrace, not even after the Court, to which he would descend.'[265] The 'not even' takes in the fact that Parnell saw no reason to resign his

---

* The wronged husband in Hartington's case was the complaisant Duke of Manchester.
† Parnell's name does not figure in the copious index to E. S. Purcell's biography of the cardinal, published in 1896.

leadership of the Irish party and had no intention of ever doing so. He felt himself strong enough in Ireland to defy both the Irish Catholic Church and British opinion.

On 21 November Gladstone recorded: 'A bundle of letters daily about Parnell: all one way. Spent the forenoon in drawing out my own view of the case.' That view was that it was no part of Gladstone's duty, 'as the leader of a party in Parliament, to form a personal judgment on the moral conduct of any other leader or fellow member'. But it was his duty that he should estimate in his own mind 'the probable results, where they are serious, which any given course of conduct, no matter whose, is likely to produce upon the public interests with which a party has to deal'. It was plain that the question arose whether Parnell could 'continue to discharge with advantage to the Irish party and people his duties as their leader'. It was also plain that the decision rested 'in the first place with the Irish Parliamentary party, and with the constituents of Mr Parnell and Irish constituencies generally'. Their 'reluctance' to depose Parnell, whom they rightly honoured for the 'inestimable services which, by his sagacity, integrity and persistence', he had done them, was understandable. 'But the great cause of constitutional Home Rule has to be decided by the free assent of the people also of Great Britain; and the Irish demand has to be pleaded in the House of Commons.' Gladstone agreed with Davitt in the *Labour World*: the key question for Parnell was 'the best course for him to adopt with a view to the forbearance of the interests of Home Rule in Great Britain'. 'And, with deep pain but without any doubt, I judge that those interests require his retirement at the present time from his leadership.'[266]

Gladstone drew up this memorandum not as a public intervention but as an opinion which he would certainly give 'if called upon from a quarter entitled to make the demand'. Gladstone deceived himself with his as yet unabated confidence in Parnell's capacity and readiness for altruistic self-sacrifice. He expected Parnell to do the decent thing. It is as if Gladstone found it impossible to accept that the man he had taken into partnership in the 'Home Rule Alliance', to whom he had confided his trust, to whom he had extended his domestic hospitality, and had vindicated against his denigrators, could be other than the man of noble principle Gladstone had decided since 1882 to take him for.

The conduct of Mr Parnell in certain instances, of which I was personally cognisant, during the period when he was acting in opposition to the Liberal Government, impressed me with a sense of his scrupulousness in matters of veracity, and have likewise left upon my mind the belief that in considering his course at the present juncture, with regard to the retention or surrender of the duties of political leadership, he will be guided principally by the question what is [best]* for the interests of the national cause of Ireland, and will include in his grounds of judgment the views of the present situation which may be taken by Liberals in the constituencies of Great Britain.[267]

Parnell was quite a different man from the one Gladstone had ingenuously taken him for. Parnell summoned a pre-sessional meeting of his party for 25 November, in the routine manner, as if nothing had happened. If it came to a fight, Parnell calculated that the most effective way of inciting popular sympathy and support in Ireland was by representing himself to the Irish as a victim of English hypocrisy in general and Gladstone's dictatorial bad faith in particular. By 23 November Gladstone was fully confirmed in his opinion that the 'present force' of the Liberal party for carrying Home Rule 'would be practically broken up were it to approve the continuance under the present circs. of Mr P.'.

On Monday the 24th he left Hawarden for London to confer with Granville, Harcourt, John Morley, and Arnold Morley. He had an interview prearranged also with Justin McCarthy, the vice-chairman of the Irish party. Rendel met Gladstone at Euston station. No sooner was he in the carriage, Rendel reported, than he 'broke out, striking my knee with his hand. Parnell now impossible! The party would not stand it! Overwhelming evidence had reached him! Parnell must go!'[268] Gladstone conveyed tactfully – too tactfully – to McCarthy to transmit this to Parnell and his colleagues. Gladstone also composed a letter for John Morley to give to Parnell before the meeting of the Irish party. McCarthy was too nervous and diffident to impart Gladstone's verbal message to his chief; and Parnell evaded Morley's attempt to thrust Gladstone's written message upon him. He strode imperiously into his party meeting and discussed the business of the session. He was unanimously re-elected its leader.

Gladstone now had to confront the dismaying fact that Parnell was going to fight. All minds were absorbed by the Parnell business, he noted on 25 November, 'which was full of sad incidents'. The letter he had written to Morley on the 24th Gladstone published on the 26th. The world now knew what Gladstone had intended the Irish party alone to know on the day previous. To the Irish this seemed 'extraordinarily precipitate'. Irish pride would react against an appearance of English dictation.[269] The Irish Catholic hierarchy, guided by Walsh, was much wiser to wait and watch, and give the Irish party time to collect itself. Gladstone's impetuousness can be explained partly by a sense of impatient grievance at having been deceived by Parnell, but mainly by the fact that he was used to treating the Liberal party with equal lack of

---

* Gladstone wrote 'most'.

consideration. If the Irish party wished to be a ready instrument for the purposes Gladstone had in mind there could be no doubt and need be no delay in doing what was needful. Gladstone put the point in a memorandum on 28 November:

The continuance of Mr Parnell's leadership means the cessation of relations and of communication between the Irish party and the Liberal party. I should not fully abandon the hope of some change which might revive the common action: but it could not be on the side of the Liberals of Great Britain. Until such change arrived, my position as the leader of the Liberal party could not continue as it is.*

Parnell on 29 November proclaimed his manifesto 'To the People of Ireland'. He attacked Gladstone for presuming to exercise a veto over the Irish party in relation to its leadership. He gave an account of his conversations with Gladstone in December 1889 ascribing to Gladstone intentions very injurious to the cause of Home Rule and the hopes of Ireland. He ignored the divorce issue.[270] Gladstone was 'astonished by Parnell's reckless and suicidal manifesto'.[271] He was now getting an astringent taste of the medicine Parnell had administered to Carnarvon. Gladstone immediately circulated to all the major newspapers his 'Reply to the Parnell Manifesto', repudiating Parnell's version of their discussions, summoning in support the shades of Grattan and O'Connell in his great battle for the Irish nation, 'in whom, even by the side of Mr Parnell, I may claim to take an interest'. Gladstone was seen looking 'very brisk and overflowing with a kind of battle glee'.[272]

Very briskly and with much of battle glee evident Gladstone disposed of attempts by members of the Irish party to negotiate through McCarthy independently of Parnell an agreement whereby in the event of the return of the Liberal party to power they would introduce a Home Rule bill conformable to the issues Parnell had raised in his Manifesto relating to the control by an Irish Executive of constabulary and judiciary and of powers to deal with the land question. Gladstone declared that he could deal with the Irish party only through its leader or persons authorized by its leader.[273] The Irish hierarchy was now on the move. Archbishop Croke of Cashel was unleashed by Walsh to inform Gladstone 'how pained we are here to think that Parnell has caused you so much trouble'. 'He must abdicate, or be deposed.' Croke had sent a 'strongly worded' telegram to Justin McCarthy which would appear in the London papers the following day, 1 December.[274]

---

* G altered the last sentence from 'the continuance of my own leadership as at present would be impossible'.

That day, 1 December, was the day Parnell's enemies in the Irish party, inspired by Timothy Healy, convened a meeting in Committee Room 15 to put Parnell at bay. Of eighty-five members, seventy-three attended. Healy put the devastating point that either Parnell's report to his party after his discussions with Gladstone was false, or his Manifesto was false. The 'necessities of Ireland' were paramount to Parnell's pride. The occasion was intense, bitter, dramatic. There was a majority against Parnell of 44 to 29. The meeting was adjourned to 3 December. Parnell did not attend. He had launched himself off to Ireland. The Irish Whips, Power and Deasy, were instructed to approach Harcourt and Morley to try to pave the way for a deputation to Gladstone to get satisfaction on the points McCarthy had earlier raised. Again, Gladstone declared to a delegation of the forty-four anti-Parnellites that he declined to consider any joint undertakings, and insisted that there could be no negotiations while Parnell remained leader, or any agreement contingent on Parnell's abdication. 'When the Irish party shall have determined upon its new leader, it will be my desire to enter without prejudice into free and confidential communication with him as occasion may require upon any particulars heretofore proposed which may be thought to require amendment, or any suggestions which may appear likely to improve the character of a measure for Home Rule.'[275] Channing assured Gladstone that 'all the best Liberals I know in the House & in the country are unanimous that the party has been enormously strengthened in the constituencies by your action and that any modification of that action wh. could be interpreted as a surrender direct or *indirect* to the duplicity and treachery and baseness of Parnell would *simply destroy the party in the country*'.[276]

Gladstone gathered together as many of his principal colleagues as could be rounded up for a meeting in his room at the Commons at 6 p.m. on the 5th to see whether there might be yet a possibility of some 'modification' to 'do something' for the forty-four Irish. This was 'not liked' by Harcourt, Morley, and Childers. At a meeting of the Irish party on 6 December the forty-four majority members seceded, with the blessing of the Irish Catholic bishops. The bitter fighting between the two Irish factions would not be healed in Gladstone's lifetime. Liberal opinion in general was in a state of great perplexity. Holyoake supportively rendered the pieties: 'On your life rest many crowns and to them the Irish crown will be added. For who has better earned the promise that "his days shall belong in the land"?'[277] Reginald Brett observed 'drooping spirits of some of your friends' and signs of 'wavering on the part of some'. 'It takes the form of suggesting the relegation of Home Rule to a secondary place in the Liberal Programme, and dwells on the impossibility of proceeding with it unless a united Irish party can be dealt with in Council.'[278] On his birthday, 29 December, Gladstone wrote a memorandum 'on the altered outlook. But the Lord God Omnipotent reigneth.' 'All my life long I have cherished from day to day the idea of "Some space between the theatre and the grave".' His hopes hitherto had been disappointed: 1875, 1880, 1885 and now in a situation in the autumn of 1890 when the conversion of the minority of 1886 into 'a large majority' had been established as a 'certainty', 'so far as an event yet contingent could be capable of ascertainment'. Then came the 'sin of Tristram with Isault, and the discovery with this of much that they did not wot of'. The case was not hopeless; but Parnell's desperate struggle to hold his position in Ireland with 'his pretended appeal to the people' had introduced into the Liberal position a dangerous uncertainty. 'Home Rule *may* be postponed for another period of five or six years.' In which case the struggle 'must survive me, cannot be survived by me'. 'Undoubtedly it is a new and aggravated condition of my life that I am finally to resign all hope of anything resembling a brief rest on this side of the grave.' But still it was Gladstone's 'duty of course to preserve the brightness and freshness of our hopes as they stood a couple of months back'. It was lawful 'to pray for success in this endeavour: but it is obligatory to pray also for meekness so as to be prepared for failure'.[279] Gladstone added later a postscript: 'This is a paper of reflex and solitary views. It does not represent but neither does it exclude the consciousness that this question affects millions, and that millions are more than one.'

CHAPTER 13

'I AM NO LONGER FIT FOR PUBLIC LIFE': APPEAL DISMISSED, 1891–3

[1]

The duty of preserving the brightness and freshness of hopes as they stood a couple of months back was greatly hindered by the difficulty Gladstone had of needing to avoid doing anything that, as Archbishop Walsh put it, could 'by any exercise even of perverse ingenuity be twisted into something like a surrender on your part to Mr Parnell'.[1] Fighting for his political life in Ireland, Parnell still looked formidable. As Gladstone pointed out, Parnell commanded about as many members in the Commons as he did in 1880. O'Brien and Dillon opened negotiations with Gladstone to secure his 'sympathy & co-operation' in helping to save Ireland from a miserable fate. Parnell's retirement could be secured on terms which would enable the movement in Ireland and America to reunite with 'full, frank and unmistakable goodwill towards yourself and towards the British people'. The 'terms' were – again – the police, judiciary, and land purchase.[2] From Gladstone's own point of view the proposals in themselves raised no insuperable obstacles in relation to another possible measure for Home Rule; but it was impossible for him to give pledges on behalf of the Liberal party.[3]

Harcourt, his hopes high that at last Home Rule was on the way out, professed outrage at this 'infamous intrigue', implying that Morley was to blame for it and insisting that the Liberal party must betray no weakness to insidious Irish. Gladstone assured him that he would 'sooner deal with a convicted swindler than with Parnell', but at the same time confessed to feeling that 'Healy & his friends have the strongest claims political & moral, on both our consideration & our support'. Though Home Rule might well be killed by Parnell, 'I am most anxious to have nothing to do with the killing of it, on public & on personal grounds', though 'nothing would be more acceptable to me as political death'.[4] He assured Morley that he remained 'extremely indisposed' to recant on a fundamental issue; yet, at the same time, in oblique answer to Morley's own question, 'How are English Liberals to fight the next election?'

Gladstone confessed that 'the relative position of Home Rule will for platforms and candidates undergo some change, but this will best be done by emphasising other matters', and 'rally ourselves by some affirmative legislation taken up by and on behalf of the party'.[5] This turn in the direction of Channing and his friends only lasted as long, however, as the unaccustomed sag in Gladstone's natural resilience.

On returning to London for the 1891 session the Gladstones settled at 18 Park Lane. By-elections meanwhile continued in their almost undeviatingly encouraging trend. An exception was the failure to wrest Nottinghamshire North from the Conservatives in December 1890, despite Gladstone's 'unprecedented' personal intervention at Retford. 'A lesson: but the reading of it not yet clear.'[6] Clarification seemed to come with the capture in January 1891 of Hartlepool, a Liberal Unionist seat in 1886. 'I congratulate you on a glorious victory,' wrote the Liberal MP for Sunderland. 'Parnell was but a factor in the election. The Liberals are well content with your action, the others said nothing against it, & the Irish all voted straight.'[7] The defection from Chamberlain's camp of W. S. Caine, who had been his Whip, was a great fillip to the Gladstonians in 1890. Caine assured Gladstone that 'the great bulk of the *Liberal* Unionists in the country feel that the Government has had its chance and lost it. We can only hope that when you are able to pronounce on the question, we may all find an amicable settlement of this weary strife & controversy.'[8] Gladstone in turn was encouraged to put the case to Carnegie that the Liberal party would be a worthwhile electoral investment.

The cruel blow struck at us by the defection of Mr Parnell, an event unexampled as far as I recollect in history, has not broken up or terrified the Liberal phalanx; and it marches steadily on to battle. Its behaviour has surpassed my most sanguine expectations. But, if the schism in Ireland keeps alive, it may deprive us of say ten seats, or take twenty votes from the majority with which alone we have to encounter the rank, wealth and so-called education of the country, with its enormous train of social influence. If we are not strong enough to win now, the cause will probably stand over for twenty years: and I, or Nature for me, must bid it farewell. *Now* is the time, or never, to strike a blow for us: and I look back with most sincere pleasure on the words you used to me in Park Lane when you were good enough to call.[9]

The parliamentary session of 1891 did not put Gladstone to any fatiguing exertions. He remained a fitful and intermittent party leader. He had the pleasure of promoting (unavailingly) a private bill to remove Roman Catholic disability in relation to the viceroyalty of Ireland and the lord chancellorship of England, and he declared that he did not see the expediency or the advantage of prolonging the controversy about disestablishing the Church in Wales. As had been the case with the Church of Ireland, it was 'the church of the few against the church of the many', and it was the 'church of the rich against the church of the comparatively poor'.[10] This gave the Liberal party a nourishing bone to chew on, and left Gladstone scope for literature. He sketched a beginning for his 'Olympian Religion' (and startled the editor of the Congregationalist *Independent* with his 'belief that the ordinary popular life of the Achaian Greek was morally higher than that of the ordinary Hebrew at the times of Moses, the Judges, and the Kings').[11] He set out his thoughts – negative – on the female suffrage question, reserving them for later publication.[12] The social lion of the moment was the prime minister of the Cape Colony, Cecil Rhodes, whom Gladstone found 'a notable man' (Morley thought 'Mr G. looked sadly white and old').[13] The scandal of the Prince of Wales's involvement in the Tranby Croft baccarat affair, and his subsequent appearance as a witness in court, Gladstone thought 'deplorable *all round*'.[14] A visit to Brighton to see Eddie Hamilton, recuperating from a serious illness, was a pleasurable interlude. 'They were delighted with the hotel (especially as they have not to pay the Bill, which Armitstead settles); and they enjoy being here.'[15]*

The signal event in the early days of the session was Granville's death at the end of March: 'my dear and fast friend'. As he wrote to Laura Thistlethwayte of the recent deaths of friends 'packed' in the last eighteen months, Granville had been 'the most intimate of them all'. 'His is a loss that can never be replaced. And it always seems to me, when persons sensibly younger than myself are taken away, as if my surviving them were a kind of fraud.'[17] Unhappily for Granville's surviving friends, he left them a parlous and tangled financial legacy to unravel. It appeared that saving his reputation from bankruptcy would require an input to his embarrassed estate of something in the order of £60,000.[18] But even sadder than Granville's case was the case of Willy. His physicians could now see no hope other than in a desperate operation in London. 'It is sad: but we are in God's hands.'[19] On 3 July 'sad news of the turn in the evening was too kindly kept from me'. By the time he arrived at Liverpool Street station from Lowestoft (where he had been staying with J. J. Colman), Gladstone was 'terribly shocked and broken down'. July the 4th was 'the day of dear Willy's entry into rest, at 5.30. A.M.', in his fiftieth year. To Laura Thistlethwayte Gladstone consoled himself that Willy's death was in its way a blessing. 'Had he lived he must have lived in agony or mental decay which only his powerful constitution warded

---

* George Armitstead, former MP for Dundee, was one of G's retinue of wealthy benefactors. Lord Armitstead 1906.[16] 'In our *host* (at this hotel) we have a prize: he is of rare modesty, courtesy, and generosity: rare in his class, or in any class.'

off so long.'[20] (A distressing and tiresome consequence of Willy's tragedy was that Lord Penrhyn, who had married Henry Glynne's daughter Gertrude, challenged – in the result unsuccessfully – the resettlement of the Hawarden estate on Willy's heir, William Glynne Charles Gladstone, then aged six.) On 8 July at Hawarden 'Our son in the prime of middle life was followed to the grave, with its wide and inspiring outlook, between twelve and one, by his mother in her 80th, and his unworthy Father in his 82nd year.'

Ever resilient, Gladstone impressed Hamilton as being 'full of *go* and vigour' when Gladstone visited his former secretary, still recuperating but now lodged temporarily in 10 Downing Street in the former Cabinet room. Gladstone could remember Peel sitting there; though he could not recall to mind the exact year – probably around 1860 – when Cabinet meetings ceased to be held at the old Foreign Office and the Cabinet migrated to Downing Street.[21] (Gladstone still had stored in the basement of Number 10, unbeknown to the then First Lord of the Treasury, W. H. Smith, papers destined for the Octagon.)

He was resilient enough also, in spite of the wounds inflicted in 1887 by the Shaftesbury biography,* to agree to compose the inscription for the series of small panels to be set around the skirt of the bronze mantle of the monument to Shaftesbury, a public fountain then to be sited in Cambridge Circus, with a design by Albert Gilbert for a statue of Christian Charity (or Divine Love – there was never an authoritative designation).†

Most resilient of all was Gladstone in his third psephological exercise in 'Electoral Facts', which came out in the September issue of the *Nineteenth Century*. The election of 1886, he declared, 'did not blind the eyes of the defeated party: for they had built their hopes, not on the humour of the moment, but on faith in the operation of principles broad and deep, and on the results of world-wide experience'. There never had been a time, he was sure, since the first Reform Act, when 'indications were so largely supplied as they now are, to aid in reckoning what was likely to be the judgment of the people at an impending General Election'. He calculated that, 'while endeavouring to rule every doubtful point against ourselves, we are landed at last in a conclusion which assigns to the Liberals at the coming election a majority, from Great Britain alone, which may probably take rank with the remarkable majorities of 1868 and 1880'. Gladstone referred back to his first attempt at psephological prediction in 1878,

* See above, page 469.

† G's words are: 'During a public life of half a century / he devoted the influence of his station / the strong sympathies of his heart / and the great powers of his mind / to honouring God / by serving his fellow men / an example to his order / a blessing to his people / and a name to be by them / gratefully remembered.' The monument was unveiled in Piccadilly Circus in 1893.

when he estimated modestly a Liberal majority of between fifty-six and seventy-six; his method thus was not one of mere sanguine temper, or the wish being father to the thought: his 'probably too low' prediction for a British majority in 1892 was ninety-seven seats.[22] Here Gladstone was predicting that the electorate would do what it had failed to do in 1885: provide him with the 'absolute necessity' of the 'perfect independence' of a majority in Britain substantially larger than the combined numbers of the two Irish factions. He had stipulated then that it would not be 'safe' for the Liberal party to enter into the question of Irish self-government with anything less than such a majority.* For reasons which seemed good to him at that time, he had nonetheless gone ahead in 1886. He did not wish to have to repeat that very unsafe operation.

[2]

All Gladstone's immense reserves of resilience were taxed to the full by the great political event of 1891, his speech to the National Conference of the Liberal Federation at Newcastle at the beginning of October. It could not be other than an important occasion. It was clear that Salisbury would advise a dissolution of the 1886 Parliament in the coming year. The only question about the general election ensuing was how large the Liberal majority in Britain would be. This was admitted on all sides. The Liberal party was in need of a steadying display of Gladstone's leadership after the shock of the Parnell crash. At the same time that shock had weakened and loosened the coils with which Gladstone had bound the party in 1886. Gladstone wanted above all to preserve his autonomy in the Home Rule policy and keep its way clear for resolution. But he did not assume thereby that his role at Newcastle would be as 'reluctant hostage' to the party's demands for British reforms to run abreast of Irish reforms.[23] If he got the majority he wanted there would be no question of his power to command the parliamentary agenda. Home Rule was no longer a startling novelty. Gladstone could tighten his coils in 1891 precisely by making it clear that his commitment to Home Rule did not blind him to the simple fact that the Liberal party and a Liberal government needed to be fully equipped with policies adequate to its post-Home Rule Act future. The big problem for Gladstone would be the House of Lords; and he had ready keenly forged arguments that resistance by the Lords to a clearly expressed will of the nation would be immensely to the advantage of the Radical 'movement'.

* See above, page 386–7.

Thus, while the tilt of Gladstone's reading of the situation remained that 'under any circumstances we must wait upon Ireland', and that 'we can take no fresh cargo aboard till that is discharged',[24] his approach to the Liberal Federation also remained very much what it had been at the time he had assisted its inauguration in 1877. He never lost sight of the view he had of it then: representing, however imperfectly, but in some authentic sense, through the Liberal party 'out of doors', the 'nation' at large; and the nation very decidedly against the parliamentary party. In 1877 Gladstone had treated Granville's and Hartington's warning about the Liberal Federation as the natural but misguided reactions of Whig parliamentarians. In 1891 he treated the anxieties of Harcourt and Morley in much the same spirit. Ever since the Federation was wrested from Chamberlain's control in 1887 Gladstone had dismayed his senior colleagues by the extent to which, as the 'great Panjandrum', he complaisantly allowed Schnadhorst to manage his appearances there. Morley in particular feared that Gladstone's obsession with Home Rule might be exploited to let loose 'the *fads* which infest the air like midges'. At Newcastle Morley was on his political home ground; and was determined to push Schnadhorst aside and make sure that the GOM did not inadvertently unleash 'Labour' fads or 'London' fads.[25]

Andrew Clark cleared Gladstone as fit for the foray, but forbade a long speech and anything in the way of a public dinner. 'My laziness regrets,' was Gladstone's own formula, 'but I think duty calls.'[26] After limbering up with a tour in Scotland taking in both Glenalmond and Fasque, the Gladstones arrived on Tyneside on 1 October. ('Great enthusiasm. Read Iliad.') Newcastle was well chosen as backdrop. Memories revived of 1862. In the north-east Gladstone's aura of 'priest-king' still radiated much of its old power. There persisted the 'zone of magnetism' which Carnegie described Gladstone's extending round all who came near him.[27]

Morley observed with disquiet that Gladstone 'had not a single note ready': in his usual way he was expecting to be guided as to what to say and what not to say in order to keep the Federation in humour, always reserving the right to select items for emphasis or relegation to the sideline. At Newcastle Gladstone reviewed an approved list of items which became known immediately as the 'Newcastle Programme': including local option, payment of MPs, registration reform and one-man-one-vote, elective parish councils, land reform, and disestablishment in Scotland and Wales. But he did not ratify them as a programme; and indeed, he entirely ignored the Nonconformist demands on elementary-education policy because of their hostility to denominational schools. He largely pleased himself in picking and choosing; he ignored also 'labour' questions and female suffrage.[28] And in his emphatic comments on the need to withdraw the British presence from Egypt and the need to reduce public expenditure he in effect rebuked the Federation managers for evading major public issues.[29] Gladstone was not unaware that he was no longer able to impose Home Rule on the party quite in the imperial style of 1886. But the point was he did not now really need to. 'As to the title of Ireland to the precedence,' he informed the Conference, 'there is no question about it at all – it is a matter fixed and determined and settled long ago, upon reasons which in my opinion – and, what is much more, in the opinion of the people – cannot be refuted, cannot even be contested.' One of the veterans of 1862, Guinness Rogers, congratulated Gladstone for putting on the old show once more: 'You have given a new inspiration to the country.'[30] In truth, Gladstone was giving an old inspiration to the country; nor was it entirely clear that Home Rule was at the heart of it.

Retreating back promptly to Hawarden ('Deo Gratias for having finished a work heavy at near 82') Gladstone was buffeted by two more deaths: W. H. Smith, First Lord and Leader of the Commons, and Parnell, disowned miserably in Ireland amid recrimination and vituperation against Gladstone, died on the same day, 6 October. ('So the Almighty bares His arm when he sees it meet . . .') Parnell's passing gave Gladstone hope that the 'healing process' in Ireland might now 'advance without a break'. He requested Labouchere to help keep Healy in check. Newcastle had confirmed for Gladstone that things generally were continuing to prosper. 'We have reached a point in the course of this long struggle, at which we are almost compelled to contemplate for the next Parliament a Liberal and Home Rule majority . . .' 'As far as I know, matters continue, in Great Britain, to move in the right direction, and rather with an accelerated than a backward force.' The great danger that the party might be 'demoralised by the Parnell catastrophe' had been 'averted by its good sense'. 'I have myself once known a majority too large for the longevity of a Government: but no majority can be too large for securing the success of a Home Rule Bill. We must not make light of a single seat that can be kept or gained.'[31] To representatives of the Labour interest who resented Gladstone's ignoring their concerns, particularly the statutory eight-hours question, at Newcastle, Gladstone unapologetically drew attention to the record of Liberalism in its engagement 'in the great task of procuring an act of justice for the fellow-labourers of the British workmen in Ireland'.[32] His obsessiveness on Ireland Rosebery found disturbing. At Hawarden Gladstone 'lost control of himself (for the third time in my experience) in speaking of the Irish rebellion of 1798. In vain did I try to keep him off and turn the subject.'[33]

A gathering at Althorp early in December of Gladstone, Morley, Harcourt and their host Spencer laid preparations for the new session. They were hardly of high moment, since Salisbury's only purpose was to dissolve once necessary public business was transacted. But Gladstone thought it important that 'complete harmony' should be seen to prevail. The difficulty was with Rosebery. Despondent at the recent death of Lady Rosebery, he resisted invitations to join the Althorp party. It was only through his great friend Hamilton's exertions that Rosebery eventually was prevailed upon to consent. Gladstone recorded on 8 December: 'Political confabulation & survey: good.' There was a 'walk with Morley and much conversation'. But behind the façade of the social amenities both Rosebery and Morley shared a premonition of Gladstone's fading into political limbo. The prospect of a new Liberal government with the octogenarian Gladstone for the fourth time at the helm dismayed them. At Mentmore earlier they had speculated on the conceivability of Gladstone's handing over the premiership to Spencer and taking office without portfolio, purely to frame and introduce a Home Rule Bill.[34] Rosebery in any case had been much occupied with his *William Pitt*, published that year, in which he gave a Seeleyan twist to an interpretation of the Act of Union somewhat different from Gladstone's. (Gladstone recorded reading *Pitt* 'with sighs at important points'.)[35] And for that matter, Morley was having grave doubts about the whole business. There was little evidence after the Newcastle rally that Home Rule commanded the attention of the British electorate. He confided to Rosebery and Hamilton that he doubted 'if Mr G. will reoccupy the conspicuous nitch in history that his admirers now accord him: he will never get over the *spills* he has given his party in 1874 and 1885'.[36]

From Althorp the Gladstones paused at Mentmore en route to London. Gladstone tried to put a stop to the widower Rosebery's talk of retirement: 'when one had attained to a certain point in politics it was impossible to retire'.[37] Hamilton talked with Catherine.

She spoke hopefully, but her hopes were rather mingled with fears, about the future. She could honestly say that, though the last 4 years might have had their disappointments, yet they would also be numbered among the happiest years of her life. She was very pleased and relieved at the prospect of Algy West being Mr G.'s right-hand man.[38]

Back in London they were lodged 'luxuriously' by Rendel at 1 Carlton Gardens before proceeding to Paris, accompanied by Helen and Morley, with West in attendance. Armitstead was the host. 'Everything most comfortable: but too sumptuous.'[39]

Thence they were 'personally *conducted* by Mr Armitstead' to the Grand Hotel, Biarritz. Gladstone responded well to the bracing ambience and the Atlantic breakers ('the sea grand and terrible'): 'full of vigour'

– until he greedily consumed large quantities of wild strawberries, and spent the following day in seclusion. Catherine shook off her deafness. There was every reason for Gladstone to declare on Christmas day: 'We are very happy with our host and otherwise.' There was invigorating talk. Among those wintering at the resort were the Lionel Tollemaches. He, the son of a former Conservative MP for Cheshire, 'though nearly blind and with a terrific stutter', as Lucy Cavendish described him, 'is clever and can be agreeable'.[40] As a professed 'student of human nature', Tollemache set out to study Gladstone. For this purpose it was helpful that Tollemache was able to observe a 'young lady' who, conversing with Gladstone, 'sprung a mine' by denouncing Walter Scott as dull, and adding that she got 'more pleasure from Thackeray and George Eliot'.[41]* It was Gladstone's turn to spring a mine under Morley in a 'long morning conversation on Locke'. It was 'a tremendous tussle, for Mr G. is of the same mind, and perhaps for the same sort of reason, as Joseph de Maistre, that contempt for Locke is the beginning of knowledge'. This startling insight into the ulterior values of a Peelite High Churchman shook Morley profoundly. 'All very well for De Maistre, but not for a man in line with European Liberalism.'[43]†

On the completion of his eighty-second year Gladstone mused on his 'singular lot': subject to the inconveniences of old age, 'but not such as to stop my work'. He was not permitted the rest he longed for. 'But I am called to walk as Abraham walked, not knowing whither he went. What an honour. Yet I long, long, long to be out of contention; I hope it is not sin.' Not the least of Armitstead's services was his companion-ableness as a player at backgammon. There were extensive excursions – Fuenterrabia, Saint-Jean de Luz, Bayonne. 'So ends the year: not rung but roared out by this magnificent sea, great alike for ear and eye.' News came of Manning's death, 'in his ripeness', following on Newman's in little more than a year. The ranks of Gladstone's generation were now thinning apace. The Gladstone party, less Helen and Morley, departed from Biarritz on 9 February, under ban from Clark against returning to London while an influenza epidemic raged.‡ The 1892 session would have to commence in Gladstone's absence. After a tour through Pau, Toulouse, and Nîmes, they took refuge at Rendel's villa at Valescure, near Saint-Raphael. Rendel could relieve Armitstead at backgammon duty. There Gladstone was cheered by the 'splendid report' of the Gladstonian success in capturing the Rossendale division of Lancashire,

---

* G had admired Ellen Terry in *Ravenswood*, a dramatic version of *The Bride of Lammermoor*, at the Lyceum in December 1890: 'fine in the great scene. But the Book, the Book!'[42]
† Comte Joseph de Maistre (1754–1821), philosopher of the clerical reaction against the French Revolution.
‡ G had suffered a bad bout of it in May 1891.

vacated by Hartington on his succeeding to the Devonshire dukedom. The Gladstones bade farewell to Rendel's 'hospitable & charming mansion' on 25 February and after an intense social round in Paris were back in London on the 29th, putting up at Rendel's other hospitable and charming mansion at 1 Carlton Gardens.

[3]

Hamilton, meanwhile, had been examining at the Treasury the financial provisions of the 1886 Home Rule Bill. 'I am convinced that the difficulties of arriving at a settlement which would be accepted by the Irishmen and would at the same time be fair to the British taxpayer are enormous.' The problems would be exacerbated by the vast layout of credit incurred by Balfour's 1891 Land Purchase Act. 'They ought to be faced at once; and Mr G., if he won't take up the question himself, ought to devolve it on some of his colleagues like Harcourt and Fowler . . .'[44] Morley, back from Biarritz, shared Hamilton's doubts about Gladstone's being able to stand the strain of prime-ministerial work again, and agreed with Hamilton that Gladstone 'ought not to be exposed to the risk of encountering insoluble difficulties at the close of his career and of making a fiasco of it'. But Morley held it 'useless to take these doubts and feelings into account, for he is certain Mr G. is bent on forming another Government if he has the chance: indeed, his mind on this head is not only made up by himself but has been made up for him by others'.[45]

Gladstone's bent was much forwarded in March 1892 by the deputy chairman of the London County Council's congratulations on the County Council elections, 'because of its immediate significance in respect of the coming General Election in London', where there were great new prospects in the 'shopkeeping class' and much more cohesion among the various sections of the Liberal party: very different from six years before.[46] Breaking the Conservative hold on the Metropolis would be an indispensable prerequisite for the big majority Gladstone would need to validate Home Rule and overawe the House of Lords. As he put it to Catherine, 'my desire is for three figures'.[47] A visit to Hawarden by the Carnegies offered yet more tantalizing prospects of electoral largesse from the 'giant millionaire'.[48] Carnegie made it clear that any largesse would depend on the future Liberal government's adopting payment for MPs.[49] The Liberal war-chest indeed, after the departure of many wealthy Liberal Unionists, was much in need of replenishment. In due course there would be embarrassing scandals attendant on Gladstone's allowing himself to be persuaded by Arnold Morley and Schnadhorst in

1891 to exchange promises of peerages to 'two insignificant but wealthy' Liberal MPs for 'substantial contributions to the Liberal party funds'.[50]*

Gladstone was lively enough in debate in the 1892 session. His complaints about Goschen's budget centred on what had by now become one of his most characteristic themes: the rudely radical manner with which the Conservative government dealt with old customs of procedure.[51] However, the new Leader of the Commons, Balfour, rendered thanks for Gladstone's *'absolutely invaluable* help' in the matter of the Clergy Discipline Bill.[52] Where Gladstone himself was in need of help was on the issue of female suffrage, which was being promoted inconveniently, and in his opinion precipitately, by Salisbury and Balfour among others. Now was the time to publish the material he had prepared in 1891: *Female Suffrage: A Letter from the Right Hon. W. E. Gladstone to Samuel Smith, MP* (11 April 1892), in which he concluded on the dangers confronting the sex: 'The fear I have is, lest we should invite her unwillingly to trespass upon the delicacy, the purity, the refinement, the elevation of her own nature, which are the present sources of its power.' Gladstone found himself voting against the Women's Suffrage Bill 'in an uncomfortably small majority of 23'.[53] He was vehemently denounced as a 'Grand Old Humbug' by the indignant Lady Florence Dixie.[54] There was the embarrassment also that Catherine was the President of the Women's Liberal Federation, the council of which, on the lead of Lady Carlisle, had voted to promote female suffrage. Catherine eventually resigned in 1893.

Compared with this problem, nimble evasion of deputations from the London Trades Council on the hours-of-work question was a matter of old habit.[55] That the Trades Council threatened to wreak electoral damage in the coming elections was a worrying portent (Gladstone's 'dishonest evasion' revealed him as 'blind to industrial life', whereas Lord Salisbury had proved a 'straightforward' enemy).[56] But Gladstone would have been much more impressed by the menaces of Hugh Price Hughes, editor of the *Methodist Times*. Methodists, Hughes pointed out, were mainly with Gladstone. There would probably be thirty Methodist candidates at the elections. The two matters which they regarded as absolutely essential were that there must be *full* Irish representation at Westminster, and that a Dublin Parliament must be really and effectively subordinate to the Westminster Parliament.[57]

But Gladstone in turn had his own menaces to display. 'We know very well', as he put it in the Commons, 'that when we are talking of the House of Lords we are talking of the Government.'[58] Behind this bold public front, however, Gladstone had to encounter the question of

---

* G's diary is opaque on the matter. See below, page 572.

octogenarian deficiencies. At one point in debate the *Hansard* record reported his finding his eyes incompetent 'readily to decipher the manuscript from which he was reading', having to turn to Morley to continue reading it.[59] This was one of the early signs of the cataract forming in his right eye. To Hamilton Gladstone confessed, believing a Liberal majority to be 'unavoidable', his anxieties about physical infirmities. 'How could he ever conduct the business of a Cabinet with his present deafness?' The only way would be by a small 'interior Cabinet'. And he was depressed too at the imminence of the problem passing the wit of man he had defined in 1882: how to have the Irish both at Westminster and Dublin: it was 'impossible now to make a "clean job of it" '. Ulster on the other hand he did not take seriously as a problem. Salisbury and Balfour were 'wicked' in talking it up; but it would all 'end in tall talk'. Ulster's claims were 'preposterous'. 'Ulster forsooth!' The province returned to Westminster as many Nationalists as Unionists.[60]

[4]

It was to be a truncated session; a June dissolution and a July general election. A Gladstonian majority was universally predicted. The Conservative Chief Whip, Aretas Akers-Douglas, estimated it at twenty-eight to thirty.[61] But Conservative Central Office was nervous. Many Liberals were known to be preparing to vote for Gladstone and the Newcastle programme, yet trusting to the House of Lords to do its plain duty with respect to Irish Home Rule. There was always the possibility that Gladstone might get his majority by accident or default. It was known that Gladstone would be content 'with nothing less than three figures'.[62]* John Morley testified that he counted on 'eighty or a hundred'.[63] Labouchere was less sanguine: 'The G.O.M. will win but not with a large majority which perhaps means losing.'[64] The Queen enquired hopefully of Cranbrook that she 'understood that Mr Gladstone said he *must* have 100 majority. How was he to obtain such a change?'[65]

The obvious answer was that Gladstone already benefited by the Unionist majority of 1886 having been whittled down from 116 to sixty-six. What was required was that the general election should confirm and extend the trend of the previous by-elections. Gladstone's problem was that for such a trend to overturn decisively the verdict of 1886 it would require in England a heave of the body politic of seismic proportions. Home Rule did not take fire in 1892. 'The difficulty is', one observer

* The *Standard* (22 July 1892, 2) claimed that G had fixed his calculation at 154.

noted, 'that the English rural constituencies are sick of the Home Rule question.' It was notorious that in the colliery districts, as another observer commented, 'Home Rule had no more to do with the result of the elections than rival theories as to the personality of Shakespeare'.[66]

Nothing of this penetrated Gladstone's fixed certitude that there should stand ultimately no obstacle to his political will as sanctified by his instrumentality to the divine will. The final triumph, as he had predicted in 1886, was certain. It was a case indeed of *'Now* is the time, or never'. A recurrence of the interest he had shown in 1876 in the Latin proverbial tag *vox populi vox dei* is curiously suggestive.[67] This was at the time he was working on *Special Aspects of the Irish Question. A Series of Reflections in and since 1886*, published in 1892 as a culminating contribution to the literary war he had waged for Ireland. Gladstone was in hopes that another 1876 would lead to another 1880. He had endeavoured to convince the English public that the whole history of the English empire in Ireland, and in particular the abolition of the Irish Parliament and the Union of 1800, had been a story of oppression and atrocity sufficiently analogous, within a Christian frame of reference, to justify a response made by the English electorate analogous to their dismissal of 'Beaconsfieldism' in 1880. His explanation for failure in 1886 had been 'the people do not know the case'. He had now, over six years, explained the case. The people would no longer be 'puzzled'. Gladstone's great endeavour between 1886 and 1892 was the most sublime example in constitutional democracy of a history lesson applied to politics.

Gladstone issued his election address on 24 June. It was avowedly, in the sixtieth year of his political life, the last that he would issue. He put the case for Irish Home Rule 'on the outlines of the proposal for which the Liberal party has unitedly contended for the last six years'. He was particularly concerned to rebut objections that the Imperial Parliament's supremacy over the self-governing colonies was a mere fiction. To Home Rule he added the consideration that in Scotland and Wales the public sense had 'conscientiously declared itself against the maintenance of the respective religious Establishments'. He favoured the setting up of representative licensing authorities to control the drink trade, the reform of registration for the franchise, the system of one-man-one-vote, and a further limitation of the hours of labour for miners. He concluded with a ritual denunciation of 'these leisured classes, these educated classes, these wealthy classes, these titled classes'. Gladstone set out from Hawarden for Midlothian on the 25th. At Chester a 'middle-aged bony woman', replete with 'spite and energy', flung from about two yards off with 'force and skill' a 'hardbaked little gingerbread say 1½ inches across' at Gladstone as he passed in his carriage, striking his left and most serviceable eye. This sent him back to Hawarden to bed and dark for four days before he could set forth again on the 29th for 'hospitable Dalmeny once more', 'dark spectacles' all the way.

At Dalmeny Acton and Algernon West were in attendance. The pattern of the campaign was much as it had been in 1879–80, 1885, and 1886. 'Vast & enthusiastic masses in our two street processions.' After his speech at Glasgow on 2 July Gladstone found 'small thin flat scales' descending in his sight; and afterwards a 'fluffy object' floating in the serviceable, but lately damaged, eye, 'with some discomfort'. Were this first indication to lead to others 'it might be grossly inconvenient'. Gladstone forswore for the time continuous reading and limited his 'eyework' upon papers and material to what was strictly necessary. 'This also is well, in the hands of God.' Gladstone was boldly prepared to risk a public pronouncement on the theme of the hands of God. At Edinburgh on 30 June he urged his audience to

go forward in the good work we have in hand and let us put our trust not in squires and peers – and not in titles nor in acres. I will go further and say not in man as such, but in the Almighty God, who is the God of justice, and who has ordained the principle of right, of equity, and of freedom to be the guides and masters of our life.[68]

There were protests against 'sacred names and holy words' being dragged into the political arena. The first results appeared on 4 July. 'At first they were even too rosy: afterwards turned down but the general result satisfactory, pointing to a gain in G. Britain of 80 seats. This may be exceeded.' That estimate would have put Gladstone very near to his desired 100 majority. But in the following days the rosy prospect faded dismally.

It was not in any case a happy gathering at Dalmeny. Rosebery still mourned, determined on not taking office in a new Liberal ministry, and unresponsive to Gladstone's overtures about men and policy in the future contingency. Catherine was never at her best in dealing with the moody and skittish Rosebery. And already the Liberal tide had slackened. The majority now looked nearer fifty than 100. 'The returns of tonight were a little improved: but the burden on me is serious: a small Liberal majority being the heaviest weight I can well be called to bear. But all is with God. His blessed will be done.' Gladstone consoled himself for the time amid the blizzard of telegrams by making a beginning on that 'quasi-Autobiography which Acton has so strongly urged upon me'.[69] By 9 July the elections 'still bear a lingering character. The pressure has been great.' Gladstone hoped that the struggle if sharp would be short; but that hope had melted away. 'But an actual minority, while a personal relief to me would have been worse in a public view. It has been a week of many searchings of heart.' The mystery of the governance of the Most High was, in its way, even more of a puzzle than in 1886.

Rosebery recorded on 8 July:

Mr G. and I drove about the park in my phaeton this afternoon. He was depressed and feeble, saying that he supposed I had no comforting consideration to offer him – which indeed I had not. He said, 'A great trial of this kind throws one back on oneself, and makes one examine oneself, and now I see how for the last six years I have been buoyed up with the belief that we should have a great majority and that the Irish business would be a very short business.' He bears up with wonderful courage.[70]

It was a time certainly of the trying of souls. John Morley, demoted to the second Newcastle upon Tyne seat, returned to Dalmeny on 12 July, to be met by his gloomy host unable to 'contain his weariness <and almost loathing> of the interior situation. They had passed a horrid week of dejection and dismay, the telegrams of the polls coming to the house all day long, and smashing to atoms the illusions of many months.' Then there was the dreadful news of Gladstone's sight. 'It was really tragic,' recorded Morley, 'as he [Rosebery] cried out in bitter intensity of repugnance to it all, "Oh, my dear M., as I sit with him half deaf & three parts blind", and see him "feverishly clutching at straws here and straws there, a downright horror comes over me."' It had come to the point of Armitstead's being summoned to conduct the Gladstone party to Braemar for a change of air. Armitstead – in Gladstone's phrase, 'old shoe, and tame cat'[71] – indeed at that moment was in the house. 'Was there anything so <abominable, so revolting> desperate?' Even the dinner bell did not release Rosebery from 'full & uncontrollable' 'pent-up bitterness severity of a fortnight's endurance'.[72]

Hamilton had received reports from Rosebery. 'Evidently things have been very unpleasant at Dalmeny. R. says he has had a terrible week of it. It is evident that Mr and Mrs G. have got on his nerves, which are not in the best of conditions, and they have been more than usually tactless.'[73] Hamilton also heard from Morley. 'Nothing (J.M. said) could have been less tactful about R. than Mr G. at Dalmeny. Mr G. went on talking and consulting with J.M. and omitting to take R. into his confidence until he was told to do so. It was extraordinary the want of *nous* which Mr G. showed about R.'[74] In fairness to Gladstone, as Rosebery later made clear to Hamilton, it was rather a case of Rosebery's not wanting to be confided in; not wishing then to return to political life, he wanted to avoid confidences 'under false pretences'.[75] Gladstone himself appears to have been to some extent aware of tensions, but not to have taken them seriously. 'Conversations with Ld Acton, most anxious, chiefly on Lord

R. who is certainly a man not on the common lines – with Lord R. himself glancing at the leadership – with J. Morley on the future policy: most satisfactory . . .'[76]*

At dinner that night Morley found himself confronted by Gladstone with his 'dark goggle-glasses on', looking 'like another man'.

He was evidently not in a confused mind. After a few common remarks on this & that, he put his hand before his mouth (a gesture of his family that does not please me) & in a deep hoarse whisper made me the confidential statement, 'I don't wish it mentioned; I should like to submit it to you; I wonder what you will think of it.' I was all ears . . . and then came the immense & commanding climax – 'I think I see my way to disestablishing the Scotch church in three clauses!!!!' Then the Old Man turned the monstrous glasses full upon me, as if to pierce my very soul with this earth-shaking announcement. I laugh at it today, but at the moment, like Rosebery, I felt something horrible & gruesome about it.

After dinner Morley accompanied Gladstone to his dressing room, 'not to compose a triumphant cabinet with a three-figure majority, but to adjust a H.R. policy to a parlt. situation with hardly a trustworthy majority at all. <Poor Old Man – it made one's heart ache.>' Gladstone duly recited his ingenious three clauses, to which Morley listened with 'seemly resignation rather than with any vivid enthusiasm'.

Then Gladstone came to Home Rule. His line of argument was that the political centre of gravity had shifted from Home Rule to 'English questions'. The relevant analogy was the Melbourne government of 1835, dependent on the Irish and giving them good administration, but dealing with English legislation. Melbourne had done this in a 'slack' method; Gladstone proposed doing it now more briskly, presenting carefully selected bills like pistols at the head of the House of Lords. The Irish would have to reconcile themselves to a supportive role in the meantime: all that could be done, once the new government had been strengthened by English legislation, was to frame a Cabinet minute about Home Rule and submit it framed as a resolution both to the Commons and Lords as the basis of future legislation.

On the following day, 13 July, Marjoribanks put the likely majority at thirty. Gladstone trusted it would be nearer forty. The Midlothian poll was to be declared. Gladstone's agent had prepared him for a modest 2,000 majority (in 1885 it had almost been 4,000). ' "Well", said Mr G., with a groan, "I confess I should have liked 3000 a deal better." ' The party waited anxiously in what Morley described as a 'fevered atmosphere',

---

* 'Leadership' was leadership of the House of Lords.

with a 'horrid pall of physical decline hanging over all, slowly immersing the scene and its great actor in dreary night', with Gladstone 'struggling, striving, wrestling, clutching', at the same time admirable for 'energetic fortitude, the indefatigable resource, the unresting fertility'. In the background was the bizarre presence of homely Armitstead: 'good fellow as he is, lumbered with much serving, in the shape of all means of preparation, trains, saloon carriages, room at Aberdeen, and all the rest of it'. Acton, in his own way just as bizarre, was pressing Morley, plainly asking 'would Mr Gladstone put him in the Cabinet?'[77] Then came shattering news from Midlothian: 'not 4,000, not 3, not 2, but 690!!' Gladstone's 'chagrin was undoubtedly intense'; but he exercised 'splendid suppression of vexation', put a brave face on it and was 'perfectly cheery all thro' luncheon'.

After luncheon Gladstone was all the more insistent that the Irish 'must be told' they would have to wait. Their quarrelling had lost the Liberals many a vote in England; and Gladstone only shrugged his shoulders at Morley's warning that unless they were carefully handled the Irish would 'put us out'.

He then talked of himself, and what talk it was. With the most complete tranquillity he informed me that a cataract had formed over one eye, that its sight was gone, and that in the other eye he was infected with a white speck. 'Only one speck', he said, almost laughing, 'I can do with, but if the one becomes many, it will be a bad business' ... All this with a quiet gravity of tone that brought the catastrophe home to my very heart.[78]

The Gladstones set off at 4.45 for Aberdeen, under Armitstead's solicitous care, and with Acton tenaciously in attendance. It was Gladstone's later impression that he left in Rosebery's hands 'provisional statements' connecting Rosebery's name with the Foreign Office and 'leaning to its association with' the leadership in the Lords, without receiving 'any adverse sign' from Rosebery.[79] Gladstone never saw 'hospitable Dalmeny' again.

[5]

The essence of Gladstone's electoral failure – his majority proving in the end to be just on forty – was that the Unionists held sufficient of their ground to preserve an English majority. In Great Britain overall the Unionist majority was fifteen, in England and Wales forty-five, in England alone seventy-one. The pivotal Conservative axis of London and

Lancashire was battered but unbreached. Conservatism remained the 'heartland' party of the British Isles. With forty-seven members returned the Liberal Unionists had secured their continued integrity as a party of consequence. Chamberlain's 'Grand Duchy' of the West Midlands survived intact. Liberalism could be seen as the party of the 'Celtic fringe' of the British Isles: as the *Standard* rather gloatingly put it, the new government's majority 'comes from the outlying extremities of the body politic – from the places where the vital force is low and the pulse beats slowly'.[80]

Gladstone's appeal against the verdict of 1886 had been dismissed. What he had failed to pull off by a *coup de tête* against his party in Parliament in 1886 he could not pull off in 1892 by a history lesson to the people. He had spoiled his case irredeemably in 1885–6, it now appeared, by trusting to Peelite heroism in shock-tactic form. Now there was nothing for it but attempt to sift through the wreckage and put the best possible face on the matter to the new Parliament. At Aberdeen and Braemar Gladstone's own thinking, understandably, did not dwell in the long ranges of what might have been. It dwelt on the damage done to his Midlothian majority by his neglect of Scottish disestablishment.[81*] Home Rule would have to be conducted 'on our coming in', as he put it to Spencer, 'which I suppose the party hardly can avoid', 'under anticipations which have not been verified', and 'in a situation which forbids simple postponement of the main Irish issue, and also forbids carrying it'.[83] To Harcourt he enlarged on the theme of how Melbourne came in in 1835 with a majority hardly touching thirty, and stayed for six and a half years. But then, of course, the Irish were led by O'Connell.[84] 'Frankly,' Gladstone recorded for himself on 15 July, 'from the condition (*now*) of my senses, I am no longer fit for public life: yet bidden to walk in it. "Lead Thou me on."' True to his belief in 'old Chatham's dictum that vacancy is worse than even the most anxious work',[85] he started on a translation of Horace's *Odes*, not being convinced that any existing English version quite caught Horace's terse compression and economy of style.

Salisbury prepared to meet the new Parliament early in August. Gladstone, reinvigorated by the Highland air, geared himself up for the battle. Being 'bold against the Lords' was ever an attractive prospect. 'Mr G. is evidently bent on coming back, no matter what happens,' sniffed Hamilton, 'and the responsibility for making the attempt must rest with himself, Mrs G., and the rest of the family.' Hamilton's thinking was no doubt influenced by his awareness at the Treasury of the sheer difficulties

---

* 'One thing is clear to me, that we ought to make a decided effort to get disestablishment in Scotland out of the political arena before the *next* General Election.'[82]

awaiting Gladstone in framing a convincing alternative version of his 1886 Home Rule Bill. It worried Hamilton also that Gladstone's neglect to humour Rosebery might lead to his losing him as he had lost Chamberlain in 1886. Besides that, there were lurking fears that the Queen might turn awkward. It was known that Victoria was alarmed and despondent at the prospect of Gladstone yet again, and was talking of asking Rosebery. It was the same danger of the fat being thrown in the fire as with her determined effort to persuade Hartington in 1880. At the Rothschild chateau at Waddesdon Hamilton concerted through Knollys and Ponsonby to keep the Queen on a straight track.[86]

At Pitlochry Gladstone turned from Horace to some consideration of the coming session, with the Scottish Church and a list of Newcastleprogramme 'English' reforms to the fore. On returning to Hawarden on 21 July he put it to Harcourt that what was needful was to cast the balance fairly between Irish and British claims, to anticipate mischief from the House of Lords, to open up therefore against that House 'as many *bouches à feu* as possible', to frame Liberal proposals with a view to getting them through the Commons, and to look particularly for issues which could be 'concisely handled' in bills.[87] At the same time Gladstone found it highly convenient that with all necessary sessional business completed, 'we shall not want our legislative programme for production' until the new session in 1893.[88] By 27 July the Gladstones were back with Rendel at Carlton Gardens, waiting to move into Downing Street. Harcourt was 'much shocked at the physical & mental change for the worse in Mr G. since he left the H. of C. in June. He thinks him confused & feeble.' Harcourt spoke very seriously to Gladstone 'about the way he (Mr G.) was & has been treating Rosebery'. Harcourt also had the Chamberlain case in mind. Harcourt's comment about G.'s confusion no doubt owed much to his exasperation at the way Home Rule had come into life again. In a 'stiff conversation' with Spencer and Morley Gladstone's proposal to be content with a resolution on the principle was sternly rebuffed: the Irish simply would not have it.[89] Spencer, after all, had always been perfectly candid that not the least of the advantages in having the Irish at Westminster was that they could provide a majority for Liberal governments.

As the grim actuality of such a majority approached nearer by the day Gladstone contemplated a task 'formidable especially at my age'. He steadied himself by beginning an article for the *North American Review* vindicating Home Rule from the criticisms of the Duke of Argyll: the last of his pieces in that genre. Getting an administration on paper ready to present to the Queen was becoming an urgent requirement. Algernon West would head the secretariat. Hamilton observed Catherine 'as keen herself as ever to return to Downing Street'. She did not allow that

Rosebery had any grounds for complaint: it would be 'monstrous' of him, after all Mr G.'s kindnesses, to make difficulties. 'I should like to give him a bit of my mind.'[90] Loulou Harcourt gathered from Mrs Gladstone and Mrs Drew and Helen Gladstone that Mr G.'s voice 'was hoarse from arguing with people' and they were protecting him from them.[91] Gladstone fortified himself on the theme of deep and hidden agencies.

Now is the time for the thoughts that wander through eternity. When I look at the task apparently before me, and at the equipment of spirit and sense with which I am furnished I cast up my eyes to heaven abashed and dismayed. A reply came from thence. My grace is sufficient for thee. O thou of little faith wherefore dost thou doubt . . . The Almighty & not any counsel of mine has brought it about: surely He will provide for it.[92]

Gladstone found it difficult to provide for Rosebery's special requirements. Hamilton noted Gladstone's 'getting his back up', and refusing to treat Rosebery as a privileged colleague.

Mr G. complains that he has never been treated so ill by any colleagues before. I hinted to Mrs G. – and she did not at all like the hint – that she and Mr G. had at Dalmeny gone the wrong way to work to capture R. Their ideas of tact are peculiar to themselves. I found more than the usual amount of confusion and fuss reigning in Carlton Gardens – Mrs G. and Helen waylaying everybody, scheming this and scheming that, intercepting letters, and almost listening at keyholes. I pity poor Algy West, who naturally complains with some bitterness. I advised his *insisting* on having everything in his own hands.[93]

Gladstone professed 'surprise' to find Rosebery apparently unaware of the dispositions relating to the Foreign Office and the leadership of the Lords which Gladstone thought he had confided before leaving Dalmeny. Rosebery in any case declined the Lords leadership; and fled abroad, to Paris, where he remained, leaving the question of the Foreign Office dangling, until 10 August.

Nor was Rosebery the only problem. Labouchere thought his talents worthy of recognition, if not in the Cabinet then as Ambassador in Washington, with a Privy Councillorship, and accused Gladstone of being an accessory to 'royal ostracism'. Gladstone's explanation that he alone was 'responsible for recommendations submitted to Her Majesty' Labouchere chose to turn to satirical admiration for Gladstone's chivalry in covering for the Queen: yet another case of Gladstone's 'perpetually bringing an ace down his sleeve, even when he has only to play fair to win the trick'.[94]* In fact it was more of a Gladstonian ostracism than a royal one that sank Labouchere's chances. Gladstone used the Queen to cover for himself. Acton also was troublesome. He was believed to have said that 'at this crisis he is going to govern England through Gladstone'. He talked openly of being in the Cabinet. 'Something in his manner repelled. To at least two of the spectators he gave the impression of grasping at office.' There was a rally of Acton's enemies to block the 'court favourite, upstart, busy-body, intruder, flatterer'. John Morley, Acton's rival for Gladstone's intimacy and confidence, was the 'chief enemy'. (Acton, for his part, was free with his opinion that Morley was 'not, in the supreme sense of the term, quite a gentleman' – which made him impossible for the Foreign Office.) Eddie Hamilton inveighed against Acton's *'meddlesomeness'*. Spencer dismissed his pretensions as those of a political unknown, without official experience. Gladstone still talked of him as a possibility for the Cabinet on 1 August. 'Morley is recorded as saying he *put his foot on this at once.'* Gladstone was coerced into sending Welby to tell Acton not to appear at Carlton Gardens. At the same time Rosebery wanted Acton – confronted with the burlesque office of Captaincy of the Yeomen of the Guard – to intervene to help secure his own objects, which included Edward Grey's getting the Foreign Under-Secretaryship.[95]†

At the opening of the session on 8 August Gladstone, spokesman for the *vox populi,* protested against the 'pointless delay' of Salisbury's going through the motions of awaiting the formal verdict of the House of Commons, and extolled by contrast the 'manly judgment' of Lord Beaconsfield in 1868, which established the precedent that Gladstone himself had followed in 1874 and 1886. (This was one area in which Gladstone was conspicuously not a defender of ancient usage.) Gladstone also insisted on having it both ways as far as the votes of the Irish contingent were concerned. There must be no impairment in the slightest degree to the 'full and plenary authority' of the House of Commons by holding that Irish votes were distinguishable from votes from Scotland or Wales. To say otherwise would be to 'strike at the root of the Constitution' of the United Parliament and 'the Constitution of the United Kingdom'. Yet at the same time there was a sense in which the 'Irish majority' *did* exist: as evidence of a decided opinion in a matter of Irish concern. This did not add to, or impair, the authority of the 'regular vote', yet it had been recognized as an element in favour of arriving at conclusions in consonance with the view expressed by the representatives of Ireland. Gladstone menaced the House of Lords with the wrath of the

* The other version of 'Labby's' quip was Gladstone's trick of 'laying upon Providence the responsibility of always placing the ace of trumps up his sleeve' (ibid.).

† In the end Acton got a Lordship in Waiting, where his expertise in the pedigrees of the German princely families stood him in good stead.

people should it transgress its proper bounds; and discoursed on the felicitous example of the Melbourne ministry of 1835–41. He concluded by warning England that it had 'a giant's strength, but must not use it like a giant'.[96] Balfour, with reference to 'Mr Parnell's Bill of 1886', took the opportunity to quote Gladstone's statements at Edinburgh in 1885 on the great problem of a Liberal government dependent on Irish votes. 'By a happy prescience the right hon. Gentleman foresaw the exact situation in which he would find himself in the year of 1892.'[97]

On 11 August Gladstone had a tense interview with Rosebery, who held to his preference against accepting office. Gladstone thought it was 'very trying & rather sad'. To Rosebery Gladstone seemed 'a splendid ruin'.[98] That night in the Commons the amendment for the Address (for which Gladstone had put up two of the prominent 'new men', Asquith and Burt) came to a huge division: the Salisbury government was defeated 350 : 310. As Salisbury went off to Osborne Hamilton observed that Gladstone was 'rather depressed and looked tired, lying down on his sofa reading a book, but quite calm and unexcited'.[99] The Queen announced pointedly that she had accepted Lord Salisbury's resignation 'with much regret'. Gladstone needed Rosebery to sustain his government; and until he could capture him for the Foreign Office many other major Cabinet dispositions were uncertain. He sent Morley and Hamilton as ambassadors. The Prince of Wales was recruited to the task. Gladstone later recalled: 'Again and again he resisted my overtures. It was only by a telegram received at Osborne on the morning of the day when I had to settle the principal appointments with the Queen ... an hour or two later, that I received from him a telegram which authorized me to put him there if I thought proper.'[100] Possibly Rosebery capitulated to Harcourt's comradely appeal: without you we will be ridiculous; with you only impossible.

That was very much the spirit of Harcourt's contribution at a 'conclave' summoned by Gladstone on 14 August. 'A storm. I am sorry to record that Harcourt has used me in such a way since my return to town that the addition of another Harcourt would have gone far to make my task impossible. All however is *well*: it comes "ανωθεν".'*[101] The exchanges were 'as unpleasant as any one could remember, with Harcourt brutally rude to Gladstone, and Gladstone pouring reproaches on Morley's head for backing Harcourt'. 'Gladstone became a chairman instead of a commander.'[102] At Osborne the following day Gladstone found the Queen 'cautiously polite. In nothing helpful. Not however captious. Perfect in temper. Not one sympathetic word on any question however detached. After dinner a little unfrozen.' To Catherine he reported: 'There is a great

* 'from above'.

change since 1886: another lurch in the direction opposed to ours . . . She inquired for you with evident sincerity, and perhaps a touch of warmth.' Gladstone sat nearer to her than usual on account of deafness. 'In all other respects the interview was carefully polite and nothing else.'[103] The Queen, doubtless prompted by Rosebery, confided to her daughter the Empress Frederick of the 'half crazy and half silly' 'O.M.' that it was 'quite idle to attempt to have any influence with him. He listens to no one and won't hear any contradiction or discussion.'[104]

In one respect Victoria was helpful. She was eager to have Rosebery at the Foreign Office, and Gladstone could take advantage of this to hold Rosebery steady. Appropriate offices were approved for the regular Whig peers: Kimberley for India and the Lord Presidency, with the lead in the Lords; Ripon for the Colonies, Spencer at the Admiralty. Herschell returned to the Woolsack. Harcourt went back to the Exchequer, Morley to the Irish Office, and Campbell-Bannerman to the War Office. Lesser offices were distributed to Mundella, Fowler, Acland, Arnold Morley, Trevelyan, Bryce, and Shaw-Lefevre. The appointments which made a stir were Asquith, direct from the backbenches, to the Home Office, and Thomas Burt as Secretary to the Board of Trade, to boost the Labour Bureau. Gladstone slotted Herbert in to be Asquith's Under-Secretary; and Rosebery got Edward Grey as his.

A Cabinet of seventeen Gladstone thought 'outrageous'; but he excused himself as being 'beset right and left'. He had thus included 'more than one man insufficient in experience or in force'. In retrospect he came to realize that his more important mistakes were 'in the persons of men whose title to Cabinet office was indisputable, and whom by my very own fault I misplaced'. In Rosebery Gladstone hoped to get another Granville. In Spencer he hoped to get a man who would face the admirals down.[105] These were to be his most grievous disappointments as far as collegiality was concerned. His new Cabinet met for the first time on 19 August at Rendel's house in Carlton Gardens. This rather incongruous setting somehow seemed to be in character. Rosebery declared: 'I thought I was at a public meeting, and nearly moved Mr Gladstone into the chair.'[106] Gladstone now decreed a new arrangement of cabinets to get around the problem of his deafness: he alone would sit at a table, with Rosebery at his right hand; all the others would sit as near as possible on whatever seating was convenient. It seemed only proper that after a cabinet at Rendel's there should be a dinner at Armitstead's. Hamilton noted his fellow guests as the Gladstones, together with Herbert and Harry,* Rosebery, Acton, and Stuart Rendel. Gladstone 'showed little

---

* Henry Neville G did secretarial work for his father when G was out of London, 1887–90, 1892–4.

or no trace of the worry or difficulties ... He is a very marvel, and certainly shows no signs of being a "ruin"."[107] Even so, Andrew Carnegie's grandiloquent salute to 'the People's "William the Fourth"' was hardly appropriate to Gladstone's circumstances. Carnegie's 'fervent wish is now that you will be spared to strengthen the United Kingdom by giving to Ireland the rights of an American State', by giving self-government to Scotland through a Grand Committee, and 'justice in religious matters' to Wales.[108]

[6]

The Hawarden season late in August was notable for an adventure that might very well have had grave consequences. Walking in the late afternoon in the park (which he would describe as 'not in the first class, but quite at the top of the second class')[109] Gladstone 'came unawares in the quietest corner of the park on a dangerous cow which knocked me down and might have done serious damage'. With great presence of mind Gladstone feigned death, according to later accounts, and then, when the animal's attention was distracted, slipped behind a tree and then escaped. All he recorded, laconically, was: 'I walked home with little difficulty & have to thank the Almighty. Early to bed.'[110] It was only, it appears, halfway through dinner, when Catherine noticed him unwell, that he recounted the incident that caused his stiffness and soreness. The wild heifer, which had found its way into the park, was shot, and its head mounted in the Glynne Arms public house in Hawarden village. It was not long before a wreath arrived at Hawarden with an inscription: 'To the memory of the patriotic cow which sacrificed its life in an attempt to save Ireland from Home Rule.'[111]

Stiffness and soreness did not prevent Gladstone's making a start two days later on his Romanes Lecture for the Michaelmas term at the University of Oxford. When Vice-Chancellor Boyd invited him in November 1891 to deliver the first lecture on this foundation, Gladstone declined, from pressure of affairs. Soon, however, the temptations of yet another academic excursion to Oxford overcame his resistance, and the date of 24 October, at the Sheldonian Theatre, was eventually fixed upon. Romanes, a Darwinian physiologist of Canadian and Cambridge provenance, wanted to endow Oxford with a prestigious public lecture on the model of the Rede Lecture at Cambridge. Gladstone's theme would be, in effect, his love for and pride in Oxford, offered in the form of a historical survey of the development of its academic spirit. He had already given a foretaste of his purpose in a piece for the June *Nineteenth Century*, 'Did Dante Study at Oxford?' Gladstone's wish that Dante, ever one of his revered 'masters', along with Aristotle, Augustine, and Butler, *had* studied at Oxford was characteristically very much father to his thought. For preparation of the Romanes lecture he let himself be guided less temerariously by the Rev. Mr Hastings Rashdall of Hertford College, who placed much of the typescript and proofs of his forthcoming *The Universities of Europe in the Middle Ages* at Gladstone's gratified disposal. Acton also was helpful.

Having originally declined the Romanes invitation while out of office on grounds of business, Gladstone then spent an inordinate amount of time while prime minister in preparing it. It kept him out of London for the International Oriental Congress: Professor Max Müller read Gladstone's paper on 'The Phoenician Elements in the Homeric Poems' to the Congress on the day on which Gladstone had Morley read his Romanes draft at Hawarden.[112] He devoted much time and energy also in the latter half of 1892 to helping to rescue the Granville estate from bankruptcy, 'with all the relentless dedication which he had shown in dealing with the Oak Farm débâcle or the embarrassed affairs of the fifth Duke of Newcastle'.[113] Yet there was time also for forward thinking on the session ahead in 1893. On 1 August Gladstone drafted a preliminary secret 'Provisional outline of Work', comprising an ambitious programme, headed by a 'Bill for the Government of Ireland', within a 'fourfold method of action': by bills to be worked by the government in Parliament, by bills to be worked through Grand Committees, by private member's bills to be supported, and by executive acts. The question of the Indian gold standard, as related to bimetallism, as in turn related to rising protectionist and 'Fair Trade' sentiment, was a matter of concern. While on an excursion to Snowdonia in mid-September there was much correspondence with Harcourt and Rosebery.

This outing was instigated by Tom Ellis, one of the Liberal Whips and the 'Welsh Parnell', aided by Herbert Gladstone, with a view to promoting north Wales interests. The Gladstones were escorted by Mary Drew, with Armitstead on hand for backgammon. The centre point was the chalet of Sir Edward Watkin, Gladstone's earlier impresario at the Paris Exposition, who was promoting the Channel-tunnel project and cultivating for this purpose Gladstone's well-known proclivity, as with the Suez Canal, for the moral beauty of international communications. There were trips to Carnarvon (where David Lloyd George did the honours with speeches which 'cheated' Gladstone of seeing the castle) and to Glaslyn ('of wonderful beauty'), where Gladstone opened a new road constructed by Watkin to Snowdon summit. He spoke rather unwillingly to a large crowd from a platform built on a great boulder, since known as 'Gladstone's Rock', accompanied by Welsh hymns in a 'grand mountainous amphitheatre'. Ensconced in the 'very pleasing domestic interior' of Watkin's chalet, Gladstone contemplated another aspect of his sessional preparations, a long memorandum to the Queen bearing on the dangers to the constitution that would be occasioned by blocking the passage of the coming Home Rule Bill.* He performed vigorously as a walker on the slopes, mounting a thousand feet in four hours on a fine day with extensive views. At the Marine Hotel at Barmouth he recorded an 'argument with Mary',[114] occasioned apparently by a speech he had made uncomplimentary to Welsh landlordism that gave great offence to a Liberal peer. The tour ended with a drive to Harlech ('a noble relic') on 20 September. It was at Barmouth that Gladstone began 'Mem. for H.M. a serious business'. He wrote also on a more immediately pressing matter: 'Mem. on Uganda'.

The Uganda question really inaugurated serious politics for Gladstone's fourth administration. It was a problem inherited from Salisbury, and had to do with whether Britain should take over responsibility for the region from the insolvent British East Africa Company, and establish a protectorate, or whether Britain should leave the Company to sink or swim. Quite apart from the merits of the case as related to the Company, there was the consideration that Uganda was the western part of the area marked in red on the maps known as 'British East Africa', which linked the Sudan to the Indian Ocean; and related therefore to the question of British security in Egypt; which in turn further related to the question of Gladstone's declared determination to get out of Egypt. To add to the complications, there was an assiduous Christian missionary interest lobbying for a continued British presence. It was, with its ramifications, an issue perfectly adapted for the purpose of pitting imperially minded Liberals against anti-imperially minded Liberals, in a situation especially where the French were known to entertain ambitions to winkle the British out of Egypt by getting in from the Congo at the Sudanese back door.

Gladstone was a natural 'scuttler' as far as Uganda was concerned; and he naturally linked getting out of Uganda with a parallel process of getting out of Egypt. In the meantime, he had to deal with a quarrel between Harcourt, an even more ardent scuttler than Gladstone himself, and Rosebery, whose policy in general was one of proclaimed 'continuity' with Salisbury's. Rosebery thus repaid Salisbury's compliment in 1886. And Rosebery was more ardent than Salisbury ever was for a British protectorate to be established in East Africa. Behind the scenes, moreover, things were much more fraught than Gladstone could have suspected. 'Continuity' with Salisbury meant continuity with the Mediterranean Agreements of 1887, secret arrangements whereby Britain linked through Italy to the Austro-German alliance in order to preserve the status quo in

---

* See below, page 532–3.

the Near East from being subverted by the Franco-Russian combination. These Agreements did not involve Britain strictly in obligations of belligerency, but they were the nearest thing to an alliance with European powers that Britain engaged itself to before 1914. Indiscretions in Italy led to questions being asked in Britain. Rosebery soothed Gladstone's suspicions away in July 1891 as to 'tangible' support or adhesion.[115] In fact, Gladstone had been nearer to the point than he realized when in 1889 he denounced 'Crispian' Italy's policy in attaching itself to the Austro-German alliance.[116] He put it to Rosebery in July 1892: 'That is the basis of my Italian ideas. Italy has not the strength to sustain the pranks which she has played since the days of Cavour, Ricasoli, and Minghetti, and this with the pope, necessarily arch-enemy, at the door.'[117]

Rosebery at the Foreign Office in 1892 took care to know as little as possible officially about the Mediterranean Agreements so that he could, should necessity arise, deny knowledge of them in some measure of good faith. But they were at the heart of 'continuity'. They linked Britain's playing the 'Great Game' against the Russians at the Straits and central Asia and what the Naval Defence Act of 1889 represented as Britain's response to the French *'guerre de course'* threat in the Atlantic, and to the combined Franco-Russian squadrons in the Mediterranean, to Britain's sticking in Egypt and protecting Egypt's back door in the Sudan which meant sticking in Uganda and East Africa. Rosebery's problem was that he could not explain why he wanted to stick in Uganda in order to stick in Egypt without blowing up the Liberal government. His strength, on the other hand, was that he was held to be indispensable to the Liberal government. At first Gladstone sympathized with Rosebery about Harcourt's 'trenchant tone'. But then Rosebery had not, as Harcourt had, gone through 'the terrible and instructive experience of the Gordon Mission, in which we adopted a ruinous decision under the most seductive appearances'.[118] However, by 26 September the point had been reached of steps being taken to avoid the 'scandal and mischief of patent differences between Foreign Sec. and Prime Minister'. As Gladstone was ultimately to conclude, the 'fatal element' in his appointment of Rosebery to the Foreign Office in 1892 was 'his total gross misconception of the relative position of the two offices we respectively held and secondly his really outrageous assumption of power apart from the First Minister and from the Cabinet'.[119]

'Rosebery has I think', Gladstone informed Spencer, 'been carried quite off his legs by the Jingoes at the Foreign Office and its agents', in what Gladstone reckoned 'as one of the very strangest occurrences' of his life of sixty years in the House of Commons.[120] Certainly the Foreign Office was playing the missionary card for all it was worth; and Gladstone found the whole business baffling ('I admit it is like gathering a history from broken Assyrian tablets'). A critical point was reached early in October when Rosebery, with only Fowler and Mundella in support, defied Gladstone and the Cabinet majority. (Rosebery accepted Gladstone's offer of a Garter on 4 October with minimum grace.) There was a furious row. Gladstone was observed as never having been seen 'more excited and more determined than he was about this Uganda business; and it took a good many plain words to make him realise that on the decision which might be taken depended a very serious Ministerial crisis'.[121] Rosebery complained: 'Mr Gladstone is always violent and unreasonable, and snubs me in Cabinet.'[122] Rosebery's indispensability told. The crisis was averted by the expedient of a postponement and a Commission. Gerald Portal was commissioned to investigate the case further and advise. Portal had been one of Cromer's entourage in Cairo. Rosebery made it clear to him that he was expected to report in favour of staying on and a protectorate in Uganda. As Rosebery put it, 'Mr G.'s hair would stand on end if he knew what was going on there.'[123] What was going on there, substantially, was the fulfilment of Gladstone's prophecy of 1877 in relation to 'Beaconsfieldism': 'our first site in Egypt, be it by larceny or be it by emption, will be the almost certain egg of a North African Empire, that will grow and grow until another Victoria and another Albert, titles of the Lake-sources of the White Nile, come within our borders'.[124]

The Uganda episode was an instructive paradigm of Gladstone's last Cabinet. For all that he commanded a majority on the issue, Gladstone could not make his will prevail. He had lost the weight his cohering role had given him in the 1880–85 government. Partly this was because of the 'spills' he had given the Liberal party. Partly it was because of his oft-proclaimed insistence, as he had again stated at the opening of the 1892 session, that 'the question of Ireland' 'is almost, if not altogether, my sole link with public life. It has been for the last seven years my primary and absorbing interest, and so it will continue to be.'[125] Gladstone was no longer strong enough to play leader of the Liberal party without actually leading it. As Hamilton observed, cabinets came to be conducted on '"prize-fight" principles'. The heavyweights – Rosebery, Harcourt, Morley, along with Gladstone himself – were 'sparring in the middle of the ring', with the rest looking on.[126] Rosebery could get his way often because of the violent antipathy that had grown between Harcourt and Morley. The Cabinet did not *pull* together enough' with so little in common between its members: relics of Palmerston's last ministry mingling with figures who were to come to the fore in the next century made up one of the most uncollegiate of Cabinets. Rosebery recorded one occasion when Gladstone walked about between Harcourt and Rosebery with 'bewildered colleagues in a knot all round'.[127]

[7]

His resentments simmering, Gladstone found relief in his preparation for the Romanes lecture. Algernon West complained that the prime minister was more concerned with the Oxford lecture than attending to Home Rule affairs, 'which don't seem to progress at all'.[128] Then came the stillness on the impact of Tennyson's death. Hallam Tennyson wrote on 4 October from Aldworth: 'My father I believe is dying . . . I should like you to know how warmly he spoke of you as a friend in his delirium today.' Among Tennyson's last words to Hallam were 'Have I not been walking with Mr Gladstone in the garden this morning and showing him my trees?'[129] On the occasion of a reading of *Maud* earlier in 1892, Tennyson had remarked on Gladstone's recantation of his criticisms of it in 1859.[130] ' "No one but a noble-minded man would have done that", my father would say of Mr Gladstone.'[131] Gladstone felt he had to decline the honour of being a pall-bearer at the Abbey because of the Romanes pressure; though he did take the opportunity to amuse the Queen by recounting an anecdote of Tennyson's remarking on Browning's death: 'I have no doubt he is a great genius; but (rather loudly) I can't read him.'[132]*

The long relationship with Tennyson ended rather as it had begun: a somewhat prickly, defensive, quasi-friendship, carefully sustained as to forms on both sides but increasingly empty of the warmth of genuine intimacy. For Gladstone there would be sombre reflections on the fate of the high ideal he had fostered in the years from 1859 of a mighty partnership of art and politics to raise the tone and hopes of the age. There was the problem, on Hallam's request for Tennyson's letters to him, of extracting them from the mass of many thousands unless their dates were known; Gladstone offered some letters but could not find time for dictated reminiscences.[133] Then there was the problem of finding a replacement for the Laureateship. Swinburne undoubtedly possessed the requisite poetical power; but he was an alcoholic, erotomaniacal republican. 'The question of the succession comes to me with very ugly features,' Gladstone told Acton. Swinburne's *Poems and Ballads* of 1866 were both 'bad & terrible'. Wordsworth and Tennyson had 'made the place great. They have also made it extremely clean.' Surveying the rather barren field of possibilities, all Acton could do was suggest Ruskin as a poet of prose. 'The objection would be that he has also written a volume of poetry.' In the end, Gladstone and the Queen agreed that it

---

* The Queen accepted eagerly Gladstone's offer to show her Arthur Hallam's letters to him.

would be best to leave the post for the present unfilled. Given Swinburne's unsuitability, a lesser appointment would lead to envy, sarcasm, and ridicule, and a disparagement of the office.[134]

Then came the great day, 24 October, for the inaugural Romanes Lecture at Oxford. There were elaborate rehearsals at Hawarden. Gladstone's text was cribbed largely from Rashdall and what remained of Gladstone's own contribution owed its accuracy largely to Acton. The Sheldonian Theatre presented an 'impressive scene – the intolerable crush without, the silent crowd within, the red-gowned figure of Oxford's greatest son as he illustrated with loyal and eloquent erudition the proud saying: *Universitas Oxoniensis aemula Parisiensis'*.[135] Many undergraduates, victims of proctorial mismanagement, fainted in the 'fearful crush' on the stairs. *An Academic Sketch*, for all that it was a 'remarkably disproportionate elaboration', succeeded well for Romanes's purpose in giving his foundation 'a unique prestige among all Oxford lectures'.[136] Gladstone offered a prime-ministerial aura and authority to the *fin de siècle* cult of the Oxford ethos. In his peroration his voice vibrated with emotion. His last words remained unspoken as he 'bowed his head in a storm of enthusiasm'.[137] Such was Gladstone's gratified relief at thus acquitting himself before his beloved Alma Mater that he promptly declined to do duty at the Lord Mayor's banquet (getting Andrew Clark to issue a sick-note) and pushed the task on to the Leader in the Lords, Kimberley.

As the time for preparatory autumnal cabinets approached the Gladstones settled in at 10 Downing Street. The 'incoherence' of their domestic arrangements, as Derby had remarked, was ever a feature of their lives. Hamilton wonderingly observed them 'I am afraid very cramped in the old house; but then they don't mind living in a sort of hugger-mugger style'. The main thing occupying Gladstone's mind on his return to London was the memorandum for the Queen he had begun working on in north Wales in September. This had something about it of the character of the 'posthumous bequest' he had sent to the Queen in May 1885 on the theme of 'some great and critical problem in the national life'. The theme then had been the question of Irish self-government as entangled with the contingency of a Parnellite sweep of the Irish constituencies. Now, in more Cassandra-like tones, it was the question of Irish self-government as entangled with the House of Lords and the 'widening of that gap, or chasm, in opinion, which more largely than heretofore separates the upper and more powerful from the numerous classes of the community'. The controversy surrounding Home Rule for Ireland raised issues going far beyond it, issues inconvenient, maybe even injurious to a safe and stable working of the constitution. Two points in particular Gladstone stressed. The first was that the widening of the chasm was aggravated by the prolongation and intensity of the Home Rule controversy. The second was that for the last sixty years the direction in which the Liberal party moved was sooner or later the direction in which the country at large moved; and the longer the struggle continued, the more the Liberal party 'will move towards democratic opinion', a movement which would greatly be enhanced by a conflict with the House of Lords. The fault for widening the chasm in opinion and laying open the working of the constitution to inconvenience and even injury lay wholly therefore with those upper and more powerful classes who wilfully misapprehended the truly 'Conservative' nature of Gladstone's proposal to resolve the Irish question by the bill he had put forward in 1886 and the bill he proposed to put forward in 1893.[138]

Possibly Victoria might have been tempted to make some pungent comments on what she described to Ponsonby as this 'curious' document, especially had she considered it side by side with its earlier counterpart of 1885. Then, the focus of Gladstone's memorandum had been Chamberlain's 'Central Board' Irish local-government scheme. That might well have been the direction in which the Liberal party at large and the country might have straggled, and which the Irish might not unitedly have been able to reject. She might have contrasted that possibility with Gladstone's sudden imposition without fair notice or preparation upon the startled Liberal party some months later of a much more radical scheme of Home Rule tailored to Irish requirements which the Liberal party, left to itself, would never have adopted. She might then have added that it was rather brazen of Gladstone, having thus himself imperiously taken the responsibility for opening that gap, or chasm, in opinion, then to complain in a kind of blackmailing manner at the failure of his opponents to surrender quickly enough to him so as to restore his definition of a safe and stable working of the constitution. It was an egregious specimen of the 'heads I win tails you lose' style of argument. She might have drawn attention to the fact, on that constitutional point, that there was nothing safe or stable in the current working, for example, of the Swedish–Norwegian constitution, which was on the brink of the wrangling conflict which would soon end their dual partnership. And as to his argument about Liberalism's historic prerogative of giving the national lead, she might have suggested the conceivability of the case that by suddenly demanding too much too soon of the Liberal party, Gladstone had driven it up a hopeless dead end; that he had done the party enormous damage in 1886, damage that had not been repaired in 1892; and that that damage most likely would be exacerbated in the next general election. That he had, in short, foisted upon his rump Liberal party a task far beyond his, or its, capacity.

However, the Queen contented herself with requesting Ponsonby to acknowledge and confined her own response to a polite intimation that she appreciated Gladstone's motives in so addressing her.[139] Salisbury, for his part, was making his own preparations for the coming work of the Lords. His 'Constitutional Revision' in the November issue of the *National Review* was a preparatory exercise in scene-setting. The British constitution, lacking the resource of a United States Supreme Court, or yet of precedent for recourse to a referendum, at least had a House of Lords which could be equipped with a doctrine, adumbrated by Salisbury in 1884, of referendal 'revision' by way of inviting an appeal to the electorate.[140]

Pre-sessional cabinets got under way on 27 October. Gladstone's colleagues assembled in his room at Downing Street expecting to hear something of plans for the Home Rule Bill, but nothing was said. 'Indeed,' commented Hamilton, 'Mr G. seems hardly to have given a thought to his Home Rule Bill; and his colleagues are not a little exercised in their minds; they feel they have been brought together under somewhat false pretences . . .'[141] Fowler soon discovered that Gladstone had not a glimmer of knowledge of the Parish Councils Bill. To Harcourt's and Hamilton's point on the estates duty question, that the principle of graduation had already been admitted by the Conservatives: ' "Yes", said he, "that was thoroughly characteristic of the Tories: they always initiate everything that is radical".'[142] Hamilton found John Morley 'very depressed politically as usual' on 2 November. Gladstone could not be brought to face the construction of the Home Rule measure. He was for putting off consideration of it till January. At this the Cabinet rebelled. It seemed clear that Gladstone no longer had his heart in his work. 'He sees he can't pass a measure and so does not exert himself to no purpose.' He agreed at least to let Morley and Spencer produce heads to be discussed in December.[143] Rosebery thought these proceedings 'rather pitiful'. Gladstone had lost his interest in almost all public affairs with the exception of foreign affairs, 'about which he was more active than necessary'. Hamilton thought it a mistake on Gladstone's part to shirk the Lord Mayor's dinner. The 'natural inference' would be that he was 'far from being *up* to the duties of Prime Minister'.[144]

On 5 November Gladstone, squeezed between Harcourt and Rosebery, reflected anxiously 'on the last & the next Cabinet'. There was a restful interlude: 'Tea with Lady Granville at Kensington: told her of *my* infinite loss in her husband.' Granville's emollient tact and disarming deftness of personal touch were much missed. Saving the Granville estate from the ignominy of bankruptcy still occupied time and effort. Gladstone passed the hat around among the Whig grandees: Westminster refused; Devonshire contributed a handsome £5,000; Spencer £3,000, others *pro rata*. Gladstone himself provided £300.[145] John Morley was the nearest thing Gladstone had to another Granville: 'He is on the whole from great readiness, joined with other qualities, about the best stay I have.' He was especially useful as 'Envoy to Rosebery'; but his effectiveness was limited when it came to the case of Harcourt. Cabinet on 11 November: 'One person outrageous.' Rosebery threatened resignation. At a cabinet on Home Rule on 21 November Rosebery and Harcourt sat ostentatiously aloof on a sofa, waving Spencer away with 'Oh no, this is the *English* bench.'[146] Two days later it was for Rosebery a 'Rembrandt *Monte Carlo* scene wh. Asquith & I viewed from a side table. Excited men round table – pale old croupier in midst with passion seething in his face – a memorable and painful scene.'[147] There was 'Something of a scene with Harcourt at the close.' Gladstone formed a Cabinet Irish Committee to shut Harcourt out.

By 18 November Gladstone was in a position to apprise the Queen that the new Home Rule Bill would retain Irish members at Westminster 'according to the apparent public desire'.[148] The difficulty on the financial side, as Hamilton discerned, would be 'to persuade Mr G. to throw over his own cherished scheme of 1886'.[149] Retention of Irish members made it redundant. 'The more one goes into the provisions generally . . . the more insurmountable do the difficulties appear to me to be,' declared Hamilton. 'Mr G's scheme of 1886 was difficult enough; but the retention of Irish members at Westminster has made what was difficult almost impracticable.' Hamilton was beginning to think that 'Home Rule may be killed by its inherent difficulties'. Gladstone himself, hating to have his hand forced into keeping Irish representation at Westminster, hated all the more having to grapple with the financial implications of it. Harcourt made a point of being worse than useless on the matter. Morley had to try amateurishly to fill in.

Restiveness in the party began to break through the surface of politics. There were demands for a Scottish Grand Committee to meet both the general strength of the Home Rule movement in Scotland and to deal with accumulated arrears of legislation otherwise. Gladstone was warned about the dangers of delay: the movement of working men since 1887 in Aberdeen, he was told, 'has culminated in the Labour party'.[150] Chamberlain, who had got free elementary education out of Salisbury in 1891, was well placed to mock the Liberal party's legislative barrenness: 'jam yesterday and jam tomorrow, but never jam today'. He was able to assert, plausibly, in the *Nineteenth Century* in November 1892 on 'The Labour Question', that 'in social questions the Tories have almost always been more progressive than the Liberals'.[151] In the years of opposition from 1887 to 1892 Gladstone had grown used to leaving the backbenchers to their own devices. Now that he was back in office there was little sign of any development at the indications evident in 1891 and 1892 about such things as old-age pensions, and friendly encouragement to the young Radicals in the LCC.* But the question was now urgent as to 'what satisfaction we can give to other wants, English, Welsh, and Scotch', in the 1893 session.

[8]

With so much to do by the beginning of the session fixed for 31 January, and so little done, ministers and officials were unnerved by Gladstone's decision, under pressure from his family, to retreat to Biarritz for a winter season. Andrew Clark so advised, Gladstone informed the Queen, on account of 'irregularity in sleep'. (Victoria took occasion to remark on how pleased she was with Acton's agreeableness as lord-in-waiting. 'He does not *force* his great learning and knowledge upon anyone . . . wh makes him particularly pleasant in society.')[152] 'The Gladstone family', observed Hamilton, 'are going to have their way to a limited extent. Mr G. is to go to Biarritz about the 20th after holding a Cabinet or two first and to return about the second week in January.' It appeared that 'the family are trying to make his colleagues write and urge his going; but I doubt there will be much response'. Algy West was 'much put out about the whole thing. The family decline to listen to anything he has to say.'[153] Gladstone's last major public appearance in 1892 was to receive the freedom of the city of Liverpool: his birthplace, and a great compliment from so Tory a corporation. Amid the classic pomp of St George's Hall he delivered 'a confident assertion of the triumph in the next century of Liverpool as the centre of world commerce'.[154] The closing cabinets Rosebery thought largely a waste of time. 'Words, words, words, and very unnecessary.'[155]

With Armitstead once more the impresario, Gladstone and Helen (Catherine elected to sit tight at home) were lodged in the Grand Hotel by 22 December. The pattern of activities was much as with the previous visit. The Tollemaches provided once more for society. Armitstead loyally plied his skills against Gladstone regularly at the backgammon table. Excursions were undertaken. Gladstone nursed his lumbago and worked on the Horace translation. 'Eighty-three birthdays!' he recorded on 29 December. 'What responsibilities have old men as such for prolonged and multiplied opportunity. And what have I, as among old men.' At the close of 1892:

* See above, page 508.

For me in some ways a tremendous year. A too bright vision dispelled. An increased responsibility undertaken, with diminished means. That *I* of all men should have come to a position which in its way is perhaps without parallel. But the *stays* are wonderful, almost incredible. The fountain of mercies still inexhaustible. *Cum Te patiar*.* Lead me through duty into rest.

His sleep quite restored, Gladstone quitted Biarritz on 9 January (having recorded his weight at 12 stone 9 pounds – *'Proh pudor'*)† and was back ready to face the session on the 12th. Both he and Catherine, Hamilton observed, 'looked well, and he was in one of his jaunty humours, entirely eschewing shop. He will avoid touching on Irish finance as long as he can. He knows I don't agree with his plan; and he has become much less tolerant of opinion differing from his own than he used to be.' The Irish wanted better terms than they had been offered in 1886. Gladstone was determined to give them worse. Morley too found Gladstone 'certainly more imperious and less open to reason than he was'.[156] If the Irish did not like his proposals, Gladstone declared, 'they must *lump* them. The question for them is whether they will have Home Rule with my finance or no Home Rule.'[157] Harcourt thought the whole business 'merely *pour rire*: it is ludicrous and impossible'. The difficulties of retention of Irish members were, as Gladstone noted, 'more & more felt: but we have no choice'.[158] At a cabinet on the 16th 'Sir W. H. pursued his usual line in the usual way'. But by 21 January Gladstone abandoned his sliding-scale quota plan and accepted the scheme put forward by Hamilton and Alfred Milner: Ireland was to have full control of stamps and taxes and to be credited with excise proceeds; but the imperial government would take customs, for good or ill, as Ireland's contribution to the imperial charges. Harcourt in the end was useful in turning Gladstone in this direction.[159]

Perhaps Gladstone was the more ready to be turned on Ireland in the circumstances of another irruption of Egyptian turmoil. A rising against the British occupation seemed to be in prospect. Cromer (erstwhile Evelyn Baring) requested reinforcements. Rosebery concurred. This put Gladstone in a 'very excited state', denouncing the demands from Cairo and the Foreign Office as 'appalling', 'preposterous'.

With such pistols as these presented at my head, my life is a perfect burden to me. I would as soon put a torch to Westminster Abbey as send additional troops to Egypt. It can't be. Such proposals make me fearful about the future. I can see nothing for it but for Rosebery to resign.[160]

---

* 'I will suffer with Thee.'
† 'For shame.'

The 21st of January was 'a day of much and varied anxiety. But some blessed words of Scripture came to me ever and anon to give the needed support.' But at a cabinet on the 23rd it was Rosebery who gained the point. He held the stronger hand, and he had the Queen solidly behind him. Cromer deftly organized a pre-emptive peaceful *coup d'état* against the Khedive, and Britain's grip on Egypt was tightened another notch. All Gladstone could do was deprecate to Campbell-Bannerman sending warships to Alexandria, 'as re-awakening the memory of the bombardment'.[161]

Sessional preparations were somewhat chilled when the Queen refused to accept Gladstone's draft wording about the new Government of Ireland Bill as conducive to 'the better Government of Ireland', and insisted on the 1886 formula to 'amend provision for the future Government of Ireland'. By 6 February the Home Rule Bill was 'pretty well finally shaped and Mr G. is hard at work on his speech'. The Crown veto on Dublin legislation, the financial arrangements, and the retention of Irish members at Westminster were the three principal cruces. Hamilton thought that if Gladstone were to get a majority of less than twenty on the second reading, he should content himself with having got the Commons to accept the principle and recognize that it would be a waste of time to fight on in committee. 'Mr G. could then make his final bow, and make it with dignity.'[162]

Gladstone relented on the matter of his social obligations to the extent of offering an 'Official dinner & evening party' on the eve of the opening of the session. 'I feel, what? much troubled & tossed about: in marked contrast with the inner attitude on former like occasions.' He was much offended by the Queen's revision on the matter of 'better Government'. After Sunday service at the Chapel Royal: 'Notwithstanding the blessings of today, in returning from the sacred precincts I felt both depression & worry.'[163] Old nagging worries about Egypt revived, with dismal memories of the 1880s, on top of the deplorable Uganda affair, and would soon stimulate in Gladstone an initiative to stipulate a definite date for withdrawal. There might not be an immediate opportunity to dispense with Britain's 'insidious though under the circumstances necessary powers'; but a target of two years would surely allow the necessary time and space. Gladstone's move in the direction of reviving an entente with the French to this end was bitterly resented and resisted by Rosebery. After nine years dealing as prime minister with the malleable Granville Gladstone was now mortified to find himself overborne by his Foreign Secretary.[164]

Gladstone was uneasy also about 'the tendency there was to embark on the perilous course of socialistic legislation, with which he was thankful that he neither would nor could have anything to do'. The impulse to such legislation came 'mainly from the party that pleased to call themselves Conservative'. The measure pressing on him which he disliked immensely was Payment of Members of Parliament. He had been pushed into accepting it for the sessional programme very reluctantly; but he would not stand for 'indiscriminate payment'. He wanted money to be available only to members who actually needed it, so as to preserve the honour of unpaid service.[165] He was to be overborne also on this point by the party's and his colleagues' unwillingness to accept the invidious implications of this. Harcourt warned that the Radical section could 'break up the united action of the party' unless it were appeased on this question. Otherwise, to pacify 'English' sentiment, Fowler had his District Councils and Asquith his Employers' Liability. The Newcastle Programme was honourably represented: local option, one-man-one-vote, shorter Parliaments, hours of labour for railwaymen, and prevention of new vested interests in ecclesiastical establishments in Scotland and Wales. But still, for Gladstone, it was a very characteristic moment early in the session when Keir Hardie's amendment to the Address about unemployment and trade depression was heavily defeated. 'An anxious evening,' recorded Gladstone, 'but with a good ending.'[166]

[9]

Apart from the Scottish Kirk matter, Gladstone scarcely bothered to conceal his lack of interest in anything but his Government of Ireland measure, the details of which he kept very close to his chest. Asquith wrote to Rosebery on a drily mocking note on Friday, 10 February: 'I understand that on Monday a Bill (to "amend the provision" for the Government of Ireland), which neither you nor I have seen, is to be introduced into the House of Commons. I send you word of this, as you may possibly like to be present, and hear what Her Majesty's Government have to propose.'[167]

   That Monday, 13 February, was the occasion of Gladstone's last performance in the heroic parliamentary role he had first established with his budgets in 1853 and 1860 and which he brought to a peak with his Irish measures of 1869 and 1870; and which he sustained with decreasing effect in 1881 and 1886. Hamilton observed Gladstone that morning 'quite calm and collected, free from all excitement', in spite of just having survived a 'Harcourtian explosion' over Irish excise duties. In the afternoon all the standard props of the drama were in place amid the atmosphere of political theatre which Gladstone relished: the cheers as Gladstone entered the packed House, the waving hats and handkerchiefs

(Hamilton deplored the new fashion of members standing to make their ovation), Gladstone's rising to speak 'amidst the loudest of renewed cheers'. But it was no longer the Gladstone of 1868 or even of 1886. The issue of Home Rule was now threadbare. There was an artificiality about the drama of the occasion. The Grand Old Man was in quest of the one great unobtainable thing.

Everyone knew how the plot of the play was to go its predictable way. Hamilton found the exposition 'not quite as clear as it usually is'. Gladstone's voice dropped at times so much that he was not easy to follow. He was received 'somewhat coldly, at any rate without any real enthusiasm on the part of Mr G.'s followers or any pronounced outcries on the part of Unionists'. Gladstone made ritually his 'very solemn appeal and impressive as well as beautiful peroration'. But it was 'not a speech that carried one away as one has so often been carried away before'. Rosebery thought the Commons scene 'most pathetic, if not tragic'.[168] Gladstone himself recorded: 'Spoke 2½ h on Introduction of Irish Bill. I felt very weak having heard every hour (or all but one) strike in the night. I seemed to lie at the foot of the Cross, and to get my arm around it. The House was most kind: and I was borne through. The later evening I spent on the sofa.'

In Selborne's opinion the second Home Rule Bill was a much better piece of legislative '*workmanship*' than the 1886 version, but the proposal to retain Irish representation at Westminster (reduced to eighty MPs, conformable to Ireland's proportion of the population of the British Isles) had now little of the effect it might have had in 1886. In any case, it simply shifted the location of the logically insoluble conundrum of Irish legislative privilege and British legislative penalty within the wider conundrum of fitting the square peg of Ireland free into the round hole of Ireland bound. Edward Clarke's brilliantly destructive response on behalf of the Unionists confirmed a general verdict that the whole subject was stale.[169] The anomaly of Irish representation was, as Gladstone admitted, serious: Irish MPs were to be restricted to voting on matters deemed 'imperial'; but they were not to be excluded from votes of confidence. Gladstone made no mention of Ulster other than to insist that the Ulster Protestants would in time come to change their minds about being governed by Dublin. The essence of his appeal was that despite anomalies and logical insolubilities the scheme would work in practice because of the sheer necessity of its so doing. This necessity of a new trust within a 'Union of hearts' would constitute a great act of indemnity and oblivion: 'cast behind you every recollection of bygone evils'; 'let the dead bury the dead' under a 'living union for power and for happiness'.[170]

The Unionist strategy was that the Conservatives would fight the bill in the Commons and leave the Liberal Unionist peers led by Devonshire to attend to its final execution in the Lords. Balfour's lead was that Gladstone's analogy of imperial supremacy over Canada or Australia was a barren and empty gesture. 'Supremacy is nothing unless it be supremacy over the unwilling as well as the willing.'[171] But Chamberlain thrust himself forward to steal the Unionist show in the Commons, challenging Gladstone to a kind of gladiatorial combat, and became the hero of the Conservative backbenches. The thrust of his objection to Gladstone's bill was that it satisfied the criteria neither of logical federalism nor of subordinate devolution. The financial provisions were relatively esoteric, but as Hamilton now had occasion to remark, great legislation ultimately lives or dies in the details. By 21 March Morley was gloomy on that aspect. Gladstone was in a great difficulty, and he 'would not appreciate or face the situation', which could well result in the bill's being wrecked in committee; which was an 'ugly confession' for him to make. 'In short, Ireland was a d—d fool to wish for Home Rule.' The Liberal party should never have embarked on it. 'We have no Parnell to deal with; and Ulster will give us more trouble than we ever had reason to expect. But, however insoluble may be the problem, I must fight it out.'[172]

That certainly was Gladstone's intention. For all his disabilities, the old Gladstone remained incomparably the greatest parliamentarian. He was no longer a commanding wielder of Cabinets or a sure constructor of intricate and epochal measures. But he still had little trouble declaiming publicly on his feet. Though half blind and half deaf the voice was still there and the mind as ready as ever in debate. He recorded for 8 April: 'Spoke I fear near one hour on compulsion. Never in my life more despondent: never more helped. I never rose with less knowledge or idea of what I should say; and it seemed to bubble up.' Some of his colleagues felt he was only too ready and too copious in debate. 'It must be rather heart-breaking for you,' Asquith told Morley. 'It's brutal to put into words, but really, if Mr G. stood aside more, we might get on better.'[173] 'Pity the sorrows of a poor old man,' Gladstone recorded of a particularly strenuous day, with a cabinet, a labour deputation, appearances twice in the Commons, with many letters and other appointments.[174] Yet a Conservative MP, who observed Gladstone closely in the 1893 session 'during the unceasing efforts he made to defy old age and rule over the House of Commons', was enormously impressed with the way Gladstone coped with his duties to the House as well as bearing the burden of the Home Rule Bill. He could appear 'as fresh as if no work had been previously attempted during the day'; 'wearing a flower in his button-hole' he 'enforced by vigour and eloquence not at this time equalled by any other disputant on this or other questions'. On one issue, the opium trade, Gladstone delivered 'denunciating oratory' of which 'those who were present declared with one accord that they had never heard any forensic effort comparable'. There was also the occasion when Gladstone, 'so pale and wan', had to announce to the Commons 'with profound emotion', the tragic loss of the battleship *Victoria*. 'The scene gave an impressive glimpse of the man as distinct from the politician.'[175]

The Easter recess gave opportunity for a return to the Lion Mansions at Brighton in Armitstead's generously hospitable care, with occasional excursions back to London or to Rosebery at The Durdans. At Brighton Gladstone found 'Pier & salt air to perfection'.[176] An odd occurrence towards the end of the stay was an interview with the Superintendent of Police about an 'intruder', one MacCurran.[177] In the following year Gladstone wrote to Mme Sadi-Carnot, widow of the assassinated French President: 'I have been the less able to remain altogether silent, because last year when I was Minister, an individual now in confinement, made his way unimpeded to the window of my Brougham, with a loaded pistol, for the purpose of dispatching me, but at the last moment relented, & abstained on account of observing, or thinking he observed in me, a likeness to his father.'[178] As with the mad-cow episode, Gladstone seems to have taken these threatening incidents without trauma.

He was much more affected by the Queen's menaces. Of an audience at Buckingham Palace on 10 March he noted: 'A form as usual, indeed I fear a sham.' To Catherine he commented on the 'formal and menacing character of my audience', though the Queen did enquire kindly after her. 'But a painful sense of unreality pervades these conversations and the public announcement of an audience hoodwinks the public.' Victoria had in fact expressed candidly her anxiety and apprehension that the Home Rule measure would 'tend towards the disruption of her Empire and the establishment of an impracticable form of Government'.[179] She seems to have been as embarrassed as Gladstone about the nullity of their meetings. She told her daughter the Empress Frederick about them: 'It is very difficult [to know] what to talk of, as Ireland is impossible and I was particularly warned by Lord Rosebery (who is my support and very open towards and much devoted to me) not to mention Uganda, so that one's political conversation was very restricted, but we talked of other things.'[180] She complained through Harcourt and Ponsonby that Gladstone did not volunteer matters of business in his conversation. Gladstone responded that etiquette obliged him to confine himself to matters raised by Her Majesty. But Her Majesty insisted that Gladstone used to speak without special invitation; and hoped that in future he would be more communicative.[181] All of which did not prevent her being awkward about birthday honours before she left in May for the Villa Palmieri in Tuscany.

For all its vulnerabilities the Home Rule Bill got through to its second-reading debate in sound shape. Gladstone addressed a rally of the party at the Foreign Office on 28 March. His lengthy harangue seems to have elicited unanimity and a degree of enthusiasm. 'Speeches seem to be no effort to him at all, even at his age,' Hamilton observed. 'It is administrative work only at which he shies.'[182] He moved the second reading on 6 April on his return from Brighton, 'sprightly and radiant', on the theme that there was once, in 1782–95, perfect unity of sentiment between Protestant and Catholic in Ireland; 'why should it not happen again?'[183] Gladstone won his second-reading division on 21 April, with a majority of forty-three ('What a poor creature I felt'). But there was 'nothing like the same excitement there was in 1886'; Hamilton noted an 'absence of all real enthusiasm even among the Irishmen'.[184] It was in the committee stage that the bill got into serious trouble. The elaborate provision for restricting the procedural scope of the Irish members did not long survive; which opened up the old problem of Irish legislative privilege. 'In 1893 Mr Gladstone and his colleagues thought themselves compelled to change clause 9 of the new bill,' as Morley recalled, 'just as they had thought themselves forced to drop clause 24 of the old bill.' Each plan, therefore, 'ended in a paradox': the Irish were either to be taxed without representation, or to be privileged 'to meddle in our affairs, while we were no longer to meddle in theirs'.[185] Hamilton knew all too well the weaknesses of the financial provisions; and he knew also Gladstone's 'delusions' about getting round these problems.[186] Gladstone took no trouble to rally his Cabinet. By 28 April there had been no cabinets for five weeks; nor would there be another till 5 May. Morley thought Gladstone treated the financial aspect with 'extraordinary indifference'. Then came disaster when it was discovered that a blunder in Belfast had put all the calculations about the Irish excise out. By 9 May Hamilton was referring to 'this wretched Home Rule Bill'. Gladstone was 'most favourably impressed' by the skills displayed in repairing the leak by Alfred Milner of the Inland Revenue Board. It is not clear whether he recognized his youthful critic at Oxford in 1878.[187]

Chamberlain led the Unionist attack with grim pertinacity. 'I have never *known* such an opposition,' Gladstone declared, 'one so detached from the merits & from rule. But it is probably suicidal.'[188] Then: 'Spoke at the dinner hour for 30m against Chamberlain. Is it fanatical to say I seemed to be held up by a strength not my own. Much fatigued.'[189] Chamberlain would have recognized some of Gladstone's old inveigling tricks. 'How can you discuss the position of the Irish Members in the British Parliament with reference to their having a Parliament established in Dublin until you have determined whether they are to have a Parliament established in Dublin or not?'[190]* How could the government be 'asked to bind ourselves before discussion as to what shall be the result of that discussion on the retention of Irish Members'?[192] Meanwhile Hamilton watched in dismay as the financial clauses crumbled. ('Mr G. won't take the trouble: Harcourt declines the task, partly from laziness and partly from pique: J. Morley can hardly be expected to get the subject up.')[193] After early church and Holy Eucharist on 23 May Gladstone recorded: 'Never I think have my needs been so heavy: but it seems as if God were lovingly minded to supply them only from day to day. "The fellowship of the Holy Ghost" is the continuing boon which seems the boon for me.' Perhaps here Gladstone was thinking of the Holy Spirit's special vocations as comforter and enemy of evil spirits: Chamberlain's 'able though almost rabid opposition to the Conservative measure of Home Rule'[194] might have seemed an appropriate occasion of such thoughts. At the end of May, after a 'very anxious & *rather* barren morning on Irish Finance', Gladstone observed, delphically: 'My present position as a whole certainly seems peculiar: but of this it is unheroic either to speak or think.' Within a month Hamilton was shocked to hear Gladstone refer to 'that confounded Bill'.[195]

[10]

Amid the heavy pounding Gladstone took relief in a regular series of refreshing excursions to Brighton, Dollis Hill, and various convenient country houses as well as Hawarden, where he retreated for the Whitsun recess. The deference accorded to ancient eminence combined with inveterate loquacity and readiness in conversation made of him increasingly a social star turn ('I had to tell many old stories of politics').[196] Lady Monkswell observed him after dinner at the Ripons'.

We found most of the party sitting round the old Prime Minister in a charmed circle. We slipped into chairs & listened to his sonorous voice. I say it with all respect – but there is something awful and almost repulsive in his grand appearance. The body so old, so very old, not like anybody else we are accustomed to; the mind burning with the fires of youth – & *those terrible eyes.*[197]

---

* Balfour pointed to the logical absurdity: how could the question of Imperial supremacy be discussed unless it was known what was to constitute the Imperial Parliament?[191]

Whatever the *terribilità* of the eyes to the outward view, for Gladstone they were a critical problem. His reading, always slow, proceeded now 'at a snail's pace'.[198] Farringdon Granger, the Chester oculist, examined them and reported hopefully. Then there were encouraging experiments with a speaking trumpet 'of a clever kind' ('This marks an onward stage').[199] Writing he found much less difficult than reading. His Horace translation ('which I find almost as fascinating as it is difficult') was a comforting, companionable task. It went well with backgammon for evening relaxation. There was little enough of literature feasible in any case at this fraught time. The irritating problems of biographers had arisen again in the case of Arthur Gordon's biography of his father, published in 1893, which Gladstone thought injurious to himself in particulars relating to his grudging attitude to Reform in the 1850s.[200]* On the other hand he was distressed to learn from Purcell that Manning's 'Anglican' letters to him, which he had returned in the exchange of correspondence in 1862, were lost: presumed destroyed by Manning. Gladstone considered them 'most valuable and might even have borne publication in extenso'.[201]† On the other hand again, having twice gone through with Lord Rothschild Disraeli's correspondence with his bene-factress Mrs Brydges Willyams, Gladstone thought it prudent to burn his box of Laura Thistlethwayte's 'older' letters to him. 'I had marked them to be returned: but I do not know what would become of them. They would lead to misapprehension: it was in the main a one-sided correspondence: not easy to understand.'[203]‡

Much more congenial was the distraction of brooding fondly over his St Deiniol's foundation. Wilfrid Scawen Blunt was one of a party who visited the 'terrible building of corrugated iron' in 1892. Blunt observed Gladstone talking about his books 'in the absorbed way he has, going on, without paying the least attention to the person he is speaking to, especially if it is his wife and she ventures to interpose a remark'.[205] He was anxious to set the trust going; and he was anxious too at yet another instance of Stephen's restlessness with his Hawarden cure. Having enjoyed, as a newly married man, a tour as Rural Dean of Mold from 1884 to 1892,¶ Stephen found his restricted scope at Hawarden uncongenial. To Gladstone it was a 'wrench and a rend', and 'from many points of view frightful' to contemplate Stephen's departure. But what he needed was

---

* G made Gordon Lord Stanmore in 1893.

† The letters were not in fact destroyed.[202]

‡ 'Mrs Brydges Williams enjoyed the same sort of relationship with Disraeli with respect to money as Mrs Thistlethwayte did to Gladstone with respect to sex.'[204]

¶ G gave consent in December 1884 for Stephen to marry Miss Annie Wilson of Liverpool. 'I promised to make up for him £10,000 at once & recommended a considerable insurance.'[206]

a transfer, not preferment; and for that there were good reasons of 'mental leisure & opportunity for refreshment & enlargement'. But if God did guide Stephen to resigning Hawarden, Gladstone had a suggestion that might fit in with Stephen's purpose. Gladstone's 'life of contention' made his unaided management of the St Deiniol's project difficult.

But while the Library is in some sense the foundation, I want to build on it an institution: a Clergy House, a Home of Rest & refreshment not rigidly confined to our own Clergy, a House of Study for the Glory of God and the culture of men, a House of Mission perhaps for Liverpool, a House of help perhaps for the parish of Hawarden, and of course a House of Prayer and worship. *Could not you* perhaps undertake the quiet & cautious modelling of all this? Could you not become the first head of my Trust?[207]

Possibly for Stephen this proposal of an even more intimate connection with his father was not quite what he was seeking, in spite of Gladstone's assurances of 'sweet Counsel': 'In association I think we could get on, and you would have a full share of influence.' Stephen remained Rector of Hawarden until 1904, when he moved to the Rectory of Barrowby in Lincolnshire.

But Gladstone's 'life of contention' was never far away. By the beginning of July thirty nights had been devoted to the committee stage of the Government of Ireland Bill. Gladstone accepted an amendment explicitly asserting Westminster's supremacy over the proposed Dublin legislature. By this he hoped to bolster his claim that 'the supremacy of the Imperial Parliament is visible from one extremity of the Empire to another'.[208] The effect, however, was all the more to put the issue in doubt. The *Hansard* shorthand writers noted on 7 July that Gladstone was sometimes inaudible.[209] Harcourt was as contemptuous as ever of the whole enterprise ('Morley, & I after him, had a disquieting conversation with Harcourt. I hope good was done').[210] Hamilton observed that Gladstone's sparrings with Chamberlain were 'a real delight to him: they possibly infuse fresh life into him'.[211] But they did not infuse fresh life into the bill which Chamberlain mauled remorselessly. And fresh life at large in the Commons was a rarity as the heats and humidities of summer exacerbated the emotions and tempers of embattled members. The very fact that the doom of the Home Rule Bill was sealed in the Lords made it necessary for the Unionists to persecute it intransigently in the Commons. Gladstone in return was obliged to resort equally intransigently to the 'guillotine' of closure of debate. Balfour on 26 July could quite plausibly damn it, after Chamberlain's savaging, as 'defunct', and a 'corpse'.[212] On 27 July, after no less than nine exhausting divisions, frayed tempers broke loose. Chamberlain denounced the Gladstonians:

'never since the time of Herod has there been such slavish adulation'. This provoked from the Irish benches cries of 'Judas!' Instantly there was a scrimmage of forty or more members swinging fists in front of the Clerks' table: 'a sad scene never to be forgotten'. The following day Gladstone summoned a conclave on 'last night's catastrophe'; and he and Balfour smoothly arranged the necessary apologies from the guilty principals and 'got the wretched incident to a close' on the 31st.

The committee stage in any case was now through. Gladstone moved the third reading on 30 August. He rehearsed old themes.* But his main concern was to vindicate the ruthless use of the closure of debate to defend the bill from the malignant pertinacity of its opponents. By the time of the final division on 2 September eighty-two sittings were devoted to the Government of Ireland Bill: 'entirely in excess of anything that has ever before happened'.[215] Gladstone got his third reading with a majority of 34. There were conscientious Liberal abstentions (Rathbone among them) on the ground that the amended privileged position of the Irish MPs was wholly unacceptable to British opinion. It was Gladstone's last achievement in the House of Commons. 'This is a great step,' he recorded. He knew it would soon be cancelled in the Lords. But it remained something that the principle of Home Rule had been accepted by the House of Commons. He always insisted on the significance of the analogy of the case of Catholic Emancipation seventy years earlier on that ground. Gladstone would not wait to see Devonshire lead the Lords to do their execution. On 4 September Gladstone moved an 'astringent' resolution that the business of the session, obstructed for so long by the Home Rule question, be resumed in the autumn, making it the longest session on record. Then he departed for the Scottish Highlands.

When the Lords did their execution early in the morning of 9 September by the devastating margin of 419 to 41, Gladstone was relaxing at Armitstead's house at Black Craig, Perthshire, working on his Horace *Odes* and playing backgammon with his host. It was as well he did not witness

---

* One of these themes was the relevance of the Sweden–Norway relationship. In a curiously apposite way, a Scandinavian sub-plot ran parallel with the Westminster debate. G's assurances as to its beneficent relevance to his case for Ireland sat ill with indications otherwise. G commented to Rosebery on 30 March 1893: 'So far as I know, Norway has a strict *right*, but is making bad use of it.' A memorandum from the Foreign Office set out the provisions of the cession of Norway to Sweden in 1814 for G's consideration.[213] Alarmed by Swedish threats of military coercion of Norway, G requested the Foreign Office to 'drop some friendly expression' of deprecation.[214] Rosebery reported on 9 June that he had instructed the Minister at Stockholm to urge 'how suicidal would be a civil war between Sweden and Norway'. 'In the race of folly in Scandinavia,' commented G, 'Sweden seems at the present moment to get ahead.' Presumably, G simply could not imagine any such 'race of folly' within his own Home Rule provisions.

the crowds outside Parliament singing 'Rule Britannia' and setting off fireworks. There could be no dissolution as in 1886. Although Gladstone would not retire, equally he did not contemplate another election. Especially was he averse to putting his Midlothian seat at risk so soon after the humiliation of 1892. The claim of the Lords that they were better exponents of the 'will of the people' than eighty Irish MPs* would be challenged in due course when the cup of their iniquities was filled. He conferred with the Queen's emissary from Balmoral, Ponsonby, on the financial complications ensuing on the Duke of Edinburgh's succeeding as Duke of Saxe-Coburg-Gotha. ('He brought me a message half-inviting me to a limited visit, which I think is well-meant.') Gladstone could make light of black looks directed at him by some Episcopalian ladies in Blairgowrie church. Burnand, the editor of *Punch*, sent him the 'capital cartoon' Tenniel had drawn, 'Over the hills and far away', with Gladstone in tartan trews and cap, watched over by a friendly stag, taking a nap with a copy of Homer by his side. (More accurately, it should have been a copy of Horace.)

---

* Hamilton thought the Lords 'clearly right on this occasion'.[216] Godley recorded walking with G at Hawarden, and venturing boldly to say that had he been in the Commons, he would not have voted for the Home Rule Bill because it allowed Irish members a share in English and Scottish affairs but no corresponding share for English and Scottish members. 'I expected an outburst, but to my great surprise he took it quite calmly and quietly, expressing regret, but neither arguing nor even hinting that I was wrong. This was so unlike him that I thought then, rightly or wrongly, that he himself in his inner consciousness, regarded this as a very weak point in the Bill.'[217]

CHAPTER 14

'VOICES FROM THE DEAD ENCOURAGING ME': ONE LAST BID, 1893–4

[1]

After a brief stop at Edinburgh, where he caused a stir by hinting that the Home Rule Bill might be reintroduced in the Lords in 1894,[1] the Gladstones were back at Hawarden for a long October season before returning to London on the eve of the reassembly of Parliament on 2 November. Labouchere, a bitter enemy since Gladstone blocked his hopes of preferment in the previous year, told Dilke apropos of Gladstone's Edinburgh hint: 'We are in the hands of an aged fetish thinking of nothing but Home Rule, senilely anxious to retain power, & fancying he can do so by tricking and dodging everyone.'[2] In fact, at Hawarden, Gladstone was much more concerned with getting the Octagon into order. Making Kosmos out of Chaos was his phrase for it. 'I am like a little mole who has cast up an enormous hill.'[3] Among family comings and goings ('Guests in full supply') he worked on his Horace translations but stopped in Ode IV i ('To Venus') in 'sheer disgust' at the pederastic final eight lines.* Among the guests was the new Home Secretary, the great 'find' of his fourth Cabinet. 'Long conversation with Mr Asquith. He will rise.'[4] Asquith, a widower, was engaged to be married to Margot Tennant. Reading was now a serious difficulty for Gladstone. 'Mary kindly read aloud to me in evg – *but.*' He made trial of his old octavo Waverley novels for their 'good type', 'but with labour & some minutes to each page'. A distressing event was that the difficulties Gladstone had been experiencing for some years with his alcoholic valet Zadok Outram had led to Outram's demotion to footman and being put out of livery. Gladstone was now obliged to engage a new valet 'after what a course of years!'[5]

Back in London for the renewed session Gladstone 'looked younger and more vigorous than ever' to Hamilton. There was no question of

---

* In the published edition of 1894 G footnoted: 'The concluding lines of the Ode are purposely omitted.'

retirement; he was evidently in one of his 'staying humours'. He would go when he wanted to, not when his colleagues wanted him to. He disliked the idea of going merely on grounds of sight and hearing. He proposed to 'take things very easily'.[6] So easily did he take things that his colleagues were soon complaining of lack of cabinets, administrative incoherence, and 'Government by Departments'. Gladstone had no interest in routine business or in his government's surviving items of legislation, Employers' Liability, Parish Councils, and Local Government (England and Wales), other than in their prospective fortunes in the House of Lords. Asquith was particularly anxious for discussion about the mode of taking some 'active steps' to put the public in possession of authentic knowledge about the real state of facts in the deplorable and disastrous dispute in the coal trade, with its attendant 'social dangers'.[7] Two men had been killed in September by soldiers at an incident at the Featherstone colliery near Wakefield. Gladstone embarked on a congenially voluminous correspondence about the financial claims on the British taxpayer of the new Duke of Saxe-Coburg-Gotha.

As the renewed session ploughed its way on in November and December Gladstone intervened little in the Commons and consulted little in Cabinet. He was restless and irritated and bored. He became increasingly detached from day-to-day affairs: 'old age, & obstructed sight and hearing,' he told Rosebery, 'have cut down very low my knowledge of the state of opinion in the House of Commons'.[8] He was much oppressed by the death of his physician, Sir Andrew Clark. 'I have repeatedly expressed my strong sense', as he put it to a Liberal MP, 'of the disadvantage at which the Liberal party is placed by my necessarily growing physical debilities.'[9] But it was clear Gladstone was unwilling to retire on a low note of failure and defeat. Catherine had told Lucy Cavendish long before that two things 'Uncle William' was 'very strong about: that he should not go without a cry (he never has) or without old colleagues'.[10] Rosebery rather felt that Gladstone's staying on to see the government out would be for the best: it would 'avoid the horrible scrimmage which will inevitably ensue over his political carcase'. Gladstone's inclination in December 1893 was that the problem about his eyesight should be known. Catherine, however, as Hamilton recorded, 'won't hear of it: so of course the matter will be kept dark. She said in effect that Mr G. with hardly any eyes is worth more than anyone else with two pairs of sound eyes – characteristic of her, and another instance of his being so much under her thumb and that of the sons and daughters.'[11]

The optimum strategy would be to re-establish the Liberal party on a footing enabling it to confront a dissolution of the 1892 Parliament with some credit and fair prospects, and to make the dissolution the fitting and proper occasion for Gladstone's departure. But how? Where was the 'cry'? Gladstone had flown his own 'kite' at Edinburgh about resuscitating Home Rule. 'Circumstances *point* to the reintroduction of the Bill in the House of Lords', he wrote cajolingly to Asquith, 'at the beginning of the [1894] session'; but it was as yet premature to decide this, and improper to indicate it.[12] If Gladstone hoped for a warmly supportive response, he was disappointed. Most of his colleagues wanted Home Rule to slide quietly out of sight and out of mind. There was always Employers' Liability and Parish Councils and Local Government. But, as ever since 1880, what were such trifles to Gladstone? Then, later in November, a new prospect of possibilities began to take shape.

[2]

Lord George Hamilton, Salisbury's former First Lord of the Admiralty, raised in the Commons on 17 November the question of the 'Naval Policy of the Government'. Gladstone responded that the House need not have 'the smallest apprehension as to the maintenance of the distinct naval supremacy of Great Britain'.[13] Behind these bland formulas lurked a congeries of critical issues linking and entangling matters of naval construction programmes, the armaments race among the Great Powers, and foreign policy, with special reference to the Franco-Russian alliance, and the specific crisis points of Egypt (and the Sudan) and the Straits. It had been Lord George's great achievement to get the 'two-power standard' of British naval supremacy established in his Naval Defence Act of 1889. Gladstone did not at that time directly challenge either the policy or the money involved.* The rolling programme of expenditure on construction of 1889 was due to end in 1894. The admirals were aware by late 1893 that the 1889 Act had not in fact established an effective naval supremacy where it was most critically needed, in the Mediterranean and the Straits. The French now had a powerful squadron at Toulon and the new Russian Black Sea fleet was in a position to reciprocate French strength at the Straits. Behind George Hamilton's question were the combined forces of the Admiralty and the Foreign Office demanding, in effect, a second Naval Defence Act to ensure that the objects of the first be realized. The immediate critical point for Gladstone was that Spencer, at the Admiralty, seemed in no doubt that his admirals had a compelling case.

Gladstone was perfectly aware of the diplomatic implications of the

* See above, page 482.

matter. 'The proceedings of the French,' he expostulated to Rosebery, 'conceived in a spirit of aggressive shabbiness, have given me extreme pain: for I retain from my youth a feeling for the old idea of French alliance, within due limits, which was so cherished by the Grey Government, & that of Peel.'[14] Within the frame of that 'aggressive shabbiness' were in fact the emerging outlines of the collapse of Salisbury's Straits policy in 1896 and the dangerous Fashoda crisis of 1898. But for Gladstone the matter never got beyond that mood of regretful reminiscence. A series of such moods began to take the form of needing to retrieve memories of conflicts with Palmerston and of conflicts with Disraeli and the 'Jingoes'. So too with evocations of his 'European' reputation as the challenger of Bismarck and the embodiment of peace, the Concert, and resister of militarism. If he had failed to give a lead against the admirals in 1889, he recurred now all the more emphatically, as if in apology, to the spirit of his rebuke to Lord Clarence Paget in 1866, on the theme of Britain's being deeply responsible to the world if we continued to set other countries the example which our enormous naval forces placed before them.* The more Gladstone came under pressure – there was a major debate in the Commons on 19 November, followed up by an intervention from the Queen on 7 December[15] – the more stubbornly he stood his ground. The country, he declared, could depend on the government's making fitting proposals in due time and measure. There was no state of danger or emergency in the present or the foreseeable future. The present agitation was wholly unwarranted and founded on fallacious arguments. To the Queen Gladstone enlarged on the 'premature' nature of demands which subverted established procedures as to estimates. She got the benefit of his views on 'immature' proposals, views which had 'varied little from those which were entertained by the leaders of both parties at the time when he had first the honour of becoming one of Your Majesty's Advisers under Sir Robert Peel'.[16]

It was Gladstone's presumption that resistance to the navalist jingoes would be the natural attitude of his party and his colleagues in accordance with hallowed principles of Liberalism. Spencer would, it was reasonable to assume, accept revised estimates once the arguments were removed from too close proximity to the admirals. Gladstone, as he told Morley, looked on a political battle with the alarmists as 'good for us from a party point of view'. A cabinet on 14 December disillusioned him. 'Rough prospects for Navy charge.' He took it hard. 'The situation almost hopeless when a large minority allows itself to panic and joining hands with the professional elements works on the susceptibilities of a portion of the people to alarm.'[17] Morley was away in Ireland; and Harcourt,

---

* See above, page 15.

who on all past form Gladstone should have been able to count upon, seemed to have capitulated to the jingoes. Gladstone found the situation particularly alarming, on his side, that the expertise of the 'professional elements' was now, in effect, usurping the prerogative of responsible politicians. It had long been his conviction, as he had warned Childers at the War Office in 1880, that 'when military men charge their so-called professional opinions with political elements', they 'thus give authority to very worthless doctrine'.[18] It had been bad enough with Barings and Portals and the Foreign Office over the Uganda matter; now it was a question of proclaiming to Europe that Britain proposed to ratchet an acceleration to the armaments race. It was in this mood of barely repressed exasperation, nursed over a Christmas break at Brighton ('Backgammon with Mr A. Worked a little on the Odes'), that Gladstone received in the House of Commons a gracious tribute from Balfour on the occasion of his birthday. Gladstone's own birthday thoughts were of gratitude for strength wonderfully maintained but of awareness also of failings in the 'digestive organs'; 'deafness is (at present) a greater difficulty, and sight the greatest'. 'Farewell, old year,' he recorded on the last day of 1893. 'Will there be another?'

The new year commenced with Gladstone's summoning Eddie Hamilton for explanations about the present state of naval expenditure and about the charges which the envisaged programme would entail. His position was that 1889 was avowedly a special case and not a benchmark for the future. The new programme would initiate a 'race for Europe for huge armaments'. Had the nation gone mad?[19] Gladstone worked on the figures; 'they seem but too conclusive'. But Harcourt revealed himself as 'rather severe'; there seemed no prospect of an accommodation with Spencer. Gladstone felt himself 'rather hard hit from a combination of circumstances. I seem to stand alone though Morley is sympathetic: my sleep is a good deal disturbed: but "it is the Lord: let him do what seemeth him good".' What seemed good was that Gladstone should retreat once more to Biarritz to repair his sleep and escape the 'savage weather'. Harcourt was under the impression that Gladstone's family were in favour of his retirement, but Hamilton had his doubts: 'it is Mrs G. who has most power with him; and I doubt if she will concur in his making his bow'. Harcourt turned very severe indeed. 'Mr G. has already twice brought the Liberal party to grief – first in 1874 and afterwards in 1886.' Mr G., declared Harcourt, 'does not care a rush for the party. So long as the party suits his purpose, he uses it. The moment the question of his own personal convenience turns up, or he finds himself out of touch with the party, he is ready to discard it regardless of consequences.'[20]

Hamilton judged by 5 January that the 'fat was in the ministerial fire with a vengeance'. Gladstone could not see how he could go on with a policy which amounted to 'a sort of challenge to France and Russia'. Harcourt thought it best Gladstone should retire. On the 7th Gladstone had 'a little conversation with C. and Mary on the sore subject'. To Morley he protested: 'I think the proposal a most alarming one. It will not be the last. It is not the largest piece of militarism in Europe, but it is one of the most virulent.'[21] Morley experienced 'one of the most uncomfortable & painful' hours of his life on 8 January when he was detained by Gladstone in a kind of Ancient Mariner mode. Morley caught the scene vividly in his diary.

'This is no ordinary occasion for me. It is not a question of a million here or a million there. It is a question of a man resisting something wh. is a total denegation [*sic*] of his whole past itself.' 'More than that', he said with suppressed passion, 'I seem to hear, if I may so say, I seem to hear voices from the dead encouraging me.' With a gesture pointing to a distant corner of the darkened room. He soon turned to what was, I verily believe, the real root of his vehemence, anger, and exaltation. 'The fact is', he sd. 'I'm rapidly travelling down the road that leads to total blindness. You are all complaining of fog. I live in a fog that never lifts. I see books, the sea, the sky, you, all through fog.' . . . But he wd. not be consoled. They said in 1886, I remember, after he had broken his party by H.R., that he wd. one day feel like Ajax, when he awoke to find the havoc he had made with the sheep-flock. Tonight, if I remember my Sophocles aright, he was in the mood of Philoctetes. This was perhaps the most painful thing about it – no piety, no noble resignation, but the resistance of a child or an animal to an incomprehensible & <incredible> torment. I never was more distressed. The scene was pure pain, neither redeemed nor elevated by any sense of majestic meekness before decrees that must be to him divine. Not the right end of a life of such power & long and sweeping triumph.[22]

A cabinet was summoned for the 9th when Gladstone intended to reassert his control. He prepared voluminous memoranda. He harangued his colleagues for fifty minutes, 'the longest speech probably ever made in Cabinet'. Morley recorded that Gladstone's 'voice was clear, grave, and steady, and he spoke slowly, without anything like heavy solemnity or anything of the sepulchral, with a sort of composed authority, that was in the highest degree impressive'. Gladstone was admirable 'in simplicity, sincerity, and the pathos of tragic reality'. Nothing could have struck 'more absolutely true'. Morley thought his most telling stroke 'was when he sd., "I cd. not help you. I cd. be of no use to you. I cd. not speak for the plan. *I shd. sit by, a silent and dishonoured man.*" '[23]

He made no impression. 'H., and in some degree R., pursued a remarkable course: different, however. In the end the matter stood over but without a ray of hope against this mad & mischievous scheme.' Harcourt's surprising course was to accept the argument that the Navy needed the money in a speech of which Morley used the words violent, spiteful, obnoxious, forced, irrelevant, ill-natured, superfluous, ungracious, malicious, and profoundly detestable. In reply, Gladstone simply 'turned and said, "Of course I can go at once if you wish it". (Sensation.) Then silence, and after a pause Rosebery, supported by Asquith, asked for a decision. Gladstone would not declare himself, but urged his ministers to continue to talk informally among themselves.'[24] Four days hence, Gladstone announced, he would be going to Biarritz, and would take the opportunity to retire after his return. He indicated that his family 'within *viva voce*, are made aware'.[25] Rosebery hinted at the convenience to all of an immediate retirement; but Gladstone was determined on going first to Biarritz. He stipulated that there should be no cabinets in his absence. Withdrawal of cabinets had ever been one of his weapons against recalcitrant colleagues.[26]

'Am I Athanasius contra mundum? Or am I Thersites, alone in the Achaian Assembly?' Gladstone would waver at Biarritz between these two models of defiance, with Athanasius coming increasingly to the fore. He could not get over the enormity of it all. 'Three only of the sixteen were in sympathy with me on the *merits* of the scheme. Thirteen against me!'[27] He identified Harcourt as the chief villain. By the 11th he was slightly calmer. 'I am now like the sea in swell after a storm, bodily affected, but mentally pretty well anchored. It is bad: but oh how infinitely better than to be implicated in that plan!' There was much manoeuvring in the background to prepare the way for Gladstone's making his decision either to agree or to go. Mary Drew, who wanted him to go, pulled Acton into the plot. She told Loulou Harcourt who sped to see Acton at the Athenaeum to rehearse his role. Acton would go with Gladstone to Biarritz.[28] Morley meanwhile tactfully prepared Catherine for what was impending. 'Poor Mrs G. is much broken down. After her talk last night with John Morley, she realizes for the first time the real picture of affairs.'[29]

Gladstone went off to Biarritz under 'friendly convoy of Mr Armitstead', with Catherine, Mrs Drew and her child, Herbert Gladstone, Acton and Algernon West in attendance. In a flourish of nepotism before departure he made his son-in-law Wickham Dean of Lincoln. He simmered with resentment both at his colleagues' failure to fall in with his views and at their evident readiness to see him go. For all that he had incessantly begged for release ever since taking office in 1880, Gladstone had never supposed or foreseen the dispiriting set of circumstances now confronting him. Could this, in the end, conceivably be the manner of the Lord's opening the door for him? Hamilton recorded on 11 January: 'There is an ingenious theory, founded mainly on surmise, that Mr G., finding to his surprise that his speech to the Cabinet made no converts, is reconsidering the position of affairs and casting about for some excuse to withdraw his threat to resign.' Hamilton thought there was something 'decidedly comic and ludicrous in this'. Morley thought 'Mr G. should never have taken office at all'.[30]

Life at Biarritz was Tollemaches, backgammon, Horace, and mainly endless gloomy talk about the iniquitous Navy estimates. Even Acton was 'not a ray'.[31] Nor was Algernon West very cheering: 'He is most kind & loyal: but weary talks cast no light whatever on the matter.' West himself reported to Hamilton there was 'such an atmosphere of moodiness and excitement about him', and that 'he never got a civil word out of Mr G., who either fulminated against everybody as if they were all criminals or treated everything with the utmost levity . . . It is the old, very old man . . .'[32] Acton reported that Gladstone still believed the others would give way. 'He was loud, unreasoning, inurbane, in proclaiming his own fixity.' Acton found Gladstone 'different at different times. Generally, he was wild, violent, inaccurate, sophistical, evidently governed by resentment. Now and then, for a moment, he collected himself, and was full of force – but never full of light, or able to see any argument but his own.'[33] West escaped and returned to London for a brief respite to tell Hamilton on 25 January that Gladstone 'intended to preserve his complete freedom of action as regards the future: – he might indeed continue to retain his seat in Parliament; and not only that, he might express his own views and disclose the real cause of his resignation in one way or another, perhaps in the House of Commons, perhaps by an appeal to his constituents, perhaps by a letter to the *Times*!' Hamilton was shocked. 'Could anything be worse? Mr G. is evidently quite beside himself. It is what I always feared – that senility would show itself in some form or another . . .' Rosebery feared the fulfilment of Palmerston's prophecy that Gladstone would ruin the Liberal party and die in a madhouse.[34]

Weary of Gladstone's obstinacy – 'Saw Ld Acton again on the dilemma (not mine)' – Acton fled the scene of desolation. He rather pointedly accepted an invitation from Drummond Wolff, then Minister at Madrid, 'by way of conveying to him [Gladstone] that I was losing my time, and thought him a little below his own level, and he quite understood, and resented it'. To Acton it was all 'a tragic and sinister catastrophe' in which 'pure reason had lost its way'.[35] He made on his return to London 'an uncomfortable report of the state of things' at Biarritz. He told Harcourt how irritable the old man grew, of his 'brusqueness and rudeness'; of how one day the Paul von Rammingens called, and 'Mr G. rang the bell for Acton to entertain them & retired to the window to read a book!'[36] Acton also warned that Gladstone was 'catching at straws, such as the idea that one or two of his colleagues (meaning Lefevre and

Trevelyan!) were still with him'. Rosebery was convinced that Gladstone's 'natural impulse' was to quit but that 'the "petticoats" around him won't allow him to give up power'.[37] Acton took revenge by sending a long memorandum to Gladstone confuting him point by point on every detail of the case, with copious references to the relevant precedents, especially that of 1859 in Palmerston's time.

[3]

The point came when Gladstone decided that Biarritz was a kind of quasi-abdication, in the mode of 1874–5, preliminary to a counter-attack and capture in the mode of 1880. That point can be identified as 31 January, when the Gladstones, returning from a visit to the Tollemaches, 'found West in a great state' with a telegram from London quoting a statement in a *Pall Mall Gazette* announcement 'that I had determined on resigning almost immediately'. Gladstone 'framed a contradiction, rather a tough business, in terms carefully weighed', and read it 'again & again to West & Herbert: we got it shortened & then despatched in West's name, on my behalf'. The difficulty was, of course, that the *Pall Mall Gazette* report was accurate. Gladstone's denial – 'pure Gladstonese', as Hamilton put it, 'sailing very dangerously to the wind of veracity' – took the form of: 'The statement that Mr Gladstone has definitely decided, or has decided at all, on resigning office is untrue. It is true that for many months past his age, and the condition of his sight and hearing have, in his judgment, made relief from public cares desirable.'[38] 'Poor dear old man!' was Hamilton's comment.[39] The news came also at this moment that the House of Lords had re-amended the Employers' Liability Bill in defiance of the House of Commons. Though ever one to menace the Lords with *bouches à feu* and to relish the notion of punitive dissolutions, Gladstone had been so obsessed with the Navy estimates issue that only now did a denial of his intention to resign click together with an entire new vista of possibility. West volunteered that the District Councils Bill was also at peril. Gladstone was much more cheerful after dinner. There was no further allusion to the Navy estimates.

Another jolt at this time also helped to trigger Gladstone's new outlook on things. Marjoribanks, the Whip, reflecting the dismay widespread in the party at the reports West had brought back about Gladstone's threatened public disclosure of the cause of his resignation, wrote suggesting to Gladstone the desirability of his retiring from the House of Commons at the same time as his resignation of the leadership.[40] This impertinence stimulated Gladstone wonderfully. More and more the pattern of counter-attack as leader of the nation against the parliamentary party as in 1877–80 suggested itself. Acton had told Mary Drew that Gladstone's colleagues were unanimous in hoping that he would repudiate them on the Navy estimates. It was clear that, far from being intimidated by Gladstone's withdrawal of his countenance, his colleagues were accustoming themselves to his absence quite comfortably. With some, 'manoeuvring for the succession and for place in a reconstituted administration intensified'.[41] Gladstone would turn the tables on them by setting aside the naval problem and by using the wickedness of the House of Lords against his party as he had once used the Eastern question. The difficulty would be convincing his colleagues to acquiesce in a coup against themselves.

The early days of February 1894 saw Gladstone galvanized into activity. He wrote to Welby at the Treasury enquiring what were the necessary number of days between dissolving a Parliament and assembling a new one and what were the minimum number of days required after reassembling a new Parliament before votes could be proposed for estimates. To Morley and Harcourt he fleshed out his new approach. 'I am looking with deep interest and anxiety at the proceedings in the Lords. Until Friday or Saturday's news came here they had not assumed the character which it now seems possible they may bear – that of a virtual destruction of the entire year's work of the Commons. If they do this it seems to raise a hard & very large question indeed: possible [sic] one large enough to carry us for the *moment* into some new current.'[42] He prepared Mundella for a change of front: 'The Lords *may* raise for us another not less urgent question crossing the scent. The unforeseen often does much in politics.'[43] He alerted his Midlothian committee chairman, James Cowan, with a gloss on his resignation statement: it would not be a decision 'irrespective of circumstances & fixing a time'.[44]

To West Gladstone announced that 'the situation has now changed'. It depended on whether the House of Lords had completed its 'tale of iniquities': if so, Gladstone would obtain a provisional vote for Army and Navy estimates first, 'and then ask the country to judge of him by the past – not the future – and to give a commission to the new Government to deal with the House of Lords'. West observed Gladstone 'brilliant at dejeuner, being full of his new idea, saying he had strength enough, and physique enough for the fight. But pointing to his eyes.'[45]

Rumours seeped back to London of an astonishing and dramatic turn of events at the Grand Hotel, Biarritz. Hamilton speculated on 5 February: Could it be that Mr G. contemplates a dissolution? A last desperate throw of the political dice? Surely his colleagues would never agree. Surely it would be political suicide. Mary Drew seemed to indicate that some volte-face on her father's part was possible, ostensibly on the grounds of the House of Lords' cruelty to the Parish Councils Bill.[46] The rumours were confirmed by telegraph from Algernon West. Gladstone proposed to dissolve the 1892 Parliament on the grounds of its representation of the people being thwarted by the Lords. It was a question of now or never to get the benefit of Gladstone's leadership of the nation. Harcourt thought it 'the act of a selfish lunatic': ' "Heads I win and tails you lose." ' He telegraphed back to West that the Biarritz proposal was 'absolutely insane'.[47] Rosebery was sure that what was 'actuating Mr G. now' was 'malevolence towards his colleagues'. Hamilton concluded that 'Mr G. has lost his sense of balance altogether, and is not really fitted to continue to be Prime Minister even in the most nominal and ornamental capacity. It is a very distressing state of things.'[48] Asquith was discouraging: there was too much yet to do. Morley dismissed the idea as 'impossible and preposterous'. Kimberley deemed it impossible to abandon the government's present measures 'and attack the House of Lords in its present aspect'. As Leader in the Lords he summarized his colleagues' responses and telegraphed that they were 'strongly and unanimously against proposal to dissolve'. Marjoribanks stressed that the party was not ready for an election. In any case the Lords had not yet gone far enough to make a convincing case. There was need either to carry a Registration Bill or to have it thrown out. There were technical problems too about delaying the consideration of estimates.[49]

Was this the great refusal of Liberalism? Was a golden opportunity let slip to retrieve the party's situation after the defeat of the second Home Rule Bill? Gladstone ever after, rather naturally, insisted so. A brilliant insight had come upon him, comparable, in his view, to his insight in August 1876 on the 'virtuous passion' of the masses about the question of the East. Indeed, Gladstone would go further. His insight in 1894 was not, as was the case in 1876, simply a discernment that public opinion had risen to a certain height needful for a given work. It was something much more profound, to be ranked along with his insights as to the 1853 budget, the Irish Church question in 1868, and Home Rule for Ireland. For Gladstone the 'desire for a dissolution of Parliament in the beginning of 1894, and the immediate determination of the issue then raised between the two Houses of Parliament' was elevated into the fourth of the series of supreme moments of political juncture, in his career, when his providentially inspired appreciation of the general situation and its result and his insight into the facts of particular eras generated in his mind a conviction that the materials existed for forming a public opinion and directing it to a particular end.[50] For Gladstone it was a play for very high stakes indeed.

For all that Gladstone returned to London on 10 February in much the same situation in which he had left it: rejected by his colleagues and bereft of a cry. The Navy estimates issue now moved back to the centre of concern. At the first cabinet, on the 12th, normal business about the Lords' amendments to the Employers' Liability and Parish Councils Bills was discussed. There were expectations that the question of resignation might be clarified, but Gladstone said nothing. 'Out we trouped', Morley recalled, 'like schoolboys dismissed from their hour of class. Never was dramatic surprise more perfect.' Harcourt afterwards was 'in fits of laughter'. It had indeed been 'an hour of dupery, and the Old Man left in the Cabinet room, as he surveyed the confusion of the 16 empty chairs might have been forgiven if he chuckled over the thought of the worse confusion of the 16 equally empty gentlemen who had just left them'. Nothing was said about the naval estimates, ostensibly the chief question before the Cabinet. Morley suspected a ruse on Gladstone's part to enable him to deny that a decision had been taken. 'This wd. be a very characteristic bit of Gladstonian subtlety as it is called – childish duplicity is what it ought to be called.'[51]

At Downing Street that evening Gladstone recorded a 'family conversation on the question'. Hamilton had talked to Catherine and the daughters. They complained that Gladstone's colleagues had never tried to meet him halfway. They did not mind his 'leaving a little early' but resented his going 'on a lie'. Hamilton feared that they were 'almost sure themselves to let the real reason be known before long, or else encourage him to allow himself to be drawn. Indeed, Helen Gladstone said that out of office her father would be uncontrolled and (by implication) a dangerous power.' Hamilton felt more sorry than he could say for Catherine. 'She feels the situation acutely; but kept on saying "My husband never has and never will sacrifice his conscience for the retention of power, for keeping the party together, or even for the sake of Ireland; and so nothing now will make him acquiesce to what he considers to be dangerous proposals".'[52] Gladstone's sense of frustration and bitterness was as fresh in November 1896 as it was in February 1894:

Had I not had cataract entailing early disability: had I not been eighty-three years old: had I not had vital controversy with my colleagues on the estimates, such as to break up or dislocate our whole relations, I might have come to London and proved the question of dissolution. But in view of the actual state of facts, and the very small amount of desire (except so far as the indication of kind feeling was concerned) the Cabinet had shown to avert my resignation, it was out of the question.[53]

Gladstone told Hamilton on the 17th: 'You see I am angry; and though I may use strong language, I am quite calm.' He even went so far as to joke to Mundella: 'But perhaps I am like the recalcitrant juryman who complained that he was associated with eleven of the most obstinate, impractical, incomprehensible fellows on the face of the earth.' Gladstone exercised his peevish humour by retaliation and prolonging the difficulty. That night he offered a Cabinet dinner. There was naturally intense expectation among his guests. Towards the end, Rosebery hinted promptingly that it would be well to close the doors. 'I believe it was expected that I should say something,' recorded the nonchalant Gladstone. 'But from my point of view there is nothing to be said.' All he did say on this occasion at which he 'regularly sold his colleagues' was that he was quite prepared to listen to anything anybody else had to say. Asquith's exasperated record of the 'dreaded dinner' was *'Rien!* '[54]

The Lords' amendments to the Employers' Liability Bill did eventually persuade Asquith to abandon it rather than accept a mutilated version. Gladstone made the announcement to the Commons on 20 February, denying that it was a question of half a loaf being better than no bread.[55] Doubtless he did so with inner reflections on the worse case of the Parish Councils Bill, and on the way he 'lay fettered if not hamstrung by the difficulties of which the most formidable lay in the disposition, and in the wants of disposition, prevailing among his immediate friends'.[56] He spoke to Harcourt two days later of retirement. To Harcourt's polite response that it would be a 'calamity', Gladstone 'bowed and said "Yes; that may be; but it is a retirement not voluntarily effected, but compelled by others." '[57] Such ultimately was the consummation of fourteen years of striving to be free of the toils of leadership. At a cabinet on the 23rd he 'alluded to his own position; but only at the end of the sitting just as everybody was leaving. So no one had a chance of saying anything and his words were received in silence . . .'[58] As Gladstone wrote in one of his autobiographical fragments later in 1894: 'Politics are like a labyrinth, from the ironic intricacies of which it is even more difficult to find a way of escape, than it was to find a way into them.' The state of his sight did more to his exchanging his 'imperious public obligations' for what seemed to him to be 'a free place on "the breezy common of humanity" '. Thus this 'operation of retirement, long ago attempted, now at length effected', must he thought 'be considered among the chief momenta' of his life. 'And like those other chief momenta which have been numerous they have been set in motion by no agency of mine, and have all along borne upon them the marks of Providential ordination.'[59]

One of the twists of the labyrinth was getting the Queen to promise strict confidentiality with respect to a forthcoming communication from her prime minister. This was a perfectly reasonable request in view of the delicate political processes still under way in the House of Lords. However, as Ponsonby had to convey, the Queen felt unable to bind herself to preserve secrecy on a matter of which she knew nothing, and asked for some intimation. On 27 February Gladstone wrote a 'preliminary intimation' of his intention to resign 'on physical grounds' when the business of the present session was disposed of.[60] He had an audience the following day, 'doubtless my last in an official capacity'. Victoria thought he looked 'very old and deaf'. They had 'much difficulty in finding topics for an adequate prolongation: but fog and rain and the coming journey to Italy all did their duty and helped'. He thought he never saw her looking better. 'She was at the highest point of her cheerfulness. Her manner was personally kind throughout.' She asked, as usual, kindly about Catherine and the family. To Gladstone she said she was 'sorry *for the cause*' which brought about his resignation. The only part of the conversation of any importance was the impression made on Gladstone that she had in mind keeping on a reconstructed Liberal government rather than turning to Salisbury; and 'further that she will not ask any advice from me as to the head, and further still that she will send for Rosebery'. For Gladstone to have ventured an initiative on a point so sensitive to the prerogative would have gone beyond her earlier invitation that he volunteer matters of business. He very much wanted to advise that Lord Spencer be sent for. It was clear to Gladstone that his going was no shock or surprise, or even a trouble dispelled; rather that she regarded it 'as the immediate precursor to an arrangement more agreeable'.[61]

[4]

A final cabinet met on Thursday, 1 March. 'A really moving scene.' Kimberley started by trying to say a few words, but broke down. Then Harcourt drew out a voluminous manuscript and read, sobbing, to the company an embarrassingly pompous *éloge*, 'which was felt', as Gladstone himself put it, 'to be nine-tenths buncrum'.[62]* At his last Cabinet Council, 'when some of the Ministers were in tears, he gave no sign of feeling & even discouraged anything of the sort in others'.[64] He would afterwards refer to it contemptuously as 'the blubbering Cabinet'. Morley recalled Gladstone going 'slowly out of one door; while we with downcast looks and depressed hearts filed out by the other; much as men walk away from the grave-side'.[65]

Gladstone made his last speech in the Commons that afternoon. The Cabinet wanted him to unloose 'a dose of very bad language' against the House of Lords. 'I tried to follow the wish of the Cabinet: with a

---

* Morley's words were horrid, grotesque, nauseous, almost obscene.[63]

good conscience. The House showed feeling: but of course I made no outward sign.' The Commons were quite unaware that this was to be Gladstone's last appearance in their chamber, after sixty-one years. He acquiesced, under protest, to the Lords' amendments to the Local Government (England and Wales) Bill. Gladstone stressed that it had become an 'intolerable' situation with the passing of the age of 'reserve and circumspection' in the Upper House. He cited the cases of Wellington, Aberdeen, and others in point. Some solution had to be found for this 'tremendous contrariety and incessant conflict upon matters of high importance between the Representatives of the people and those who fill a nominated or non-elective chamber'. Gladstone declared that his duty terminated by calling the attention of the House to the fact that 'a question enormously large, a question which has become profoundly acute', will demand a settlement 'from the highest authority', an authority higher than the authority of the House of Commons: 'It is the authority of the nation which must in the last resort decide.'[66]

Thus, in Asquith's words, 'the legacy which he left to his party'.[67] No one present took this declaration of war on the House of Lords as Gladstone's swansong. Quite apart from the pathos of his circumstances, there was a hollowness in his protestations. There were too many in the Commons who could perfectly well see that it was Gladstone himself, by presenting his hopeless second Home Rule Bill as a sacrificial offering to have its throat cut by the House of Lords, who exposed the vulnerable flank of his government. No one doubted that the House of Lords would get the endorsement of the British constituencies at the next general election. Lord Randolph Churchill responded with a tribute to Gladstone's 'vigour and eloquence', and his opening the way to a 'battle royal' on the constitution. Balfour declared that he would like nothing better than for Gladstone to attempt to stir up the people against the Lords. Gladstone departed quietly from the arena in which so often he had heard roars of acclamation. 'He took up his little box, & walked out, & gave us no sign of emotion. The old man seemed to have *steeled* himself for all those last days.'[68]

At Windsor the following day the Gladstones dined and slept. 'The Queen, long & courteous, but of little meaning on "fundamentals".' He had two interesting conversations 'with the Empress Frederick, & Duchess of Albany: both *low*, one on European matters, the other domestic. Household circle and Acton afterwards.'[69]* On his way to St George's Chapel next morning Gladstone fell in with Ponsonby, who was 'much impressed with the movement among a body of Members

---

* Victoria, former German Crown Princess, widow of Emperor Frederick III, 1888; Princess Helen of Waldeck, widow of Leopold, Duke of Albany, 1884.

of Parliament against having any peer for Prime Minister'. Gladstone 'signified briefly' that he did not think there should be 'too ready submission to such a movement', and on seeing Ponsonby again after chapel repeated the point, adding that there was advantage in strengthening the small Liberal minority in the Lords with the weight of office.[70] Thus Harcourt was paid back, with interest.

The train full of ministers for a meeting of the Privy Council later that morning arrived. Gladstone joined them in the drawing room and there it was arranged that he would see the Queen after the Council but before luncheon. 'I carried in with me a box containing my letter of resignation.' The 'only incident of any interest in this, perhaps rather memorable audience', which closed a service near to fifty-three years since Gladstone himself had been sworn as Privy Councillor in September 1841, was that when he came near 'to take the seat she has now for some time courteously commanded, I did think she was going to "break down"'. She did not, as it happened, and conducted a conversation that was neither here nor there: 'not one syllable on the past'; except reiterated gratitude for his services in the matter of the Duke of Saxe-Coburg's affairs. There were kind remarks about Catherine, whom she had previously seen. 'And various nothings.' There was 'no touch on the subject of the last Ponsonby conversation'.

Was I wrong in not tending orally my best wishes? I was afraid that anything said by me should have the appearance of *touting*. A departing servant has some title to offer his hopes and prayers for the future: but a servant is one who has done, or tried to do service in the past. There is in all this a great sincerity. There also seems to be some little mystery as to my own case with her. I saw no sign of embarrassment or preoccupation.[71]

No doubt the saddest feature of Gladstone's thinking there was 'some little mystery' as to his own case with Victoria was his failing in awareness of the enormous difficulty she had, as a person of naturally rather transparent candour, of dissembling her honest detestation of him. Gladstone reported to Catherine that it was 'thought there had been some suggestion from the Queen' of a title in her own right for Catherine. The offer was 'politely declined'.[72]* Arthur Balfour replied to Gladstone's intimation as to what was about to happen with words which represented accurately the feelings of every one of his fellow members: 'I can hardly realise what the House of Commons will be without you.'[73]

---

* The precedent presumably was that of Mary Anne Disraeli. G much preferred the idea of Catherine's regaining dormant peerages to which she was 'supposed to have a good claim'.

'A SURVIVAL FROM THE TIME OF SIR ROBERT PEEL': LAST YEARS, 1894–8

[1]

There was much to do in receiving and acknowledging visits and messages of condolence and tribute and good wishes. There was a peerage for Reginald Welby, whose parsimony at the Treasury had always recommended him to Gladstone. ('He and Mr Gladstone delighted in each other, and thoroughly enjoyed the financial discussions which they frequently had together when Mr Gladstone was in office.')[1] There was a peerage also for Stuart Rendel, in gratitude for 'infinite personal kindness, I might indeed say tenderness which you have shown me since the first opportunity for it was afforded in these last years: & which has had a real warming & cheering influence on my public as well as private life'.[2] His former Private Secretaries (Welby, Godley, West, Meade, Carmichael, Hamilton, Primrose, Leveson Gower, Seymour, Lyttelton, Murray, and Shand) gave Gladstone a dinner at Brooks's Club. It was George Murray who supervised the removal of Gladstone's effects from Downing Street to Dollis Hill. A sharp attack of bronchial hoarseness prevented acceptance of an invitation to dine from the Duke and Duchess of York.[3] Catherine attended alone.

But always there was the rankling sense that his farewell from the Queen was not as it should have been. He was put in mind of the manner of his own leave-taking from the mule which had borne him uncomplainingly but uncomfortably around Sicily in 1838. He complained that her response to his formal letter of resignation was in the manner of 'settling a tradesman's bill'.[4] To Ponsonby he wrote that the 'first entrance of a man to Windsor Castle, in a responsible character is a great event in his life; and his last departure from it not less moving'. But 'in & during the process which has led up to this termination on Saturday, my action has been in the strictest sense sole, & it has required me in circumstances partly known to harden my heart into a flint'.[5] Gladstone was greatly upset that Rosebery, who sat by Catherine at the Yorks' dinner, pressed her about her husband: 'he hates the Queen, doesn't he?' This provoked Gladstone into setting out in a memorandum a 'clean breast' of his feelings on the matter. 'I am as I hope loyal to the Throne.' He admired the 'many fine qualities' possessed by the Queen. But he used to admire her more than he did now: 'frankly I do not see that the Queen has improved in the last twenty years'. Taking her relations to himself 'since 1844, as a whole, there is in them something of a mystery, which I have not been able to fathom, and probably never shall'.[6] Stiffly obstinate in this respect, as in almost every other respect throughout his career, Gladstone simply lacked the imaginative sympathy with other workings of other minds adequate to comprehending that the Queen might not see it her duty to 'improve' herself conformably with Gladstone's requirements. Gladstone had a way of docketing people after conversation as 'satisfactory' or 'most satisfactory' as showing evidence, presumably, of having attained to a standard of outlook or opinion rather severely preordained by himself. The other female who suffered under this air of supervision, Gladstone's sister Helen, might have contributed valuable insights into Gladstone's inability to fathom the mystery of the Queen's resentment at the manner in which, as she felt it, Gladstone imposed himself upon her.

It was natural that, in the immediate aftermath of the frustration of a passionate wish to dissolve the 1892 Parliament and launch out on a crusade to rouse the nation against the House of Lords, Gladstone should have found retirement not an easy condition to cope with. 'By the resignation of office, which the superintendence of the Almighty so notably and quietly enabled me to bring about, I have passed into a new state of existence.' For the first time in his life Gladstone was thus awarded 'by the Providence of God a period of compulsory leisure'. Such a period 'drives the mind in on itself, and invites, almost constrains, to recollection, and the rendering at least internally an account of life'. Further, 'it lays the basis of a habit of meditation, to the formation of which the course of my existence, packed and crammed with occupation outwards, never stagnant and oft times overdriven, has been extremely hostile'. There were certain practical matters to be attended to. He conversed with Catherine 'on our funeral arrangements'.* He gave Harry 'a financial retrospect & prospect of my life and affairs'. He could get on with the autobiographical writings he had started at Dalmeny in 1892. By September 1894 Gladstone could declare that he was 'thoroughly content' with his retirement: 'I cast no lingering look behind. I pass onward from it *oculo irretorto.*' He saw plenty of work before him,

---

* The essence of the matter was that G did not stipulate against a public funeral, provided Catherine could eventually, on the assumption of his predeceasing her, be interred with him. The case of Disraeli, a widower, was not analogous.

'peaceful work, and work directed to the supreme, i.e. the spiritual, cultivation of mankind, if it please God to give me time and vision to perform it'.[7]

Within a few days of resignation Gladstone recorded: 'Read 10 pages Butler.' A week later: 'Dipped in Bp Butler on Necessity.' This was the resumption of a task he had long before set himself: to assert Butler's theological greatness and to restore his reputation as Christianity's most potent apologist in a time of growing scepticism. But to undertake an edition of Butler's works and provide an accompanying commentary would be a heavy call on eyesight. Consultation in March 1894 with the eye surgeon Nettleship of Wimpole Street disclosed that the cataracts which had first been diagnosed in 1892 had further developed, though the eyes otherwise were sound and good. An operation at the proper time would be feasible. The right, worse, eye was in fact ripe for surgery immediately, but it would be best to delay because of the present infection of bronchial catarrh. The left eye would not be ripe for surgery for a while yet. Gladstone could thus hope that the fog closing in on him might soon be materially dispersed. Hamilton came upon him 'in his shirt sleeves arranging his papers and turning out his drawers' at Downing Street on 22 March, declaiming against the Navy estimates, professing himself 'astonished' at how 'quietly' those 'mad or drunk' proposals had been accepted. 'Today', Hamilton mused, 'was presumably the last occasion on which I shall ever see that great man inside the walls of Downing Street.'[8]

The *oculo irretorto* applied most necessarily to the world of politics, particularly when Gladstone's resignation had been on an issue of policy which the reconstructed Liberal government under a new leader, Rosebery, was preparing to pursue. It was a matter material to this consideration also that Gladstone's successor as prime minister was not at all a man he would have recommended for the post. 'Rosebery has been under no obligation to give me his confidence,' Gladstone observed in July 1894, 'and he has entirely withheld it as to inner matters, while retaining unimpaired all his personal friendliness. He does not owe his present position in any way to me, and has no sort of debt to pay.' It was true, of course, that Gladstone's bringing Rosebery to the front at the Foreign Office in 1886 'was indeed an immense advancement'; but it was done 'with a belief, not sustained by subsequent experience, in his competency and wisdom'.[9]

Rosebery had not endeared himself to many in his party when, on 12 March, he inaugurated his premiership by quite gratuitously echoing Salisbury's pronouncement in defence of the Lords' veto on the Home Rule Bill in the previous year that no great constitutional change could be made without the consent of the 'deciding judge' of the United

Kingdoms, England. Rosebery declared his 'entire accord' with Salisbury 'that before Home Rule is concluded by the Imperial Parliament, England as the predominant member of the partnership of the three Kingdoms will have to be convinced of its justice and equity'.[10] From Gladstone's point of view Rosebery thus represented a Liberalism prepared to go ahead on the 'outrageous mischief' of the Navy estimates and not prepared to go ahead with the struggle to accord justice and self-government to the Irish. In one sense Salisbury's point was one of brute electoral fact: in another sense one of his 'blazing indiscretions', injudiciously offensive to the Scots and Welsh as well as the Irish. The implied menace to the Welsh on the issue of Church disestablishment was unmistakable. Mutinous Harcourtians immediately organized a Liberal counterstroke aimed equally at Rosebery and the House of Lords. Gladstone, recuperating at Brighton under Armitstead's care, 'unbosomed' himself to Acton on 'R's very imprudent declaration'.[11] Apart from the public restraint incumbent upon him, Gladstone in any case could hardly have much room for sympathy with Harcourt's plight, subordinate to, as Gladstone himself put it, 'one who is his junior by a score of years in age, and by nearly half that term in official life: who was moreover at no very [distant] date his own Undersecretary'.[12]* Gladstone undoubtedly was confirmed in his judgement that Spencer would have been the best man, in spite of his initiating at the Admiralty the estimates crisis. And it was a further problem for Gladstone that when Harcourt did exact his revenge on Rosebery with his budget, it was a matter in which Gladstone's sympathies were decidedly on the side of Rosebery and the fiscal conservatives among the Liberals.

George Murray at the Treasury wrote to Gladstone early in April telling him that Harcourt was 'much pleased with his budget; and read to the Cabinet . . . copious extracts from the speech which he is going to deliver'.[13] Harcourt was much in need of a more expansive revenue from direct taxation. The burden of expansion he imposed upon an aggressive new system of death duties, by which estates were to be valued on their actual capital value and taxed at death on a graduated scale. Land was thus to be treated in the same way as unsettled personal property. Ten years previously Gladstone had discussed with Chamberlain and Dilke this 'financial *knot*': the 'very great importance of the proposal to establish equality in principle between realty and personalty as to death duties'. This must in all likelihood, Gladstone then thought, 'lead to a very serious struggle with the Tories for it strikes at the very heart of class-preference, which is the central point of what I call the lower & what is the now prevalent, Toryism'.[14] In 1888, to upstage Chamberlain, he had in fact

---

* G wrote 'recent', though his sense indicates the contrary.

recommended that very principle to the House of Commons.* But now that the Liberal government had adopted this equality for the very purpose of striking at the 'heart of class-preference', Gladstone found it 'too violent'. He thought it involved 'a great departure from the methods of political action established in this country, where reforms, and especially fiscal reforms, have always been considerate and even tender'. That this new graduated tax on land he held to be inconsiderate and harsh was but the beginning of a long critique of Harcourt's budget by Gladstone: 'I can find nothing to give me satisfaction.' And in general Gladstone found little satisfaction in the way Rosebery and Harcourt were conducting the Liberal government. 'I have had very free communication with Tweedmouth [erstwhile Marjoribanks] and with J. Morley. From them I gather we have a prospect of an anarchical Cabinet, abundant pledges, obstructive opposition, compulsory acquiescence in small achievement, and an apathy and languor in the general mind curiously combined with a decided appetite for novelties and for promises apart from the prospect of performance.'[15]

All this was much in accordance with his Peelite nostalgia. 'In some & some very important respects', he wrote to G. W. E. Russell, 'I yearn for the impossible revival of the men and the ideas of my first 20 years which immediately followed the first Reform Act.'[16]† But then, as Gladstone allowed, it was not his purpose 'to arraign the politics or politicians of the day'. His immediate public purpose on 10 May was to assist at the celebrations of the marriage of Asquith to Margot Tennant at St George's, Hanover Square. He was one of the four past, present, and future prime ministers who signed the register; the others were Rosebery, Balfour, and Asquith himself. Margot had invited Gladstone in characteristic mode: '*Please* come to my wedding – May 10th & give me – or rather *us* – your final blessing.'[17] Margot was a 'forward' young woman of whom Gladstone did not entirely approve. 'She has very fine qualities & capacities. I should be glad were she to add to them more of humility and dependence. He has a great future.'[18] A. C. Benson, the Archbishop's son, observed Gladstone, 'very toothless and hairless', talking at length to Arthur Balfour on the vestry stairs, 'with the pathetic reverence of old age for youth and success'.[19] At the reception at Grosvenor Square Gladstone proposed the toast to the bride and groom (though not standing on a chair, as he had done in 1885 on the occasion of Margot's tragic sister Laura's wedding to Alfred Lyttelton).

Gladstone's pathos on this brilliant occasion perhaps was partly

* For the 1888 episode see page 477.
† Russell, a Liberal MP and man of letters, was at that time Under-Secretary at the India Office.

explained by the fact that he was shortly due to undergo his operation for cataract. That operation, on 24 May, at Dollis Hill, went well as far as could immediately be ascertained. It gave Gladstone also 'a good opportunity for breaking off the commonly dry daily journal, or ledger as it might be called, in which for seventy years I have recorded the chief details of my outward life'.[20]* Henceforward Gladstone would note only 'principal events or occupations'. On that new basis Gladstone resumed entries on 19 July, proceeding then 'by leaps and bounds' to September and then December 1894, remarking on his sense of 'relief from small grind of the Daily Journal'.[21] Thus it was that Gladstone made no record, on 30 May, of the death of Laura Thistlethwayte at Woodbine Cottage in Hampstead. There was immense relief also in the 'great revolution' in the incidence of correspondence, which had been 'for many years a serious burden, and at times one almost intolerable'.[22] But if Gladstone himself could do no reading and little writing at this time, he had Murray working on comparative tables of Cabinet colleagues. Murray calculated that Palmerston had seventy-six, Lansdowne seventy-five; but as for Gladstone, 'I cannot get the number above 70'.[23]

The most daring excursion that summer of 1894 was to Scotland, again under Armitstead's care. At Pitlochry in July they were visited by Lady Aberdeen, on leave from helping her husband to be Governor-General of Canada. She was surprised at finding both Gladstones 'looking so well'. Gladstone now had 'considerable colour in his cheeks, instead of the extreme pallor of last year'. He was vehement in criticism of her brother-in-law Arthur Gordon, Lord Stanmore; but generally was cheerful and 'very playful most of the time'. His mind often dwelt on the past.

Say what you will, I am a survival – a survival from the time of Sir Robert Peel – think of what that means. My colleagues were very good to me but they felt this – they were all men twenty, thirty, forty years younger than myself. Could I break with all the associations of my middle life and of the men I then served with and under? It *could* not be and the others felt the time had come when I was best away. – I cannot sympathise with much of the talk of the present day and they knew it.

As for Rosebery: 'He never consults me.'† He remained a closed book. Gladstone felt he understood Rosebery less than he had twelve or fifteen years before. Gladstone much appreciated the attentions of her brother Tweedmouth: 'a matter in which he has evidently differed from the

---

* The first entry in G's diary was for 16 July 1825.
† Murray knew well that G would be 'horrified' to learn that Rosebery was to install 'the Electric Light in Downing St'.[25]

others'. Gladstone assured Lady Aberdeen that he had never felt the dispensations of Providence 'more clear in any of the events of my life than in the past four months, when I have been laid on my back – tied – forced to think – it has supplied a need in my life – it has forced an overdriven man to understand something of what meditation may mean – it has supplied a link' – 'and then about Kemble's farewell and how the line "a period between the theatre and the grave" runs in his head'.[24]

September at what Sir William Fraser alluded to Gladstone as 'your shrine at Hawarden'[26] was marked by a fête, which Gladstone found a severe disturbance. 'Numbers are put at 54000: it strained me a little.'[27] The condition of his right eye was now much improved. This 'new form of vision' would enable him to 'get through in a given time about half the amount of work which would have been practicable under the old'.[28] Gladstone was active still as a controversialist. The novelist Hall Caine requested his thoughts on 'Moral Aim in the novel & the drama'. *The Green Carnation*, the skit on the daring aesthetic fashions of the time, published anonymously in September 1894, was the current literary sensation, widely attributed to Oscar Wilde.* Caine was concerned to hit back at the 'art for art's sake' challenge to Victorian mores.[30] Just as with Tennyson's vituperation against the naturalistic horrors of 'Zolaism' in *Locksley Hall Sixty Years After*, Gladstone reserved his highest praise for works of fiction infused with moral uplift, 'written with so high an aim, & with such evident & entire integrity of intention'.[31] Praise for a work of autobiography, on the other hand, was not bestowed upon the Theosophist Annie Besant. Her son protested that it was 'painful to find that you of all people should attribute to her faults and littlenesses impossible to such a character'.[32]†

[2]

The great world intruded from time to time. An American Invitation Committee, in consideration of Gladstone's 'far reaching and beneficent influence upon our common race of your long and brilliant course', offered to arrange an autumn tour of the United States in 1894.[33] Gladstone contented himself with having provided a proxy in the form of an axe exhibited in the Forestry Building at the Chicago World's Fair.[34] The great

---

* It was written by Robert Hichens. Wilde disclaimed authorship: 'The flower is a work of art. The book is not.'[29]

† The offending piece was G's 'True and False Conceptions of the Atonement' in the September *Nineteenth Century*.

world intruded also in ways much less congenial. Extensive massacres of Armenian Christians by the Turks in that autumn of 1894 set off an agitation of moral outrage in British public opinion reminiscent of Bulgaria and 1876. Naturally Gladstone's name was much invoked. Armenian bishops pleaded for the succour of his voice and reputation. At Hawarden on his eighty-fifth birthday, 29 December 1894, he received an Armenian deputation who presented a chalice for use at the parish church and heard him urge the need for Europe to intervene with deeds as well as words.

Winter came to Hawarden cruelly in 1894. Fierce gales toppled Gladstone's favourite beech trees. (He felled himself stunningly by tripping over an opened drawer in his writing desk on Christmas eve.) It was a bitter blow when Alfred Lyttelton, the most brilliant scion of his clan, came to Gladstone to declare his Unionist allegiance.[35] Mary Drew shared her parents' 'utter misery' at Alfred's defection, preparatory to his standing (successfully) as a Unionist candidate in the coming general election.[36]

If spacious touring in America was not to be contemplated, a dash to the south of France in the new year most decidedly was. After 34¾ hours non-stop, 'admirably engineered by Harry', the Gladstones were received at Rendel's hospitable Château de Thorenc, or 'palazzetto' as Gladstone gratefully named it, near Cannes. The Riviera climate again exercised a beneficial stimulus to Gladstone's and Catherine's constitutions; for Gladstone particularly in the 'peccant' 'bowel department', where his proneness to diarrhetic upsets had lately been aggravated by influenza. Rendel was interested to observe that when Gladstone mentioned that he had kept a diary for seventy years, 'To all his family this seemed news.'[37]

The Gladstones varied Rendel's splendid hospitality by sojourns in Cannes. Later they moved to Cap Martin at Menton. It happened that the Emperor Francis Joseph of Austria was also wintering at Cap Martin that season. He reported on 13 February to his *amie amoureuse*, the actress Kathi Schratt, that the hotel was full, mainly of English, and that the 'famous old Gladstone, with his elderly wife, has been staying in the place for several days, right above us. I saw him yesterday in the garden from a distance.'[38] The two men, both in their time eminent for longevity, had never met. It is likely that the Gladstones were quite unaware of such august observation. In his garden promenades, in any case, Gladstone would have been preoccupied with a matter decidedly not august. It was at Cap Martin that a rather discreditable episode from his past caught up with Gladstone. The parties who had purchased promises of peerages in 1891 now demanded that the undertakings be honoured. Rosebery was disconcerted thus to be importuned. He 'naturally demurred until he had received a written request from Gladstone'. Arnold Morley, the original broker, was deputed to communicate with Gladstone at Cap Martin putting to him the necessity of writing to Rosebery to confirm the undertakings and to accept responsibility for enriching the House of Lords with the baronies of Ashton (for James Williamson, MP for Lancaster) and Wandsworth (for S. J. Stern, MP for North-West Suffolk).*[39]

After a detour to visit Wickham and Agnes in their new decanal splendour at Lincoln, the Gladstones were back at Hawarden by the beginning of April. Having got his Horace translation off his hands, Gladstone settled down to completing his edition of Butler. Ever since his first grapplings with the great bishop in 1845,[40] for Gladstone Joseph Butler's *Analogy of Religion, Natural and Revealed, to the Constitution and Course of Nature* of 1736 had been his theological lodestar. An edition, with an appended volume of *Studies Subsidiary to the Works of Bishop Butler*, would be his intellectual valediction to a world which, in Gladstone's view, stood greatly in need of being reminded of Butler's supreme value and utility as a remedy for its spiritual ills. Much of his talk with Lionel Tollemache was about the 'chief fault' of the Oxford theological liberals that they 'do not appreciate Butler'.[41] Dean Mansel's Bampton lectures of 1858 were 'Butler writ plain', but since then Oxford had puzzled and grieved Gladstone by its neglect of Butler.[42] It was Butler's 'bold unshrinking declaration as to the use & authority of reason' which most recommended him to Gladstone. 'I accept it without reserve & I think you can desire nothing beyond it.' It was in 'that free use of reason, applied to religion as to all matters of life & conduct that I embrace & adopt with all my mind the Christian Faith only wishing I was less unworthy to be numbered among its professors'.[43] An edition testifying his reverence would make Gladstone a little less unworthy.

Acton had always been an obstacle in this matter. Gladstone was unimpressed by Acton's opinion that Butler had been superseded by Kant. 'Kant is the macrocosm of Butler,' insisted Acton. 'He is Butler writ very large.'[44] Gladstone, for his part, had a low opinion of the utility of German metaphysics to the spiritual needs of man.† It was precisely the Englishness of Butler, his stress on probability and the primacy of 'reason and of the common sense which we rightly accept as our guide' as opposed to the absolutism of German 'right reason', which so recommended him to Gladstone. Compared with Kant, Butler seemed to Gladstone 'a great moral discoverer'. 'I want to know', he demanded of Acton, 'when did Time produce a greater – perhaps not so great – a

* See above, page 512–13.
† See above, page 117.

teacher on the laws of moral action as between God & Man? And all action (not 75%, as M. Arnold says) is moral.'[45]* At all events Oxford University would not disown its inaugural Romanes Lecturer on the matter of a new edition. Henry Frowde, the publisher at the Clarendon Press, could assure Gladstone that the Delegates attached importance to 'keeping up the connection of the Press with Butler'; and Frowde himself professed that he personally valued most highly the privilege of publishing Gladstone's edition.[46]

By the summer of 1895 Gladstone had his two volumes of the Butler text prepared. There was time for a fortnight's cruise in June on Currie's *Tantallon Castle* around the Baltic, with Mary and Harry in attendance. 'We did not see the places we mainly wished, but the weather was very good, the hotel incomparable & the sanatory effect admirable!'[47] One of the places they did see was Kiel, on the occasion of the opening of the Kiel Canal connecting the Baltic with the North Sea. As the Emperor William reviewed his glittering fleet, Gladstone is said to have 'remarked coldly to those standing near him, "This means war!" '[48] No doubt he interpreted the event as a vindication of his warnings about the naval estimates. 'I dread the effect which the proposals may have on Europe. The peace of Europe is my primary consideration,' as he had impressed upon Hamilton.[49]† Harry delivered an oak sapling from Prince Bismarck's estate at Friedrichsruhe, which he planted in the park on returning to Hawarden at the end of June.[50]‡

'I am now', Gladstone noted on 13 July, 'beyond expectation, at the level reached at Cannes. D.G.' The 1892 Parliament had come to its end. Gladstone had played no part in the session other than to arrange a pair with the Father of the House, Charles Villiers. However, certain reservations about the Welsh Church Disestablishment Bill caused Gladstone to cancel the pair for the committee stage. Rendel's henchman A. C. Humphreys-Owen was much disturbed at this, as it was being interpreted as 'some constraint on your support of the Bill'. Humphreys-Owen much desired some reassurances as to Gladstone's position.[51] Although Herbert explained at Leeds that his father did not disagree with the policy of his late colleagues, only with certain details in a complex measure which had been drawn without his participation, Gladstone's action undoubtedly compromised Rosebery's government and contributed to its collapse in a footling division on cordite supplies on 21 June. Ministers decided on resignation rather than dissolving the

---

* Rosebery made Acton Regius Professor of Modern History at Cambridge in succession to Seeley in 1895, having knighted Seeley the previous year.
† Of course, it was open to those who opposed him on this issue to interpret the matter in an entirely contrary direction, perhaps with better reason.
‡ 'It is today a fine tree.'

Parliament. That would be the quickest way of extricating themselves from further embarrassments on the Welsh Disestablishment Bill. Rosebery resigned immediately. He recorded calling on Gladstone on 24 June, 'old and cold'. But that evening, together with the Tweedmouths and George Murray, the Gladstones and Mrs Drew dined with the fallen prime minister. Mary described Gladstone and Rosebery as being 'merry as boys out of school'.[52]

Salisbury formed a coalition government of Conservatives and Liberal Unionists. Devonshire was Lord President and Chamberlain Colonial Secretary. Henry James and Lansdowne were the two other Liberal Unionists in the new Cabinet. Already Gladstone was anticipating the dissolution by writing to his Midlothian chairman, bringing to 'final form the prospective farewell I addressed last year to the Midlothian constituency'.[53] For the first general election since 1832 Gladstone was not a candidate. There was a general presumption that the Conservatives and Liberal Unionists would emerge with a majority. The best guess was that they would end up by capturing thirty or so Liberal seats, providing a majority of between thirty and forty. 'How foreign to all minds', as the Conservative *National Review* put it, 'was the notion of the utter smash-up of the Home Rule Party.'[54] A smash-up indeed it turned out to be. The Liberal party lost seventy-three seats net to Conservatives and twenty-three to Liberal Unionists. John Morley was ousted from his Newcastle seat. Astonished at the Liberal collapse, Gladstone could only console himself with the thought that 'should the Tories obtain a majority really heavy, how Chamberlain will shake in his shoes!'[55] This was wishful thinking on Gladstone's part. Chamberlain's partnership with Balfour would see Gladstone out. The supreme irony of Chamberlain's career would be that, having ultimately vindicated himself as a dissenter from Gladstone's attempt to impose Home Rule by overweening statesmanship on an unwilling nation in 1886, he proceeded to attempt very much the same thing himself with Tariff Reform in 1903.

[3]

Gladstone made no comment in his *Autobiographica* on the question raised by the 1895 general election for his assumption as to the nation's habitual assent to the Liberal party. Nor did he advert to the extent to which his certainty about the ultimate triumph of the Home Rule cause, bound up in that assumption, had possibly compounded the withdrawal of that assent. It is plausible to speculate that for Gladstone any notion of going back over that ground would have raised issues too deeply painful to be readily subjected to examination or analysis in a historical spirit. If the high necessity to respond to the Parnellite revolution in Ireland had been squandered away by imperious imposition too soon and too far, then such examination and analysis might conclude that it was a case of profoundly deluded overconfidence as to what was possible and how it would be possible. It seems that Gladstone was content simply to leave the question as a great mystery, or, as he had put it in 1886, when his enterprise first began seriously to fall apart, a 'puzzle'.* He made no allusion to the Home Rule question in his lists of 'Recorded Errors'. His only reference to it in these last years was his defiant listing of 'The proposal of Home Rule for Ireland' in his 'General Retrospect' of 1896 or 1897, in which he claimed for it an origin in a providentially assigned 'insight' which linked it in a grand series passing from the renewal of the income tax in 1853 to the 'proposal of religious equality for Ireland' in 1868 through ultimately to his desire to dissolve in 1894 and challenge the House of Lords. Gladstone then did record his intention to 'consider these four junctures severally'; but he got no further than that statement of intent.[56]

What Gladstone did go on about in his autobiographical writings after 1895, perhaps inordinately, were his rankling resentments at what he felt was the shabbiness of the Queen's treatment of himself and Catherine. Psychoanalytic investigation might diagnose this as an exercise in 'displacement'. Being himself 'conscious without mistrust of having invariably rendered to her the best service that I could', Gladstone could account for the 'signs perfectly unequivocal if partly negative' in the Queen's attitude to him only in some defect of understanding and response on her part. Gladstone did, however, scrupulously make allowance for the influence of rumours widely circulating in the world of politics concerning his 'rescue work' and his well-known association with Mrs Thistlethwayte.

I do not speak lightly, when I state my conviction that the circumstances of my farewell, which I think were altogether without parallel, had serious causes, beyond the operation of political disagreements, which no doubt went for something, but which were insufficient to explain them. Statements, whether true or false must have been carried to her ears which in her view required (and not merely allowed) the mode of proceeding which was actually adopted.[57]

These broodings rumbled on beneath a surface of life busy enough with such affairs as finishing off the Butler text, addressing a meeting at

---

* See above, page 449.

Chester in aid of the Armenians, and completing arrangements for the St Deiniol's Trust. Harry Drew had returned after a spell in South Africa to restore his health and was now taking on helpfully the kind of managerial role that Gladstone had earlier projected for Stephen. Stephen himself, having declined ecclesiastical preferment from Rosebery,[58] devoted his filial energies to the Grand Old Couple at Hawarden. On 21 November Gladstone made over to Harry and the financial trustees of St Deiniol's all his bondholdings supplemented with various other stocks together with the library and furniture. 'I am now nearly 40m[ille] poorer than this day week. All right: & may God prosper the work.' Various threads were snapped. Lord De Lisle and Dudley much regretted Gladstone's resignation, after thirty-five years, of his trusteeship of the National Portrait Gallery.[59] Gladstone indignantly resigned from the Folk-Lore Society because of what he felt was flippancy about religion in the president's address.[60] He was helpful to R. Barry O'Brien with his biography of Parnell, setting Parnell next to O'Connell, and judging him a more masculine and stronger character than Grattan. 'I set the Home Rule question on foot, exclusively in obedience to the call of Ireland, that call being in my judgment constitutional & conclusive.' He put the '*sum total*' of his interviews on business with Parnell at 'under two hours. He was wonderfully laconic and direct.'[61]* Rosebery called, 'finding his host very well, and ready to talk till midnight'.[62] Sir Walter and Lady Phillimore visited Hawarden in November 1895. 'The G.O.M. is just as energetic as ever . . . He spoke for four hours one day much as usual.' They noted however that Catherine showed signs of failing; she did 'not seem to thirst after active life in the way she used'.† Margot Asquith found the Gladstones 'demanding and crotchety' when they visited Glen. 'Everything had to be just as it was at home, and Margot was worn out protecting the servants.' She thought Catherine 'had reached the end of everything'.[63]

It was in December of 1895 that the Armenian question began seriously to obtrude itself on Gladstone. Already at Chester in August 1895 he had made a public declaration as to the necessity of the government's acting. (The Duke of Westminster had chaired that meeting: Gladstone was much gratified that Hawarden and Eaton should be back on terms.) It was not a question, as in 1876, of fighting a hostile government. Salisbury was entirely in accord with Gladstone. The problem, as he pointed out, was that of 1876 turned upside down: it was the European

---

* This brief time hardly squares with the accounts given by Morley and G himself. See above, pages 424, 435, 472, 485, 489.
† Walter P. was the son of G's old friend Sir Robert P. Walter's daughter-in-law Lucy was 'an admirable friend nurse' to Catherine.

concert of France, Germany, and Russia which sustained the Sultan. In such circumstances Britain could do little. Public opinion, however, would not be content with helpless explanations. Gladstone was much in demand to put himself at the head of another moral crusade. Dr Clifford wanted him to say a few words at the City Temple.[64] The Bishop of Hereford wanted him to say a few words at St James's Hall.[65]

Having, with some reluctance, been pushed out of the life of contention, Gladstone was now reluctant to be pulled back into it. In any case, with the winter setting in, swift retreat once more to Cannes was in order. Once enfolded in the warm luxury of Rendel's palazzetto, Gladstone looked forward to imminent publication of his two-volume edition of *The Works of Joseph Butler*. He relapsed into more rankling memories 'Incidental to Resignation', in which he recounted dreams he had been having of Parliament and the Court. Of the latter he concluded that their 'sole force and effect' was to show that 'the subject of my personal relation to the Queen, and all the unsatisfactory ending of my over half a century of service, had more hold on me, down at the root, than I was aware'. One particular resentment he now nourished was at the Queen's failure to acknowledge Catherine's claims on her regard. 'What a fine opportunity of conveying by language and by token to this wife herself some voluntary offering, which would have been so well merited and appropriate, and would have furnished a conclusive answer to any criticism which might have been suggested by the cold negation of her conduct to me.'[66] He seems quite to have forgotten the Queen's offer of a peerage to Catherine. He added a note in his now sporadic journal: 'While it is on my mind, I place on record here . . . my strong desire that after my decease my family shall be most careful to keep in the background all information respecting the personal relations of the Queen and myself during these later years, down to 1894 when they died a kind of natural death: relations rather sad in themselves though absolutely unattended with the smallest ruffle on their surface.'[67]

'My own case is this,' he recorded at Cannes. 'Hearing goes downward. Sight is on the whole wonderfully effective for reading & writing, more than for any other purpose: and these purposes are for me most essential. My walking power is *very* much gone down: and is my weakest point.' Gladstone left himself 'wonderfully blessed in the love and care' around him. He was 'out of the wild', his 'temptations' 'more inward', but as he hoped 'losing somewhat of their force'. 'I anxiously try, while faculty remains, to get on with my work.'[68] A copy of Purcell's *Manning* arrived, with the author's profuse thanks for Gladstone's 'kind interest' and 'invaluable aid'. Gladstone felt he had cause, nonetheless, for complaint at what he considered the misrepresentation of his position relating to his refusal to sign the Declaration of protest against the Gorham

Judgment in 1850.[69]* 'I entirely disavow and disclaim Manning's statement *as it stands*.'[70] In all other respects, however, Gladstone was perfectly satisfied with the rather damaging impact Purcell's volumes made on the ultramontane stance of Manning's successors in the English hierarchy. 'The Purcell storm still rages in England,' Gladstone observed gleefully at Cannes, 'and will rage. But his position is essentially strong and unassailable. The book is a real fact in Church History & in psychology.'[71]

Rather less gratifying were the questions raised in the January *Nineteenth Century* by Leslie Stephen as to the strength and unassailability of Bishop Butler's arguments and Gladstone's fervent endorsement of them. In 'Bishop Butler's Apologist'[72]† Stephen, a scholar who had rejected Christian belief, and, partly for that reason, immensely learned in eighteenth-century English literature, theology, and culture, set out to demolish Butler's credibility and to expose Gladstone as, like Butler, 'a man of powerful intellect working within the shackles of a preconceived system' of which 'we can perceive at each step why it seems plausible to him; but directly one looks at it from outside . . . it falls into ruins'. Stephen represented a younger Victorian generation for whom Butler was an interesting specimen in an exhibition of reasons why Christian belief could never be convincingly founded on grounds of reason. 'In spite of what I take to be his fallacies,' Stephen allowed, 'I can understand why his argument should be treated with a respect more than proportioned to its logical merits, especially among gentlemen who have had the advantage of an Oxford education.' Stephen, famously an embodiment of the 'Cambridge ethos' (and father of Virginia Woolf, who took a long step further with the 'Bloomsbury Group'), addressed both Butler and Gladstone in his ultimate dismissal: 'your whole elaborate structure, with its perfectly good deity, who appears to act unjustly, and the omnipotent being who appears to be unable to make a satisfactory system, is so much waste of labour'.

Gladstone, who, after all, had gone through the experience of being badly reviewed by Macaulay, and who had suffered for his Homeric theories at the hands of the cream of classical scholarship of the high nineteenth century,[73] would not have been too cast down by such objections. Besides, Stephen had not had the benefit of reading Gladstone's supplemental volume of commentary, with which he was hoping to finish with the Clarendon Press by April 1896.[74] In any case, there were matters enough to occupy him at Cannes and later at Hawarden that season. Hirsch of *Le Figaro* wanted his views on the sharp deterioration

---

* Purcell undertook to have the matter corrected in the fourth edition. G promptly wrote to the *Month* and the *Nineteenth Century*.

† Stephen had written on Butler's *Analogy* in his *History of English Thought in the Eighteenth Century* (1876), which G read in 1884.

of Anglo-French relations following from Edward Grey's sensational declaration in the Commons on behalf of the Foreign Office in March 1895 that any French penetration from central Africa through to the upper Nile would be regarded as an 'unfriendly act'. Gladstone reiterated the views he had held for over forty years redolent of the *'entente cordiale'* days of Grey and Aberdeen.[75] Gladstone was engaged also in lexicographical intercourse with James Murray of the *New English Dictionary on Historical Principles* projected by the Clarendon Press. With great respect for Murray's 'Herculean labours', Gladstone was involved with citations of his usages of 'dogmatize' and 'dogmatization', in relation to Pope Pius IX's *Syllabus* of 1864. He had opinions also about the spelling of 'forgo'. But what most oppressed him, he confided to Murray, was his need of more light and more time. 'The worst of it is that the more one has the more one wants, and greatly should I be indebted to anyone who would now give me whole sight instead of half, and 48 hours instead of 24. Such are my modest askings. But Deo Gratias.'[76]

By this time the Gladstones, after three nights under Harry and Maud's hospitable roof in London, were back in Hawarden to enjoy the coming of spring. 'My limitations necessarily continue with a tendency to grow slowly: but my general health, the health of my trunk, is excellent. Dearest Catherine's is also according to the doctors obstinately good although she continues to have her sleep very uncertain and much interrupted.'[77] The marriage of the Prince of Wales's daughter Maud to Prince Charles of Denmark brought the Gladstones briefly into the ambience of the Court. The Waleses were particularly attentive. Gladstone could not suppress a suspicion that 'they do so much towards us from a sense of the Queen's deficiencies'.[78]*

A matter much before Gladstone's attention now was the question of the Roman Church's view of the validity of Anglican orders. Pope Leo XIII had set up a commission to investigate the case in 1895. High Anglican aspirations having thus been encouraged, Gladstone was foremost in hoping for a better frame of mind in the Vatican. He wrote a letter to the Archbishop of York in May 1896, which, with Gladstone's approval, the Archbishop made public.† 'Your letter on Anglican Orders', Purcell assured him, 'goes to the root of the vital question – the necessity of closer relations, of cordial co-operation between the Mother Church and the Church of England in defence of Christianity against the common enemy.'[79]

Yet it was curiously appropriate that one of the foremost embodiments

---

* The royal couple eventually became King and Queen of Norway when the Sweden–Norway union broke up in 1904.

† G republished it in 1897 in his volume of *Later Gleanings*, under the title 'Soliloquium'.

of the 'common enemy', Herbert Spencer, should at this moment appear as a comrade-in-arms with Gladstone as exponent of high Victorian cultural and intellectual values. Spencer and Gladstone, divided deeply on every crucial issue in their time other than defence of the ideal of the minimal anti-imperial state, found themselves by the 1890s survivors together in terrain where the familiar contours and landmarks were shifting and dissolving. They were both under fire from the generation represented by Leslie Stephen, who could find no solace in grand systems of human hope, whether of divine providence or social evolution. Spencer had received from Huxley, in the second Romanes Lecture in 1893, 'Evolution and Ethics', much the same kind of dismissal that Gladstone had just received from Stephen. Thus their exchange of books in 1896 was more than merely an occasion of polite literary amenity: it was almost a solemn joint profession of faith. Spencer thanked Gladstone for his valedictory *Studies Subsidiary to the Works of Bishop Butler*; and arranged to send in return the forthcoming third volume of *The Principles of Sociology*, 'with the completion of which my life-long task will be ended'.[80] There were literary occasions less amenable. Sophia Palmer, daughter of the late Roundell, Earl of Selborne, pleaded in vain that Gladstone relax his rule about defending himself from having his own biography being written 'piecemeal' by refusing permission to publish his letters. She was in process of preparing the final volume of her father's *Memorials*. She quoted Selborne on the split with Gladstone in 1886: 'he said to me with tears in his eyes – "I can meet and talk with others from whom I am parted but Gladstone is different. With him it is like a woman you have been desperately in love with and have parted – You cannot meet and talk of art and politics and weather – Your heart is too full."' According to Sophia, over the last three years the 'acute pain' had passed, 'and I think he would have liked to meet again'.[81] Such a meeting might well have been feasible in the atmosphere being generated by the Armenian problem. It had brought Argyll as well as Westminster back on terms; it might well also have revived some warmth of feeling in Tennyson. As it was, Hallam Tennyson proposed coming up to Hawarden to go through with Gladstone the proofs of his memoir of his father and explain what he had put in and why, with the aim of avoiding anything 'fulsome or false'.[82]

[4]

Gladstone was now under pressure to make some signal public intervention in the Armenian case. He resisted on the grounds that 1876 could not be repeated. He was now a private individual without any authority due to special knowledge. There was the difficulty of discerning clearly the line of duty; but the mode of proceeding 'à la 1876' was 'beyond and distinct from this'. A step back into the arena of contention could not be a single step.[83] However in a letter to the *Daily Chronicle* on 13 September Gladstone put it to the public that there was a conspiracy of the powers at the expense of the Armenians, led by Russia. As to the impending state visit of the new Tsar Nicholas II, Gladstone allowed that one could sympathize with him for his youth; but 'I should like to see him received here, unless he shall have given tokens of an altered course, as in a city of the dead'. Gladstone much wanted Lord Salisbury to be encouraged to break through the diplomatic obstacles.[84] It was a curious reversion to his encouragement at the Eastern Question Conference in 1876 to Salisbury's mission to Constantinople.*

Eventually Gladstone was enticed as far as Hengler's Circus, Liverpool, the scene of his dramatic declaration in 1886 that he would, all the world over, back the masses against the classes. Now, in what was to prove his last grand public appearance, on 24 September, he denounced the 'moral infamy' of the Sultan and the Turks in an echo of the evangelical spirit of 1876. Rosebery eagerly seized on the occasion to resign the Liberal leadership on the grounds of his not being willing to play the Granville role to a rampant 'leader of the nation'. Rosebery's rather petulant act flattered Gladstone more than a little. He decided, at Penmaenmawr, that there would be no harm in causing more turmoil with a letter to the Bishop of Rochester† to be read out at a big meeting at St James's Hall on 19 October. As one who 'cannot escape or disclaim the moral responsibility of one who, for a period of forty-five years from the year 1850, frequently had an active concern in the foreign affairs of this country', Gladstone again denounced the Sultan Abdul Hamid as the 'Great Assassin' and fomentor of systematic massacre. He called on the meeting to strengthen the hand of Lord Salisbury.[85]

Far from being strengthened, Salisbury's hand was weakened in 1896 to the point of Britain's abandonment of her traditional 'eastern policy'. It was a case of falling back from the Straits to Egypt, and the consequent 'Fashoda' confrontation with France. But for Gladstone in any case

---

* See above, pages 190, 192.
† E. S. Talbot, the former Warden of Keble College, Oxford.

attention to the Armenian case was diverted by the shock of Leo XIII's encyclical *Apostolicae Curae*, issued on 13 September, which condemned Anglican Orders as invalid through defect of both form and intent. This insult set off an immense furore reminiscent of the 'Papal Aggression' of 1850, and triggered a 'Protestant' and anti-ritualist and anti-popery frenzy which lasted beyond the end of the century. Gladstone shared fully the sense of smarting disappointment among High Churchmen at what they felt to be a failure of ecumenical spirit at the Vatican and a retrogression to the narrowest sacerdotalism of the time of Pius IX.

Lady Grosvenor, who was present at Hawarden on 10 October when the Archbishop of Canterbury and Mrs Benson arrived for tea on their way back from an Irish tour, observed Gladstone plunge straight away into the Pope's 'Bull'. 'I had never heard him so excited; what with Armenia, Lord Rosebery and most of all the Pope, all in one moment, the Archbishop sat with his teacup in his hand, I suppose for three quarters of an hour, waiting to drink.' Gladstone felt he had been deceived by the Pope's instructing his commission '*not* to examine into the past'. Had he known this, he would never have intervened as he did, or written to the Archbishop of York as he did. 'He was very hot on it,' as Mrs Benson noted, 'and talked most delightfully.'[86]

The following morning, at service in the parish church, the Archbishop slumped dead. His body was carried down to the Rectory. Later, the coffin in the church was covered in a 'magnificent white embroidered pall', provided by Catherine, which would be used for the same purpose at the lying-in-state and funeral of Gladstone himself.[87] The shock left Gladstone white-faced as the funeral train pulled out of Sandycroft station.

That season at Hawarden was marked by a third arrangement for dividing his property among the children. The three sons were each to receive a share worth £37,000, the three daughters a share each of £20,000. The complex matter of drawing up a new will was not finally completed until the Gladstones had returned to their 'old haunt' at Penmaenmawr to 'fortify ourselves against the coming winter'.[88]* It was between returning to Hawarden late in November and departing for Cannes in January 1897 that Gladstone drew up the statement later known as his 'Declaration', signed and dated 7 December:

With reference to rumours which I believe were at one time afloat, though I know not with what degree of currency: and also with reference to the times when I shall not be here to answer for myself, I desire to record my solemn declaration and assurance, as in the sight of God and before His Judgment

---

* The will was signed and dated 26 November 1896.

Seat, that at no period of my life have I been guilty of the act which is known as that of infidelity to the marriage bed.

I limit myself to this negation, and I record it with my dear son Stephen, both as the eldest surviving of our sons, and as my pastor. It will be for him to retain or use it, confidentially unless necessity should require more, which is unlikely: and in any case making it known to his brothers.[89]*

Gladstone placed this in an envelope which he sealed and addressed to Stephen, adding his initials and the instruction: '*Only to be opened after my death.*' Gladstone was never an approver of auricular confession.

'My long and tangled life', Gladstone recorded on 29 December, 'this day concludes its 87th year.'

My father died four days short of that term. I know of no other life so long in the Gladstone family, and my profession has been that of politicians, or more strictly Ministers of State, an extremely short-lived race, when their scene of action has been in the House of Commons: Lord Palmerston being the only complete exception.

In the last twelve months, eyes and ears may have declined, but not materially. The occasional constriction of the chest is the only inconvenience that can be called new. I am not without hope that Cannes may have a mission to act upon it. Catherine is corporally better than she was twelve months ago.

As to my work I have finished my labours upon Butler, have made or rather remade my Will, have made progress with 'Olympian Religion' and good progress with a new Series of Gleanings, and have got St. Deiniol's very near its launch upon the really difficult and critical part of the undertaking. The blessings of family life continue to be poured in the largest measure upon my unworthy head. Even my temporal affairs have thriven . . .

As to politics, I think the basis of my mind is laid principally in finance and philanthropy. The prospects of the first are darker than I have ever known of them. Those of the second are black also: but with more hope of some early dawn.

I do not enter upon interior matters. It is so easy to write, but to write honestly nearly impossible.

Lady Grosvenor gave me today a delightful present of a small Crucifix. I am rather too independent of symbol.

Adieu old year. Lord have mercy.[91]†

This was Gladstone's last diary entry.

* In a legal case involving accusations against Gladstone in 1927, counsel for the Gladstone family advised that the Declaration be not cited.[90]
† Sibell, Lady Grosvenor, was President of the League of Mercy. Her son succeeded his grandfather as second Duke of Westminster in 1899.

The new year of 1897 opened with touching evidence that Gladstone's name and reputation counted still with a young Liberal generation. F. W. Hirst, writing on behalf of five other young Oxford graduates who were projecting a volume of essays on the themes of individual freedom versus collectivism, Home Rule for Ireland, and a more democratic conception of foreign policy, requested a few words of preface.[92]* The Gladstones left for Cannes at the end of January, heading for the 'palazzetto of Lord Rendel'. All things considered, Gladstone thought, particularly in relation to Catherine's being not at all well, 'it had become plain that Mr Armitstead had acted most wisely in detaching himself from us, we had become too great an armful even for his kindness'.[93] Illness drove them for a while up to Grasse. Gladstone found it difficult to face up to working on 'The Olympian Religion' (which was not in fact completed). But he pushed on with his *Autobiographica*. He was glad to be of service to Bodley's Librarian, E. W. B. Nicholson, however, in the matter of pressing for money from Carnegie.[94] He was glad to be of service too to the Greeks in their war with the Turks. 'God help your efforts', he telegraphed to a meeting in a pathetically old and scrawling hand, 'to stop all coercion against Greece and so avert disgrace from England.'[95]

It was the Greek issue which as it happened made a firm connection between Gladstone and the Queen's daughter Princess Louise, Marchioness of Lorne. Gladstone told the Princess that he scrupled to discuss the Greek and Cretan subject 'because my opinions were so violent'. It soon appeared that her own opinions were no less so. The Queen and her party were wintering at Cimiez outside Nice; and there were what Gladstone called 'a batch of Hanoverian Royalties' at the Hôtel du Parc in the English quarter of Cannes. The Princess was instrumental, after complicated negotiations in which Gladstone was concerned to do 'nothing which could possibly wear the appearance of an endeavour to lay myself in the Queen's way or to force myself upon her', in arranging that the Queen and the Gladstones should appear for tea at the Hôtel du Parc. 'We were shown into a room tolerably but not brilliantly lighted, much of which was populated by a copious supply of Hanoverian Royalties including the Queen of Hanover, the Duke of Cumberland and others. *The* Queen was in the inner part of the room, and behind her stood or sat the Prince of Wales with the Duke of Cambridge.' Gladstone found the Queen's manner entirely lacking in her old and usual vitality. Ten minutes' entirely desultory conversation convinced him that she had become more feeble and constitutionally 'now more nearly a cypher'.

* The others were J. S. Phillimore, Hilaire Belloc, P. J. McDonald, J. L. Hammond, and J. A. Simon. Both Hirst and Hammond became noted journalists and Gladstone scholars. Phillimore became a Professor at Glasgow. Simon became Foreign Secretary. Belloc of course became Belloc.

He found the Prince of Wales 'had become a more substantial personage, so to speak, in her presence'. He predicted, in fact, that he was witnessing 'forethought and preparation for an abdication' and for 'the beginning of the reign of Edward VII'.[96]

[5]

For much of the rest of 1897 Gladstone's 'ordinary life from day to day, though of diminished power', suffered no interruption. The Queen soon quashed all notions of abdication. From Osborne she sent two Jubilee medals to the Gladstones as if to emphasize the point. Gladstone distributed copies of *Later Gleanings*. Bram Stoker, Irving's manager, sent his *Dracula*, on the theme of 'immortaliability', trusting that Gladstone would find nothing irreverent or base in it.[97] Hall Caine sent his *The Christian* ('You will see that I have drawn upon you in more places than one . . .').[98] Hallam Tennyson sent his *Memoir* of his father. There were now fewer incursions from the great world. A visit in May by the Prince and Princess of Wales, up at Eaton for the Chester Races, escorted by the Duke and Duchess of Westminster, was for Gladstone a doubly gratifying occasion. H. W. Massingham of the *Daily Chronicle* wanted Gladstone's opinion of the Canadian proposal of imperial preference at Chamberlain's Colonial Conference, and the proposed denunciations of the commercial treaties with Germany and Belgium.[99] Indeed, Gladstone received the Colonial premiers, escorted by the Prince of Wales, at Hawarden in July.[100] In August Arthur Benson, writing the biography of his late father the archbishop, dined at Hawarden with a family party. As he came in he saw Gladstone and Catherine 'sitting on a sofa, side by side, hand in hand, like two lovers'. There was a 'slight jostling for places at the dinner table', with Gladstone insisting that Benson be at his right hand – ' "My left ear is useless", he said, touching it.' Gladstone talked much of Eton and Hallam. ' "The story of M. Gaskell's friendship with Hallam was curious; you know" – with a smile – "people fell in love very easily in those days".' Perhaps Benson took the point of this rather coy displacement allusion; in any case he made no comment. He observed Gladstone closely at table.

He ate and drank little – a glass of champagne and a curious little cut glass full of port – his own particular glass – with cheese. He ate soup – but spilling much of it and rather vague with his spoon. Fish and some bread pudding only handed to him. He took no coffee but another glass of port (it was rough light new port, not good), asking the butler loudly 'Which is the port? Is it this?' He had on a rather high dress waistcoat, unbuttoned, a watchguard round his neck – a tie tied very badly into a kind of flat knot on one side and high collars ... He was most animated and talked the *whole* of dinner. They told me it needed a *visitor* and a *topic* ... After dinner he played backgammon with Stephen, saying sternly and loudly to Stephen when his attention wandered, his own last score 'Three and one, three and one'. He played with great concentration, his face puckered up, rattling the dice vigorously and jamming the dice box down. Once or twice when the conversation grew loud, he said suddenly and severely 'Don't *chatter* there, chatter not'. Everyone laughed, and talked on quietly.[101]

It was early in September that the first painful pangs of the cancer that was to kill Gladstone came upon him.

It was a question at first of a numbness in the cheek, on the left side of his face, thought to be an attack of catarrh, leading to neuralgic pains in the nose and cheekbone. Dr Dobie of Chester diagnosed that the pain in the head, ear, and eye were 'connected with some local irritation affecting the great sensory nerve of the face', which he trusted would soon subside with warm applications and nasal spray.[102] By 17 September he was advising that there was no risk in laudanum being freely used. Ten drops of Nepenthe would ensure a comfortable night. Under Armitstead's care once more, at Butterstone, in Perthshire, Gladstone complained of excruciating pains in his eye, but seemed otherwise quite hale and loquacious. George Curzon, fishing on the Tay, drove over to visit. He found Gladstone 'immensely old and a good deal bent', with both hearing and eyesight failing him. 'He talked, however, with perfectly clear and resonant voice', descanting on a wide variety of topics. After luncheon he rested and later in the afternoon went for a drive. 'He wished me all success in fishing; but betrayed not the faintest interest in my public life or career.'[103]* Gladstone was much interested, on the other hand, in the inscription for the memorial tablet in Durham Cathedral which, through Lord Northbourne's generosity, was being set up in honour of Bishop Butler.[104]

By November it seemed that Gladstone's symptoms showed signs of abatement. Nettleship was clear that the trouble in the left eye, not the 'working eye', was probably not ocular at all. It was decided that the balms of the Riviera climate would once more be resorted to. Hamilton and Arnold Morley went down to Bishop Talbot of Rochester's house at Kennington, where the Gladstones were staying on their way south.

---

* Curzon at the time was Salisbury's Under-Secretary at the Foreign Office. He became Viceroy of India in 1898.

When I began talking to Mr G. and asking him about himself he was very glum, put on his well known black-look, and complained that the neuralgia which had taken hold of one side of his face was most distressing and completely incapacitated him for serious writing or reading. He has always made the most of his ailments, partly due to the extraordinary immunity from troubles which he has enjoyed during his long life; so one must make allowance for some exaggeration; and I tried to persuade him that all his neuralgia would fly at the sight of Cannes. Apart from glumness and depression, I could see no sign of increased failure either mentally or physically. His voice was strong, and he was quite ready to talk. What is now uppermost in his mind is what he calls the spirit of Jingoism under the name of Imperialism which is now so prevalent.

'It was enough', Gladstone declared, 'to make Peel and Cobden turn in their graves.'[105]

The Gladstones stayed at Rendel's Château Thorenc from the end of November 1897 to 16 February 1898. Gladstone's condition worsened steadily. Paroxysms of agony – the 'roaring pains', as Gladstone called them – attacked frequently and ever more severely. He and Catherine drove out occasionally when the weather was fine. But the decline was remorseless. Rendel's daughter Daphne recalled how 'music was almost his only pleasure & how dreadful it was, poor old Mrs Gladstone being at times almost off her head, indeed had it not been for Miss Phillimore, who looked after her almost entirely, I really don't know what they would have done'.[106] Something of Gladstone's old pertinacity survived. He was not ready to let the Tennysons' view of Arthur Hallam's poetical and other shortcomings go unchallenged. In a long article for the *Daily Telegraph* of 5 January 1898 Gladstone offered one last public exercise in making distinctions. While accepting with reluctance Tennyson's opinion that Hallam would not have attained the highest standard of excellence as a poet, Gladstone yet insisted that this was not to affirm that Hallam, had he lived, would have been 'less than a great poet, but that the bent and bias of his powers lay in a different, though an allied, direction . . . he resembled a passing emanation from some other and less darkly chequered world'. The Chaplain at the Embassy in Vienna, taking up the cue, sent details of the house at Vienna where Hallam died, 'Zur goldenen Birne', still standing. A dedication tablet was planned; and he sent a copy of the death certificate of 'Hallan'.[107]

Even the fondest old memories, if perhaps a solace, could not heal. Nor had Cannes worked its accustomed beneficial influence. It was decided to return to England. He stayed briefly in London, not neglecting to sign his and Catherine's names in the Prince of Wales's visitors' book at Marlborough House. Hawarden was ruled out as unsuitable in winter conditions. Bournemouth was fixed upon: a kind of reversion, in its way, to that nomadic life in southern resorts which Gladstone's father had imposed upon his family when Gladstone was at Eton and Oxford. It was at Bournemouth that cancer of the palate was first diagnosed: inoperable and mortal. A public announcement was made, and Gladstone determined to go back to Hawarden to die. The sentence of death was for him a promise of blessed release.

On 22 March he left Bournemouth, speaking a few words to the crowd at the station: his last public utterance. At Hawarden the blessed release was agonizingly long in coming. His body, the 'health of his trunk', remained too strong to allow a quick and merciful death. He chanted his favourite Biblical passages and hymns, especially Newman's 'Praise to the Holiest in the Height'. To the condolences of the University of Oxford he replied: 'There is no expression of Christian sympathy that I value more than that of the ancient University of Oxford, the God-fearing and God-sustaining University of Oxford. I served her perhaps mistakenly, but to the best of my ability. My earnest prayers are hers to the uttermost and to the last.' After 9 April he was no longer able to walk outside the Castle. After 18 April he was no longer able to come downstairs. For much of the time he was in drugged semi-consciousness or unconsciousness. Rosebery and John Morley paid their respects. The end came on Ascension Day, Thursday, 19 May. He was perfectly calm, having ceased to feel pain for the while. He had made his farewells. Shortly before five o'clock that morning, Stephen read to him two of his favourite hymns and offered a prayer; all the family kneeling round the bed. At the end of the prayer Gladstone was, so the official family version had it, heard to 'murmur a distinct "Amen!"' At ten minutes to five his breathing ceased.[108]*

Gladstone's body was laid out in his Oxford doctoral robes in the 'Temple of Peace'. Unlike Disraeli, Gladstone had not ruled out a public funeral. Balfour in the Commons moved an adjournment and gave notice of an Address to the Queen praying for a public funeral in Westminster Abbey. 'We felt it very much,' recorded Lady Monkswell, 'for he has been the background to our entire lives. There is no loss we shall ever feel so much as this, except when the good old Queen goes. When I read of his peaceful blessed death I could not help shedding tears. How glad I feel that I have talked to him & often shaken hands with him.'[110] This testimony spoke eloquently. Lady Monkswell, unlike her husband, was hostile to Home Rule; her feelings, quite transcending the old bitterness of party, were very representative of the general public response to the passing of someone iconic for the century. Tributes in both Houses of

---

* 'He had probably been unconscious for several hours.'[109]

Parliament, as the Address to the Queen was approved, reflected this sense of a dispensation from anything like conventional sentiments. Herbert Gladstone, speaking for the family, gratefully accepted Parliament's offer to pay honour to its grandest figure. Harry Gladstone negotiated with the Dean of Westminster. It was the 'good old Queen', the only person who shared with Gladstone that iconic status and thus did not share the sentiments attached to it, who was inclined to be captious. She could not agree with her daughter the Empress Frederick that Gladstone was 'a great Englishman'. She allowed that he was a 'clever man, full of talent', and a 'good and very religious man'.[111] She took the Prince of Wales to task, along with his son the Duke of York, for agreeing, without precedent, to be pall-bearers at the Abbey. The Prince replied that the circumstances were unprecedented.[112] Although the Queen's respect for truth was too intense to allow her to make a hypocritical announcement in the *Court Circular*, she sent a gracious telegram to Catherine.[113]

After a communion service in the presence of Gladstone's coffin was held in Hawarden church, his remains passed from Broughton Hall station, pulled by the locomotive 'Gladstone', to Willesden, where they were transferred on the London Underground to Westminster station, and thence to Westminster Hall. Although it was a state funeral, there was no long procession in state. The family wanted something prompt and on a simple scale. The full pomp of state would take too long to arrange. Gladstone's remains lay in state for an unprecedented two days, 26–27 May, while more than a quarter of a million mourners filed through Westminster Hall. The funeral in the Abbey on 28 May was 'a most wonderful sight'. 'It was more than wonderful, it was quite unique,' thought Mary Monkswell. 'Never again . . . will such violent, new, painful & extraordinary emotions go thro' and thro' me, giving me strength to get through it at the time, & letting me down to a pretty low place when it was all over.'

A figure in deepest mourning came slowly up the aisle. 'A sort of murmur ran through the crowd, & then it dawned on me that here was indeed poor dear old Mrs Gladstone. I think she was leaning on Mr Drew's arm as close behind her came Mrs Drew & the charming little Dorothy.' 'To see that erect pathetic figure with her expression half dreaming & half wild but triumphant, & to remember her immense age, 86, & what she had gone through & what she had lost – & then close behind her the charming jolly child (aged about 8) whose mourning could not look anything but smart & pretty, with her beautiful curly hair hanging round her, & positively *tripping* down the aisle.' The ten pall-bearers were the Prince of Wales and the Duke of York representing the royal family, Rosebery, Harcourt (the present leader of the Liberal party), Salisbury and Balfour, Kimberley, Rutland (the former Lord John Manners, standing in for Argyll, who could not be present), and Gladstone's steadfast 'old shoes', Rendel and Armitstead. The music Lady Monkswell thought most beautiful; 'a multitude of voices singing very softly' *Rock of Ages*, the old edition with four verses. 'When the coffin was removed from under the Lantern to where it will be throughout the ages in the N. transept we could only catch the sound of the last two prayers. While the coffin was put into the grave we sang the hymn from Cardinal Newman's "Dream of Gerontius" – "Praise to the Holiest in the height" a hymn which is quite beyond me but which I shall love for his sake.' The service finished with Stainer's 'fourfold Amen, & the hymn *"O God our help in ages past"*, Ps XC in which we all joined like the voice of many waters. We all stood reverently while the *"Dead March"* was played, & then it was all over.'[114]

At the close of the service, Catherine rested for a few minutes in the chair provided, having hitherto preferred to stand or kneel. She expressed a wish to Harry that she might shake hands with the pall-bearers. 'The most striking and touching of all the features of the ceremony', thought Hamilton, 'was the presence of Mrs G. I am truly glad she lived to see the day. It was far more striking than all the tributes of love [and] veneration paid to Mr G. when alive; and it is doubtful whether any public man ever had so great a tribute paid to his memory.'[115]*

---

* Catherine joined G in the grave in the north transept on 19 June 1900. The Queen recorded that the account of the funeral 'and above all one from Mrs Gladstone was very touching'.[116]

References

Abbreviations Used in References

AR	*The Annual Register*
BL	The British Library
D	*The Gladstone Diaries, 1825–1896*, M. R. D. Foot and H. C. G. Matthew (eds.), 14 vols. (Oxford, 1968–94)
G	W. E. Gladstone
GBA	R. T. Shannon, *Gladstone and the Bulgarian Agitation, 1876* (1963)
G & G, 1	*The Political Correspondence of Mr Gladstone and Lord Granville, 1868–1876*, A. Ramm (ed.), *Transactions of the Royal Historical Society*, 2 vols. (1952)
G & G, 2	*The Political Correspondence of Mr Gladstone and Lord Granville, 1876–1886*, A. Ramm (ed.), 2 vols. (Oxford, 1962)
Gladstone	R. T. Shannon, *Gladstone, 1809–1865* (1984)
GP	The Gladstone Papers, British Library
H(3), (4)	*Hansard's Parliamentary Debates*, Third, Fourth Series
Hamilton, i, ii	*The Diary of Sir Edward Walter Hamilton, 1880–1885*, D. W. R. Bahlman (ed.) (Oxford, 1972)
Hamilton, iii	*The Diary of Sir Edward Walter Hamilton, 1885–1906*, D. W. R. Bahlman (ed.) (Hull, 1993)
HJ	*The Historical Journal* (Cambridge)
M & B	W. F. Monypenny and G. E. Buckle, *The Life of Benjamin Disraeli, Earl of Beaconsfield* (2 vol. edn, 1929)
Morley	J. Morley, *The Life of William Ewart Gladstone* (2 vol. edn, 1905)
PMP	*The Prime Ministers' Papers: W. E. Gladstone*, J. Brooke and M. Sorenson (eds.), 4 vols. (1971–81)
Q & G	*The Queen and Mr Gladstone*, P. Guedalla (ed.), 2 vols. (1933)
TRHS	*Transactions of the Royal Historical Society*

CHAPTER 1:
'MAKING HISTORY': 1865–6

1. *Gladstone*, 548.
2. A. West, *Recollections* (1899), i, 306; *Gladstone*, 511.
3. *Gladstone*, 274.
4. H. Butterfield, 'Lord Acton's Correspondence with Döllinger', HJ, 1966, 143.
5. *Gladstone*, 530.
6. ibid., 547.
7. M & B, ii, 158.
8. *Gladstone*, 428.
9. ibid., 428–9.
10. ibid., 496.
11. ibid., 550–51. See D, 12 March 1892.
12. G, *A Chapter of Autobiography* (1868), 7.
13. *Gladstone*, 555.
14. ibid., 547.
15. ibid., 320.
16. ibid., 339.
17. ibid., 276–7.
18. ibid., 270.
19. D. M. Schreuder, 'The Making of Gladstone's Posthumous Career: The Role of Morley and Knaplund as "Monumental Masons,"', 1903–1927', in B. Kinzer (ed.), *The Gladstonian Turn of Mind* (Toronto, 1985), 107.
20. H. C. G. Matthew, *Gladstone, 1875–1898* (Oxford, 1995), 53. G, 'Postscriptum on the County Franchise', *Gleanings from Past Years* (1879), i, 199–202.
21. *Gladstone*, 523.
22. G & G, 2, i, 42.
23. C. Harvie, 'Gladstonianism, the Provinces, and Popular Political Culture, 1860–1906', in R. Bellamy (ed.), *Victorian Liberalism. Nineteenth Century Political Thought and Practice* (1990).
24. *Gladstone*, 519.
25. G to Bedford. 17 December 1884 (copy). GP, 44488, 277.

26. R. T. Shannon, 'Tennyson and Gladstone', *The Times Literary Supplement*, 2 October 1992, 4–6.
27. *Gladstone*, 389.
28. J. Prest, *Lord John Russell* (1972), 403.
29. ibid., 402.
30. F. B. Smith, *The Making of the Second Reform Bill* (Cambridge, 1966), 60.
31. *Gladstone*, 451.
32. Bright to Hargreaves, 23 October 1865. BL, 62079, 83.
33. G, 'Place of Ancient Greece in the Providential Order', *Gleanings of Past Years* (1879), vii, 79, 89.
34. D, 3 November 1865.
35. D, 1 December 1865. See also Delane (of *The Times*) to G, 16 January 1866. GP, 44409, 86.
36. GBA, 206–9.
37. J. Fraser to G, 16 October 1865. GP, 44408, 34.
38. G to *Star*, 4 October (1865). Ibid., 10.
39. Gibson to G, 3 October 1865. GP, 44408, 5.
40. T. Wemyss Reid, *Life of . . . William Edward Forster* (1888), i, 391.
41. G. M. Trevelyan, *The Life of John Bright* (1913), 359.
42. Glynne-Gladstone MSS, Clwyd Record Office, Hawarden, Box 94/11, Rough Book A, Accounts, 103.
43. G, 'On Ecce Homo', *Gleanings of Past Years* (1879), iii, 90–92.
44. D, 10 January 1866.
45. G to Rathbone, 12 January 1866 (copy). GP, 44409, 62.
46. G to Rathbone, 17 January 1866 (copy). Ibid., 96.
47. *Gladstone*, 556.
48. Q & G, i, 129.
49. G. I. T. Machin, 'Gladstone and Nonconformity in the 1860s: The Formation of an Alliance', HJ, 1974, 355–6.
50. D, 3 March 1866.
51. AR, 1866, 102.
52. H(3), clxxxii, 22–59.

53. Earl of Selborne, *Memorials*. Part II, *Personal and Political, 1865–1895* (1898), i, 56.

54. 1 Sam. 22: 1, 2, referring to the enemies of King Saul who gathered around David.

55. H(3), clxxxii, 2095 (26 April 1866).

56. ibid., 873.

57. H(3), clxxxi, 1688 (7 March 1866). O. Anderson, 'Gladstone's Abolition of Compulsory Church Rates: A Minor Political Myth and Its Historical Career', *Journal of Ecclesiastical History*, 1974, 187.

58. *Gladstone*, 479. P. F. McHugh, *Prostitution and Victorian Social Reform* (1980), 42.

59. G to Paget, 2 January 1866 (copy). GP, 44409, 26.

60. *Gladstone*, 352–4, 379, 439–40, 484–6.

61. H(3), clxxxi, 1519, 5 March 1866. Bratiano to G, 19 March 1866. GP, 44409, 260.

62. G, 'The War in Italy', QR, 1859, 559.

63. G to Bratiano, 16 May 1866 (draft). GP, 44410, 186.

64. Matthew, *Gladstone*, i, 141. D, 6 April 1866.

65. See above, page xii.

66. *The Times*, 7 April 1866, 9.

67. H(3), clxxxii, 1124–48.

68. ibid., 2089–90, 26 April 1866.

69. H. Maxwell, *Life of . . . Clarendon* (1913), ii, 314.

70. G to Bruce, 26 April 1866 (copy). GP, 44410, 102.

71. H(3), clxxxiii, 103–13 (27 April 1866).

72. G, 'Place of Ancient Greece in the Providential Order', *Gleanings of Past Years* (1879), vii, 33.

73. H(3), clxxxiii, 113–51.

74. *Gladstone*, 206.

75. G. Barnett Smith, *Life of . . . Gladstone* (1883), 344.

76. ibid., 344–5.

77. Ly Trevelyan to G, 1 May 1866. GP, 44410, 128.

78. H(3), clxxxiii, 365.

79. H(3), clxxxiii, 1341 (28 May 1866).

80. ibid., 1488 (30 May 1866).

81. ibid., 1525–6 (30 May 1866).

82. Selborne, *Memorials*, i, 65–7.

83. H(3), clxxxiii, 1900 (4 June 1866).

84. D, 4 June 1866.

85. Smith, *Making of the Second Reform Bill*, 103.

86. ibid.

87. R. B. Wilson (ed.), *Sir Daniel Gooch* (Newton Abbot, 1972), 112.

88. D, 18 June 1866.

89. Smith, *Making of the Second Reform Bill*, 114.

90. D, 26 June 1866.

91. D, 2 June 1886.

92. Smith, ibid.

CHAPTER 2:
'IN THE PATH OF RIGHT': 1866–8

1. H(3), clxxxiv, 1144–5.

2. F. B. Smith, *The Making of the Second Reform Bill* (Cambridge, 1966), 133.

3. M. St J. Packe, *John Stuart Mill* (New York, 1954), 454.

4. H(3), clxxxiv, 1939 (2 August 1866).

5. J. Prest, *Lord John Russell* (1972), 415.

6. F. W. Hirst, 'Mr Gladstone as Leader of the House and Reformer, 1865–68', in T. W. Reid (ed.), *Life of W. E. Gladstone* (1899), 491.

7. D, 22 October 1866.

8. Hirst, ibid., 492.

9. *Gladstone*, 181–2.

10. See F. E. Hamer (ed.), *The Personal Papers of Lord Rendel* (1931), 116.

11. Smith, *Making of the Second Reform Bill*, 165.

12. Morley, i, 856.

13. Smith, 135.

14. K. Robbins, *John Bright* (1979), 188.

15. H. Maxwell, *Life . . . of Clarendon* (1913), ii, 325.

16. M & B, ii, 218.

17. Earl of Selborne, *Memorials*. Part II, *Personal and Political, 1865–1895* (1899), i, 64.

18. D, 28 November 1880.

19. Selborne, 87.

20. H(3), clxxxv, 69 (5 February 1867).

21. ibid., 441–3 (15 February 1867).

22. Paget to G, 10 March 1867. GP, 44412, 116.

23. Stratford to G, 13 March 1867. Ibid., 123.

24. H(3), clxxxv, 486–7 (18 February 1867).

25. Smith, 166.

26. ibid., 982, 988–9 (25 February 1867).

27. H(3), clxxxv, 1355 (5 March 1867).

28. Smith, 154.

29. ibid., 159.

30. H(3), clxxxv, 1358 (5 March 1867).

31. ibid., 1346, 1349 (5 March 1867).

32. G to Elcho, 7 March 1867 (copy). GP, 44412, 109.

33. H(3), clxxxvi, 6–16 (18 March 1867).

34. ibid., 53, 57 (18 March 1867).

35. ibid., 39–40 (18 March 1867).

36. M & B, ii, 256.

37. H(3), clxxxvi, 45 (18 March 1867); 476–7, 499 (25 March 1867).

38. ibid., 89 (18 March 1867).

39. ibid., 41 (18 March 1867).

40. ibid., 577 (26 March 1867).

41. ibid., 664 (26 March 1867).

42. Smith, 172.

43. H(3), clxxxvi, 1143, 1291 (4 April 1867).

44. Smith, 174. M. Cowling, *1867. Disraeli, Gladstone and Revolution* (Cambridge, 1967), 195.

45. Cowling, 196.

46. D, 8 April 1867.

47. Smith, 176.

48. Morley, i, 866.

49. Smith, 178.

50. H(3), clxxxvi, 1687–8 (12 April 1867).

51. Morley, i, 866.

52. D, 12 April 1867.

53. Temple to G, 17 April 1867. GP, 44412, 217.

54. Smith, 181, 183.

55. Hughes to G, 13 April 1867. GP, 44412, 209.

56. Denman to G, 1 May 1867. Ibid., 259.

57. Duke of Argyll, *Autobiography and Memoirs* (1906), ii, 236.

58. Morley, i, 866.

59. D, 1 May 1867.

60. Selborne, i, 70.

61. Morley, i, 868–9.

62. H(3), clxxxvii, 715 (17 May 1867).

63. D, 9 May 1867.

64. G, 'The Session and Its Sequel', *Edinburgh Review*, October 1867, 565.

65. H(3), clxxxvii, 303–4 (9 May 1867).

66. Hirst, in Reid, *Gladstone*, 494.

67. H(3), clxxxvii, 719.

68. ibid., 719 (17 May 1867).

69. Smith, 197, 201; Cowling, 235.

70. Smith, 197.

71. G, *Edinburgh Review*, October 1867, 554.

72. H(3), clxxxvii, 738, 756 (17 May 1867); M & B, ii, 283.

73. D, 28 May 1867.

74. H(3), clxxxvii, 1231 (28 May 1867).

75. H(3), clxxxvii, 1548 (15 July 1867).

76. Selborne, *Memorials*, i, 72.

77. D, 7 July 1867. See *Gladstone*, 416, 443.

78. Morley, i, 868.

79. H(3), clxxxviii, 1549 (15 July 1867).

80. Bright to Hargreaves, 19 August 1867. BL, 62079, 111.

81. D, 8 August 1867.

82. H(3), clxxxvii, 1459 (31 May 1867).

83. *Gladstone*, 531.

84. H(3), clxxxvii, 121, 130.

85. G, *Edinburgh Review*, October 1867, 543, 556, 577, 578, 581, 584.

86. H. C. G. Matthew, 'Gladstone, Vaticanism and the Question of the East', *Studies in Church History*, xv, ed. D. Baker (1978), 420.

87. G to Disraeli, 16 December 1865 (copy). GP, 44408, 219.

88. Disraeli to G, 20 November 1867. GP, 44413, 242.

89. Hirst, in Reid, *Gladstone*, 495.

90. Prest, *Russell*, 417.

91. Hirst, in Reid, *Gladstone*, 596–7.

92. H(3), cxcv, 1545–6 (26 April 1869). See also Grey to G, 27 April 1869. GP, 44420, 182, on Granville's 'virtual admission that it was the Fenian outrages which led you last year to make your move against the Irish Establishment'.

93. G. E. Buckle (ed.), *The Letters of Queen Victoria*, 2 series, *1862–1878* (1926), i, 562.

94. S. Walpole, *Lord John Russell* (1891), ii, 446–7.

95. Prest, *Russell*, 417.

96. Argyll, *Autobiography and Memoirs*, ii, 240–41.

97. Lord E. Fitzmaurice, *Life of . . . Lord Granville* (1905), i, 518–19.

98. P. M. H. Bell, *Disestablishment in Ireland and Wales* (1969), 75.

99. R. T. Shannon, *The Age of Disraeli* (1992), 37.

100. H(3), clxxxx, 1288–9.

101. ibid., 1771 (16 March 1868).

102. ibid., 1758, 1759, 1767.

103. J. Parry, *Democracy and Religion. Gladstone and the Liberal Party, 1867–1875* (Cambridge, 1986), 269.

104. *Gladstone*, 149.

105. Selborne, *Memorials*, i, 93.

106. Fitzmaurice, *Granville*, i, 254.

107. Shannon, *Disraeli*, 41.

108. Fitzmaurice, *Granville*, ii, 522–3.

109. H(3), clxxxxi, 474 (30 March 1868); ibid., 932 (3 April 1868).

110. G to Cook, 19 May 1868 (copy). GP, 44415, 62.

111. D, 12 April 1868.

112. H(3), clxxxxi, 1686, 1694.

113. N. E. Johnson (ed.), *The Diary of Gathorne Hardy, later Lord Cranbrook, 1866–1892* (Oxford, 1981), 72.

114. Shannon, *Disraeli*, 45.

115. ibid., 44.

116. Bessborough to G, 28 May [1868]. GP, 44415, 104.

117. Shannon, *Disraeli*, 29.

118. Maxwell, *Clarendon*, ii, 346.

119. See O. Anderson, 'Gladstone's Abolition of Compulsory Church Rates: A Minor Political Myth and Its Historical Career', *Journal of Ecclesiastical History*, 1974.

120. Parry, *Democracy and Religion*, 274–5; G. I. T. Machin, *Politics and the Churches in Great Britain, 1832–1868* (Oxford, 1977), 353–4.

121. GP, 44415, 306 (18, 25 July 1868).

122. Rathbone to G, 4 May 1868. GP, 44415, 10.

123. D, 1 August 1868.

124. G, *A Chapter of Autobiography* (1868), 40.

125. Fitzmaurice, *Granville*, i, 534.

126. Maxwell, *Clarendon*, ii, 351.

127. Butler to G, 19 December 1868. GP, 44416, 74.

128. A. P. Robson, 'A Bird's Eye View of Gladstone', in B. L. Kinzer (ed.), *The Gladstonian Turn of Mind* (Toronto, 1985), 68–70; H(3), cci, 618–19 (12 May 1870).

129. D, 28 October 1868.

130. D, 3 November 1868.

131. Gibson to G, 19 November 1868. GP, 44416, 206.

132. Bilson to G, 25 November 1868. Ibid., 238.

133. Maxwell, *Clarendon*, ii, 351–2.

134. H(3), cc, 1128 (1 April 1870).

135. G to Disraeli, 6 December 1868 (copy). GP, 44416, 315.

136. D, 1 December 1868.

137. E. Ashley, *National Review*, June 1898, 536. See Hirst in Reid, *Gladstone*, 541, for the romantic engraving of the incident, by J. H. Bacon, depicting Gladstone in shirtsleeves and almost unbuttoned waistcoat. Ashley misdated the occasion to 4 December.

138. D, 6 December 1868; PMP, i, *Autobiographica*, 96.

139. D, 6 December 1868.

140. Q & G, i, 145–6.

141. D, 4 December 1868.

142. B. L. Kinzer, *The Ballot Question in Nineteenth Century English Politics* (New York, 1982), 146–7.

143. Brougham to G, 26 November 1868. GP, 44416, 249.

144. *Letters of . . . Henry Austin Bruce, Lord Aberdare* (Oxford, 1920), i, 325.

145. G to Delane, 6 December 1868 (copy). GP, 44416, 313.

146. T. A. Jenkins (ed.), *The Parliamentary Diaries of Sir John Trelawny, 1868–1873* (1994), 345.

147. Parry, *Democracy and Religion*, 278–9.

148. J. Winter, *Robert Lowe* (Toronto, 1976), 244–5.

149. Hamilton, iii, 150.

150. ibid., 105–6.

151. Aberdare, i, 258.

152. J. Parry, *The Rise and Fall of Liberal Government in Victorian Britain* (Yale, 1993), 229.

153. G & G, 1, i, 6.

154. D, 13 December 1868.

155. G to Trench, 14 December 1868 (copy). GP, 44417, 138.

156. G to Lady Salisbury, 16 December 1868 (copy), ibid., 161.

157. G to Lansdowne, 15 December 1868 (copy), ibid., 146.

158. G to Mrs Stonor, 24 December 1868 (copy), ibid., 245.

CHAPTER 3:
'THE ALMIGHTY SEEMS TO SUSTAIN ME': 1869–71

1. G, 'The Session and Its Sequel', *Edinburgh Review*, October 1867, 576.

2. A. West, *Recollections, 1832–1886* (1899), i, 331.

3. G, 'The Session and Its Sequel', *Edinburgh Review*, October 1867, 576–8, 579–80.

4. D, 24 October 1868. GP, 44756, 157.

5. *Gladstone*, 527–8, 531, 534, 552, 556.

6. D, 31 December 1868.

7. O. Chadwick, *Acton and Gladstone* (1976), 18.

8. Q & G, i, 152–3, 157.

9. G to Disraeli, 18 February 1869 (copy). GP, 44419, 89.

10. D, 11 June 1869.

11. Q & G, i, 147, 150–51.

12. T. A. Jenkins (ed.), *The Parliamentary Diaries of Sir John Trelawny, 1868–1873* (1994), 346.

13. G to Sullivan, 1 January 1869 (copy). GP, 44418, 4.

14. G to Sullivan, 11 January 1869 (copy). Ibid., 127.

15. G & G, 1, i, 11.

16. G to Sullivan, 7 January 1869 (copy). Ibid. G to Delane, 27 February 1869 (copy). GP, 44419, 132. Gloucester to G, 8 March 1869, ibid., 179.

17. *Trelawny*, 347.

18. H(3), cxciv, 412, 414, 416, 424, 458–62, 465–6.

19. D, 1 May 1869.

20. G to Ramsden, 20 March 1869 (copy). GP 44419, 243.

21. *Trelawny*, 351–2.

22. Cullen to G, 18 March 1869. GP, 44419, 198.

23. H(3), cxcv, 2009–17 (30 April 1869).

24. D, 30 April 1869.

25. H(3), cxcv, 2022–7 (30 April 1869).

26. H(3), cxcvi, 1069.

27. *Trelawny*, 354.

28. ibid., 364.

29. ibid., 365.

30. G & G, 1, i, 29.

31. D, 12 July 1869.

32. D, 17 July 1869.

33. D, 15 July 1869.

34. Derby Diaries (15th Earl), Liverpool Record Office, 16 July 1869.

35. G & G, 1, i, 74.

36. D, 23 August 1869.

37. D, 13 August 1869.

38. R. Fulford (ed.), *Your Dear Letter. Private Correspondence of Queen Victoria and the Crown Princess of Prussia, 1865–1871* (1971), 248.

39. J. Vaio, 'Gladstone and the Early Reception of Schliemann in England', in *Heinrich Schliemann nach hundert Jahren*, ed. W. M. Calder and J. Cobet (Frankfurt am Main, 1992), 417.

40. GP, 44422, 5.

41. *Gladstone*, 278–83.

42. Lowe to G, 10 November 1869. GP, 44537, 149.

43. D, 23 November 1869.

44. G & G, 1, i, 56–7. Q & G, i, 195–7.

45. D, 4 August 1869.

46. Grote to G, 9 November 1869. GP, 44423, 54.

47. D. W. R. Bahlman, 'The Queen, Mr Gladstone, and Church Patronage', *Victorian Studies*, 1959–60, 357.

48. G & G, 1, i, 44.

49. D, 28 August 1869.

50. D, 3 January 1870.

51. J. R. Seeley, 'The Church as a Teacher of Morality', in W. L. Clay (ed.), *Essays on Church Policy* (1868).

52. D, 16 October 1869.

53. D, 9 October 1869.

54. G to Döllinger, 25 March 1870 (copy). GP, 44426, 15. Newman to Ullathorne, 28 January 1870 (copy). GP, 44424, 197.

55. G to Döllinger, 25 March 1870 (copy). GP, 44426, 15.

56. D, 1 December 1869. H. Jenkins, 'The Irish Dimension of the British Kulturkampf, 1870–75', *Journal of Ecclesiastical History*, 1979.

57. Morley, ii, 707.

58. *Gladstone*, 468. D, 1 April 1869. G to Dss of Argyll, 18 May 1869 (copy). GP 44420, 281.

59. G & G, 1, i, 25. Dss of Argyll to G, 19 May 1869.

60. GP, 44430, 286.

61. D, 24 August 1869.

62. D, 21 October 1869.

63. D, 2 October 1869.

64. H(3), cxcix, 333 (15 February 1870).

65. R. T. Shannon, *The Age of Disraeli, 1868–1881* (1992), 94.

66. D, 7 September 1869.

67. M. J. Winstanley, *Ireland and the Land Question, 1800–1922* (1984), 36. See in more detail E. D. Steele, *Irish Land and British Politics. Tenant-Right and Nationality, 1865–1870* (Cambridge, 1974).

68. D, 17 September 1869.

69. D, 23 October 1869.

70. G to Sullivan, 28 December 1869 (copy). GP, 44423, 356.

71. D, vii, ciii.

72. D, 13 December 1869.

73. D, 18 February 1870.

74. D, xii, 435–6 (31 August 1870).

75. D, viii, 575–6.

76. ibid. (1 November 1869).

77. D, xii, 467.

78. D, xii, 441.

79. D, 29 December 1869.

80. H(3), cc, 996 (31 March 1870), 1714, 1716 (12 April 1870).

81. ibid., 134, 1358 (5 April 1870).

82. ibid., 1927 (27 April 1870).

83. H(3), cci, 618–19 (12 May 1870).

84. *Trelawny*, 414.

85. C. S. Parker, *Sir James Graham* (1907), ii, 295.

86. Fulford, *Your Dear Letter*, 259, 261.

87. *Trelawny*, 385.

88. D, 24 March 1870.

89. G to Mrs Cardwell, 22 April 1870 (copy). GP, 44426, 149.

90. *Trelawny*, 388.

91. H(3), cc, 292–3, 299 (18 March 1870).

92. J. Parry, *The Rise and Fall of Liberal Government* (Yale, 1993), 262.

93. D. Hudson, *Munby, Man of Two Worlds* (1972), 288.

94. H(3), cciii, 745–8 (22 July 1870).

95. Derby Diaries, 24 July 1871.

96. H(3), ccii, 202, 268 (16 June 1870).

97. ibid., 285–7 (16 June 1870).

98. *Trelawny*, 410.

99. ibid., 374.

100. Steele, *Irish Land and British Politics*, 221.

101. D, 21 September 1869.

102. *Trelawny*, 374, 389.

103. H(3), cxcv, 1014 (15 April 1869).

104. Selborne, *Memorials*, i, 135.

105. ibid., 147, 148, 153.

106. D, 12 April 1870.

107. *Trelawny*, 397.

108. G & G, 1, i, 77.

109. D, 12 April 1870.

110. D, 16 April 1870.

111. D, 17 April 1870.

112. Steele, *Irish Land and British Politics*, 305.

113. D, 2 April 1870.

114. *Trelawny*, 393.

115. D, 20 June 1870.

116. G & G, 1, i, 114–15.

117. Steele, 310.

118. G & G, 1, i, 76.

119. Winstanley, *Ireland and the Land Question*, 37.

120. Steele, 313.

121. Selborne, *Memorials*, i, 135.

122. Steele, 315.

123. *Gladstone*, 425, 454, 552.

124. G & G, 1, i, 21–2.

125. ibid., 89.

126. H(3), cc, 1901 (26 April 1870).

127. G & G, 1, i, 73.

128. For the Clarendon convention of 14 January 1869 see H. Maxwell, *Life of . . . Clarendon* (1913), ii, 357–8, 364–5.

129. D, 10 February 1870.

130. D, xii, 434.

131. H(3), cciii, 1303 (1 August 1870).

132. *Gladstone*, 516–17.

133. H(3), ccx, 1178 (12 April 1872).

134. G & G, 1, i, 117. Q & G, i, 248.

135. H(3), cciii, 1576–7 (5 August 1870).

136. ibid., 1776–89.

137. D, 14 May 1890.

138. G & G, 1, i, 130.

139. ibid., 135.

140. Northcote to Derby, 28 May 1877. BL, Iddesleigh 50022, 149.

141. D, 30 September 1870.

142. GP, 44759, 166.

143. G & G, 1, i, 137, 140.

144. G, 'Germany, France and England', *Edinburgh Review*, October 1870, 554–93. D. Schreuder, 'Gladstone as "Troublemaker" ', *Journal of British Studies*, 1977–8, 111–12.

145. Fulford, *Your Dear Letter*, 320.

146. P. Knaplund, *Gladstone's Foreign Policy* (1935), 61.

147. G & G, 1, i, 166.

148. *Gladstone*, 315.

149. H(3), cc, 1817 (26 April 1870).

150. H(3), cciii, 1366 (6 March 1871).

151. *Trelawny*, 427.

152. Thorold Rogers to G, 3 January 1878. GP, 44454, 4.

153. D, 16, 19 November 1870.

154. D, 26 November 1870.

155. D, 10 April 1870. St Albans to G, 13 April 1869. GP, 44420, 89. White to G, 13 April, 17 April, 4 May 1869. ibid., 90, 139, 212.

156. D, 22 February 1870.

157. G & G, 1, i, 133.

158. ibid., 170–71. For Disraeli's very similar fears, Shannon, *Age of Disraeli*, 87.

159. H(3), ccvii, 1342 (10 July 1871).

160. H(3), cciv, 2 (9 February 1871).

161. D, 13 April 1871.

162. D, 4 December 1871.

163. D, 21 September 1871.

164. H(3), cciv, 7 (9 February 1871).

165. *Trelawny*, 419.

166. Shannon, *Age of Disraeli*, 104.

167. D, 21 March 1871.

168. *Trelawny*, 420, 422.

169. Parry, *Rise and Fall of Liberal Government*, 230.

170. Shannon, *Age of Disraeli*, 107.

171. H(3), cciv, 1998.

172. H(3), ccv, 1336 (20 April 1871).

173. ibid., 1460 (20 April 1871).

174. D, 29 June 1871. H(3), ccvii, 831, 838 (29 June 1871).

175. H(3), ccvii, 406 (22 June 1871).

176. ibid., 1130 (4 July 1871).

177. H(3), ccv, 148 (6 March 1871).

178. *Trelawny*, 428.

179. ibid., 429.

180. Derby Diaries, 27 April 1871.

181. ibid., 29 April 1871.

182. Howell to G, 14 July 1873. GP, 44439, 163.

183. *Trelawny*, 431.

184. ibid.

185. H(3), ccvi, 1593 (5 June 1871).

186. *Trelawny*, 433.

187. ibid., 434.

188. G. Woodridge, *The Reform Club, 1836–1978* (1978), 145.

189. *Trelawny*, 439.

190. H(3), ccvii, 1078 (4 July 1871).

191. H(3), ccviii, 35 (20 July 1871).

192. D, 15 July 1871.

193. H(3), ccvii, 1069 (3 July 1871).

194. ibid., 1890 (17 July 1871).

195. H(3), ccviii, 20 (20 July 1871).

196. D, 23 August 1871.

197. D, 26 July 1871.

198. *Trelawny*, 441.

199. D, 11 August 1871.

200. A. T. Bassett (ed.), *Gladstone to His Wife* (1936), 188.

201. Derby Diaries, 22 August 1871.

202. Shannon, *Age of Disraeli*, 97, 105.

203. Derby Diaries, 14 June 1871. 'Repealer': of the Act of Union, 1800.

204. D, 23 August 1871.

205. G & G, 1, ii, 256.

206. F. W. Hirst, 'Mr Gladstone as Leader of the House and Reformer, 1865–68', in T. W. Reid (ed.), *Life of W. E. Gladstone* (1899), 574.

207. T. Wemyss Reid, *Life of Richard Monckton Milnes, Lord Houghton* (1891), ii, 253; D, 13 September 1871.

208. AR (1871), 106.

209. G & G, 1, ii, 274–5; D, 19 October 1871; Hirst, in Reid, *Gladstone*, 576.

210. Bright to Hargreaves, 18 November 1871. BL, 62079, 144.

211. Hirst, in Reid, *Gladstone*, 578.

212. G & G, 1, ii, 258.

213. *Letters of . . . Henry Austin Bruce, Lord Aberdare* (Oxford, 1902), 318–19.

214. Tenterden to G, 20 December 1871. GP, 44432, 294.

215. *Gladstone*, 190–92.

216. D, 16 May 1871.

217. D, 29 December 1871.

218. D. M. Schreuder, *Gladstone and Kruger. Liberal Government and Colonial 'Home Rule', 1880–1885* (1969), 49.

219. Shannon, *Age of Disraeli*, 134.

220. G & G, 1, ii, 291. D, 21 December 1871.

221. D, 29 December 1870.

222. D, 29 December 1871.

CHAPTER 4:
'THE FUTURE OF POLITICS HARDLY EXISTS FOR ME': 1872–5

1. H(3), ccxviii, 80–82 (19 March 1874).

2. ibid., 83.

3. D, 13 March 1873.

4. D, 21 March 1873. Earl de Grey created Marquess of Ripon 1871.

5. D, 14 August 1873.

6. D, 10 January 1874.

7. H(3), ccxviii, 1121 (24 April 1874).

8. ibid., 82 (19 March 1874).

9. Derby Diaries (15th Earl), Liverpool Record Office, 7 February 1872.

10. D, 16 September 1872.

11. D, 13 December 1871.

12. Disraeli to Barrington, 1 January 1872. BL, 51280, 17.

13. T. A. Jenkins (ed.), *The Parliamentary Diaries of Sir John Trelawny, 1868–73* (1994), 448, 449.

14. G & G, 1, ii, 281.

15. Derby Diaries, 29 April 1872.

16. N. E. Johnson (ed.), *The Diary of Gathorne Hardy, later Lord Cranbrook, 1866–1892* (Oxford, 1981), 23 February 1872.

17. Tennyson to G, 5 February 1872. GP, 44433, 130.

18. Bright to Hargreaves, 11 February 1872. BL, 62079, 150.

19. Q & G, i, 332.

20. G & G, 1, ii, 299, 323. Schenck to G, 19 March 1872. GP, 44434, 1.

21. D, 27 February 1872.

22. A. Ellis to G, 25 January 1872: *Memorandum on Employment for the Prince of Wales*, GP, 44433, 90–103.

23. D, 9 March 1872.

24. Q & G, i, 340–41.

25. D, 2 July 1872. Q & G, i, 351–8, 361–6.

26. D, 28 August 1872.

27. G to Cambridge, 29 August 1872 (copy). GP, 44435, 155.

28. F. Harcourt, 'Gladstone, Monarchism and the "New Imperialism"', 1868–74', *Journal of Imperial and Commonwealth History*, 1985–86, 21.

29. R. Fulford (ed.), *Darling Child. Private Correspondence of Queen Victoria and the German Crown Princess, 1871–1878* (1976), 29.

30. Derby Diaries, 29 January 1872.

31. D, 27 November 1872.

32. D, 1 December 1872.

33. R. T. Shannon, *The Age of Salisbury, 1881–1902. Unionism and Empire* (1996), 458–9.

34. AR (1872), 8–9.

35. R. T. Shannon, *The Age of Disraeli* (1992), 143.

36. Bright to Hargreaves, 7 December 1872. BL, 62079, 157.

37. D, 6 July 1872.

38. *Age of Disraeli*, 144.

39. Bright to Hargreaves, 24 March 1872. BL, 62079, 152.

40. Morley, i, 1024–5.

41. D, xii, 454–5.

42. G & G, 1, iii, 306.

43. ibid., 327.

44. ibid., 329.

45. D, 13 June 1872.

46. D, 15 June 1872.

47. F. W. Hirst, 'Mr Gladstone's First Premiership', in T. W. Reid (ed.), *Gladstone* (1899), 582.

48. Q & G, i, 339.

49. H(3), ccxi, 912 (31 May 1872).

50. R. Robinson, J. Gallacher, and A. Kenny, *Africa and the Victorians. The Official Mind of Imperialism* (1963), 30.

51. G & G, 1, ii, 340, 342.

52. ibid., 382.

53. H(3), ccxvii, 76–7, 82 (8 July 1873).

54. D, 21 August 1872.

55. Derby Diaries, 13 August 1872.

56. G to Osborne Morgan, 12 December 1872 (copy). GP, 44436, 120.

57. G & G, 1, ii, 340.

58. *Gladstone*, 407, 424.

59. G. Battiscombe, *Mrs Gladstone* (1956), 153.

60. D, 15 August 1872.

61. G & G, 1, ii, 361.

62. H. C. G. Matthew, 'Gladstone, Vaticanism, and the Question of the East', in *Studies in Church History*, xv, ed. D. Baker (Oxford, 1978).

63. D, 1 April 1872.

64. D, 17 January 1872.

65. R. MacLeod, 'The Ayrton Incident: A Commentary on the Relations of Science and Government in England, 1870–73', in *Science and Values*, ed. A. Thackray and E. Mendelsohn (1974), 47.

66. D, 24 December 1872. For Gladstone's earlier discipleship to Bishop Butler see *Gladstone*, 177–80.

67. D, 16 February 1873.

68. D, 21 April 1874.

69. G to Vance Smith, 28 June 1874 (copy). GP, 44443, 319.
70. Balfour to G, 20 January 1875. GP, 44446, 102.
71. GP 44444, 38. For earlier exercises, *Gladstone*, 448.
72. O'Dell to G, 16 February 1875. GP, 44446, 198.
73. For G's easy relationship with the anti-Darwinian Professor Richard Owen of the Natural History division of the British Museum see *Gladstone*, 465.
74. Spencer to G, 4 December 1873; G to Spencer, 12 January 1874 (copy); Spencer to G, 14 January 1874. GP, 44441, 171; 44442, 35, 43.
75. G to Jevons, 10 May 1874 (copy). GP, 44443, 229.
76. See p. 202 (1896 edn), International Scientific Series (11th edn).
77. e.g., *Trelawny*, 454, 459.
78. Kenny to G, 17 January 1870. GP, 44425, 1.
79. H(3), cc, 1127 (1 April 1870).
80. H(3), ccvii, 1164 (5 July 1871).
81. J. P. Parry, *Democracy and Religion. Gladstone and the Liberal Party, 1867–1875* (Cambridge, 1986), 353.
82. Cairns to G, 19 February 1870. GP, 44425, 15–19.
83. Cullen to G, 25 February 1870. GP, 44433, 287.
84. G & G, 1, ii, 361.
85. ibid., 424.
86. D, 7–9 December 1872.
87. G to Disraeli, 19 January 1873 (copy). GP, 44437, 41. Disraeli to G, 24 January 1873. Ibid., 65.
88. D, 8 February 1873.
89. H(3), ccxiv, 416.
90. ibid., 1240, 1254–5 (3 March 1873).
91. D, 22 February 1873.
92. *Letters of Henry Austin Bruce, Lord Aberdare* (Oxford, 1902), i, 354.
93. *Trelawny*, 478.
94. Shannon, *Age of Disraeli*, 149.

95. Q & G, i, 393.
96. D, 8 March 1873.
97. H(3), cciv, 1630–31.
98. *Trelawny*, 479.
99. D, 13 March 1873.
100. Q & G, i, 397–8.
101. Fulford, *Darling Child*, 81.
102. *Trelawny*, 480.
103. D, 19 March 1873. For Disraeli's 'educating' his party, see Shannon, *Age of Disraeli*, 24.
104. E. Drus (ed.), *A Journal of Events during the Gladstone Ministry, 1868–74. By John, First Earl of Kimberley* (1958), 37.
105. D, 7 April 1873.
106. *Trelawny*, 484.
107. D, 14 April 1873.
108. D, 19 May 1873.
109. *Trelawny*, 487.
110. Peel to G, 26 August 1873. GP, 44270, 289.
111. Derby Diaries, 23 September 1873.
112. D, 12 July 1873.
113. *Trelawny*, 491–2, 499, 500.
114. D, 19, 20 July 1873.
115. *Trelawny*, 501.
116. Derby Diaries, 18 September 1873. For John Bright on the 'revolt of the labourers' (led by Joseph Arch and the Agricultural Labourers' Union) as a 'great event', see Bright to Hargreaves, 21 June 1873. BL, 62079, 163.
117. D, 3 September 1873.
118. Q & G, i, 424.
119. D, 13 August 1873.
120. R. R. James, 'Gladstone and the Greenwich Seat', *History Today*, 1959.
121. Jessel, 15 August 1873 (copy). GP, 44439, 300–301.
122. J. Vaio, 'Schliemann and Gladstone: New Light from Unpublished Documents', in *Heinrich Schliemann. Grundlagen und Ergebnisse moderner Archäologie 100 Jahre nach Schliemanns Tod*, ed. J. Herrmann, Akademie Verlag (Berlin, 1992), 74.
123. G & G, 1, ii, 397.

124. D, 29 August 1873.

125. G & G, 1, ii, 405.

126. D, 15 August 1873.

127. M. R. Temmel, 'Gladstone's Resignation of the Liberal Leadership', *Journal of British Studies*, 1976, 162.

128. D, 11 August 1873.

129. H(3), ccxv, 942 (24 April 1873).

130. ibid., 1034 (28 April 1873).

131. ibid., 1056 (28 April 1873).

132. ibid., 1390 (1 May 1873).

133. D, 30 April 1873.

134. D, 27 August 1873. Bright to Hargreaves, 16 October 1873. BL, 62079, 174.

135. G to Stansfeld, 7 November 1872 (copy). GP, 44436, 8.

136. Bright to Hargreaves, 14 October 1873. BL, 62079, 174.

137. D, 30 October 1873.

138. Newton to G, 9 October 1873. GP, 44440, 176.

139. G to Crawford, 16 February 1874 (copy). GP, 44442, 264.

140. Scott to G, 8 December 1873. GP, 44441, 198.

141. D, 31 December 1873.

142. D, 18 August 1873.

143. D, 3 January 1874.

144. G & G, 1, ii, 438. Morley, ii, 479–82.

145. D, 10 January 1874.

146. D, 19 January 1874.

147. D, 17 January 1874.

148. ibid.

149. D, 16 January 1874. As noted on page 135 above, no response from Peel appears to be extant in the Gladstone Papers.

150. D, 18 January 1874.

151. H(3), ccxviii, 83 (19 March 1874).

152. D, 9 February 1874.

153. D, 20 January 1874.

154. Lord Kilbracken, *Reminiscences* (1931), 98.

155. Hirst, in Reid, *Gladstone*, 589.

156. G & G, 1, ii, 445.

157. D, 23 January 1874.

158. H(3), ccxviii, 83 (19 March 1874).

159. F. Harrison, 'The Conservative Reaction', *Fortnightly Review*, March 1874, 296.

160. Derby Diaries, 24 January 1874.

161. G & G, 1, ii, 441.

162. D, 28 January 1874.

163. D, 6 February 1874. G to Peel, 26 February 1874. GP, 44270, 297.

164. D, 6 February 1874.

165. H(3), ccxviii, 84 (19 March 1874).

166. D, 23 February 1874.

167. G & G, 1, ii, 446–7.

168. D, 7 February 1874.

169. Q & G, i, 446.

170. *Letters of Henry Austin Bruce, Lord Aberdare*, i, 361–2.

171. ibid., 362.

172. Q & G, i, 447.

173. D, 19 February 1874.

174. D, 20 February 1874.

175. D, 23 February 1874.

176. *Gladstone*, 196–7.

177. G to Fielden, 26 February 1874 (copy). GP, 44443, 37.

178. G to Pringle, 27 February 1874 (copy). ibid., 41.

179. G to Fielden, as above.

180. D, 25 February 1874.

181. D, 9 February 1874.

182. G memo, 7 March 1874. GP, 44762, 37.

183. D, 13 March 1874.

184. G & G, 1, ii, 449–50. For a psycho-historical interpretation of G's 'strategy of withdrawal', see T. L. Crosby, *The Two Mr Gladstones. A Study in Psychology and History* (Yale, 1997), 145, 150.

185. Temmel, 156.

186. D, 21 April 1874.

187. Peel to G, 30 April 1874. GP, 44270, 361.

188. Temmel, 156.

189. H(3), ccviii, 42–3 (19 March 1874).

190. ibid., 46.

191. ibid, 83 (19 March 1874).

192. D, 16 March 1874.

193. H(3), ccxviii, 83, 90, 1101–21 (19 March, April 1874).

194. ibid., 130 (20 March 1874).

195. H(3), ccxxi, 1285–7 (4 August 1874).

196. Kilbracken, *Reminiscences*, 84.

197. D, 15 May 1874.

198. D, 30 May, 1 June 1874.

199. *Contemporary Review*, May 1974.

200. D, 22 July 1874.

201. D, 3 March 1874.

202. D, 12 May 1874.

203. Martin to G, 24 December 1874. GP, 44445, 264.

204. D, xii, 465–6.

205. Pringle to G, 12 August [1874]. GP, 44444, 200.

206. *Gladstone*, 553–4.

207. D, 18 June 1874.

208. H(3), ccxx, 1372, 1376, 1381, 1386, 1391 (9 July 1874).

209. H(3), ccxxi, 1361 (5 August 1874).

210. Derby Diaries, 1 April 1873.

211. G & G, 1, ii, 457.

212. Selborne, *Memorials*, i, 334.

213. Ly Ripon to CG, 20 August 1874. GP, 44444, 219.

214. G to Ly Ripon, 21 August 1874 (copy). ibid., 222.

215. D, 13 September 1874. G, 'Ritualism and Ritual', *Contemporary Review*, October 1874, 674.

216. G to Mazzari, 11 December 1873 (draft, copy). GP, 44441, 215.

217. G & G, 1, ii, 458.

218. Emly to G, 3 October [1874]. GP, 44152, 235. Emly to G, 10 October [1874]. Ibid., 241.

219. *The Vatican Decrees in Their Bearing on Civil Allegiance* (1874), 6–7.

220. ibid., 21.

221. D, 30 September 1874.

222. D, 6 October 1874.

223. *A Letter Addressed to His Grace the Duke of Norfolk on the Occasion of Mr Gladstone's Recent Expostulation* (1875).

224. *Vatican Decrees*.

225. Fulford, *Darling Child*, 162.

226. D, 16 November 1874.

227. D, 16 December 1874.

228. Münster to G, 25 November 1874. GP, 44445.

229. R. T. Shannon, 'Gladstone, the Roman Church, and Italy', in M. Bentley (ed.), *Public and Private Doctrine* (Cambridge, 1993).

230. Bismarck to G, 1 March 1875. GP, 44445, 293.

231. G & G, 1, ii, 458–9.

232. G to Bismarck, 5 March 1875 (copy). GP, 44445, 294.

233. H. Jenkins, 'The Irish Dimension of the British Kulturkampf: Vaticanism and Civil Allegiance, 1870–1875', *Journal of Ecclesiastical History*, 1979, 358–60. Jenkins draws attention to a similar evasion by Newman.

234. *Vatican Decrees*, 46.

235. Hudson to G, 22 March 1875. GP, 44446, 338.

236. D, 30 December 1874; also see pages 351–2.

237. G memo. GP, 44762, 168.

238. Stansfeld to G, 23 November 1874. GP, 44445, 91.

239. G & G, 1, ii, 460–61.

240. ibid., 461–2.

241. A. T. Bassett (ed.), *Gladstone to His Wife* (1936), 208.

242. G & G, 1, ii, 463.

243. ibid., 465.

244. GP, 44762, 148.

245. G & G, 1, ii, 464–5.

246. Temmel, 'Gladstone's Resignation', *Journal of British Studies*, 1976, 176–7. GP, 44762, 162–6.

247. D, 18 January 1875.

248. GP, 44762, 169.

249. G. E. Marindin (ed.), *Letters of Frederic Lord Blachford* (1896), 360.

250. H. E. Carlisle (ed.), *A Selection from the Correspondence of Abraham Hayward QC. From 1834 to 1884* (1886), ii, 258.

251. Mundella to Leader 1, 19 March

1875. Mundella Papers, Sheffield City Library.
252. Strafford to G, 16 January 1875. GP, 44446, 64.
253. Derby Diaries, 28 January 1875.
254. Lord E. Fitzmaurice, *Life of . . . Granville* (1905), ii, 149.
255. ibid., ii, 149.
256. ibid., 154.
257. ibid., 153.
258. Manners to G [8 February 1875]. GP, 44446, 169.
259. D, 2 April 1875.
260. D, 14 April 1875.
261. D, 2 April 1875.
262. D, 31 March 1875.

CHAPTER 5:
'A VIRTUOUS PASSION': 1875–7

1. H(3), ccxxiv, 297–8 (7 May 1875).
2. Caird to G, 31 December 1875. GP, 44448, 357.
3. *The Life and Letters of . . . Friedrich Max Müller*, edited by his wife (1902), i, 417.
4. G. Battiscombe, *Mrs Gladstone* (1956), 153.
5. D, 25 November 1875.
6. D, xii, 478–9.
7. ibid., 475.
8. Farley to G, 19 August 1875. GP, 44447, 364; enclosed pamphlet, *The Decline of Turkey, Financially and Politically*.
9. See, e.g., G & G, 1, ii, 359. H. C. G. Matthew, 'Gladstone, Vaticanism, and the Question of the East', in D. Baker (ed.), *Studies in Church History*, xv (1978), 440.
10. GBA, 92.
11. D, 26 November 1875.
12. G & G, 1, ii, 473–4.
13. R. T. Shannon, *The Age of Disraeli* (1992), 275.
14. Disraeli to Barrington, 29 November 1875. BL, 58210, 43.
15. Levy to G, 29 November 1875. GP, 44448, 257.
16. G & G, 1, ii, 476.
17. D, 9 December 1875.
18. D, xii, 434–5.
19. P. Magnus, *Gladstone* (1954), 229.
20. D, 23 March 1876. H(3), ccxxvii, 734, 746 (9 March 1876).
21. H(3), ccxxvii, 102–4 (8 February 1876).
22. GP, 44790, 112–14.
23. R. T. Shannon, 'Gladstone and British Balkan Policy', in *Der Berliner Kongress von 1878*, ed. R. Melville and H.-J. Schröder (Wiesbaden, 1982), 173.
24. GBA, 92.
25. D, 14 May 1876. On the question of the status of Lyttelton's life-assurance policy, see Talbot of the Guardian Assurance Office to G, 3 May 1876. GP, 44450, 14.
26. G & G, 1, ii, 485.
27. GBA, 93.
28. *Gladstone*, 513–14.
29. Derby Diaries, Liverpool Record Office, 7 September 1876.
30. Stratford to G, 29 June 1876. GP, 44450, 219.
31. G to Granville, 27 June 1876. PRO, 30/29/29.
32. GBA, 46–7.
33. ibid., 48.
34. D, 3 July 1876.
35. D, 12 July 1876.
36. GBA, 43.
37. For the ultimate fate of Farley's League, see GBA, 250–51.
38. GBA, 94–5.
39. G to Granville, 26 July 1876. PRO, 30/29/29A.
40. G to Granville, 27 July 1876, ibid.
41. GBA, 51–2. H(3), ccxxxi, 174–203.
42. GBA, 91–2, on Freeman's aborted effort to clear Gladstone over accusations in the Cretan case of 1866–7.
43. GP, 44790, 112–14.
44. ibid.

45. H(3), ccxxxi, 215, 1146 (7, 11 August 1876).

46. GBA, 59.

47. ibid., 98.

48. ibid.

49. ibid., 99.

50. G to Granville, 7 August 1876. PRO, 30/29/29A.

51. For G's pen-portrait of Olga Novikov to Laura Thistlethwayte, see D, xii, 517.

52. GBA, 86.

53. GP, 44790, 112–14.

54. ibid. Morley's version (ii, 158): 'the question was alive'.

55. G to Broadhurst, 20 September 1896. Broadhurst Papers, LSE, V, i.

56. GP, 44790, 112–14.

57. GP, 44698, 367.

58. D, 19 August 1876.

59. G & G, 2, i, 1.

60. ibid.

61. GBA, 79.

62. GBA, 106.

63. *The Times*, 30 August 1876, 7.

64. G & G, 2, i, 3.

65. GBA, 107–8.

66. G to Elliot, 3 September 1876 (copy). GP, 44451, 116.

67. GBA, 112.

68. G & G, 2, i, 26.

69. G to Acton, 16 October 1876. GP, 44093, 192.

70. GBA, 108.

71. D, 27 April 1877.

72. M & B, ii, 933.

73. GBA, 109.

74. *Gladstone*, 361–2.

75. ibid., 352–4.

76. See R. W. Seton-Watson, *Britain in Europe, 1789–1914* (Cambridge, 1937), 102, 520. G would probably not have read the original reference; and Stratford undoubtedly quoted it to G in their conversations of May and June 1876. See also S. Lane-Poole, *The Life of . . . Viscount Stratford de Redcliffe* (1888), i, 307.

77. Disraeli to Barrington, 11 September 1876. BL, 58210, 60.

78. See also G's controversy with Sir Henry Elliot on this point: G to Elliot, 26 February 1877 (copy). GP, 44453, 134, 136.

79. Derby Diaries, 7 September 1876.

80. Magnus, 242.

81. GBA, 108.

82. M & B, ii, 929.

83. Morley, ii, 156–7.

84. GBA, 100.

85. *Gladstone*, 320 (1856), *Gladstone*, 270 (1896).

86. GBA, 90.

87. Magnus, 239.

88. For Freeman's sensitivity to the way in which the blurring of events in time led to G's being credited with unmerited promptitude in the Bulgarian case see GBA, 90.

89. *Gladstone*, 292.

90. Shannon, *Age of Disraeli*, 279.

91. GBA, 113.

92. ibid., 114.

93. ibid., 115.

94. ibid., 116.

95. Holyoake to Gladstone, 9 September 1876. GP, 44451, 157–8. See also *The Life of Hugh Price Hughes* by his daughter (1905), 113; G. Lansbury, *My Life* (1928), 40; *A Memoir of the Right Hon. William Edward Hartpole Lecky* by his wife (1909), 112.

96. *Northern Echo*, 11 September 1876, 2. *Daily Telegraph*, 11 September 1876, 2.

97. *Daily Telegraph*, ibid.

98. GBA, 116–17.

99. ibid., 118–19.

100. ibid., 119–20.

101. ibid., 120–21.

102. ibid., 123.

103. ibid., 124.

104. ibid., 126.

105. ibid., 127–8.

106. D, 6 October 1876.

107. M & B, ii, 930.

108. GBA, 130.
109. Chapman to G, 10 August 1876. GP, 44457, 198.
110. G to Stead, 21 September 1876 (copy). GP, 44303, 235, 237.
111. R. Fulford (ed.), *Darling Child. Private Correspondence of Queen Victoria and the German Crown Princess, 1871–1878* (1976), 222–3.
112. GBA, 128.
113. ibid., 132.
114. D, 2 October 1876.
115. GBA, 132.
116. D, 23 September 1876.
117. GBA, 133.
118. ibid., 134.
119. D, 9 October 1876.
120. GBA, 135.
121. Hall to Gladstone, [13] September [1876]. GP, 44188, 150.
122. GBA, 247. 'Russian Policy and Deeds in Turkestan', *Contemporary Review*, November 1876. E.g. *Methodist*, 10 November 1876, 9; *The Times*, 1 November 1876, 9.
123. GBA, 248.
124. ibid., 249–50.
125. D, 1 November 1876.
126. *Gladstone*, 474–5. R. T. Shannon, 'Gladstone and the Hellenic Factor in the Eastern Question', in *Actes du Symposium Historique International, 'La Dernière Phase de la Crise Orientale et l'Hellénisme (1878–1881)'* (Athens, 1983), 449–51.
127. G, *Gleanings*, iv, 277, 302.
128. G & G, 2, i, 18.
129. GBA, 257.
130. F. E. Hamer (ed.), *The Personal Papers of Lord Rendel* (1931), 113.
131. GBA, 257–8.
132. ibid., 259.
133. ibid., 260.
134. D, 8 December 1876.
135. F. Cavendish to Hartington, 22 December 1876. Devonshire Papers, Chatsworth, 8th Duke, 340/691.

136. G to Negropontis, 9 January 1877 (copy). GP, 44453, 18.
137. G & G, 2, i, 28.
138. ibid.
139. G to Bryce, 29 January 1877. Bryce Papers, Bodleian, Oxford, E.6.
140. ibid.
141. G to Schuyler, 30 January 1877 (copy). GP, 44453, 62.
142. G to Novikov, 6 February 1877 (copy). GP, 44268, 148.
143. G & G, 2, i, 29.
144. Lord E. Fitzmaurice, *Life of . . . Earl Granville* (1905), ii, 167.
145. G to Novikov, 6 February 1877 (copy). GP, 44268, 148.
146. H(3), ccxxxii, 111, 113, 118 (8 February 1877).
147. ibid., 554–5 (18 February 1877).
148. D. Hudson, *Munby, Man of Two Worlds* (1972), 389.
149. G & G, 2, i, 31.
150. D, 10–11 March 1877. Morley's account: Morley, ii, 170. See also Morley to G, 7 April 1880. GP, 44255, 13. He describes Huxley's (and Tyndall's) anti-Liberal position.
151. Memorandum 'in anticipation of General Ignatieff', 'but not read to him', 21 March 1877. GP, 44763, 85.
152. GP, 44763, 43–4.
153. Parliamentary Papers, xc, *Turkey* (1877), No. 221.
154. M. MacColl, *The Eastern Question. Its Facts & Fallacies* (1877), 413.
155. G, *Lessons in Massacre* (1877), 76.
156. G to Granville, 2 March 1877. Devonshire Papers, Chatsworth, 8th Duke, 340/700.
157. G to Elliot, 28 February 1877 (copy). GP, 44453, 152. Elliot to G, 2 March 1877. Ibid., 159.
158. G & G, 2, i, 34.
159. H(3), ccxxxiii, 605.
160. Watson to G, 28 February 1877. GP, 44453, 157.
161. Fitzmaurice, *Granville*, 168–9.

162. G & G, 2, i, 35.

163. F. W. Hirst, in T. W. Reid (ed.), *The Life of . . . Gladstone* (1899), 622.

164. James, Rylands, and Chamberlain to G [7 May 1877]. GP, 44454, 111.

165. H(3), ccxxxiv, 366–435.

166. *Spectator*, quoted Morley, ii, 174.

167. Morley, ibid.

168. G & G, 2, i, 38.

169. D, 16 May 1877.

CHAPTER 6:
'*A GREAT ELECTION OF GOD*':
1877–80

1. D, xii, 482.

2. D, 4 June 1877.

3. Spencer to G, 17 June [1877]. GP, 44454, 203.

4. Wilde to G [14, 17 May 1877]. GP, 44454, 124–5, 126, 137–8.

5. GBA, 269–70.

6. G & G, 2, i, 42.

7. ibid.

8. ibid., 43.

9. D, 31 May 1877.

10. *The Times*, 1 June 1877, 10. It is noteworthy that Gladstone did not cite Seeley. For Merivale see page 209. See also Morley, ii, 169.

11. Morley, ii, 178.

12. G & G, 2, i, 44.

13. D, 21 June 1877.

14. Hill to G, 22 June 1877. GP, 44454, 213.

15. Hartington to Devonshire, 28 June 1877. Devonshire Papers, Chatsworth, 8th Duke, 340/695.

16. GP, 44454, 226.

17. G, 'Aggression in Egypt and Freedom in the East', *Nineteenth Century*, August 1877. *Gleanings of Past Years, 1843–1879* (1879), iv, 357.

18. G to Shuvalov, 20 July (copy). GP, 44453, 270.

19. G to Negropontis, 21 July 1877 (copy). Ibid., 281.

20. Transvaal Deputies to G, 24 July 1877. GP, 44454, 285.

21. G to Hill, 11 August 1877. Ibid., 322.

22. Salisbury to G, 15 September 1877. GP, 44455, 52.

23. D, 16 August 1877.

24. D, 4 August 1877.

25. D, 20 August 1877.

26. D, 1 September 1877.

27. *The Times*, 20 August 1877, 12.

28. D, xii, 483.

29. *The Times*, 21 August 1877, 7.

30. GBA, 271–2.

31. H(3), ccliv, 1287 (23 July 1880).

32. G to Liddon, 22 August 1877. Liddon Papers, Keble College, Oxford.

33. G to Shuvalov, 2 September 1877. GP, 44455, 15.

34. G to Negropontis, 7 September 1877. Ibid., 33, G & G, 2, i, 52–3.

35. G to Bryce, 6 October 1877. Bryce Papers, Bodleian Library, Oxford, E.6. For G's own version of 'perfect calmness' see *Gladstone*, 489. Also A. Austin to G, 2 June 1877. GP, 44454, 295. For regrets at the break between G and the *Telegraph*, Lawson to G, 20 June [1877]. Ibid., 207.

36. GBA, 277.

37. G & G, 2, i, 54.

38. *Daily Express* (Dublin), 8 November 1877.

39. G & G, 2, i, 54.

40. GBA, 162–4.

41. ibid., 275.

42. ibid., 159.

43. GP, 44763, 96.

44. M & B, ii, 885.

45. GBA, 278–9.

46. ibid., 160.

47. *Gladstone*, 177.

48. *The Times*, 2 June 1877, 12.

49. GBA, 277.

50. ibid.

51. G to Errington, 14 September 1877 (copy). GP, 44455, 49.

52. D, 18 October 1877.

53. GBA, 279.

54. G to Novikov, 31 October 1877 (copy). GP, 44268, 169.

55. Lord Eversley, *Gladstone and Ireland* (1912), 79–80.

56. *Daily Express* (Dublin), 8 November 1877.

57. G to Novikov, 31 October 1877 (copy). GP, 44268, 169.

58. G & G, 2, i, 65.

59. G to Forsyth, 22 December 1877 (copy). GP, 44455, 334.

60. Rogers to G, 27 December [1877]. Ibid., 350.

61. Rogers to G, 3 January 1878. GP, 44456, 4.

62. D, i, xxxix. L. March-Phillips and B. Christian (eds.), *Some Hawarden Letters* (1917), 21.

63. G to Bath, 4 January 1878 (copy). GP, 44456, 10.

64. G & G, 2, i, 66–7.

65. D, 17 January 1878.

66. D, 26 January 1878.

67. G & G, 2, i, 68.

68. *The Times*, 31 January 1878, 10–11.

69. *The Times*, 4 February 1878, 8.

70. G, 'The Hellenic Factor in the Eastern Problem', *Contemporary Review*, December 1876, 290.

71. *The Times*, ibid.

72. GBA, 213.

73. D, 5 February 1878.

74. H(3), ccxxxvii, 933–4, 938–9.

75. D, 10 February 1878.

76. AR (1878), 15.

77. D, 4 March 1878.

78. *Nineteenth Century*, March 1878, 598–9.

79. P. Metcalf, *James Knowles, Victorian Editor and Architect* (Oxford, 1980), 262.

80. D, 10 March 1878.

81. D, 2, 18 March 1878.

82. *The Times*, 4 February 1878, 6.

83. D, 19 March 1878.

84. D, 22 March, 18 April, 29 May, 2 June 1878.

85. D. Hudson, *Munby. Man of Two Worlds* (1972), 393–4.

86. G to Novikov, 1 April 1878 (copy). GP, 44268, 173.

87. H(3), ccxxxix, 871.

88. G & G, 2, i, 70–71.

89. D, 18 April 1878.

90. D, 25 April 1878.

91. D, 3 June 1878.

92. D, 1 June 1878.

93. ibid.

94. H. C. G. Matthew, *Gladstone, 1875–1898* (Oxford, 1995), 267–9; and see page 233.

95. D, 23 May 1878.

96. D, 21 May 1878; G, 'Liberty in the East and West', *Nineteenth Century*, June 1878, 1155, 1163, 1168.

97. GP, 44763, 130 (26 May 1878).

98. GP, 44697, 142, 145.

99. H(3), ccxl, 1069–70, 1616 (3, 17 June 1878).

100. Metcalf, *Knowles*, 282.

101. G, 'Postscriptum on the County Franchise', *Gleanings*, i, 199–202. Matthew, *Gladstone*, 95, draws attention to the possibility of Newman's influence on this point.

102. Barrington to Beaconsfield, 11 July 1878. Hughenden Papers, Bodleian Library, Oxford, B/xx/Ba/67.

103. D, 21 July 1878.

104. AR (1878), 96.

105. H(3), ccxlii, 672c (30 July 1878).

106. G to Beaconsfield, 30 July 1878 (copy). GP, 44457, 166. See *Gladstone*, 486, and page 478.

107. H(3), ccxlii, 672, 693, 716.

108. G, 'England's Mission', *Nineteenth Century*, August 1878, 562.

109. G to Layard, 22 August 1878 (copy). GP, 44457, 219.

110. Metcalf, *Knowles*, 282.

111. D, 7 October 1878.

112. Morris to G, 17 March 1879. GP, 44459, 197.

113. G & G, 2, i, 78.

114. ibid., 85. 'Electoral Facts' appeared in the November *Nineteenth Century*.

115. G & G, 2, i, 78.

116. H(3), ccxliii, 904 (16 December 1878).

117. Beaconsfield to Barrington, 30 November 1878. BL, 58210, 94.

118. D, 14 October 1878.

119. Morley, ii, 190.

120. D, 1 November 1878.

121. D, 25 November 1878. *Gladstone*, 397.

122. D, 16 September 1878.

123. Morley, ii, 247.

124. G to Potter, 22 October 1878 (copy). GP, 44458, 83.

125. N. E. Johnson (ed.), *The Diary of Gathorne Hardy, Later Lord Cranbrook, 1866–1892* (Oxford, 1981), 394.

126. R. T. Shannon, *The Age of Disraeli* (1992), 334–8.

127. Hill to G, 24 December 1878. GP, 44458, 256.

128. G to Hill, 24 December 1878 (copy). Ibid., 258.

129. *Gladstone*, 473.

130. G to Hill, 26 December 1878 (copy). Ibid., 264.

131. D, 7 December 1877.

132. G & G, 2, i, 85.

133. G to 'Working Men & Free Trade', 6 December 1877 (copy). GP, 44454, 301.

134. *Gladstone*, 101.

135. ibid., 44.

136. ibid., 45.

137. ibid., 55.

138. ibid., 166.

139. G to McCormick, 12 August 1894 (copy). GP, 44519, 9.

140. D, 29 December 1878.

141. Smith to G, 14 January 1879. GP, 44459, 36.

142. Moncrieff to G, 27 December 1878. GP, 56444.

143. Rosebery to G, 9 January 1879. Ibid.

144. Adam to G, 10 January 1879. Ibid.

145. G to Adam, 11 January 1879. Ibid.

146. G to Cowan, 30 January 1879. GP, 44763, 142–3.

147. H(3), ccxlv, 540, 543 (17 April 1879). 'Greece and the Treaty of Berlin', *Nineteenth Century*, June 1879, 1121–34. Again, H(3), ccxlviii, 1061–77 (22 July 1879).

148. D, 8 July 1879.

149. H(3), ccxlv, 1596, 1622 (2 May 1879).

150. D, 27 February 1879.

151. D, 19 April 1879.

152. D, 24 March 1879.

153. D, 26 January 1878. For Gladstone's hopes of getting a knighthood for Irving see Matthew, *Gladstone*, ii, 277.

154. Balfour to G, 16 June 1879. GP, 44460, 60.

155. *Nineteenth Century*, May 1879.

156. Shore to G, 21 May 1879. GP, 44460, 60.

157. D, 6 March 1879.

158. Fagan to G, 9 April 1879. GP, 44459, 235.

159. D, 16 April 1879. *Gladstone*, 42.

160. Johnson, *Diary of Gathorne Hardy, Lord Cranbrook*, 409.

161. GP, 44461, 72 (10 October 1879); 253 (17 December 1879).

162. D, 7 July 1879. J. G. Rogers, 'The Union of the Liberal Party', *Nineteenth Century*, August 1879.

163. D, 28 October 1879.

164. Verney to G, 2 June 1879. GP, 44460, 116.

165. Verney to G, 22 June 1879. Ibid., 179.

166. D, September 1879.

167. G & G, 2, i, 101.

168. O. Chadwick, *Acton and Gladstone* (1976), 11.

169. Lord E. Fitzmaurice, *Life of . . . Earl Granville* (1905), ii, 182.

170. Adam to G, 18 November 1879. GP, 56444.

171. G & G, 2, i, 99.

172. Rosebery to G, 17 November 1879. GP, 56444.

173. Hollowell to S. Morley, [November 1879]. GP, 44461, 121.

174. P. Magnus, *Gladstone* (1954), 264.

175. C. Harvie, 'Gladstonianism, the Provinces, and Popular Political Culture, 1860–1906', in R. Bellamy (ed.), *Victorian Liberalism. Nineteenth-century Political Thought and Practice* (1990), 170.

176. ibid., 154.

177. E. F. Biagini, *Liberty, Retrenchment and Reform. Popular Liberalism in the Age of Gladstone, 1860–1880* (Cambridge, 1992), 369ff.

178. M. R. D. Foot (ed.), *Midlothian Speeches, 1879. W. E. Gladstone* (Leicester, 1971), 32.

179. ibid., 27–8.

180. ibid., 48.

181. ibid., 86–8.

182. ibid., 117.

183. GP, 44461, 306.

184. *Gladstone*, 292.

185. Morley, ii, 159.

186. H. Paul (ed.), *Letters of Lord Acton to Mary Gladstone* (1904), 202.

187. *Gladstone*, 292–3.

188. G, 'The Friends and Foes of Russia', *Nineteenth Century*, January 1879.

189. Foot, 118.

190. *Gladstone*, 314–15.

191. Foot, 115–17.

192. D, 11 December 1879.

193. *Gladstone*, 157.

194. ibid., 219.

195. D, 31 December 1879.

196. Foot, 42.

197. Fitzmaurice, *Granville*, ii, 186.

198. G to Wemyss Reid, 1 February 1892. GP, 56445.

199. Fitzmaurice, *Granville*, ii, 182–3.

200. ibid., 185.

201. ibid., 187.

202. GP, 44763, 152 (19 August 1879).

203. Lord Kilbracken, *Reminiscences* (1931), 108. Cf. *Gladstone*, 428: G in 1860, his fifty-second year: 'I cannot believe it. I feel within me the rebellious unspoken word, I will not be old.' Ibid., 451: G in 1861: 'rebellion (I know not what else to call it) against growing old'.

204. D, 12 December 1879. See also D, 25 June 1879.

205. D, 28 December 1879.

206. Transvaal Deputies to Gladstone, 4 January 1880. GP, 44462, 38.

207. Foot, 209.

208. ibid., 63.

209. D, 18 January 1880. See PMP, *Autobiographica*, iv, 41. D, 8 February 1880: 'Wrote a long memorandum on the evidence in regard to Dear Helen's religious profession.' (Ibid., 37.)

210. Kilbracken, *Reminiscences*, 110.

211. D, 16 March 1880.

212. D, 23 March 1880.

213. N. St John-Stevas (ed.), *The Collected Works of Walter Bagehot*, xv (1986), 140.

214. W. E. Gladstone, *Political Speeches in Scotland, March and April 1880* (Edinburgh, 1880), i, 30.

215. AR (1880), 47.

216. Hamilton, i, 13.

217. BL, Iddesleigh, 50020, 1.

218. Morley, ii, 218–19.

219. Foot, 50.

220. Morley, ii, 221, 223.

221. G to Plimsoll, 11 April 1880 (draft). GP, 44463, 107.

222. Q & G, ii, 16.

223. R. Fulford (ed.), *Beloved Mama. Private Correspondence of Queen Victoria and the German Crown Princess, 1878–1885* (1981), 73.

224. R. Blake, *Disraeli* (1966), 716.

225. Magnus, 272.

226. G to Wemyss Reid, 1 February 1892. GP, 56445.

227. ibid. G to Wemyss Reid, 1 February 1892 (copy). GP, 44514, 50.

228. Morley, ii, 229.
229. D, 12 April 1880.
230. B. Holland, *Life of . . . 8th Duke of Devonshire* (1911), i, 273–6, 276–8. Holland comments that Algernon West's assumptions as to Hartington's alleged 'vain attempt to form a Cabinet' (A. West, *Recollections, 1852–1886* (1899), ii, 103) were expressive of the mood of the 'Gladstonian entourage'. Holland, i, 278.
231. Morley, ii, 223.
232. Holland, i, 273.

CHAPTER 7:
'THE ALMIGHTY HAS EMPLOYED ME . . .': 1880–81

1. R. Fulford (ed.), *Beloved Mama. Private Correspondence of Queen Victoria and the German Crown Princess, 1878–1885* (1981), 75.
2. 'Second Cabinet of 1880–5'. GP, 56445 (27 September 1897).
3. Karolyi to G, 1 May 1880. GP, 44464, 50. G to Karolyi, 4 May 1880 (copy). Ibid., 48.
4. Cardwell to G, 27 April 1880. GP, 56445.
5. Fulford, *Beloved Mama*, 130.
6. A. B. Cooke and J. Vincent (eds.), *Lord Carlingford's Journal. Reflections of a Cabinet Minister, 1885* (Oxford, 1971), 109.
7. D, 27 April 1882.
8. Lord Kilbracken, *Reminiscences* (1931), 119.
9. J. Chamberlain, *A Political Memoir, 1880–1892*, ed. C. H. D. Howard (1953), 58.
10. R. T. Shannon, *The Age of Disraeli* (1992), 400.
11. Hamilton, i, 3.
12. G, 'Second Cabinet of 1880–5'. GP 56445 (27 September 1897).
13. D, 29 September 1881. See page 281.
14. *Gladstone*, 550.
15. H(3), cclxix, 1713 (26 May 1882).
16. D, 16 June 1885.
17. Shannon, *Age of Disraeli*, 406–7.
18. A. L. Thorold, *The Life of Henry Labouchere* (1913), 144. See also A. G. Gardiner, *The Life of Sir William Harcourt* (1923), i, 457. The Queen made satirical reference to it: Fulford, *Beloved Mama*, 148.
19. GP, 56445 (27 September 1897). See page 262.
20. G. Battiscombe, *Mrs Gladstone* (1956), 181.
21. D, 22 October 1880.
22. D, 24 May 1880.
23. H(3), cclii, 65 (29 April 1880).
24. G memo, 14 May 1880. GP, 56445.
25. H(3), cclii, 65 (29 April 1880).
26. W. N. Medlicott, *Bismarck, Gladstone, and the Concert of Europe* (1956), 1.
27. Kruger and Joubert to G, 10 May 1880. GP, 44464, 97.
28. D. M. Schreuder, *Gladstone and Kruger* (1969), 66–8; C. F. Goodfellow, *Great Britain and South African Confederation, 1870–1881* (1966), 188–9.
29. Rathbone to G, 17 April 1880. GP, 44463, 142.
30. E. C. F. Collier (ed.), *A Victorian Diarist. Later Extracts from the Journals of Mary, Lady Monkswell, 1895–1909* (1946), 15.
31. A. Lang, *Life . . . of Sir Stafford Northcote, First Earl of Iddesleigh* (Edinburgh, 1891), 327.
32. *Memoirs of an Old Parliamentarian* (1929), i, 8.
33. G to O'Brien, 10 December 1895. GP, 56445.
34. H(3), cclii, 150, 157 (20 May 1880).
35. D, 14 June 1880.
36. D, 16 March 1882.
37. Shannon, *Age of Disraeli*, 400.
38. H(3), ccliii, 1652, 1656 (5 July 1880); ccliv, 1437 (26 July 1880).
39. D, 17 July 1880.

40. Shannon, *Age of Disraeli*, 406.

41. G, 'Second Cabinet of 1880–5'. GP, 56445 (27 September 1897).

42. Dicey to Maxse, 1 January 1895. Maxse Papers, West Sussex Record Office, 443/693.

43. H(3), cclii, 459 (25 May 1880).

44. D, 15 June 1880.

45. D, 29 June 1880.

46. Schreuder, *Gladstone and Kruger*, 66ff.

47. Q & G, ii, 167.

48. Hamilton, i, 32. On the insanitary state of No. 10 Downing St see G. Leveson Gower, *Years of Content* (1940), 153.

49. Fulford, *Beloved Mama*, 84, 88.

50. Hamilton, i, 37, 39.

51. *Gladstone*, 133. D, 29 August, 4 September 1880.

52. D, 18 September 1880.

53. D, 19 September 1880.

54. D, 10, 19 September 1880.

55. GP, 44776, 145–53.

56. R. T. Shannon, 'Gladstone and the Hellenic Factor in the Eastern Question', *Actes du Symposium Historique International, 'La Dernière Phase de la Crise Orientale et l'Hellénisme (1878–1881)'* (Athens, 1983), 440.

57. Northcote to Beaconsfield, 7 October 1880. BL, Iddesleigh, 50018, 230.

58. GP, 44776, 145–53.

59. ibid.

60. A. T. Bassett (ed.), *Gladstone to His Wife* (1936), 234.

61. ibid.

62. Kilbracken, *Reminiscences*, 131–2.

63. Bassett, *Gladstone to His Wife*, 234.

64. D, 23 October 1880. E. Hughes, 'The Changes in Parliamentary Procedure, 1880–1882', in R. Pares and A. J. P. Taylor (eds.), *Essays Presented to Sir Lewis Namier* (1956), 296–7.

65. G, 'Second Cabinet of 1880–5'. GP, 56445 (25 September 1897).

66. Morley, ii, 169.

67. D, 25 October 1880.

68. Lord Eversley, *Gladstone and Ireland* (1912), 147.

69. D, 27 November 1880.

70. Bassett, *Gladstone to His Wife*, 237.

71. Hamilton, i, 46.

72. D, xii, 496.

73. Tennyson to G, 3 November 1880. GP, 44466, 251.

74. Hamilton, i, 71. D, 23 January 1881.

75. S. Gladstone to Liddon, 26 October 1880. Liddon Papers, Keble College, Oxford, Misc. Box.

76. Schreuder, *Gladstone and Kruger*, 88–9.

77. Hamilton, i, 94.

78. Richard to G, 9 February 1881. GP, 44468, 86.

79. H(3), cclvii, 3–7.

80. Beaconsfield to Rowton, 29 January 1881. Hughenden Papers, Bodleian Library, Oxford, B/XX/D/314.

81. See Abbott to G, [21 April 1888]. GP, 44503, 146.

82. H(3), cclvii, 870 (17 January 1881); 1690 (28 January 1881).

83. Spurgeon to G, 1 March 1881. GP, 44468, 86.

84. D, 1 February 1881.

85. D, 12 March 1881.

86. P. Magnus, *Gladstone* (1954), 298.

87. Hamilton, i, 125.

88. D, 13 April 1881.

89. H(3), cclx, 601 (4 April 1881).

90. Morley, ii, 293.

91. Shannon, *Age of Disraeli*, 416. On the vindictiveness theme, ibid., 402–3: 'Cardinal Manning had once told him that he knew Gladstone well and that he thought him the most revengeful man he ever knew.' For explanatory and corrective interpretations of G's moral targeting of Palmerston and Disraeli/ Beaconsfield see *Gladstone*, 244, 250, 254, 256–8, 336–7.

92. D, 28 March 1881. Allon to G, 30 March 1881. GP, 44095, 379.

93. Q & G, ii, 153.
94. D, 21 April 1881.
95. D, 24 April 1881.
96. Magnus, 280–81.
97. Kilbracken, *Reminiscences*, 131–2.
98. D, 10 May 1881.
99. R. Blake, *Disraeli and Gladstone* (1969), 3; *Disraeli* (1966), 739–41.
100. D, 21 April 1881.
101. Hamilton, i, 61, n5.
102. Morley, ii, 294.
103. D, 29 April 1881.
104. H(3), cclxiii, 594 (11 July 1881).
105. Hamilton, i, 156.
106. D, 25 May 1885. G. Shaw-Lefevre, 'The Duke of Argyll and the Irish Land Bill', *Nineteenth Century*, June 1881, 1044–5.
107. H(3), cclxiv, 267 (1 August 1881). See also Lansdowne's comments, ibid., 279–80.
108. H(3), cclxxx, 449–54 (12 June 1883). See also cclxvii, 752 (13 March 1882); cclxx, 661–2 (9 June 1882) and 1266 (15 June 1882).
109. Hamilton, i, 162.
110. D, 29 August 1881.
111. D, 30 August 1881.
112. Wilde to G, [21 July 1881]. GP, 44470, 239.

CHAPTER 8:
'AN AUTHOR OF UNBOUND INTELLIGENCE': 1881–2

1. Citizens of Volo to G, 15 November 1881. GP, 44473, 64. *Gladstone*, 474–5.
2. GP, 44226, 76, 78; 44492, 191, 197.
3. Gov. of Cyprus to G, 12 April 1881. GP, 44226, 74.
4. H(3), cclxii, 1287–8, 1326 (24 June 1881).
5. Q & G, ii, 161.
6. ibid., 165–6.
7. D. Schreuder, *Gladstone and Kruger* (1969), 203. Dillwyn to G, 10 June 1882,

GP, 44475, 253, on Liberal dissatisfaction at the progress of Zulu resettlement on their lands and restoration of King Cetawayo.
8. Schreuder, ibid.
9. H(3), cclxiii, 1862–3 (25 July 1881).
10. G to Cowper, 22 August 1881. GP, 56453.
11. G to Cowper, 1 September 1881. Ibid.
12. G to Cowper, 9 September 1881. Ibid.
13. Hamilton, i, 166.
14. F. S. L. Lyons, *Charles Stewart Parnell* (1977), 166.
15. D, 29 September 1881.
16. D, 22 September 1881.
17. Hamilton, i, 173.
18. Q & G, ii, 169–70.
19. Lyons, *Parnell*, 167–8.
20. Lady F. Cavendish to Morley, 31 January 1902. GP, 56553.
21. AR (1881), 196.
22. D, 13 October 1881. Law to G, 25 October 1881. GP, 44472, 166–7.
23. D, 19 October 1881.
24. Lyons, 168.
25. Lord E. Fitzmaurice, *Life of . . . Lord Granville* (1905), ii, 301.
26. Hamilton, i, 193.
27. D, 11 November 1881; 19 November 1881.
28. D, 13 November 1881.
29. D, 18 November 1881.
30. D, 21 November 1881.
31. Hamilton, i, 187.
32. ibid., 188.
33. ibid., 185, 186, 189.
34. ibid., 170.
35. W. Partington, *Thomas Wise in the Original Cloth* (1947), 227.
36. Hamilton, i, 128.
37. D, 27 March 1881.
38. Hamilton, i, 166.
39. D, 10 May 1880.
40. G to Newman, 18 December 1881 (copy). GP, 44473, 185.

41. Hamilton, i, 190–91.
42. D, 4 November 1881.
43. D, 18 January 1882.
44. D, 16, 18, 19 December 1881.
45. D, 2 December 1881.
46. D, 26 December 1881.
47. Ellen O'Connell to G, 27 January 1882. GP, 44474, 97. No such bust is known now at Hawarden.
48. D, 20 January 1882.
49. H(3), cclxvi, 3–4, 6.
50. D, 6 February 1882.
51. D, 8 February 1882.
52. H(3), cclxvi, 203 (8 February 1882).
53. ibid., 260–63.
54. ibid., 266.
55. ibid., 273 (9 February 1882), 521 (13 February 1882).
56. ibid., 865 (16 February 1882).
57. Q & G, ii, 176.
58. ibid., 176–7.
59. ibid.
60. H(3), cclxvi, 866 (16 February 1882).
61. H(3), cclxviii, 1229, 1297, 1304.
62. D, 20 February 1882.
63. D, 17 March 1882, 12 April 1882; H. Maxwell, *Life of . . . W. H. Smith* (1893), ii, 57–61, 347–53.
64. D, 12 April 1882.
65. D, 11, 14 March 1882.
66. H(3), cclxvii, 1468 (21 March 1882).
67. G. M. Trevelyan, *John Bright* (1913), 432.
68. G & G, 2, i, 326–7.
69. ibid., 348.
70. R. Robinson, J. Gallagher, A. Denny, *Africa and the Victorians* (1963), 101.
71. G & G, 2, i, 363.
72. D, 28 March 1882.
73. D, 2 April 1882.
74. Hamilton, i, xlix–xlx.
75. D, 25 April 1882.
76. Lady F. Cavendish to Morley, 31 January 1902. GP, 56453.
77. Lord Eversley, *Gladstone and Ireland* (1912), 198. On the question of G and land purchase see A. Warren, 'Gladstone, Land and Social Reconstruction in Ireland, 1881–1887', *Parliamentary History*, 1983.
78. H(3), cclxviii, 1965.
79. Cowper to G, 2 May 1882. GP, 44475, 84.
80. Cross to G, 3 May 1882. Ibid., 89.
81. J. Chamberlain, *A Political Memoir, 1880–1892*, ed. C. H. D. Howard (1953), 60.
82. B. Holland, *Life of . . . the Eighth Duke of Devonshire* (1912), I, 352.
83. Chamberlain, 58. See page 251.
84. G. Battiscombe, *Mrs Gladstone* (1956), 184.
85. Hamilton, i, 188.
86. Lady F. Cavendish to Morley, 31 January 1902. GP, 56453.
87. D, xii, 500–501.
88. H(3), cclxix, 121.
89. D, 15 May 1882. Chamberlain, *Political Memoir*, 50, 59.
90. Battiscombe, *Mrs Gladstone*, 185.
91. R. Kee, *The Laurel and the Ivy* (1993), 455. Hamilton, i, 269–70, thought the story much 'dressed up'.
92. E. C. F. Collier (ed.), *A Victorian Diarist. Extracts from the Journals of Mary, Lady Monkswell, 1873–1895* (1944), 242.
93. R. Fulford (ed.), *Beloved Mama. Private Correspondence of Queen Victoria and the German Crown Princess, 1878–1885* (1981), 119.
94. H(3), cclxix, 836 (16 May 1882).
95. D, 17 May 1882. Talbot to Balfour, 12 July [1882]. BL, Balfour, 48789, 24.
96. D, 9 May 1882.
97. G & G, 2, i, 371.
98. G to Ly Derby, 17 May 1882 (copy). GP, 44475, 156.
99. H(3), cclxix, 1404–5 (23 May 1882).
100. ibid., 1715, 1718 (26 May 1882).
101. ibid., 1711 (26 May 1882).
102. Holland, *Devonshire*, i, 356.
103. Hamilton, i, 290.
104. G & G, 2, i, 373.

105. Hamilton, ii, 138.
106. D, 23 May 1882.
107. D, 8 June 1882.
108. Holland, *Devonshire*, i, 356.
109. Lyttelton to CG, 9 June 1882. GP, 44475, 251.
110. Terry to G, 20 June [1882]. Ibid., 305.
111. Fitzmaurice, *Granville*, ii, 301.
112. D, 16 June 1882.
113. Gregory to G, 8 June 1882. GP, 56450.
114. G to Gregory, 9 June 1882 (copy). Ibid.
115. D, 29 June 1882.
116. S. Gwynn and G. M. Tuckwell, *Life of . . . Sir Charles W. Dilke* (1917), i, 446, 447.
117. M. E. Chamberlain, 'Sir Charles Dilke and British Intervention in Egypt, 1882: Decision-making in a Nineteenth-century Cabinet', *British Journal of International Studies*, 1976, 237.
118. D, 23 June 1882.
119. G & G, 2, i, 383.
120. Robinson *et al.*, *Africa and the Victorians*, 111.
121. G & G, 2, i, 380.
122. Harrison to G, 5 July 1882. GP, 44476, 10.
123. H. C. G. Matthew, *Gladstone, 1875–1898* (Oxford, 1995), 375.
124. Holland, *Devonshire*, I, 365.
125. G & G, 2, i, 391.
126. Robinson *et al.*, *Africa and the Victorians*, 111.
127. Gwynn and Tuckwell, *Dilke*, i, 468–9.
128. D, 14 July 1882.
129. G to Queen, 15 July 1882 (copy). GP, 56450.
130. Gwynn and Tuckwell, *Dilke*, i, 471–2.
131. G, memo, 14 September 1882. GP, 56450.
132. G to Richard, 31 August 1882 (draft). Ibid.

133. D, 6 September 1882.
134. Gosscevic to G, 1 August 1882. GP, 56450.
135. G, memo, 14 September 1882. Ibid.
136. ibid.
137. Abbott to G, 16 September 1882. GP, 56450.
138. G, memo, 14 September 1882. Ibid.
139. D, iii, 521.
140. G to York, 16 September 1882 (draft). GP, 56450.
141. D, 26 October 1882.
142. D, 16 September 1882.
143. Q & G, ii, 236.
144. D, 14 August 1882.
145. G, memo on 'Control in Egypt', 20 October 1882. GP, 56450.
146. G on F.O. Memorandum on the Control, 19 September 1882. Ibid.
147. E. Hughes, 'The Changes in Parliamentary Procedure, 1880–1882', in R. Pares and A. J. P. Taylor (eds.), *Essays Presented to Sir Lewis Namier* (1956), 317.
148. D, 24 October 1882.
149. G & G, 2, i, 458.
150. D, 10, 15 December 1882.
151. D, 18 November 1882.
152. D, 5 December 1882.
153. D, 4 December 1882.
154. Q & G, ii, 221–2.
155. A. G. Gardiner, *The Life of Sir William Harcourt* (1923), i, 467.
156. D, 28 December 1882.
157. R. R. James, *Rosebery* (1963), 145–6.
158. D, 30 November 1882.
159. T. A. Jenkins, *Gladstone, Whiggery and the Liberal Party, 1874–1886* (Oxford, 1988), 183.
160. D, 30 December 1882.
161. D, 20 October 1882.
162. D, 11 September 1882.
163. King George to G, 13 December 1882. GP, 44478, 82; Tricoupis to G, 13 December 1882. Ibid., 92.

CHAPTER 9:
'WE HAVE THE INTERESTS OF
JUSTICE IN OUR HANDS': 1883–5

1. D. Schreuder, *Gladstone and Kruger* (1969), 369.
2. Hamilton, i, li.
3. T. A. Jenkins, *Gladstone, Whiggery, and the Liberal Party, 1874–1886* (Oxford, 1988), 233–4.
4. H(3), cclxxxv, 122 (28 February 1884).
5. Hamilton, i, 2.
6. D, 1 January 1883.
7. D, 19 February 1884.
8. GP, 44768, 84.
9. D, 3 February 1883.
10. L. Masterman (ed.), *Mary Gladstone (Mrs Drew), Her Diaries and Letters* (1930), 280.
11. D, 6, 8, 22 February 1883.
12. D, 27 February 1883.
13. D, 17 May 1883.
14. D, 18, 23 May 1883.
15. Jenkins, *Gladstone, Whiggery, and the Liberal Party*, 234–5.
16. Rathbone to G, 16 April 1883. GP, 44480, 192.
17. Firth to G, 13 April 1883. Ibid., 157.
18. Rathbone to G, 9 May 1883. Ibid., 309.
19. D, 29 March 1883.
20. Q & G, ii, 233–4; D, 22 June 1883.
21. D, 2 July 1883.
22. P. McHugh, *Prostitution and Victorian Social Reform* (1980), 42. *Gladstone*, 479.
23. D, 14 June 1883. See Bennett to G, 4 June 1883, GP, 44481, 121, on Evangelical grievance at not getting 'a fair share of recognition at your hands'.
24. D, 11 July 1883.
25. H(3), cclxxxiii (21 August 1883).
26. D, 29 June 1883.
27. H(3), cclxx, 446–7 (12 June 1883).
28. G to Dufferin, 3 August 1883 (copy). GP, 56450.
29. *Pall Mall Gazette*, 4 August 1883, 1–2.
30. Baring to Granville, 9 October 1883;
Granville to Baring, 9 October 1883. GP, 56450.
31. D, 15 November 1883.
32. H. Lord Tennyson, *Alfred, Lord Tennyson* (1897), ii, 281.
33. C. Tennyson, *Six Tennyson Essays* (1954), 60.
34. Tennyson to G, 2 October 1883. GP, 44483, 188.
35. GP, 44483, 206.
36. D, 27 December 1883.
37. D, 8 August 1883.
38. G. Watson, *Politics and Literature in Modern Britain* (1977), 151–2.
39. Owen to G, 8 February 1884. GP, 44485, 156.
40. Tennyson, *Tennyson*, ii, 303.
41. R. T. Shannon, *The Age of Salisbury* (1996), 53–4.
42. ibid., 69.
43. D, 10 October 1883.
44. GBA, 278–81.
45. Rathbone to G, 23 October 1883. GP, 44483, 266.
46. ibid.
47. AG for Ireland to G, 3 November 1883. GP, 44483, 388.
48. D, 23 October 1883.
49. D, 7 November 1883.
50. Salisbury to Cairns, 29 November 1883. PRO, Cairns, 30/51/6.
51. Jenkins, *Gladstone, Whiggery, and the Liberal Party*, 236–7.
52. D, 29 December 1883.
53. G & G, 2, ii, 130. Jenkins, 181–2.
54. D, 26 December 1883.
55. ibid.
56. D, 29 December 1883.
57. D, 26 October 1883.
58. D, 1 January 1884.
59. D, 18 January 1884.
60. Schreuder, *Gladstone and Kruger*, 430.
61. G & G, 2, ii, 84.
62. Schreuder, 363.
63. D, 27 November 1883.
64. Verney to G, 24, 30 April 1881. GP, 44469, 164, 211.

65. Granville to G, 11 March 1888. GP, 56452.

66. D, 13 April 1884.

67. Hamilton, ii, 825. G, memo, 9 April 1885. GP, 56452.

68. D, 18 January 1884.

69. D, 2 February 1884.

70. Hamilton, ii, 559.

71. G to Victoria, 9 February 1884 (copy). GP, 56451.

72. D, 12 February 1884.

73. GP, 56451.

74. Hamilton, ii, 559.

75. Memo for G by E. W. Hamilton, 9 April 1885. GP, 56452.

76. Hamilton, ii, 566.

77. Lord Zetland, *Lord Cromer* (1932), 120–21.

78. GP, 56451, 'Cabinet'.

79. Zetland, *Cromer*, ibid.

80. H(3), ccxciv, 1072 (23 February 1885).

81. H(3), cclxxxvi, 1534, 1539.

82. ibid., 1540, 41.

83. Q & G, ii, 264–5.

84. H(3), cclxxxvii, 138.

85. e.g., GP, 44503, 27.

86. *Gladstone*, 486.

87. H(3), cclxxxiii, 69 (12 May 1884).

88. H(3), ccxciv, 1058 (23 February 1885).

89. ibid., 1058. H(3), cclxxxiii, 64–5 (12 May 1884).

90. S. Gwynn and G. M. Tuckwell, *Life . . . of Sir Charles W. Dilke* (1917), ii, 48.

91. D, 12 May 1884.

92. Hamilton, ii, 611.

93. H(3), cclxxxii, 1057, 1059 (1 May 1884); 1852 (9 May 1884).

94. H(3), cclxxxiii, 216 (13 May 1884); ccxciv, 1221 (24 February 1885).

95. H(3), cclxxxviii, 55.

96. ibid., 65, 71.

97. H(3), cclxxxiii, 672–3 (19 May 1884); ccxci, 1765 (5 August 1884).

98. G to Victoria, 1 June 1884 (copy). GP, 56451. D, 28 May, 30 May, 2 June 1884.

99. G to Ponsonby, 18 May 1884. GP, 56451.

100. Zetland, *Cromer*, 121.

101. D, 8 June 1884.

102. Gwynn and Tuckwell, *Dilke*, ii, 57.

103. G, memo, 9 May 1884. GP, 44768, 37.

104. G, memo, 13 June 1884. Ibid., 51–2. For a feminist reading of Gladstone's 'duplicity, betrayal, and arbitrary opposition', see A. P. Robson, 'A Bird's Eye View of Gladstone', in B. L. Kinzer (ed.), *The Gladstonian Turn of Mind* (Toronto, 1985), 92. See Courtney to G, 2 April 1884, GP, 44486, 1; Woodall to G, 9 June 1884, ibid., 238, forwarding a circular signed by seventy-six Liberal MPs urging that women's suffrage be made an open question.

105. C. C. Weston, 'Salisbury and the Lords, 1868–1895', HJ, 1995; Shannon, *Age of Salisbury*, 14.

106. Tennyson to G, 4 July 1884. GP, 44487, 42.

107. D, 6 July 1884.

108. Tennyson to G, 7 July 1884. GP, 44487, 52.

109. Q & G, ii, 283.

110. ibid., 284–5.

111. D, 22 March 1882.

112. G, GP, 44769, 35, 28 February 1885.

113. D, 14 August 1882.

114. Shannon, *Age of Salisbury*, 107.

115. Hamilton, i, xxix. See also G, 'Hereditary Principle', August or September 1884. GP, 44768, 117.
'1. I attach value to it.
2. *And* am averse to adding to this controversy.
3. Its worst enemies – those who pit it against the representative principle.
4. Or agst. the nation.
5. Obj. Then you extinguish it.
6. No. Nation so rare to rouse.
7. Ample scope – aye for doing mischief within this limit.
8. Proof – the history of 52 years

Shows 1. They have vast power without provoking it.
Shows 2. They suffer when they provoke the conflict.'

116. G, 'The Franchise Bill and the Present Situation', *Secret*, 19 August 1884. GP, 44768, 93–107.

117. ibid., 98–9.

118. D, 10 September 1884.

119. GP, 44488, 31.

120. Shannon, *Age of Salisbury*, 94.

121. D, 30 July 1884.

122. D, 13 September 1884.

123. G, 'Reform & Redistribution', 3 January 1884. GP, 44768, 5–6.

124. R. Fulford (ed.), *Beloved Mama. Private Correspondence of Queen Victoria and the German Crown Princess, 1878–1885* (1981), 158, 168.

125. Q & G, ii, 311.

126. Shannon, *Age of Salisbury*, 94.

127. GP, 44768, 137. 13 November 1884.

128. Brett to Hamilton, 18 November 1884. GP, 44488, 81.

129. H(3), ccxciv, 157 (21 November 1884).

130. PMP, *Autobiographica*, i, 106.

131. A. Jones, *The Politics of Reform, 1884* (Cambridge, 1972), 223.

132. D, 28 September 1884. See page 343.

133. G to Bedford, 17 December 1884 (copy). GP, 44488, 277.

134. D, 10 May 1880; G to Newman, 18, 23 December 1881 (copies). GP, 44473, 184, 208.

135. Q & G, ii, 306.

136. D, 27 September 1884.

137. *Gladstone*, 448.

138. D, 18 November 1884.

139. GP, 44768, 128–31.

140. H. C. G. Matthew, *Gladstone, 1875–1898* (Oxford, 1995), 293.

141. A. B. Cooke and J. Vincent (eds.), *Lord Carlingford's Journal. Reflections of a Cabinet Minister, 1885* (Oxford, 1971), 46.

142. ibid., 49–50.

143. ibid., 60.

144. Glynn and Tuckwell, *Dilke*, ii, 95.

145. ibid., 99.

146. ibid., 97.

147. Cranbrook to Cairns, 9 January 1885. PRO, Cairns, 30/51/7.

148. Elliot to G, 5 February 1885. GP, 44489, 191. Elliot was later the biographer of Goschen.

149. Glynn and Tuckwell, *Dilke*, ii, 105.

150. ibid.

151. Carlingford, 54.

152. Jenkins, *Gladstone, Whiggery, and the Liberal Party*, 235.

153. G, 29 January 1885. GP, 56451. For G's condemnation of Chamberlain and Dilke as the 'only two men to whom he could impute betrayal of Cabinet secrets and avowed communications with the Press', Hamilton, iii, 150–51.

154. Jenkins, *Gladstone, Whiggery, and the Liberal Party*, 236.

155. D, 5 February 1885.

156. Q & G, ii, 326.

157. GP, 44489, 20,

158. Fulford, *Beloved Mama*, 182–3.

159. Hamilton, ii, 794.

160. H. Lloyd Jones, 'Gladstone on Homer', *The Times Literary Supplement*, 3 January 1975, 16.

161. Carlingford, 67.

162. Hamilton, ii, 794.

163. ibid., 797.

164. E. F. C. Collier (ed.), *A Victorian Diarist, 1873–1895. Extracts from the Journals of Mary, Lady Monkswell* (1944), 168.

165. D, 11 February 1885.

166. D, 17 February 1885.

167. H(3), ccxciv, 874–5.

168. ibid., 1080, 1088, 1091.

169. G, memo [1885]. GP, 56451.

170. GP, 56452.

171. Carlingford, 74.

172. ibid., 77.

173. D, 11 April 1885.

174. GP, 56452.

175. Hamilton, ii, 817–18.

176. D, 22 March 1995.

177. D, 6 March 1885.

178. Carlingford, 81.

179. ibid., 74, 76.

180. ibid., 68.

181. A. B. Cooke and J. Vincent, *The Governing Passion. Cabinet Government and Party Politics in Britain, 1885–86* (1974), 30.

182. Fulford, *Beloved Mama*, 184.

183. D. Wormald, *Sir John Seeley and the Uses of History* (Cambridge, 1980), 10–11.

184. ibid., 165–6.

185. M. McDonagh, *The Life of William O'Brien* (1928), 81–2. See page 356.

186. Report of Proceedings in Cabinet, 12 March 1885. GP, 56452.

187. D, 24 March 1885.

188. Report of Proceedings in Cabinet, 12 March 1885, GP, 56452.

189. Carlingford, 82.

190. ibid., 85.

191. ibid., 87.

192. Brett to G, 11 April 1885. GP, 44490, 117.

193. D, 8 April 1885.

194. G to Victoria, 13 April 1885 (copy). GP, 56452.

195. G to Victoria, 20 April 1885 (copy). Ibid.

196. *Grillion's Club. A Chronicle, 1812–1913* (1913), 96. Norton to G, 21 April [1885]. GP, 44490, 141.

197. Carlingford, 89.

198. H(3), ccxcvi, 1162 (9 April 1885), 1863, 1866 (16 April 1885).

199. H(3), ccxcvii, 860–61 (27 April 1885).

200. ibid., 1127–8 (30 April 1885). For the 1878 occasion, see page 216.

201. Gwynn and Tuckwell, *Dilke*, ii, 62.

202. D, 2 May 1885.

203. H(3), ccxcvii, 1508–9.

204. GP, 44769, 101.

205. D, 2 May 1885.

206. *The Times*, 9 October 1913, 8. For O'Brien's speech demanding the return of the Irish Parliament see *Freeman's Journal* (Dublin), 2 March 1885.

207. G, *The Irish Question* (1886), 7–8.

208. J. Chamberlain, *A Political Memoir, 1880–92*, ed. C. H. D. Howard (1953), 109.

209. ibid., 136.

210. ibid., 141.

211. ibid., 144.

212. H(3), ccxcviii, 971 (20 May 1885).

213. D, 6 May 1885.

214. Carlingford, 96–7.

215. ibid., 100.

216. D, 9 May 1885.

217. Chamberlain, 149.

218. Gwynn and Tuckwell, *Dilke*, ii, 132.

219. Morley, ii, 437–8.

220. D, 6 July 1885.

221. D, 29 May 1885.

222. Q & G, ii, 354–8.

223. Carlingford, 106–7.

224. D, 9 May 1885.

225. D, 25 May 1885.

226. D, 18 June 1885.

227. D, 30 June 1885.

228. D, 10 June 1885.

229. G, memo, 26 June 1885. GP, 44769, 152.

230. D, 18 June 1885.

231. D, 30 June 1885.

232. GP, 44769, 181–2. D, 30 June 1885.

233. Leighton to G, 16 June 1885. GP, 44491, 130.

234. Labouchere to G, 9 June 1885. GP, 44491, 77. G to Granville and Hartington, 12 June 1885 (copy). GP, 44769, 189.

235. GP, 44469, 183.

236. D, 18 June 1885.

CHAPTER 10:
'SUCH A SUPREME MOMENT':
1885–6

1. Hamilton, iii, 197.

2. Q & G, ii, 352–3.

3. GP, 44126, 91.

4. J. Loughlin, *Gladstone, Home Rule and the Ulster Question, 1882–93* (1986), 33, 45.

5. D, 1 July 1885; D. Chadwick, *Acton and Gladstone* (1976), 31.

6. R. T. Shannon, *The Age of Salisbury* (1996), 156.

7. Morley, ii, 476.

8. Shannon, *Age of Salisbury*, 161.

9. ibid., 157.

10. D, 17 July 1885.

11. D, 8 August 1885.

12. K. O'Shea to G, 5 August 1885. GP, 56446.

13. D, 30 June 1885.

14. S. Walsh to G, 30 May 1887. GP, 44501, 39.

15. G to Walsh, 1 June 1887 (copy). Ibid., 46.

16. Evans to G, 28 November 1890. GP, 44511, 199.

17. A. B. Cooke and J. Vincent, *The Governing Passion. Cabinet Government and Party Politics in Britain, 1885–86* (Brighton, 1974), 282.

18. Shannon, *Age of Salisbury*, 154.

19. D, 8 August 1885.

20. Hamilton, iii, 1.

21. D, 8 August 1885.

22. Hamilton, iii, 2–3.

23. D, 5 August 1885.

24. R. Barry O'Brien on 'Irish Wrongs and English Remedies', *Nineteenth Century*, November 1885; 'Federal Union with Ireland', ibid., January 1886.

25. David Kay, Lord Edmond Fitzmaurice, and G. Shaw-Lefevre contributed items on Austria–Hungary, Sweden–Norway and Russia–Finland in *Nineteenth Century*, vol. xl (January–June 1886).

26. GP, 44769, 218–19 (6 August 1885).

27. B. Holland, *Life of . . . the Eighth Duke of Devonshire* (1911), ii, 77–8.

28. Q & G, ii, 379.

29. Lorange to G, 21 October 1885. GP, 44769, 225.

30. D, 29 August 1885. G. Leveson Gower, *Years of Content, 1858–1886* (1940), 226–7.

31. GP, 44769, 233.

32. D, 30 August 1885.

33. J. Chamberlain, *A Political Memoir, 1880–92*, ed. C. H. D. Howard (1953), 122.

34. Holland, *Devonshire*, ii, 81.

35. PMP, *Autobiographica*, i, 136.

36. F. S. L. Lyons, *Charles Stewart Parnell* (1977), 294–5.

37. Holland, *Devonshire*, ii, 99.

38. I. Ker, *John Henry Newman* (Oxford, 1988), 51.

39. Holland, *Devonshire*, ii, 81.

40. ibid., 82–3.

41. L. Masterman, *Mary Gladstone (Mrs Drew): Her Diaries and Letters* (1930), 362.

42. Holland, *Devonshire*, ii, 83–5.

43. D, 16 June 1885. See page 253.

44. Holland, *Devonshire*, ii, 88.

45. ibid., 89.

46. ibid.

47. ibid., 86.

48. G to Granville, 9 December 1885. GP, 56446.

49. D, 12 September 1885.

50. D, 23 September, 10 October 1885.

51. R. F. Foster, 'History and the Irish Question', TRHS, 1983, 181.

52. G to O'Brien, 10 December 1895. GP, 56445.

53. AR (1885), 158.

54. GP, 44769, 49–51.

55. A. B. Cooke and J. Vincent (eds.), *Lord Carlingford's Journal, 1885* (Oxford, 1971), 134.

56. G to Chamberlain, 26 September 1885 (copy). GP, 44126, 107.

57. Chamberlain to G, 28 September 1885. Ibid., 109.

58. D, 8 October 1885.

59. Chamberlain to G, 24 October 1885, GP, 44126, 112. G to Chamberlain, 25 October 1885 (copy). Ibid., 114.

60. *Gladstone*, 41.

61. D, 25 October 1885.

62. J. L. Garvin, *The Life of Joseph Chamberlain* (1932–4), ii, 114.

63. Chamberlain to G, 26 October 1885. GP, 44126, 116.

64. D, 10 October 1885.

65. Holland, *Devonshire*, ii, 90.

66. D, 11, 18 October 1885.

67. D, xii, 513–14.

68. D, 9 October 1885. GP, 56446. 'Autumn 1885'.

69. Holland, *Devonshire*, ii, 91.

70. H. Lord Tennyson, *Tennyson* (1897), ii, 302.

71. Oxford to G, 4 November 1885. GP, 44493, 34.

72. G to Chamberlain, 6 November 1885 (copy). GP, 44126, 118.

73. H. Paul (ed.), *Letters of Lord Acton to Mary Gladstone* (1904), 328–9.

74. G to Southesk, 1 November 1885 (copy). GP, 44493, 15.

75. Holland, *Devonshire*, ii, 90–91.

76. ibid., 86.

77. ibid., 91.

78. AR (1885), 176.

79. Carlingford, 140.

80. ibid., 141.

81. *The Times*, 10 November 1885, 7.

82. Hamilton, iii, 69.

83. *The Times*, 10 November 1885, 7.

84. Morley, ii, 479–80.

85. ibid., 481–2.

86. GP, 56446, 'Sketch', Secret No. 3. 14 November 1885.

87. Walker to Travers, 19 November 1885. GP, 44493, 123.

88. T. A. Jenkins, *Gladstone, Whiggery and the Liberal Party* (Oxford, 1988), 244.

89. Paul, *Letters of Lord Acton*, 327.

90. D, 18 November 1885.

91. AR (1885), 180.

92. Holland, *Devonshire*, ii, 94–5.

93. ibid., 99.

94. D, 27 November 1885.

95. D, 3 July 1885.

96. P. F. Clarke, 'Electoral Sociology of Modern Britain', *History*, 1972, 48.

97. Hill to G, 6, 7 January 1886. GP, 44494, 20.

98. Channing to G, 15 December 1885. GP, 44493, 225.

99. G to Granville, 9 December 1885. GP, 56446.

100. Cooke and Vincent, *Governing Passion*, 53. The article was 'Proem to Genesis: a Plea for a Fair Trial', *Nineteenth Century*, January 1886.

101. Bryce to G, 11 December 1885. GP, 44740, 5.

102. Grosvenor to G, 14 December 1885. GP, 56446.

103. G to Jenkinson, 11 December 1885 (copy). Ibid.

104. Hill to G, 14 December 1885. GP, 44493, 220.

105. G to Hill, 15 December 1885 (copy). GP, 44493, 231.

106. D, 15 December 1885.

107. A. J. Balfour, *Chapters of Auto-biography*, ed. B. Dugdale (1930), 211–12.

108. G to R. Grosvenor, 7 January 1886 (copy). GP, 56447.

109. Loughlin, 41–5.

110. Carlingford, 141.

111. G to Balfour, 20 December 1885 (draft). GP, 44493, 252.

112. G to Balfour, 23 December 1885 (copy). Ibid., 265.

113. H(3), cccii, 635–6 (18 February 1886).

114. G, memo, 12 December 1885. GP, 44770, 15.

115. Holland, *Devonshire*, ii, 97.

116. Hamilton, iii, 13.

117. G to Granville, 22 December 1885 (copy). GP, 56446.

118. HG memo, 31 December 1885. GP, 56445. See page 288–9.

119. HG memo, 31 December 1885. GP, 56445.

120. D, July 1885.

121. Press cutting, 19 December 1885. GP, 44740, 17.

122. Hamilton, iii, 13–14.
123. Shannon, *Age of Salisbury*, 190–91.
124. G & G, 2, ii, 415.
125. D, 19 December 1885.
126. G to Chamberlain, 18 December 1885 (copy). GP, 44126, 125.
127. G & G, 2, ii, 416–17.
128. Holland, *Devonshire*, ii, 98.
129. ibid., 101.
130. ibid.
131. ibid., 102.
132. ibid., 104–5.
133. Chamberlain to G, 19 December 1885. GP, 44126, 127.
134. Holland, *Devonshire*, ii, 105.
135. G, memo, 26 December 1885. GP, 56446. 'Sent to Ld Granville and Ld Spencer'. The full text is given in Morley, ii, 510–12.
136. ibid.
137. Hamilton, iii, 217. See page 553.
138. ibid., 421.
139. G & G, 2, ii, 419.
140. E. Fitzmaurice, *Life of . . . Earl Granville* (1905), ii, 472.
141. Holland, *Devonshire*, ii, 106.
142. ibid., 106–7.
143. ibid., 108–9.
144. D, 30 December 1885.
145. G to Granville, 31 December 1885. GP, 56446.
146. ibid.
147. Holland, *Devonshire*, ii, 110.
148. G, memo, 31 December 1885, GP, 56446.
149. G to Granville, 31 December 1885. GP, 56446.
150. Holland, *Devonshire*, ii, 110.

CHAPTER 11:
'HOLD THOU MY GOINGS': 1886

1. Hamilton, iii, 15.
2. B. Holland, *Life of . . . the Eighth Duke of Devonshire* (1911), ii, 111.
3. D, 5 January 1886.
4. D, 3 January 1886.
5. G to Grosvenor, 7 January 1886 (copy). GP, 56447.
6. D, 15 February 1886. Morley's abbreviations disabbreviated.
7. Holland, *Devonshire*, ii, 112.
8. G to Granville, 18 January 1886 (copy). GP, 56447.
9. E. Hamilton to HG, 14 January 1886. GP, 56447.
10. Holland, *Devonshire*, ii, 113.
11. To G, 15 January 1886. GP, 44494, 48, 49.
12. Buchanan to G, 20 January 1886. GP, 56447.
13. J. Vincent (ed.), *The Later Derby Diaries* (1981), 55.
14. H(3), cccii, 10–19 (21 January 1886).
15. Russell to G, 23 January 1886. GP, 44494, 68.
16. K. O'Shea to G, 23 January 1886. GP, 44269, 280.
17. G to O'Shea, 24 January 1886 (copy). GP, 56447.
18. Hamilton, iii, 233.
19. Hamilton, iii, 17.
20. Davitt to Labouchere, 29 January 1886. GP, 44494, 89.
21. Hamilton, iii, 21.
22. G to K. O'Shea, 29 January 1886 (copy). GP, 56447.
23. Davitt to Labouchere, 29 January 1886. GP, 44494, 89.
24. D, 23 December 1885.
25. G, memo, 30 January 1886. GP, 44771.
26. R. T. Shannon, 'Gladstone and Home Rule, 1886', in *Ireland after the Union* (Oxford, 1989), 54.
27. A. B. Cooke and J. Vincent, *The Governing Passion* (Brighton, 1974), 339.
28. Chamberlain to G, 30 January 1886. GP, 44126, 132.
29. G to Wolverton, 31 January 1886 (copy). GP, 56447.
30. G to Harcourt, 31 January 1886. GP, 56447.

31. Hamilton, iii, 6. Hamilton rejoiced that the 'cocky' Shaw-Lefevre had lost his seat.

32. Cooke and Vincent, *Governing Passion*, 367–8.

33. Hamilton, iii, 21.

34. Hamilton, iii, 23.

35. Q & G, ii, 390.

36. ibid., 391.

37. G to Argyll, 27 January 1886 (copy). GP, 56447.

38. GP, 44771, 1–2.

39. D, 12 February 1886.

40. ibid.

41. D, 16 February 1886.

42. Walsh to G, 17 February 1886. GP, 56447.

43. Shannon, 'Gladstone and Home Rule, 1886', 54.

44. H(3), cccii, 581–636; 1917 (4 March 1886).

45. H(3), cccii, 173 (21 January 1886).

46. Salis-Schwabe to G, 6 March 1886. GP, 44495, 153.

47. O. Browning to G, 8 March 1886. Ibid., 176.

48. Bryce to G, 12 March 1886. GP, 56447.

49. *Gladstone*, 531.

50. Shannon, 'Gladstone and Home Rule, 1886', 55.

51. Cooke and Vincent, *Governing Passion*, 54.

52. Hamilton, iii, 29.

53. ibid., 26.

54. R. E. J. Walling (ed.), *The Diaries of John Bright* (1930), 535.

55. Chamberlain to G, 15 March 1886. GP, 44126, 154, quoting Gladstone's 'own words'.

56. Caird to G, 7 March 1886. GP, 44495, 116.

57. G to Chamberlain, 15 March 1886 (copy). Ibid., 160.

58. D, 23 March 1886.

59. *Diaries of John Bright*, 535.

60. Tennyson to G [14 March 1886]. GP, 44495, 259.

61. Shannon, 'Gladstone and Home Rule, 1886', 55.

62. *Diaries of John Bright*, 536–7 (20 March 1886).

63. D, 23 March 1886.

64. G to Morley, 22 March 1886 (copy). GP, 44255, 65.

65. D, 23 March 1886.

66. A. V. Dicey, *England's Case against Home Rule* (1886), 226.

67. D, 25 March 1886.

68. D, 26 March 1886.

69. Harcourt to G, 26 March 1886. GP, 56445.

70. Hamilton, iii, 31.

71. ibid., 4.

72. Hamilton, iii, 31.

73. G, *The Irish Question* (1886), 16.

74. Heneage to G, 29 March 1886. GP, 44496, 90.

75. *Diaries of John Bright*, 538.

76. Hamilton, iii, 32.

77. D, 1 April 1886.

78. Herschell to G, 5 April 1886. GP, 44496, 71.

79. *Diaries of John Bright*, 538.

80. Sandhurst to G, 2 April 1886. GP, 44496, 162.

81. D, 5 April 1886.

82. F. S. L. Lyons, *Charles Stewart Parnell* (1977), 343.

83. ibid.

84. Psalm 17:5.

85. P. Magnus, *Gladstone* (1954), 356.

86. Shannon, 'Gladstone and Home Rule, 1886', 57.

87. J. L. Hammond, *Gladstone and the Irish Nation* (1938), 489.

88. Hamilton, iii, 33–4.

89. J. Chamberlain, *A Political Memoir, 1880–1892*, ed. C. H. D. Howard (1953), 212.

90. H(3), ccciv, 1038–85. See, on the theme of G's problems about federalism, J. Kendle, *Ireland and the Federal Solution,*

1870–1921 (McGill, Montreal, 1989), 47.
91. Fischer to Primrose, 15 April 1886. GP, 44496, 251.
92. H(3), ccciv, 1053–4.
93. Lyons, *Parnell*, 305–6.
94. Cooke and Vincent, *Governing Passion*, 403.
95. D, 14 April 1886.
96. ibid.
97. Labouchere to HG, 20 March 1886. GP, 56447.
98. AR (1886), 148. See Shaw-Lefevre's comment: Lord Eversley, *Gladstone and Ireland* (1913), 305.
99. Cooke and Vincent, *Governing Passion*, 404.
100. ibid., 403.
101. D, 20, 21 April 1886.
102. Cooke and Vincent, *Governing Passion*, 410.
103. D, 20 April 1886.
104. Hamilton, i, l.
105. GP, 44493, 1.
106. D, 26 April 1886.
107. D, 28 April 1886.
108. See G to Tricoupis, 18 October 1885. GP, 44492, 197.
109. *The Times*, 4 May 1886, 7.
110. Labouchere to HG, 20 March [1886]. GP, 56447.
111. A. Morley to G, 9 May 1886.
112. D, 1 May 1886.
113. D, 7 May 1886.
114. Stansfeld to G, 5 May 1886. GP, 44497, 134.
115. Stansfeld to G, 6 May 1886. Ibid., 176.
116. R. Jay, *Joseph Chamberlain* (Oxford, 1981), 142.
117. R. T. Shannon, *The Age of Salisbury* (1996), 198.
118. Whitbread to G, 11 May 1886. GP, 44497, 199.
119. Illingworth to G, 12 May 1886. Ibid., 201.
120. G to Illingworth, 12 May 1886 (copy). Ibid., 203.
121. Morley, ii, 567–9.
122. Pease to G, 14 May 1886. GP, 44497, 223.
123. D, 14 May 1886.
124. G to Pease, 15 May 1886 (copy). GP, 44497, 231.
125. Shannon, *Age of Salisbury*, 201.
126. D, 18 May 1886.
127. Pease to G, 20 May 1886. GP, 44497, 246.
128. G to Pease, 21 May 1886 (copy). Ibid., 258.
129. Hamilton, iii, 37–8.
130. ibid., 39.
131. D, 24 May 1886.
132. Brassey to G, 24 May 1886. GP, 44497, 267.
133. AR (1886), 194–6.
134. Raleigh to Stedman, 23 October 1889. GP, 44508, 91.
135. *John Bright* (1913), 454. See page 501.
136. Chamberlain, *Political Memoir*, 225.
137. Shannon, 'Gladstone and Home Rule, 1886', 55.
138. *Gladstone*, 91.
139. Shannon, ibid.
140. G. P. Gooch, *Life of Lord Courtney* (1920), 259.
141. H(3), cccvi, 1218–40.
142. Ly Russell to G, 9 June 1886. GP, 44497, 368.
143. Morley, ii, 581.

CHAPTER 12:
'NOW BEGINS THE GREAT STRUGGLE': 1886–90

1. G to Duffy, 11 December 1886. GP, 44499, 237.
2. PMP, i, *Autobiographica*, 75 (1894).
3. *Gladstone*, 495–6.
4. ibid., 101.
5. B. Hilton, 'Gladstone's Theological Politics', in M. Bentley and J. Stevenson

(eds.), *High and Low Politics in Modern Britain* (1983), 41.

6. *Gladstone*, 101.

7. P. Magnus, *Gladstone* (1954), 365–6.

8. R. T. Shannon, 'Gladstone and Home Rule, 1886', in *Ireland after the Union* (Oxford, 1989), 53.

9. *Gladstone*, 179.

10. Q & G, ii, 416.

11. Morley, ii, 570.

12. M. Weber, 'The Nature of Charismatic Domination', in W. G. Runciman (ed.), *Max Weber. Selections in Translation* (Cambridge, 1978), 248.

13. M. Tennant to G, 11 June 1886. GP, 44498, 13.

14. *The Times*, 19 June 1886, 8.

15. W. S. Churchill, *Lord Randolph Churchill* (1905), Appendix v.

16. Rogers to G, 19 June [1886]. GP, 44498, 40.

17. D, 15 June 1886.

18. D, 1 July 1886. P. Jalland, 'Mr Gladstone's Daughters: The Domestic Price of Victorian Politics', in B. Kinzer (ed.), *The Gladstonian Turn of Mind* (Toronto, 1985), 97, 116–17.

19. T. L. Crosby, *The Two Mr Gladstones* (Yale, 1997), 96.

20. D, 24 June, 30 June, 3 July 1886.

21. D, 23 June 1886.

22. G to A. Morley, 9 July 1886. GP, 56445.

23. Fyffe to G, 5 May 1890. GP, 56445.

24. D, 10 July 1886.

25. Primrose to G, 3 July 1886. GP, 56445.

26. G. M. Trevelyan, *John Bright* (1913), 453.

27. Morley, ii, 582.

28. D, 2 July 1886.

29. *The Times*, 10 November 1885, 7.

30. Rogers to G, 6 July 1886. GP, 44498, 149. See T. W. Heyck, 'Home Rule, Radicalism, and the Liberal Party, 1886–1895', *Journal of British Studies*, 1974–5.

31. G to Bailey, 5 July 1886. GP, 44498, 131.

32. D, 10 July 1886. G. Leveson Gower, *Years of Content, 1858–1886* (1940), 248–9.

33. Primrose to G, 7 July 1886. GP, 56445.

34. Ivory to G, 10 July 1886. GP, 44498, 174.

35. D, 8 July 1886.

36. GP, 44505, 14.

37. D, 9 July 1886.

38. G to Morley, 9 July 1886 (copy). GP, 56445.

39. ibid.

40. Primrose to G, 12 July 1886. GP, 44498, 191.

41. Foster to G, 12 July 1886. Ibid., 185.

42. G to Morley, 9 July 1886 (copy). GP, 56445.

43. Morley, ii, 587–8.

44. R. Hough (ed.), *Advice to a Granddaughter. Letters from Queen Victoria to Princess Victoria of Hesse* (1975), 81.

45. Sharp to G, 12 November 1885. GP, 44493, 73, 81.

46. D, 16 July 1886.

47. D, 31 July 1886.

48. Hamilton, iii, 58.

49. F. W. Hirst, 'Mr Gladstone and Home Rule, 1885–1892', in T. W. Reid (ed.), *Gladstone* (1899), 708.

50. G, memo, 12 July 1886 (copy). GP, 56445.

51. G, draft, 29 November 1890. GP, 56448.

52. Hamilton, iii, 8.

53. G to HG, 16 July 1886 (copy). GP, 56445.

54. D, 3 August 1886.

55. J. Vincent (ed.), *The Later Derby Diaries* (1981), 64–5.

56. D, 2 August 1886.

57. H(3), cccviii, 105 (19 August 1886).

58. ibid., 106.

59. G to Pressensé, 9 January 1889 (copy). GP, 44506, 19.

60. See F. E. Hamer (ed.), *The Personal Papers of Lord Rendel* (1931), 61.
61. G, *The Irish Question* (1886), 32–3.
62. G. Leveson Gower, *Years of Endeavour, 1886–1907* (1942), 1–2.
63. D, xii, 516.
64. G, *The Irish Question*, new edn, 13 October 1886, 29.
65. G to Editor of *Blackwood's*, 30 October 1886 (copy). GP, 44499, 110.
66. G to Dicey, 12 November 1886 (copy). Ibid., 162. C. Harvie, 'Gladstonianism, the Provinces, and Popular Political Culture, 1860–1906', in R. Bellamy (ed.), *Victorian Liberalism* (1990), 170.
67. K. Robbins, *John Bright* (1979), 259.
68. D, 16 October 1886.
69. D, xii, 517.
70. H. C. G. Matthew, *Gladstone, 1874–1898* (Oxford, 1995), 364.
71. D, 12 October 1886.
72. Kay-Shuttleworth to G, 29 November 1886. GP, 44499, 206.
73. G to Duffy, 11 December 1886 (copy). GP, 44499, 237.
74. See for example Charles Tennyson's account in *Six Tennyson Essays* (1954), 68.
75. P. Metcalf, *James Knowles* (Oxford, 1980), 316–17.
76. Tennyson to G, 4 January 1887. GP, 44500, 1.
77. J. Chamberlain, *A Political Memoir, 1880–1892*, ed. C. H. D. Howard (1953), 233–4.
78. D, 23 December 1886.
79. Brett to G, 25 December 1886. GP, 44499, 262.
80. Rogers to G, 30 December 1886. Ibid., 311.
81. Chamberlain, *Political Memoir*, 234–5.
82. G to Labouchere, 29 December 1886 (copy). GP, 44499, 304.
83. Chamberlain, *Political Memoir*, 238.
84. D, 29 December 1886.
85. Q & G, ii, 359. See memo of conversation between Knollys and Hamilton, 12 May 1885 (GP, 44769, 115–17). Hamilton, iii, 254, on 'Mr G's custom of communicating to H.R.H. the gist of his report of Cabinet proceedings to the Queen'.
86. The full story is told by M. Hurst, *Joseph Chamberlain and Liberal Reunion. The Round Table Conference, 1887* (1967).
87. Hurst, 278.
88. Acland to G, 27 February 1887. GP, 44500, 135.
89. Hurst, 284.
90. Chamberlain, *Political Memoir*, 252–3.
91. G to *Baptist*, 23 February 1887 (copy). GP, 44500, 129.
92. Hamilton, iii, 55. It is now in the National Portrait Gallery.
93. ibid., 57–8.
94. H(3), cccxiii, 1825 (25 April 1887).
95. ibid., 1203 (18 April 1887).
96. Chamberlain, *Political Memoir*, 268.
97. Psalm 116: 4.
98. H(3), cccxiv, 989 (5 May 1887).
99. Kay-Shuttleworth to G, 15 May 1887. GP, 44501, 10.
100. Whitbread to G, 20 May 1887. Ibid., 21.
101. D, 24 May 1887.
102. *Western Mail* (Cardiff), 6 June 1887.
103. R. T. Shannon, *Mr Gladstone and Swansea, 1887* (Swansea, 1982).
104. D, 4 June 1887.
105. *The Times*, 5 June 1887, 9.
106. Hubbard to G, 10 October 1889. GP, 44508, 53.
107. Ecclus. 39: 12.
108. D, 13 June 1887. G to Carnegie, 18 July 1887 (copy). GP, 44501, 193. Carnegie to G, 25 January 1886. GP, 44494, 71.
109. D, 15 June 1887.
110. G. St-Aubyn, *The Royal George* (1963), 233–4.
111. H(3), cccxvii, 85, 100–101 (7 July 1887).

112. D, 13 August 1887.

113. G to Brunner, 15 August 1887 (copy). GP, 44501, 222.

114. H(3), cccxix, 1843 (25 August 1887).

115. D, 9 September 1887.

116. H(3), cccxxii, 755–6 (17 February 1888).

117. H(3), cccxxi, 354 (12 September 1887).

118. GP, 44508, 182 (19 November 1889).

119. Hamilton, i, xxii.

120. Hamilton, iii, 75.

121. T. W. Reid to G, 24 June 1887. GP, 44501, 95.

122. D, 19 March 1887. G to Hodder, 30 April 1887 (copy). GP, 44500, 273. Hodder to G, 29 April 1887. Ibid., 269.

123. D, 23 January 1888; 1 February 1888.

124. Hamilton, iii, 67.

125. Purcell to G, 24 May 1887. GP, 44501, 29. See Purcell's expansive acknowledgements to Gladstone in the preface to his Manning biography (1895).

126. G to Reid, 6 July 1888 (copy). GP, 44504, 85.

127. G to Ly Rothschild, 27 October 1888 (copy). GP, 44505, 70.

128. *Gladstone*, 366–72.

129. M. E. Chamberlain, *Lord Aberdeen. A Political Biography* (1983), 1–2.

130. Hamilton, iii, 82–3.

131. P. Metcalf, *James Knowles* (1980), 319–21. Reprinted later in G's *Special Aspects of the Irish Question* (1892).

132. G, 'Electoral Facts of 1887', *Nineteenth Century*, October 1887, 435, 440, 444.

133. D, 16 November 1887.

134. Hamilton, iii, 67.

135. ibid., 75.

136. ibid., 49.

137. ibid., 73.

138. ibid., 75.

139. D, 9 February 1888.

140. White to G, 23 January 1888. GP, 44503, 73.

141. e.g., H(3), cccxxii, 776 (17 February 1888).

142. ibid., 747–51.

143. Hamilton, iii, 1.

144. F. S. L. Lyons, *Charles Stewart Parnell* (1977), 403.

145. H(3), cccxxviii (23 July 1888).

146. D, 8 March, 30 April 1888.

147. D, 8 March 1888.

148. W. S. Petersen, 'Gladstone's Review of *Robert Elsmere*: Some Unpublished Correspondence', *Review of English Studies*, 1970, 442–61.

149. D, 11 June 1888.

150. D, 2 May 1888.

151. G to Pomeroy, 23 October 1888 (draft). GP, 44505, 40.

152. D, xii, 523.

153. Rogers to G, 2 July [1888]. GP, 44504, 69.

154. Ivory to G, 17 July 1888. GP, 44504, 118.

155. McCarthy to G, 14 July 1888. Ibid., 100.

156. Walsh to G, 25 October 1888. GP, 44505, 61.

157. Haldane to G, 21 November 1888. Ibid., 140.

158. Ivory to G, 19 July 1888 (enclosure). GP, 44504, 124.

159. Ivory to G, 25 October 1888. GP, 44505, 47.

160. Hamilton, iii, 122.

161. H(3), cccxl, 64 (25 November 1890).

162. Hamilton, iii, 81.

163. GP, 44509, 249.

164. Mackenzie to G, 1 February 1891. GP, 44512, 72. On the phrenological aspect of G's concern with head shape see *Gladstone*, 533.

165. ibid.

166. G to Laing, 9 September 1888 (copy). GP, 44504, 249.

167. D, 14 August 1888.

168. D, 12 November 1888.

169. D, 7 November 1888. For the death-

duties issue see H(3), cccxxv. GP, 190–214 (23 April 1888); and 568–9.

170. Newman to G, [6 November 1888]. GP, 44505, 103.

171. D, 9 November 1888.

172. D, 19 November 1888.

173. H(3), cccxxxi, 892, 908 (3 December 1888).

174. D, 8 December 1888.

175. GP, 44505, 228 (18 December 1888).

176. D, 22 November 1888.

177. D, 19 December 1888.

178. Hamilton, iii, 85.

179. See *Gladstone*, 484.

180. D, 11 January 1889.

181. G to Schilizzi, 7 November 1891 (copy). GP, 44513, 248.

182. G to Labouchere, 12 January 1889 (copy). GP, 44506, 21.

183. Ffrench to G, 11 March 1889. GP, 44506, 93.

184. Lyons, *Parnell*, 424.

185. H(3), cccxxxv, 102–3, 108 (9 April 1889).

186. Tennyson to G, 17 June 1889. GP, 44507, 17.

187. D, 7 May 1889.

188. *Gladstone*, 133.

189. D, 18 June 1889.

190. D, 27 June 1889.

191. Corelli to G, 24 May 1889. GP, 44507, 6.

192. B. Masters, *Now Barabbas was a Rotter. The Extraordinary Life of Marie Corelli* (1978), 87–8; B. Vyner, *Memoirs of Marie Corelli* (1930), 105–6.

193. D, 4 June 1889.

194. Corelli to G, [4 June] 1889. GP, 44507, 6.

195. Blind to G, 15 October 1889. GP, 44508, 66.

196. G, 'Journal de Marie Bashkirtseff', *Nineteenth Century*, October 1889.

197. Hamilton, iii, 94.

198. ibid., 100; D, 7 July 1889.

199. ibid., 102.

200. G to Parnell, 30 August 1889 (copy).

GP, 44507, 203. On the problems of getting the Liberal party to accept Roman Catholic claims to the funding of denominational education, see Archbishop Walsh to G, 18, 20 October 1889. GP, 44508, 79, 81.

201. Freeman to G, 18 August 1889. Ibid., 171.

202. Freeman to G, 22 August 1889. Ibid., 183.

203. Raleigh to Stedman, 23 October 1889. GP, 44508, 91. See page 437.

204. D, 2 September 1889.

205. Q & G, ii, 432.

206. D, 4 October 1889.

207. ibid.

208. Matthew, *Gladstone*, ii, 366.

209. ibid., 365.

210. D, 13 October 1889.

211. Hubbard to G, 7 October 1889. GP, 44508, 22.

212. Freeman to G, 14 October 1889. Ibid., 64.

213. Channing to G, 11 October 1889. Ibid., 55.

214. D, 3 December 1889.

215. G to Wood, 30 October 1889 (copy). GP, 44508, 102.

216. G to Parnell, 4 October 1889 (copy). Ibid., 10.

217. Lyons, *Parnell*, 467–8.

218. Parnell to G, 12 October 1889. GP, 44508, 62.

219. Clayden to G, 13, 16 November 1889. Ibid., 140–66.

220. Ivory to G, 25 November 1889. Ibid., 160.

221. Lyons, *Parnell*, 448.

222. G, memo, 12 January 1891 (copy). GP, 56449.

223. Anson to G, 28 December 1889. GP, 44508, 259.

224. D, 29 December 1889.

225. GP, 44509, 148.

226. Peel to G, 25 January 1890. Ibid., 85.

227. A. T. Bassett (ed.), *Gladstone to His Wife* (1936), 254.

228. C. R. L. F[letcher], *Mr Gladstone at Oxford, 1890* (1908), 29–39. C. W. Oman, *Memories of Victorian Oxford* (1941), 140–41.
229. Hamilton, iii, 119.
230. D, 8 February 1890.
231. H(3), cccxli, 63, 67 (11 February 1890).
232. H(3), cccxli, 721–2 (19 February 1890).
233. Hamilton, iii, 112. D, 21 March 1890.
234. Freeman to G, 22 August 1889. GP, 44507, 171; Freeman to G, 14 October 1889. GP, 44508, 84.
235. H(3), cccxlvii, 1765–6 (4 August 1890).
236. K. O. Morgan, *Lloyd George Family Letters* (1973), 28. D, 7 June 1890.
237. Hamilton, iii, 111.
238. G to Schilizzi, 7 November 1891 (copy). GP, 44513, 248.
239. D, 30 April 1890.
240. D, 4 July 1890.
241. E. F. C. Collier (ed.), *A Victorian Diarist. Extracts from the Journal of Mary, Lady Monkswell, 1873–1895* (1944), 160.
242. Carrington to G, 9 June 1890. GP, 44510, 70.
243. D, 23 June 1890.
244. D, 14 May, 9 June 1890. Carnegie to G, 10 June 1890. GP, 44510, 81.
245. D, 24 June 1890.
246. Hamilton, iii, 115.
247. D, 2 April 1890.
248. Matthew, *Gladstone*, ii, 322.
249. Caine to G, 8 July 1890. GP, 44510, 143.
250. Hamilton, iii, 121.
251. D, 29 May 1887.
252. GP, 44510, 256. 15 August 1890.
253. D, 21 September 1890.
254. G, 'On Books and the Housing of Them', *Nineteenth Century*, March 1890.
255. Walsh to G, 5 March 1890. GP, 44509, 227.
256. D, 30 October 1890.

257. D, 17 October 1890.
258. D, 21 October 1890.
259. D, xii, 525–6.
260. MacColl to G, 19 November 1890. GP, 56448.
261. Channing to G, 19 November 1890. GP, 56448.
262. Stead to G, 19 November 1890. Ibid.
263. Stead to G, 20 November 1890. Ibid.
264. Lyons, *Parnell*, 489.
265. G to Labouchere, 31 December 1890 (copy). GP, 56449.
266. G, 21 November 1890. GP, 56448.
267. G, memo, 22 November [1890]. GP, 56448.
268. F. E. Hamer (ed.), *The Personal Papers of Lord Rendel* (1931), 26.
269. Lyons, *Parnell*, 500–501.
270. Lyons, *Parnell*, 504–5.
271. D, 29 November 1890.
272. Lyons, *Parnell*, 510.
273. D, 30 November 1890.
274. Croke to G, 30 November [1890]. GP, 44511, 208.
275. G, memo, 6 December 1890. GP, 56449.
276. Channing to G, 5 December 1890. GP, 44511, 220.
277. Holyoake to G, 31 December 1890. Ibid., 265.
278. Brett to G, 31 December 1890. Ibid., 262.
279. D, 29 December 1890. GP, 56449.

CHAPTER 13:
'I AM NO LONGER FIT FOR PUBLIC LIFE': 1891–3

1. Walsh to G, 28 January 1891. GP, 44512, 65.
2. Dillon to G, 20 January 1891. GP, 56449.
3. G to Dillon, 21 January 1891 (copy). Ibid. G, memo, 31 January 1891. Ibid.
4. Harcourt to G, 17 January 1891; G to Harcourt, 19 January 1891. Ibid.

5. M. Barker, *Gladstone and Radicalism, 1885–1894* (Brighton, 1975), 205.
6. D, 16 December 1890.
7. Storey to G, 22 January [1891]. GP, 44512, 52.
8. Caine to G, 24 June 1891. Ibid., 328.
9. G to Carnegie, 3 July 1891 (copy). GP, 44513, 1.
10. H(3), cccxl, 1264 (20 February 1891).
11. G to Editor of *Independent*, 7 February 1891 (copy). GP, 44512, 102.
12. D, 30 April 1891.
13. D, 19 February 1891.
14. D, 4 June 1891.
15. Hamilton, iii, 139.
16. D, 26 March 1891.
17. D, xii, 526–7.
18. Meade to G, 12 October 1891. GP, 44513, 208; West to G, 2 June 1892. GP, 44515, 7.
19. D, 4 June 1891.
20. D, xii, 528.
21. Hamilton, iii, 144–5.
22. G, 'Electoral Facts, No. III', *Nineteenth Century*, September 1891, 330, 331, 337–8, 340.
23. Barker, *Gladstone and Radicalism*, 160–61.
24. Caine to G, 24 September 1891. GP, 44513, 181. D. A. Hamer, *Liberal Politics in the Age of Gladstone and Rosebery* (Oxford, 1972), 173–4.
25. Barker, *Gladstone and Radicalism*, ibid.
26. D, 14 September 1891.
27. Carnegie to G, 28 March 1892. GP, 44514, 155.
28. Hamer, *Liberal Politics*, 229.
29. Barker, *Gladstone and Radicalism*, 162.
30. Rogers to G, 8 October 1891. GP, 44513, 202.
31. G to Labouchere, 24 November 1891 (draft). GP, 56449.
32. G to Perry, 5 December 1891 (copy). GP, 44513, 293.
33. Lord Crewe, *Lord Rosebery* (1931), ii, 375.
34. Hamilton, iii, 148.
35. D, 26 November 1891. See G's comments to Rendel. F. E. Hamer (ed.), *The Personal Papers of Lord Rendel* (1931), 93–4.
36. Hamilton, iii, 148.
37. D, 10 December 1891.
38. Hamilton, iii, 151.
39. D, 15 December 1891. H. G. Hamilton (ed.), *The Private Diaries of Sir Algernon West* (1922), 23–31.
40. J. Bailey (ed.), *The Diary of Lady Frederick Cavendish* (1927), i, 193.
41. L. A. Tollemache, *Talks with Mr Gladstone* (1898), 44. The third edition of Tollemache's *Talks* (1903) was reprinted with an introduction by A. Briggs: *Gladstone's Boswell: Late Victorian Conversations by Lionel A. Tollemache* (Brighton, 1984).
42. D, 2 December 1890.
43. Morley, ii, 716.
44. Hamilton, iii, 153.
45. ibid.
46. Stuart to G, 6 March 1892. GP, 44514, 114.
47. D, 1 April 1892.
48. D, 21, 22 April 1892.
49. Carnegie to G, 28 March 1892. GP, 44514, 155.
50. H. J. Hanham, *Elections and Party Management* (1959), 375.
51. H(4), iii, 1170, 1672 (11, 29 April 1892).
52. Balfour to G, 28 April 1892. GP, 44514, 215.
53. D, 27 April 1892.
54. Dixie to G, 22 April 1892. GP, 44514, 191.
55. G to Shipton, 29 April 1892 (copy). Ibid., 219.
56. Press clippings, June 1892. GP, 44515, 75.
57. Hughes to G, 30 April 1892. GP, 44514, 225.
58. H(4), v, 1484 (17 June 1892).
59. H(4), iv, 1692 (24 May 1892).
60. Hamilton, iii, 157.

61. R. T. Shannon, *The Age of Salisbury* (1996), 372.
62. PMP, i, *Autobiographica*, 116.
63. Morley, ii, 730.
64. Shannon, *Age of Salisbury*, 372.
65. ibid.
66. Shannon, *Age of Salisbury*, 376.
67. Marsham to G, 24 June 1892. GP, 44515, 70. See page 172.
68. D. McCartney, *W. E. H. Lecky: Historian and Politician* (Dublin, 1994), 125.
69. D, 8 July 1892. See also Carnegie to G, 12 January 1891 (GP, 44512, 200), urging that with one good stenographer G could make £50,000. The Editor of the *Century Magazine* was much interested in 'the duty you owe posterity in this matter'. D, 3 March 1891: 'Literary proposals from America, promising from 100 gns to £25,000!' G had in view the enticing prospect of extinguishing the Hawarden estate debt.
70. Crewe, *Rosebery*, ii, 391–2.
71. A. T. Bassett (ed.), *Gladstone to His Wife* (1936), 256.
72. D, xiii, 431. The < > marks indicate passages deleted in Morley's diary.
73. Hamilton, iii, 158–9.
74. ibid., 162.
75. ibid., 188–9.
76. D, 12 July 1892.
77. O. Chadwick, *Acton and Gladstone* (1976), 5.
78. D, xiii, 431–3.
79. D, 4 August 1892.
80. *Standard*, 22 July 1892, 2.
81. G to J. B. Balfour, 18 July 1892 (copy). GP, 44515, 110.
82. ibid.
83. D, 13 July 1892.
84. D, 14 July 1892.
85. Morley, ii, 718.
86. Hamilton, iii, 160–61.
87. D, 22 July 1892.
88. Barker, *Gladstone and Radicalism*, 239.
89. D, 28 July 1892.
90. Hamilton, iii, 164.
91. D, 28 July 1892.
92. D, 31 July 1892.
93. Hamilton, iii, 164–5.
94. A. Thorold, *Labouchere* (1913), 375.
95. Chadwick, *Acton and Gladstone*, 34–5, 37–42.
96. H(4), vii, 196, 199, 200, 212, 215 (9 August 1892).
97. ibid., 218, 223.
98. Hamilton, iii, 168.
99. ibid., 169.
100. PMP, i, *Autobiographica*, 135.
101. D, 16 August 1892: 'from above'.
102. Chadwick, *Acton and Gladstone*, 46.
103. D, 15 August 1892.
104. A. Ramm (ed.), *Beloved and Darling Child. Last Letters between Queen Victoria and Her Eldest Daughter, 1886–1901* (Stroud, 1990), 146–7.
105. PMP, i, *Autobiographica*, 134.
106. R. R. James, *Rosebery* (1963), 254.
107. Hamilton, iii, 172.
108. Carnegie to Gladstone, 17 August 1892. GP, 44515, 187.
109. Lord Kilbracken, *Reminiscences* (1931), 139.
110. D, 29 August 1892.
111. P. Magnus, *Gladstone* (1954), 402–3.
112. D, 7 September 1892.
113. R. Jenkins, *Gladstone* (1995), 594.
114. D, 15 September 1892.
115. Crewe, *Rosebery*, ii, 374–5.
116. G, 'The Triple Alliance and Italy's Place in It', *Contemporary Review*, October 1889.
117. D, 19 July 1892. PMP, i, *Autobiographica*, 121.
118. D, 21 September 1892.
119. PMP, i, *Autobiographica*, 135.
120. D, 26 September 1892.
121. Hamilton, iii, 174, 176–7.
122. James, *Rosebery*, 274.
123. ibid., 272.
124. See page 205.
125. H(4), vii, 212 (9 August 1892).
126. Hamilton, iii, 191.

127. James, *Rosebery*, 267.
128. Hamilton, iii, 177.
129. Hallam Tennyson to G, 4, 9 October 1892. GP, 44516, 114, 142.
130. *Gladstone*, 397.
131. J. D. Jump, *Tennyson. The Critical Heritage* (1967), 214.
132. Q & G, ii, 443.
133. Hallam Tennyson to G, 5 December 1892. GP, 44516, 300. G to Hallam Tennyson, 7 December 1892 (copy). GP, 44549, 49. D, 7 December 1892.
134. Q & G, ii, 453.
135. F. W. Hirst, 'Mr Gladstone's Fourth Premiership and Final Retirement, 1892–1897', *Gladstone*, ed. T. W. Reid (1899), 724.
136. Jenkins, *Gladstone*, 593.
137. L. Masterman (ed.), *Mary Gladstone (Mrs Drew): Her Diaries and Letters* (1930), 420.
138. Q & G, ii, 447–50.
139. See Ramm, *Beloved and Darling Child*, 150, for the Queen's comments to the Empress Frederick on her snubbing response to G: '*He* it is who has done all he could to set class against class . . . and *he* only.'
140. C. C. Weston, 'Salisbury and the Lords, 1868–1895', HJ, 1982, 124–5.
141. Hamilton, iii, 176.
142. ibid., 177.
143. ibid.
144. ibid., 177–8.
145. Currey to G, 25 January 1893. GP, 44517, 26.
146. James, *Rosebery*, 275.
147. ibid., 276.
148. Q & G, ii, 458.
149. Hamilton, iii, 178–9.
150. Hunter to G, 14 December 1892. GP, 44516, 318.
151. R. Jay, *Joseph Chamberlain* (Oxford, 1981), 171, 173.
152. Q & G, ii, 457–8.
153. Hamilton, iii, 179.
154. D, 3 December 1892.
155. James, *Rosebery*, 276.
156. Hamilton, iii, 183.
157. ibid., 184.
158. D, 13 January 1892.
159. Hamilton, iii, 186.
160. ibid., 186–7.
161. G to Campbell-Bannerman, 23 January 1893 (copy). GP, 44517, 20.
162. Hamilton, iii, 188.
163. D, 5 February 1893.
164. PMP, i, *Autobiographica*, 135–6.
165. Hamilton, iii, 189.
166. D, 7 February 1893.
167. James, *Rosebery*, 283.
168. Hamilton, iii, 190–91.
169. Shannon, *Age of Salisbury*, 386.
170. H(4), viii, 1260–62, 1275.
171. ibid., 1412 (14 February 1893).
172. Hamilton, iii, 194–5.
173. J. Spender and C. Asquith, *Life of Lord Oxford and Asquith* (1932), i, 78–9.
174. D, 23 February 1893.
175. P. M. Thornton, *Some Things We Have Remembered* (1912), 259–61.
176. D, 3 March 1893.
177. D, 5 April 1893.
178. G to Mme Sadi-Carnot, 26 June 1894 (copy). GP, 44518, 244.
179. Q & G, ii, 463–4.
180. Ramm, *Beloved and Darling Child*, 150.
181. ibid., 467.
182. Hamilton, iii, 195.
183. H(4), x, 1603–4.
184. Hamilton, iii, 199.
185. Morley, ii, 738.
186. Hamilton, iii, 196.
187. See pages 215–16.
188. D, 8 May 1893.
189. D, 11 May 1893. Gladstone wrote 'It is'.
190. H(4), xii, 354–5 (8 May 1893).
191. ibid., 358.
192. ibid., 691 (11 May 1893).
193. Hamilton, iii, 204.
194. D, 23 May 1893.
195. Hamilton, iii, 205.

196. D, 9 August 1893.
197. E. F. C. Collier (ed.), *A Victorian Diarist. Extracts from the Journal of Mary, Lady Monkswell, 1873–1895* (1944), 223–4.
198. D, 12 May 1893.
199. D, 9 June 1893.
200. *Gladstone*, 376; D, 17 February 1893.
201. D, 29 May 1893.
202. See D, xiii, 244.
203. D, 25 February 1893.
204. H. C. G. Matthew, *Gladstone, 1875–1898* (Oxford, 1995), 364–5.
205. W. S. Blunt, *My Diaries. Being a Personal Narrative of Events, 1888–1914* (1921), i, 73.
206. D, 20 December 1884.
207. D, 8 April 1893.
208. H(4), xiii, 1552 (20 June 1893).
209. H(4), xiv, 1114.
210. D, 21 July 1893.
211. Hamilton, iii, 209.
212. H(4), xv, 548.
213. GP, 44517, 131 (26 April 1893).
214. D, 10 May 1893.
215. H(4), xvi, 1458, 1463.
216. Hamilton, iii, 212.
217. Lord Kilbracken, *Reminiscences* (1931), 80.

CHAPTER 14:
'VOICES FROM THE DEAD': 1893–4

1. D, 7 October 1893.
2. P. Stansky, *Ambitions and Strategies. The Struggle for the Leadership of the Liberal Party in the 1890s* (Oxford, 1964), 17.
3. D, 23 October 1893.
4. D, 28 October 1893.
5. D, 10 October 1893. The tragic outcome was that Outram drowned himself in the Thames on or shortly after 1 December 1893. See G to CG, 23 December 1893: 'Am also missing Zadok at every turn: in all these years he had fitted into the nooks & crannies of one's life.'
6. Hamilton, iii, 213.
7. Asquith to G, 9 November 1893. GP, 44517, 305.
8. D, 5 November 1893.
9. D, 19 October 1893.
10. S. Brown, 'One Last Campaign from the GOM: Gladstone and the House of Lords in 1894', in B. Kinzer (ed.), *The Gladstonian Turn of Mind* (Toronto, 1985), 156.
11. Hamilton, iii, 213–15.
12. D, 7 October 1893.
13. H(4), xviii, 1149, 1151.
14. D, 18 September 1893.
15. Q & G, ii, 478.
16. ibid., 479–80.
17. D, 19 December 1893.
18. D, 18 September 1880.
19. Hamilton, iii, 216.
20. ibid., 217–18. See N. Gash, *Sir Robert Peel* (1972), 709: 'Gladstone once said [to Lionel Tollemache] that Peel's two conspicuous attributes as a statesman were his sense of public duty and his sense of measure. For the latter he instanced his concept of the relations between the leader of his party and his followers. It was not an example which would occur to most critics of Peel's career.'
21. D, 7 January 1894.
22. D, xiii, 434.
23. ibid., 436.
24. Stansky, 28.
25. D, 9 January 1894.
26. For this supreme example of 'escape-avoidance coping' see T. L. Crosby, *The Two Mr Gladstones. A Study in Psychology and History* (Yale, 1997), 220.
27. PMP, i, *Autobiographica*, 122.
28. Stansky, 29.
29. Hamilton, iii, 220–21.
30. ibid., 221–2.
31. D, 18 January 1894.
32. Hamilton, iii, 226–7, 234.

33. Stansky, 30.
34. Hamilton, iii, 226.
35. Stansky, 30–31.
36. D, 8 January 1894.
37. Hamilton, iii, 229.
38. D, 31 January 1894.
39. Hamilton, iii, 229.
40. Brown, *Gladstonian Turn of Mind*, 157–8.
41. Stansky, 41–56.
42. D, 4 February 1894.
43. D, 6 February 1894.
44. D, 8 February 1894.
45. Brown, 157–8.
46. Hamilton, iii, 232.
47. ibid., 233.
48. ibid., 226, 233.
49. Brown, 159–60.
50. PMP, i, *Autobiographica*, 136.
51. D, 12 February 1894.
52. Hamilton, iii, 236.
53. PMP, i, *Autobiographica*, 120.
54. Hamilton, iii, 238–9. Stansky, 62–3.
55. H(4), xxi, 851–2.
56. PMP, i, *Autobiographica*, 120.
57. Hamilton, iii, 241.
58. ibid., 242.
59. PMP, i, *Autobiographica*, 121–2.
60. Q & G, ii, 491.
61. D, 28 February 1894.
62. J. B. Conacher, 'A Visit to the Gladstones in 1894', *Victorian Studies*, 1958–9, 158.
63. D, 1 March 1894.
64. E. F. C. Collier (ed.), *A Victorian Diarist. Extracts from the Journal of Mary, Lady Monkswell, 1873–1895* (1944), 241.
65. D, 1 March 1894.
66. H(4), xxi, 1151–2.
67. Lord Oxford and Asquith, *Fifty Years of Parliament* (1926), i, 212.
68. Collier, *Journal of Lady Monkswell*, 241.
69. D, 2 March 1894.
70. D, 3 March 1894.
71. D, 3 March 1894; written 5 March.
72. A. T. Bassett, *Gladstone to His Wife* (1936), 260.
73. Balfour to G, 2 March 1894. GP, 44517, 65.

EPILOGUE:
'I AM A SURVIVAL': 1894–8

1. Lord Kilbracken, *Reminiscences* (1931), 94.
2. D, 2 March 1894.
3. Later King George V (1910–1936) and Queen Mary.
4. D, 10 March 1894.
5. D, 5 March 1894.
6. D, 10, 11 March 1894.
7. PMP, i, *Autobiographica*, 162–3.
8. Hamilton, iii, 253.
9. PMP, i, *Autobiographica*, 164.
10. H(4), xxii, 22–3, 32; Lord Crewe, *Lord Rosebery* (1931), 444; R. R. James, *Rosebery* (1963), 338. R. T. Shannon, *The Age of Salisbury* (1996), 390–91.
11. D, 15 March 1894.
12. PMP, i, *Autobiographica*, 164–5.
13. Murray to G, 4 April 1894. GP, 44517, 157.
14. D, 24 April 1885.
15. PMP, i, *Autobiographica*, 165–7.
16. D, 6 March 1894.
17. M. Tennant to G, 22 March 1894. GP, 44517, 135.
18. D, 17 February 1894. For Catherine's being an 'interfering hen' on these matters see D. Bennett, *Margot* (1984), 123.
19. D. Newsome, *On the Edge of Paradise* (1980), 50.
20. PMP, i, *Autobiographica*, 164.
21. D, 17 December 1894.
22. D, 25 July 1894.
23. Murray to G, 11 July 1894. GP, 44518, 258.
24. J. B. Conacher, 'A Visit to the Gladstones in 1894', *Victorian Studies*, 1958–9, 156–60.
25. Murray to G, 11 September 1894. GP, 44519, 68.

26. Fraser to G, 25 September 1894. GP, 44519, 99.

27. D, 1 September 1894.

28. D, 1 October 1894.

29. R. Hart-Davis (ed.), *The Letters of Oscar Wilde* (1962), 372–3.

30. Caine to G, 8 October 1894. GP, 44519, 132.

31. G to Watson, 14 September 1894 (copy). Ibid., 74.

32. Digby Besant to G, 2 October 1894. Ibid., 118.

33. AIC to G, 4 July 1894. GP, 44518, 265.

34. Shurick to G, 12 December 1894. GP, 44519, 272.

35. D, 24 December 1894; J. Ridley and C. Percy (eds.), *The Letters of Arthur Balfour and Lady Elcho, 1885–1917* (1992), 118.

36. L. Masterman (ed.), *Mary Gladstone (Mrs Drew): Her Diaries and Letters* (1930), 426.

37. F. E. Hamer (ed.), *The Personal Papers of Lord Rendel* (1931), 110.

38. J. de Bourgoing (ed.), *The Incredible Friendship. The Letters of the Emperor Franz Joseph to Frau Katharina Schratt* (English eds. E. M. Kienostand and R. Rie, New York, 1966), 250.

39. R. R. James, *Rosebery* (1963), 380.

40. *Gladstone*, 177–80.

41. Tollemache to G, 10 March 1891. GP, 44512, 167.

42. L. A. Tollemache, *Talks with Mr Gladstone* (1903), 26.

43. G to Watts, 17 June 1891 (copy). GP, 44512, 317.

44. D, 19 September 1892.

45. D, 26 September 1892.

46. Frowde to G, 6 May 1895. GP, 44518, 204.

47. D, xiii, 423.

48. P. Magnus, *Gladstone* (1954), 429.

49. Hamilton, iii, 253.

50. Magnus, 429. See I. Thomas, *Gladstone of Hawarden. A Memoir of Henry Neville, Lord Gladstone of Hawarden* (1936), 154.

51. Humphreys-Owen to G, 27 June 1895. GP, 44520, 222.

52. Crewe, *Rosebery*, ii, 507. James, *Rosebery*, 384.

53. G to Cowan, 1 July 1895 (copy). GP, 44520, 240.

54. Shannon, *Age of Salisbury*, 406.

55. ibid., 419.

56. PMP, i, *Autobiographica*, 136.

57. ibid., 171.

58. Murray to G, 29 October 1894. GP, 44519, 178.

59. De Lisle and Dudley to G, 5 December 1895. GP, 44521, 177.

60. G to Milne, 11 May 1896 (copy). GP, 44522, 212.

61. G to O'Brien, 10 December 1895. GP, 56445.

62. Crewe, *Rosebery*, ii, 515.

63. E. C. F. Collier (ed.), *A Victorian Diarist. Later Extracts from the Journals of Mary, Lady Monkswell, 1895–1909* (1946), 1. Bennett, *Margot*, 145.

64. Clifford to G, 13 December 1895. GP, 44521, 208.

65. Hereford to G, 13 December 1895. Ibid., 212.

66. PMP, i, *Autobiographica*, 169.

67. D, 2 January 1896.

68. ibid.

69. *Gladstone*, 218. E. S. Purcell, *Life of Cardinal Manning* (1895), i, 528–30.

70. D. C. Lathbury (ed.), *Correspondence on Church and Religion of W. E. Gladstone* (1910), ii, 338.

71. G to Webster, 3 March 1896 (copy). GP, 44522, 88.

72. L. Stephen, 'Bishop Butler's Apologist', *Nineteenth Century*, January 1896, 106–22. J. Garnett, 'Bishop Butler and the *Zeitgeist*: Butler and the Development of Christian Moral Philosophy in Victorian Britain', in C. Cunliffe (ed.), *Joseph Butler's Moral and Religious Thought* (1922).

73. *Gladstone*, 82–5, 350–51, 360–61.

74. *Studies Subsidiary to the Works of Bishop Butler*. It should be noted that *The Oxford Dictionary of the Christian Church* (ed. F. L. Cross, 1957), 47, 211, listed G's edition as the best modern edition of the *Analogy*, and his edition of the *Works* similarly.

75. G to Hirsch, 13 February 1896 (copy). GP, 44522, 65.

76. G to Murray, 16 March, 14 April 1896 (copies). ibid., 115, 164.

77. D, 25 March 1896.

78. D, 27 July 1896.

79. Purcell to G, 2 June 1896. GP, 44522, 206.

80. Spencer to G, 11 August 1896. GP, 44523, 187.

81. S. Palmer to G, 22 June 1896. Ibid., 47.

82. Tennyson to G, 7 September 1896. ibid., 240.

83. G to Crossley, 7 September 1896. ibid., 236.

84. G to *Daily Chronicle*, 13 September 1896 (copy). Ibid., 264.

85. GP, 44524, 124.

86. A. C. Benson, *The Life of Edward White Benson, Sometime Archbishop of Canterbury* (1899), ii, 733.

87. ibid., 778.

88. D, 20 October 1896.

89. D, 7 December 1896.

90. See H. C. G. Matthew, *Gladstone, 1874–1898* (Oxford, 1995), 377–8.

91. D, 29 December 1896.

92. Hirst to G, 1 January 1897. GP, 44525.

93. PMP, i, *Autobiographica*, 171.

94. G to Carnegie, 22 February 1897 (copy). GP, 44525, 103.

95. GP, 44776, 180. [17] March 1897.

96. ibid., 173–5.

97. Stoker to G, 24 May 1897. GP, 44525, 221.

98. Caine to G, 31 July 1897. GP, 44526, 42.

99. Massingham to G, 14 June 1897. GP, 44525, 256.

100. For a charmingly informal photograph of the occasion see L. March-Phillips and B. Christian (eds.), *Some Hawarden Letters, 1878–1893* (1917), opp. 82.

101. Newsome, *On the Edge of Paradise, 96–7*.

102. Dobie to G, 6, 8 September 1897. GP, 44526, 74, 78.

103. Lord Ronaldshay, *The Life of Lord Curzon* (1928), i, 249–50.

104. Dean of Durham to G, 18 September 1897. GP, 44526, 97.

105. Hamilton, iii, 344–5.

106. Collier, *Later Monkswell Journals*, 59.

107. Hechler to G, 1 February 1898. GP, 44526, 243.

108. F. W. Hirst, 'Mr Gladstone's Last Days', in T. W. Reid (ed.), *Gladstone* (1899), 742.

109. H. C. G. Matthew, *Gladstone, 1875–1898* (Oxford, 1995), 382.

110. Collier, *Later Monkswell Journals*, 44.

111. A. Ramm (ed.), *Beloved and Darling Child. Last Letters between Queen Victoria and Her Eldest Daughter, 1886–1901* (Stroud, 1990), 215.

112. Hamilton, iii, 356.

113. Magnus, 438.

114. *Monkswell*, 45–8.

115. Hamilton, iii, 357.

116. Ramm, *Beloved and Darling Child*, 215.

Bibliographical Notes

As yet the only bibliography of publications about Gladstone is that of Caroline J. Dobson, *Gladstoniana: A Bibliography of Material Relating to W. E. Gladstone at St. Deiniol's Library, Hawarden* (Hawarden, n.d., c1981). It contains 501 items, many of them, valuably, from obscure contemporary sources. This can be supplemented by consulting the indexes of H. J. Hanham (ed.), *Bibliography of British History, 1851–1914* (Oxford, 1976), and B. Chaudhiri (ed.), *Cumulative Bibliography of Victorian Studies: 1970–1984* (2 vols., Edmonton, Alberta, 1988) and *Cumulative Bibliography of Victorian Studies: 1985–1989* (Edmonton, Alberta, 1990). These four compilations will answer pretty well all requirements. There is serviceable material also in G. Lewis, *British Politics, 1800–1930: A Bibliography of Pamphlets at St. Deiniol's Library* [1985]. What is offered here is a selection of works published in English, mostly books but with a fair sprinkling of articles, designed to equip the general reader with a reasonably comprehensive notion of the range of the literature essential for appreciating the scope of Gladstone scholarship. (The manuscript sources, mostly the vast body of material deposited at the British Library and in the Glynne–Gladstone deposit at Hawarden, together with the diaries at Lambeth Palace Library, have been commented on in the preface to the first volume of this biography.) Biographies and memoirs of Gladstone's political colleagues and contemporaries are not listed. Place of publication is London unless otherwise designated.

Gladstone's Publications

A bibliography of material published by Gladstone was compiled at Hawarden in 1977 by Patricia M. Long: *A Bibliography of Gladstone's Publications at St Deiniol's Library*. This is described in the preface to the first volume of this study. It includes 348 titles of books, articles, and addresses. St Deiniol's Library contains thirty-eight volumes of speeches and pamphlets and eleven volumes of *Speeches and Writings*, mostly press clippings. And *Hansard's Parliamentary Debates* contain 15,000 columns of Gladstone's utterances in the House of Commons in 366 volumes between 1833 and 1894.

A selection of Gladstone's more illuminating and representative publications would include his early books on restoring an identity between established religion and national institutions: *The State in Its Relations with the Church* (1838) and *Church Principles Considered in Their Results* (1841). Then at the Board of Trade he explored the links between Christian morality and state policy as applied to 'general rules and reasons' about tariffs, in 'The Course of Commercial Policy at Home and Abroad' in the *Foreign and Colonial Review*, January 1842. The Gorham-case crisis of 1850 was marked by *Remarks on the Royal Supremacy as It is Defined by Reason, History and the Constitution* (1850). Anguished retreat to Naples led inadvertently to an explosive intervention in foreign affairs: *A Letter to the Earl of Aberdeen on the State Prosecutions of the Neapolitan Government* (1851). Post-Crimean frustrations incited frantic diatribes against Palmerston: 'The Declining Efficiency of Parliament', *Quarterly Review*, September 1856, and 'The Past and Present Administrations', *Quarterly Review*, October 1858. The leisure of being long out of office provided time for *Studies on Homer and the Homeric Age* (3 vols., 1858), with its concise revised form, *Juventus Mundi: The Gods and Heroes of the Heroic Age* (1869). Gladstone signalled the fulfilment of his financial vocation in *The Financial Statements of 1853, 1860–1863* (1863), and the opening of a new epoch in *Speeches on Parliamentary Reform, 1866* (1866).

Gladstone's failures on the Reform question inspired a vision of future vindication and Peelite renewal: 'The Session and Its Sequel', *Edinburgh Review*, 1867. Irish Church disestablishment elicited *A Chapter of Autobiography* (1868), explaining his change of opinion since his resignation over Maynooth in 1845. Foreign affairs intruded once more with the anti-Bismarckian diatribe, incognito, 'Germany, France and England', *Edinburgh Review*, October 1870. Foreign affairs and religion mingled explosively in *The Vatican Decrees in Their Bearing on Civil Allegiance* (1874). Then the eruption of the Eastern question brought forth the volcanic *Bulgarian Horrors and the Question of the East* (1876) and 'England's Mission', *Nineteenth Century*, August 1878, together with consideration of its implications for popular politics: 'The County Franchise and Mr. Lowe Thereon', *Nineteenth Century*, November 1877. 'Aggression on Egypt and Freedom in the East', *Nineteenth Century*, August 1877, has a special ironic resonance in relation to later events. The climax of that epoch for Gladstone were the *Midlothian Speeches* (1879) edited by M. R. D. Foot (Leicester, 1971). In *Gleanings of Past Years* (7 vols., 1879) Gladstone gathered together most of his more important earlier pieces. Then his bid to provide Ireland with Home Rule he defended in *The Irish Question* (1886) and *Special Aspects of the Irish Question* (1892). He defended also the Christian faith in which he saw his politics providentially accredited: *The Impregnable Rock of Holy Scripture* (1890). Gladstone's valediction was his edition of *The Works of Bishop Butler* (2 vols., Oxford, 1896), on which he had started work in 1845, supplemented by *Studies Subsidiary to the Works of Bishop Butler* (Oxford, 1896).

Speeches, Autobiographica, and Diaries

There is no satisfactory edition of Gladstone's speeches. The project edited by A. W. Hutton and H. J. Cohen produced only two volumes covering the period 1892–4, published in 1902. A. T. Bassett's *Gladstone's Speeches. Descriptive Index and Bibliography* (1916) prints a very restricted number of speeches, fourteen in all, between 1850 and 1886.

A valuable selection of Gladstone's writings, mainly autobiographical, was edited for the Stationery Office in four volumes between 1971 and 1981 by J. Brooke and M. Sorenson, *The Prime Ministers' Papers: W. E. Gladstone*. Between 1968 and 1994 Gladstone's diaries at Lambeth Palace have been edited for and published by the Oxford Press: the first two volumes (1825–39) by Professor M. R. D. Foot, the next two (1840–54) jointly by Professor Foot and Professor H. C. G. Matthew, and the next nine (1855–97) by Professor Matthew, together with a concluding fourteenth volume of lists and indices. The diaries are for the most part arid accounts of the expenditure of time. But they are intermittently of unsurpassed importance because of their revelations of Gladstone's interior life. Their value is enhanced by additional material: Cabinet minutes and political correspondence, and Gladstone's surviving letters to the most intensely consequential of his 'rescue' cases, Laura Thistlethwayte. The diaries are not especially revealing in macroscopic political matters such as, for example, Gladstone's conversion to Irish Home Rule. His citing elsewhere in this respect the impact upon him of W. O'Brien's speech of 1 March 1885 is not reflected in his entries at that time. Likewise, at the microscopic level, H. J. Hanham's supposition that the circumstances of the sale of peerages in 1891 would be clarified by the publication of Gladstone's diaries (H. J. Hanham, 'The Sale of Honours in Late Victorian Britain', *Victorian Studies* (Bloomington, Ind.), 1959–60, 284) has not been sustained in the event: Gladstone maintained a studied reticence on the affair.

The Gladstone Family

The prime text is S. G. Checkland, *The Gladstones. A Family Biography, 1764–1851* (Cambridge, 1971), followed by P. Gladstone, *Portrait of a Family. The Gladstones, 1839–1889* (1989). Catherine Gladstone, née Glynne, figured earlier in G. Battiscombe, *Mrs. Gladstone* (1956) and J. Marlow, *Mr. and Mrs. Gladstone. An Intimate Biography* (1977). There is valuable matter also in A. T. Bassett, *Gladstone to His Wife* (1936).

Two of Gladstone's children offered important testimony. Mary Drew produced *Catherine Gladstone* (1919) and *Acton, Gladstone, and Others* (1924). L. Masterman edited *Mary Gladstone (Mrs Drew): Her Diaries and Letters* (1930), with much illuminating detail. Letters to Mary Drew are edited by L. March-Phillips and B. Christian, *Some Hawarden Letters, 1878–1893* (1917), with interesting family photographs. Herbert, Viscount Gladstone, 'manifested pious pugnacity on behalf of his father's reputation' in *After Thirty Years* (1928). I. Thomas, *Gladstone of Hawarden. A Memoir of Henry Neville, Lord Gladstone of Hawarden* (1936) includes matter of interest. Gladstone as Victorian patriarch is at the centre of P. Jalland's 'Mr. Gladstone's Daughters: the Domestic Price of Victorian Politics', in B. Kinzer (ed.), *The Gladstonian Turn of Mind* (Toronto, 1985).

Acton's special relationship with Mary made him virtually a member of the family: H. Paul (ed.), *Letters of Lord Acton to Mary Gladstone* (1904). Acton's special relationship to Gladstone himself is attended to by O. Chadwick, *Acton and Gladstone* (1976). The diaries of Catherine Gladstone's niece Lucy Cavendish, née Lyttelton, were edited by S. J. Bailey, *The Diary of Lady Frederick Cavendish* (2 vols., 1927). Her father, the fourth Lord Lyttelton, contributed anonymously a study of Gladstone–Glynne family lore with his *Contributions Towards a Glossary of the Glynne Language* (privately published

1851, reprinted 1904). Another person who was practically 'family', Stuart, Lord Rendel, Henry Neville's father-in-law, left serviceable material edited by F. E. Hamer, *The Personal Papers of Lord Rendel* (1931). There is a familial atmosphere also in Lionel Tollemache's records of his conversations with the aged Gladstone, the third edition of which was enhanced by A. Briggs, *Gladstone's Boswell: Late Victorian Conversations with Lionel A. Tollemache* (Brighton, 1984).

Also counting rather as 'family' were the four official private secretaries who published or have been published. A. West's *Recollections, 1832–1886* (1899) were supplemented by H. G. Hamilton (ed.), *The Private Diaries of Sir Algernon West* (1922). A. Godley produced *Reminiscences of Lord Kilbracken* (1931); and G. Leveson Gower *Years of Content 1858–1886* (1940) and *Years of Endeavour, 1886–1907* (1942). But unquestionably the cream of secretarial writings is the diary of E. W. Hamilton, edited by D. W. R. Bahlman: *The Diary of Sir Edward Hamilton, 1880–1885* (2 vols., Oxford, 1972) and *The Diary of Sir Edward Hamilton, 1885–1906* (Hull, 1993). In a general way, Hamilton's diaries are much more revealing of Gladstone than Gladstone's own diaries. Hamilton also published a short tribute after Gladstone's death, *Mr. Gladstone, A Monograph* (1898): insightful, affectionate, skirting the religious dimension, but distinctly critical of Gladstone's 'springing' Home Rule on his party.

Royalty

Gladstone's increasingly disastrous relationship with Queen Victoria does not much obtrude itself in the discreet series of *Letters of Queen Victoria*, edited in nine volumes between 1907 and 1932 by A. C. Benson, Viscount Esher, and G. E. Buckle. Something of it emerges in the correspondence of the Queen and Lord Palmerston, edited by B. Connell, *Regina v. Palmerston* (1962). Even more is evident in *The Queen and Mr. Gladstone*, edited by P. Guedalla (2 vols., 1933). But the stark scale of the disaster is disclosed in the correspondence of the Queen with her eldest daughter Victoria, successively Crown Princess of Prussia, German Crown Princess, German Empress, and the widowed Empress Frederick. R. Fulford edited three relevant series: *Your Dear Letter*, covering the years 1865–71 (1971), *Darling Child*, 1871–8 (1976), and *Beloved Mama*, 1878–85 (1981). A. Ramm completed the series with *Beloved and Darling Child*, 1886–1901 (Stroud, 1990). It should be noted that the Princess and Empress Victoria, like her brother the Prince of Wales, by no means shared her mother's animus against Gladstone. These are supplemented by R. Hough (ed.), *Advice to a Grand-daughter. Letters of Queen Victoria to Princess Victoria of Hesse* (1975). There is a little, but priceless, matter in G. St-Aubyn's study of the Queen's cousin, the Duke of Cambridge: *The Royal George* (1963).

General Biographies

Some early items in this genre are of interest. G. Barnett Smith's *Life* of 1879 (with several later editions) is noteworthy because of Gladstone's close personal involvement in the propagandist venture. J. McCarthy's *Life* of 1898 is an Irish tribute. The ample illustrated *Life* edited in 1899 by T. Wemyss Reid is very useful, mainly because F. W. Hirst contributed twelve of the twenty chapters. Goldwin Smith's *My Memory of Gladstone* (1904) is of interest because of his early insights into the problematic nature of Gladstone's Liberalism.

The genre is conventionally held to take developed and mature form with J. Morley's authorized classic *Life*, published in three volumes in 1903, with a cheaper two-volume edition in 1905. Morley's depiction of Gladstone as a 'wonderful pilgrim' questing from Tory darkness to Liberal light by no means reflected accurately his private and candid opinions about Gladstone's later career. Morley's skilfully crafted celebration fulfilled its purpose as an inspiration to the distraught Liberal party in its travails at the beginning of the twentieth century. If Gladstone himself inflicted dire wounds on Liberalism, Morley's biography of him was a healing balm. A notorious 'secularist', Morley was prohibited by the Gladstone family from dealing with Gladstone's religion. His interpretation of Gladstone was a secular one, which has suited the twentieth century all too well. Morley set entirely new standards both of literary and intellectual excellence for the political-biographical genre. His *Gladstone* was deservedly a brilliant success, and its influence has permeated Gladstone studies to the present time. See J. Powell, *Art, Truth, and High Politics. A Bibliographic Study of the Official Lives of Queen Victoria's Ministers in Cabinet, 1843–1969* (Folkestone, 1996), 102–6; M. R. D. Foot, 'Morley's Gladstone: A Reappraisal', *Bulletin of the John Rylands Library*, 1969; and D. M. Schreuder, 'Morley and Knaplund as "Monumental Masons" ', in B. Kinzer (ed.), *The Gladstonian Turn of Mind* (Toronto, 1985). There is shrewd comment on Morley and Gladstone also in G. M. Young's Romanes Lecture of 1944, 'Mr. Gladstone', in his *Victorian Essays* (1962).

Notable biographical landmarks following Morley are E. Eyck's *Gladstone* (1938), expressive of a central European admiration for the great enemy of Bismarck; an angle of view which informs also E. J. Feuchtwanger's *Gladstone* (1975, with a new edition 1989). J. L. L. B. Hammond and M. R. D. Foot, *Gladstone and Liberalism* (1952), reflected a collaboration of an older generation of Gladstone scholarship (Hammond died in 1949) with a younger. P. Magnus, *Gladstone* (1954), was allowed access to hitherto reserved materials, and this, combined with winning readability, inaugurated a new era in Gladstonian biographica. Representative specimens of new approaches are D. A. Hamer, 'Gladstone: The Making of Political Myth', *Victorian Studies*, 1978, and B. Kinzer (ed.), *The Gladstonian Turn of Mind* (Toronto, 1985), already cited, which includes pieces from a sharply feminist angle by A. P. Robson on Gladstone's enmity to female suffrage, P. Jalland (already cited), and a view of Gladstone's last, flailing, months in office by S. Brown. P. Stansky, *Gladstone: A Progress in Politics* (1981), is concise; as is A. Ramm, *William Ewart Gladstone* (Cardiff, 1989), and pithy. A refreshingly unorthodox interpretation of Gladstone as 'control freak' is offered by T. L. Crosby, *The Two Mr Gladstones. A Study in Psychology and History* (Yale, 1997): an interpretation of 'dualism' first explored by G. T. Garratt in *The Two Mr Gladstones* (1936).

Gladstone studies in the 1980s and 1990s have been influenced enormously by the steady publication of the diaries, completed in 1994. Professor H. C. G. Matthew's two volumes of 'biographical studies', *Gladstone, 1809–1875* (Oxford, 1986) and *Gladstone, 1875–1898* (Oxford, 1995), based on his introductions to his editions of the diaries, reconstruct an essentially Morleyan and secular Gladstone, with Gladstone as prophet of the twentieth-century 'progressive' politics of Liberalism, Social Democracy, and

New Labour. On these issues see R. T. Shannon, 'Matthew's Gladstone', *Parliamentary History*, xv, part 2, 1996. Lord (Roy) Jenkins's *Gladstone* (1995) gives an extra Asquithian twist to this celebratory-progressive story, with more than a hint of the Social Democratic ethos. P. J. Jagger (ed.), *Gladstone* (1998), is a collection of thirteen essays on a wide variety of Gladstoniana.

Religion and the Church

The scene here is set by D. Lathbury's edition in two volumes of 1910, *Correspondence on Church and Religion of W. E. Gladstone*. Lathbury was engaged to do the job from which Morley was warned off. Thus was established and consecrated the split between Gladstone's religion and his politics which has bedevilled Gladstone studies ever since. The convention was set in place that everyone stresses how profoundly important religion was to Gladstone, but no one does much about it. J. Barnett's 'Bishop Butler and the *Zeitgeist*: Butler and the Development of Christian Moral Philosophy in Victorian Britain', in C. Cunliffe (ed.), *Joseph Butler's Moral and Religious Thought* (1922), set Gladstone's obsession with Butler in its historical-intellectual context. A. R. Vidler, *The Orb and the Cross* (1945), examined his early Church and State doctrine with a view to its mid-twentieth-century implications. This doctrine was further examined by P. Butler, *Gladstone: Church, State and Tractarianism, 1809–1859* (1982); D. M. Schreuder, 'Gladstone and the Conscience of the State', in P. Marsh (ed.), *The Conscience of the Victorian State* (Syracuse, NY, 1979); B. Hilton, 'Gladstone's Theological Politics', in M. Bentley and J. Stevenson (eds.), *High and Low Politics in Victorian Britain* (1983); and A. Ramm, 'Gladstone's Religion', *Historical Journal* (Cambridge), 1985. Gladstone's links with Nonconformity have been analysed by G. I. T. Machin, 'Gladstone and Nonconformity in the 1860s: The Formation of an Alliance', *Historical Journal*, 1974, and D. W. Bebbington, 'Gladstone and the Nonconformists: a Religious Affinity in Politics', in *Studies in Church History*, xii, ed. D. Baker (Oxford, 1975). Gladstone's fraught relationship with the Roman Catholic Church is examined by J. Altholz, 'Gladstone and the Vatican Decrees', *Historian*, 1963; H. C. G. Matthew, 'Gladstone, Vaticanism, and the Question of the East', in *Studies in Church History*, xv, ed. D. Baker (Oxford, 1978); and R. T. Shannon, 'Gladstone, the Roman Church, and Italy', in M. Bentley (ed.), *Public and Private Doctrine* (Cambridge, 1993). Other aspects worth attention are J. Bentley, *Ritualism and Politics in Victorian Britain* (Oxford, 1978), D. W. R. Bahlman, 'The Queen, Mr. Gladstone, and Church Patronage', *Victorian Studies*, 1960, and O. Anderson, 'Gladstone's Abolition of Compulsory Church Rates: A Minor Political Myth and Its Historical Career', *Journal of Ecclesiastical History*, 1974. J. D. Bastable (ed.), *Newman and Gladstone Centennial Essays* (Dublin, 1978), opens up consideration of the world in which Gladstone knew Keble, Pusey, and Liddon. I. Ker, *John Henry Newman* (Oxford, 1988), is indispensable; as are indeed R. Ornsby, *Memoirs of James Hope-Scott* (2 vols., 1884), A. R. Ashwell and R. G. Wilberforce, *Life of Samuel Wilberforce* (3 vols., 1881), E. Hodder, *Life of Shaftesbury* (2 vols., 1887), and E. S. Purcell, *Life of Cardinal Manning* (2 vols., 1896). See also V. A. McLelland, 'Gladstone and Manning: a Question of Authority', in *Gladstone, Politics and Religion*, ed. P. Jagger (1985).

Literary and Intellectual Interests

P. Metcalf's *James Knowles, Victorian Editor and Architect* (Oxford, 1980) is a mine of information about Gladstone's connection with the Metaphysical Society, with the *Contemporary Review* and the *Nineteenth Century*, to both of which, especially the latter, he contributed copiously, and generally for the life of the mind in Victorian Britain. Consult also A. W. Brown, *The Metaphysical Society, 1869–1880* (New York, 1947). F. M. Turner, *The Greek Heritage in Victorian Britain* (Yale, 1981), covers the ground of Gladstone's Homeric studies. A conveniently concise guide to Gladstone's Homerology is provided by H. Lloyd Jones in *Blood for the Ghosts. Classical Influences in the Nineteenth and Twentieth Centuries* (1982). Much fresh information about Gladstone's intense interest in Schliemann, the celebrated excavator of 'Troy', is provided by J. Vaio: 'Gladstone and the Early Reception of Schliemann in England', in W. M. Calder and J. Cobet (eds.), *Heinrich Schliemann nach hundert Jahren* (Frankfurt am Main, 1992), and 'Schliemann and Gladstone: New Light from Unpublished Documents', in J. Herrmann (ed.), *Heinrich Schliemann, Grundlagen und Ergebnisse moderner Archäologie 100 Jahre nach Schliemanns Tod* (Berlin, 1992).

Gladstone's intimate relationship with the ex-Carbonarist Principal Librarian of the British Museum is recorded by M. R. D. Foot, 'Gladstone and Panizzi', *British Library Journal*, 1979. Two pamphlets at St Deiniol's are serviceable here: M. Drew, *Mr Gladstone's Library at St Deiniol's, Hawarden* (1906), and E. W. B. Nicholson, *Mr Gladstone and the Bodleian* (1898). As connoisseur he is scrutinized by M. Pointon, 'W. E. Gladstone as Art Patron and Collector', *Victorian Studies*, 1975. His special and difficult partnership with Tennyson is outlined in R. T. Shannon, 'Tennyson and Gladstone', *The Times Literary Supplement*, 2 October 1992. His fabled week at All Souls College, Oxford, is recorded by C. R. L. Fletcher, *Mr Gladstone at Oxford, 1890* (1908). The story of how Gladstone had alienated most of the Fellows he mingled with at Oxford is told classically by J. Roach, 'Liberalism and the Victorian Intelligentsia', *Cambridge Historical Journal*, 1957, reprinted in P. Stansky (ed.), *The Victorian Revolution* (New York, 1973).

Gladstone's Earlier Political Career up to the 1860s

A. F. Robbins, *The Early Public Life of Gladstone* (1894), is still useful. F. W. Hirst made of Gladstone a model for depressed times in *Gladstone as Financier and Economist* (1931). F. E. Hyde, *Mr Gladstone at the Board of Trade* (1934) and L. Brown, *The Board of Trade and the Free-Trade Movement, 1830–1842* (1958), covered the ground of Gladstone's lieutenancy to Peel in the 1840s. Gladstone as Peelite has been comprehensively delineated by J. B. Conacher: *The Peelites and the Party System, 1846–52* (Newton Abbot, 1992), 'Mr Gladstone Seeks a Seat', *Canadian Historical Association*, 1962, and *The Aberdeen Coalition, 1852–1855* (Cambridge, 1968). J. R. Jones, 'The Conservatives and Gladstone, 1855', *English Historical Review*, 1962, adds illuminating details; as does A. B. Hawkins, *Parliament, Party and the Art of Politics in Britain, 1855–59* (Basingstoke, 1987), and T. A. Jenkins (ed.), *The Parliamentary Diaries of Sir John Trelawny, 1858–65* (1990).

Gladstone's work at the Treasury from 1853 is attended to in: E. Hughes, 'Civil

Service Reform, 1853–55', *History*, 1942; O. Anderson, 'Loans versus Taxes: British Financial Policy in the Crimean War', *Economic History Review*, 1963–4, and *A Liberal State at War* (1967); J. M. Hart, 'Sir Charles Trevelyan at the Treasury', *English Historical Review*, 1960; R. J. Moore, 'The Abolition of Patronage in the Indian Civil Service', *Historical Journal*, 1964; H. C. G. Matthew, 'Disraeli, Gladstone, and the Politics of Mid-Victorian Budgets', *Historical Journal*, 1979; and M. W. Wright, *Treasury Control of the Civil Service, 1854–1874* (1969).

Gladstone's uneasiness as ally of the Whigs is brought out by E. D. Steele, 'Gladstone and Palmerston, 1855–65' in P. Jagger (ed.), *Gladstone, Politics and Religion* (1985); P. Guedalla (ed.), *The Palmerston Papers: Gladstone and Palmerston, being the Correspondence of Lord Palmerston with Mr Gladstone, 1851–1865* (1928); J. M. Prest, 'Gladstone and Russell', *Transactions of the Royal Historical Society*, 1966; D. F. Krein, *The Last Palmerston Government* (Iowa, 1978); and P. Gurowich, 'The Continuation of War by Other Means: Party and Politics, 1855–1865', *Historical Journal*, 1984. Gladstone's getting ahead of the Whigs is the theme of W. E. Williams, *The Rise of Gladstone to the Leadership of the Liberal Party, 1859–68* (Cambridge, 1934), and of J. Vincent, *The Formation of the Liberal Party, 1857–1868* (1966). W. Bagehot's shrewd insights into the 'adaptiveness' of Gladstone's Liberalism are to be had in N. St John-Stevas (ed.), *The Collected Works of Walter Bagehot*, iii, *Historical Essays* (1968). Valuable for the issues raised by the American Civil War is M. Ellison, *Support for Secession. Lancashire and the American Civil War* (1972). A dispassionate and acute observer of Gladstone was Lord Stanley, later fifteenth Earl of Derby. His earlier diaries have been edited by J. Vincent, *Disraeli, Derby and the Conservative Party, 1849–1869* (Brighton, 1978).

Colonial and Foreign Affairs

The groundwork in both aspects was laid by P. Knaplund: *Gladstone and Britain's Imperial Policy* (1927) and *Gladstone's Foreign Policy* (1935). A. J. P. Taylor, *The Trouble Makers* (1957), is a lively account of Gladstone's role as challenger of Foreign Office orthodoxy. See also M. Schwartz, *The Politics of Foreign Policy in the Era of Disraeli and Gladstone* (New York, 1985). On Italy key works are S. Gopal, 'Gladstone and the Italian Question', *History*, 1956; D. Beales, *England and Italy, 1859–1860* (1961); D. M. Schreuder, 'Gladstone and Italian Unification: the Making of a Liberal?', *English Historical Review*, 1970, and O. Chadwick, 'Young Gladstone and Italy', *Journal of Ecclesiastical History*, 1979. For the crisis of 1870: D. M. Schreuder, 'Gladstone as "Troublemaker": Liberal Foreign Policy and the German Annexation of Alsace–Lorraine, 1870–71', *Journal of British Studies* (Chicago), 1977–8, and 'The Gladstone–Max Müller Debate on Nationalism and German Unification', *Historical Journal, Australia and New Zealand* (Melbourne), 1979.

For Gladstone and the Eastern question consult: R. W. Seton-Watson, *Disraeli, Gladstone and the Eastern Question* (1935); R. T. Shannon, *Gladstone and the Bulgarian Agitation, 1876* (1963); A. P. Saab, *Reluctant Icon: Gladstone, Bulgaria, and the Working Classes, 1856–1878* (Cambridge, Mass., 1991); R. Harrison, 'Marx, Gladstone and Olga Novikov', *Bulletin of the Society for the Study of Labour History* (1976); W. N. Medlicott, 'Gladstone and the Turks', *History*, 1928, and 'Gladstone and the Cyprus Convention', *Journal of Modern History* (Chicago), 1940. On the later phase see R. T. Shannon, 'Gladstone and

British Balkan Policy', in R. Melville and H.-J. Schröder, *Der Berliner Kongress von 1878* (Wiesbaden, 1982), and 'Gladstone and the Hellenic Factor in the Eastern Question', *Actes du Symposium International, 'La Dernière Phase de la Crise Orientale et l'Hellénisme, 1878–1881* (Athens, 1983). W. N. Medlicott, *Bismarck, Gladstone, and the Concert of Europe* (1956), winds up that story.

On the theme of Gladstone's difficulties with Empire see F. Harcourt, 'Gladstone, Monarchism and the "New Imperialism"', 1868–74', *Journal of Imperial and Commonwealth History*, 1985–6. For both Egypt and South Africa there is much in R. Robinson, J. Gallagher, and A. Denny, *Africa and the Victorians* (1963). See also A. Ramm, 'Great Britain and France in Egypt, 1876–1882', in P. Gifford and W. R. Lewis (eds.), *France and Britain in Africa* (Yale, 1971), M. E. Chamberlain, 'Sir Charles Dilke and the British Intervention in Egypt, 1882', *British Journal of International Studies*, 1976, and 'British Public Opinion and the Invasion of Egypt, 1882', *Trivium* (Lampeter), 1981. On the Gordon affair see D. H. Johnston, 'The Death of Gordon: a Victorian Myth', *Journal of Imperial and Commonwealth History*, 1982. On Gladstone at the Colonial Office see K. Fitzpatrick, 'Mr Gladstone and the Governor', *Historical Studies, Australia and New Zealand*, 1940. On South Africa key texts are C. F. Goodfellow, *Great Britain and South African Confederation, 1870–1881* (1966), and D. M. Schreuder, *Gladstone and Kruger* (1969).

Ireland

The Irish aspect of Gladstone's concerns is best introduced by J. Lee, *The Modernisation of Irish Society, 1848–1918* (Dublin, 1973), R. Foster, *Modern Ireland, 1600–1972* (1988), K. T. Hoppen, *Ireland Since 1800* (1989), and *Elections, Politics and Society in Ireland, 1832–1885* (Oxford, 1984). R. F. Foster, 'History and the Irish Question', *Transactions of the Royal Historical Society*, 1983, is valuably suggestive. R. D. C. Black, *Economic Thought and the Irish Question, 1817–1870* (Cambridge, 1960), is indispensable. A concise survey is M. J. Winstanley, *Ireland and the Land Question, 1800–1922* (1984). The Church question is set forth in E. R. Norman, *The Catholic Church in the Age of Rebellion, 1859–73* (Yale, 1971), and P. M. H. Bell, *Disestablishment in Ireland and Wales* (1969).

The most influential interpretation of Gladstone's relationship to Ireland still remains J. L. L. B. Hammond, *Gladstone and the Irish Nation* (1938). That relationship is critically examined by E. D. Steele, 'Gladstone and Ireland', *Irish Historical Studies* (Dublin), 1970, and J. Vincent, 'Gladstone and Ireland', *Proceedings of the British Academy*, 1977. Lord Eversley (G. Shaw-Lefevre), *Gladstone and Ireland* (1912), forbore to reveal the extent to which Gladstone ignored his advice to adopt a thoroughgoing policy of land purchase by tenants. See thus E. D. Steele, *Irish Land and British Politics* (Cambridge, 1974), and A. Warren, 'Gladstone, Land and Social Reconstruction in Ireland, 1881–1887', *Parliamentary History*, 1983.

On the neglected Irish aspect of 'Vaticanism' see H. Jenkins, 'The Irish Dimension of the British Kulturkampf, 1870–75', *Journal of Ecclesiastical History*, 1979. D. A. Hamer investigates the ways in which Ireland derailed Liberalism in 'The Irish Question and Liberal Politics, 1880–1894', *Historical Journal*, 1969. The role of Parnell is central: C. C. O'Brien, *Parnell and His Party, 1880–90* (Oxford, 1957); F. S. L. Lyons, *The Fall of Parnell*,

1890–91 (1960). Consult also D. G. Boyce, *The Irish Question and British Politics, 1868– 1986* (1988), and *Nationalism in Ireland* (1982). L. P. Curtis, *Coercion and Conciliation in Ireland, 1880–1892* (Princeton, NJ, 1963), remains a standard text. Gladstone's way to Home Rule is marked by R. Hawkins, 'Gladstone, Forster and the Release of Parnell, 1882–8', *Irish Historical Studies*, 1969. The Ulster problem is introduced by J. Loughlin, *Gladstone, Home Rule and the Ulster Question, 1882–93* (Dublin, 1986). That Gladstone's motives in 1886 were part of a larger series of his motivations is argued by R. T. Shannon, 'Gladstone and Home Rule, 1886', in *Ireland after the Union (Proceedings of the Royal Irish Academy and the British Academy, 1986)* (Oxford, 1989). A neglected aspect of the Home Rule problem is put forward by J. Kendle: *Ireland and the Federal Solution, 1870–1921* (1989).

Gladstone's Later Political Career

The most important primary materials are the two series of *The Political Correspondence of Mr Gladstone and Lord Granville* edited by A. Ramm: 1868–76 (2 vols., 1952) and 1876– 86 (2 vols., Oxford, 1962). The most illuminating study which connects Gladstone's earlier political career with his later leadership of the Liberal party is J. P. Parry, *The Rise and Fall of Liberal Government in Victorian Britain* (Yale, 1993). For the 1868 election see A. F. Thompson, 'Gladstone's Whips and the General Election of 1868', *English Historical Review*, 1948. Other recommendable works covering most of this latter period are H. J. Hanham, *Elections and Party Management: Politics in the Time of Disraeli and Gladstone* (1959), M. Bentley, *The Climax of Liberal Politics: British Liberalism in Theory and Practice, 1868–1918* (1987), D. A. Hamer, *Liberal Politics in the Age of Gladstone and Rosebery* (Oxford, 1972), T. A. Jenkins, *Gladstone, Whiggery and the Liberal Party, 1874– 1886* (Oxford, 1988), E. F. Biagini, *Liberty, Retrenchment and Reform. Popular Liberalism in the Age of Gladstone, 1860–1880* (Cambridge, 1992), and C. Harvie, 'Gladstonianism, the Provinces, and Popular Political Culture, 1860–1906', in R. Bellamy (ed.), *Victorian Liberalism. Nineteenth-century Political Thought and Practice* (1990). Two conveniently concise surveys are P. Adelman, *Gladstone, Disraeli, and Later Victorian Politics* (1970), and M. J. Winstanley, *Gladstone and the Liberal Party* (1990).

Gladstone's part in the Reform issue in 1866–7 is examined by F. B. Smith, *The Making of the Second Reform Bill* (Cambridge, 1966) and M. Cowling, *1867: Disraeli, Gladstone and Revolution* (Cambridge, 1967). The first Gladstone ministry of 1868–74 is reviewed in various aspects by J. P. Parry, *Democracy and Religion: Gladstone and the Liberal Party, 1867–1875* (Cambridge, 1986), a brilliant study which retrieves and restores religion's centrality to high Victorian politics, E. Drus (ed.), *A Journal of Events During the Gladstone Ministry, 1868–74 by John First Earl of Kimberley* (1958), A. Ramm, 'The Parliamentary Context of Cabinet Government, 1868–1874', *English Historical Review*, 1984, W. L. Arnstein, 'Gladstone and the Bradlaugh Case', *Victorian Studies*, 1962, T. A. Jenkins (ed.), *The Parliamentary Diaries of Sir John Trelawny, 1868–1873* (1994), P. McHugh, *Prostitution and Victorian Politics* (1980), P. Adelman, 'Gladstone and Education', *History Today*, 1970, R. R. James, 'Gladstone and the Greenwich Seat', *History Today*, 1959, and W. H. Maehl, 'Gladstone, the Liberals, and the Election of 1874', *Bulletin of the Institute of Historical Research*, 1963.

Gladstone's resignation of the Liberal leadership in 1875 is investigated by M. R. Tebbel, *Journal of British Studies* (Chicago), 1976. The way to 1880 is explored by R. Kelley, 'Midlothian, a Study in Politics and Ideas', *Victorian Studies*, 1960, and T. A. Jenkins, 'Gladstone, the Whigs, and the Leadership of the Liberal Party, 1879–80', *Historical Journal*, 1984. T. Lloyd, *The General Election of 1880* (Oxford, 1968), is a psephological analysis of the elements of the Gladstonian triumph. Aspects of Gladstone's 1880–85 ministry are handled by E. Hughes, 'The Changes in Parliamentary Procedure, 1880–1882', in R. Pares and A. J. P. Taylor (eds.), *Essays Presented to Sir Lewis Namier* (1956), A. Jones, *The Politics of Reform, 1884* (Cambridge, 1972), and W. A. Hayes, *The Background and Passage of the Third Reform Act* (New York, 1982). Invaluable insights are provided in A. B. Cooke and J. Vincent (eds.), *Lord Carlingford's Journal, Reflections of a Cabinet Minister, 1885* (Oxford, 1971). Important also is J. Chamberlain's account of his relationship with Gladstone: *A Political Memoir, 1880–1892*, ed. C. H. D. Howard (1953).

M. R. D. Foot, 'The Hawarden Kite', *University of Leeds Review*, 1986–7, introduces the emergence of the Irish Home Rule question. The Parliament of 1885–6 is scrutinized by W. C. Lubenow, *Parliamentary Politics and the Home Rule Crisis* (Oxford, 1988). A view of Gladstone's machinations in that Parliament is offered with idiosyncratic verve by A. B. Cooke and J. Vincent, *The Governing Passion. Cabinet Government and Party Politics in Britain, 1885–86* (Brighton, 1974). The attempt to patch together the broken Liberal party is dealt with by M. Hurst, *Joseph Chamberlain and the Liberal Reunion: The Round Table Conference, 1887* (1967). M. Barker investigates the implications of the party's not being patched together: *Gladstone and Radicalism, 1885–1894* (Brighton, 1975). For a Welsh dimension see R. T. Shannon, *Mr Gladstone and Swansea, 1887* (Swansea, 1982). J. Vincent's editions of the later Derby diaries, *Derby Diaries, 1869–78* (Cambridge, 1995), and *Home Rule, Liberal Unionism, and Aristocratic Life in Late Victorian England* (Bristol, 1981), include much relevant matter. P. Stansky looks at the last days in office: *Ambitions and Strategies: The Struggle for the Leadership of the Liberal Party in the 1890s* (Oxford, 1964). Occasional vivid glimpses of Gladstone in this latter phase are to be had in E. C. F. Collier (ed.), *A Victorian Diarist. Extracts from the Journals of Mary, Lady Monkswell, 1873–1895* (1944), and *Later Extracts, 1895–1909* (1946), and in J. B. Conacher, 'A Visit to the Gladstones in 1894', *Victorian Studies*, 1958–9.

Index

694